www.wadsworth.com

wadsworth.com is the World Wide Web site for Wadsworth Publishing Company and is your direct source to dozens of online resources.

At *wadsworth.com* you can find out about supplements, demonstration software, and student resources. You can also send e-mail to many of our authors and preview new publications and exciting new technologies.

wadsworth.com
Changing the way the world learns®

FROM THE WADSWORTH SERIES IN SPEECH COMMUNICATION

Adams/Clarke   *The Internet: Effective Online Communication*

Adler/Towne   *Looking Out/Looking In,* Media Edition, Tenth Edition

Albrecht/Bach   *Communication in Complex Organizations: A Relational Perspective*

Babbie   *The Basics of Social Research,* Second Edition

Babbie   *The Practice of Social Research,* Tenth Edition

Benjamin   *Principles, Elements, and Types of Persuasion*

Berko/Samovar/Rosenfeld   *Connecting: A Culture Sensitive Approach to Interpersonal Communication Competency,* Second Edition

Bettinghaus/Cody   *Persuasive Communication,* Fifth Edition

Braithwaite/Wood   *Case Studies in Interpersonal Communication: Processes and Problems*

Brummett   *Reading Rhetorical Theory*

Campbell/Huxman   *The Rhetorical Act,* Third Edition

Campbell/Burkholder   *Critiques of Contemporary Rhetoric,* Second Edition

Conrad/Poole   *Strategic Organizational Communication,* Fifth Edition

Cragan/Wright/Kasch   *Communication in Small Groups: Theory, Process, Skills,* Sixth Edition

Crannell   *Voice and Articulation,* Third Edition

Dwyer   *Conquer Your Speechfright: Learn How to Overcome the Nervousness of Public Speaking*

Freeley/Steinberg   *Argumentation and Debate: Critical Thinking for Reasoned Decision Making,* Tenth Edition

Geist Martin/Ray/Sharf   *Communicating Health: Personal, Cultural and Political Complexities*

Goodall/Goodall   *Communicating in Professional Contexts: Skills, Ethics, and Technologies*

Govier   *A Practical Study of Argument,* Fifth Edition

Griffin   *Invitation to Public Speaking,* Preview Edition

Hall   *Among Cultures: Communication and Challenges*

Hamilton   *Essentials of Public Speaking,* Second Edition

Hamilton/Parker   *Communicating for Results: A Guide for Business and the Professions,* Sixth Edition

Hoover   *Effective Small Group and Team Communication*

Jaffe   *Public Speaking: Concepts and Skills for a Diverse Society,* Third Edition

Kahane/Cavender   *Logic and Contemporary Rhetoric: The Use of Reason in Everyday Life,* Eighth Edition

Knapp/Hall   *Nonverbal Communication in Human Interaction,* Fifth Edition

Larson   *Persuasion: Reception and Responsibility,* Ninth Edition

Liska/Cronkhite   *An Ecological Perspective on Human Communication Theory*

Littlejohn   *Theories of Human Communication,* Seventh Edition

Lumsden/Lumsden   *Communicating with Credibility and Confidence: Diverse Peoples, Diverse Settings,* Second Edition

Lumsden/Lumsden   *Communicating in Groups and Teams: Sharing Leadership,* Third Edition

Metcalfe   *Building a Speech,* Fourth Edition

Miller   *Organizational Communication: Approaches and Processes,* Third Edition

Morreale/Bovee   *Excellence in Public Speaking*

Morreale/Spitzberg/Barge   *Human Communication: Motivation, Knowledge, and Skills*

Orbe/Harris   *Interracial Communication: Theory Into Practice*

Peterson/Stephan/White   *The Complete Speaker: An Introduction to Public Speaking,* Third Edition

Rothwell   *In Mixed Company,* Fourth Edition

Rubin/Rubin/Piele   *Communication Research: Strategies and Sources,* Fifth Edition

Samovar/Porter   *Communication Between Cultures,* Fourth Edition

Samovar/Porter   *Intercultural Communication: A Reader,* Tenth Edition

Sellnow   *Public Speaking: A Process Approach,* Media Edition

Sprague/Stuart   *The Speaker's Handbook,* Sixth Edition

Thomas   *Public Speaking Anxiety: Conquering the Fear of Public Speaking*

Ulloth/Alderfer   *Public Speaking: An Experiential Approach*

Verderber/Verderber   *The Challenge of Effective Speaking,* Twelfth Edition

Verderber/Verderber   *Communicate!,* Tenth Edition

Westra   *Active Communication*

Williams/Monge   *Reasoning with Statistics: How to Read Quantitative Research*

Wood   *Communication Mosaics: An Introduction to the Field of Communication,* Second Edition

Wood   *Communication in Our Lives,* Third Edition

Wood   *Communication Theories in Action: An Introduction,* Second Edition

Wood   *Gendered Lives: Communication, Gender, and Culture,* Fifth Edition

Wood   *Interpersonal Communication: Everyday Encounters,* Third Edition

Wood   *Relational Communication: Continuity and Change in Personal Relationships,* Second Edition

Gendered Lives

COMMUNICATION, GENDER, AND CULTURE

FIFTH EDITION

Julia T. Wood

LINEBERGER DISTINGUISHED PROFESSOR OF HUMANITIES
THE UNIVERSITY OF NORTH CAROLINA
AT CHAPEL HILL

THOMSON
WADSWORTH

Australia · Canada · Mexico · Singapore · Spain
United Kingdom · United States

THOMSON
WADSWORTH ™

Executive Editor: Deirdre Anderson
Publisher: Holly J. Allen
Assistant Editor: Nicole George
Editorial Assistant: Mele Alusa
Technology Project Manager: Jeanette Wiseman
Marketing Manager: Kimberly Russell
Marketing Assistant: Neena Chandra
Advertising Project Manager: Shemika Britt
Project Manager, Editorial Production: Mary Noel
Print / Media Buyer: Robert King

Permissions Editor: Elizabeth Zuber
Production Service: Vicki Moran, Publishing Support
   Services
Text Designer: Seventeenth Street Studios
Copy Editor: April Wells-Hayes
Cover Designer: Gopa and Ted2
Cover Image: "Landscape: Homage to DeStael" by
   Gopa and Ted2
Compositor: G & S Typesetters, Inc.
Printer: Webcom, Ltd.

Printed in Canada
1   2   3   4   5   6   7   06   05   04   03   02

For more information about our products,
contact us at:
Thomson Learning Academic Resource Center
1-800-423-0563

For permission to use material from this text,
contact us by:
Phone: 1-800-730-2214   **Fax:** 1-800-730-2215
Web: http://www.thomsonrights.com

Library of Congress Cataloging-in-Publication Data
Wood, Julia T.
   Gendered lives : communication, gender, and culture
/ Julia T. Wood.—5th ed.
      p.   cm.
   Includes bibliographical references and index.
   ISBN 0-534-58163-3
   1. Sex role.   2. Communication—Sex differences.
3. Gender identity.   I. Title.
HQ1075 .W69 2002
305.3—dc21
                                        2002016796

Wadsworth / Thomson Learning
10 Davis Drive
Belmont, CA 94002-3098
USA

Asia
Thomson Learning
5 Shenton Way #01-01
UIC Building
Singapore 068808

Australia
Nelson Thomson Learning
102 Dodds Street
South Melbourne, Victoria 3205
Australia

Canada
Nelson Thomson Learning
1120 Birchmount Road
Toronto, Ontario M1K 5G4
Canada

Europe / Middle East / Africa
Thomson Learning
Berkshire House
168-173 High Holborn
London WC1V 7AA
United Kingdom

Latin America
Thomson Learning
Seneca, 53
Colonia Polanco
11560 Mexico D.F.
Mexico

Spain
Paraninfo Thomson Learning
Calle / Magallanes, 25
28015 Madrid, Spain

This book is dedicated to:

Emma Goldman, Elizabeth Cady Stanton, Susan B. Anthony, Margaret Sanger, Sojourner Truth, Mary Wollstonecraft, Charlotte Perkins Gilman, Frederick Douglass, and other women and men who began the conversation about gender in this country;

and to:

Betty Friedan, Ella Baker, Marilyn French, Bill McCartney, Gloria Steinem, Jackson Katz, Ellen Goodman, Michael Kimmel, Evelyn Fox Keller, bell hooks, James Doyle, Sandra Harding, Nancy Chodorow, Robert Bly, Susan Faludi, Karlyn Campbell, Mary Daly, Madonna, and other women and men who have added to the cultural dialogue about gender;

and to:

Cam McDonald, Michelle Wood Wilco, Samuel Keenan Bingman Cox, Daniel Wood Wilco, Harrison Wood Wilco, Dylan Tyler Reich, and other boys and girls whose voices will shape the next generation's understanding of women and men, masculinity and femininity, and the meaning of gender in our society.

CONTENTS

CHAPTER 9

Gendered Organizational Communication   226

ACKNOWLEDGMENTS

One of the most gratifying aspects of writing a book is the opportunity to thank those who have offered support, insight, and advice. First and foremost, I thank my students. The undergraduate women and men in my classes are unfailing sources of education for me. Their questions and ideas, their willingness to challenge some of my notions, and their generosity in sharing their perceptions and experiences have shaped the pages that follow—sometimes in obvious ways, sometimes subtly.

My thinking about gender reflects my interaction with many students. In classes and conversations, we have taught each other about intersections among communication, gender, and culture. Undergraduate students who have pushed me to think in new ways about gender, communication, and culture are Cutler Andrews, Leigh Raynor, Erin Karcher, and especially Christina Davis. Among the graduate students who have influenced my thinking are Phaedra Pezzullo, Nina Reich, Chris Inman, Sharon Varallo, Chuck Grant, Scarlet Wynns, Richard Danek, LindaBecker Bourne, Allison Howry, Deborah Austin, Walter Carl, Amanda Granrud, Tim Muehl hoff, Rachel Hall, Ted Striphas, Lynn O'Brien Hallstein, Drew Davidson, Nathan Epley, Natalie Fixmer, and Kate Willink.

I am fortunate to have enjoyed the professional and personal support of Holly Allen and Deirdre Anderson, my editors at Wadsworth. They have been active partners in developing each edition of *Gendered Lives*. Holly's and Deirdre's creativity, insights, and continuous involvement with this book have enhanced it immeasurably. Along with Holly and Deirdre, others at Wadsworth have contributed in important ways to this edition of *Gendered Lives*. They are April Wells-Hayes, manuscript editor; Elizabeth Zuber, permissions editor; Mary Noel, project editor; and Vicki Moran, project manager.

I also thank the individuals who reviewed the first, second, third, fourth, and fifth editions of this book and who offered generous responses and insightful suggestions, which are reflected in the pages that follow. Reviewers for the first edition were Sandra Albrecht, University of Kansas; Victoria DeFrancisco, University of Northern Iowa; Bonnie Dow, University of Georgia; Valerie Downs, California State University, Long Beach; Cheris Kramarae, University of Illinois at Urbana-Champaign; Larry Lance, University of North Carolina at Charlotte; Suzanne McCorkle, Boise State University; Edward Schiappa, University of Minnesota; and

Patricia Sullivan, State University of New York, the College at New Paltz. Reviewers for the second edition were Dan Cavanaugh, Southwest Texas State University; Judith Dallinger, Western Illinois University; Bonnie Dow, University of Georgia; Kathleen Galvin, Northwestern University; Jim Hasenauer, California State University at Northridge; and Diane Umble, Millersville University. Reviewers for the third edition were Cynthia Berryman-Fink, University of Cincinnati; Pamela Cooper, Northwestern University; Jill Rhea, University of North Texas; Ralph Webb, Purdue University; and Gust A. Yep, San Francisco State University. Reviewers for the fourth edition were Bernardo Attias, California State University at Northridge; Pamela Dawes-Kaylor, Ohio State University; Michael R. Elkins, Texas A&M University at Kingsville; Maureen Keeley, Southwest Texas State University; Kelly Morrison, Michigan State University; Trevor Parry-Giles, University of Maryland at College Park; and Carol Thompson, University of Arkansas at Little Rock. Reviewers for the fifth edition were Rick Buerkel, Central Michigan University; Steve Duck, University of Iowa; Victoria Leonard, College of the Canyons; Jennifer Linde, Arizona State University; Kaye J. Nubel, Saddleback College; Bruce Riddle, Kent State University; and Eva Rose, Chaffey College. And, always, I thank Robbie —the love of my life.

Julia T. Wood
The University of North Carolina at Chapel Hill

Courtesy of Dan Sears

Julia T. Wood
**The University of North
Carolina at Chapel Hill**

J ulia T. Wood joined the Department of Communication Studies at the University of North Carolina at Chapel Hill at the age of 24. She is now a professor in that department, where she teaches courses and conducts research on gender, communication, and culture, and on communication in personal relationships. During her career, she has authored 15 books and edited 8 others. In addition, she has published more than 70 articles and book chapters and has presented numerous papers at professional conferences. She has won 8 awards for undergraduate teaching and 8 awards for her scholarship.

Professor Wood lives with her husband, Robert Cox, who is a professor of communication studies, also at the University of North Carolina at Chapel Hill. Filling out their family are Madhi "the wonder dog" and two cats, Sadie and Wicca. When not teaching or writing, Professor Wood enjoys traveling to other countries, working with prisoners in a stop violence program, interacting with students, friends, and family members, and consulting with attorneys on cases involving sex and gender issues.

GENDERED LIVES

Introduction

Opening the Conversation

Most textbooks open by discussing the area of study, but I'd like to launch our conversation a bit differently. I think you're entitled to know something about the person behind the words you'll be reading, so I want to introduce myself.

We tend to think books are impersonal sources of information. Like anything people create, however, books reflect the experiences and identities of those who compose them. Authors influence books when they decide to include certain topics and to disregard others, to rely on particular theories, and to include some issues and exclude others. Choices about topics, writing style, and theoretical stance shape the content and overall meaning of a book. This doesn't mean books are not informative or reliable, but it does mean they reflect authors' points of view. Like all books, *Gendered Lives* is personal. By telling you a little about who I am, what I believe, and why I wrote this book, I am inviting you to recognize how my background, experiences, beliefs, and values have shaped the book you're reading.

Let's start with some simple demographic information. I am a European American, middle-aged, heterosexual, spiritually engaged, middle-class woman who has been in a committed relationship with Robert (Robbie) Cox for 27 years. Yet, if you think about it, this information isn't simple at all, because it implies a great deal about my identity and my experiences. For instance, I am privileged in many ways—my race, class, and sexual orientation are approved by mainstream Western culture. I am also socially disadvantaged by my sex, because women are valued less than men in Western culture. I did not earn the privileges conferred by my skin, sexual orientation, and class, nor did I earn the inequities that come with being female in America. That is the nature of privilege and inequity—they are unearned. They do not reflect the achievements, efforts, or failings of individuals who enjoy or suffer them.

THE SOCIAL CONSTRUCTION OF INEQUALITY

To speak of being privileged in some ways and devalued in others does not mean I take either for granted. The fact that my sex makes me vulnerable to job discrimination, violence, devaluation, and exploitation is not something I accept as unchangeable. In fact, one reason I wrote this book is that I believe we *can* bring about changes in our society. I also do not accept my privileges unreflectively. Our society constructs inequality by assigning different value to various skin colors, genders, sexual orientations, and classes. The realization that my personal and professional life are contoured by whether I fit what our culture arbitrarily designates as normal or superior makes me keenly aware that sex, gender, race, sexual orientation, and class profoundly influence individuals' knowledge, experience, and possibilities.

If we don't want to be limited to the horizons of our social position, we can try to learn about the experiences, feelings, and views of people in other social positions — the anger and hurt gay men and lesbians experience in a society that defines heterosexuality as normal; the resentment that heterosexual White men sometimes feel toward efforts to instigate changes that might reduce the privileges they enjoy; the frustration women experience in knowing they cannot venture out at night without risking assault; what it means to be a person of color in a sea of Whiteness. Yet we should not delude ourselves into thinking we understand fully the lives of others who differ from us in some important ways. Sensitivity and earnest efforts to understand are important, yet they cannot yield complete knowledge of the daily reality of others' lives.

What we can do is stretch ourselves to realize that our feelings, identities, values, and perspectives are not everyone's. Realizing the limits of our own standpoint encourages us to learn from people whose standpoints differ from ours. We do this by respecting the different conditions that shape their lives and by recognizing that only they can define the meanings of their experiences, feelings, thoughts, hopes, beliefs, problems, and needs. We cannot speak for them, cannot appropriate their voices as our own. But to listen is to learn, and to learn is to broaden our appreciation of the range of human experiences and possibilities.

In addition, realizing that inequality is socially constructed empowers us to resist participating in it. We have choice in whether to accept our culture's designations of who is valuable and who is not, who is normal and who is abnormal. We don't have to treat light skin, heterosexuality, maleness, and the middle class as superior or right. Instead, we may challenge social views that proclaim arbitrary values for differences and that limit human opportunities.

Three features distinguish this book and support the views I've just discussed. First, I include discussion of diverse classes, ethnicities, races, and sexual orientations whenever research is available. Unfortunately, what I can include is constrained by the limited study of some groups in our society. Regrettably, there is not a great deal of research on men's issues, transgendered and intersexed people, gay and lesbian lives, and other topics that lie outside of what our society defines as the norm. I hope *Gendered Lives* reflects the diversity of human beings better than many current books do.

A second feature of this book is language that includes all readers. I use terms like *he and she, women and men,* and *feminine and masculine* in preference to *he, mankind,* and *men.* Yet inclusive language means more than including women. It also means using language that recognizes other groups our culture has marginalized. For instance, I refer to individuals in intimate relationships as *partners* rather than *spouses,* and I generally refer to *committed relationships* rather than *marriages.* The terms *spouse* and *marriage* exclude lesbians and gay men because our society denies gays and lesbians the legal, material, and social legitimacy accorded to heterosexuals. The terms *spouse* and *marriage* also fail to acknowledge the intimate connection between people who cohabit but choose not to formalize their relationship through marriage. My use of inclusive language is not an effort to be politically correct. Rather, it reflects my unwillingness to contribute to sustaining inequities, even in subtle ways. If I use noninclusive terms such as *spouses,* then I participate in oppressing those whose commitments our society refuses to recognize.

A third way in which *Gendered Lives* reflects awareness of my own limited standpoint and my respect for those whose standpoints differ is the narratives that punctuate this book. In the pages that follow, you'll meet a lot of students—some like you, some quite different. In my course on gender and communication, students keep journals in which they write about issues that arise in our class conversations. Many of my students were kind enough to give me permission to include their ideas in this book. In addition, students at other campuses around the country have written to respond to previous editions of *Gendered Lives,* and some of their comments appear in this edition. I've tried to return their generosity by including a range of individuals and viewpoints, including ones with which I personally disagree. In fact, including ideas with which I disagree—both from students' journal entries and from scholars—is necessary if this book is to reflect the range of ideas about gender and communication that circulate in our culture. A student from a Northeastern college wrote me a letter commenting on this choice.

Hannah's comment reflects a critical openmindedness that fosters learning. As you read this

 HANNAH

When I was reading *Gendered Lives,* I had to keep reminding myself that you were presenting information and that not all points were your personal values and beliefs. I didn't agree with all of your statements or the ideas of others, like the students in their commentaries, but I learned a lot about the ways others see gender. I also learned a lot about how I think about gender by seeing what ideas I agreed with and disagreed with.

book, think about research findings and students' voices, and reflect on how they are like or different from your own beliefs and values. To encourage you to think independently about other students' ideas, I have refrained from evaluating or interpreting the reflections that appear in this book. The students write clearly and eloquently, and I don't want to muffle their voices with my analysis. The student commentaries, my ideas, and your responses to what you read create a circle of learning in which we collaboratively explore gender, communication, and culture.

FEMINISM—FEMINISMS

Finally, in introducing myself to you, I inform you that I am a feminist. The word *feminist* is often misunderstood. Many people, like my student Andrea (see commentary), associate feminism with antimale attitudes or radical acts of protest. Andrea is not alone. Many of my students reject the term *feminist* to describe themselves. Fewer than 20% of college-age women say that they definitely think of themselves as feminists (Fox-Genovese, 1996). Ironically, although most women do not align themselves with feminism, more than two-thirds of women in polls say that the women's movement has made life better, and more than 80% say the movement is still enhancing women's lives (Kaminer, 1993). When feminism is defined as a movement for social, political, and economic equality of women and men, 71% of women and 61% of men say they agree with the movement (Baumgardner & Richards, 2000). This suggests that there is greater reservation about the label "feminist" than about the actual goals, values, and achievements of feminists.

When I talk with students who say they don't consider themselves feminist, we often discover that we agree on most issues relevant to gender but disagree on what feminism means. There's good reason for this. First, feminism is not one single belief or stance but many. Chapter 3 discusses a variety of feminist positions as well as different stances within men's movements. Most people's impressions of feminism have been influenced by media's portrayals of feminism and feminist movements. Beginning with the inaccurate report in the 1960s that feminists burned bras as a protest (which did not occur then), media have consistently misrepresented feminists as man-hating, tough, shrill extremists. Yet that stereotype fails to fit many women and men who define themselves as feminists. Like me, many feminists have good relationships with both women and men, and most are generous and compassionate as well as vocal in challenging inequities in our society. Many women who label themselves feminists are also feminine in many ways: They enjoy wearing femi-

ᕼ ANDREA

I would never call myself a feminist, because that word has so many negative connotations. I don't hate men or anything, and I'm not interested in protesting. I don't want to go around with hacked-off hair and no makeup and sit around bashing men. I do think women and men are equal and should have the same kinds of rights, including equal pay for equal work. But I wouldn't call myself a feminist.

On Feminism

Katha Pollitt is a nationally prominent writer whose columns on current issues have appeared in *The New Yorker, The Nation,* and the *New York Times.* She is also a poet whose first book of poetry won a National Book Critics Circle Award. Here are some of her thoughts on what feminism is—and is not:

> To me, to be a feminist is to answer the question "Are women human?" with a yes. It is not about whether women are better than, worse than or identical with men. . . . It's about justice, fairness and access to the broad range of human experience. . . . It's about women having intrinsic value as persons . . . human beings, in other words. No more, no less. (pp. xii–xiv)

Jennifer Baumgardner and Amy Richards, who define themselves as new feminists, say this about what feminism means:

> Feminism [is] a word that describes a social-justice movement for gender equity and human liberation. . . . By feminists we mean each and every politically and socially conscious woman or man who works for equality within or outside the movement. (pp. 50, 54)

Sources: Baumgardner, J., & Richards, A. (2000). *ManifestA.* New York: Farrar, Straus, & Giroux; Pollitt, K. (1994). *Reasonable creatures: Essays on women and feminism.* New York: Knopf.

nine clothes, experimenting with hairstyles and makeup, and engaging in traditionally feminine activities such as baking bread (one of my favorites), gardening, and interacting with children. Being feminist does not conflict with being feminine.

I define feminism as an active commitment to equality and respect for life. For me, this includes respecting all people, as well as nonhuman forms of life and the earth itself. Simply put, my feminism means I am against oppression, whether it be oppression of women, men, lesbians, African Americans, Jewish individuals, gay men, elderly people, children, animals, or our planet. I don't regard oppression and domination as worthy human values. I believe there are better, more humane and enriching ways to live, and I am convinced we can be part of bringing these alternatives into existence. That is the core of feminism as I define it for myself. During the course of reading this book, you will encounter varied versions of feminism, which should shatter the myth that feminism means the same thing to all people, and should invite you to consider where to position yourself among diverse viewpoints.

Feminism does not just happen. It is an achievement and a process. My own feminism began in the 1970s when a friend first introduced me to some readings that made me aware of discrimination against women. My initial response to this knowledge was denial; I tried to rationalize inequities or repress my knowledge of them, perhaps because recognizing them would be too painful. When denial failed to work, I entered an angry phase. I was bitter about my growing understanding of ways women, including me, were devalued. This anger led me to strike out, sometimes in inappropriate ways and at inappropriate targets. It was a deep anger, directed both toward discrimination against women and toward myself for having been ignorant of it for so long. This angry and embittered phase was necessary for me to absorb what I was learning, but it could not lead me forward in any constructive sense.

Finally, I transformed the anger into an abiding commitment to being part of change, not so much for myself as for future generations. I want our society to be fairer, to respect differences, and to affirm all people more than it has historically. Years later, when I began to study gender issues, I learned that the path I had traveled to achieve my feminist identity is not uncommon: Denial, anger, and transformation to constructive commitment are stages many individuals undergo as they dislodge one identity and understanding of how the world operates and move forward to alternate ones.

Becoming Aware

Reading this book will enlarge your awareness of gender—how it is shaped and expressed in contexts ranging from the political arena to intimate relationships. The awareness you gain will enable you to understand yourself and society better. At the same time, you may be unsettled as you read this book and discuss gender, culture, and communication in your course. If you are a woman, you may find it disturbing to learn the extent to which Western culture discounts your experiences and limits your opportunities. I also realize a number of those reading this book—both women and men—have been raped, sexually abused, sexually harassed, or battered. Some of you have eating disorders; some have suffered job discrimination; some of you have been taunted for not embodying current social expectations about being male or female. Reading *Gendered Lives* is likely to stir up these issues in your personal life. If you don't wish to deal with these, then you may choose to forgo or delay study in this area. If, however, you are ready to wrestle with serious personal matters, then this book should help you understand more about why issues in your life are not only personal but also political. They reflect widespread cultural biases that define unrealistic expectations for both men and women, marginalize women, condone violence and aggression, and promote inequities.

If you are a man, reading this book may increase your awareness of ways in which cultural views of masculinity constrain your options. You may be uncomfortable learning about social expectations for men to perform, succeed, be self-sufficient, repress feelings, and put work ahead of family. You may also be surprised to learn how your sex advantages you in ways that you may not have noticed. As a

Julia—the Author—Comments

I want to comment directly on an issue that may occur to you as you read this book. Occasionally, a student says that *Gendered Lives* "bashes men." When I hear such a comment, I am genuinely puzzled, because I don't think of myself as a male basher. For 27 years I've been married to a wonderful man; I have many male friends and colleagues whom I like and admire, and I've done as much to mentor male students as female ones. When I ask students to explain why they think the book bashes men, they tell me it's because *Gendered Lives* gives more attention to discrimination against women than to discrimination against men. They are correct in this observation, but the difference in coverage is not because I am promoting a particular agenda.

Like any other scholar, what I write depends largely on the research and facts available. Frankly, there is a great deal more information on discrimination against women than against men, and this is reflected in the book's content. It's also the case that in general (and there are exceptions) women face more discrimination than men do. For example, although both men and women experience violence from an intimate partner, 95% of people who are known to be physically abused by a romantic partner are women (Hasenauer, 1997, National Coalition Against Domestic Violence, 1999, Wood, 2001b). It would be inaccurate to give equal space to discussion of men and women who are physically abused by their partners. The same is true of sexual harassment: Although members of both sexes are sexually harassed, most victims are women. The only way I could present an absolutely gender-balanced discussion of sexual harassment would be to misrepresent the facts.

In this book, I have included information about men and men's issues—more, in fact, than any other book for a course in gender and communication. In the chapters that follow, you'll find information about men's movements and men's increased investment in fathering, pressures men face to be successful and make money, and stereotypes that limit men in the workplace and in personal relationships.

I think gender roles limit all of us—both men and women. Research I've included throughout this book shows how we are all restricted by some social expectations of women and men. I hope that as you read this book you'll perceive that the coverage is fair and that it reflects current research and social patterns.

result of what you read, you may decide that you don't want to be part of a social system that values some people more than others.

Becoming aware of inequities in social life may prompt you to criticize practices and attitudes that sustain discrimination and disadvantage. Yet some people will dismiss thoughtful criticisms as whining or unjustified complaining. Women who call attention to attitudes and practices that disadvantage women are sometimes accused of male bashing. Men who speak out against discrimination against women are sometimes regarded as wimps or disloyal to men. These are immature responses because they do not reflect a willingness to engage the substance of the criticism. If you want to be part of improving social life, you must be willing to be

I don't want to be lumped with all men. I am not sexist; I don't discriminate against women; I believe in gender equality and try to practice it in my relationships with women. It really makes me angry when people bash males as if we are all oppressors or something. I don't oppress women or anyone else, and I don't want to be blamed for unfair things that others do.

open-minded about your own views and those of others.

In his commentary, Patrick makes an important point when he says that he personally doesn't discriminate against women. We need to distinguish between the actions and attitudes of individuals and the social practices and values of our culture. This book doesn't suggest that individual men are bad, oppressive, or sexist. The point is that Western culture as a whole has constructed inequalities between women and men, and this continues in our era. The problem, then, is not individual men or women. Rather, it is the social system that accords unequal value and opportunity on the basis of sex, skin color, sexual orientation, and other factors. This kind of prejudice diminishes us all. It limits our appreciation of human diversity by falsely defining a very restricted zone of what is good, normal, and worthy of respect. Regardless of whether you are privileged or oppressed by social evaluations of what is normal and good, studying gender, communication, and culture may be unsettling. If you are seriously disturbed by what you read, you might find it helpful to talk with your instructor or to visit the counseling center at your school.

WHY I WROTE THIS BOOK

I invested the time and energy to write *Gendered Lives* because I believe that change in how we view and enact gender is needed and possible and that the knowledge in this book can empower individuals to change their personal lives and our shared world. Since the first edition appeared, I've received many positive responses from students in my classes as well as from students around the nation. I am most gratified when readers like Carlotta (see p. 9), who attends a Southwestern university, tell me the book made a difference in their lives.

In addition to continuing to emphasize our potential as agents of change, this edition of *Gendered Lives* includes research that has been published since the Fourth Edition went to press or that I had not read at that time. For example, this edition offers an enlarged discussion of women's sports and media coverage of them. Chapter 3 now includes expanded coverage of the third wave of U.S. feminism, which has gained visibility and coherence since I wrote the last edition. New research on the roles of fathers is included in Chapters 4 and 6, and recent scholarship on gendered violence, including violence against men, appears in Chapter 11. At the request of readers, I've added more research on gender in non-Western cultures and more biographical information on major historical figures such as Betty Friedan and Sojourner Truth. This edition also identifies Web sites that may be of interest to readers. Punctuating each chapter are FYI inserts that highlight important information about gender. I call your attention to this information to emphasize that knowledge is a critical basis for sound opinions, attitudes, and behavior regarding gender.

Change is needed. In the chapters that follow, you'll learn about the extent to which our society creates inequities by defining men, light skin, middle- and upper-class status, and heterosexuality as superior to women, darker skin, lower-class status, and lesbian and gay orientations. I hope to make you more aware of the impact of these inequities on the psychological, interpersonal, professional, economic, and material circumstances of people's lives. Is it right, for instance, that at least 50% of women working outside of the home experience sexual harassment in their jobs? Is there any way to justify the fact that every 12 seconds, every day in the United States, a woman is battered by her intimate partner, or that each day four women die from battering? Is it fair that men who want to spend time with their families may be judged negatively in professional contexts? Is there any reason why a typical woman working full time outside the home earns less than a typical man working full time (Steinberg, 2001)? Is it right that mothers have an advantage over fathers in gaining custody of children?

If you were unaware of these issues and you think they should be changed, then read on. Becoming aware of the ways in which our culture establishes and communicates inequities is necessary, but that alone does not lead to progress. In fact, concentrating exclusively on what is wrong tends to depress us and paralyze impulses toward reform. Awareness of gender inequities must be coupled with belief that change is possible. A bit of historical perspective should convince us of this. In the 1800s, women weren't allowed to vote — they had no voice in the government and in making laws that affected them. They also had no access to a university education, could not own property if they married, and were barred from participating in many professions. Through individual action and social movements, many of these blatant sex inequities have been changed. Since 1972, schools receiving federal funds have been required not to discriminate against women. When my mother had a child in 1958, her employer dismissed her because he believed that a mother should not be actively engaged in a profession. She had no voice and no legal recourse. We now have laws to protect women against unfair employment practices. In the last decade, sexual harassment has been named and brought to public awareness, and in February 1992, the courts ruled that victims of sexual harassment may sue institutions for compensatory as well as punitive damages.

Paralleling these legal changes are substantial transformations in how we view

 CARLOTTA

What I learned from your book and my class has changed my life. I see so much now about women and men that I never even saw before. It's like I can see clearly now, and I can be critical of things that I took for granted before taking this course. And I understand that I have choices about how I will act and what I will believe. The knowledge I've gained will help me make more informed choices throughout the rest of my life.

ourselves and each other as women and men. Our culture once defined women as too frail and delicate for hard manual or intellectual work. Today, women pursue careers in business, construction, science, education, politics, and the military. Despite lingering barriers, women are doing things and defining themselves in ways not previously possible for women in the United States. Views of men, too, have changed. At the turn of the century, our society defined manliness in terms of physical strength and bravery. Following the Industrial Revolution, the ability to earn a good salary became the social standard of manliness. Today, many men are challenging social definitions of men as income producers and seeking greater opportunities to participate in family life and personal relationships. You have options for what you will do and who you will be that were not available to your parents. Recognizing that views of gender have evolved fuels our conviction that further changes can be realized.

COMMUNICATION AS THE FULCRUM OF CHANGE

Change comes about through communication, which is the heart of social life and social evolution. Through communication we identify and challenge current cultural views that constrain individuals and create inequities. We also rely on communication to define alternatives to the status quo and persuade others to share our visions. For example, in 1848 Elizabeth Cady Stanton galvanized support for the women's rights movement through her eloquent speeches. Public discourse sparks and guides collective efforts at political reform. Yet other kinds of communication also instigate change. Perhaps you talk with a friend about gender inequities, and as a result your friend alters her perceptions. Maybe a teacher discusses sexual harassment with his class, and a student is empowered to bring charges against a man who has been harassing her. You talk with your father about ways in which current leave policies disadvantage working mothers, and he persuades his company to revise its policies. Wherever there is change, we find communication. Through your public, social, and interpersonal communication, you are a powerful agent of change—someone who can bring about transformations in yourself and the society in which we jointly participate.

Information is a key part of the foundation for being an effective change agent. Before you can define what needs to be different, you must first know what exists now and what it implies. To be a credible catalyst for change, you must be informed about gender inequities and how they are created and sustained by communication within our culture. You must understand how conventional views of masculinity and femininity lead to inequities, how they reflect cultural values, and how institutional, social, and personal communication sustain the status quo. In addition, you should consider diverse perspectives on gender issues rather than assuming there is one single truth. Reading *Gendered Lives* and taking this course will inform you about these issues and provide a range of viewpoints on them. Then you can make informed choices about what you believe and about what identity you wish to fashion for yourself. You may want to change your identity and how you view gender, or you may be entirely satisfied with your identity and with traditional gender arrangements in our culture. Either stance is grounded if it is an *informed* choice, but no choice is wise if it is not based on information and serious reflection.

THE CHALLENGE OF STUDYING COMMUNICATION, GENDER, AND CULTURE

Studying communication, gender, and culture requires courage because it involves us in unsettling questions about our culture and our personal identities. We have to be willing to consider new ideas openly and to risk values and identities that are familiar to us. Further, with awareness comes responsibility. Once we are informed about gender and communication, we can no longer sit back passively as if this were not our concern. It is our concern both because it affects each of us directly and because we are part of a collective world. Thus, how we act—or fail to act—influences our shared culture.

Because studying communication, gender, and culture is unsettling, it is not easy. Yet it can be very worthwhile. By questioning constructed inequality, we empower ourselves to do more than unthinkingly reproduce the cultural patterns we have inherited. By involving ourselves in communication that enlarges others' awareness and revises cultural practices, we assume active roles in creating personal and collective lives that are fairer, more humane, and infinitely more enriching than what might otherwise be possible. That is the goal of *Gendered Lives*.

DISCUSSION QUESTIONS

1. I state that books do not present objective information. Do you agree or disagree? If books aren't neutral and unbiased, how do we know what to believe and what to do with ideas in books? Could an objective, neutral book be written?

2. I explained that who I am affects what I have written. What is your image of me based on the information I've provided? How does that image affect your perceptions of the book? How do you think my identity shaped my thinking about issues of communication, gender, and culture?

3. What is your own standpoint? Using my self-description as a guideline, discuss how your identity influenced your choice to take this course, as well as how it may affect your perceptions of topics in the book and the course. Have you been privileged and disadvantaged by your membership in various groups designated by our society? How have your privileges and disadvantages affected your opportunities, knowledge of issues, interests, abilities, goals, and so on?

4. This is a good time to familiarize yourself with InfoTrac® College Edition. Access the InfoTrac College Edition Web page at *http://www.infotrac-college.com/wadsworth*. Type in the password from the card you received with your free subscription. You will be at the opening screen. Select Keywords and type "women and language." Read several of the articles that appear, to see the kind of current research in the area of gender, communication, and culture.

5. If each of us is informed and constrained by our own standpoint, to what extent is it possible to understand others? Can someone who is White, in the upper socio-economic class, heterosexual, and Protestant really understand the experiences of a Hispanic man, a Latina, a gay person?

6. I explain why I use language that is inclusive. What do you think of modifying language to reduce exclusion? Is *partner* preferable to *spouse?* Is *he or she* better than *he?* Does language make a difference in how we think?

7. Write out *your* definition of feminism. What differences has it made and can it make in your personal life and our society? When you've completed this course, review this definition to see if it still expresses what feminism means to you.

8. I discuss change as one of my goals for writing *Gendered Lives.* What changes do you think are most needed in our society? How are these related to issues of communication, gender, and culture?

1

The Study of Communication, Gender, and Culture

I f you tune into *Oprah* or other popular talk shows, the chances are good that you'll see guests discussing gender and communication. If you go to a bookstore, you'll find dozens of popular advice books that promise to help men and women communicate with each other. The public's fascination with gender and communication is mirrored by college students' interest. Gender and communication is a rapidly expanding area of study in colleges and universities around the nation. Many campuses, like mine, cannot meet the high student demand for enrollment in these courses.

This chapter introduces communication, gender, and culture as an area of study. After discussing how learning about relationships among gender, communication, and culture can empower you personally and professionally, we will look at the key concepts that form the framework of this book. This will provide us with a common vocabulary for the chapters that follow.

COMMUNICATION, GENDER, AND CULTURE AS AN AREA OF STUDY

Two reasons explain skyrocketing enrollments in gender and communication courses: (1) expanding knowledge about intersections among gender, communication, and culture and (2) student interest.

▪ Knowledge of Gender, Communication, and Culture

Had you attended college in the 1970s, you would not have found a textbook like this one. Classes that explore various aspects of gender have become widespread only in the last fifteen years. Before this, research on gender and communication was limited and offered no extensive understanding of how both interact with culture. An explosion of interdisciplinary scholarship has generated rich insight into how gender is created and sustained through communication within cultures. Research has also shown us how gender shapes individuals' communication and how, in turn, communication influences culture, including its views of women and men. In *Gendered Lives*, you'll encounter much of this research, which will allow you to appreciate the profound connections among gender, communication, and culture.

▪ Student Interest

A second reason for rising enrollment in courses in gender and communication is students' interest in the subject. Differences between women's and men's communication show up, for example, when heterosexual intimate partners try to work through problems using distinct styles of conflict management, when male and female co-workers have different preferences for how to lead a meeting, when teachers interact differently with female and male students, when media represent men and women in sex-stereotyped ways, when female and male political candidates say similar things but the public evaluates them differently. In these areas as well as others, gender affects how we interact, and social views of gender influence how women and men are perceived. Given the pervasiveness of gender and communication in our lives, it's little wonder students seek courses to help them be more effective in all their interactions.

▪ The Value of Studying Communication, Gender, and Culture

Learning about relationships among communication, gender, and culture serves two important goals. First, it enhances your appreciation of complex ways in which communication, gender, and culture interact to affect society and your personal life. Reading this book should increase your understanding of the extent to which cultural values and habits influence your views of masculinity and femininity. In addition, you will become more aware of ways in which cultural expectations of gender are communicated to you in your daily life. In turn, this should expand your insight into how your own communication affirms or challenges prevailing cultural prescriptions for gender. This enables you to be reflective and active as you craft your personal identity and participate in cultural conversations about gender.

Second, studying communication, gender, and culture should strengthen your effectiveness as a communicator. Once you understand how culture shapes gender and gender shapes communication, you'll find you listen more perceptively to what others say. By extension, learning about general differences in how women and men communicate should enlarge your ability to appreciate the distinct validity of diverse communication styles. This allows you to interact more constructively and insightfully with others whose ways of communicating may differ from your own. A broad and flexible repertoire of communication skills is especially important today because we are a global community in which diversity is a constant. Effective participation in contemporary life demands that we understand varied individuals with whom we interact and that we cultivate a range of communication skills in ourselves.

THE MEANING OF GENDER IN A TRANSITIONAL ERA

These days we hear a lot about problems between the sexes and about the gender gap. We're told that men and women misunderstand each other and don't speak the same language. Talk shows feature guests who discuss women who love too much and whether women should have active roles in combat duty. In magazines we read about the new fathers who are actively involved with their children. Men are often confused when women want to continue talking after an issue is settled; some women become frustrated when men seem not to listen or respond to what they say. What men and women expect of each other and themselves is no longer clear.

Confusing Attitudes

If you are like most people who have been socialized in the United States in the past 25 years, then you have a number of attitudes about gender and what it means. You probably don't subscribe to your grandparents' ideals of manhood and womanhood. It is likely that you think both women and men should be able to pursue careers and both should be involved in homemaking and child care. You probably have taken classes taught by women and by men, and some were quite good whereas others were not so interesting. You are not surprised when a woman knows something about car maintenance or a man prepares a good meal. These experiences and your attitudes about them depart from those of former generations. Americans as a whole have enlarged their perspectives on women's and men's roles and abilities.

 MICHAEL

The other day in class we were talking about whether women should have combat duty. I'm really uncomfortable with where I stand on this, since I *think* one way but I *feel* another. I do think women should have to serve just as much as men do. I've never thought it was right that they didn't have to fight. And I think women are just as competent as men at most things, and could probably be good soldiers. But then when I think about my mom or my sister or my girlfriend being in the trenches, having to kill other people,

(continued)

(Michael continued)

maybe being a prisoner who is tortured and assaulted, I just feel that's wrong. It doesn't seem right for women to be involved in killing when they're the ones who give life. Then, too, I want to protect my girlfriend and sister and mom from the ugliness and danger of war. But then this other part of me says, "Hey, guy, you know that kind of protectiveness is a form of chauvinism." I just don't know where I stand on this except that I'm glad I don't have to decide whether to send women into combat!

Yet, if you're like most of your peers, there are also a number of gender issues about which you are confused. Many people believe women should have equal opportunities in public and work life, but they think women should not be involved in actual wartime combat. Although a majority of young adults believe both parents should participate in childrearing, most people also assume the mother, not the father, should take time off from a career to be with a child during the early years of life. You may support equal opportunity in education, but you think colleges should be able to offer more and bigger scholarships to male athletes. You may believe women are as effective as men in management, yet perhaps you're still more comfortable with a man as your supervisor.

FYI

Changing Traditions

Remember the media hubbub in 1995, when the first woman joined the Corps at The Citadel, which had been all male for 151 years? Those who said women didn't belong at the prestigious military school felt their opinions were justified when she left after only six days. But that woman was just the first, and others have stayed the course that she initiated. According to Major General John Grinalds, a faculty member at the school, "The Citadel has emerged from its troubled beginnings with coeducation. . . . Those challenges have made The Citadel stronger than ever." Consider these facts:

In May of 1999, the first female cadet graduated from The Citadel. She completed the training in only three years.

In December of 1999, an African American woman was the first woman to graduate from The Citadel and enter full-time military service as a second lieutenant in the Marines.

In the summer of 1999, a woman led the military training for new cadets.

In 2000, the admissions office at The Citadel reported an increase of 33% in the number of women applicants since the previous year.

In 2000, the 1650-member Corps at The Citadel included 63 women.

 Visit the Citadel's home page at **http://www.citadel.edu.** Click on Cadets on Video, Webcam, and Photopage. Do these features of the site suggest that women have been well integrated into life at the Citadel?

Source: Grinalds, J. (2000, February 15). New look, proven values at The Citadel. *Raleigh News and Observer,* p. 9A.

When we grapple with issues like these, we discover that our attitudes are less than clear even to ourselves. On one level, many of us think women and men are equal in all important respects; yet on another level, where deeply ingrained values and beliefs reside, we have some very traditional feelings and views. Conflicts in our own attitudes and values make us unsure of what we really believe and of who we really are. We live in a transitional time in which we no longer embrace former views of men and women, yet we haven't become comfortable with alternative images of the sexes. This makes our lives and our relationships interesting, unsettled, and sometimes very frustrating!

Differences Between Women and Men

Are women and men really as different as pop psychologists would have us believe? Certainly there are some important differences between the sexes that we need to understand. There is also a great deal of variation within the sexes with regard to diverse experiences, sexual orientations, races, and classes. And there are a great many similarities between women and men—ways in which the two sexes are more alike than different.

Because there are similarities between the sexes and variations within each, it is difficult to come up with language for discussing general differences in communication patterns. Terms like *women* and *men* are troublesome because they imply a sameness across all women and all men. When we say, "Women's communication is more personal than men's," the statement is true of most, but not all, women and most, but not all, men. Certainly not all women engage in personal talk and not all men avoid it. Thinking and speaking as if there is some stable essence to women and some stable, distinct essence to men is referred to as **essentializing**,* the tendency to reduce something or someone to certain essential characteristics. When we essentialize, we distort by implying that all members of a sex are alike in basic respects

---

*Boldfaced terms appear in the Glossary at the end of the book.

I read John Gray's book, and I could identify men and women who were just like he described them—you know, from Mars or Venus. But I also know some men who aren't at all like the ones in his book—they don't go into "caves," which Gray says all men do. And I know some women, myself included, who do go into caves—just retreat from others and conversation to sort stuff out. But Gray says women don't go into caves—they talk with others. What I think is that you can't say anything about all women or all men. There may be generalizations, but there are also exceptions.

and that they are distinct from the other sex in these respects (Spelman, 1988; Wood, 1993c; Young, 1992). Essentializing obscures the range of characteristics possessed by individual women and men and conceals differences among members of each sex. In this book we will discuss generalizations about women and men, but this does not imply any essential, universal qualities possessed by all members of a sex. We'll also take time to notice exceptions to generalizations about gender—a point Elaine makes in her commentary.

To think constructively about differences and similarities, we need to understand what gender and sex are, how they are influenced by the culture in which we live, and how communication reflects, expresses, and re-creates gender in our everyday lives. In *Gendered Lives,* we'll consider different images of masculinity and femininity and examine why such diverse views exist and what practical implications they have. To explore this, we'll need to consider more than gender alone. We will also examine both how communication creates our gender identity and how we use communication to express our masculinity or femininity in interaction with others. A third focus of our attention will be culture, because gender is embedded within culture and reflects the values and assumptions of the larger society. To begin our study, we need some preliminary definitions of the central concepts in this book: sex, gender, culture, and communication.

RELATIONSHIPS AMONG GENDER, CULTURE, AND COMMUNICATION

When asked to discuss a particular aspect of nature, John Muir, who founded the Sierra Club, said he could not discuss any single part of the natural world in isolation. He noted that each part is "hitched to the universe," meaning it is connected to all other parts of nature. Gender, culture, and communication are interlinked, and they are "hitched to the whole universe." Because this is so, we cannot study any one of them without understanding a good deal about the other two. What gender means depends heavily on cultural values and practices; the ways a culture defines masculinity and femininity lead to expectations about how individual women and men should act and communicate; and how individuals communicate establishes meanings of gender that, in turn, influence cultural views. Clearly, sex, gender, culture, and communication interact in elaborate, ongoing patterns. These concepts are complex, so we will clarify them in the following sections. This will allow us to share common meanings and vocabulary in the chapters that follow.

Gender and Sex

Although many people use the terms *gender* and *sex* interchangeably, the two terms have very distinct meanings (Reeder, 1996). Sex is a designation based on biology, whereas gender is socially and psychologically constructed. Each of us has some qualities that our culture labels feminine and some it defines as masculine. How much of each set we have indicates our gender within the current social order. Often the two go together so that most men are primarily masculine and most women are primarily feminine. In other cases, a male is more feminine than most men, or a woman is more masculine than the majority of women. Sex and gender are inconsistent for transsexual individuals, who feel they are trapped in the body of one sex but identify strongly with the other sex (Money, 1988). The term *gender* refers to how an individual sees himself or herself and how he or she acts in terms of masculine and feminine tendencies. In many respects, your gender represents an area of potential choice for you, because you can change it more easily than your sex. Because sex is the less complex concept, we'll explain it first, then discuss gender.

Sex. Sex is classified by biological characteristics. Our society uses genetic and biological qualities to define whether a person is male or female. Designation of sex is usually based on external genitalia (penis and testes in males, clitoris and vagina in females) and internal sex organs (ovaries and uterus in females, prostate in males). Sex is determined by chromosomes, which program how a fetus develops. Of the 23 pairs of chromosomes that direct human development, only one pair determines sex. The chromosome pair that affects sex usually has two chromosomes, and one of these is always an X. The presence or absence of a Y chromosome determines whether a fetus will develop into what we recognize as male or female. Thus, an XX creates female sex, whereas an XY creates male sex. Genetic research indicates that the X chromosome has a more complex molecular structure. This may explain why males, who typically have only a single X chromosome, are more vulnerable to a number of X-linked recessive conditions.

You might have noticed that I qualified discussion of genetic determination of sex by using words like *usually* and *typically.* That's because there are occasional departures from the standard XX or XY structure. Some sex chromosomes are XO, XXX, XXY, or XYY. As long as there is a single Y chromosome, a fetus will develop into what we label male, although he may differ in some respects from males with the more standard XY pattern. For instance, men with XYY chromosomes may be more aggressive than men with XY chromosomes.

Sex is also influenced by hormones, another biological factor. Even before birth, hormones affect us. Beginning only seven weeks after conception, hormones influence sexual differentiation in the fetus. They determine the development of internal sex organs, which control reproductive capacities. In most cases, biology works smoothly so that the hormones direct development of female or male reproductive organs that are in line with external genitalia. Occasionally, however, fetal development doesn't proceed routinely, and a child is born with ambiguous or

Most of us think of male and female as categories that are both clear and adequate. However, sometimes the categories aren't so clear cut. For instance, intersexuals are born with ambiguous genitals and may differ from most people in hormonal, chromosomal, and physiological ways. For many years, infants who were born with ambiguous genitals routinely underwent "clarifying surgery," which reconstructed genitals to appear more typically male or female. Doctors have decided which sex the child was "meant to be" and advised parents to authorize "clarifying surgery" and then bring the child up as the sex it was "meant to be."

But is it possible that intersexed people aren't "abnormal" or in need of fixing? Recently, a number of scholars, scientists, doctors, and laypersons have advocated acceptance of intersexuality. Adult intersexuals within the transgender movement want to change society's view that they are abnormal. To further their goal, they have formed the Intersex Society of North America (ISNA). According to ISNA, genital variability is not a disease or "problem"; it's just another form of human variation. In other words, as Suzanne Kessler says, "There is no one best way to be male or female or any other gender possibility" (p. 132).

Sources: Kessler, S. (1998). *Lessons from the intersexed.* NJ: Rutgers University Press; Lorber, J. (2001). *Gender inequality: Feminist theories and politics,* 2nd ed. Los Angeles: Roxbury.

mixed sex—the child has some biological characteristics of each sex. People whose internal and external genitalia are inconsistent are called **hermaphrodites.**

When pregnancy proceeds routinely, fetuses with a Y chromosome are bathed in androgens that ensure development of male sex organs, and fetuses without a Y chromosome receive relatively little androgen, so female sex organs develop. In some cases, however, a pregnant woman does not produce the hormones conducive to conventional sexual development of a fetus. More typically, when customary hormones are not present, it is due to outside intervention. Hormones may be administered externally, as when doctors give a synthetic form of progesterone to lessen the likelihood of miscarriage. Because this stimulates male sex organs to develop, a genetically female fetus (XX) who is exposed to excessive progesterone (progestin is the synthetic form) may develop male genitalia. The opposite is also true: If a male fetus is deprived of progesterone during the critical period of sexual differentiation, his male genitalia may not develop and he will appear physically female (Money, 1986; Pinksy, Erickson, & Schimke, 1999).

The influence of hormones does not end with birth. They continue to affect our development by determining whether we will menstruate, how much body hair we will have and where it will grow, how muscular we will be, and so forth. Because male fetuses receive heavier amounts of hormones, they become sensitized to hormonal influence. Researchers currently think this may be why males are more sensitive than females to hormonal activity, especially during puberty (Jacklin, 1989; Tavris, 1992).

Because research on biological sexuality is still relatively new, there are many questions for which we lack conclusive answers. For instance, among scientists opinion is divided about whether sex hormones affect sexual orientation (Adler, 1990; Money, 1988) and cognitive abilities (Adler, 1989; Bleier, 1986). Also, there is controversy over whether high levels of testosterone result in aggression and violence. For many years it was widely believed that males' higher levels of testosterone caused aggression. Recent research, however, suggests the connection between hormones and behavior is not direct but mediated by social factors. It appears that both boys and girls are fairly aggressive and engage in rough play until about age 3, when most children figure out that they are male or female. Once young girls realize they are female and understand social expectations of females, they tend to become less aggressive. On the other hand, when boys realize they are male and grasp social expectations of males, they often become more physically aggressive (A. Campbell, 1993; Fagot, Leinbach, & Hagan, 1986). This suggests that biological sex does not directly determine levels of aggression.

What we do know with confidence is that, however strong the influence of biology may be, it seldom, if ever, determines behaviors. It *influences* behavior in greater or lesser amounts, but it doesn't *determine* behavior, personality, and so on. Biology also doesn't determine the meaning that members of a culture assign to particular behaviors—which ones are valued, which ones devalued. More important than whether biological differences exist is how we treat differences. There is consensus among researchers that environment is at least as great an influence on human development as biology, and a majority of researchers conclude environment is the stronger of the two factors in influencing what we think, feel, and do. Awareness of environment in shaping our identities moves us into discussion of a second concept: gender.

Gender. Gender is a considerably more complex concept than sex. There is nothing a person does to acquire her or his sex. It is a classification based on genetic and physical factors and one that is enduring. Gender, however, is neither innate nor necessarily stable. It is acquired through interaction in a social world, and it changes over time. One way to understand gender is to think of it as what we learn about sex. We are born male or female—a classification based on biology—but we learn to be masculine and feminine. Gender is a social construction that varies across cultures, over time within a given culture, and in relation to the other gender. We'll elaborate on this definition in our discussion.

Gender is a social, symbolic creation. Mary Wollstonecraft may have been the first to recognize the social character of gender when, in 1792, she declared that most differences between the sexes are socially created, not natural. The meaning of gender grows out of a society's values, beliefs, and preferred ways of organizing collective life. A culture constructs and sustains meanings of gender by investing

BISHETTA

I remember when I was very little, maybe 5 or so. My brother and I were playing outside in the garden and Mom saw us. Both of us were coated with dirt—our clothes, our skin, everything. Mom came up to the edge of the garden and shouted, "Bishetta, you get out of that garden right now. Just look at you. Now what do you think folks will think of a dirty little girl? You don't want people to think you're not a lady, do you?" She didn't say a word to my brother, who was just as dirty.

BOB

What I always thought was unfair in my family was the way my folks responded to failures my sisters and I had. Like once my sister Maryellen tried out for cheerleader, and she wasn't picked. So she was crying and upset, and Mom was telling her that it was okay and that she was a good person and everyone knew that and that winning wasn't everything. And when Dad came home he said the same things—telling her she was okay even if she wasn't picked. But when I didn't make the junior varsity football team, Dad went bonkers! He asked me what had gone wrong. I told him nothing, that other guys were just better than I had been. But he'd have none of that. He told me I couldn't give up and had to work harder, and he expected me to make the team next season. He even offered to hire a coach for me. It just wasn't okay for me not to succeed.

biological sex with social significance. Consider current meanings of masculinity and femininity in America. To be masculine is to be strong, ambitious, successful, rational, and emotionally controlled. Although these requirements are perhaps less rigid than they were in earlier eras (House, Dallinger, & Kilgallen, 1998), they remain largely intact. Those we consider "real men" still don't cry or need others to help them; "real men" are successful and powerful in their professional and public lives (Kimmel, 2000a, 2000b).

Femininity in the 1990s is also relatively consistent with earlier views, although there is increasing latitude in what is considered appropriate for women. To be feminine is to be physically attractive, deferential, unaggressive, emotional, nurturing, and concerned with people and relationships. Those who embody the cultural definition of femininity still don't outdo men (especially their partners), disregard others' feelings, or put their needs ahead of others'. Also, "real women" still look good (preferably very pretty and/or sexy), adore children, and care about homemaking. For all of the changes in our views of women and men, the basic blueprint remains relatively constant (Cancian, 1989; Kerr, 1997, 1999; Riessman, 1990; Wood, 1993a).

Gender, by definition, is learned. Socially endorsed views of masculinity and femininity are taught to individuals through a variety of cultural means. From infancy on, we are encouraged to conform to the gender that society prescribes for us. Young girls are often cautioned "Don't be selfish— share with others," "Be careful— don't hurt yourself," and "Don't get messy." They are praised for looking pretty, expressing emotions, and being nice to others. Young boys, in contrast, are more likely to be admonished "Don't be a sissy," "Go after what you want," and "Don't cry." Usually they are reinforced for strength, independence, and success, particularly in competitive arenas. When socialization is effective in teaching us to adopt the gender society prescribes for our sex, biological males learn to be masculine and biological females become feminine.

"Sex brought us together, but gender drove us apart."

So far we've focused on how individuals learn gender, yet gender is not a strictly personal quality. Rather, it is a complex set of interrelated cultural ideas that stipulate the social *meaning* of sex. Because social definitions of gender permeate public and private life, we see them as normal, natural, and right. When the practices and structures that make up social life constantly represent women and men in particular ways, it is difficult to imagine that masculinity and femininity could be defined differently. Later chapters show how a range of institutional structures and communicative processes sustain social views of masculinity and femininity.

The fact that the social meanings of gender are taught to us does not mean we are passive recipients of cultural meanings. We evaluate cultural meanings, and we can influence them (West & Zimmerman, 1987). In our choices to accept cultural prescriptions or to reject them, we affect the meanings our society endorses. Those individuals who internalize cultural prescriptions for gender reinforce traditional views by behaving in ways that support prevailing ideas about masculinity and femininity. Other people, who reject conventional prescriptions and step outside of social meanings for gender, often provoke changes in cultural expectations. In the early part of the 19th century, for instance, many women challenged social views that asserted women were not entitled to vote or pursue higher education. In voicing their objections through marches, organizing, and political action, these suffragists departed from conventional expectations of women as quiet and unassertive (Simon & Danziger, 1991). In defying their era's definition of women, these individuals transformed social views of women and the rights to which they are entitled.

The Gender Blur

Cross-dressing is not new to our era. Throughout history, a number of people have dressed and behaved other than was typical for their biological sex (Griggs, 1998). For example, the novelist known as George Sand was actually Amandine Aurore Lucile Dudevant, a very stylish cross-dresser and an aficionado of fine cigars.

Mary Edwards Walker was the first woman commissioned as a surgeon in the Union Army in the American Civil War. To practice medicine on the field, she abandoned her petticoats for a modified version of the uniform male officers wore. Walker discovered she preferred the comfort and freedom of men's clothes, so after the war she appeared in full drag with bow tie and top hat to advocate dress reform for women. Unfortunately for Walker, public attitudes were not in her favor, and she was arrested numerous times for appearing in public when not dressed appropriately for a woman!

And then there's Parinyua Kiatbusaba, a Thai gay transvestite who is called *kratoey*, which means "lady boy." Kiatbusaba also happens to be a champion kickboxer who wears lipstick, eye shadow, and pink nail polish when he goes in the ring to pummel his opponents. "Inside, I'm a woman," he says (Spayde, 1998, p. 55).

Meanings of gender are also changed by communication less public and less collective than social movements. Role models, for instance, provide individuals with visible alternatives to traditional views. Two of my colleagues have infants, whom they sometimes bring to the office. When students see a female professor teaching with her baby nearby, and when they confer with a male faculty member while he rocks his baby, the students encounter an alternative definition of professionalism—one that recognizes that men and women can be professionals and parents simultaneously. Concrete embodiments of alternatives to conventional roles create new possibilities for our own lives. We also influence ideas about gender as we interact casually with friends. When one woman encourages another to be more assertive and to confront her supervisor about problems, she may instigate change in what her friend sees as appropriate behavior for women. Similarly, when one man tells another that time with his family is a top priority, his friend has to rethink and perhaps change his own views of men's roles. As these examples indicate, there is a reciprocal relationship between individual communication and cultural views of gender: Each influences the other in an ongoing spiral that creates and re-creates the meanings of masculinity and femininity.

A good example of the way we remake the meaning of gender is the concept of **androgyny**. In the 1970s, researchers coined the word *androgyny* by combining the Greek word *aner* or *andros,* which means "man," and the Greek word *gyne,* which means "woman." As you may know, androgynous individuals reject rigid sex roles and embody qualities that the culture considers feminine and masculine. For example, androgynous women and men are both nurturing and assertive, both strong and sensitive. Many of us don't want to be restricted to the social prescriptions of a single gender, and we cultivate both masculine and feminine qualities in ourselves. As Miguel points out in his commentary, we should value the full range of human qualities—those the culture labels feminine and those it labels masculine.

To realize the arbitrariness of the meanings of gender, we need only consider varying ways different cultures define masculinity and femininity. Many years ago, anthropologist Margaret Mead (1935/1968) reported three distinctive gender patterns in New Guinea societies she studied. Among Arapesh people, both women and men conform closely to what we consider feminine behavior. Both are passive, peaceful, and deferential, and both nurture others, especially young children. The Mundugumor tribe socializes both women and men to be aggressive, independent, and competitive. Mothers are not nurturant and spend very little time with newborn babies, weaning them early instead. Within the Tchambuli society, genders are the converse of current ones in America: Women are domineering and sexually aggressive, whereas men are considered delicate and are taught to wear decorative clothes and curl their hair so that they will be attractive to women.

In some cultures, a person's gender is considered changeable (Kessler & McKenna, 1978), so someone born male may choose to live and be regarded as female, and vice versa. In other societies, notably some Native American groups, more than two genders are recognized and celebrated (Garbarino, 1976; Olien, 1978). Individuals who have qualities of multiple genders are highly esteemed. I personally realized the arbitrariness of gender definitions in America when I spent some time living with Tamang villagers in the hill country of Nepal. I discovered that both women and men did what we consider sex-specific tasks. For instance, men do much of the cooking and child care, and they seem especially nurturing and gentle with young children. Women also do these things, as well as engaging in heavy manual labor and working as porters carrying 70-plus pounds of trekking gear for Western travelers. In the United States, gender varies across racial–ethnic groups. In general, African American women are more assertive than European American women, and African American men tend to be more communal than White men (Gaines, 1995; Rothenberg, Schafhausen, & Schneider, 2000; V. Smith, 1998).

Even within a single culture, the meaning of gender varies over time. Views of gender in the United States were not always as distinct as they are today. Prior to the Industrial Revolution, family and work life were intertwined for most people (Ryan, 1979). Thus, men and women participated in the labor of raising crops or running businesses, and both were involved in homemaking and childrearing. Affection and expressiveness were considered normal and natural in men as well as in women (Degler, 1980); industriousness and strength were attractive in women just

MIGUEL

I like to be strong and to stand up for myself and what I think, but I would not want to be only that. I am also sensitive to other people and how they feel. There are times to be hard and times to be softer; there are times to be strong and times to let others be strong.

He Was a She

AP/Wide World Photos

Jazz musician Billy Tipton was born on December 29, 1914. Early in life, Billy discovered jazz, and it became a lifelong passion. In the 1950s, Billy played saxophone and piano with popular bands that performed in nightclubs throughout the West and Midwest. Eventually Billy headed up his own band, the Billy Tipton Trio.

Tipton married Kitty Oakes in 1960, and the couple raised three adopted sons. They had a traditional family life, complete with Boy Scouts, PTA, and church. In the late 1970s, Oakes and Tipton separated but remained friends. Soon after Tipton's death in 1989, it was learned that he had four other common-law wives. However, the discovery of common-law wives was not the most amazing secret about Tipton that surfaced at his death: It was discovered that Billy Tipton was actually a female.

Donald Ball of the Ball & Dodd Funeral Home reported that the morticians had discovered Tipton was female in the process of preparing the body for burial. Ball broke the news to Jon Clark, one of Tipton's adopted sons, who was stunned. Clark said it had never occurred to him that his father was a woman.

Clark wasn't the only one who was fooled. Dick O'Neill, who played drums with the Billy Tipton Trio for a decade, said, "I never suspected a thing." Neither did Duke Ellington or others with whom Billy played. Although some people who had attended live performances remarked that Billy had a high singing voice, none of them ever questioned that Tipton was male.

Why did Tipton live as a man—both publicly and privately? Kitty Oakes provides some answers to this question. According to Oakes, social norms in the mid-20th century stipulated that only men could be jazz musicians and travel around the country with bands. To follow his love of jazz, Billy had to appear to be male. As an adolescent, Billy Tipton (who was born Dorothy Lucille Tipton) bound his breasts so that he could appear to be male and get jobs with the big bands. Later, Billy wore his hair in a crewcut and dressed in men's suits. In his private life, Billy told Kitty Oakes when they married that he'd been injured in an automobile accident and that he couldn't engage in conventional sexual activities. Obviously, these answers only begin to explain the mysterious life of Billy Tipton.

Sources: Holt, P. (1998, June 29). Unraveling the secret life of a man who was a woman. *San Francisco Chronicle*, pp. D1, D5; Middlebrook, D. (1998). *Suits me: The double life of Billy Tipton.* New York: Houghton Mifflin; (1989, February 2). Musician's death at 74 reveals he was a woman. *New York Times.*

as they were in men (Cancian, 1989; Douglas, 1977). During that era, both women and men were expected to show initiative and caring.

The Industrial Revolution gave birth to factories and to paid labor outside the home as a primary way of making a living. With this came a division of life into separate spheres of work and home. As men took jobs away from home, women increasingly assumed responsibility for family life. Consequently, femininity was redefined as being nurturant, dependent on men for income, focused on relationships, and able to make a good home. Masculinity was also redefined to mean emotional reserve, ambition, success at work, and, especially, ability to provide income (Cancian, 1989; Risman & Godwin, 2001). In her commentary, Emma, a 58-year-old, part-time student, reflects on changes in how women see themselves.

 EMMA

In my day, women were a lot different than they are today. We were quieter, and we put other people ahead of ourselves. We knew our place, and we didn't try to be equal with men. Today's women are very different. Some of the younger women in my classes put their careers ahead of marriage, some don't want children, and many think they should be as much the head of a family as the man. Sometimes I feel they are all wrong in what they want and how they are, but I have to admit that a part of me envies them the options and opportunities I never had.

As another example of how meanings of gender change, consider how ideals of beauty for women have varied over time in the United States. In the 1950s, Marilyn Monroe was widely considered the most beautiful, sexiest woman alive. Yet by today's standards of excessive slimness in women, Marilyn Monroe would be considered fat! In our era, supermodels look anorectic, and painfully thin superstar Calista Flockhart is a size zero (Hicks, 1998a, 1998b). As these examples indicate, what we take for granted as masculine and feminine is really quite arbitrary. Meanings of gender vary across cultures and over time in any given society.

Changing views of gender as well as sex are also evident in increasing recognition of individuals who don't fit conventional definitions of male or female, masculine or feminine. Intersexed individuals have biological characteristics of both males and females. Transgendered individuals are people who feel their biological sex is wrong—that they are really women trapped in men's bodies or men trapped in women's bodies. In the movie *Boys Don't Cry*, Hillary Swank gave a compelling portrayal of a transgendered person.

We should also realize that gender is a relational concept, because femininity and masculinity make sense in relation to each other. Our society defines femininity in contrast to masculinity and masculinity as a counterpoint to femininity. As meanings of one gender change, so do meanings of the other. For instance, when social views of masculinity stressed physical strength and endurance, femininity was defined by physical weakness and dependence on men's strengths. Perhaps you've read in older novels about women's fainting spells and the "vapors" they kept nearby to bring them out of faints. With the Industrial Revolution, sheer physical strength was no longer as important to survival, so masculinity was redefined as intellectual ability and success in earning income. Simultaneously, women's fainting spells seemed virtually to disappear, as did their former acumen at business and family finances. In part, this happened because society relied less on physical strength to distinguish between women and men.

Today in the United States, many women are reclaiming ambition and intelligence as qualities consistent with femininity, and they are exercising these in careers and civic and social involvements. As women become more assertive and active in public life than their foremothers, many men are changing their roles as well. Some men are learning skills in homemaking and child care that formerly were regarded as "women's work," and many are creating relationships in which partners have equal power and status. These illustrations remind us that the way one gender is defined influences expectations of the other; consequently, our views of femininity and masculinity continuously interact.

Let's summarize this extended discussion of gender. We have noted that gender is a social, symbolic category that reflects the meanings a society confers on biological sex. These meanings are communicated through structures and practices of cultural life that pervade our daily existence, creating the illusion that they are the natural, normal ways for women and men to be. Yet we've also seen that what gender means varies across cultures and over time in a particular culture, and how we conceive each gender is related to our views of the other. In other words, gender is the meaning that a culture—including individuals who belong to it—attaches to sex. This reminds us that, even though what our society defines as feminine and masculine may seem natural to us, there is nothing necessary about any particular meaning given to gender. By extension, this insight suggests we have more choice than we sometimes realize in how we define ourselves and each other as men and women.

Culture

A **culture** consists of structures and practices that uphold a particular social order by legitimizing certain values, expectations, meanings, and patterns of behavior (Weedon, 1987). To explore this idea, it may be helpful to consider how our culture creates and sustains one of its most basic values, democracy, and then examine how it upholds meanings of gender.

Our republic places a high value on representation, participation, and equality of opportunity and rights. Although inequity and inequality still persist in the United States, they are less pronounced than in less democratic cultures. Social structures, or institutions, reflect democratic values and seek to ensure they are enacted. We have a Congress to "represent the will of the people," and we have open voting in which each person's ballot is equal to everyone else's. Social structures such as laws protect freedom of speech and equality of rights and opportunities for all citizens. To make sure all citizens are represented, our judicial system guarantees everyone the right to counsel, regardless of whether she or he can pay for it. Schools cannot exclude students on the basis of age, race, sex, national origin, or other criteria, because we want to furnish educational opportunities for all citizens.

Normative practices of our culture also reflect its democratic values. We have "open meetings" so that policymaking can be understood and influenced by those not directly responsible for developing policy. Most businesses have complaint departments so that consumers have a place to air grievances and receive a hearing. Lobbying, protesting, and striking are protected activities by which people may dissent from the will of those in power. And those in power are subject to recall or impeachment should enough people object to them and their activities. Thus, we see that many of our society's structures and practices reflect and sustain democratic values.

Now consider how meanings of gender are reflected in and promoted by social structures and practices. One of the primary practices that structures society is discourse, or communication (Weedon, 1987). We are surrounded by communication that announces social images of gender and seeks to persuade us these are natural, correct ways for men and women to be and to behave. We open a magazine and see a beautiful, sexy woman waiting on a man who looks successful and in charge; we turn on our television and watch a prime-time program in which a husband tells of a big business coup while his wife prepares dinner for them; the commercials interspersed in the show depict women cleaning toilet bowls and kitchen floors and men going for the gusto after a pickup basketball game; we go to dinner, and our server presents the check to the man; we meet with a group of people on a volunteer project, and one of the men assumes leadership; a working woman receives maternity leave, but her husband cannot get paternity leave. Each of these practices communicates our society's views of men and women and the "proper" roles of each.

Consider additional examples of cultural practices that uphold gendered meanings. The custom whereby a woman gives up her name and takes her husband's on marriage, although no longer universal, still prevails. It carries forward the message that a woman is defined by her relationship to a man rather than by her individual identity. Within families, too, numerous practices reinforce social views of gender. Parents routinely allow sons greater freedom and behavioral latitude than they grant daughters, a practice that encourages males to be independent and females not to be. Daughters, much more than sons, are taught to do housework and care for younger siblings, thus reinforcing the idea that women are supposed to be concerned with home and family. These and other practices we take for granted support social prescriptions for gender and provide guidelines for how we are supposed to live as individual men and women.

Socially endorsed meanings are also communicated through structures such as institutions, which serve to announce, reflect, and perpetuate gendered cultural views. Because gender is important in our society, our institutions uphold preferred meanings and encourage individuals to conform to what is collectively endorsed as "appropriate" masculine and feminine behavior. Schools, for instance, are institutions that often reinforce established cultural prescriptions for gender. Research has shown that some teachers tend to encourage dependence, quietness, and deference and frown on assertiveness in female students. Contrast this with the

---

DYMPNA

"In 1974 I traveled to New York for my college education. . . . I'm a member of the Ibo tribe of Nigeria, and although I've lived in the United States most of my adult life, my consciousness remains fixed on the time and place of my upbringing. . . . When I left Nigeria at 18, I had no doubts about who and what I was. I was a woman. I was *only* a woman. . . . My role was to be a great asset to my husband. . . . I was, after all, raised within the context of child brides, polygamy, clitorectomies and arranged marriages. . . . I've struggled daily with how best to raise my daughter. Every decision involving Delia is a tug of war between Ibo and American traditions."

Published as: Ugwu-Oju, Dympna (2000, December 4). My turn: Should my tribal past shape Delia's future? *Newsweek*, p. 14.

finding that teachers generally reward independence, self-assertion, and activity in boys (Krupnick, 1985; Sadker & Sadker, 1984). Further, studies consistently report that teachers are more likely to encourage academic achievement in male students than in female students and that both teachers and guidance counselors tend to foster career ambitiousness in male students but encourage it less in female students (Sandler & Hall, 1986; Wood & Lenze, 1991a). Thus, schools are institutions that reinforce the feminine prescription for low achievement and deference and the masculine prescription for aggressiveness and ambition.

Another institution that upholds gender ideology is the judicial system. The view of women as sexual objects is supported in some states by legal codes that do not allow a wife to sue her husband for rape, because intercourse is regarded as a "husband's right." Men's rights are abridged by judicial views of women as the primary caretakers of children, views which are expressed in the presumption that women should have custody of children if divorce occurs. Thus, it is difficult for a father to gain child custody even when he might be the better parent or have a better situation for raising children.

Through its structures and practices, especially communication practices, societies create and sustain perspectives on what is normal and right. We are saturated with these culturally legitimized viewpoints, which punctuate our lives at every turn. Because messages that reinforce cultural views of gender pervade our daily lives, most of us seldom pause to reflect on whether they are as natural as they have come to seem. Like the air we breathe, they so continuously surround us that we tend to take them for granted and not question them. Learning to reflect on cultural prescriptions for gender (and other matters) empowers you as an individual. It increases your freedom to choose your own courses of action and identity by enlarging your awareness of the arbitrary and not always desirable nature of cultural expectations.

Communication

The last key term we define in this chapter is **communication**. Scholars have proposed well over a hundred different definitions of *communication*. This suggests that communication is very complex and difficult to define. Still, we need some working understanding of what communication is if we are to study how it interacts with gender and culture. *Communication is a dynamic, systemic process in which two levels of meanings are created and reflected in human interaction with symbols* (Wood, 2002). This rather complicated definition can be understood by focusing on one part of it at a time.

Communication is a dynamic process. Central to understanding communication is recognizing it as a highly dynamic process. This means that it continuously changes, evolves, and moves on. Because communication is a process, there are no definite beginnings or endings of communicative interactions. Suppose a friend drops by while you're reading this chapter and asks what you are doing. "Reading about gender, communication, and culture," you reply. Your friend then says, "Oh, you mean about how men and women talk differently." You respond, "Not exactly—you see, gender isn't really about males and females; it's about the meaning our culture attaches to each sex." Did this interaction begin with your friend's question, or with your instructor's assignment of the reading, or with other experiences that led you to enroll in this class? Think also about when this communication ends. Does it stop when your friend leaves? Maybe not. What the two of you talk about may influence what you think and do later, so the influence or effect of your communication continues beyond the immediate encounter. All communication is like this: It is an ongoing, dynamic process without clear beginnings and endings.

Communication is systemic. All communication occurs in particular situations or systems that influence what and how we communicate and especially what meanings we attach to messages. For example, assume you observe the following interaction. In an office building where you are waiting for an appointment, you see a middle-aged man walk to the secretary's desk and put his arm around her shoulders and say, "You really do drive me crazy when you wear that outfit." She doesn't look up from her work but responds, "You're crazy, period. It has nothing to do with what I'm wearing." How would you interpret this interaction? Is it an instance of sexual harassment? Are they co-workers who are comfortable joking about sexuality with each other? Is he perhaps not an employee but her friend or romantic partner? The only reasonable conclusion to draw is that we cannot tell what is happening or what it means to the communicators because we don't understand the systems within which this interaction takes place.

When we say communication is systemic, we

 TERESA

The stuff we talked about in class last time about contexts of communication helped me understand something that happens a lot. I really hate it when people call me "girl." I mean, I'm an adult, and that means I am a woman, not a little girl. People don't call 22-year-old guys "boys," do they? So it grates on me when folks say that. Except it doesn't bother me when older folks like my grandfather call me a girl. I think that doesn't irritate me because I know that "girl" means something different to him and he's of a different generation. I can't really expect someone 66 years old to understand this issue and to change a whole lifetime's habit. So I know he doesn't mean it as an insult, and I don't take it as one. But if a 20- or 30-year-old calls me "girl," I'll call them on it!

mean more than that its contexts affect meaning. As John Muir said, each part of communication is "hitched to the universe." As a system, all aspects of communication are interlinked and interactive. Who is speaking affects what is said and what it means. In the foregoing example, the secretary would probably attach different meanings to the message "You drive me crazy when you wear that outfit" if it was said by a friend or by a co-worker with a reputation for hassling women. Communication is also influenced by how we feel: When we're low, we're more likely to be irritated and abrupt than when we feel good. If you were just assaulted by lewd remarks from construction workers, you might take offense at a comment that ordinarily wouldn't bother you. The time of day and place of interaction may also affect what is communicated and how our words and actions are interpreted.

The largest system affecting communication is our culture, which is the context within which all of our interactions take place. As we saw in the preceding section, all societies have routine ways of regarding and treating men and women, and these change over time. Thirty years ago, it would have been rude for a man not to open a car door for his date and not to stand when a woman entered a room. Today most people would not regard either as rude or ungentlemanly. Even a decade ago, sexual harassment was largely unnamed and not considered cause for grievance or legal action. Today, however, laws and policies prohibit sexual harassment, and employees may bring charges against harassers. The same behavior now means something different, and it may have different results than it did 10 years ago. The systems—situation, time, people, culture, and so on—within which communication occurs interact so that each part affects all others and what they mean.

Communication has two levels of meaning. Perhaps you noticed that our definition of communication referred to meanings, not just a single meaning. That's because communication has two levels or dimensions of meaning. Years ago, a group of clinical psychologists (Watzlawick, Beavin, & Jackson, 1967) noted that all communication has both a content and a relationship level of meaning.

The **content level of meaning** is its literal meaning. If Ellen says to her partner Ed, "It's your turn to fix dinner tonight," the content level of her message is a rule about sharing cooking responsibilities and a reminder of whose turn it is. The content level also indicates what response is expected to follow from a message. In this case, both Ellen and Ed may assume he will get busy working on dinner. The content level of meaning involves a literal message and implies what response is appropriate.

The **relationship level of meaning** is not so obvious. This level defines the relationship between communicators by defining each person's identity and indicating who they are in relation to each other. In our example, Ellen seems to be defining the relationship as an equal one in which each partner does half of the cooking. The relationship level of meaning in her comment also suggests that she regards it as her prerogative to remind her partner when it's his turn. Ed could respond by saying,

"I don't feel like cooking. You do it tonight." Here the content level is again clear. He is describing how he feels and suggesting this implies he will not cook. On the relationship level, however, he may be arguing about the power balance between him and Ellen. He is refusing to accept her reminder that it's his turn to cook. If she agrees and fixes dinner, then she accepts Ed's definition of the relationship as not exactly equal. She affirms his right not to fix some of their meals and his prerogative to tell her to cook.

The relationship level of meaning is the primary one that reflects and influences how people feel about each other. It underlies and serves as a context for the content level of meaning because it tells us how to interpret the literal message. Perhaps when Ed says he doesn't feel like fixing dinner, he uses a teasing tone and grins, in which case the relationship level of meaning is that Ellen should not take the content level seriously, because he's joking. If, however, he makes his statement in a belligerent voice and glares at her, the relationship level of meaning is that he does mean the content level. Relationship levels of meaning tell us how to interpret content meaning and how communicators see themselves in relation to each other.

Relationship levels of meaning are particularly important when we try to understand gendered patterns of communication. A good example is interruptions. Elyse is telling Jed how her day went. He interrupts and says, "Let's head out to the soccer game." The content level of an interruption is simply what Jed said. The more important meaning is usually on the relationship level, which declares that Jed has the right to interrupt Elyse, dismiss her topic, and initiate his own. If he interrupts and she does not protest, they agree to let him control the conversation. If she does object, then the two may wind up in extended negotiations over how to define their relationship. We speak of meanings in communication because all messages have two levels of meaning.

Meanings are created through human interaction with symbols. This premise suggests two final important understandings about communication. First, it calls our attention to the fact that humans are symbol-using creatures (Blumer, 1969; Burke, 1966; Cassirer, 1978). Symbols are abstract, arbitrary, and ambiguous ways of representing phenomena. For example, X and Y are symbols for *female* and *male* respectively. Words are also symbols, so *woman* and *man* are symbols of particular physical beings. Humans rely on symbols to communicate, and that is largely responsible for their distinction from other creatures. In contrast, animals think and interact on a concrete, nonsymbolic level. A snarl is an unambiguous warning one dog gives to another; there is nothing abstract or uncertain about the action. The other dog doesn't need to reflect on what the snarl means. No real thinking need occur for the two animals to understand each other through their concrete behaviors.

Because human communication is symbolic, it requires mediation, or thought. Rather than reacting in automatic or instinctive ways to communication, we usually reflect on what was said and what it means before we respond. Symbols require thought to be interpreted. Symbols are also ambiguous; that is, what they mean is not clear-cut. Recall our earlier example in which a man tells a secretary, "Your outfit drives me crazy." To interpret what he said, she has to think about their relationship, what she knows about him, and what has occurred in their prior interactions. After thinking about all of these things, she'll decide whether his comment was a joke in poor taste, a compliment, sexual harassment, or a flirtatious show of interest from someone with whom she is romantically involved. Sometimes people interpret what we say in a manner other than what we intended because symbols are so abstract that more than one meaning is plausible.

The second implication of the premise that we create meanings through interaction with symbols is that the significance of communication is not in words themselves. Instead, humans *create* meanings in the process of communicating with one another. Our verbal and nonverbal behaviors are not simply neutral expressions of thoughts but imply values and judgments. How we express ourselves influences how we and others feel about what we communicate. "You're a feminist" can create distinctive impressions depending on whether the inflection is one suggesting interest, shock, disdain, or admiration. Calling a woman "aggressive" conjures up an impression that is different from the impression created by calling her "assertive." A man who interacts lovingly with his child could be described as either "nurturing" or "soft," and the two descriptions suggest quite distinct meanings. People differ in how they interpret identical messages. One woman is insulted when a man opens a door, whereas another considers it rude if a man doesn't hold a door for her. One person finds it entirely appropriate for a woman manager to give orders, but another employee thinks she's acting unfeminine. The meaning of communication depends on much more than verbal and nonverbal behavior; it arises from human interpretations of what is communicated.

The fact that symbols are abstract, ambiguous, and arbitrary makes it impossible to think of meaning as inherent in symbols themselves. Each of us constructs an interpretation of communication by drawing on our past experiences, our knowledge of the people with whom we are interacting, and other factors in a communication system that influence our interpretations. Because the meaning we attach to communication is heavily influenced by our personal experiences, values, thoughts, and feelings, we inevitably project our own thoughts, feelings, desires, and so forth onto messages to interpret what they mean. This certainly makes communication interesting, but it can be very confusing and frustrating as well. Differences in how we interpret messages are the source of much misunderstanding between people. However, you can become a more effective communicator if you keep in mind that people differ in how they perceive and interpret communication. Reminding yourself of this should prompt you to ask for clarification of what another person means rather than assuming your interpretation is correct. Similarly, we should check with others more often than we sometimes do to see how they are interpreting our verbal and nonverbal communication.

SUMMARY

In this chapter, we began to explore the nature of communication, gender, and culture. Because each of us is a gendered being, it's important to understand what gender means and how we can be more effective in our communicative interactions within a culture that is also gendered. The primary focus of this chapter was introducing four central concepts: sex, gender, culture, and communication.

Sex is a biological classification, whereas gender is a social, symbolic system through which a culture attaches significance to biological sex. Gender is something individuals learn, yet because it is constructed by cultures, it is more than an individual quality. Instead, it is a whole system of social meanings that specify what is associated with men and women in a given society at a particular time. We also noted that meanings of gender vary over time and across cultures. Finally, we found that gender is relational, because femininity and masculinity gain much of their meaning from the fact that our society juxtaposes them.

The third key term, culture, refers to structures and practices, particularly communicative ones, through which a society announces and sustains its values. Gender is a particularly significant issue in our culture, so there are abundant structures and practices that serve to reinforce our society's prescriptions for women's and men's identities and behaviors. To understand what gender means and how meanings of gender change, we must explore cultural values and the institutions and activities through which those are expressed and promoted.

Finally, we defined communication as a dynamic, systemic process in which meanings are created and reflected in human interaction with symbols. In examining the dimensions of this definition, we emphasized the fact that communication is a symbolic activity, which implies that it requires reflection and that meanings are variable and constructed rather than inherent in symbols themselves. We also saw that communication can be understood only within its contexts, including the especially important system of culture.

This chapter provides a foundation. In the following chapters, we will examine ways in which individuals learn gender, the differences and similarities in feminine and masculine communication, and a range of ways in which gendered communication and identities punctuate our lives.

DISCUSSION QUESTIONS

1. How different do you think men and women are? Drawing on your experiences as a man or woman and on your knowledge of both sexes, do you think men and women are more like each other (with a few differences) or more different from each other (with a few similarities)?

2. Use your InfoTrac College Edition to access Mary Hale's 1999 article, "He says, she says: Gender and the workplace." What does Hale identify as primary differences

between gender issues for women and men in the workplace? Do you foresee these changing in the next decade?

3. I discuss generational changes in attitudes about gender. How are your views of women and men, gays and lesbians, minority and majority peoples different from those of your parents and grandparents? How do you think the next generation's views about communication, gender, and culture may differ from yours?

4. Why are communication, gender, and culture intimately interwoven? How do cultural beliefs shape communication and gender? How does gender shape communication and culture? How does communication influence gender and culture?

5. Use the EasyTrac option on your InfoTrac College Edition. Type in the keyword "transgender," and scroll through the listings until you find an article in the September 25, 2000, issue of *Time* entitled "His name is Aurora." What would you have done if you had been Aurora's (or Zach's) parents?

6. Think about your sex and your gender. Deciding which sex you are won't be difficult. Identifying your gender, however, is more complicated. How closely do you conform to society's views of masculinity and femininity? Do you have what our culture defines as masculine and feminine qualities in yourself?

7. What are current cultural prescriptions for femininity and masculinity? As a class, discuss what society today defines as masculine and feminine, and write the ideas on a chalkboard. How comfortable are you with current views of masculinity and femininity? Which ones do you find restrictive? Are you doing anything to change them in society's view or to resist them in defining your own personal identity?

2

Theoretical Approaches to Gender Development

A student of mine named Jenna recently told me that she didn't like studying theory because it had nothing to do with "real life." This wasn't the first time I'd heard a student dismiss theories as impractical. But I had to disagree with Jenna. Years ago, a premier social psychologist, Kurt Lewin, said, "There is nothing so practical as good theory." What he meant, and what I tried to explain to Jenna, is that theories are very practical. They help us understand, explain, and predict what happens in our lives and the world around us. Although we sometimes think theories are removed from the real world, actually they pertain directly to our everyday lives. A **theory** is simply a way to describe, explain, and predict relationships among phenomena. Each of us uses theories to make sense of our lives, guide our attitudes and actions, and predict others' behavior. Although our theories are not always conscious, they still shape our conduct and expectations.

Among the theories that each of us has are ones that we use to make sense of men's and women's behaviors. For instance, assume you know Kevin and Carlene, who are 11-year-old twins. In many ways they are alike, yet they also differ. Carlene is more articulate than Kevin, and she tends to think in more synthetic, creative, and integrative ways. Kevin is better at solving analytic problems, especially mathematical ones. He also has better-developed muscles, although he and Carlene spend equal time in athletics. How you explain the differences between these twins reflects your implicit theory of gender.

If you subscribe to biological theory, you would note that different cognitive strengths result from differential hemispheric specialization in male and female brains. You might also reason that Kevin's greater muscle development results from androgens, which encourage musculature, whereas estrogen programs the body to develop more fat and soft tissue.

Then again, perhaps you think there is another reason for the differences between Kevin and Carlene. Knowing that researchers have shown that teachers and parents tend to encourage analytic problem solving in boys and creative thinking in girls, you might explain the twins' different cognitive skills as the result of learning and reinforcement. The same explanation might be advanced for disparity in their muscle development, because you could reason that Kevin is probably more encouraged and rewarded than Carlene for engaging in activities that build muscles.

A third way to explain differences is to point out the likelihood that each twin identifies with same-sex role models. If so, we would predict that Kevin will imitate the behavior of men he chooses as models—physical strength and logical thinking. Identifying herself with women, Carlene is more likely to emulate feminine models.

These are only three of many ways we could explain the differences between Kevin and Carlene. Each represents a particular theoretical viewpoint—a way of understanding the relationship between gender and people's behaviors and abilities. None of the three is clearly right or even more right than the others. Each viewpoint makes sense, yet each is limited, which suggests that an adequate explanation may involve several theories.

It's important to realize that theories do more than provide explanations. Our theories about sex and gender affect our thoughts and behaviors. How we explain the twins' differences is likely to influence how we treat them. If you think the differences in muscle development are determined by biology, then you probably would not push Carlene to work out more in order to cultivate muscles. On the other hand, if you think differences result from learning and role models, you well might encourage Carlene to develop her muscles and Kevin to think more integratively and creatively. If you believe women have a natural maternal instinct (biological theory), then you might not expect fathers to be equal caretakers. A different set of expectations would arise if you theorize that women are taught to nurture and that men can learn this too. If you think males are more aggressive because of their higher levels of testosterone, then you are apt to tolerate rowdiness in boys and men and to discourage it in girls and women. The theories you hold consciously or unconsciously influence how you see yourself as a woman or man, what you expect of women and men generally, and what kinds of changes you attempt to bring about in gendered behavior. Because the theories we hold do affect our perceptions, behaviors, and expectations, it's important to examine them carefully. That is the goal of this chapter.

THEORETICAL APPROACHES TO GENDER

There are many theories about gender and its relationship to culture and communication. Because each theory attempts to explain only selected dimensions of gender, different theories are not necessarily in competition with one another to produce *the* definitive explanation of how gender develops and what it implies. Instead, theories often complement one another by sharpening our awareness of multiple ways in which communication, sex, gender, and culture interact. Thus, as we survey alternative theoretical approaches, you shouldn't try to pick the best or right one. Instead, focus on identifying the limitations and appreciating the particular insights of each theory's account of gender development. Not all theories are equally sound, and some theories are incompatible with others. Understanding a range of theories about sex and gender will allow you to decide which are stronger and which can fit together to provide a richly layered account of the gendering process and the critical role of communication in it.

Theories about gender development and behavior can be classified into three types: those that focus on biological bases of gender, those that emphasize interpersonal origins of gender, and those that concentrate on cultural influences on gender development. Within these broad categories, a number of specific theories offer insight into factors and processes that contribute to gendering individuals. As we discuss these, you will probably notice both how they differ in focus and how they work together to create an overall understanding of gender development.

■ Biological Influences on Gender

Perhaps the first attempt to explain general differences between women and men was **biological theory.** This approach maintains that biological characteristics of the sexes are the basis of gender differences. Biologically based theories focus on how X and Y chromosomes and hormonal activities influence a range of individual qualities from body features to thinking and motor skills.

Although in recent years biological explanations have been increasingly over shadowed by theories that emphasize socialization, it would be unwise to discount biological factors altogether. The jury is still out on some of the connections theorized to exist between biology and gender, but research clearly demonstrates some biological influences on human behavior.

One focus of biological theories is the influence of sex chromosomes. Most males have an XY chromosome structure because they inherit an X chromosome from their mothers and a Y chromosome from their fathers. Most females have an XX chromosome structure because they inherit an X chromosome from each parent. In 1996, geneticists reported evidence that several genes controlling intelligence are located only on X chromosomes (Tanouye). This implies that the genetic aspect of males' intelligence is inherited from their mothers, whereas females may inherit their genetic intelligence from either or both parents. Of course, socialization profoundly influences how genetically transmitted intelligence develops. Genetic researchers have also reported that the primary gene responsible for social skills is active only on the X chromosome (Langreth, 1997). This may explain why women are generally more adept and comfortable than men in social situations. Only females inherit X chromosomes from both parents; males inherit only the single X chromosome from their mothers.

A second focus of biological theories is the role of hormonal activity in shaping sex-related behaviors. Sex hormones affect development of the brain as well as the body. For instance, estrogen, the primary female hormone, causes women's bodies to produce "good" cholesterol and to make blood vessels more flexible than those of men (Ferraro, 2001; Shapiro, 1990). Estrogen also strengthens the immune system, making women generally less susceptible to immune disorders and more resistant to infections and viruses. Thus, it is not surprising that, from the fetal stage throughout life (Jacklin, 1989), men are more vulnerable to some physical problems than are women. Estrogen also accounts for fat tissue around women's hips, which provides cushioning to a fetus during pregnancy, and there is some preliminary support for the claim that estrogen impedes liver functioning so that women eliminate alcohol more slowly than men and thus may react more quickly to alcohol consumption (Lang, 1991).

Male sex hormones also have some documented effects, as well as some controversial possible influences. After surveying an extensive amount of research on sex hormones, Carol Tavris (1992) concludes that men, like women, have a hormonal cycle. And, like women, men's hormonal cycles affect their behavior. Males who use drugs, engage in violence and abusiveness, and have conduct disorders tend to be at their cycle's peak level of testosterone, the primary male hormone. A study of 1,706 men from ages 39 to 70 found that men with higher levels of testosterone had personalities researchers described as "dominant with some aggressive behavior" ("Study Links High Testosterone," 1991). Higher levels of testosterone are linked to jockeying for power, attempts to influence or dominate others, and physical expressions of anger (Schwartz & Cellini, 1995). Another study ("Study Links Men's Cognitive Abilities," 1991) reported that fluctuations of testosterone affect men's cognitive functioning so that men have better spatial abilities at low points in their hormonal cycle. A second male hormone, androgen, has also been linked to aggressiveness and even to an instinct for killing in animals ("Male Hormone," 1991). Whether these findings also apply to humans remains open to question.

A third focus of biological theories of difference is brain structure and development, which appear to be linked to sex. Research indicates that, although both women and men use both lobes of the brain, each sex tends to specialize in one. Men generally have greater development of the left lobe of the brain, which controls linear, conventionally logical thought, sequential information, and abstract, analytic thinking. Specializing in the right lobe, women tend to have greater aptitude for imaginative and artistic activity, for holistic, intuitive thinking, and for some visual and spatial tasks (Hartlage, 1980; Lesak, 1976; Walsh, 1978). Research indicates that women tend to use both sides of their brains to do language tasks, whereas men are more likely to use only the left sides of their brains. Further, women's brains do not have to work as hard as men's brains to figure out others' emotions (Begley, 1995; "Gender Difference," 1995).

Linking the two lobes of the brain is a bundle of nerves and connecting tissues called the corpus callosum (Figure 2.1). Women generally have greater ability to use

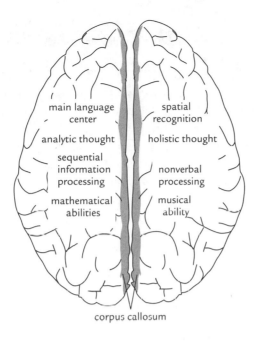

Figure 2.1 Structure of the Human Brain

this structure and to access the distinct capacities of both lobes. For instance, a recent report ("Men Use Half a Brain to Listen," 2000) involving brain scans showed that men used mostly the left lobes of their brains when they were listening, whereas women used both lobes of the brain to listen. This finding does not mean that men listen less fully or less well than women. It means only that women and men, in general, use different parts of their brains when they engage in listening.

It is tempting to see differences in how we use our brains as indisputable evidence of the force of biology, but another study suggests this conclusion is not warranted. M. Hines (1992) found that within the corpus callosum there is a thick, rounded fold of connecting tissues, which she labeled the splenium. Her preliminary work indicates women have thicker splenii (pronounced "splĕn'-ēē-ēē"), which may account for their greater verbal abilities. However, Hines cautions us not to interpret this as demonstrating innate difference due to biology. She stresses that the splenium changes as a result of experience, which implies that we can develop it by using it, just as we use exercise to develop other muscles in our bodies.

Research on brain development also suggests there may be differences between the brains of heterosexuals and gays. The National Academy of Sciences (Elias, 1992) reports that sexual orientation may be strongly influenced by biology. Examinations of brains revealed that a band of fibers called the anterior commissure, which is part of the tissues connecting brain lobes, is significantly larger in gay men than in heterosexual men or women. Dean Hamer headed a National Cancer Insti-

Biological Differences That Make a Difference

For many years, physicians as well as laypersons assumed that, except for reproduction, men and women were basically alike from a biological perspective. Yet new research (Ferraro, 2001; Hales, 1999; Legato, 1998; Reiss, 2000; Wheeler, 1998) suggests there are some significant biological sex differences. Consider these findings:

- Women are more likely than men to experience pain. They are also more able to cope with pain and tend to have higher tolerances for pain than men do.

- Women are more likely than men to suffer from migraine headaches and lupus; men are more likely than women to suffer from cluster headaches.

- Men's livers metabolize drugs, including alcohol, more quickly than women's.

- Women and men typically have different symptoms of heart attack. Women's symptoms include backache, profuse sweating, and extreme fatigue. Men's primary symptom is usually chest or arm pain.

- Men's digestive systems work more quickly than women's.

- Both women and men develop diabetes, yet women of all ages who have diabetes are two to three times more likely than their male counterparts to develop heart disease.

- Women develop more cases of melanoma, but men are more likely to die from this skin cancer.

- Women are more likely to suffer from depression and anxiety, whereas men are more subject to violent behavior and abuse of drugs, including alcohol.

tute research project that examined the genes of 40 pairs of gay brothers. Only 7 of the 40 pairs did not have a genetic marker on the tips of their X chromosomes (Allman, 1993). The researchers hypothesize that prenatal hormones may influence development of the anterior commissure. We don't yet know if, like the splenium, the size of the anterior commissure is influenced by use. If it is, then biology alone doesn't account for differences in anterior commissures or, perhaps, sexual orientation.

In summary, biological theories of gender attribute masculine and feminine qualities and abilities to genetics and biology. Specifically, it appears that chromosomes and hormones affect brain development, physiology, thinking, and behavior. A value of this theory is the identification of ways in which our choices are influenced by innate and relatively stable factors. Yet, biological theories tell us only about physiological and genetic qualities of men and women *in general.* They don't necessarily describe individual men and women. Some men may have less testosterone and may be less aggressive than most men, whereas some women, like Luanne, may have the mental and physical qualities necessary to play football.

Used by permission of Johnny Hart and Creators Syndicate Inc.

Although virtually no researchers dispute the influence of biology on gender, there is substantial controversy about how strong and how immutable biological forces are. Those who hold an extreme version of biological theory maintain that our chromosomes and other biological factors program, or determine, masculine and feminine behavior. Allan Bloom (1987), for instance, argues that women should stay home with babies because women's breasts produce milk. Attitudes like Bloom's echo Freud's claim that biology is destiny. A greater number of research-ers argue that biology is substantially edited by environmental factors. Based on a 12-year study of adolescent males and females, psychologist David Reiss stated emphatically, "Biology is not destiny" (Reiss, 2000; Begley, 2000, p. 64). By extension, many claim that biology is most accurately understood as an influence on, not a determinant of, gender (Martin & Doka, 2000; Reiss, 2000). To consider how environmental forces may mitigate biological endowments, we turn to theories of interpersonal and cultural influences on gender.

■ Interpersonal Influences on Gender

A number of theorists have focused on interpersonal factors that influence development of masculinity and femininity. From their work, two major theoretical views have emerged to explain how individuals become gendered. Psychodynamic theory emphasizes interpersonal relationships within the family that affect a child's sense of identity, particularly his or her gender. Psychological theories stress learning and role modeling between children and a variety of other people, including parents. I'll introduce both theories here and pursue them in greater detail in subsequent chapters.

LUANNE

When I was in high school, I wanted to play football. My folks were really cool about it, since they'd always told me being a girl didn't mean I couldn't do anything I wanted to. But the school coach vetoed the idea. I appealed his decision to the principal as sex discrimination (my mother's a lawyer), and we had a meeting. The coach said girls couldn't play football as well as guys because girls are less muscular, weigh less, and have less dense bodies to absorb the force of momentum. He said this means girls can be hurt more than guys by tackles and stuff. He also said that girls have smaller heads and necks, which is a problem in head-to-head contact on the field. My dad said the coach was talking in generalizations, and he should judge my ability by me as an individual. But the coach's arguments convinced the principal, and I didn't get to play just because women's bodies are generally less equipped for contact sports.

The Claims of Sociobiology

One of the more controversial theories of sex and gender differences is sociobiology (also called evolutionary theory) (Segerstråle, 2000). According to sociobiology, differences between women and men are the inevitable result of genetic factors that aim to ensure survival of the fittest. Put plainly, Harvard entomologist E. O. Wilson, who founded sociobiology, explains that it is "the systematic study of the biological basis of all social behavior" (1975, p. 4).

A key claim of sociobiology is that women and men follow distinct reproductive strategies in an effort to maximize the chance that their genetic lines will continue (Buss, 1994, 1995, 1996, 1999; Buss & Kenrick, 1998). For men, the best strategy is to have sex with as many women as possible in order to father many children with their genes. Because men produce millions of sperm, they risk little by impregnating multiple women. Women, however, usually produce only one egg during each menstrual cycle during their fertile years, so the best evolutionary strategy for them is to be highly selective in choosing sex partners and potential fathers of their children (Barash, 1979).

Sociobiology has at least as many critics as proponents. Some scholars (Futuyama & Risch, 1984) point out that the theory fails to account for sexual behavior that occurs without the goal of reproduction—and sometimes in an active effort to avoid that outcome! Also, note critics of the theory, social evolution is not the same thing as biological evolution. Cynthia Fuchs Epstein reminds us that "as humans are ordered by nature, so too do they order it" (1988, p. 71).

Psychodynamic theory of gender development. Originally advanced by Sigmund Freud (1957), **psychodynamic theory** focuses on family and psychic dynamics that influence individuals' development of gender identity. More recent work has refined psychodynamic theory to compensate for some of Freud's blind spots, particularly his misunderstanding of women's development.

Object-relations theory, one of the most widely endorsed branches of the psychodynamic perspective, claims that relationships are central to the development of human personality and, specifically, gender identity. According to this theory, early relationships are the primary basis of our sense of identity. For most children, the single most important early relationship is with the primary caretaker, typically the mother. That relationship is thought to be the most fundamental influence on how an infant comes to define herself or himself and on how she or he understands interactions with others.

Psychodynamic theorists think that development of a sense of self and a gender identity occurs as an infant internalizes the views of others around him or her. So, for example, infants who are lovingly nurtured by parents tend to incorporate the parents' view into their own sense of self, and they regard themselves as valuable and worthy. In addition, the parents' tendencies to nurture, to be attentive, to express affection, and so forth are internalized so that the child develops these capacities as part of herself or himself. Internalizing others is not merely acquiring roles; instead, it creates the basic structure of the psyche—the core self.

Psychodynamic theory explains the development of masculine or feminine identity as the result of different kinds of relationships that typically exist between mothers and children of each sex. According to Nancy J. Chodorow (1989), one of the most widely respected psychodynamic theorists, the key to understanding how family psychodynamics create gender lies in realizing that "we are all mothered by women, ... [and] women rather than men have primary parenting responsibilities" (p. 6). Because the mother herself is gendered, she forms distinctly different relationships with sons and daughters. Consequently, male and female infants follow different developmental paths depending on the specific relationship each has with the mother.

Between a mother and daughter there is a fundamental likeness, which encourages close identification between them. Mothers generally interact more with daughters and keep them physically and psychologically closer than sons. In addition, mothers tend to be more nurturing and to talk more about personal and relationship topics with daughters than with sons. This intense closeness allows an infant girl to import her mother into herself in so basic a way that her mother becomes quite literally a part of her own self. Because this internalization occurs at a very early age, a girl's first efforts to define her own identity are suffused with the relationship with her mother. The fact that girls generally define their identities within a relationship may account for women's typical attentiveness to relationships (Lorber, 2001; Surrey, 1983).

The relationship between a mother and son typically departs from that between a mother and daughter. Because they are not the same sex, full identification may not be possible. Theorists (Chodorow, 1978, 1999; Miller, 1986; Surrey, 1983) suggest that infant boys recognize in a primitive way that they differ from their mothers. More important, mothers realize the difference, and they reflect it in their interactions with their sons. In general, mothers encourage more and earlier independence in sons than in daughters, and they interact less closely with sons. Also, mothers are more likely to discuss impersonal topics with sons and to talk less about personal and relationship matters. Thus, mothers tend to encourage autonomy in sons at very early ages.

How do most young boys formulate a masculine gender identity? Because they cannot define it through the relationship with their mothers as daughters typically do, boys pursue a different path. To establish his identity, a boy must differentiate

JENNIFER

I remember when Marilyn was born. She was our second; the first was Bobby. From the moment Marilyn entered our lives, I felt connected to her in a way I never had to my son. I love Bobby just as much, but the connection is different. When I look at Marilyn, I sometimes feel there is a circle connecting us—a kind of private union so that we are one. I encourage Marilyn to be with me and do things with me, whereas I let Bobby go off on his own a lot more. It's just a different kind of connection—almost a fusion between Marilyn and me.

himself from his mother—declare himself unlike her. Some psychodynamic theorists argue that boys actually negate and reject their mothers in order to define an independent self. The idea that a boy must renounce his mother to establish masculine identity underlies the puberty rites of many cultures. To enter into manhood, boys are required to distance themselves from their mothers and, more broadly, from femininity (French, 1992; Gaylin, 1992). Whether a boy rejects his mother or merely differentiates himself from her, becoming independent of others is central to a boy's initial sense of self. Distancing himself from others and defining himself apart from them becomes a fundamental anchor of masculine identity.

Identity, of course, is not static and fixed completely in the early years of life. The initial self that we construct out of primary relationships continues to grow and change throughout life as we interact with others and revise our sense of who we are. Yet, object-relations theorists maintain that the identity formed in infancy is fundamental. They see it as the foundation on which later views of the self are erected. Thus, although identity clearly evolves, it does so on a foundation laid in infancy.

According to psychodynamic theorists, as infants mature, they carry with them the basic identity formed in the pivotal first relationship with their mothers. As girls become women, they elaborate their identity in connections with others, and relationships tend to figure prominently in their values and lives. As boys grow into men, they too elaborate the essential identity formed in infancy, making independence central to their values and lives. This major difference in self-definition suggests that close relationships may mean quite different things to masculine and feminine persons. For someone who is feminine, intimate relationships may be a source of security and comfort, and they may affirm her (or his) view of self as connected with others. In contrast, someone with a masculine orientation may feel that relationships stifle the independence essential to selfhood and security (Gilligan, 1982; Lorber, 2001; Rubin, 1985; Wood & Lenze, 1991b).

A primary value of this theory of gender development is that it highlights the importance of relationships in creating and sustaining human identity. Thus, this perspective offers us insight into the role that connections with others play in cultivating gender. Whether or not we agree with the extent of influence psychodynamic theorists accord to relationships, their insights into this area are important to overall understandings of gender. As we will discover later in this chapter, a number of other scholars, who represent distinct theoretical schools of thought, also focus on relationships.

Psychological theories of gender development. Psychological theories also focus on interpersonal bases of gender, but they do not emphasize intrapsychic processes as do psychodynamic explanations. Instead, psychological theories of gender highlight the role of communication on gender through individual learning and cognitive development.

Social learning theory, developed by Walter Mischel (1966) and others (Bandura & Walters, 1963; Lynn, 1969), claims that individuals learn to be masculine and feminine (among other things) through observation, experimentation, and responses from others. Children notice how others behave, and imitate the communication they see on television and in parents, peers, and others. At first, young children are likely to mimic almost anything that catches their eyes or ears. However, other people will reward only some of a child's behaviors, and those behaviors that are reinforced tend to be repeated. Thus, social learning suggests that others' communication teaches boys and girls which behaviors are appropriate for them. Because children prefer rewards to punishments or neutral responses, they are likely to develop behavioral patterns that others approve.

Social learning theory does not regard biological sex as the basis of gender identity. Instead, it argues that children learn gender by imitating others and continuing to imitate those behaviors that bring them positive responses from others. Young girls tend to be rewarded when they are polite, considerate, quiet, loving, emotionally expressive, and obedient—all qualities associated with femininity. They tend to get less positive responses if they are boisterous, independent, unconcerned with others, or competitive—qualities associated with masculinity. As parents and others reinforce in girls what is considered feminine and discourage behaviors and attitudes that are masculine, they shape little girls into femininity. Similarly, as parents communicate approval to boys for behaving in masculine ways and curb them for acting feminine—for instance, for crying—they influence little boys to become masculine.

Mark Breedlove, a behavioral endocrinologist, says, "We're born with predispositions, but it's society that amplifies them, exaggerates them" (Blum, 1998, p. 46). In other words, tendencies to be aggressive or nurturing are shaped and elaborated by parents, peers, and other people. A good example of this comes from a report by Deborah Blum, a Pulitzer Prize–winning science writer. Blum calls our attention to studies of girls with a condition called congenital adrenal hypoplasia, which means they have higher levels of testosterone than is typical for girls. These girls are more interested in trucks and toy weapons than most little girls are, and they engage in rougher play. Yet, as they interact with other girls, their peers socialize them toward behaviors, games, and preferences more traditional for girls (Blum, 1997, 1998).

You may have noticed that social learning theory views children as relatively passive in the learning process. It suggests they more or less absorb a gender identity in response to external stimuli such as rewards and punishments from parents and other important people in their world. Social learning theory also suggests that the reinforcement process continues throughout life with messages that reinforce femininity in women and masculinity in men.

 VICTORIA

When I was little—like 4 or 5 maybe—if I got dirty or was too loud, Mama would say, "That's no way for a lady to act." When I was quiet and nice, she'd say, "Now you're being a lady." I remember wanting Mama to approve of me and trying to act like a lady. But sometimes it as hard to figure out what was and wasn't ladylike in her book. I had to just keep doing things and seeing how she responded until I learned the rules.

Cognitive development theory also focuses on how individuals learn from interaction with others to define themselves, including their gender. Unlike social learning theory, however, this approach assumes children play active roles in developing their own identities. Researchers claim that children use others to define themselves because they are motivated by an *internal desire* to be competent, which includes knowing how to act feminine or masculine in Western culture.

Within this school of thought, theorists like Lawrence Kohlberg (1958), Jean Piaget (1932/1965), and Carol Gilligan and her associates (1982, 1988) have offered models of how children develop gendered views of themselves, relationships, and moral orientations. Central to the development of identity is communication, which is the primary way children learn what is considered feminine and masculine, as well as the principal means by which they practice their own gender behaviors. Work in this area suggests that children go through several stages in developing gender identities (Wadsworth, 1996). From birth until about 24 to 30 months, they search others' communication for labels to apply to themselves. When they hear others call them a "girl" or "boy," they learn labels for themselves. Then children actively look for same-sex models they can imitate.

A key developmental juncture occurs very early in life, by age 3 or earlier (A. Campbell, 1993). At this point, a child develops **gender constancy,** which is the understanding that they are male or female and that this will not change. Given this, say cognitive development theorists, children develop a high internal motivation to learn how to be competent in the sex and gender assigned to them. Boys and girls now devote themselves to identifying behaviors and attitudes others consider masculine and feminine and to learning to enact those. Same-sex models become extremely important as gauges whereby young children figure out what behaviors, attitudes, and feelings go with their gender. If Mommy is identified as the same gender as a little girl, then whatever Mommy does and is communicates information about feminine gender. Likewise, little boys study their fathers and other important males in their world to learn what counts as masculine. Actively using others as models allows children to mold themselves into the gender their culture expects of them.

As children mature, they continue to seek role models to become competent at being masculine and feminine (Martin, 1994, 1997). Perhaps you, like many adolescents, studied teen magazines and watched movies and television to figure out how to be successful as a boy or girl. Everything from how to style your hair and do the latest dances to how to feel various things is learned, and often what is considered appropriate differs for the sexes. It's feminine to squeal or scream at the sight of bugs or mice, but boys who do so are quickly labeled sissies.

𝒞 DERRICK

Over break I was visiting my sister's family, and her little boy attached himself to me. Wherever I went, he was my shadow. Whatever I did, he copied. At one point, I was dribbling a basketball out in the driveway, and Derrick got it and started dribbling. I egged him on, saying "Attaboy! What a star!" and stuff like that, and he just grinned real big. The more I praised him for playing with the ball, the harder he played. It was really weird to see how much influence I had over him.

It's acceptable—if not pleasant to everyone—for adolescent boys to belch, but a teenage girl who belched would most likely be criticized.

In studying how senses of morality and relationships develop, Carol Gilligan and her colleagues (1982; Gilligan & Pollack, 1988) theorized that most females are socialized to value connections with others, to communicate care and responsiveness, and to preserve relationships. According to cognitive development theory (Kohlberg, 1958), males are more likely to value autonomy and to communicate in ways that preserve their independence from others. Each has learned what is appropriate for her or his sex, and each guides her or his own communication to be consistent with social prescriptions for gender.

Some researchers think gender constancy is established well before the third birthday. It may even be set within the first year of life. Once established, gender constancy seems very difficult to change. The firmness of gender constancy is evident in efforts to change the sex of children. Perhaps the most famous case is that of Joan-John (Leo, 1997). When John was only 8 months old, his penis was destroyed in a surgical accident. Following doctors' advice, John's parents decided to change him into a girl. His testicles were removed, a vagina was surgically created, and John was renamed Joan. Joan did not take to being a girl. Her preferred toys were trucks and guns, and she routinely ripped off the dresses her parents made her wear. Joan also insisted on urinating standing up. Even hormonal treatments and therapists could not convince Joan to accept being a girl. Finally, at age 14, Joan was told by her father she had been born a boy. For Joan-John, things now made sense. John had a mastectomy, took male hormone shots, and began living as a male. At age 25, John married a woman with children, and he continues to live as a man.

In summary, psychological theories focus on how individuals learn gender through interpersonal communication. Whether you think children are more or less active in the learning process, it's clear from this perspective that others' com-

---

FYI

Where's the Boy's/Girl's Bathroom?

Amy Kathryn May has a problem. So does Lane Community College in Oregon. Amy wants to use the women students' locker room to shower and dress after her physical education classes. Because Amy has male anatomy, school officials say it would be inappropriate for her to shower and change with female students. Amy is a transgendered person who is physically becoming a woman. She takes hormones and undergoes electrolysis to remove hair. Despite her male anatomy, Amy says she is female and would feel uncomfortable in a men's locker room. In May 2001, Lane College came up with a compromise. A custodian's closet between two women's locker rooms was converted into a private shower and changing room for Amy.

Source: Evelyn, J. (2001, June 1). Changing times. *Chronicle of Higher Education*, p. A6.

---

munication both teaches lessons about gender and provides models of how to enact masculinity and femininity. Once gender constancy is established, most children strive for communication, attitudes, goals, and self-presentations consistent with the gender they consider theirs.

Cultural Influences on Gender

A third group of theorists focuses on understanding gender from a cultural perspective. Scholars in this area do not necessarily dispute biological and psychological factors but assume that these are qualified by the larger influence of culture. The ways that mothers, fathers, and other models for children behave, for instance, embody socially approved views of masculinity and femininity. Thus, interpersonal influences on gender are part of a broad system of cultural views and values. Because it incorporates other theories, the cultural perspective is a particularly comprehensive approach to understanding the development of gender and what it means in any society at a specific time.

Of the many cultural contributions to knowledge about gender, we will focus on three. First, we'll look at findings from anthropology to discover what cross-cultural research tells us about gender. Next, we will explore symbolic interactionism, which concentrates on how individuals acquire cultural values so that most of us adopt the identities our culture designates as appropriate for our gender. Finally, we'll look at standpoint theory, which is a recent approach that augments the insights of symbolic interaction and anthropology.

Anthropology. Anyone who has been outside the United States knows that traveling prompts you to learn not only about those countries but also about your own. When confronted with different values and ways of doing things in a foreign culture, you see the norms of your own society in a new and usually clearer light. This holds true of gender. Our understanding of gendered identities and the meaning of gender in America are clarified by considering what it means elsewhere—how other cultures view gender and how women and men in other cultures express gendered identities.

In Chapter 1, I mentioned the pioneering anthropological work of Margaret Mead (1935/1968), in which she discovered distinct meanings of gender in three different societies. One reversed what is considered masculine and feminine in our culture; one encouraged extremes of what we consider masculine in both sexes; and the third promoted what we regard as feminine in men and women. This provided an early clue to the arbitrary nature of gender by demonstrating that different cultures create quite distinctive gender arrangements and identities.

Much work has followed Mead's. Charlotte G. O'Kelly and Larry S. Carney (1986) analyzed the gender arrangements and assumptions characteristic of different kinds of cultures. In foraging or hunter-gatherer societies, there is the least gender division and, therefore, the greatest equality between women and men. Horticultural and pastoral societies tend also to be egalitarian, although less so than purely foraging cultures. Agrarian peoples generally have a pronounced system of gender stratification in which women are subordinate to men in status and rights. Finally, industrial-capitalist societies like ours distinguish sharply between the genders and confer different value on women and men.

There are many examples of societies that have different views of gender from those in the United States. Tahitian men tend to be gentle, mild tempered, and nonaggressive, and it is entirely acceptable for them to cry, show fear, and express pain (Coltrane, 1996). The Mbuti, a tribe of pygmies in central Africa, don't discriminate strongly between the sexes. Both women and men gather roots, berries, and nuts, and both hunt (Coltrane, 1996). Another example comes from a group of villages in the Dominican Republic where it is common for children to be born without the ability to produce the enzyme that concentrates testosterone to develop genitalia. Boys born with this condition have undescended testes and an underdeveloped penis. Because this condition is not rare, the society does not pathologize it. Instead, boys born with this condition are raised as "conditional girls," who wear dresses and are treated as girls. At puberty, a secondary tide of androgens causes the testes to descend, the penis to grow, and muscle and hair typical of males to appear. At that point, the child is considered a boy—his dresses are discarded, and he starts dating girls. Members of the society call the condition *guevedoces,* which means "testes at 12" (Blum, 1998).

Further evidence of the cultural nature of gender comes from a classic study conducted by Beatrice Whiting and Carolyn Edwards (1973). They investigated gender identities in children from 3 to 11 years old in three cultures. They found that the nurturing inclinations and skills we associate with femininity are taught to whomever a society labels caregivers. One African group is structured so that young boys are responsible for taking care of babies. In this society, unlike our own, young boys are actually more nurturant than young girls.

Native American tribes offer yet another cultural construction of gender. According to Angela Gonzales and Judy Kertész (2001), prior to contact with Western Europeans, many (but not all) Native American groups had long-established matrilineal systems of inheritance, property ownership, and social status. These tribes were not necessarily matriarchal (in which females have greater power than males), but they were matrilineal because lines of kinship were traced through females, not males. Many of the tribes also viewed women as relatively autonomous, in direct contrast to the views of Western Europeans who colonized the United States.

Perhaps the most important lesson we can draw from anthropological studies is that cultures profoundly shape gender identity. Amazingly few sex differences have been found across a range of societies, and the ones that have been documented tend to be very small (Adler, 1991). For instance, both boys and girls in most cultures show tendencies to nurture and to be aggressive. What usually differs is the extent to which particular cultures encourage these qualities in children of each sex.

Symbolic interactionism. Cultural perspectives on gender also inform us about the intricacies of gender arrangements within our own society. **Symbolic interactionism** is a very broad theory developed by George Herbert Mead that holds that individuals learn to participate competently in their society and to share its values through communication (symbolic interaction) with others. His theory covers socialization in general and can be applied specifically to how we learn gender through interaction with others.

According to Mead (1934), awareness of personal identity arises out of communication with others who pass on the values and expectations of a society. Because newborns do not enter the world with a sense of self as distinct from the world, they learn from others how to see themselves. As parents and others interact with children, they literally tell them who they are. A child is described as big or dainty, delicate or tough, active or quiet, and so on. With each label, others offer the child a self-image, and children internalize others' views to arrive at their own understandings of who they are. Communication is the central process whereby we gain a sense of who we are. From the moment of birth, we engage in interaction with others, especially parents, who tell us who we are, what is appropriate for us, and what is unacceptable.

Gender is one of the primary aspects of identity that we learn through conversations with others. In Western society, gender is extremely important and is tied to the social order as a whole (Fox-Genovese, 1991; Riessman, 1990; Wood & Lenze, 1991b). Research has shown that views of gender are communicated by parents through their responses to children (Chodorow, 1978, 1989; Safilios-Rothschild, 1979; Shapiro, 1990), through play activities with peers (Maccoby, 1998; Maltz & Borker, 1982), and through teachers' interactions with students (Sandler & Hall, 1986; Wood, 1996b; Wood & Lenze, 1991b). The intensity of focus on gender may explain why this is one of the first clear senses of self that children develop. Before they know their nationality, religion, or social status, most children develop gender constancy and see themselves as gendered beings.

Let's look more closely at exactly how cultures communicate norms and expectations for gender to children. The process occurs as others define them by sex or gender and as those others link gender to particular activities and feelings. "You are Mommy's helper in the kitchen," mothers may say to daughters, using a label that defines young girls as both connected to their mothers and appropriately involved in domestic activities. This and similar labels encourage young girls to define themselves through helping activities and care for others. When young boys carry in packages after shopping, parents often praise them by saying, "You're such a strong little man." This defines the child as a man and links strength with manhood and praise. At school, young girls are likely to be reprimanded for roughhousing as a teacher tells them, "That's not very ladylike." Boys engaged in similar mischief more often hear the teacher say with some amusement, "You boys really are rowdy today." Notice that responses from others, such as teachers, not only reflect broad cultural values but also provide positive and negative rewards, consistent with social learning theory. In play with peers, gender messages continue. When a young girl tries to tell a boy what to do, she may be told, "You can't boss me around. You're just a girl." Girls who fail to share their toys or show consideration to others may be told, "You're not being nice," yet this is considerably less likely to be said to young boys. Thus, children learn what is expected of them and how that is related to being masculine or feminine.

Symbolic interactionism makes it clear that the process of defining a personal self is inevitably a social process that reflects the views of others we have incorporated into our own perspectives. Our thinking about ourselves never occurs from some absolutely personal, idiosyncratic perspective but from the viewpoints of others and the cultural values they embody (Wood, 1993b). Having studied the process by which we learn to conceive of ourselves, George Herbert Mead was able to answer his question, How is it that society gets into individuals? His conclusion was that, through communication with others, we learn who we are and what that means in the culture into which we have been born.

An important contribution to a cultural theory of gender is the concept of role and, specifically, how our society defines roles for women and men. A role is a set of expected behaviors and the values associated with them. In an insightful analysis, Elizabeth Janeway (1971) discusses two dimensions of roles. First, roles are external to individuals because a society defines them in general ways that transcend particular individuals. Roles are assigned to individuals by the society as a whole. Thus, for each of us there are certain roles we are expected to fulfill.

Within our culture, one primary way to classify social life is through gender roles. Women are still regarded as caretakers (Wood, 1994b), and they are expected to provide most of the care for infants, elderly relatives, and others who are sick or disabled. If a child is sick, the mother is generally expected to take time from work or other activities to care for the child (Hewlett, 1986, 1991; Hochschild, 1989; Okin, 1989). If a parent or in-law needs help, it is the daughter or daughter-in-law who is expected to, and who generally does, provide the help, regardless of the costs to her personal and professional life (Aronson, 1992; Wood, 1994b). Even in work outside the home, the feminine role is evident. Women remain disproportionately represented in service sectors and human relations divisions of companies, whereas men are moved into executive positions. Women are still asked to take care of

---

✆ MARK

I see how gender roles work in my own family. My mother works full time, and she's still the one who fixes all the meals and does all the shopping and most of the housework. Both she and Dad seem to accept that as the way things are supposed to be. Last year her mother had a stroke, and since then Mom's been doing another job—taking care of her mother. Every day she goes by to see how Grandma is, and she shops for her and cleans her house as well as ours. Dad has told her she's doing too much, and it's clearly taking a toll on Mom. But I don't think she feels she can do less. And it doesn't seem to have occurred to Dad that he could do more to help. When I asked her why she was doing so much, she told me Grandma expected her help and needed it, and she felt that way too. I don't know how long Mom can keep taking care of everybody else without breaking down herself.

---

social activities on the job, but men in equivalent positions are seldom expected to do this.

Men are still regarded as the primary breadwinners for families. Thus, it is seen as more acceptable for a woman than a man not to have an income-producing job. Some women today regard a career as an option, something they may or may not do or might do for a while and then focus full time on raising a family. Very few young men regard working as optional. To fulfill the masculine role successfully, a man must work and bring in an income; the feminine role does not require this.

Not only are roles assigned by society, but their value is defined as well. Within Western culture, the feminine role remains subordinate to the masculine role. Men are still regarded as the heads of families, even if their wives earn more money than they do. Men, more often than women, are seen as leaders and given opportunities to lead. Further, the work that men do is more highly regarded by the society than is the work assigned to women. Janeway noted that the roles assigned to women—caring for families, keeping a home, and so on—have low prestige in our culture. Society teaches women to accept the role of supporting, taking care of, and responding to others. Yet that is a role clearly devalued in the United States. Competing and succeeding in work life and public affairs are primary roles assigned to men, and to those roles prestige is attached.

A second important dimension of role is that it is internalized. For social specifications of behaviors to be effective, individuals must internalize them. At very young ages, girls understand that they are supposed to be nice, put others' needs ahead of their own, and be nurturing, whereas boys understand that they are supposed to take command and assert themselves. As we take cultural scripts for gender inside of ourselves, we learn not only that there are different roles for men and women but also that unequal values are assigned to them. This can be very frustrating for those who are encouraged to conform to a role that will not be esteemed.

Symbolic interactionism clarifies the ways in which gender reflects meanings widely endorsed by a culture. Although gender is clearly influenced by family psychodynamics, learning, and cognitive development in interpersonal settings, those relational contexts themselves are part of a larger society whose values they echo and perpetuate. Symbolic interactionism underlines the fact that gender is socially created and sustained through communication that teaches us to define ourselves as gendered and to adopt the roles that society prescribes for us.

Standpoint theory. A final contribution from the cultural perspective is **standpoint theory** (Collins, 1986; Harding, 1991, 1998), which offers insights into how a person's location within a culture shapes his or her life. Standpoint theory focuses on how gender, race, and class influence the circumstances of individuals' lives, especially their positions in society and the kinds of experiences those positions foster. To symbolic interactionism's emphasis on how we are socialized into a common social world, standpoint theory adds that the common social world consists of very different positions within social hierarchies. We may all understand that our culture defines people by class and race and values those differently; yet each of us experiences being only in a certain race and class. The particular standpoint that an individual has in a society guides what she or he knows, feels, and does and directs an individual's understanding of social life as a whole.

Although modern theorists have developed standpoint theory, it began some time ago with Georg Wilhelm Friedrich Hegel's reflections on the institution of slavery. Hegel (1807), a prominent 19th-century German philosopher, noted that society as a whole recognized that slavery existed but that the nature of that institution was perceived quite differently depending on whether one's position was that of master or slave. From this insight, Hegel reasoned that in any society where power re-

 KIM

My mother never finished college, but she sure understands the standpoint theory we talked about. The thing she drilled into us as kids was "Don't ever judge others until you've been in their shoes." She said that all the time, and I still hear it in my head whenever I start to judge somebody who's different from me. I think there's a lot to this idea, since the situations people are in do affect how they think and what they are like, and if you haven't been in a situation, you can't judge somebody who has. You can't even understand him or her really.

lationships exist, there can be no single perspective, no correct understanding of social life. Each person sees society as it appears from the perspective of his or her social group, and every perspective is limited. All views are partial because each reflects a particular standpoint within a culture stratified by power.

A particularly important implication of standpoint theory is that although all perspectives on social life are limited, some are more limited than others. Those in positions of high power have a vested interest in preserving their place in the hierarchy, so their views of social life are more distorted than the views of persons who gain little or nothing from existing power relationships. Another reason that those in groups labeled subordinate may have fuller understandings is that they have to understand both their own perspective and the viewpoints of persons who have more power. To survive, subjugated persons have to understand people with power, but the reverse is not true. From this, it follows that marginalized groups have unique insights into the nature and workings of a society. Women, minorities, gays and lesbians, people of lower socioeconomic class, and others who are outside of the cultural center may see the society from a perspective that is less distorted, less biased, and more layered than those who occupy more central standpoints. Marginalized perspectives can inform all of us about how our society operates. María Lugones and Elizabeth Spelman (1983) point out that one of the privileges of dominant groups is the freedom not to try to understand the perspective of less privileged groups. They don't need to learn about others in order to survive.

According to standpoint theory, different social groups like women and men develop particular skills, attitudes, ways of thinking, and understandings of life as a result of their standpoint within society. Patricia Hill Collins (1986, 1998) uses standpoint theory to show that Black women scholars have special insights into Western culture because of their dual standpoints as "outsiders within," that is, as

No Maternal Instinct

In some small Brazilian towns, mothers routinely let sickly children die, even when a simple solution of sugar and salt could save them (Cordes, 1994). During the Renaissance, parents of all classes frequently abandoned babies—900 children a year were left in just three foundling homes in Florence (Thurer, 1994).

Maternal instinct is a cherished ideal in modern Western society, but there is no convincing evidence that women have the alleged maternal instinct. Instead, recent research increasingly suggests that society constructs views of what counts as good mothering, and these views vary across time and cultures.

Scholars who have studied the social construction of motherhood warn that the current Western expectations of mothers can be harmful to real-life mothers (Kaplan, 1992; Roth, 1994; Scheper-Hughes, 1994). Many women with children find it impossible to meet the romanticized views of mothers as unselfish, always nurturing, and uninterested in anything but their families. At the same time, prevailing social expectations fail to define a central role for fathers in caring for children. Whether we look in Brazil or in the United States, it's important to remember that mothering—and fathering—are socially shaped.

members of a minority group (African Americans) who hold membership in majority institutions (higher education).

Another application of standpoint logic came from Sara Ruddick's (1989) study of mothers. She claims that the demands of their role lead mothers to develop what she calls "maternal thinking," which consists of values, priorities, and understandings of relationships that are specifically promoted by the process of taking care of young children. Ruddick argues that what we often assume is a maternal instinct that comes naturally to women is actually a set of attitudes and behaviors that arise out of women's location in domestic, caregiving roles. Supporting Ruddick's finding is work by Sandra Bem (1993), who claims that what we view as maternal instinct is really the result of placing women in roles requiring caregiving. Ruddick's view of learned maternal inclinations is limited by race and class bias because she focused on the mothering of middle-class White women. In a study of African American mothering, Alison Bailey (1994) found that ethnicity also shapes perspectives on mothering.

The impact of standpoint on nurturing ability is further demonstrated by research on men in caregiving roles. In her research on single fathers, Barbara Risman (1989) found that men who are primary parents are more nurturing, attentive to others' needs, patient, and emotionally expressive than are men in general and as much so as most women. Other studies (Downey, Ainsworth-Darnell, & Dufur, 1998; Kaye & Applegate, 1990) found that men who care for elderly people enlarge their capacities for nurturing.

Standpoint research also calls into question the extent to which biology influences gendered behavior. When we discussed biological theory earlier in this chapter, I noted findings ("Study Links Men's Cognitive Abilities," 1991) that men's testosterone levels seemed to affect their aggressiveness and their ability to perform certain cognitive tasks. Yet those findings must be qualified by noting that men in higher socioeconomic classes did not display more aggression when their testosterone was high. This suggests that their standpoint in society included socialization that it is inappropriate to behave aggressively. Even when their testosterone rose, they had learned not to react by being violent and aggressive.

It would be incorrect to think that an individual is shaped by a single standpoint. All of us occupy multiple standpoints that overlap and interact. For example, an African American man's knowledge and identity are shaped by both race and gender standpoints. Because standpoints interact and affect one another, this man's masculine gender identity is different from that of a European American man. As cultural studies scholar Craig Calhoun (1995) notes, no person is determined by a single category.

The cultural perspective broadens our understandings by demonstrating that gender is not merely a quality of individuals. Instead, it entails social expectations that define the meaning of sex and that are systematically taught to individuals. Cultural views of gender reflect three related research traditions. From anthropology, we gain insight into the arbitrary and variable nature of gender by seeing how variably it is defined in diverse cultures. Symbolic interactionist theory offers an understanding of culture as a whole and the key role of communication in socializing new members into the understandings and values of a common social world. Finally, standpoint theory adds the important realization that individuals' positions within a society influence how they see social life and how they define their roles, activities, priorities, and feelings. This is a particularly important point, because Western culture is decisively stratified by gender, race, and class. Women and men typically occupy different standpoints in our society, which profoundly influence how they understand and act in the world as well as how they define themselves.

SUMMARY

In this chapter, we have considered different theories that offer explanations of relationships among communication, gender, and culture. Rather than asking which is the *right* theory, we have tried to discover how each viewpoint contributes to overall understandings of how gender develops. By weaving together the different theories' focus on individual, interpersonal, and cultural influences, we gain a powerful appreciation of the complex origins of gender identity. The cultural perspective seems broadest, because it incorporates interpersonal and biological theories yet also goes beyond their foci. The remainder of this book reflects the view that gender (not sex) is culturally constructed and that the meanings a culture assigns to femininity and masculinity are expressed and sustained through communication.

A key point to keep in mind is that the theories work together to explain both gender and sex differences. For instance, more girls and women, particularly those who are athletes, suffer knee injuries, especially one known as ACL (anterior cruciate ligament). In an N.C.A.A. study of ACL problems in basketball players from 1994 to 1998, women players were nearly three times more likely to suffer ACL injuries than men. For soccer players, the risk for females is even greater (Jacobson, 2001). The fact that women suffer more ACL injuries than men suggests that there may be a sex difference—a biologically based difference between women's and men's knees. However, socialization may also be a factor. Dr. William Garrett, a sports medicine surgeon, has studied films of women and men engaged in sports. In an interview with me (Garrett, 2001), he noted that women and men athletes hold their bodies differently. Men, he says, are looser and tend to move and stand with their knees slightly bent. Women are more likely to keep their legs and knees straight and to maintain more rigid posture. Loose posture and bent knees reduce stress on the knee and thus reduce the risk of ACL injury. There seems to be no biological reason for the difference in posture and knee positioning. It's likely that both result from early socialization in how girls and boys are supposed to act, stand, sit, run, and so forth. Thus, what seems a purely biological effect may also reflect interpersonal and social influences.

Most of us are born biologically male or female. What sex means and what it implies for participation in life, however, are matters of social convention that are communicated to us. Various societies attach different meanings to masculinity and femininity, so what gender means depends on the society in which one lives and the particular position one occupies in that society. Families, schools, peers, and others teach children the cultural dictates of gender. Thus, in the process of becoming socialized, we are encouraged to internalize gendered identities that shape how we understand the common life of a culture and our own places, opportunities, and priorities within it.

With this theoretical background, we are now ready to consider contexts in which gender is formed and communicated, as well as ways in which individuals accept or resist cultural directives for masculinity and femininity. The next chapter builds on this one by exploring how communication within rhetorical movements redefines socially shared views of men and women.

DISCUSSION QUESTIONS

1. What are your assumptions about gender as you begin this course? Do you think gender is influenced more by biology, by society, or by interpersonal relationships? How do your implicit theories affect your own actions and your interpretations of other people's attitudes and behaviors?

2. Using your InfoTrac College Edition, go to PowerTrac and type "search by author name" for the 2000 article by Jayne Stake, "When situations call for instrumentality and expressiveness: Reason appraisal, coping strategy choice and adjustment." What does Stake's research suggest about the value of both instrumentality (conventionally a masculine style) and expressiveness (conventionally a feminine style)?

3. What are the implications of research indicating that men have hormonal cycles that affect their moods and behaviors? Women's hormonal cycles have long been used to justify not trusting women's judgment and excluding them from important roles in decision making. If men too are influenced by their hormones, should we distrust their judgment and actions?

4. Think about your relationship with your parents. How were your connections to your father and mother different? How were they similar? How did sex and gender influence each relationship? If you have siblings of the other sex, were their relationships with your parents different from yours?

5. To learn how Sandra Bem developed the Bem Sex Role Inventory for measuring psychological sex, go to http://www.garysturt.free-online.co.uk/bem.htm.

6. Standpoint theory maintains that a person's social location affects what she or he can know and be. Do you agree or disagree? How have your gender and race affected your standpoint in society? In turn, how has your standpoint affected how you see yourself, others, and social life? As a man or a woman, what do you think you understand particularly well? About what do you not have much insight? Relate this to standpoint theory.

7. Watch men and women athletes as they play their sports. Do you see the differences in posture and knee position that Dr. Garrett found in his research?

8. To learn more about the range of sex and gender identities that people have, go to the Intersex Society of North America's site at http://www.isna.org/faq. There you will find information about transsexual, transgendered, and intersexed people. There are superior faqs and excellent links to related sites.

3 The Rhetorical Shaping of Gender: Women's, Men's, and Gender Movements in America

I n the last chapter, we saw that communication in society influences individuals' gender identities. Equally important is how individuals' communication influences society and its views of masculinity and femininity. Although it's true that gender is socially created, it's also true that individuals make up society and have an impact on how it views men and women.

In the early 1800s, masculinity was equated with physical potency, but today masculinity is tied to economic power and success. Views of femininity have also changed such that women are no longer seen as frail and too uninformed to vote. Changes like these do not just happen. Instead, they grow out of rhetorical movements that alter cultural understandings of gender and, with that, the rights, privileges, and perceptions of women and men. For this reason, insight into relationships among gender, communication, and culture must be informed by knowledge of how rhetorical movements sculpt social meanings of men and women.

Rhetoric is persuasion. Rhetorical movements are collective efforts to change existing attitudes, laws, and policies. In examining U.S. rhetorical movements concerned with gender, we will explore how each movement defined gender and whom it sought to persuade. We will first consider a number of women's movements that have altered the meaning, roles, status, and opportunities of women in America. Second, we'll explore the more recent phenomenon of men's movements, through which men are attempting to redefine what masculinity means on both personal and social levels. We will then discuss two movements that respond to branches of women's and men's movements. As we survey these rhetorical movements, you'll discover that collective efforts to alter views of women and men are anything but uniform. Both women's and men's efforts reflect diverse views of gender and pursue varying goals. Insight into the range of rhetorical movements about gender allows us to appreciate the complexity of the ongoing cultural conversation about the meanings of masculinity and femininity. Further, it may allow you to define more clearly where your own values and goals place you within the range of movements about gender.

WOMEN'S MOVEMENTS

A widely held misconception is that feminism began in the 1960s. This, however, disregards over a century's history in which women's movements had significant impact. It also implies that feminism is one thing, when actually there have been and are many forms of feminism.

Beginning in the 1800s, rhetorical movements to define women's nature and rights have occurred in three waves. During each wave, two distinct ideologies have informed movement goals and efforts at change. One tradition, called **liberal** or **equality feminism** (Crawford, 1988; Hare-Mustin & Marecek, 1988; Yellin, 1990), holds that women and men are basically alike and equal in most respects. Therefore, goes the reasoning, they should have the same rights, privileges, and opportunities to participate in various aspects of life. A second, quite different ideology, which is referred to as **cultural, structural,** or **difference feminism,** holds that women and men are essentially unlike each other. If women differ from men in important ways, then different roles, rights, and activities should be assigned to each. As we survey women's movements, we'll see how these conflicting ideologies lead to diverse rhetorical goals and strategies.

The First Wave of Women's Movements in the United States

Roughly spanning the years from 1840 to 1925, the first wave of women's movements included both liberal and cultural branches. As we will see, the contradictory views of women implicit in these two movements ironically worked together to change the status and rights of women in society.

The women's rights movement. What we now call the **women's rights movement**—activism aimed at enlarging women's rights—grew out of women's efforts in other reform movements (Behling, 2001; Campbell, 1989a). Prior to focusing on women's rights as such, many women in the early 1800s engaged in other reform movements such as abolition and temperance (Yellin, 1990). These early reformers discovered that their efforts to instigate changes were hampered by their lack of a legitimate public voice. Thus, a prerequisite for effective political action about any issue was securing their own rights, most particularly the right to speak and to be counted in public and civic arenas.

In 1840, Lucretia Coffin Mott was chosen as one of the U.S. representatives to the World Anti-Slavery Convention in London (Campbell, 1989a), but she was not allowed to participate, because she was a woman. At the convention, Mott met Elizabeth Cady Stanton, who accompanied her husband (who was a delegate), and the two women discussed the indignity and unfairness of Mott's exclusion. Later, Mott, Stanton, and other women in America who believed women were entitled to rights denied by law organized the first women's rights convention. Held in New York in 1848, the Seneca Falls Convention marked the beginning of women's vocal efforts to secure basic rights in America—ones granted to White men by the Constitution. Lucretia Coffin Mott, Martha Coffin Wright, Mary Anne McClintock, and Elizabeth Cady Stanton collaboratively wrote the keynote address, titled the "Declaration of Sentiments." Ingeniously modeled on the Declaration of Independence, the speech, delivered by Stanton, proclaimed (Campbell, 1989b, p. 34):

> We hold these truths to be self-evident: that all men and women are created equal; that they are endowed by their Creator with certain inalienable rights, that among these are life, liberty, and the pursuit of happiness.

Continuing in the language of the Declaration of Independence, Cady Stanton catalogued specific grievances women had suffered under the "unjust government of men," including denial of the right to vote, exclusion from nearly all types of higher education, restriction on employment, and denial of property rights upon marriage. Following Cady Stanton's stirring oratory, 32 men and 68 women signed a petition supporting specific rights for women except the right to vote. Instrumental to passage of this resolution were the persuasive pleas of former slave Frederick Douglass (Campbell, 1989b).

Although Douglass's support of women's suffrage was critical for ratification at Seneca Falls, it does not signify widespread participation of Black citizens in the women's rights movement. In fact, although there were originally strong links between abolitionist efforts and women's rights, these dissipated. Believing that, if slavery could be abolished, so could women's disenfranchisement, women's rights activists initially connected their campaign to efforts to enfranchise Black men. That initial linkage broke down because many abolitionists believed that the movement for Black men's voting rights had to precede women's suffrage. In addition, many Black women thought White women had defined women's problems in terms of issues that mattered more to Whites and had ignored grievous differences caused by race. Forced to choose between allegiance to their race and allegiance to their sex, most Black women of the era chose race. Thus, the women's rights movement became almost exclusively White in its membership and interests.

The Seneca Falls Convention did not have immediate political impact. Women's efforts to secure the right to vote based on the argument that the Constitution defined suffrage as a right of all individuals fell on deaf ears. At that time in America's history, women were still not considered individuals but rather the property of men. In 1872, two years after Black men received the right to vote, Susan B. Anthony and other women registered and attempted to cast votes, but they were

Ain't I a Woman?

Sojourner Truth was named Isabella Van Wagenen when she was born as a slave in Ulster County, New York, in the late 1700s. After she was emancipated, Van Wagenen moved to New York City and explored various spiritual practices before becoming a Pentecostal preacher at the age of 46. She preached throughout Northern states, using the new name she gave herself: Sojourner of God's Truth. Her preachings called for reforms, including temperance, women's rights, and the abolition of slavery.

On May 28, 1951, Truth attended a women's rights meeting in Akron, Ohio. Throughout the morning, she listened to speeches that focused largely on white women's concerns. Here the historical account splits. Some scholars (Painter, 1996) state that Sojourner did not speak at the meeting and someone else gave the speech that is widely credited to Truth. Other accounts state that Sojourner Truth rose to speak and walked forward despite hisses of disapproval. Soon the audience quieted in the face of this tall woman who stood with her head erect and her eyes piercing. The speech, "Ain't I a Woman?"—whether given by Truth or another person—pointed out the ways in which White women's situations and oppression are different from those of Black women. With a voice like rolling thunder, Sojourner Truth eloquently gave voice to the double oppression suffered by Black women in the 1800s (Folb, 1985; Hine & Thompson, 1998; hooks, 1981):

> "That man over there says that woman needs to be helped into carriages, and lifted over ditches, and to have the best place everywhere. Nobody ever helps me into carriages or over mud-puddles, or gives me any best place. And ain't I a woman?
>
> I have ploughed, and I planted, and gathered into barns. . . . And ain't I a woman?
>
> I have borne thirteen children and seen them most all sold off into slavery, and when I cried out with a mother's grief, none but Jesus heard. And ain't I a woman?"

turned away at the polls and arrested. Only 48 years later would women win the right to vote, and that occurred in part as a result of a second ideology within the first wave of women's movements.

The cult of domesticity. Many women of this era disagreed with the basic claim that women and men are equal and alike in important respects. Instead, these women argued that women belong in the domestic sphere and that women and men differ in fundamental ways. They believed that, compared with men, women were purer, more moral, nurturing, concerned about others, and committed to harmony. Unlike women's rights activists, cultural feminists of this period did not challenge the domestic roles assigned to women; in fact, they celebrated the "cult of domesticity" as the ideal of femininity or "true womanhood" (Welter, 1966). Belief in women's moral virtue led cultural feminists to form various reform organizations such as the Women's Christian Temperance Union and to fight for child labor laws, rights of women prisoners, and policies of peace. It's important to realize that the cult of domesticity, like other women's movements in the 1800s, focused on the lives and concerns of middle-class White women. White women were concerned about political and educational rights, whereas nearly all Black women confronted far more basic injustices and suffered fundamental deprivations of liberty, food, shelter, and medical care.

Cultural feminists' belief in women's higher morality reflected highly conservative views of women. Ironically, this ideology—not the more liberal one—was critical to securing women's right to vote. Cultural feminists gave speeches arguing that women should be allowed to vote because it would curb the corruption of political life. Women's moral virtue, they claimed, would reform the political world that had been debased by the control of immoral men. This rhetorical strategy

---

FYI

Reproductive Rights

Birth control was a major issue in the first and second waves of women's movements. In the 19th century, Elizabeth Cady Stanton raised the idea of "voluntary motherhood" as a prerequisite to women's freedom (Gordon, 1976). Later, Margaret Sanger emerged as the most visible proponent of women's access to birth control. Sanger's work as a nurse and midwife made her painfully aware that many women, particularly immigrants and poor women, were dying in childbirth or as a result of illegal abortions (Chesler, 1992). Sanger crusaded relentlessly for birth control for women, arguing the cause in speeches all over America and Europe. In her periodical publication, *The Woman Rebel,* Sanger wrote many articles, including one in which she declared, "A woman's body belongs to herself alone. It is her body. It does not belong to the Church. It does not belong to the United States of America or any other government on the face of the earth. . . . Enforced motherhood is the most complete denial of a woman's right to life and liberty" (1914, p. 1).

During the second wave of feminism in the United States, feminists again protested for safe, accessible birth control and abortion for all women. In 1969, a group of feminists disrupted the New York State legislature's expert hearing on abortion reform—the experts who had been invited to address the legislature consisted of 14 men and one nun (Pollitt, 2000). The feminists insisted that none of the so-called experts had any personal experience with what reproductive choices mean. Although this protest didn't lead to immediate abortion reform, four years later the landmark case of *Roe v. Wade* established the right to abortion as a woman's right. Yet, 25 years after that case was decided, abortion is still not available to all women who are citizens of the United States. Although the courts have upheld women's right to abortion, legislation has progressively restricted access to abortion. In 1997, the 105th Congress banned access to privately funded abortions at overseas military hospitals, prohibited insurance for federal employees from covering abortion, and greatly restricted abortions for Medicaid recipients ("*Roe v. Wade* at Twenty-five," 1998).

Even among feminists, abortion is controversial. Although feminist groups such as NOW support women's right to choose, other groups such as Feminists for Life argue that abortion is wrong and antithetical to feminine values.

---

eventually carried women to victory in their struggle to gain political franchise. On August 26, 1920, the constitutional amendment granting women the right to vote was passed and ratified.

Although the combined force of the cultural and liberal women's movements was necessary to win suffrage, the deep ideological chasm between these two groups was not resolved. Nor did securing voting rights immediately fuel further efforts to enlarge women's rights, roles, influence, and opportunities. Few women exercised their hard-won right to vote, and in 1925 an amendment prohibiting child labor failed to be ratified, signaling the close of the first wave of women's movements.

After this, women's movements in the United States were relatively dormant for nearly 35 years. This time of quiescence in women's movements resulted from several factors. First, America's attention was concentrated on two world wars. During that time, women joined the labor force in record numbers to maintain the economy while many men were at war. Between 1940 and 1944, 6,000,000 women went to work—a 500% increase in the number of women in paid labor (Harrison, 1988; Klein, 1984). When the wars were over, women's and men's energies focused on creating families and enjoying America's premier status in the world. In postwar America, men's economic opportunities expanded tremendously, and the government encouraged women to return to their homes and leave paid labor to men. The view of the man as the breadwinner for the family became the ideal. During these years, only 12% of married women with children under the age of 6 were employed outside of their homes (Collins & Coltrane, 1995; Risman & Godwin, 2001).

■ The Second Wave of Women's Movements in the United States

Between 1960 and roughly 1995, a second wave of women's movements emerged in America. As in the first wave of women's movements, both liberal and cultural ideologies coexisted in the second wave, sometimes in harmony, often in tension. Also like the first era of women's activism, the movements of the second wave sprang from different sources, sought diverse goals, and pursued distinct rhetorical strategies.

Radical feminism. The first form of feminism to emerge in this century was **radical feminism.** In the United States, this grew out of New Left politics, which focused on protesting the Vietnam War and fighting for civil rights for Blacks. As women participated side by side with men in objecting to U.S. involvement in Vietnam and egregious racial injustices at home, it became clear that the women were not being treated equally. They did the same work as their male peers and risked the same hazards of arrest, beatings, and expulsion, but women were treated as subordinate. Men dominated and kept a monopoly on New Left leadership, whereas women activists were expected to make coffee, type news releases and memos, do the menial work of organizing, and be ever available for the mens' sexual recreation.

Women were generally not allowed to represent the movement in public—their voices were not recognized or respected.

In 1964, women in the Student Nonviolent Coordinating Committee (SNCC) who argued for female equality within the New Left movement were met with rigid, sexist attitudes. Stokely Carmichael, a major leader for civil rights, responded to women's demands for equality by telling them that "the position of women in SNCC is prone." (He actually meant *supine*—on their backs.) In 1965, women in the Students for a Democratic Society (SDS) found no receptivity to their demands for equality (O'Kelly & Carney, 1986).

Outraged by men's total disregard for their rights and men's refusal to extend to gender equality the democratic, egalitarian principles they preached, many women withdrew from the New Left organizations and formed their own organizations. The most basic principle of radical feminism was that oppression of women is the fundamental form of oppression on which all others are modeled (Dow, 1995; Du Plessis & Snitow, 1999; Willis, 1992).

The crux of radical feminism was confronting women's oppression with revolutionary analysis, politics, and action (Barry, 1998). Whereas other branches of second-wave feminism aimed for reform, radical feminists demanded revolutionary change in women's place in society and relationships between women and men.

In 1968, women organized and held the first national meetings, where they began to chart the principles and practices that would define radical feminism. Central to what they created were new forms of communication, which became the heart of radical feminism. A primary radical feminist communication technique was "rap" groups or consciousness-raising groups, in which women gathered to

---

FYI

The Famous Bra Burning (That Never Happened!)

One of the most widespread perceptions of feminism is based on the bra burning of 1968, in which media reported that a number of radical feminists burned their bras to protest the Miss America Pageant's focus on women as sexual objects.

In planning a response to the pageant, protesters considered a number of guerrilla theater techniques to dramatize their disapproval of what the pageant stood for and how it portrayed women. They decided to protest by throwing false eyelashes, bras, girdles, and so forth into a trash can in front of reporters. They also put a crown on a large pig labeled Miss America and led it around the pageant. In early planning for the protest, some members suggested burning bras, but this idea was discarded (Hanisch, 1970). However, a reporter heard of the plan and reported the event on national media. Millions of Americans accepted it as a fact, and even today many people refer to feminists as "bra-burners."

It made a great story, it captured public interest, and it supported media caricatures of radical feminists as crazy, extremist, man-hating women. The truth is, not a single bra was burned at that time!

---

talk informally about personal experiences with sexism. Radical feminists' commitment to equality and their deep suspicion of stratification led them to practice communication that ensured equal participation by all members of rap groups. For instance, some groups used a system of chips in which each woman was given an equal number of chips at the outset of a rap session. Each time she spoke, she tossed one of her chips into the center of the group. When her chips were all cashed in, she could not contribute further, and other, less outspoken women had an opportunity to speak. This technique was valuable because it recognized the importance of women's voices, encouraged individual women to find and use their voices, and taught women to listen to and respect each other.

Consciousness-raising groups were leaderless, as were working committees in radical feminist organizations. Reflecting disillusion with formal organizations like SDS and SNCC, in which members vied for power, leaderless discussions allowed each woman to contribute to conversations without anyone being in charge of anyone else. A third innovative communication form that radical feminists employed was guerrilla theater, in which they engaged in public communication to dramatize issues and arguments. Although public rhetoric was not a primary focus of radical feminism, it occurred occasionally. Protests against the Miss America pageants in 1968 and 1969, for instance, included throwing cosmetics and constrictive under-

---

FYI

The Guerrilla Girls

Radical feminists are not confined to history. Some radical feminists continue to operate, using shock, outrageousness, and bravado to challenge sexism, racism, and other kinds of discrimination. The best-known radical feminist group on the contemporary scene is the Guerrilla Girls, an anonymous organization that campaigns against sexism, racism, and elitism in the art world. They first captured public attention in 1985 when they were outraged by the Museum of Modern Art's exhibit titled "International Survey of Contemporary Art." The Guerrilla Girls plastered posters throughout public places in New York City. Armed with equal measures of information, sarcasm, and humor, the posters asked "Do women have to be naked to get into Metropolitan Museum?" Following the question were statistics on the number of women artists (5) and women nudes (85) in the museum's exhibit. The press appreciated the media-savvy tactics of the Guerrilla Girls and gave them good coverage. The Guerrilla Girls are an anonymous group, insisting that their identities are irrelevant and that they want to focus on the issues, not on themselves. This mystery, of course, enhanced public interest in the Guerrilla Girls, who are invited to appear on talk shows, give public lectures, and otherwise educate the public—all done without removing their masks. Periodically the Guerrilla Girls issue new dramatic statements in response to sexism and racism.

Sources: Guerrilla Girls (1995). *Confessions of the guerrilla girls.* New York: Harper Perennial; Smith, N. (1998).

---

wear for women into trash containers to demonstrate rejection of a view of women as sex objects.

The radical feminist movement has achieved some notable results. Perhaps the most important outcome of this movement was identifying the structural basis of gender differences and opportunities. The connection between individual women's situations and social practices was captured in the movement's declaration that "the personal is political." Through consciousness raising and collective efforts, radical feminists organized a women's health movement, which has helped women recognize and resist sexist and dictatorial attitudes of doctors and become knowledgeable about their own bodies (Boston Women's Health Club Book Collective, 1976; The Diagram Group, 1977). Although radical feminists' refusal to formally organize limits their ability to affect public policies and structures, they offered—and continue to offer—the most profound and far-reaching critique of sexual inequality.

 Liberal feminism. A second major form of liberal feminism in our era goes by various labels: middle-class feminism, **liberal feminism,** and equality feminism. At the heart of this movement were women's demands for full participation in the world outside of the home, especially the workplace. Two distinct issues gave rise to this demand. First, the costs of living and home ownership rose, and many working-class families found it difficult or impossible to make ends meet on just one person's (the husband's) salary (England & Farcas, 1980; Stacey, 1990).

The second source of women's desire to participate in the labor force came from a very different form—middle-class, White women who were economically comfortable but who were not entirely fulfilled by their domestic roles. Surrounded by their children and hardworking husbands, with matching appliances in their three-bedroom, suburban ranch houses and station wagons in the driveways, these women were told they were living the American Dream. They were supposed to be happy and feel gratified. But many of these middle-class homemakers were not happy. They loved their families and homes, but they also wanted an identity outside of the home. So they were not only unhappy, but they felt guilty about their malaise. Most women, in fact, felt so guilty about their dissatisfaction that they kept their feelings to themselves. Consequently, most individual women didn't realize that many other women had the same feelings.

The liberal feminist movement crystallized in 1963, when Betty Friedan published her landmark book, *The Feminine Mystique.* Friedan's book highlighted "the problem that has no name," by which

---

✎ ANNA

I remember when the second wave of feminism started. I was in college then. I'd never thought about women being oppressed. I'd never questioned women's place in society. Two of my close friends and I were protesting for civil rights. The men in our group always asked us to go get coffee or food or whatever. We started talking about that—why was it that we were supposed to wait on them? If all of us were working to end discrimination based on race, why were they practicing discrimination based on sex? That was when I first became aware of sexism and when I became a feminist.

Who Was Betty Friedan?

Born Bettye Naomi Goldstein in Peoria, Illinois, in 1921, Betty Friedan would engage in nightly dinner-table conversations with her father. They discussed politics while her beautiful, fashionable mother looked on disappointedly at Betty's physical appearance.

Bettye Goldstein enrolled in Smith College, where she blossomed intellectually and became the star student in the psychology department. After dropping the "e" from her name, Betty Goldstein became the editor-in-chief of the Smith College newspaper, which she used as a platform for espousing her views on issues such as Smith's secret societies, pacifism, and international politics. In 1942, Goldstein graduated with highest honors and began graduate studies at the University of California at Berkeley. Within her first year, she was offered the most prestigious graduate fellowship in the field of psychology.

Betty Goldstein declined the scholarship, left school, and moved to New York City, where she continued her dating relationship with a physicist. That relationship eventually ended, and Betty met Carl Friedan, a witty, handsome theatrical director whom she married. The marriage was not happy, and there were incidents of violence.

Friedan worked as a journalist until 1952, when she was pregnant with her second child and McCarthyism had eclipsed feminism and leftist politics. She was compelled to withdraw to the suburbs, where she wrote for women's magazines. But Friedan was unhappy with her life in the suburbs. She questioned other Smith graduates and discovered that they too were discontented with having given up their careers for their families.

It was nine years later that her most famous book, *The Feminine Mystique,* was published. In that book, she addressed "the problem that has no name," thus giving it a name and giving impetus to the second wave of feminism in the United States.

Sources: Hartman, S. (1998). *The other feminists: Activists in the liberal establishment.* New Haven, CT: Yale University Press; Hennesee, J. (1999). *Betty Friedan: A biography.* New York: Random House; Horowitz, D. (1998). *Betty Friedan and the making of the feminine mystique: The American left, the cold war, and modern feminism.* Amherst, MA: University of Massachusetts Press.

she meant the vague, chronic discontent that many middle-class American women felt. Friedan named the problem and defined it as a political issue, not a personal one. She pointed out that the reasons women were not able to pursue personal development were political: American institutions, including laws and prevailing values, kept women confined to domestic roles that squelched fulfillment in arenas outside of home life.

Acting from the liberal tenet that women and men are alike in important respects and, therefore, entitled to equal rights and opportunities, the movement spawned by Friedan's book is embodied in NOW, the National Organization for Women, which works to secure political, professional, and educational equity for women. Founded in 1966 with Betty Friedan acting as an organizer, NOW is a public voice for equal rights for women. It has been extremely effective in enacting

The National Organization for Women was established on June 30, 1966, in Washington, DC, by people attending the Third National Conference on the Commission on the Status of Women. Among the 28 founders of NOW were Betty Friedan, its first president, and the Reverend Pauli Murray, an African American woman who was an Episcopal minister. Murray co-authored NOW's original mission statement, which begins with this sentence:

> The purpose of NOW is to take action to bring women into full participation in the mainstream of American society now, exercising all privileges and responsibilities thereof in truly equal partnership with men.

 Visit the NOW Web site at **http://www.now.org.**

Email NOW at **now@now.org.**

rhetorical strategies that have brought about concrete changes in laws and policies that enlarge women's opportunities and protect their rights. Consider some of the advances for women that liberal feminism has achieved:

- The 1963 Equal Pay Act was passed.

- The Civil Rights Act of 1964 was amended to include sex, along with race, religion, and nationality, as an illegal basis for employment discrimination.

- Executive Order 11246 was modified to prohibit gender discrimination in employment by holders of federal contracts.

- NOW supports federally financed child-care centers, which make it possible for many women to be employed.

- NOW documents sexism in children's books and programs and publishes its findings so that parents and teachers can make informed choices about media for their children.

- NOW, along with other organizations, has stimulated reforms in credit and banking practices that disadvantage women.

- NOW has enlarged equity in sports so that women have greater opportunities, especially through support of Title IX.

- In 1971, NOW formed the National Women's Political Caucus to support women who seek elective and appointive public office.

Liberal feminism, particularly as exemplified by NOW, identifies and challenges institutional practices, policies, and laws that exclude women from positions of

Reprinted with special permission of North American Syndicate.

influence in public and professional life (Brownmiller, 2000; Rosen, 2001). The rhetorical strategies of this movement include lobbying, speaking at public forums, drafting legislation, and holding conventions where plans are formed and further strategies are developed. For those women who want equal opportunities to participate in the existing structures of our society, this form of feminism has been liberating.

Yet liberal feminism has little to offer other women who endorse the belief that women are distinct from men and therefore have different needs and abilities and deserve different opportunities. For those endorsing this ideology, various forms of cultural feminism are more compelling.

Separatism. Some women believe, as first-wave cultural feminists did, that women are fundamentally different from men in the value they place on life, equality, harmony, nurturance, and peace. Finding that these values gain little hearing in a capitalist society that is wedded to competition and power mongering, some women adopt the revolutionary goal of forming all-women communities in which feminine values can flourish without intrusion from men and the aggressive, individualistic, oppressive values of capitalism. They strive for lifestyles and communities in which people are interdependent and live in mutual respect and harmony.

Herland

Herland is a feminist utopian novel published in 1915 and reissued in 1979. In it, author Charlotte Perkins Gilman describes a matriarchal society in which feminine traditions infuse personal and social life. Motherlove is the religion of Herland, and Maternal Pantheism is the prime goddess.

All women inhabitants of Herland live in a communal fashion in which everyone is committed to helping others and the collective society. They are peace loving, life affirming, and vegetarian, avoiding at all costs activities that harm any life form, including the earth itself.

The drama of the story begins when a small group of men accidentally enter Herland and try to make sense of a culture in which competition gets them nowhere, power is not coveted, and individual self-interest only hampers personal happiness.

Separatists believe it is impossible or a poor use of their generative energies to attempt to reform the male-oriented culture of America. Instead, they simply choose to remove themselves from the mainstream and live in tune with communal values and respect for life, including life of people, animals, and the earth. In adopting this course of action, separatists not only remove themselves from mainstream culture but also foreclose opportunities to alter dominant social values. They do not assume a public voice to critique the values they find objectionable, so they have no real impact on social views. In this sense, they exercise little pragmatic or political influence. Yet their very existence defines an alternative vision of how we might live—one that speaks of harmony, cooperation, and peaceful coexistence of all life forms.

Cultural feminists. Beginning in the 1970s, a women's renaissance emerged in the United States as well as in parts of Europe, Asia, Latin America, and Africa. The mainstream, second-wave feminism had torn down some of the barriers to women and had paved the way for appreciating women in their own right and on their own terms. This led to an outpouring of music, literature, and art by women, whose creative, artistic work had been silenced or ignored for centuries (Aptheker, 1998). Operating from standpoint theory, which we considered in Chapter 2, **cultural feminists** argue that women's experiences are different from men's and, thus, what women know, believe, and create is also different. Although cultural feminists contend that women are different from men, most are skeptical of claims that the differences are innate or biological (Donovan, 1985). Instead, a majority of cultural feminists believe that women's traditional position in the domestic sphere of life has led them to develop more nurturing, supportive, cooperative, and life-giving values than those that men learn through participation in the public sphere. Sara Ruddick (1989), for instance, claims that the process of mothering young children cul-

Socialist and Marxist Feminism

Both **Marxist** and **socialist feminism** offer alternatives to Western and capitalist versions of feminism. There are similarities between Marxist and socialist feminism. Both draw heavily on the works of the German philosophers and intellectual companions Karl Marx (1818–1883) and Friedrich Engels (1820–1895). Also, both branches of feminism assume that economic and material conditions are powerful sources of oppression. Finally, both assume that capitalism is important in creating and reproducing a sexual division of labor and resulting political and economic inequities between women and men.

There are also notable differences between Marxist and socialist feminism. Whereas the Marxist branch focuses on how capitalism sustains itself by subordinating many people, the socialist branch emphasizes the inequality that grows out of women's unpaid and unappreciated labor in the home and family.

Marxist theory assumes that members of the privileged class (the bourgeoisie) oppress members of the working class (the proletariat) by forcing working-class people to sell their labor at whatever price is offered by people who have the means to produce goods and services. Thus, the proletariat is forced to serve the interests of the bourgeoisie. Applying this idea to relations between the sexes, Marxist feminism regards the sexual division of labor as an effect of capitalism.

Socialist feminism, on the other hand, sees the sexual division of labor as intrinsic to capitalist modes of production but does not assume that capitalism alone is responsible. Socialist feminists regard patriarchy as an oppressive system that is inseparable from racism and class oppression. Because systems of oppression are interlinked, creating a more equitable social system requires a complete transformation of the present system. For example, abolishing the system of private property would transform race, class, and gender.

Socialist feminists regard the family as a key site of the oppression of women and the reproduction of that oppression. For this reason, changing how families operate is a major focus of socialist feminism. Objectives include eliminating the sexual division of labor; fully valuing homemaking, housework, and child care; and requiring full participation of fathers in childrearing.

Both oppression and the possibilities of change must be understood within specific historical contexts because gender and other aspects of human nature are constructed differently at different times and in different social locations.

tivates in women "maternal thinking," which is marked by attentiveness to others and personal involvement with others' health, happiness, and development. Because of their different standpoint, women also produce distinct forms of art.

Cultural feminists engage in several kinds of communication. Some cultural feminists enter into legal debates in an effort to secure unique legal rights for women because of their sex. For instance, they argue that laws need to recognize that only women bear children and thus have special needs that must be legally protected. Other cultural feminists seek to persuade others and society as a whole to incorporate women's perspectives and experiences into public awareness in order to enhance the quality of politics, professional activity, and cultural life in general. A third form of communication by cultural feminists is public shows and festivals that focus on women's experiences and creative expression. Perhaps the best-known example of this is the Lilith Fair, an annual music festival.

Lesbian feminists. Arguing that only women who do not orient their lives around men can be truly free, **lesbian feminists** define themselves as woman identified. Although not all lesbians ally themselves with feminism, many do so because of a shared commitment to ending discrimination against women. Many lesbian feminists are also committed to political activism designed to improve the conditions of women's lives. They join groups ranging from mainstream to radical (Taylor & Rupp, 1998). Some people argue that lesbians should keep their sexual lives private, just as heterosexuals do. In response, lesbian feminists point out, "That's exactly the point: We don't think employers and others should be able to pry into our private lives and deny us jobs and housing because of the gender of our sweethearts" ("A New Court Decision," 1992).

Lesbian feminists are united in the focus on certain core issues that specifically affect lesbians' lives. High in priority is fighting for basic civil rights through passage of legislation that prohibits job discrimination on the basis of sexual orientation. Lesbian feminists are also concerned with discrimination in insurance coverage, housing, and property rights. Battles over these issues currently are being waged in legislative chambers across the nation. For instance, in *Soroka v. Dayton Hudson Corporation* (1991), the California Court of Appeals ruled that questions about sexual orientation may not be included on job applications, because this violates applicants' rights to privacy. For lesbian feminists, the primary goals are to live as woman-identified women and to make it possible for women in committed, enduring relationships to enjoy the same property, insurance, and legal rights granted to heterosexual spouses. The rhetoric of lesbian feminists has two characteristic forms. First, much communication by lesbian feminists is responsive to criticism from the culture. Second, some lesbian feminists adopt proactive rhetorical strategies to assert their value, rights, and integrity.

Revalorists. Some modern feminists, who may endorse liberal or cultural ideologies, are committed to valuing traditionally feminine skills, activities, and perspectives that have been marginalized in this society. The members of this group are often called **revalorists** because they seek to revalue women and their contributions to cultural life. In addition, revalorists want to "re-cover" women whose contributions to public life have been excluded from histories of America. Revalorists often use unusual language to call attention to what they are doing. For instance, they talk about re-covering, not recovering, women's history to indicate they want to go beyond the prevailing male perspectives that have created history and views of women. Instead, their goals are to recover the contributions of women and to precipitate cultural acknowledgment of their values and validity.

Examples of revalorists' efforts include Karlyn Khors Campbell's series of books entitled *Man Cannot Speak for Her* (1989a, 1989b), in which her goal (1989a) is "to restore one segment of the history of women" (p. 1). Another example, from a different field, is physicist Evelyn Fox Keller's (1983, 1985) efforts to make known Barbara McClintock's brilliant work in genetics, which science books have disregarded. In re-covering women's contributions, revalorists contribute to a more complete, more accurate history of North America and the people composing it.

Other revalorists focus on celebrating women's traditional activities and skills. Carol Gilligan (1982), for instance, highlights women's commitment to caring. Following Gilligan's work, Mary Belenky and her colleagues (1986) identify ways of knowing that seem more characteristic of women than of men. All of these revalorist efforts aim to give women and their values and activities equal time and equal value in public awareness and recognition. The broad goal of revalorists, then, is to increase the value and salience of skills, activities, and philosophies derived from women's traditional roles (Donovan, 1985).

Revalorist rhetoric is consistent with the goal of heightened public awareness of and respect for women's ways. Some revalorists seek public forums in which to raise the status of activities and roles traditionally associated with women. Through speeches and other symbolic forms such as art, the integrity of women's traditional roles and their contributions to social life are affirmed. Exhibitions of women's traditional arts such as weaving and quilting are examples of rhetorical strategies that rely on symbols other than words to persuade.

Some scholars warn that celebrating women's traditional activities and inclinations has repressive potential, because it seems to value what results from oppression (Boling, 1991; Wood, 1994b). For instance, caring for others may reflect skills women developed to please those who controlled their lives—sometimes literally. Revalorists respond to this criticism by arguing that not to celebrate women's traditional activities is to participate in widespread cultural devaluations that have long shaped perceptions of women. This controversy is part of the ongoing cultural conversation about the meaning and value of femininity.

Womanists. Another group of second-wave activists calls themselves **womanists** to differentiate themselves from other feminists. Picking up the first-wave criticism of feminism as being White, middle-class feminism, many African American women have defined a viewpoint that embodies their racial and gender identities. Their

---

REGINA

If I had to put myself in one or another of the feminist categories, I guess I'd say that I'm more of a structural feminist. I don't see much to be gained by having equal rights to participate in institutions that are themselves all wrong. I don't believe dog-eat-dog ethics are right. I don't want to be part of a system where I can advance only if I slit somebody else's throat or step on him or her. I don't want to prostitute myself for bits of power in a business. I would rather work for different ways of living, ones that are more cooperative like win-win strategies. Maybe that means I'm a dreamer, but I just can't motivate myself to work at gaining status in a system that I don't respect.

goals are to make others aware of the exclusionary nature of feminism as it has been articulated by middle-class White women and to educate others about the ways in which gender and race oppression intersect in the lives of women of color. Liberal feminism, say the womanists, speaks only to the experiences, concerns, and situations of members of a privileged race in America. bell hooks (1990), among other womanists, notes that African American women's oppression is bound up with both race and gender and cannot be addressed by a middle-class feminist agenda that is ignorant of how racism and sexism come together in the lives of minority women. For this reason, many Black women remain loyal to Black men out of a commitment to racial unity (Collins, 1996).

Women of color have a distinctive cultural history that is seldom recognized, much less addressed, by the White, middle-class women who have dominated women's movements of both waves. In remaining ignorant of experiences of non-White, nonmiddle-class women, White feminists may inadvertently participate in the very kind of oppression they claim to oppose (Joseph & Lewis, 1981; Rothenberg, Schafhausen, & Schneider, 2000). Some general differences related to race in women's situations are that Black women as a group are more often single, have less formal education, bear more children, are paid less, and assume more financial responsibility for supporting families. Differences such as these lead many women of color to feel they don't belong in feminist groups, because those groups have agendas that ignore their experiences (Findlen, 1995; Logwood, 1997).

Beginning in the 1970s, a number of African American women who were disenchanted with White, middle-class feminism but who were committed to women's equality began organizing their own groups (B. Smith, 1998). Feminist organizations such as Black Women Organized for Action and the National Black Feminist Organization sprang up and quickly attracted a number of members. These organizations were more effective than mainstream liberal feminism in cutting across class lines to include working-class women and to address issues of lower-class African American women in their agendas. Their goals included reforming welfare organizations so they respond more humanely to poor women and increasing training and job opportunities so that women of color can improve the material conditions of their lives (Hertz, 1977). Primary rhetorical strategies employed by womanists include consciousness-raising and support among women of color, lobbying decision makers for reforms in laws, and community organizing to build grassroots leadership of, by, and for women of color.

In 1997, African American women organized a

𝒞 LASHENNA

NOW's answer to African American women is just a trickle-down theory. Whatever big gains and changes NOW makes in the lives of middle-class White women are supposed to trickle down to us so we get a little something too. Well, thanks, but no thanks, I say. NOW and all those White feminist movements ignore the issues in Black women's lives. We have to deal not only with gender, but with race as well. Unlike a majority of White women, many African American women are faced with economic disadvantages, single parenthood, factory or housekeeping jobs, and little education. I have family members who face one or more of these problems. I don't want White women's trickle-down theory. I want a bottom-up theory!

To Be Womanish, to Be a Womanist

Alice Walker is credited with coining the term *womanism* as a label for Black women who believe in women's value, rights, and opportunities. According to Walker, Southern Black women often said to their daughters "You acting womanish," which meant the daughters were acting boldly, courageously, willfully, and in ways that White females typically don't act. Womanish girls are definitely not girlish, silly, or trivial in their thoughts and actions. Instead, to be womanish is to demand to know more than others say is good for you—to explore, demand, and stretch beyond what is prescribed for a woman or girl (Collins, 1998). In her 1983 book *In Search of Our Mothers' Gardens*, Walker writes, "Womanist is to feminist as purple is to lavender" (p. xii).

march to celebrate and nourish community among African American women. Following the second Million Man March, which we'll discuss later in this chapter, the **Million Woman March** was held in Philadelphia on October 24 and 25, 1997. The Million Woman March was powered by grassroots volunteers, who worked to drum up support in their localities. The steering committee was made up not of celebrities but of average women who worked at unglamorous jobs and lived lives outside of the spotlight. The march reflected the grassroots organizing by de-emphasizing media hype in favor of woman-to-woman sharing of experiences, hopes, and support. Perhaps the spirit of the Million Woman March is best summed up by Irma Jones, a 74-year-old woman who had marched with Dr. Martin Luther King, Jr., from Selma to Montgomery. After the Million Woman March, Jones said, "I'm glad we did this before I died. People say black women can never get together. Today, we got together, sister" (Logwood, 1998, p. 19).

Multiracial feminism. Womanism established a foundation for **multiracial feminism**, an emerging movement that recognizes that women and men are located in a range of systems of domination (Lorber, 2001). Leaders of this movement prefer the term *multiracial* to *multicultural* because they believe that race is a particularly potent power system that shapes identities and opportunities (Zinn & Dill, 1996). The work of this movement is carried on largely by scholars such as Patricia Hill Collins (1990, 1998) who work to show how race cuts across other differences, such as those of culture, class, and sexual orientation. At the same time, multiracial feminists insist that race cannot be viewed in isolation. Although especially important from their perspective, race intersects other systems of domination in ways that affect what race means. For instance, an Asian American will experience his or her race differently, depending on whether he or she is unemployed or a member of the professional class, the working class, or the middle class. Also central to the multiracial feminist project is emphasis on women's agency. Despite the constraints of systems of domination, women of color have often resisted those who sought to oppress them. Even when they operated within abhorrent systems of power such as slavery, women of color found ways to care for themselves and their families and to contribute to their communities. In highlighting how women of color have resisted oppression, multiracial feminists seek to value the strengths of all women.

A second important emphasis in multiracial feminism is challenging and changing some of the categories that structure how we think about gendered identities. Most notably, these feminists assert that gender does not have universal meaning— instead, what gender means and how it affects our lives varies as a result of our locations in different cultures, economic classes, and social-political communities. Gloria Anzaldúa (1999), a Chicana feminist, resists being categorized according to just her sex or just her race-ethnicity or just her sexual orientation. She insists that, on its own, each category misrepresents her identity because her race-ethnicity affects the meaning of being a woman and a lesbian; her sex affects the meaning of her race-ethnicity and sexual orientation; and her sexual orientation affects the meaning of being a woman and a Chicana. Yen Le Espiritu (1997) makes the same argument about Asian American women and men, as does Minh-ha Trinh (1989) about being a Vietnamese woman. For these multiracial feminists, the key to understanding anyone's identity lies in the *intersection of and interaction among* multiple categories such as gender, race-ethnicity, sexual orientation, and social class. This leads multiracial feminists to write and talk, not about women or men as broad groups, but about more precise and complex categories such as black working-class heterosexual men and middle-class Chicana lesbians.

Multiracial feminists have contributed significantly to feminist theory and practice by demonstrating that members of subordinate groups are often disadvantaged by multiple systems of domination or the "matrix of domination" (Zinn & Dill, 1996). This important insight compels us to recognize how the intersection of multiple social locations or standpoints shapes individual lives and structures society.

Power feminism. The 1990s gave birth to a new movement called **power feminism.** Although this movement labels itself feminist, it is actually antagonistic to enduring concerns of many feminists and, some argue, to women themselves. Writing in 1993, Naomi Wolf argued that feminism is wrong to emphasize women's victimization and oppression. According to Wolf, it is self-defeating to focus on social causes of inequities and harm that women suffer. As an alternative, Wolf advocates power feminism, which contends women have personal responsibility for what happens to them, including their success in traditionally male activities. Power feminism claims that women are not victims unless they choose to be; They simply need to empower themselves to be socially, professionally, and politically equal to men.

Wolf urges women to "stop thinking of themselves as victims" and to capitalize on using the power inherent in their majority status ("What About This Backlash?" 1994). To add credibility to her views, Wolf links herself with the Reverend Jesse Jackson, a passionate champion of those who have not had power in society. Wolf quotes Jackson as having said, "You're not responsible for being down, you are responsible for standing up" ("What About This Backlash?" 1994, p. 15). She then explicitly draws on the language of the civil rights movement to advise women to "use the master's tools—such as money, votes, and political embarrassment"—to raise their status in society. Although Wolf's rhetorical tactics are clever, the validity of her argument doesn't necessarily depend on whether others made similar arguments. It's true that Jesse Jackson and before him, the Reverend Martin Luther King, Jr., exhorted African Americans to resist oppression. They did not, however, claim that racial oppression is sustained only by the passive acceptance of those who have suffered it.

The message of power feminism is more closely linked to the ideas of Shelby Steele (1990), a conservative African American who claims that racial discrimination is no longer part of society but only a paranoid victim psychology in the heads of Blacks and other minorities. Following in Steele's footsteps, Wolf counsels women that the only thing holding them back from equality is their own belief that they are victims. She claims that women can achieve and be everything that men are simply by seizing the power that is already theirs.

Power feminism may work for women like Naomi Wolf, who is White, upper class, successful, well educated, and physically attractive. It is less helpful or relevant to a great many women who do not enjoy Wolf's privileges. Feminist theorist and social critic bell hooks ("What About This Backlash?" 1994) says power feminism is endorsed by "people who have access to power. Naomi presents herself as speaking for the masses, but she is speaking first and foremost for her own class interests" (p. 15).

Along with Wolf, Katie Roiphe is a visible proponent of power feminism. In her 1993 book, *The Morning After: Sex, Fear, and Feminism on Campus,* Roiphe denies the existence of a rape epidemic on campuses and in society. She believes that sex does and should involve power, pursuit, and struggle and that the term *rape* is being misused to describe normal sexual relations. Roiphe derides Take Back the Night marches, annual nonviolent protests that began in 1978 to speak out against rape on many college campuses. To Roiphe, march participants are "whining," and marches are self-defeating because "proclaiming victimhood" does not project strength. Roiphe apparently doesn't realize that Take Back the Night marches and other public denunciations of violence against women reflect and fuel activism, not victimhood.

The attraction of power feminism is its focus on individual women's power to control their lives and identities. Yet, many scholars and activists regard power feminism as misguided and dangerous in implying that women have the ability to control their sexual, economic, and social well-being (Bowman, 1994; Franek, 1994; hooks, 1994). Critics of power feminism note that excessive emphasis on women's personal choices ignores pervasive social influences that historically and currently aggrieve women as a group. As *New York Times* columnist Anna Quindlen (1994) points out, "No one should ever discount the reason so many women can so easily see themselves as victims. It is because, by any statistical measure, they so often are"

(p. A23). Women are disproportionately the targets of violence, ranging from rape and sexual abuse to genital mutilation and murder (see Chapter 11, "Gendered Power and Violence"). It is naive to think that, by exercising personal will, individual women always can avoid being targets of violence. Women are not natural victims, but they are often victimized in our society.

There is a big difference between identifying a moment in which one was a victim, on the one hand, and adopting the status of victim as an identity, on the other hand. Bryn Panee, a student of mine, clarified this distinction when she reported on her experiences as a rape crisis counselor: "Every turnaround case, where a woman is able to make the transformation from a helpless victim to an empowered survivor, could not have happened if she did not recognize she was a victim of a horrible crime" (1994, n.p.).

In (over)emphasizing individual control, power feminism diverts attention from continuing and severe injustices that many women and minorities experience. Makini Hammond, an African American woman who is a deputy city attorney in San Diego, points out that ideas like those espoused by Wolf and other power feminists don't speak to the circumstances of minority women's lives. Hammond says, "The feminist movement for black women is about survival, while for white women it's about power" (Griffin, 1993, p. E1). Perhaps that is why power feminism is espoused mainly by White, middle- and upper-class individuals who have little or no personal experience with devaluation, discrimination, and sexual violation (Wood, 1996a).

One of the most pressing challenges before women today is building coalitions among different kinds of women. Women of diverse backgrounds and in varying circumstances need to talk with one another to discover shared concerns and work toward shared goals. Together women can build a truly inclusive movement in which attention to common struggles and oppressions does not obscure awareness of real and important differences among women.

The Third Wave of Women's Movements in the United States

A **third wave of feminism** has emerged in the United States. It goes by several names: the third wave, girl power, and girlie feminism. Although still in its formative stage, certain definitive features of this movement are evident. Among these is the belief that feminism must include women of different ethnicities, abilities and disabilities, classes, appearances, and sexual orientations. Rather than treating women as a homogeneous group, third-wave feminists recognize and even celebrate differences among women—differences based on race, class, sexual orientation, body shape and size, and (dis)ability. "We are not all the same," they insist. This rising generation of feminists is figuring out how to speak about and for women as a group while simultaneously recognizing differences among women.

Another prominent facet of third-wave feminism is insistence that it is not simply an extension of the goals, principles, and values of the second wave (Bailey, 1997; Ehrenreich, 1990; Findlen, 1995; Howry, 1999; Howry & Wood, 2001; Orr, 1997; Tobias, 1997). Although built on the foundations of earlier waves of women's movements, third-wave feminists believe that the second wave did not create a "complete package of entitlement" (Griffin, 1996, p. 116). They see a primary goal of the third wave as addressing the gap between the second-wave goal of unlimited possibilities for all people and the glaring inequities and exclusions that mar social life as we begin a new millennium.

Some third-wave feminists also claim to be more interested in action than in ideology and politics. Kim Allen, one of the creators of the 3rd WWWave Web site, contends that her generation of feminists is "more practical and less ideological than our second-wave predecessors" (Allen, 1999). Despite Allen's claim that second-wave feminists were not pragmatic enough, we should remember that they brought about a great many very concrete changes, including securing reproductive freedom and laws against sex discrimination. Other third-wave feminists point out that the politics that will be effective in this era are not those of the 1970s. More local, concrete organizing and activism are the new order of the day.

NATALIE

I really appreciate what the women's movement that started in the [19]60s has done to make my life better, but I can't personally identify with its issues. My life is different than my mother's was, so naturally my issues are different. She was fighting just to get a job. I want a job that pays well and lets me advance. She worked really hard trying to get better day care for her children and other children. I want to have a marriage and a job that allows me not to have to rely on day care. Her generation fought to make it okay for women not to marry. My generation wants to figure out how to make marriages work better, more fairly. Different generations. Different issues.

KATIE

I like the ideas of the multiracial feminists. I agree that race cuts across everything else. I'm middle class, but my life isn't the same as a White middle-class girl's, because I'm Asian American. It's like the issues in my life aren't just about my sex; they're also about my race. I can talk to Black or Hispanic girls, and we have a lot in common—more than I have in common with most White girls. You just can't get away from the issue of race unless if you're White.

A fourth feature of third-wave feminism is an embrace of some aspects of traditional "girl culture." The most visible and effective branches of second-wave feminism were very critical of cultural emphasis on feminine beauty. The second wave denounced advertising's efforts to sell girls and women makeup, clothes, and other products designed to help them comform to the cultural ideal of femininity. They claimed that women were being "duped by Madison Avenue" if they cared about makeup, fashion, and "girlified glamor" (Karp & Stoller, 1999, p. 42).

In contrast, many third-wave feminists celebrate their femininity and sexuality.

For instance, some third-wavers say Madonna has shown that "the trappings of femininity could be used to make a sexual statement that was powerful, rather than passive" (Karp & Stoller, 1999, p. 45). In a conversation I had with the authors of *ManifestA* (2001), they pointed out that the second wave of the movement disparaged pop culture, but this generation seeks to engage it and shape it to their own purposes. The blending of serious issues and "girl culture" is one of the earmarks of new magazines for girls and women. Alongside articles about glitter nail polish and cool clothes is serious advice about issues such as racism, eating disorders, and self-empowerment (Kuczynski, 2001). For the rising generation of feminists, it's possible—and fun—to be both fashionable and feminist (Waggonner & Hallstein, 2001).

A final defining feature of third-wave feminism is explicit interest in affirming and improving connections between women and men. The second wave focused primarily on the needs and rights of women, which was necessary at that time. That focus inevitably fueled some tensions between women and men. Today, many young feminists are committed to building positive connections with men as their friends, romantic partners, co-workers, brothers, and fathers. But, warn these women, "We can't do the work for men, and we won't try. Social change requires efforts from *both* sides. We want to meet men in the middle, not do all the adjusting ourselves" (3rd Wave, 1999).

Insistence that men get involved in working out equitable gender arrangements for the next millennium is a major theme in Debbie Stoller and Marcelle Karp's writing for third-wave feminists. They call their zine *Bust* and their book *The Bust Guide to the New Girl Order* (1999). The titles both play on traditional views of women and proclaim that women today are busting out of old images. Stoller and Karp observe that trying to balance work and family has been almost exclusively a concern of women. They argue that it should equally be a concern of men

Don't agree

because women and men are in it together (Stoller & Karp, 1999).

Unlike women in the second wave, today's young feminists don't coalesce around an agreed-upon agenda. They are not motivated by a shared realization that they suffer from the feminine mystique or any other single kind of oppression. Instead, young feminists come from widely diverse backgrounds, and they bring with them equally diverse visions of how feminism should evolve. Energetic, humorous, thoughtful, angry, sassy, hopeful, and passionate— the new feminists are dreamers and fighters who are committed to activist feminist work (Heywood, 1998; Heywood & Drake, 1997). As they voice their concerns and discuss ideas with others, they will carry feminism forward, remaking it to reflect the priorities of their generation.

⚲ MARCELLA

I'm totally into nail polish and all the other stuff that girlie feminism is about. Until I learned about it, I would have said I'm not a feminist, but now I think maybe I am. All the women of my mother's generation seem to think that nobody will take you seriously if you wear makeup or sexy clothes. That probably was true for them, but I don't think it's true today. The cool thing about girlie feminism is that it says we don't have to quit being girls to be serious about ourselves and other things.

As we have seen, the "women's movement" is really a collage of many movements that span over one and a half centuries and include a range of political and social ideologies as well as diverse understandings of women's identities, needs, and values. The different goals associated with feminism are paralleled by a broad scope of rhetorical strategies, ranging from private empowerment through consciousness-raising and support to public lobbying and stump speaking. The issue of whether a person is a feminist is considerably more complicated than it first appears. Whether you define yourself as a feminist or not, you have some views of women's identities, rights, and nature. It may be that each of us needs to ask not just whether we are feminists but *which* kind of feminist we are.

MEN'S MOVEMENTS

Men's voices have only recently joined the cultural conversation about gender. During the first wave of U.S. feminism, men were largely uninvolved with issues of gender. Most opposed women's efforts to gain rights, although a few like Frederick Douglass actively supported women's struggles for equality and are considered feminists. During the second wave, a number of men supported liberal feminism, many joining NOW to work with women for equality. Only in the last two decades have men in any number begun to question the nature and effects of social views of masculinity and to define issues in men's lives.

Like the women's movement, the men's movement is really a collection of different movements with different views of men and diverse, sometimes conflicting, political and personal goals and rhetorical strategies. Also like their feminist parallels, men's movements are evolving, with new ones constantly emerging. Diverse views of men and masculinity are considered in umbrella forums such as men's studies courses, increasingly popular on many campuses, and the Men's Studies Association. In addition, in August 1992, *The Journal of Men's Studies* was launched to report research on men and to explore various approaches to masculinity (D. Gross, 1990). Another important scholarly journal devoted to men's lives is *Men and Masculinities,* which began publication in July 1998. Men's movements include branches that have diverse viewpoints and goals and adopt particular communication practices. To gain appreciation of the range of issues and ideologies entailed in men's movements, we will discuss various branches.

■ Profeminist Men's Movements

Only one sector of men's movements shares the liberal or egalitarian ideology of liberal feminism. Referred to as **male feminists** or profeminist men, this branch of men's movements emerged from the upheaval of the 1960s. Although many men in student activist organizations like SNCC and SDS ridiculed women who accused them of sexism, not all New Left men responded negatively. A number of them recognized truth in the women's charges, and they were ashamed when confronted with the hypocrisy of their political efforts to end discrimination while discriminating against women. These men worked to reform their own attitudes and behavior to bring them in line with the egalitarian ideology they espoused. Male feminists believe that women and men are basically alike in important respects and therefore should enjoy the same privileges, opportunities, rights, and status in society. For the most part, these men have linked themselves and their rhetoric to mainstream liberal feminism. Out of this perspective, two distinct concerns emerge—one focused on women and the other on men.

Because they believe in the equality of the sexes, male feminists support women's battles for equitable treatment in society (Doyle, 1997). They participated in efforts to increase women's rights during the second wave of U.S. feminism. During the 1972 campaign to ratify the ERA (Equal Rights Amendment), many men gave time, effort, and resources to the battle to gain legal recognition of women's equality. They joined women in seeking public platforms from which to advocate women's equality and rights. After Congress approved the amendment in 1972, it was quickly ratified by 28 states, and its passage seemed assured.

However, a Stop ERA campaign, led by Phyllis Schlafly and generously financed by conservative political and business interests, stymied progress of the legislation. By 1973, of the needed 38 states, 35 had ratified the amendment, but the remaining ones—conservative Southern and Western states—refused to support passage, and the ERA was defeated. Throughout struggles to gain ratification, male feminists worked alongside women. They lobbied, canvassed neighborhoods, made speeches in public settings, and helped organize the campaign to gain legal recognition of women's equality.

One rhetorical strategy used by some profeminist men is performing a "traitorous identity," which is to voice criticism of particular attitudes and actions that are common among members of a group. For example, a Christian man of my acquaintance often speaks out at Christian conferences about ways in which many Christians discriminate against gays. Another example comes from Larry May, author of *Masculinity and Morality* (1998a). May notes that at meetings he attends male speakers sometimes make sexist jokes or statements. He points out that if a woman comments on the sexism, many men roll their eyes or dismiss her as being "unable to take a joke." However, May says that when he or other men comment on the sexism, both the speaker and other men in the audience look ashamed. According to May, men find it easy to dismiss women's criticism of sexism but difficult to dismiss the same criticism when it comes from "one of us."

Male feminists also support issues embraced by women feminists. For instance, men who consider themselves feminists generally endorse efforts to gain equal pay for equal work, to end discrimination against qualified women in academic and professional contexts, and to increase parental leaves and child-care facilities that are necessary for families in which both parents work. An important kind of communication employed by many male feminists is personal persuasion, used to convince particular others to alter discriminatory attitudes and practices. For instance, one of my friends who considers himself a feminist talked with several of his colleagues about his disapproval of his firm's policy of paying women less than it paid men in equivalent positions. He thought the action was wrong, and he used his voice and his credibility to speak out to other individuals.

Another interest of male feminists is their personal growth beyond restrictions imposed by society's prescriptions for masculinity. Because they believe that men and women are alike in most ways, male feminists want to develop the emotional capacities that society approves in women but discourages in men. Specifically, many male feminists claim that social expectations of masculinity force men to repress their feelings, and this diminishes men's humanity and makes their lives less satisfying than they could be (Avery, 1999; Hudson & Jacot, 1992).

Agreeing with liberal feminist women, men in this movement regard cultural prescriptions for gender as toxic to both sexes. Whereas for women social codes have restricted professional development and rights, for men they often seal off feelings (Brod, 1987; Hearn, 1987). Male feminists think that in restricting men's ability to understand and experience feelings, society has robbed them of an im-

The National Organization for Men Against Sexism defines itself as an activist organization that promotes positive changes in men. NOMAS is pro-men, pro-women, and pro-gay in its philosophy. Through formal and informal efforts, NOMAS attempts to bring about personal, political, and social changes designed to foster equality of men and women and gay and straight people.

For several years, NOMAS's spokesperson has been Michael Kimmel, a professor of sociology at SUNY at Stony Brook and the author of many books and articles about men, masculinity, and men's movements.

Information on the organization's goals, activities, and membership procedures may be obtained by contacting the national organization:

NOMAS 798 Pennsylvania Avenue, Box 5, Pittsburgh, PA 15221

 Visit the NOMAS Web site at
http://sh.lh.vix.com/~throop/men/orgs/writeups/nomas.html.

portant aspect of what it means to be human. A major goal of male feminists is changing this. They encourage men to get in touch with their feelings and to be more sensitive, caring, and able to engage in meaningful, close relationships.

The male feminist movement includes both informal, interpersonal communication and more organized political efforts. Formal, public action in this movement dates to 1975, when the first Men and Masculinity Conference was held in Tennessee. The conference has met annually since then to discuss the meaning of masculinity, to establish a network of support for men, and to identify and talk about problems and frustrations inherent in how our culture defines masculinity (Doyle, 1997; Messner, 2001). The most prominent male feminist organization is NOMAS, the National Organization for Men Against Sexism, which has more than 1,000 members. This association sponsors workshops with speakers and group discussions to expand men's awareness of ways in which their emotional development has been hindered by restrictive social views of masculinity. In addition, the workshops attempt to help men change this state of affairs by offering men guidance in how to become more feeling and sensitive. Often these groups serve as safe testing grounds in which men can experiment with expressing their feelings, needs, and problems.

NOMAS makes discriminations in its judgment of human qualities. Although members argue that some qualities traditionally associated with masculinity, such as courage and ambition, are valuable in all humans (women as well as men), it condemns other conventionally masculine qualities such as aggression, violence, and emotional insensitivity. One of the most important achievements of NOMAS is its Fathering Task Group; this group issues a newsletter called *Fatherlove*, which promotes nurturance of children and involvement of fathers (Doyle, 1989).

For almost 25 years, NOMAS has held an annual conference on men and masculinity. Three issues consistently arise as priorities for discussion and action at these conferences: ending men's violence, developing profeminist men's studies, and supporting homophobia education. NOMAS's annual conferences allow members to work on social change through political and educational activism.

Equally important are informal group discussions where men meet to explore the joys, frustrations, privileges, and problems of being men. Modeled after the consciousness-raising groups popular with radical feminists, these groups encourage men to talk about what our society expects of men and what problems this creates for them. Through discussion, men pursue their goal of getting in touch with their emotions. They try to learn how to talk openly with other men about feelings, fears, concerns, and frustrations. Topics like these are ones men are socialized to avoid, because such subjects increase vulnerability and reflect a need for others, violating social expectations for independence. The communication of this men's movement, then, includes public rhetoric in support of women's rights and men's personal development, public and interpersonal challenges to sexist attitudes and practices, and more private, small-group communication in which men explore with one another what they feel and how they might change attitudes and behaviors they find unworthy.

Promasculinist Men's Movements

A number of men's groups fit within the second camp of men's movements. These groups, labeled **promasculinist** (Fiebert, 1987), see feminism as in conflict with men's interests (Freedman, 1985). Many promasculinist men demean profeminist men by calling them "soft" or "male-bashers" and by accusing them of fueling negative stereotypes of men. A primary rhetorical strategy of the promasculinists is attacking those men who define themselves as male feminists. Promasculinists and profeminist men also split in their attitudes toward homophobia and gay men. The promasculinist camp does not focus on homophobia, which profeminist men see as underlying all men's—gay and straight alike—inability to form close relationships with other men. The issue of gay rights is not a primary concern for most promasculinist men, who tend to either ignore or denigrate gay men. Profeminist men, in contrast, are committed to supporting gay concerns and to eliminating oppression faced by gay men (Lingard & Douglas, 1999).

Free Men. In sharp distinction to male feminists, one branch of the men's movement calls itself **Free Men** and includes specific organizations such as MR, Inc. (Men's Rights, Incorporated); the National Coalition for Free Men; and NOM (National Organization of Men). Free Men aim to restore men's pride in being "real men." By "real men," this group means men in the traditional macho image—tough, rugged, invulnerable, and self-reliant. Free Men see male feminists as soft and unmanly and denigrate them with epithets such as "the men's auxiliary to the women's movement" (D. Gross, 1990, p. 12). In fact, Free Men say that profeminist men are not part of the men's movement at all. Interestingly, when men of this movement took the name NOM, the feminist men who had originally called *their* organization NOM changed its name to NOMAS to emphasize that they were in favor of *changing* traditional men's roles, not reinforcing them.

Free Men think that discrimination against men is far greater and worthy of more attention and correction than the discrimination women face. These men say that "it is actually *women* who have the power and *men* who are most oppressed by the current gender arrangements" (Messner, 1997, p. 41). The oppression of men includes being subject to the draft, shorter life spans, health problems, and custody laws that favor women (Whitaker, 2001). According to this group, the primary burden of masculinity is the provider role. Assigning that to men, they argue, makes men little more than meal tickets whose worth is measured by the size of their paychecks and their titles. Warren Farrell (1991), for instance, claims that men are relentlessly oppressed by the "24-hour-a-day psychological responsibility for the family's financial well-being" (p. 83). Farrell claims that "almost all men see bringing home a healthy salary as an obligation, not an option." Many men believe a woman will not love them if they are not successful and good providers.

Specific issues such as the provider burden, however, are subordinate to Free Men and NOM members' greater concern that men are being robbed of their masculinity. Targeting feminism as the primary source of men's loss of their masculinity, promasculine men claim that "men have been wimpified. They've been emasculated" (D. Gross, 1990, p. 13). Given this perspective, it's not surprising that members of NOM oppose affirmative action, forced collection of alimony and child support, and a single-sex military (Kimmel, 1996a). Longing for the return of traditional roles and men's unquestioned supremacy, Free Men want women to return to positions of subordination and attitudes of deference toward men. With this, they believe, men will regain their rightful places as heads of families and unquestioned authorities. To advance this agenda, Free Men engage in rhetoric ranging from lobbying for reform of laws they claim discriminate against men to condemning feminist men and women in public and private communication.

Have American Men Been Betrayed?

In 1991, prize-winning journalist Susan Faludi published *Backlash: The Undeclared War Against American Women,* in which she documented cultural practices that demean women and thwart their progress. Eight years later, she published *Stiffed: The Betrayal of the American Man,* in which she argues that a significant number of men today feel that the United States has betrayed them. Based on interviews, observations, and other research, Faludi concludes that many men feel that society has broken its contract with them. No longer can they count on loyalty from a company that they commit to—they might be fired if economic conditions change. No longer do many men engage in work that has immediate meaning and satisfaction for them—too often they are pushing papers and dealing with abstractions whose impact they never see. No longer is being a breadwinner enough to be considered a good man—now they must also be involved fathers and husbands. Faludi argues that the traditional rules for being a man no longer hold, yet a new set of rules hasn't emerged. The result, she claims, is confusion, frustration, and resentment.

Source: Faludi, S. (1999). *Stiffed: The betrayal of the American man.* New York: Morrow.

Mythopoetic men. Another branch of the men's movements that has garnered much publicity is the **mythopoetic movement,** founded by poet Robert Bly. Blending neoconservative politics with some of the ideology of the Free Men, the mythopoetic movement is less interested in social change than in men's personal growth and wholeness (Silverstein, Auerbach, Grieco, & Dunkel, 1999). Mythopoetics want men to rediscover the deep, mythic roots of masculine thinking and feeling, which will restore men to their primordial spiritual, emotional, and intellectual wholeness (Keen, 1991).

Mythopoetics agree with feminist women and men that the male role is toxic, yet they argue it was not always so. They claim ideal manhood existed during ancient times and the Middle Ages, when men were self-confident, strong, and emotionally alive and sensitive. As exemplars of ideal manhood, mythopoetics cite King Arthur, Henry David Thoreau, Walt Whitman, and Johnny Appleseed (D. Gross, 1990). Mythopoetics think men's former connections to the earth and to other men were ripped asunder by modernization, the Industrial Revolution, and feminism. Men were taken away from their land and, with that, from ongoing con-

SAM

I know it's not politically correct these days to say it, but I agree with a lot of what promasculinist men believe. I think families were stronger when the man was the head and the woman knew to follow. Families can't work if both spouses want to lead. There can be only one leader. I think the country was a lot stronger too before women started getting into business and government. I think women and men have different abilities. They're equal, but they're different, and there's no point in pretending otherwise. As far as gays go, I'm not homophobic or anything, but I don't see protecting their rights as a priority.

FatherLoss

Do social prescriptions for masculinity undermine men's ability to mourn the loss of their fathers? Neil Chethik thinks there may be a connection between socialization that teaches men to be strong and to avoid close ties with other men and men's difficulty in grieving when their fathers die. Chethik surveyed more than 300 men and conducted in-depth interviews with 70 men to learn how they dealt with their fathers' deaths. He found that, no matter how many years have passed since the father died, sons continue to yearn deeply for connections with their fathers. Chethik found that many men try to follow social prescriptions for masculinity: They don't talk about their grief, don't cry, and don't show how much they hurt. Instead, they buck up and carry on, keeping their grief silent. Chethik reports that many men grieve and heal by reflecting quietly or by taking up hobbies that give them a sense of connection with their fathers. Some men turn to fishing, woodworking, or gardening because their fathers engaged in those activities. In doing these things, the sons keep their fathers' traditions alive.

Source: Chethik, N. (2001). *FatherLoss: How sons of all ages come to terms with the deaths of their dads.* New York: Hyperion.

tact with life itself and their roles as stewards of the land (Kimbrell, 1991). At the same time that men were isolated from their earthy, natural masculinity (D. Gross, 1990), industrialization separated men from their families. When men began working outside of the home, young boys lost fathers who could initiate them into manhood and teach them how to relate spiritually and emotionally to other men.

Although mythopoetics do believe that men have been separated from their feelings, their views depart dramatically from those of profeminist men (Keen, 1991; Mechling & Mechling, 1994). Like Free Men, Bly and his followers conceive of feminism as having caused men's emotional deficits. Feminism is seen as making men soft and decidedly unmasculine because it robs them of emotional virility. Bly finds male feminists troublesome because he thinks they are moving down a counterproductive path. In "soft males," Bly says, "there's not much energy" (Wagenheim, 1990, p. 42). Stating this view more strongly, some mythopoetics (Allis, 1990) charge that "the American man wants his manhood back. Period. . . . [F]eminists have been busy castrating American males. They poured this country's testosterone out the window in the 1960s" (p. 80). So one rhetorical strategy of mythopoetics is to debunk and put down male feminists and to provide a counterstatement to male feminists' public arguments about masculinity.

What do mythopoetics advocate for masculinity? They insist men need to recover the *distinctly male mode of feeling*, one that is fundamentally different from female feelings endorsed by profeminist men. Men need to reclaim courage, aggression, and virility as masculine birthrights and as qualities that can be put to the service of bold and worthy goals as they were when knights and soldiers fought for causes. Central to modern man's emotional emptiness, argues Bly, is **father hunger,** a grief born of yearning to be close both to actual fathers and to other men and to build deep, spiritual bonds between men. To remedy this, Bly and other leaders of the movement urge men to get in touch with their grief and, from there, to begin to rediscover their deep masculine feelings and spiritual energies. An especially influential form of persuasion by mythopoetics is Robert Bly's book *Iron John*, which is the major rhetorical text of this movement. This book, which explains mythopoetic views and recounts ancient myths of manhood, was a national bestseller for over 30 weeks, making it a rhetorical message that captured a wide audience.

To facilitate this process, there are workshops and retreats that allow men to "come together in nature alone, in the absence of women and civilization" (D. Gross, 1990, p. 14). In the natural world, men can recover their sense of brotherhood and distinctively male feelings, ones repressed by industrialization and feminism. At nature retreats, men gather in the woods to beat drums, chant, and listen to poetry and mythic stories, all designed to help them get in touch with their father hunger and to move beyond that to positive masculine feeling. As this suggests, favored mythopoetic forms of communication are storytelling, chanting, and affirming what it considers the deep roots of distinctively masculine feelings.

ℰ CHUCK

Bly's ideas sound pretty strange to me. I can't identify with chanting in the woods with a bunch of other guys to find my manhood. Heck, I didn't know I'd lost it! But if I were to be serious about this stuff, I guess I'd say there might be something to it. I mean I do like to get together with brothers in my fraternity, and being with a group of just men does have a different kind of feeling than being with women or women and men. Like we're more uninhibited, more rough, and more loud than when girls are around. I guess I do feel more manly or something in those groups.

Another thing that interests me about what Bly says is the stuff about absent fathers. I'm not sure I'd go so far as to say I have the father hunger he talks about or that I have deep grief, but I do feel my father and I should have been closer. I never saw much of him when I was growing up. He worked all day and wanted to relax at night, not spend time with us kids. I wish I'd known him better—in fact, I still do wish it. I think a lot of guys feel that way.

The mythopoetic movement is not without critics. Michael Schwalbe's book, *Unlocking the Cage* (1996), offers an inside look at the mythopoetic movement. For three years, Schwalbe belonged to a men's support group, attended another men's group that was devoted to drumming, and participated in week-long men's retreats. Schwalbe concludes that many of these men had been harmed by distance and sometimes abuse from fathers and were drawn to the mythopoetic movement because it offered primitive rites of masculinity that their fathers had not provided. Schwalbe criticizes mythopoetics for being unwilling to confront issues of gender inequality and for their participation in sustaining that inequality (Avery, 1999).

In the 1990s, two new branches of men's movements emerged. The Promise Keepers and the Million Man March depart from the secular branches of men's movements to offer distinctively religious movements about manhood.

FYI

Facts About the Mythopoetic Movement

- Well over 50,000 men have participated in nature retreats at a cost of more than $200 per participant.

- *MAN!,* the national quarterly devoted to the movement, has more than 3,500 subscribers.

- *Wingspan,* another national quarterly of the movement, has a (free) circulation of more than 125,000 readers.

- In the Northeast alone, over 163 mythopoetic groups have formed in communities.

- Robert Bly's book *Iron John* enjoyed over 30 weeks on the best seller list.

- Mythopoetics are largely White and middle class and so do not include or represent all men.

 You can visit Robert Bly's page at
http://dist.woodstock.edu/~dcox/ohenry/bly.html.

Sources: Adler, J., with Duignan-Cabrera, A., & Gordon, J. (1991). Drums, sweat, and tears. *Newsweek,* pp. 46–54; Bonnett, A. (1996). The new primitives: Identity, landscape and cultural appropriation in the Mythopoetic men's movement. *Antipode, 28,* 273–291; Messner, M. (1997). *Politics of masculinity: Men in movements.* Thousand Oaks, CA: Sage.

Promise Keepers. In 1990, Bill McCartney, who was then head football coach at the University of Colorado, and his friend Dave Wardell were on a three-hour car trip to a meeting of Christian athletes in Pueblo, Colorado. On that trip, the two men conceived the idea of filling a stadium with Christian men. Later that year, McCartney and Wardell motivated 72 men to pray and fast about the idea of men coming together in Christian fellowship. The first **Promise Keepers** event in 1991 drew 4,200 men. Two years later, McCartney achieved his goal of filling the 50,000-seat Folsom Field. In 1994, the Promise Keepers were ready to spread out. They had seven sites at which more than 278,000 men came together to pray and commit themselves to being Promise Keepers. Each year, increasing numbers of men attend Promise Keepers meetings across the nation (Shimron, 1997; Wagenheim, 1996).

According to Bill McCartney, many men have fallen away from responsible lives. He says, "Men have been irresponsible. They have abandoned the home. They've chased careers. Their word wasn't good anymore. They've been unfaithful" ("Promise Keepers," 1997, p. 14A). Whereas mythopoetics see nature as the solution to men's disconnection from their true nature, Promise Keepers see the Bible as the solution. Based on evangelical Christian ideology, the movement urges men to be the leaders of their families because that reflects the "God-given division of labor between women and men" (Messner, 1997, p. 30). Following the Christian path also requires men to be good husbands, fathers, and members of communities. Each Promise Keeper makes seven promises (Shimron, 1997):

1. To honor Jesus Christ through worship, prayer, and obedience to God's word through the power of the Holy Spirit.

2. To pursue vital relationships with a few other men, understanding that he needs brothers to help him keep his promises.

3. To practice spiritual, moral, ethical, and sexual purity.

> ☎ KATHY
>
> I really don't know what to think of the Promise Keepers. I like what they say about men committing to family values and to strong spirituality. I'm Christian, so I agree with a lot of what they stand for. But I don't like the idea that men have to be *the* leader in relationships. I won't be led by a man, and I don't want to lead a man either. I want a relationship where we're equal in all respects. This makes me identify with only parts of what the Promise Keepers stand for.

4. To build strong marriages and families through love, protection, and biblical values.

5. To support the mission of his church by honoring and praying for his pastor and by actively giving his time and resources.

6. To reach beyond any racial and denominational barriers to demonstrate the power of biblical unity.

7. To influence his world, being obedient to the Great Commandment (see Mark 12:30–31) and the Great Commission (see Matthew 28:19–20).

Supporters of Promise Keepers believe that the movement is good for men and families. They say it champions values that build strong families and strong communities. In their opinion, Promise Keepers is a call for male responsibility (Whitehead, 1997). Furthermore, a number of women who are married to Promise Keepers say their marriages have improved since their husbands joined the movement (Cose, 1997; Griffith, 1997; Whitehead, 1997).

Yet others voice reservations about the Promise Keepers. Patricia Ireland, past president of NOW, asks why women aren't allowed to attend Promise Keepers meetings. Why can't husbands and wives be equals? (Ingraham, 1997). McCartney responds, "When there is a final decision that needs to be made and they can't arrive at one, the man needs to take responsibility" ("Promise Keepers," 1997, p. 14A). Critics charge that "taking responsibility" is a code term for taking away women's voices and rights.

Another reservation about Promise Keepers is that the group might be elitist. The great majority of Promise Keepers are White and middle- or upper-class economically. Gay men and those who support gays are uncomfortable with the Promise Keepers' view that homosexuality is a sin and gays therefore are leading

Getting to Know Promise Keepers

The Promise Keepers maintains an active Web site on which leaders of the organization offer their views of who they are, what they stand for, and how men can participate in the organization. The Web site also offers texts of key documents, including its mission statement, speeches, and members' comments. To find out more, go to the Web site at **http://www.promisekeepers.org.**

You can also find information critical of the Promise Keepers on the Web. One thoughtful assessment of what's right and not so right about the Promise Keepers is offered in a speech by Congressman Jesse L. Jackson, Jr., "Watch as Well as Pray." In this speech, Jackson disputes the Promise Keepers' claim that the organization is not political. According to Jackson, "Coach McCartney has been politically active in anti-gay and anti-choice campaigns. . . . This is really the third wave of the religiously-based conservative political movement. First, there was Rev. Jerry Falwell's Moral Majority. Then there was Rev. Pat Robertson and Ralph Reed's Christian Coalition. Now there is Coach Bill McCartney's Promise Keepers." To read the full text of Jackson's speech, go to **http://www.now.org/issues/right/promise/jackson.html.**

immoral lives. Finally, some critics regard Promise Keepers as more of a conservative political movement than a social and spiritual movement (Cose, 1997; Whitaker, 2001). In response to criticism, Promise Keepers has made efforts to broaden its membership to men of different races and to soften its rhetoric about husbands leading wives.

Million Man March. Just as many African American women feel that feminism doesn't speak to or for them, many African American men feel that mainstream men's movements don't fit their histories and lives (Hammer, 2001). In the fall of 1995, Minister Louis Farrakhan, leader of the Nation of Islam, and the Reverend Benjamin Chavis, Jr., organized the first **Million Man March.** Their goal was to have Black men of all religions and classes fill the Mall of the nation's capital. The goals for the 1995 meeting were for Black men to atone for sins and to reconcile with one another. Spike Lee's film *Get on the Bus* (1997) commemorates this first march.

At the march, organizers encouraged men to pledge themselves to spiritual transformation and political action. Specifically, organizers called for the men to register to vote, fight drugs in their lives and communities, and stand against unemployment and violence. Men were asked to recommit themselves to their wives and families and to active involvement in their churches and communities.

The Million Man March was not a one-time event. Additional marches were held in years following, and each time the crowd stretched from the steps of the

Capitol nearly to the Washington Monument. Those who attended found something they could identify with in this movement—something that could guide their lives and give them meaning.

The Million Man March has been widely praised as a positive, uplifting movement for Black men. Yet there have been criticisms. One is that women are excluded from Million Man Marches. Some women think there is irony in asking men to leave home and be with other men in order to commit to their wives and families. Another criticism was advanced by Glenn Loury (1996), who is African American and a professor of economics. He is concerned that this movement encourages Black men to base their rage on the racial identity of those who suffer rather than to rage against suffering and inequity no matter who is the victim. Finally, some people criticize the Million Man March for being anti-feminist and antigay and for holding overly conservative views of families and women (Messner, 1997).

MICHAEL

I attended the Million Man March a couple of years ago, and it was the most important event of my life. It was wonderful to see so many Black men in one place—all there to unite with one another and to change our world. The whole mood was one of total brother-hood. It strengthened my pride in be-ing a Black man and my feeling that I can build a life around strong spiritual values.

The inaugural Million Man March in 1995 seemed to strike a chord with other groups. Since that march, America has seen a Million Woman March in Phila-delphia, a Million Youth March in Harlem, a Million Mom March in Washing-ton, and most recently, in 2000, a Million Family March ("Million Family March," 2000).

Men's movements, like those focused on women's issues, are diverse and even contradictory. Some men consider themselves feminists and work with women for gender equality in society as well as attempt to become more sensitive themselves. Other men see feminism as a primary source of men's problems, and they feel threatened by women's progress toward more equal status. Men's movements range from efforts to advance women's rights and status to active attacks on women's re-sistance to traditional, subservient roles. Members of men's movements engage in public and private forms of communication that contribute to the cultural conver-sation about gender—what it means and how it affects the individual men and women who live under its edicts.

OTHER MOVEMENTS FOCUSED ON GENDER

Before concluding our survey of rhetorical movements about gender, we should consider two that are not branches of women's or men's movements. One of these, the backlash, attempts to discredit and disable feminism. The other, ecofeminism, seeks to integrate a range of positions held by women and men into a single humanistic movement committed to a more just, life-affirming philosophy of living.

■ The Backlash

Feminist movements have brought about substantial changes in women's lives. Their economic opportunities and rewards are better, although still not equal to men's; laws now prohibit discrimination in educational and work contexts; and many women's self-esteem has grown with the positive image of femininity promoted by women's movements. In fact, the very successes of feminism have led to an intense countermovement called the **backlash** against feminism.

Unlike other gender movements we have considered, the backlash is not formal or organized. Instead, it consists of assorted, disparate kinds of communication that attempt to demean feminism and obstruct efforts to achieve further equality between the sexes. Included within the backlash are media misrepresentations of women's successes and problems, judicial rulings that reduce women's freedoms, business practices that covertly restrict women's opportunities, governmental actions that make it difficult for women to gain economic security without abandoning motherhood responsibilities, and popular book writers who scapegoat feminism as the source of problems ranging from loneliness to delinquent children. In 1994, *Backlash* magazine debuted with the announced goal of returning women and men to their traditional roles. Two years later, in 1996, David Gelernter wrote an article in a mainstream magazine titled "Why Mothers Should Stay Home." In this article, Gelernter argues that mothers who work outside the home are selfish and irresponsible, and he claims that many problems in families are the direct result of women's employment outside the home. Gelernter and others who engage in backlash rhetoric assume that keeping a home and raising children are exclusively the responsibilities of mothers.

The first clear examples of efforts to undermine feminism emerged in the 1970s, when Marabel Morgan launched the Total Woman movement and Helen Andelin founded the Fascinating Womanhood movement, both of which advocated women's return to traditional attitudes, values, and roles in life. The Total Woman movement (Morgan, 1973) stressed the conventional social view of women as sexual objects and urged women to devote their energies to making themselves sexually irresistible to men. One example of advice given to women was to surprise their husbands by meeting them at the door dressed only in Saran Wrap. Fascinating Womanhood (Andelin, 1975) was grounded in conservative interpretations of biblical teachings, and it emphasized women's duty to embody moral purity and submit to their husbands.

Although feminists found the goals of Fascinating Womanhood and the Total Woman movements laughable and regressive, many women and men found them attractive. Over 400,000 women paid to take courses that taught them to be more sexually attractive and submissive to their husbands (O'Kelly & Carney, 1986). Primary support for these courses and the ideologies behind them came from women who were economically dependent on husbands and who embraced conservative values. The same ideas resurfaced in the 2001 book, *The Surrendered Wife: A Practical Guide for Finding Intimacy, Passion, and Peace with Your Man* (L. Doyle). This book, like the earlier two that it echoes, counsels women to abandon the myth of equality if they want happy marriages (Clinton, 2001). Women are advised to let their husbands lead the family and to accommodate their husbands.

Another instance of backlash was the Stop ERA movement in the 1970s. Taking to the public platform, the most prominent spokesperson for Stop ERA, Phyllis Schlafly, traveled around the nation to persuade people that feminism was destroying femininity by turning women into men. She told women to return to their roles as helpmates and homemakers and affirmed men's traditional roles as heads of families. Ironically, although Schlafly argued that women should be deferential and that their place was in the home, her own activities belied this advice. In speaking forcefully in public, she violated her own advice on feminine style. Further, her speaking schedule kept her on the road or writing much of the time, so she was unable to devote much time to being a homemaker or mother.

The scope and intensity of this movement are described in depth by Susan Faludi in her 1991 book, *Backlash: The Undeclared War Against American Women* (see FYI on page 89). Faludi correctly notes that there are two levels of the broad backlash against feminism, and these levels are internally contradictory. On one hand, substantial contemporary rhetoric defines feminism as the source of women's problems as well as broken homes, tension between spouses, and delinquent children. In encouraging women to become more independent, feminism is portrayed as an evil force that turns women into fast-track achievers who have nothing to come home to but microwave dinners. We saw a good example of backlash rhetoric in the 1992 presidential race. Many conservatives criticized Hillary Rodham Clinton for being an assertive, achieving, intelligent woman, and Bill Clinton was ridiculed as unmanly for letting his wife have so much power and voice. Backlash rhetors argue that, rather than helping women, feminism has created more problems for them and has made their lives miserable. They conclude that the obvious answer to the problems is to renounce feminism.

A second backlash theme directly contradicts the first one by arguing that women have never had it so good. The media proclaim that women have won their battles for equality, they have made it, all doors are open to them, and they can have it all. Pointing to the gains in status and opportunities won by feminists, the backlash announces that all inequities have disappeared and that there is no longer any need for feminism. This line of rhetoric has been persuasive with some people, because many individuals in their twenties think gender discrimination is history. Yet, as Faludi insightfully asks, "How can American women be in so much trouble at the same time that they are supposed to be so blessed? If the status of women has never been higher, why is their emotional state so low? If women got what they asked for, what could possibly be the matter now?" (p. x). Faludi concludes her study by pointing out that the backlash has not convinced women to return to traditional roles. Because of their numeric advantage and what Faludi calls the "justness of their cause," she believes women will continue to fight for equality in personal, professional, legal, and social arenas.

■ Ecofeminism

An entirely different response to women's movements is **ecofeminism.** Although there are historical roots in first-wave American feminism, ecofeminism's official inception is usually dated to 1974, when Françoise d'Eaubonne published *La Feminisme ou la Mort,* which translates to mean *Feminism or Death.* This book, although not widely noted at the time, provided the philosophical foundation for ecofeminism and inspired further work that did achieve some visibility. A key event was the first ecofeminist conference, "Women and Life on Earth: Ecofeminism in the 1980s," which was held in 1980.

Foundations for the emergence of ecofeminism came both from U.S. feminist thinkers such as Rosemary Radford Reuther and from influential French feminists, including Françoise d'Eaubonne, Luce Irigaray, and Hélène Cixous. Feminists on both continents highlight the connection between efforts to control and subordinate women and desires to dominate nature, which perhaps not coincidentally is called Mother Earth. Rosemary Radford Reuther (1974, 1983, 2001), a Christian and theological scholar, argues that the lust to dominate has brought the world to the brink of a moral and ecological crisis in which there can be no winners. According to Reuther, the quest to exploit and control is ultimately destructive and must end.

Ecofeminism unites the intellectual and political maturity of feminist thought with larger concerns about oppression and life itself. According to Judith Plant, a fortuitously named early proponent of ecofeminism (Sales, 1987, p. 302), this movement

> *gives women and men common ground. . . . The social system isn't good for either—or both—of us. Yet we are the social system. We need some common ground . . . to enable us to recognize and affect the deep structure of our relations with each other and with our environment.*

Perhaps the idea most central to ecofeminism is that oppression, so valued and encouraged by modern civilization, is wrong and destructive of all

🕐 MILLY

Personally I relate to ecofeminism since it is most consistent with my own values about life and mutuality. I am a great lover of nature, especially animals. I've rescued a few animals over the years and placed a number into good homes. I also help wounded people. You might think I'm just a tree-hugging, liberal do-gooder, but my small-scale activism demonstrates my values and, in turn, blesses me. I don't jump behind every cause, but I will stand up for what I believe and put my dollar and my shoulder behind those beliefs. Every improvement or change in the world begins as a thought in the mind of a dreamer . . . or an ecofeminist.

forms of life, including the natural world. From ecofeminists have come radical critiques of modern social values and the ends to which they lead us. Reuther (1975), for instance, claims that "the project of human life must cease to be seen as one of 'domination of nature,' or exploitation. . . . We have to find a new language of ecological responsiveness, a reciprocity between consciousness and the world system in which we live" (p. 83). For ecofeminists, oppression itself, not particular instances of oppression, is the primary issue. They believe that, as long as oppression is culturally valued, it will be imposed on anyone and anything that cannot or does not resist. Thus, women's oppression is best understood as a specific example of an overarching cultural ideology that idolizes oppression. A number of individuals who stood against specific types of oppression have redefined themselves as ecofeminists (Chase, 1991). For instance, many vegetarians, animal rights activists, and peace activists have joined the ecofeminist movement.

The goals of this movement flow directly from its critique of cultural values. Ecofeminists seek to bring themselves and others to a new consciousness of humans' interdependence with all other life forms. Although some ecofeminist writing relies on essentialist assumptions about "woman's nature" (Stearney, 1994), essentialist views do not define this movement. Rather, its central goal is to speak out against values that encourage exploitation, domination, and aggression and to show how these oppress women, men, children, animals, plants, and the planet itself. Ecofeminists argue that the values most esteemed by **patriarchal** culture are ones that will destroy us (Diamond & Orenstein, 1990; Gaard & Murphy, 1999; Mellor, 1998; Warren, 2000). (The term *patriarchy* means, literally, "rule by the fathers"; it generally refers to systems of ideology, social structures, and practices, created by men, that reflect the values, priorities, and views of men as a group.)

SUMMARY

Contributing to the cultural conversation about gender are rhetorical movements, which aim to change social views, policies, and perceptions regarding men and women. We've discussed a wide range of women's and men's movements, as well as the backlash and ecofeminism.

Communication in private and public settings delineates multiple versions of femininity and masculinity and seeks to persuade us to adopt certain points of view. As the conversation evolves, new voices will join existing rhetorical efforts to define the meaning of masculinity and femininity and the rights, roles, and opportunities available to women, minorities, men, lesbians, and gay men. It's up to you to define your role in the cultural conversation about gender. Some people will be passive listeners. Others will be critical listeners who reflect carefully on others' communication. And still others will claim a voice in the conversation and will be part of active rhetorical efforts to define gender. What role will you choose?

DISCUSSION QUESTIONS

1. Before you read this chapter, did you know that there were three waves of the feminist movement in the United States? Did you realize that there are so many and such diverse forms of feminism? Many people are not aware that feminism is anything larger than the liberal branch of contemporary United States feminism (for example, NOW). What does limited knowledge of women's movements imply about biases in education?

2. Choose the PowerTrac search option in your InfoTrac College Edition. Select title and type in "Seneca Falls Revisited." Then view the text of Lisa Marsh Ryerson's speech, "Seneca Falls Revisited: Reflections on the Legacy of the 1948 Women's Rights Convention." Pay particular attention to the excerpts from Elizabeth Cady Stanton's speech that appear in Ryerson's speech. Next, select the EasyTrac search option, and, using the keywords "Seneca Falls," read the excerpts from the speech and one of the related articles that are accessed.

3. For suffragists in the 1800s, the big issues were voting, education, and access to employment. What do you see as the most important issues for liberal feminism in the 1990s in the United States? What kinds of discrimination and oppression still limit women economically, personally, educationally, professionally, and politically?

4. With which form or forms of feminism do you most agree? With which are you least comfortable? Do you think it's more the case that women should work to have equal rights and opportunities within existing systems (liberal feminism) or that they should work to change the systems so that they incorporate traditionally feminine values and concerns (cultural feminism)?

5. Which of the men's movements do you find most consistent with your own values? Do you think men should work to restore traditional male prerogatives and social power, become more sensitive themselves, or change society?

6. Follow up on the discussion of men's movements presented in this chapter by visiting the Web sites of one branch of the men's movement. Addresses for the sites appear in the FYI boxes in various sections of the chapter.

7. Is the mythopoetic movement incorrect in arguing that most men suffer from father hunger—an unmet need to be deeply connected to fathers and other men? What are the implications of men not having close and enduring ties to other men?

8. Speculate about gender movements in the next decade. Do you see cultural trends that will influence women's and men's movements as well as broad phenomena like the backlash and ecofeminism? Do you think current social issues such as rising emphasis on cultural diversity will recontour some of the movements that now exist? Do you think new movements will arise?

4 Gendered Verbal Communication

I now pronounce you man and wife.

Bob baby-sat his son while his wife attended a meeting.

Anna Kournikova is sports' hottest pinup girl.

Freshmen find it difficult to adjust to college life.

We reached a gentlemen's agreement on how to proceed.

These five sentences reflect cultural assumptions about women and men—who they are and what they are supposed to do and not do. In the first one, did you notice that "man" is portrayed as an individual, whereas "wife" is defined only by her relationship to the man? In the second sentence, the use of the word *baby-sat* implies that the father was performing a special service, one we usually pay for; have you ever heard a mother's care for her children called baby-sitting? The third sentence defines a highly accomplished tennis player in terms of appearance and deflects attention from her athletic skills and sports victories. Unless the fourth sentence refers to first-year students at an all-male school, the word *freshmen* erases first-year female students. Finally, the term *gentlemen's agreement* reflects the cultural association between men and professional activities.

Throughout previous chapters, we've discussed relationships among communication, gender, and culture. In this and the following chapter, we add depth to those discussions by concentrating specifically on how communication reflects and expresses cultural views of gender. This chapter focuses on how verbal communication interacts with social life and gender, and Chapter 5 traces relationships among nonverbal communication, culture, and gender. We will probe how verbal and nonverbal communication reflect and shape cultural understandings of masculinity and femininity. In addition, we will consider how individuals embody cultural expectations about communication—that is, how individual women's and men's communication reflects or challenges socially prescribed gendered identities. In concert, these two themes highlight the cyclical process whereby cultural views of gender are communicated to individuals, who exemplify them personally and thereby perpetuate cultural expectations of masculine and feminine identities and styles of interacting.

THE NATURE OF HUMAN COMMUNICATION

Communication is symbolic behavior. Unlike other animals, which rely primarily on signal communication, humans interact using symbols. Signal communication is concrete and unambiguous, and therefore doesn't require interpretation. For instance, when I point to the floor, my dog Madhi knows to lie down. The hand signal has a definite, unvarying meaning, so she reacts automatically without having to think. Life gets considerably more complex when we enter the realm of symbolic activity. In fact, many philosophers and scientists who have tried to understand how we differ from other animals believe that the ability to think symbolically is the distinguishing quality of humans. It is what allows us to plan, invent, envision new possibilities, and remake ourselves and our world. (Sagan and Druyan, 1992, offer an excellent and readable summary of research on this topic.)

Not all symbols are linguistic or verbal. For instance, art is symbolic (Langer, 1953), as is dance (Langer, 1979). Both represent feelings and sensations, and both require interpretation. In this chapter, our focus is language, and all language is symbolic; in fact, language is one of the most complex symbol systems we have. Our nature as symbolic beings transforms us from biological creatures, who respond to the concrete world as it exists, into thinking beings who interpret, interact with, and remake our world through symbols (Langer, 1953, 1979). This implies that the symbols we use shape our understandings of the world and our own places within it.

VERBAL COMMUNICATION EXPRESSES CULTURAL VIEWS OF GENDER

In his analysis of humans' use of symbols, philosopher Ernst Cassirer (1978) noted that the power of symbols lies in the kinds of thought and action they enable. Cassirer identified five implications of symbolic ability: symbols allow us to define, organize, and evaluate phenomena, to think hypothetically, and to reflect on ourselves. Discussing these implications of symbolic behavior will illuminate ways in which verbal communication expresses cultural views and expectations of women and men.

Language Defines Gender

The most fundamental implication of symbolic ability is that symbols define phenomena. We use symbols to name objects, people, feelings, experiences, and other phenomena. Because symbols are not concrete or tied naturally to things, the language we use shapes our perceptions selectively. The names we apply emphasize particular aspects of reality and neglect others. We cannot describe things in their total complexity, so the labels we choose highlight only certain qualities. What we emphasize is guided in part by cultural values, so that we name those things or aspects of things that are important in society's perspective. Western society includes language that devalues women and sometimes erases them. In so doing, it represents men and their experiences as the norm—and women and their ways as a departure from what is normal.

Male generic language excludes women. **Male generic language** purports to include both women and men yet specifically refers only to men. Examples are nouns such as *businessmen, chairmen, mailmen,* and *mankind,* and pronouns such as *he* used to refer to both women and men. Some people think it is understood that women are included in terms such as *mankind* and *chairmen.* This viewpoint, however, is not supported by research on how people interpret male generic language.

Research demonstrates that many people interpret masculine generics as referring predominantly or exclusively to men. When people hear or read male generic language, they think first or only of men, not women. In an early study of the effects of male generics (Schneider & Hacker, 1973), children were asked to select photographs for a textbook with chapter titles of "Urban Man" and "Man in Politics" or "Urban Life" and "Political Behavior." The children nearly always chose pictures of men when the titles included male generics. When the titles did not refer to men only, the children chose more photographs that portrayed both sexes. What they saw as appropriate to include in the chapters was shaped by the language in titles.

Other researchers (Gastil, 1990; Hamilton, 1991; Switzer, 1990; Todd-Mancillas, 1981) have conducted similar studies and found that male generic language tends to lead people to perceive males and not females as included. In a particularly interesting study, students from first grade through college were asked to make up a story about an average student. When the instructions referred to the average student as "he," only 12% of students composed a story about a female. However, when the instructions defined the average student as "he or she," 42% of the stories were about females (Hyde, 1984). Another study found that female students took longer to process male generic pronouns (*he, him*) than inclusive pronouns (*they, he or she*). It seems that we have to ponder whether male terms do or do not include females, so it takes longer to comprehend language that explicitly refers only to men (Martyna, 1978).

One of the effects of male generic language is to make men seem more prominent and women less prominent than in real life. Speaking to this concern, a woman wrote of her experiences as a mother (Sheldon, 1990). She had noticed that her 6-year-old daughter used male generic language to describe her stuffed toys. When she asked her daughter why she called a stuffed animal "he," her daughter responded that "there are more he's than she's" (p. 4). In making us think there are more he's than she's, Sheldon contends, our language "is tricking us all" (p. 5) into perceiving as dominant a group that is less than 50% of the population.

According to Nancy Henley (1989), male generic language reduces awareness of women and tends to result in our perceiving women as excluded or exceptions to the rule. This affects comprehension of language, views of personal identity, and perceptions of women's presence in various spheres of life. Exclusionary language in classrooms may inhibit women's learning if they perceive themselves as not included in discussions of "businessmen" and so forth.

Because there is convincing evidence that male language is not perceived as generic, most authorities on writing style don't allow male generic language. Since 1991, *Webster's Dictionary* ("No Sexism Please," 1991) has followed a policy of avoiding male generics and other sexist language. In addition to avoiding man-linked words, the new dictionary cautions against other ways of defining men as the standard and women as the exception. For instance, it discourages **spotlighting**— the practice of highlighting a person's sex. Terms such as *lady doctor* and *woman lawyer* define women as the exception in professions and thereby reinforce the idea that men are the standard.

Language defines men and women differently. A second way that language expresses cultural views of gender is by defining men and women in different ways. Women are frequently defined by appearance or by relationships with others, whereas men are more typically defined by activities, accomplishments, or positions.

Media offer countless examples of defining women by their physical qualities. Headlines announce "Blonde Wins Election," causing us to focus on the candidate's sex and physical appearance rather than her qualifications and plans for office. Coverage of women's sports, which is disproportionate compared with that of men's sports, frequently focuses on women players' appearance rather than their athletic skills. Stories on female athletes often emphasize wardrobes ("Chris is changing her

ANDY

For a long time, I thought all of this stuff about generic *he* was a bunch of junk. I mean, it seemed really clear to me that a word like *mankind* obviously includes women or that *chairman* can refer to a girl or a guy who chairs something. I thought it was pretty stupid to hassle about this. Then last semester I had a woman teacher who taught the whole class using *she* or *her* or *woman* whenever she was referring to people, as well as when she meant just women. I realized how confusing it is. I had to figure out each time whether she meant women only or women and men. And when she meant women to be general, I guess you'd say generic for all people, it still made me feel left out. A lot of the guys in the class got pretty hostile about what she was doing, but I kind of think it was a good way to make the point.

style with a snappy new outfit"), bodies ("She's gotten back in shape and is looking good on the field"), and hairstyles ("When she stepped on the court, fans noticed her lightened hair"), whereas stories about male athletes focus on their athletic abilities ("He sunk two dream shots"). In the opening of this chapter you read the statement: *Anna Kournikova is sports' hottest pinup girl.* That statement appeared in Frank Deford's article about Kournikova, published in the June 2000 issue of *Sports Illustrated.* In that article, photos showed Kournikova in a long black dress with a slit and in a sultry pose with a pillow. In addition to calling her "sports' hottest pinup girl" (p. 98), Deford referred to her as "the Jezebel of sweat" (p. 98) and stated that "on the court she is like a trim sloop, skimming across the surface" (p. 99). Kournikova is physically stunning, and she herself highlights that. However, that isn't why she was featured in *Sports Illustrated.* In focusing more on her sex appeal and beauty than her skill on the courts, Deford defines her as a woman more than as a tennis player. Can you imagine such descriptions of any male athlete featured in *Sports Illustrated*?

Similarly, coverage of women in professional and political life regularly directs attention to appearance, which influences readers to notice women's looks more than issues germane to their occupations. Even when describing women who have been raped or abused, media reports often include extraneous and irrelevant information on the victims' appearance and dress (Carter, 1998; Meyers, 1997, 1999). The bias in descriptions of women reinforces the cultural view of women as decorative objects whose identity hinges on physical appeal. Language in media and everyday conversations reflects social views of women as more passive than men in

---

FYI

What's in a Name?

During the 1970s, several states declared that they did not require women to assume their husbands' last names on marrying. Other states, however, insisted that a woman must assume her husband's last name on marrying (Scheuble & Johnson, 1993). Only in 1975 was the issue of whether a woman is legally required to assume her husband's last name resolved. Then, a Hawaiian statute requiring women to give up their birth names on marriage was ruled unconstitutional (Schroeder, 1986).

Research by Laura Stafford and Susan Kline (1996) shows that some men are not comfortable being married to a woman who keeps her birth name. They report that men, more than women, say they would question a woman's commitment to her husband if she did not adopt his name. Although men felt more strongly about this than women, a majority of both sexes surveyed favored a woman's taking her partner's last name. Additional research (Klein, Stafford, & Miklosovik, 1996) revealed that women's decisions to retain their birth names or adopt their husbands' last names are influenced by a variety of factors, including the value attached to heritage and tradition, the importance of professional identity, desire for a new personal identity, views of marriage and family, practical issues.

---

relationship contexts. Think about discussions of sexual activity that you've heard or in which you've participated. Have you noticed that people commonly say, "He laid her," "He balled her," "He screwed her," "She got laid," and "He made love to her"? Each of these phrases suggests that in sexual activity men are active whereas women are passive.

Our language also reflects society's view of women as defined by their relationships rather than as independent agents. News reports are more likely to include personal information, such as marital status and family topics, when covering women newsmakers than when covering men newsmakers (Carter, 1998; Foreit et al., 1980). In prime-time television, even professional women are often depicted primarily in interpersonal contexts, and their appearance is highlighted (Lott, 1989; Merritt, 2000). For instance, Ally McBeal's legal knowledge and ability are overshadowed by emphasis on her appearance and personal life.

The cultural association of women with relationships is explicitly expressed in the words *Miss* and *Mrs.*, which designate marital status. There are no parallel titles that define men in terms of whether they are married. The alternative term *Ms.* to designate a woman without identifying her by her marital status is a relatively new addition to the language and not yet fully accepted. It was not until 1987 that the *New York Times* would print "Ms." if a woman preferred that title (Stewart, Stewart, Friedley, & Cooper, 1996). The extent to which our society defines women by marriage and family is further evidenced in the still prevalent tradition of a wife adopting her husband's name upon marrying. Symbolically, she exchanges her individual identity for one based on her relationship to a man: Mrs. John Smith.

There are a number of alternatives to the traditional ways of naming ourselves (Foss, Edson, & Linde, 2000; Fowler & Fuehrer, 1997). Some women choose to retain their birth names when they marry. A number of men and women adopt hyphenated names such as Johnson-Smith to symbolize the family heritage of both partners. In some countries, such as Spain, both the mother's and father's family names are used to construct children's family names. Another alternative, less often practiced so far, is renaming oneself to reflect **matriarchal** rather than patriarchal lineage. (The term *matriarchy* means, literally, "rule by the mothers"; it generally refers to systems of ideology, social structures, and practices, created by women, that reflect the values, priorities, and views of women as a group.) This involves

SANDRA

It has never occurred to me that I wouldn't take my husband's name when I marry. It just seems right to me for us to have the same last name once we become our own family. I want us to be one, and the best way to express that is by taking his name.

BRIAN

I never considered whether my wife would take my name. I just assumed she would. I'm proud of my family and I feel tied to who we are, and my family name represents that. I always thought it would be a great honor for a woman to have my family name. But my fiancé doesn't feel the same way. She says she's proud of her name too, that it's who she is too. I can understand that in a way, but still it seems like she should want to take my name. She turned the tables on me by asking if I would take her name.

 SUSAN

When we were talking about how naming makes us aware of things, it rang a bell for me. My first semester here, I had a lab instructor who made me really uncomfortable. I was having trouble with some of the material, so I went to see him during office hours. He moved away from his desk and sat beside me. Then he sort of touched my arm and knee while I was trying to show him my work. I felt really bad. I kept trying to edge away, but he just moved too. Then he started cornering me after class and suggesting we get lunch together. I didn't know what to do. I wondered if I was doing some-

(continued)

changing a last name from that of the father's family to that of the mother's. Because that course of action, however, still reflects male lineage—that of the mother's father—some women use their mothers' first names to create a matrilineal last name: for example, Lynn Edwards's daughter, Barbara, might rename herself Barbara Lynnschild. In coming years, doubtlessly we will see other alternatives to traditional naming practices. Their existence reminds us of the importance we attach to naming and of our power to use language creatively.

Language names what exists. Finally, consider the pivotal power of language to name what does and does not exist. We notice what we name and tend not to recognize or reflect on phenomena we leave unnamed. Spender (1984b) argues that not to name something is to deny that it exists or matters—to negate it. The power of naming is clear with sexual harassment and date rape. Only recently has the term *sexual harassment* entered our language. For most of history, sexual harassment occurred frequently (see

---

FYI

Language: Victims, Survivors, or . . .

How should we refer to people who are raped or physically assaulted? Should we call them *victims*? Should we call them *survivors*? For most crimes, there is no controversy about language—the target of the crime is called a victim. With sex-related crimes, however, there is a heated debate about language and its effects. Some scholars, counselors, and activists think that the term *victim* is dangerous because it reinforces sex stereotypes of women as powerless and vulnerable. It also fuels criticism of feminism as too focused on women as victims. The term *survivor,* on the other hand, emphasizes the fact that the target of a sex-related crime survived, which suggests strength and resilience. Others who study or work with targets of violent sex-related crimes, say the term *victim* is appropriate at the time of the violence. The person was a victim when the violence happened. Also, they note, *victim* is more useful for getting funds—groups such as rape crisis centers and battered women's shelters can qualify for "victim services funds," but there are no funds for "survivor services."

It may be that we need to devise language that can represent different points in a person's experience. Someone who is raped may be a victim at one moment and a survivor later. Alone, neither word may accurately represent the total of a person's experience.

Source: Lamb, S. (Ed.) (1999). *New versions of victims.* New York: New York University Press.

Wood, 1992b, 1993f for a summary), but it was un-named. Because it wasn't named, sexual harassment was not visible or salient, making it difficult to recognize, think about, stop, or discipline.

Why was sexual harassment unnamed for so long? Scholars suggest that the world is named by those who hold power, and what affects those people is what they notice and acknowledge with names (Coates, 1997; Kramarae, Thorne, & Henley, 1978; Spender, 1984a). Because historically men have held most of the power in professional life and because sexual harassment was rarely a problem for them, it was unnamed. If sexual harassment was discussed at all, it was with language that obscured its violating nature and its ugliness. Phrases such as "making advances," "getting out of line," and "being pushy" fail to convey the abusiveness of sexual harassment. Only when the term *sexual harassment* was coined did we start calling attention to the wrongness of unwanted behavior that objectifies and humiliates individuals and ties sexuality to security and advancement. And only with this awareness were efforts to redress sexual harassment devised.

(Susan continued)
thing that made him think I was interested or maybe I was overreacting to him, but I just know I felt uncomfortable. Finally, one day he stopped me after class and told me that he might be able to help me with my grade if I would go out with him that weekend. And you know what? I still didn't understand what was happening. I knew I didn't want to date him, and I knew he could hurt my grade, but I didn't know it was sexual harassment. If that happened again today, I'd know what to call it, and I'd also know I could do something about it. So I understood the stuff about names being important.

Similarly, the term *date rape* did not exist a decade ago. Although a number of women engaged in sex against their wishes, there was no term to describe what occurred. Women who experienced date rape had no socially recognized way to name what happened to them. They had to deal with their experience without language that acknowledged that a date could commit rape. Consequently, it was not much discussed, and victims were left without ways to define and think about grievous violations that often had lifelong repercussions (Wriggins, 1998). These two examples make clear the power of naming—it allows us to see more clearly what exists and to think about it in ways possible only with symbolic designation.

Verbal communication is a primary means by which cultural definitions of gender are expressed and sustained. By excluding women, defining them as exceptions to the male standard, or depicting them in terms of appearance and relationships, language reinforces cultural stereotypes of femininity. In defining men by their activities and achievements and not by their relationships, language fortifies the traditional view of men as independent, assertive agents.

Language Organizes Perceptions of Gender

A second implication of humans' symbolic nature is that we use language to organize experience and perceptions. Because language is abstract, not concrete, we can classify phenomena and think in terms of generalizations. Suzanne Langer (1979), one of the most influential philosophers of language, recognizes that humans inevitably construct understandings by abstracting from their experiences and feelings. Calling symbols "vehicles for the conceptions of objects" (p. 60), Langer points out that symbols allow us to translate concrete sense data into symbolic forms so that we can conceive and reflect on them. The organizing function of language expresses cultural views of gender by stereotyping men and women and by encouraging polarized perceptions of gender.

Stereotyping gender. Because symbols are abstract, they allow us to think in general ways and to understand broad concepts like democracy, freedom, religion, and gender. Although our ability to think in broad categories is useful in many ways, it is also the source of stereotypes, which sometimes misrepresent individuals. A **stereotype** is a broad generalization about an entire class of phenomena based on some knowledge of some aspects of some members of the class. When we stereotype, we use a general label to define specific members of a class. For example, if most women you know aren't interested in sports, you might conclude that women don't like sports. This stereotype could keep you from noticing that many women engage in sports and enjoy attending athletic events. Relying on stereotypes can lead us to overlook important particularities of individuals and to perceive them only in terms of what we consider common to a general category.

Verbal communication groups men and women, masculine and feminine into broad, stereotypical categories. Women tend to be classified as emotional, whereas men are usually classified as rational; men are defined as strong, whereas women are stereotyped as physically weaker ("the weaker sex"). Because cultural stereotypes promote these views of men and women, they restrict perceptions of others and of ourselves. For instance, women's arguments are sometimes dismissed as being emotional when, in fact, they entail evidence and reasoning (Mapstone, 1998). The stereotype of women as emotional provides a framework that can lead people to judge women's ideas in terms of the stereotype, not the reality. Similarly, a man who accepts the cultural view of masculinity may be unable to recognize, much less act on, strong emotions because they don't fit his stereotype of what it

> **BEA**
>
> When I was 13 years old, I started having blackouts, where I'd just shut down for a few minutes, although I stayed conscious. When I came out of the spells I wouldn't remember what happened, but others would tell me I had been babbling. My mother took me to a doctor, who said not to worry about it. He said it was normal for teenage girls to be flighty and hysterical. He didn't do any tests or even examine me. He just told Mother it would go away when I matured.
>
> My mother was furious and called him an idiot. She then took me to another doctor and another, and they both agreed with the first one. She didn't buy it, and we kept making the rounds until we found one doctor who wanted to run some tests before making any diagnosis. He did a CAT scan, which showed that I had a rare form of epilepsy. It is a condition that develops in early adolescence and causes blackouts, sometimes with odd talking during them. He put me on a medicine that stopped them. But if we had listened to those other doctors, I wouldn't have been treated—except as a *normally* hysterical young girl.

means to be a man. Thinking of others stereotypically can cause us to misperceive them, which can have severe consequences.

Encouraging polarized thinking. A second implication of language's organizing function is the encouragement of **polarized thinking.** Polarized or dichotomous thinking involves conceiving of things as opposites. More than many languages, English emphasizes polarities. Something is right or wrong, good or bad, appropriate or inappropriate. Our vocabulary emphasizes all-or-none terms and includes few words that indicate degrees. This makes it difficult for us to think in terms of variation and range (Bem, 1993).

Polarized language and thought are particularly evident in how we think about gender: People are divided into two realms—male and female. Then we are all expected to conform to the stereotyped molds or suffer the consequences of negative social judgments. Research indicates that women who use assertive speech associated with masculinity are frequently perceived as arrogant and rude, whereas men who employ emotional language associated with femininity are often perceived to be wimps or gay (Rasmussen & Moley, 1986). Activities and feelings are either feminine or masculine. A man is what a woman is not; a woman is what a man is not. In reality, of course, most of us have a number of qualities, some of which our society designates as feminine and some of which it defines as masculine. Our culture's binary labels for sexual identity encourage us not to notice how much variation there is among women and among men (Lorber, 2001). By being aware of the tendencies to stereotype and think in polar terms, we enhance our capacity to question and resist limiting conceptions of masculinity and femininity.

■ Language Evaluates Gender

Language is not neutral. It reflects cultural values and is a powerful influence on our perceptions. Related to gender, language expresses cultural devaluations of females and femininity. It does this by trivializing, deprecating, and diminishing women and things defined as feminine.

Women are often trivialized by language. They are frequently demeaned by terms that label them as immature or juvenile (*baby doll, girlie, little darling*) or

DILBERT reprinted by permission of United Feature Syndicate, Inc.

Until we talked about language in class, I hadn't really thought about the double standard for sexually active girls and guys. Or if I had thought about it, I probably would have said that the double standard doesn't exist anymore. Our discussion got me thinking, and that's not really true. Guys who have sex with a lot of girls are *studs* or *players*. Girls who have sex with a lot of guys are *sluts* or *easy*. It's not as bad as it used to be, but I guess there still is kind of a double standard.

equate them with food (*dish, feast for the eyes, good enough to eat, sugar, sweet thing, cookie, cupcake, hot tomato, honey pie*) and animals (*chick, pig, dog, cow, bitch*). They are described as possessions (*his wife, my secretary, my girl*). Susan A. Basow (1992) notes that history books' accounts of how this country was settled include statements such as "Pioneers moved West, taking their wives and children with them" (p. 142). This description portrays only men as the pioneers and women and children as possessions the pioneers took along.

Language sometimes trivializes women's accomplishments or activities. For instance, not long ago on my campus, two administrators—one woman and one man—spoke out sharply against a particular proposal under consideration. The local newspaper reported that the male administrator "expressed deep concern and outrage," whereas the woman "was piqued." To label her reaction *piqued* is to imply that it was frivolous, lightweight, or otherwise not to be taken seriously.

Women are also deprecated by language that devalues them. One researcher (Stanley, 1977) found 220 terms for sexually permissive women but only 22 for sexually promiscuous men. Although there are derogatory terms for men (*wimp, bastard*), there are fewer of them, especially terms that devalue promiscuity in men. Women are further deprecated when topics of particular importance to women are marginalized and treated as insignificant. Frequently, women newsmakers and issues that affect women are not covered or are sequestered in the leisure or lifestyle sections of newspapers (Danner & Walsh, 1999).

In addition, women and what is feminine are diminished by language. This happens in a number of ways. Quite often, diminutive suffixes are used to designate women as deviations from the standard form of the word: *suffragette, majorette.* Calling women "girls" (a term that technically refers to a female who has not gone through puberty) diminishes them by defining them as children, not adults. Conservative media commentator Rush Limbaugh demeans feminists by calling them "feminazis" and "fembots" (as in *robots*).

■ Language Enables Hypothetical Thought

Particularly important to our thinking about gender is the fact that symbols allow **hypothetical thought,** which is consciousness of things that do not exist in the moment. Because symbols are abstract, they allow us to think not only about what is but also about what will or might be and what has been. In turn, this enables us to think of past, present, and future and to conceive of alternatives to current states of affairs. To understand the power of hypothetical thought, consider your own com-

If Men Are Guys, Then Women Are . . . Gals

During the early years of the second wave of feminism, many women objected to being called *girls*. The term, they argued, portrayed adult women as childlike. Similarly rejected was the term *lady* because it suggested a prim, upper-class, Emily Post image. *Chicks, dames,* and similar terms were also renounced.

But there's a problem. Many females who are past puberty feel the term *woman* is too formal and fussy. They want a term that's more casual, relaxed, snazzy—an equivalent to what men have with the term *guy*.

According to Natalie Angier, reporter for the *New York Times* (1995), the new choice may be *gal*. In 1995, the prestigious *Washington Post* used *gal* 85 times. Progressive columnist Kate Clinton describes herself as a "gal comedian," and she talks often about her "gal pals." And Charles S. Mechem, who is commissioner of the Ladies Professional Golf Association, doesn't call the members *ladies*. Nope, he refers to them as *gals*—fierce, sassy, talented gals.

mitment to earning a college degree and launching a career. Although these ideas have no material basis in the actual world, they are real enough to you to motivate years of work.

Humans do not accept the world as it is. We continuously imagine alternatives to what currently exists, which is why humans invent things (electricity, computers, refrigeration), devise systems (transportation, banking, education), develop technologies (wireless phones, the Web), and improve medical treatments (immunizations, CAT scans). When we see a disease such as AIDS or cancer, we don't just accept it; instead, we imagine finding a cure and effective treatments. Our ability to name alternatives to what exists is the source of much progress in human life.

Hypothetical thought has been very influential in defining what gender means. As we saw in Chapter 3, many of the first-wave feminists envisioned the day when women could vote, attend universities, and own property. It was imagining these possibilities that inspired the courage and effort required to instigate changes in social views of women and activities appropriate for them. Years later, in the second wave of feminism, many liberal feminists imagined laws that would prohibit sex discrimination on the job, and this idea motivated them to actions that made this a reality. Those involved with the backlash, too, rely on hypothetical thinking in their efforts to define gender. They recall former times when women were subservient, and they try to persuade others to reclaim that vision of womanhood. Whether pushing to move forward or backward in time, people engage in hypothetical thinking to define and work toward alternatives to prevailing views of genders.

Hypothetical thought is important in individuals' gender identity as well as in rhetorical movements. Each of us has to decide what it means to be a woman or a man. We understand society's views and expectations, yet we are not compelled to accept them as given. Sometimes we challenge cultural definitions of gender and define our personal identities outside of culturally approved prescriptions. Imagine your ideals of women and men. What are they like? How might you realize them? In entertaining these questions, you are engaging in hypothetical thought, which gives you possibilities for defining yourself that transcend those defined by society.

■ Language Allows Self-Reflection

This final implication of symbolic ability is especially relevant to thinking about our own gendered identities. Because we are symbol users, we name not only phenomena around us but also ourselves. If we don't like the self we see, we are able to change it—to alter how we act and how we define our identity. We do this by combining our capacities to think hypothetically and to self-reflect. For instance, one alternative to traditional sex-typing is androgyny (see Chapter 1). Androgynous people possess qualities the culture defines as masculine and feminine, instead of possessing only those assigned to one sex. Androgynous women and men are, for example, both assertive and sensitive, both ambitious and compassionate (Bem, 1993).

Many people reflect on cultural views of gender and decide they don't want to limit themselves only to those qualities prescribed for one sex. They believe they are more flexible in attitudes and behaviors than is recognized by polarized views of gender. A number of women choose not to be as passive as the culture prescribes for femininity, and they work to be more assertive. Men also may decide to resist social prescriptions for masculinity by showing sensitivity and vulnerability in appropriate situations as well as strength and toughness in others.

FYI

The Report Card on Androgynous Communication

Androgynous communication, which incorporates qualities associated with both masculinity and femininity, seems linked to personal and professional success. Androgynous women and men have higher self-esteem and more advanced psychological development and personal adjustment than sex-typed individuals (Heilbrun, 1986; Heilbrun & Han, 1984; Hemmer & Kleiber, 1981; Jackson, 1983; Lamke, 1982; Waterman & Whitbourne, 1982). In the workplace, androgynous individuals are more flexible and more effective in interacting with a range of people (Heath, 1991; Wheeless, 1984). It seems especially the case that women who possess both masculine and feminine qualities are effective in work settings (Hall & Taylor, 1985; Mills & Bohannon, 1983).

A long-term study of adults reports that androgynous people are more likely to be successful in their professional and personal lives than are sex-typed individuals (Heath, 1991). Androgynous individuals are able to communicate in a range of ways and to respond to diverse others with flexible skills that meet the demands of various situations.

Androgyny is not the only alternative to rigid sex-typing. Based on his experiences and his studies of men, Larry May (1998b) does not favor androgyny. He thinks androgynous men and women are too much alike. Instead, he suggests that men should define themselves within what he calls a "progressive male standpoint" that encourages men to adopt some traditionally masculine qualities, such as ambition and competitiveness, but to reject other traditionally masculine qualities, such as domination and violence. May's vision of ideal masculinity calls on men to "accept responsibility for the men they are and to strive toward the men they can become" (p. 151). Because May's research focuses on men, he has not defined a parallel progressive female standpoint. You might want to think about which traditionally feminine qualities would and would not fit within a progressive female standpoint.

Language Is a Process

We've seen that language expresses cultural views of gender and tends to reproduce them. Yet language is not static. Instead, we continuously change language to reflect our changing understandings of ourselves and our world. When we find existing language inadequate or undesirable, we change it. We reject terms we find objectionable (*girl*, male generics), and we create new terms to define realities we think are important (*sexual harassment, Ms., androgyny, third-wave feminism*). As we modify language, we modify how we see ourselves and our world.

We become empowered when we realize how profoundly language influences perceptions of men and women, masculinity and femininity. Awareness of the power of language generates choices about what language we will use and support others in using. The choices we make affect not only our personal identities and lives but also social expectations and perceptions of gender. Thus, in being reflective about language, we assume an active role in shaping our culture.

GENDERED INTERACTION: MASCULINE AND FEMININE STYLES OF VERBAL COMMUNICATION

Language not only expresses cultural views of gender but also constitutes individuals' gender identities. The communication practices we use define us as masculine or feminine; in large measure, we create our own gender through our communication. Because language constitutes masculinity and femininity, we should find generalizable differences in how women and men communicate. Research bears out this expectation by documenting rather systematic differences in the ways men and women typically use language.

If you are like most people, you've sometimes felt uncomfortable or misunderstood or mystified in communication with members of the other sex, but you've not been able to put your finger on what was causing the difficulty. In the pages that follow, we'll try to gain greater insight into masculine and feminine styles of speech and some of the confusion that results from differences between them. We want to understand how each style evolves, what it involves, and how to interpret verbal communication in ways that honor the standpoints of those using it.

■ Gendered Speech Communities

Writing in the 1940s, Suzanne Langer introduced the idea of "discourse communities." Like George Herbert Mead, she asserted that culture, or collective life, is possible only to the extent that a group of people share a symbol system and the meanings encapsulated in it. This theme recurs in Langer's philosophical writings over the course of her life (1953, 1979). Her germinal insights into discourse communities prefigure later interest in the ways in which language creates individual identity and sustains cultural life. Since the early 1970s, scholars have studied speech communities. William Labov (1972) extended Langer's ideas by defining a speech community as existing when a group of people shares a set of norms regarding communicative practices. By this, he meant that a **speech community** exists when people share understandings about goals of communication, strategies for enacting those goals, and ways of interpreting communication.

It's obvious that we have entered a different speech community when we travel in countries whose language differs from our own. Distinct speech communities are less apparent when they use the same language but use it in different ways and to achieve different goals. The communication of traditional African Americans who have not adopted the dominant pattern of North American speech, for instance, relies on English yet departs in interesting and patterned ways from the communication of middle-class White North Americans. The fact that diverse groups of people develop distinctive communication patterns reminds us again of the continuous interaction of communication and culture. As we have already seen, the standpoint we occupy in society influences what we know and how we act. We now see that this basic tenet of standpoint theory also implies that communication styles evolve out of different standpoints.

Studies of gender and communication (Campbell, 1973; Coates, 1986, 1997; Coates & Cameron, 1989; Johnson, 2000) convincingly show that most girls and women and boys and men are socialized into distinct speech communities that have dissimilar assumptions about the goals and strategies of communication. Given this, it seems appropriate to consider masculine and feminine styles of communicating as embodying two distinct speech communities. To understand these different communities and the validity of each, we will first consider how we are socialized into feminine and masculine speech communities. After this, we will explore divergence in how women and men typically communicate. Please note the importance of the word *typically* and others that indicate we are discussing generalizable differences, not absolute ones. Some women are not socialized into feminine speech, or they are and later reject it; likewise, some men do not learn or choose not to adopt a masculine style of communication. What follows describes gendered speech communities into which *most* women and men are socialized.

■ The Lessons of Childplay

Initial insight into the importance of children's play in shaping patterns of communication come from a classic study by Daniel Maltz and Ruth Borker (1982). As they watched young children engaged in recreation, the researchers were struck by two observations: Young children almost always play in sex-segregated groups, and girls and boys tend to play different kinds of games. Maltz and Borker found that boys' games (football, baseball) and girls' games (school, house, jump rope) cultivate distinct understandings of communication and the rules by which it operates. More recent research on young children's play confirms Maltz and Borker's original findings that children tend to prefer others of their sex as playmates and that girls and boys develop and use different kinds of communication (Austin, Salehi, & Leffler, 1987; Goodwin, 1990; Kovacs, Parker, & Hoffman, 1996; Maccoby, 1998).

Boys' games. Boys' games usually involve fairly large groups—nine individuals for each baseball team, for instance. Most boys' games are competitive, have clear goals, and are organized by rules and roles that specify who does what and how to play. Because these games are structured by goals, rules, and roles, there is little need to discuss how to play, although there may be talk about strategies to reach goals. In boys' games, an individual's status depends on standing out, being better, and often dominating other players. Observations of children at play show that boys initiate more activity and engage in communication to get attention (Austin et al., 1987). In their games, boys engage in more heckling, storytelling, interrupting, and commanding than girls typically do. From these games, boys learn how to interact in their communities. Specifically, boys' games cultivate three communication rules:

1. Use communication to assert yourself and your ideas; use talk to achieve something.

2. Use communication to attract and maintain an audience.

3. Use communication to compete with others for the "talk stage," so that they don't gain more attention than you; learn to wrest the focus from others and onto yourself.

These communication rules are consistent with other aspects of masculine socialization that we have already discussed. For instance, notice the emphasis on individuality and competition. Also, we see that these rules accent achievement—doing something, accomplishing a goal. Boys learn they

> ### ♪ ALAN
>
> I got the message about not letting other guys beat me when I was just 10. Every day on my way home from school, this other boy who was 4 or 5 years older would wait for me so that he could beat on me. I got tired of this, so I talked to my dad about it, hoping he'd help me. But he just lit into me some kind of bad. He told me not to ever, ever come to him again saying some other guy was beating up on me. He told me if that guy came after me again, I should fight back and use something to hit him if I had to.
>
> Sure enough, the next day that dude was waiting for me. When he hit me, I picked up the nearest thing—a two-by-four on the ground—and hit him on the head. Well, he had to go to the hospital, but my dad said that was okay because his son had been a man.

must *do things* to be valued members of the team. It's also the case that intensely close, personal relationships are unlikely to be formed in large groups. Finally, we see the undercurrent of masculinity's emphasis on being invulnerable and guarded: If others are the competition from whom you must seize center stage, then you cannot let them know too much about yourself and your weaknesses.

Girls' games. Turning now to girls' games, we find that quite different patterns exist, and they lead to distinctive understandings of communication. Girls tend to play in pairs or in very small groups rather than large ones. Also, games like house and school do not have preset, clear-cut goals, rules, and roles. There is no analogy for the touchdown in playing house. Because girls' games are not structured externally, players have to talk among themselves to decide what they're doing and what roles they have. Observations of young girls at play reveal that they spend more time talking than doing anything else—a pattern that is not true of young boys (Goodwin, 1990; Maccoby, 1998). Playing house, for instance, typically begins with a discussion about who is going to be the daddy and who the mommy. This is typical of the patterns girls use to generate rules and roles for their games. The lack of stipulated goals for the games is also important, because it tends to cultivate in girls an interest in the process of interaction more than its products. For their games to work, girls have to cooperate and work out problems by talking: No external rules exist to settle disputes. From these games, girls learn normative communication patterns of their speech communities. Specifically, girls' games teach three basic rules for communication:

1. Use collaborative, cooperative talk to create and maintain relationships. The *process* of communication, not its content, is the heart of relationships.

2. Avoid criticizing, outdoing, or putting others down; if criticism is necessary, make it gentle; never exclude others.

3. Pay attention to others and to relationships; interpret and respond to others' feelings sensitively.

Despite changes in sex roles and children's play, the findings we've discussed continue to apply to children's typical interaction and the communication patterns it cultivates. After reviewing 40 years of research on male and female patterns of interaction, Anne Campbell (1993) concludes that "play groups of girls are less structured than those of boys, display less conflict and verbal efforts at control, and deny status differences" (p. 34). Campbell believes that the typically smaller size of girls' play groups fosters cooperative discussion and an open-ended process of talking to organize activity, whereas the larger groups in which boys usually play encourage competition and external rules to structure activity. In another investigation of preschoolers, boys used talk primarily to exert control and give orders, whereas girls were more likely to make requests (Weiss & Sachs, 1991). Finally, one scholar recorded 9- to 14-year-old African Americans engaged in interaction in neighborhood play groups. Girls in the groups typically used inclusive and nondirective language, whereas boys tended to issue commands, used talk to compete, and worked to establish status hierarchies in their groups (Goodwin, 1990).

Psychologist Campbell Leaper (1991, 1994, 1996) has conducted many studies of children's interaction. Consistent with other research, Leaper's investigations show that girls tend to engage in more affiliative, cooperative play, whereas boys tend to interact in more instrumental ways. Along with other scholars (Fabes, 1994; Harris, 1998), Leaper reports that gendered communication styles are more pronounced in same-sex than in mixed-sex groups, a finding that is supported by other scholars. The tendency for same-sex groups to foster highly gendered ways of communicating is particularly important when we realize that children's play tends to be strongly sex segregated (Clark, 1998; Maccoby, 1998; Moller & Serbin, 1996). Even children as young as 2 or 3 years old (about the time that gender constancy develops) show a preference for same-sex playmates (Martin, 1991, 1994, 1997; Ruble & Martin, 1998).

These basic patterns in communication echo and reinforce other aspects of gender socialization. Girls' games stress cooperation, collaboration, and sensitivity to others' feelings. Also notice the focus on process encouraged in girls' games. Rather than interacting to achieve some outcome, girls learn that communication itself is the goal. Whereas boys learn they have to do something to be valuable, the lesson for girls is *to be.* Their worth depends on being good people, which is defined by being cooperative, inclusive, and sensitive. The lessons of child's play are carried forward. In fact, the basic rules of communication that adult women and men employ turn out to be refined and elaborated versions of the very same ones evident in girls' and boys' childhood games (Clark, 1998; Mulac, 1998).

■ Gendered Communication Practices

Many communication scholars have studied men's and women's communication and concluded that there are some patterned, general differences (Bate, 1988; Hall & Langellier, 1988; Kramarae, 1981; Treichler & Kramarae, 1983; Wood, 1993a). In some instances, women and men tend to engage in distinctive styles of communication with different purposes, rules, and understandings of how to interpret talk. We will consider features of women's and men's speech that have been identified by a number of researchers. As we do, we will discover some of the complications that arise when men and women operate by different rules in conversations with each other.

Feminine speech. People who are socialized in feminine speech communities— many women and some men—tend to regard communication as a primary way to establish and maintain relationships with others. They engage in conversation to share themselves and to learn about others (Johnson, 1996). This is an important point: For many women, talk *is* the essence of relationships. Consistent with this primary goal, women's speech tends to display identifiable features that foster connections, support, closeness, and understanding.

Scholarship Versus Popular Psychology

Deborah Tannen, author of books on differences in women's and men's communication (1990a, 1990b, 1995), declares that "communication between men and women can be like cross-cultural communication, prey to a clash of conversational styles (1990b, p. 42). John Gray goes even further, claiming that women and men are so different, they are from different planets (1992, 1995, 1996a, 1996b, 1998). Both Tannen and Gray have sold millions of books. Should we believe what they say about communication between the sexes?

When trying to determine the worth of their claims, we might first ask about their credentials as experts in communication. Tannen is a linguist who holds a Ph.D. Gray has no graduate education from a creditable school. Tannen bases her claims on her studies and those of others. Gray bases his on anecdotes from his personal experience.

Second, we should compare their claims with the findings of good research. When we do this, we discover gaps between what these popular psychologists tell us and what scholarship documents. Tannen's claims fare better than Gray's. Although Tannen generalizes too broadly from limited and unrepresentative samples, her claims are not wholly without support. Gray, on the other hand, portrays women and men in extreme and dichotomous stereotypes that are not supported by credible research.

If you want to learn about how these popular psychology books measure up to research, read these articles: Goldsmith, D., & Fulfs, P. (1999). "You just don't have the evidence": An analysis of claims and evidence in Deborah Tannen's *You Just Don't Understand*. In M. Roloff (Ed.), *Communication Yearbook, 22* (pp. 1–49). Thousand Oaks, CA: Sage. Wood, J. T. (2001a). A critical essay on John Gray's portrayals of men, women, and relationships. *Southern Communication Journal, 67,* 201–210.

Establishing equality between people is generally important in women's communication. To achieve symmetry, women often match experiences to indicate "You're not alone in how you feel." Typical ways to communicate equality would be saying, "I've done the same thing many times," "I've felt just like that," or "Something like that happened to me, too, and I felt like you do." Growing out of the quest for equality is a participatory mode of interaction in which communicators respond to and build on each other's ideas in the process of conversing (Hall & Langellier, 1988). Rather than a rigid "You tell your ideas, then I'll tell mine" sequence, women's speech more characteristically follows an interactive pattern in which different voices weave together to create conversations.

Also characteristic of many women's speech is showing support for others. To demonstrate support, women often express understanding and sympathy with a friend's situation or feelings. "Oh, you must feel terrible," communicates that we understand and support how another feels. Related to these first two features is women's typical attention to the relationship level of communication (Wood, 1993a, 1993b; Wood & Inman, 1993). You will recall that the relationship level of

Feminine Communication Style in Politics

Jane Blankenship and Deborah Robson (1995) analyzed women's political communication between 1990 and 1994 in debates, speeches, televised congressional hearings, and other political contexts. They identified five features of feminine political style:

1. Political judgments were based in part on concrete experiences.

2. Communication valued and reflected inclusivity and awareness of relationships among people.

3. Women speakers viewed power as the ability to get things done and empower others.

4. Policy judgments were approached holistically.

5. What are typically regarded as women's issues were moved to the forefront of public discussion.

talk focuses on feelings and the relationship between communicators rather than on the content of messages. In conversations between women, it is common to hear a number of questions that probe for greater understanding of feelings and perceptions surrounding the subject of talk (Beck, 1988). "How did you feel when it occurred?" "Do you think it was deliberate?" "How does this fit into the overall relationship?" are probes that help a listener understand a speaker's perspective.

A fourth feature of women's speech style is conversational "maintenance work" (Beck, 1988; Fishman, 1978). This involves efforts to sustain conversation by inviting others to speak and by prompting them to elaborate their experiences. Women, for instance, ask a number of questions that initiate topics for others: "How was your day?" "Did anything interesting happen on your trip?" "What do you think of the candidates this year?" Communication of this sort maintains interaction and opens the conversational door to others.

Inclusivity also surfaces in a fifth quality of women's talk, responsiveness. Women usually respond in some fashion to what others say. A woman might say "Tell me more" or "That's interesting"; perhaps she will nod and use eye contact to signal she is engaged; perhaps she will ask a question such as "Can you explain what you mean?" Responsiveness reflects learned tendencies to care about others and to make them feel valued and included (Chatham-Carpenter & DeFrancisco, 1998; Kemper, 1984). It affirms another person and encourages elaboration by showing interest in what was said.

☾ YOLANDA

With my boyfriend, I am always asking, "How was your day? Your class? Your jam session? Did you get such and such done? Did you talk to so and so?" He answers my questions, usually with just a few words, but he almost never asks questions about my day and my life. When I do talk about myself, he often interrupts and sometimes listens, but he doesn't say much in response. I'm tired of doing all the work to keep a conversation going in our relationship.

A sixth quality of women's talk is personal, concrete style (Campbell, 1973; Hall & Langellier, 1988). Typical of women's conversation are details, personal disclosures, anecdotes, and concrete reasoning. These features cultivate a personal tone in women's communication, and they facilitate feelings of closeness by connecting communicators' lives. The detailed, concrete emphasis prevalent in women's talk also clarifies issues and feelings so that communicators are able to understand and identify with each other. Thus, the personal character of much of women's interaction sustains interpersonal closeness.

A final feature of women's speech is tentativeness. This may be expressed in a number of forms. Sometimes women use verbal hedges such as "I kind of feel you may be overreacting." In other situations they qualify statements by saying "I'm probably not the best judge of this, but . . ." Another way to keep talk provisional is to tag a question onto a statement in a way that invites another to respond: "That was a pretty good movie, wasn't it?" Tentative communication leaves the door open for others to respond and express their opinions.

There has been controversy about tentativeness in women's speech. Robin Lakoff (1975), who first noted that women use more hedges, qualifiers, and tag questions than men, claimed these represent uncertainty and lack of confidence. Calling women's speech powerless, Lakoff argued that it reflects women's socialization into subordinate roles and low self-esteem. Since Lakoff's work, however, other scholars have suggested different explanations of women's tentative style of speaking. Dale Spender (1984a), in particular, points out that Lakoff's judgments of the alleged inferiority of women's speech were based on using male speech as the standard, which does not recognize the distinctive validity of different speech communities. Rather than reflecting powerlessness, the use of hedges, qualifiers, and tag questions may express women's desires to keep conversation open and to include others (Bate, 1988; Mills, 1999; Wood & Lenze, 1991b). It is much easier to jump into a conversation that has not been sealed with absolute, firm statements. It is important to realize, however, that people outside of feminine speech communities may misinterpret women's intentions in using tentative communication.

Masculine speech. Masculine speech communities tend to regard talk as a way to exert control, preserve independence, entertain, and enhance status. Conversation is often seen as an arena for proving oneself and negotiating prestige. This leads to two general tendencies in many men's communication as well as the communication of women who adhere to norms of masculine speech communities. First, men often use talk to establish and defend their personal status and their ideas by asserting their ideas and authority, telling jokes and stories, or challenging others. Second, when they wish to comfort or support another, men may be more likely than women to show respect for the other's independence and avoid communication they regard as condescending.

To establish their status and value, men often speak to exhibit knowledge, skill, or ability. Equally typical is the tendency to avoid disclosing personal information that might make a man appear weak or vulnerable (Lewis & McCarthy, 1988;

Saurer & Eisler, 1990). For instance, if someone expresses a problem, a man might say, "The way you should handle that is . . . ," or "Don't let your boss get to you." This illustrates the masculine tendency to give advice. On the relationship level of communication, giving advice does two things. First, it focuses on instrumental activity—what another should do or be—and does not acknowledge feelings. Second, it expresses superiority and maintains control. It says "I know what you should do" or "I would know how to handle that." The message may be perceived as implying that the speaker is superior to the other person. Between men, advice giving seems understood as a give-and-take, but it may be interpreted as unfeeling and condescending by women whose rules for communicating differ.

> ✆ **JOANNE**
>
> My boyfriend is the worst at throwing solutions in my face when I try to talk to him about a problem. I know he cares about me; if he didn't, he wouldn't use up all that energy thinking up solutions for me. But I'm the kind of person who prefers a good ear (and maybe a shoulder) when I have a problem. I would like it so much better if he would forget about solutions and just listen and let me know he hears what's bothering me.

A second prominent feature of men's talk is instrumentality—the use of speech to accomplish instrumental objectives. In conversation, this is often expressed through problem-solving efforts to get information, discover facts, and suggest solutions. Again, between men this is usually a comfortable orientation, because both speakers have typically been socialized to value instrumentality. However, conversations between women and men are often derailed by the lack of agreement on what this informational, instrumental focus means. To many women it feels as if men don't care about their feelings. When a man focuses on the content level of meaning after a woman has disclosed a problem, she may feel he is disregarding her emotions and concerns. He, on the other hand, may well be trying to support her in the way that he has learned to show support—by suggesting ways to solve the problem.

A third feature of men's communication is conversational command. Despite jokes about women's talkativeness, research indicates that in most contexts, men tend to talk more often and at greater length than women. This tendency, although not present in infancy, is evident in preschoolers (Austin, Salehi, & Leffler, 1987). Compared with girls and women, boys and men talk more frequently (Eakins & Eakins, 1976; Thorne & Henley, 1975) and for longer periods of time (Aries, 1987; Eakins & Eakins, 1976; Kramarae, 1981; Thorne & Henley, 1975). Further, men engage in other verbal behaviors that sustain prominence in interaction. They may reroute conversations by using what another said as a jumping-off point for their own topic, or they may interrupt. Although both sexes engage in interruptions, most research suggests that men do it more frequently (Beck, 1988; Johnson, 2000; Mulac, Wiemann, Widenmann, & Gibson, 1988; West & Zimmerman, 1983).

Not only do men seem to interrupt more than women, but they may do so for different reasons. Lea P. Stewart and her colleagues (1996) suggest that men use interruptions to control conversation by challenging other speakers or wresting the talk stage from them, whereas women interrupt to indicate interest and to respond.

This interpretation is shared by a number of scholars who note that women use interruptions to show support, encourage elaboration, and affirm others (Anderson & Leaper, 1998; Aries, 1987; Mulac et al., 1988). A different explanation is that men generally interrupt more than women because interruptions are considered normal and good-natured within the norms of masculine speech communities (Wood, 1998). Whereas interruptions that reroute conversation might be viewed as impolite and intrusive within feminine speech communities, the outgoing, give-and-take character of masculine speech may render interruptions just part of normal conversation.

Fourth, men tend to express themselves in fairly direct, assertive ways. Compared with women, their language is typically more forceful and authoritative. Tentative speech such as hedges and disclaimers is used less frequently by men than by women. When another person does not share that understanding of communication, however, speech that is absolute and directive may seem to close off conversation and leave no room for others to speak.

Fifth, in general, men communicate abstractly more often than women. Men frequently speak in general terms that are removed from concrete experiences and distanced from personal feelings (Johnson, 2000; Schaef, 1981; Treichler & Kramarae, 1983). The abstract style typical of many men's speech reflects the public and impersonal contexts in which they often operate and the less personal emphasis in their speech communities. Within public environments, norms for speaking call for theoretical, conceptual, and general thought and communication. Yet, within more personal relationships, abstract talk sometimes creates barriers to knowing another intimately.

Finally, men's speech tends to be less emotionally responsive than women's, especially on the relationship level of meaning. Men, more than women, give what are called "minimal response cues" (Parlee, 1979), which are verbalizations such as "yeah" or "umhmm." In interaction with women, who have learned to demonstrate interest more vigorously, minimal response cues may inhibit conversation because they are perceived as indicating lack of involvement (Fishman, 1978; Stewart et al., 1996). Men's conversation also often lacks self-disclosures as well as expressed sympathy and understanding (Saurer & Eisler, 1990). Within the rules of men's speech communities, sympathy is a sign of condescension, and the revealing of personal problems is seen as making one vulnerable. Yet women's speech rules count sympathy and disclosure as demonstrations of equality and support. This creates potential for misunderstanding between women and men.

■ Gender-Based Misinterpretations in Communication

In this final section, we explore what happens when men and women interact, each operating out of a distinctive gender speech community. In describing features typical of each gender's talk, we already have noted differences that provide fertile ground for misunderstandings. We now consider several examples of recurrent misreadings between masculine and feminine individuals.

Showing support. The scene is a private conversation between Martha and George. She tells him she is worried about her friend. George gives a minimal response cue, saying only, "Oh." To Martha, this suggests he isn't interested, because women make and expect more of what Deborah Tannen (1986) calls "listening noises" to signal interest. Yet, if George operates according to norms of masculine speech communities, he is probably thinking that, if Martha wants to tell him something, she will. Masculine rules of speech assume people use talk to assert themselves (Bellinger & Gleason, 1982). Even without much encouragement, Martha continues by describing the tension in her friend's marriage and her own concern about how she can help. She says, "I feel so bad for Barbara, and I want to help her, but I don't know what to do." George then says, "It's their problem, not yours. Just butt out and let them settle their own relationship." At this, Martha explodes: "Who asked for your advice?" George is now completely frustrated and confused. He thought Martha wanted advice, so he gave it. She is hurt that George didn't tune into her feelings and comfort her about her worries. Each is annoyed and unhappy.

The problem here is not so much what George and Martha say and don't say. Rather, it's how they interpret each other's communication—actually, how they *misinterpret* it, because each relies on rules that are not familiar to the other. They fail to understand that each is operating by different rules of talk. George is respecting Martha's independence by not pushing her to talk. When he thinks she directly requests advice, he offers it in an effort to help. Martha, on the other hand, wants comfort and a connection with George—that is her purpose in talking with him. She finds his advice unwelcome and dismissive of her feelings. He doesn't offer sympathy, because his rules for communication define this as condescending. Yet the feminine speech community in which Martha was socialized taught her that showing sympathy is how a person shows support.

"Troubles talk." Talk about troubles, or personal problems, is a kind of interaction in which hurt feelings may result from the contrast between most men's and women's rules of communication. A woman might tell her partner that she is feeling down because she did not get a job she wanted. In an effort to be supportive, he might respond by saying, "You shouldn't feel bad. Lots of people don't get jobs they want." To her this seems to dismiss her feelings—to belittle them by saying lots of people experience her situation. Yet within masculine speech communities,

Reprinted with special permission from King Features Syndicate.

this is a way of showing respect for another by not assuming that she or he needs sympathy.

Now let's turn the tables and see what happens when a man feels troubled. When he meets Nancy, Craig is unusually quiet because he feels down about not getting a job offer. Sensing that something is wrong, Nancy tries to show interest by asking, "Are you okay? What's bothering you?" Craig feels she is imposing and trying to get him to show a vulnerability he prefers to keep to himself. Nancy probes further to show she cares. As a result, he feels intruded on and withdraws further. Then Nancy feels shut out.

But perhaps Craig does decide to tell Nancy why he feels down. After hearing about his rejection letter, Nancy says, "I know how you feel. I felt so low when I didn't get that position at Datanet." She is matching experiences to show Craig that she understands his feelings and that he's not alone. According to the communication rules that Craig learned in a masculine speech community, however, this is demeaning his situation by focusing on her, not him. When Nancy mentions her own experience, Craig thinks she is trying to steal the center stage for herself. Within his speech community, that is one way men vie for dominance and attention. Yet Nancy has learned to share similar experiences as a way to build connections with others.

The point of the story. Another instance in which feminine and masculine communication rules often clash and cause problems is in relating experiences. Typically, men have learned to speak in a linear manner, in which they move sequentially through major points in a story to get to the climax. Their talk tends to be straightforward without a great many details. The rules of feminine speech, however, call for more detailed and less linear storytelling. Whereas a man is likely to provide rather bare information about what happened, a woman is more likely to embed the information within a larger context of the people involved and other things going on (Wood, 1998, 2000). Women include details, not because all of the specifics are important on the content level of meaning, but because they matter on the relationship level of meaning. Recounting details is meant to increase involvement between communicators and to invite a conversational partner to be fully engaged in the situation being described.

Because feminine and masculine rules about details differ, men often find women's way of telling stories wandering and unfocused. Conversely, men's style of storytelling may strike women as leaving out all the interesting details. Many a discussion between women and men has ended either with his exasperated demand, "Can't you get to the point?" or with her frustrated question, "Why don't you tell me how you were feeling and what else was going on?" She wants more details than his rules call for; he is interested in fewer details than she has learned to supply.

Relationship talk. "Can we talk about us?" is the opening of innumerable conversations that end in misunderstanding and hurt. In general, men are inclined to think a relationship is going fine as long as there is no need to talk about it. They are interested in discussing the relationship only if there are particular problems to be addressed. In contrast, women generally think a relationship is working well as long as they can talk about it with partners (Acitelli, 1988). The difference here grows out of the fact that men tend to use communication to do things and solve problems, whereas women generally regard the *process* of communicating as a primary way to create and sustain relationships with others. For many women, conversation is a way to be with another person—to affirm and enhance closeness. Men's different rules stipulate that communication is to achieve some goal or fix some problem. No wonder men often duck when their partners want to "discuss the relationship," and women often feel a relationship is in trouble when their partners are unwilling to talk about it.

CATHY

When I broke up with Tommy, my dad tried so hard to help me through it. He took me to games and movies, offered to pay for it if I wanted to take horseback riding lessons. He just kept trying to *DO* something to make me feel better. That's how he's always been. If mom's down about something, he takes her out or buys her flowers or something. It used to really bother me that he won't talk to me about what I'm feeling, but now I understand better what he's doing. I get it that this is his way of showing love and support for me.

These are only four of many situations in which feminine and masculine rules of communication may collide and cause problems. Women learn to use talk to build and sustain connections with others. Men learn that talk is to convey information and establish status. Given these distinct starting points, it's not surprising that women and men often find themselves locked into misunderstandings.

Interestingly, research (Sollie & Fischer, 1985) suggests that women and men who are androgynous are more flexible communicators who are able to engage comfortably in both masculine and feminine styles of speech. The breadth of their communicative competence enhances the range of situations in which they can be effective. On learning about different speech rules, many couples find they can improve their communication. Each partner has become bilingual, and so communication between them is smoother and more satisfying. When partners understand how to interpret each other's rules, they are less likely to misread motives. In addition, they learn how to speak the other's language, which means women and men become more gratifying conversational partners for each other, and they can enhance the quality of their relationships.

Public speaking. Differences in feminine and masculine communication patterns also surface in public contexts. In Western society, the public sphere traditionally has been considered men's domain. From Chapter 3, you'll recall that one of the constraints on women's efforts to gain legal rights in the 1800s was the proscription of women from speaking in public. Although many women are now active and vocal in public life, feminine forms of communication are still devalued. The assertive, dominant, confident masculine style is the standard for public speaking, whereas the more collaborative, inclusive feminine style of communicating is considered less effective. This male generic standard for public speaking places feminine speakers at a disadvantage in public life. Their style of speaking is judged by a standard that neither reflects nor respects their communication goals and values (Campbell & Jerry, 1988). Women such as former Texas governor Ann Richards who are considered effective public speakers manage to combine the traditionally feminine communication style (which includes personal compassion and use of anecdotal information) with more masculine qualities such as assertiveness and instrumentality (Dow & Tonn, 1993). Even today, a conventionally feminine communication style is usually devalued because masculine standards of public speaking still prevail.

SUMMARY

In this chapter, we have explored a range of ways in which verbal communication intersects with gender and culture. The first focus we pursued highlighted how language reflects and sustains cultural views of masculinity and femininity. By defining, classifying, and evaluating gender, language reinforces social views of men as the standard and as more valuable than women and femininity. From generic male terms to language that demeans and diminishes women, verbal communication is a powerful agent of cultural expression. We also saw, however, that symbolic abilities allow us to think hypothetically and therefore to imagine alternatives to existing patterns of meaning. In addition, the self-reflexivity promoted by our symbolic capacity invites us to examine critically how we have defined masculinity and femininity in general and our own gender identities in particular. We have the capacity to revise cultural perspectives through the language we use and the identities we express in our own communication.

The second theme of this chapter is that women and men express gendered identities through their styles of communication. Because males and females tend to be socialized into distinct gender speech communities, they learn different rules about the purposes of communication and ways to indicate support, interest, and involvement. Because many women and men have some dissimilar rules for talk, they often misread each other's meanings and misunderstand each other's motives. This frequently leads to frustration, hurt, and tension between people who care about each other and to misjudgments of people speaking in public settings. Appreciating and respecting the distinctive validity of each style of communication is a foundation for better understanding between people. Further, learning to use different styles of communication allows women and men to be more flexible and effective in their interactions with each other.

DISCUSSION QUESTIONS

1. How important is language in influencing how we think about gender in general and our own gender identity in particular? For instance, do you think inclusive language (*he or she, mail carrier*) is important and should be used? Why?

2. Read several newspapers—front pages, sports sections, etc.—and find examples of differences in how language describes women and men. Do you find examples of women being described by appearance, marital status, and family life? Are such descriptions pertinent to why they are featured in news stories?

3. Think about naming, specifically about naming yourself. If you are a woman, do you plan to keep your name if you marry? If you are a man, do you expect (or want) your partner to change hers? Would you consider adopting her name instead? What do conventions governing women's names tell us about cultural views of gender?

4. Think back to your childhood games. Which games did you play? What rules for using talk were implicitly promoted in the games you tended to play? Do you see how engaging in childhood activities may have affected your style of verbal communication?

5. Use the PowerTrac option on your InfoTrac College Edition. Access the 1999 article by Laura Madson and Robert Hessling, "Does alternating between masculine and feminine pronouns eliminate perceived gender bias in texts?" How does alternating pronouns affect readers' perceptions of gender bias and credibility? Do the authors of the article think this method is better than using ungendered plural terms such as "they"?

6. Try to follow the rules of talk generally *not* typical for your sex. Can you develop proficiency in another style of talking? How might enlarging your communication repertoire affect your relationships?

7. The next time you have a conversation in which you feel that gendered rules of talk are creating misunderstandings, try to translate your expectations to the person with whom you are talking. For instance, if you are a woman talking with a man about a problem, he might try to help by offering advice. Instead of being frustrated by his lack of attention to your feelings, try saying to him, "I appreciate your suggestions of what I might do, but I'm not ready to think about how to fix things yet. It would be more helpful to me if you'd help me work through my feelings about this issue." Discuss what happens when you explain what you need or want from others.

8. Visit Deborah Tannen's home page at **http://www.georgetown.edu/tannen.** What do you learn about her academic work as well as her popular writing?

9. Use the PowerTrac option on your InfoTrac College Edition to access Kristen Anderson and Campbell Leaper's 1998 article, "Meta-analyses of gender effects on conversational interruptions." How does their analysis of numerous studies of interruptions complement or challenge the patterns identified in this chapter?

5

Gendered Nonverbal Communication

The nonverbal dimension of communication is extensive and important. Some scholars, in fact, consider it more significant than verbal language because our nonverbal behaviors are estimated to carry from 65% (Birdwhistell, 1970) to 93% (Mehrabian, 1981) of the total meaning of communication. Like language, nonverbal communication is related to gender and culture in two ways: It expresses cultural meanings of gender, and men and women construct their gender identities through differences in their nonverbal communication. In this chapter, we will consider some of the ways in which nonverbal behaviors express and sustain meanings of gender in our society.

Nonverbal communication consists of all elements of communication other than words themselves. It includes not only visual cues (gestures, appearances), but also vocal qualities (inflection, volume, pitch) and environmental factors (use of space and color) that affect meanings. Like language, nonverbal communication is learned through interaction with others. Also like verbal communication, nonverbal behaviors reflect and reinforce social views of gender and encourage individuals to embody them in distinctive feminine and masculine styles. According to Judith Butler (1990, p. 270), "Gender is instituted through the stylization of the body." In other words, we perform, or enact, gender through nonverbal communication that is ritualized according to cultural norms and meanings. As we will see, nonverbal communication frequently reinforces and embodies cultural views of masculinity and femininity. We will identify functions and types of nonverbal communication and then concentrate on gender-related patterns of nonverbal communication to understand how cultural views of masculinity and femininity are embodied in the nonverbal styles of men and women.

FUNCTIONS OF NONVERBAL COMMUNICATION

Researchers who have studied nonverbal communication identify a number of functions it can serve. It supplements verbal communication, regulates interaction, and conveys the bulk of the relationship level of meaning in interaction. In each of these areas, there are some consistent gender differences.

■ Nonverbal Communication Can Supplement Verbal Communication

Communication scholars have identified five ways in which nonverbal behaviors interact with verbal messages to influence meanings (Malandro & Barker, 1983). First, nonverbal communication may *repeat* words, as when you say "right" while pointing to the right. Second, we may nonverbally *contradict* a verbal message. For example, the statement "I'm fine" would be contradicted if a speaker were trembling and on the verge of tears. Nonverbal behavior may also *complement* or augment verbal communication by underlining a verbal message. The statement "I never want to see you again" is more forceful if accompanied by a frown and a threatening glare. Fourth, sometimes we use nonverbal behaviors to *replace* verbal ones. Rather than saying "I don't know," you might shrug your shoulders. Finally, nonverbal communication may *highlight* or accent verbal messages, telling us which parts are important. "I love *you*" means something different from "*I* love you" or "I *love* you," because different words are emphasized with cues of volume and inflection.

Because masculine socialization emphasizes self-assertion and dominance, we would expect most men to use more nonverbal behaviors than most women to complement, repeat, and highlight their verbal messages. Instruction in femininity highlights relationships, deference, and expressiveness, so women specialize in nonverbal functions such as complementing and highlighting that add personal emphasis and feeling to their communication.

■ Nonverbal Communication Can Regulate Interaction

Nonverbal communication often regulates verbal interaction. We use body posture, eye contact, and vocal inflection to signal others that we wish to speak or that we are through speaking (Drummond & Hopper, 1993; Eckman, Friesen, & Ellsworth, 1971). Whereas women frequently use nonverbal signals to invite others into conversation, men more frequently use them to sustain control of interaction. For instance, if a man who is talking does not ever establish eye contact with others, they are unlikely to jump into the conversation. In classrooms, raised hands announce a desire to talk, and averted gazes are often silent requests that teachers not call on people.

■ Nonverbal Communication Can Establish the Relationship Level of Meaning

A final and particularly important function of nonverbal communication is to convey relationship levels of meaning that define identities and relationships between communicators. As Aino Sallinen-Kuparinen (1992) notes, "Nonverbal communication is a relationship language" (p. 163). In most cases, the overall feeling or style of relationships is expressed nonverbally (Burgoon, Buller, Hale, & deTurck, 1988; Burgoon & Le Poire, 1999). Women and men in general differ in the relationship messages they communicate. Three primary dimensions of relationship-level communication are responsiveness, liking, and power (Mehrabian, 1981), each of which is linked to gender.

Responsiveness. The first dimension of the relationship level of meaning in communication refers to how aware of and responsive to others we seem. Nonverbal cues of responsiveness include lively gestures, inflection, eye contact, and attentive body posture that express interest and involvement. Lack of responsiveness may be signaled by bored looks and posture and averted eyes. Jon Nussbaum (1992) reports that students learn more when they have teachers who use nonverbally responsive behaviors such as vocal expressiveness, relaxed body posture, eye contact, and smiling.

Both women and men display responsiveness, yet they tend to do so in rather distinctive ways. Socialized to be affiliative, women tend to engage in responsive nonverbal communication that indicates engagement with others, emotional involvement, and empathy. Men, on the other hand, are socialized to focus on status and power, and this is mirrored in their nonverbal responsiveness. More than women, men use gestures and space to command attention, and vocal inflection and volume to increase the strength of their ideas and positions (Hall, 1987; Major, Schmidlin, & Williams, 1990). Laura Guerrero (1997) observes distinctively masculine and feminine styles of responsiveness. She reported that females showed responsiveness by maintaining more eye contact and direct body orientation. Males displayed responsiveness by leaning forward and adopting postures congruent with that of the person speaking.

There are also general differences in how overtly men and women respond to others. Women tend to be more overtly expressive of emotions than men—a finding reflective of the socialization that promotes this in women and discourages it in men. Men are encouraged to assert themselves, whereas women are taught to react, listen, and respond (Cegela & Sillars, 1989; LaFrance & Mayo, 1979). Brenda Ueland (1992) observes that women have developed skill at listening, whereas many men have less well-developed listening skills because they are socialized to give greater priority to asserting themselves than to listening and responding to others.

Women are expected to respond expressively to others. Smiling sends the message "I am approachable, interested, friendly," which conforms to cultural ideals of femininity. Yet gender alone doesn't shape our responsiveness (Hall, 1998). Other aspects of identity, such as race-ethnicity, interact with gender to shape our communication. For instance, African American women generally don't smile as much as Caucasian women. Similarly, attentive eye contact is practiced less by many African American women than by Caucasian women (Halberstadt & Saitta, 1987), reminding us that gender varies across standpoints. In general, if a White woman does not smile and maintain eye contact, others are likely to think something is wrong with her or that she is angry with them. Conversely, a man who *does* smile a lot and look steadily at others may be suspect (Chesler, 1972; Henley, 1977).

Women not only tend to display feelings more overtly than men, but they also seem to be more skilled than men at interpreting others' emotions. Researchers report that females exceed males in the capacity to decode nonverbal behaviors and more accurately discern others' emotions (Stewart, Cooper, Stewart, & Friedley, 1996).

One explanation of women's generally strong ability to read feelings is sex-related brain differences (Begley, 1995). In addition to possible biological influences, women's skill in interpreting others may reflect one or both of two social factors. One hypothesis is that women are socialized to be more attentive to feelings (Noller, 1986; Rosenthal & DePaulo, 1979). From childhood on, most females are encouraged to be sensitive to others and to relationships. Further, the contexts of women's socialization—relationships—provide them with more opportunities to refine their skills in reading nonverbal cues. Related to this is women's standpoint as caregivers who often take care of children, the elderly, and sick people. Women also far outnumber men in caring professions such as social work, counseling, nursing, and human resources. Women's involvement in caring provides them with a standpoint different from those whose lives do not routinely center on nurturing.

✆ ELAINE

I never thought it would be so hard not to smile. When you challenged us in class to go one day without smiling except when we really felt happy, I thought that would be easy. I couldn't do it. I smile when I meet people, I smile when I purchase things, I even smile when someone bumps into me. I never realized how much I smile—all the time.

What was most interesting about the experiment was how my boyfriend reacted. We got together last night, and I was still working on not smiling. He asked me what was wrong. I told him nothing. I was being perfectly nice and talkative and everything, but I wasn't smiling all the time like I usually do. He kept asking what was wrong, was I unhappy, had something happened—even was I mad. I pointed out that I was being as friendly as usual. Then he said, yeah, but I wasn't smiling. I told him that I just didn't see anything particular to smile about, and he said it wasn't like me. I talked with several other women in our class, and they had the same experience. I just never realized how automatic smiling is for me.

A second explanation that many scholars (Deaux, 1976; Leathers, 1986; Major, 1980; Willis, 1966) find credible is that women's decoding skill results from their standpoint as subordinate members of society. Scholars (Janeway, 1971; Miller, 1986; Tavris, 1992) have amassed considerable evidence in support of the idea that those who are oppressed learn to interpret others in order to survive. Nancy Henley (1977) analyzed the nonverbal behaviors of people in subordinate positions and found consistent patterns for minorities, women, and individuals in subservient roles.

The argument that people in subordinate positions learn to interpret others' moods and feelings is supported by substantial research. Many years ago, Bruno Bettelheim (1943) showed that prisoners in concentration camps learned to interpret their captors' feelings and moods. More recently, Bill Puka (1990) demonstrated consistency between the emotional sensitivity typical of women and that found in prisoners, slaves, and other oppressed groups. For women, minorities, and others who are oppressed, decoding is a survival skill. Women's decoding skills probably result from a combination of socialization and ways power is distributed in society.

Liking. A second dimension of the relationship level of meaning is liking. We use nonverbal behaviors to signal that we like or dislike others. Nonverbal cues of liking include vocal warmth, standing close to others, touching, and holding eye contact. Because females are socialized to be nice to others and to form relationships, they tend to employ more nonverbal communication that signals liking than do men (LaFrance & Mayo, 1979; Stewart et al., 1998). For instance, when conversing, two women typically stand or sit more closely than two men (Rosengrant & McCroskey, 1975), and women, particularly Caucasian ones, generally engage in more eye contact with others than do men (Cegela & Sillars, 1989; Henley, 1977).

Power or control. The third aspect of the relationship level of meaning in communication is power or control, which involves dominance and power relationships between communicators that are defined through interaction. Control issues in conversations include who defines topics, who directs conversation, who interrupts, and who defers. Although many nonverbal behaviors convey control messages, three are especially important: vocal qualities, touch, and use of space. In all three categories, men generally engage in more nonverbal efforts to exert control

"I love being a partner Mr. Jenkins! There's just one problem."

From *The Wall Street Journal*—permission, Cartoon Features Syndicate.

than do women. For instance, compared with women, men tend to use greater volume and stronger inflection to highlight their ideas and add to the force of their positions (Eakins & Eakins, 1978). Men also tend to touch women more in nonaffiliative or aggressive ways that indicate and reinforce status differences (Deaux, 1976; Leathers, 1986; Major, 1980; Spain, 1992). In addition, men command and use more personal space than women; they take up more space in sitting and standing, a difference not attributable to body size alone. Even at very young ages, boys are taught to seek and command more space than girls (Harper & Sanders, 1975; Mills, 1985), a finding that reflects the emphasis on independence in male socialization. In terms of nonverbal cues of power, then, men generally exceed women in behaviors that communicate dominance and control in relationships.

Now that we have seen how nonverbal communication functions to supplement verbal communication, regulate interaction, and define relationships, we are ready to explore how it reflects and sustains cultural definitions of gender.

FORMS OF NONVERBAL COMMUNICATION

Cultural views of gender are evident in nonverbal communication about males and females as well as in nonverbal messages directed toward them. In addition, the nonverbal styles of interaction that men and women typically learn are distinctive in many respects and function to constitute gendered identities for individuals. Examining these topics will illuminate further means by which culture constructs gender.

■ Artifacts

Artifacts are personal objects that influence how we see ourselves and express the identity we create for ourselves. Beginning with the pink and blue blankets used by many hospitals, personal objects for children define them as female or male. Parents send artifactual messages through the toys they give to sons and daughters. Typically, boys are given toys that invite more active, rougher play, whereas girls are given playthings that emphasize nurturing, domestic activities, and appearances (Caldera, Huston, & O'Brien, 1989; Pomerleau, Bolduc, Malcuit, & Cossette, 1990). One implication of sex-differentiated toys is that they cultivate different cognitive and social skills (Miller, 1987). Despite evidence that sex-typing restricts development, many parents continue to favor sex-differentiated toys. Parents, especially fathers, tend to discourage children's interest in toys and activities that are judged not to be sex appropriate (Antill, 1987; Fagot, 1978; Lytton & Romney, 1991). These artifacts are powerful communicators of what males and females are supposed to be and do.

One clear indicator of cultural meanings attached to the sexes is toy catalogues. Even in 2002, as I was writing this book, catalogues for children's gifts feature pages titled "For Girls," with play kitchen appliances, makeup and hair accessories, and pink tutu outfits! The pages labeled "For Boys" show soldiers and science equipment, swords and shields, and building sets. Most of the girls' pages are predominantly pink with splashes of other pastel colors, whereas the pages displaying items for boys use darker, bolder colors. Carrying cultural views of gender, these catalogues and those who purchase from them tell girls they are supposed to be pretty, soft, and nurturing, whereas they instruct boys to be active, adventurous, and aggressive.

Beyond childhood, artifactual communication continues to manifest and promote cultural definitions of masculinity and femininity. Although clothing has become less sex distinctive than in former eras (Abdullah, 1999), there are still differences in fashions for women and men. Men's clothes generally are not as colorful or bright as women's clothing (although this has attenuated in recent years), and they are designed to be functional. Pockets in jackets and trousers allow men to carry wallets, change, keys, and miscellany. The relatively loose fit of men's clothes and the design of men's shoes allow them to move quickly and with assurance. Thus, men's clothing deemphasizes physical appearance and enables activity.

Women's clothing is quite different. Reflecting social expectations of femininity, women's clothing is designed to call attention to women's bodies and to make them maximally attractive to viewers.

👣 DAN

I don't care what the experts say about bringing kids up, no son of mine will get any dolls. I think that's just stupid. Boys aren't supposed to play with dolls and stuff like that. I didn't, and I turned out okay. I played with normal guy toys like model planes and cars and erector sets and computers. I did have a G.I. Joe, though. I guess it would be okay with me if my son played with one of them, but no Barbies.

Form-fitting skirts, materials that cling to the body, and details in design contribute to making women look decorative. Many women's clothes have no pockets or ones not large enough to hold wallets and keys without distorting the line of the garment. Further, most shoes for women are designed to call attention to their legs at the cost of comfort and safety—how quickly can you run in 2-inch heels?

Other artifactual communication reinforces cultural views of women and men. Advertisements for food, homemaking, and childrearing feature women, reiterating the view of women as mothers and the view of men as uninvolved in parenting. Products associated with heavy work, cars, and outdoor sports feature men (or women in seductive poses, designed to appeal to men). Also, consider the artifacts that women are encouraged to buy to meet the cultural command to be attractive: The cosmetics industry alone is a multimillion-dollar business in the United States; products to condition, straighten, curl, color, and style hair are similarly thriving. Women are taught to like and want fashionable clothes and jewelry, reflecting and reinforcing images of women as decorative objects. In Chapter 10 on media, we will pursue in greater detail how advertising reinforces social views of women and men.

 BETH

Women's clothes—that's my pet peeve. I mean, why is it I have to choose between being comfortable and looking nice? Guys don't have to. I'm interviewing for jobs this semester, so I have to wear suits a lot of days, and they make me miserable. The jackets are cut close and don't let me move freely, and the skirts are made to ride up when I sit down. And shoes! They're the pits. To wear nice-looking shoes—ones that look professional—I have to be masochistic. Even in the good lines of shoes, the toes on pumps cramp my toes. There's no way I can walk fast when my body is strapped in a suit and my feet are bound.

FYI

Cross-Cultural Norms for Women's Nonverbal Communication

Imagine that you are a successful American businessperson who travels to Saudi Arabia to negotiate a major deal. Would you expect to have your visa rejected, to be barred from restaurants, and to be ordered to change your dress before attending a business lunch? That's what happened to Kay Ainsley of Detroit when she went to Saudi Arabia to sell the rights to open Domino's Pizza shops there (Steinberg, 1999). Her business visa was twice rejected, and she was allowed to enter the country only when the Saudi businessman with whom she was meeting intervened with the authorities. Wearing a conservative business suit, Ainsley was asked to change into an *abaya*, a long black robe that Saudi women traditionally wear. Trying to get lunch, she discovered that women were not allowed in a sandwich shop, so she had to ask a male colleague to get lunch for her. When Ainsley had successfully negotiated the deal, she found that she was barred from the signing ceremony and a male colleague had to sign for her.

■ Proximity and Personal Space

In 1968, Edward T. Hall coined the word **proxemics** to refer to space and our use of it. As researchers began studying space, they realized it is a primary means through which cultures express values and shape patterns of interaction. Early work revealed that different cultures have different norms for how much space people need and how closely they interact. For instance, in Latin American countries, people interact at closer distances than in reserved societies like the United States (Hall, 1959, 1966; Samovar, Porter, & Stefani, 1998). Different cultures also have distinct understandings of personal space. In some countries, houses for big families are no larger than small apartments in the United States, and the idea of private rooms for individual members of families is unheard of. As these examples indicate, cultural views are evident in proxemic behavior.

Proxemics offers keen insight into the relative power and status accorded to various groups in society. Space is a primary means by which a culture designates who is important, who has privilege. In societies that have been slow to recognize women's value, women may not be allowed to own property. Thus, women are literally denied space. Only in the mid-1990s did India's legislature pass a measure that allows daughters to inherit property in the same manner that sons have always enjoyed.

Consider who gets space in our society. You'll notice that executives have large offices, although there is little functional need for so much room. Secretaries, however, are crowded into cubbyholes that overflow with file cabinets and computers. Generally there is a close correlation between status and the size of a person's home, car, office, and so forth. Who gets space and how much space they get indicate power. In fact, both Daphne Spain (1992) and Leslie Weisman (1992) have shown in detail how the use of space in the United States designates lesser status for women

---

FYI

Gendered Proxemics

Virginia Valian (1998) is a professor of psychology and linguistics who is interested in how gender stereotypes shape perceptions. She conducted an experiment to find out whether college students are equally likely to perceive women and men as leaders. Students were asked to identify the leader in photos of people seated around a conference table. When the people in the photo were all men or all women, students overwhelmingly chose the person at the head of the table as the leader. Students also selected the person at the head of the table as the leader when the photo showed both women and men and a man was seated at the head of the table. However, when both women and men were in the photo and a woman was at the head of the table, students selected the woman at the head as the leader only half of the time.

---

and minorities. Now think about the amount of space women and men typically have in our society. As we have seen, early socialization encourages boys to go out on their own and girls to stay closer to adults and home.

Gender-differentiated use of space continues in adult life. Think about your family. Did your father have his own room, space, or chair? Did your mother? Many men have private studies, workshops, or other spaces that others do not enter freely, but few women with families have such spaces. My students initially disagreed with this report and informed me their mothers had spaces. When we discussed this, however, it turned out that most of their mothers' spaces were kitchens and sewing rooms—places where they do things for other people! Students who said their mothers had home offices noted that their mothers' workspaces were usually parts of other rooms (a corner in the living room) or moveable (using the dining-room table for work when it's not needed for meals). Many years ago, Virginia Woolf gave a famous lecture titled "A Room of One's Own," in which she argued that women's ability to develop and engage in creative, independent work is hampered by not having an inviolate space for themselves.

Proxemics also concerns how space is used. Again, think of your family. Who sat at the head of the table—the place reserved for a leader? In most two-parent families, that position belongs to the man and symbolizes his leadership of the family. Now consider the extent to which men's and women's spaces are invaded by others. We have already seen that men are more likely than women to have spaces that are off limits to others. Yet this is not the only way in which men's territory is more respected than women's.

Territoriality refers to our sense of personal space or our private area that we don't want others to invade. Yet not everyone's territory is equally respected. People with power tend to enter the spaces of those with less power (Henley, 1977). Paralleling this is the finding that men go into women's spaces more than women enter men's spaces and more than men enter other men's spaces (Evans & Howard, 1973; Willis, 1966). Going into others' private space sometimes is interpreted as sexual harassment, because too much closeness communicates a level of intimacy that may be perceived as inappropriate in work and education situations (Le Poire, Burgoon, & Parrott, 1992).

What happens when a person's private territory is invaded? This question has intrigued many researchers, including Judee Burgoon and her colleagues (Burgoon, Buller, Hale, & deTurck, 1988; Burgoon & Hale, 1988; Le Poire et al., 1992). One way people respond is to engage in behaviors themselves that attempt to restore their privacy zones (Burgoon & Hale, 1988; Le Poire et al, 1992). For instance, if someone moves too close for comfort, you might step back to create distance. Similarly, there is the well-known elevator phenomenon in which people are often crowded more closely than they like, so everyone looks up or down as if to say "I'm really not this close to you, and I am not trying to intrude." Further, we know that when personal territory is invaded, men tend to respond negatively and sometimes aggressively to defend their territory (Fisher & Byrne, 1975), whereas women tend to yield space or flee their territory rather than challenge the intruder (Polit & LaFrance, 1977). These patterns reflect cultural teachings that tell men to be aggressive in protecting their turf and instruct women to defer.

■ Haptics (Touch)

The first of our senses to develop, touch is an important form of nonverbal behavior. **Haptics,** or touch, from parents and other adults communicates different messages to boys and girls. Studies of parent-child interaction reveal that parents tend to touch sons less often and more roughly than they touch daughters (Condry, Condry, & Pogatshnik, 1983). Daughters are handled more gently and protectively. Early tactile messages encourage boys to touch others to assert themselves, whereas girls learn to expect touching from others and to use touch affiliatively—for example, holding hands or hugging.

Although women are more likely than men to initiate hugs and touches that express support, affection, and comfort, men more often use touch to direct others, assert power, and express sexual interest (Deaux, 1976; Leathers, 1986; Pearson, West, & Turner, 1995). The meaning of touching, of course, depends on more than touch per se. As Judee Burgoon and her colleagues have shown (Burgoon, Buller, & Woodall, 1989), how we interpret touch depends on factors such as its duration, intensity, and frequency and the body parts touching and being touched. Because masculine socialization encourages men to enter the private spaces of others, particularly women, and to use touch to establish power, they may engage in touching that women co-workers will perceive as harassing (Le Poire et al., 1992). Men are more likely to invade others' spaces and to use touch to assert power, even when their interest is unwelcome. Women's training to be nice to others can make them reluctant to speak forcefully to a boss or co-worker whose touches are unwanted.

Finally, in discussing haptic communication, we must recognize the different degrees of sheer strength men and women in general can exert. Because men are generally larger and stronger than women, they tend to have more physical confidence and to be more willing to use physical force than women (May, 1998a). Some men are unaware of how strong they are, especially in relation to others who have less physical strength.

ℰ ROSEANNE

I'm not paranoid or anything, but men really do have more physical strength, and they can use it against me. A few months ago, I was out with this guy I'd been seeing for a while. We weren't serious or anything, but we had gone out a few times. Well, we were at his place listening to music when he started coming on to me. After a while, I told him to stop because I didn't want to go any further. He grinned and pinned my arms back and asked what I was going to do to stop him. Well, I didn't have to, thank goodness, because he didn't really push, but just the same I had to think there really wasn't anything I could have done if he had. That's always there when I'm with a guy—that he could overpower me if he wanted to.

Janet Lee Mills

The man and the woman in these photos are in identical postures. Do you have different perceptions of them based on gendered expectations in our culture?

Kinesics (Facial and Body Motion)

Kinesics refers to face and body movements. This area of nonverbal communication reflects a number of gendered patterns. For instance, women tend to tilt their heads in deferential positions, condense their size, and allow others to invade their spaces. Men too tend to enact patterns they were taught by displaying less emotion through smiles or other facial expressions, using larger gestures, taking more space, and being more likely to encroach on others' territories. In combination, these gender-differentiated patterns suggest that women's facial and body motions generally signal they are approachable, friendly, and unassuming. Men's facial and body communications, in contrast, tend to indicate they are reserved and in control.

A particularly interesting area of facial behavior is communication with the eyes. Called by poets the "mirrors of the soul," eye expressions indicate love, anger, fear, interest, challenge, and a range of other emotions. Men and women tend to differ in how they use their eyes to communicate. Women signal interest and involvement with others by sustaining eye contact, whereas men generally do not sustain eye contact during conversations. These pat-

> ### ℰ RANDALL
>
> It sounds kind of stupid when we talk about it, but it's true that a guy has to return another guy's stare if he wants to hold his own. It's like a staring contest. Sometimes on a street, another guy will meet my eyes. When I notice, then he's locked into holding the stare, and that means that I have to, too. It's like that old joke about the first one to blink loses. It's kind of dumb, but I'd feel strange not returning another guy's gaze. Like a wimp or something.

terns reflect lessons from childhood in which girls learned to maintain relation-ships and boys learned to vie for status—to give attention to others may jeopardize your own position. Consistent with the image of women as interactive, researchers have shown that women not only give but also receive more facial expressions of interest and friendliness (Feldman & White, 1980). There is one exception to males' generally low eye contact. Among primates, the eyes are used to challenge and threaten. Particularly challenging is a prolonged stare, especially when accompanied by a scowl. Although women seldom engage in staring, men sometimes use it to challenge others, particularly other men, and to assert their status (Pearson, 1985). Men in my classes tell me that they cannot refuse to return a stare without losing face and appearing cowardly.

■ Paralanguage

Vocal cues that go along with verbal communication are called **paralanguage.** Although there are some physiological differences in male and female vocal organs (the larynx and pharynx), these do not account fully for differences in women's and men's paralanguage. For instance, the larger, thicker vocal folds of male larynxes do result in lower pitch, but the difference between the average pitch of male speakers and the pitch of female speakers exceeds that explained by physiology. To understand why women and men tend to have divergent paralanguage, we must once again consider socialization processes. What vocal cues would you expect of someone taught to be deferential, polite, and caring? What would you expect of someone encouraged to be assertive, emotionally reserved, and independent? Your expectations probably closely match identified differences in male and female paralanguage. In general, women use higher pitch, softer volume, and a lot of inflection. Men tend to use their voices to assert themselves and command the conversation, which means they use lower pitch, greater volume, and limited inflection. Further, men discourage others from talking, by interrupting and responding with minimum and delayed "umms" (Zimmerman & West, 1975).

A classic study shed light on cultural stereotypes of men and women (Addington, 1968). A researcher asked participants to judge the personalities of people on the basis of vocal qualities, which he experimentally manipulated. Women with breathy, tense voices were judged to be pretty, feminine, petite, shallow, immature, and unintelligent. Men with throaty, tense voices were judged to be mature, masculine, intelligent, and sophisticated. The researcher concluded that, when women are perceived as feminine, other aspects of the feminine gender stereotype—such as being pretty, immature, and unintelligent—are attributed to them. Perceptions of men as masculine are accompanied by the assumption that they are intelligent and mature.

■ Physical Characteristics

Physical characteristics refer to aspects of personal appearance, which are evaluated according to cultural standards. In other words, our appearance itself is less the issue than how well it fits—or fails to fit—with cultural ideals for femininity and masculinity. Because our society promotes unrealistic images of physical attractiveness, it's not surprising that members of both sexes tend to be dissatisfied with their bodies (Bordo, 1999; Chaiken & Pliner, 1987; Davison & Birch, 2001; Mishkind, Rodin, Silberstein, & Striegel-Moore, 1987). The extent of dissatisfaction, however, differs between the sexes. Men who are dissatisfied with their weight or muscularity—cultural expectations for masculine attractiveness—tend to compartmentalize their concerns. They may dislike physical features, but that seldom affects how they feel about their overall competence, worth, and abilities (Mintz & Betz, 1986). For women, dislike of their bodies often affects overall self-esteem, especially for Caucasian women. In other words, women generalize from the specific idea that their bodies don't meet the cultural standard to the broad evaluation that they are unworthy or undesirable (AAUW, 1991; Mintz & Betz, 1986).

The difference between women's and men's feelings about their bodies makes sense when we consider cultural definitions of the two sexes. Women's greater concern about physical appearance reflects our culture's emphasis on physical attractiveness in women (Silverstein, Perdue, Peterson, & Kelly, 1986; Spitzack, 1993; Wolf, 1991). Unfortunately, women who fall short of cultural ideals are judged more harshly and negatively than men who do not meet the cultural benchmark (Basow & Kobrynowicz, 1990; Feingold, 1990; Tiggemann & Rothblum, 1988).

What is designated as the ideal female form, however, is not constant. Like other aspects of gender, attractiveness varies across cultures and over time within any single society. The intense emphasis on thinness is a relatively new standard of feminine beauty, and it prevails more among European Americans than among people of color. Some of the most famous art (for instance, Peter Paul Rubens's paintings) features women with more voluptuous, fleshier bodies than would be favorably regarded today.

How serious is the problem? Recent investigations reveal that European American culture's message to women that they must be thin to be successful has precipitated severe problems. Many women think constantly about appearance, particularly weight. In one survey (Wooley & Wooley, 1984), a majority of adult women rated losing 10 to 15 pounds more important than success in work or love. In her book *The Beauty Myth*, Naomi Wolf

---

⛯ WENDY

All my life, I've had to live with the "dumb blonde" label. I am blonde, pretty, and petite, and this makes others perceive me as dumb and immature. That's what people always think before they get to know me. They act toward me as if I were dumb, and they don't expect me to be mature. What really gets me is that sometimes I get hooked into their impression of me, and I start *acting* the part of the dumb blonde. Why can't a woman be feminine and smart both?

Beauty: His and Hers

Q: Isn't it mainly women who have cosmetic surgery?

A: Not anymore. Today, both sexes have cosmetic surgery. Women most often have facial surgeries and fat reduction operations. Men have surgeries to enhance muscles, implant hair, and enlarge penises. Both sexes are turning more often to surgery to make them appear younger. From 1992 to 1998, surgeries to lift buttocks increased 328% to 1,246; eyelifts increased 102% to 120,001; removing forehead wrinkles rose 172% to 36,777; tummy tucks grew 177% to 46,597; and liposuctions accelerated from 47,212 to 172,070.

Q: Is there anything wrong with having plastic surgery to look better?

A: All of us care about our appearances, and most of us make efforts to look good by eating well, exercising, and choosing attractive clothes and hairstyles. However, it isn't healthy to have excessive concerns about how we look or unrealistic ideals for appearance. Many plastic surgeons report that prospective patients come to them with pictures of celebrities they want to look like. Others come with pictures of themselves 20 or more years ago and ask to be restored to how they looked then. These aren't realistic goals. Even more troublesome are reasons some people seek cosmetic surgery. Many think others will like them better if they "fix" how they look. They haven't learned to value themselves for qualities more important than physical appearance.

Q: So what's the big deal? Maybe appearance shouldn't matter so much, but if you can afford to pay for cosmetic surgery, why not do it?

A: There are some risks. Injections to hide wrinkles and smile lines can shrink and distort the face or other areas. Skin resurfacing can cause inflammation and discoloration of skin. Eyelift surgeries can make it difficult or even impossible to close eyes completely. Scarring sometimes happens, as do pain, nerve damage, and other complications.

(1991) reported that on any given day 25% of the women in America are dieting, and an additional 50% are just finishing or just starting diets.

For girls, weight concerns start early and often become enduring (Nichter, 2000). A recent study by Kirsten Davison and Leann Birch (2001) reported that by the age of 5 many girls have negative self-images based on their weight. Dieting is rampant among girls in the fourth and fifth grades (Seligmann, Joseph, Donovan, & Gosnell, 1987). In high school, as many as 75% of women report being preoccupied with losing weight ("Nearly Half," 1991). Today an estimated one in four college women has an eating disorder; without treatment, as many as 20% of those with eating disorders die (Hicks, 1998a,b).

The cultural mandate to be thin has a number of serious effects on women who internalize that value. Women who have negative body images are more likely to be depressed and have low self-esteem (Davison & Birch, 2001; Mintz & Betz, 1986). Further, the pressure to be thin has ushered in an epidemic of eating disorders, of

Eating Disorders

Q: How many females and males have eating disorders?

A: The National Association of Anorexia Nervosa and Associated Disorders estimates that 8 million females and 1 million males suffer from eating disorders. A new disorder, so far specific to males, has been identified: bigorexia, an unhealthy preoccupation with muscularity and activities designed to increase muscularity.

Q: Is there any way to get help for eating disorders?

A: Yes. If you or someone you know has an eating disorder, there are resources. The following Web sites provide information on symptoms and consequences of eating disorders, personal accounts of living with and recovering from eating disorders, and treatment programs:

Ability's Bulimia Page: **http://www.ability.org.uk/bulimia.html**

Pale Reflections: **http://members.aol.com/paleref/index.html**

Sources: Gross, M. (2000, June). The lethal politics of beauty. *George*, pp. 53–59, 99–100. Saunders, B. (2001, March 4). The stomach grumbles at equal-opportunity eating ills. *Raleigh News and Observer*, p. 17A.

which women are the primary sufferers. These disorders affect more than 5 million Americans, a majority of whom are girls and women (Brumberg, 1988; Hicks, 1998).

Cultural emphasis on thinness as ideal for women carries a second danger. When they are encouraged to focus so intensely on their bodies, women may give less attention to more important aspects of identity. Historian Joan Brumberg's book, *The Body Project: An Intimate History of American Girls* (1997), claims that for many young women in America the body has become an all-consuming project—one that takes precedence over all others. Brumberg says that "girls have moved from basing their identities on good works to good looks" (Winkler, 1997, p. A15).

Based on her studies of women and weight, Christiane Northrup concludes that "the concept of an 'ideal' body weight is extremely destructive for many women" (1995, p. 573). The ideal leads many women to deny themselves the normal pleasures of nourishment and leads some women to engage in very dangerous behaviors in an effort to achieve an unrealistic and unhealthy ideal.

Awareness of the perils of ultra-thin body ideals for women has motivated some resistance. *Mode* is a women's fashion magazine that challenges the waif look so prevalent in many women's magazines. Debuting in 1997, *Mode* portrays women who are sizes 12, 14, and 16. The full-figured models in *Mode* disprove the idea that only thin women can look good (Navarro, 1998). And then there's Emme, a plus-

Women's Body Ideals and Realities

The average Miss America weighed 134 pounds in the 1950s. By the early 1980s, her average weight had dropped to 117. Today, the average Miss America weighs even less.

In 1962, leading fashion models weighed only 8% less than the average woman in the United States. Thirty years later, in 1992, the highly sought-after fashion models weighed a whopping 25% less than the average woman in the United States. That's a 300% increase in the difference between models and average women ("The Wrong Weight," 1997). In 1998, the average American woman was 5'4" tall, weighed 130, and wore a size 12 or larger dress. Contrast that with the size 0 that is worn by *Ally McBeal*'s star Callista Flockhart (Hicks, 1998a,b).

Given ideals of extreme thinness, it's no wonder that so many women diet. And it's not just women. Girls too diet. A 1997 report by researchers at the University of Florida found that 42% of 6- and 7-year-old girls wanted to lose weight. Another study reported that nearly half of the girls surveyed were dieting by age 9 and on any given day, 25% of girls and women in the United States are dieting.

size fashion diva. Emme is 5'11" tall, weighs 190 pounds, and wears a size 14 with style. In 1994, *People* magazine listed Emme as one of the 50 most beautiful people (McDowell, 1998). Although full-figured models (and women) aren't yet as valued as super-slim ones, they are gaining increasing respect.

Perhaps you are wondering if there is some kind of profile for those likely to become obsessed with weight or to develop eating disorders. Women are more likely than men to be preoccupied with weight and physical attractiveness ("An All-Consuming Passion," 1991). Women who are highly sex typed (they have internalized the culture's views of femininity) are more susceptible to cultural ideals for women's weight than are androgynous women (Franzoi, 1991). Women who resist contemporary standards of excessive thinness are more able to accept themselves regardless of how much they weigh. A number of studies (Levinson, Powell, & Steelman, 1986; Thomas, 1989; Thomas & James, 1988) indicate that African American women tend to be less dissatisfied and less extreme in punishing themselves for a few extra pounds. Also, African American women less often develop eating disorders than Caucasian women, perhaps because weight is judged less negatively by African Americans than by Caucasians (Root,

NIKKI

When I was growing up, my mother and grandmother were always on diets. They think being ultra-thin is essential. Four years ago when I came to college, I gained the "freshman 15." When I went home for the summer, my mother and grandmother commented on how much weight I'd gained and how bad I looked. Mother got her doctor to put me on FenPhen, the diet pill. I'd heard it could be dangerous (you've probably read about the lawsuits against it), but I took the pills for

(continued)

1990). Linda Villarosa (1994) explains that traditional African societies admire full-figured bodies as symbols of wealth and prosperity. African American women who identify strongly with their ethnic heritage are less vulnerable to obsessions with thinness than African American women who leave their communities or who don't have strong Black identities (Villarosa, 1994). Adding to Villarosa's explanation are the insights of a Black student from a northern college. In a letter to me, Daneen described the ideology behind the views of physical beauty that she and other Black women in her community learned:

> *My family and my African American culture instilled pride in me. I was told that my full lips, round body, and rough hair encompassed the beauty and pride of my history. To want to be skinny or have straight hair or thin lips would be to negate my identity as a Black woman.*

Because our culture is increasingly emphasizing men's bodies, more and more men are exercising and working out with weights to develop the muscularity promoted as ideal (Mishkind et al., 1987; Tucker, 1983). Although women, particularly heterosexual Caucasian women, are most likely to develop eating disorders, increasing numbers of men too are developing eating disorders (Seligmann, 1994). The greater risk for men is compulsive exercising or use of potentially lethal steroids to attain the cultural ideal of strength. One group of men, however, is particularly likely to be concerned about appearance and to develop eating disorders: gay men. Physical appearance is linked more closely to self-worth for gay than straight men, perhaps because gay men, like straight women, want to attract men (Siever, 1988).

In summary, sex-related differences in nonverbal behavior reflect culturally constructed views of masculinity and femininity. In general, women are more sensitive to nonverbal communication; display more overt interest, attention, and affiliation; constrict themselves physically; are given and use less space; use touch for affiliative purposes but are touched more; and restrict body gestures more than men. Reflecting cultural messages to them about how to enact masculinity, men's nonverbal communication tends to be used to signal power and status, to assert themselves and their agenda, to command territories, and to veil their emotions from public display.

(Nikki continued)

two months and lost a lot of weight—more than the 15 pounds I'd gained. Then I started having echoing sounds in my ears. I went to a doctor and he found out the fluid in my ear had drained out as a result of taking Fen-Phen. The ringing is with me all the time, even though I've quit taking that pill. Being thin is fine, but it's not worth risking your health. I actually feel sorry for my mother and grandmother because they obsess over their weight and never enjoy eating food.

JILL

Eating disorders are epidemic, all right. What's more, they aren't even hidden. A lot of us just accept it as a way to keep from gaining weight. In my sorority, it's almost a joke by now that most of us will be in the bathroom right after dinner throwing up. Nobody thinks anything about it anymore. Sometimes I worry when I hear about people who die from it, but I think that's pretty rare, isn't it?

Race and Views of Physical Beauty

What's thin? What's fat? Is weight attractive on women? It turns out that the answers to these questions often depend on the race of the person answering. There is growing evidence that Black and White girls and women view their bodies in different ways, and that they have different ideals of feminine beauty.

In a survey of young women in junior high and high school, 90% of White students said they were dissatisfied with their bodies, but 70% of Black students were satisfied with their bodies. Nearly two-thirds of the White students were dieting or had dieted in the past year, whereas fewer Black students dieted or tried to control weight in a sustained way (Ingrassia, 1995).

At early ages, White girls learn that being slender or even thin is considered desirable. When asked to describe a perfectly shaped female, young White women said she would be 5′9″ tall and weigh 100 to 110 pounds. Young Black women offered more realistic descriptions of the perfect body form: full hips, thick thighs. Young Black women also emphasized that beauty is about more than weight and appearance: It's having the "right attitude." These differences in feminine ideals shed insight on the reasons why anorexia and bulimia are less common among Black girls and women, especially those who are strongly identified with African American culture (Bocella, 2001; Molloy & Herzberger, 1998; Vobejda & Perlstein, 1998).

Thinness is not the only aspect of physical attractiveness that is race related. For years, European American features have been represented as the only standard of female beauty (Edrut, 2000; Finstein, 1993; hooks, 1995; Shandler, 1999). Tyra Banks, Naomi Campbell, and other women of color who are successful models have skin color, hair, and features that are more like those of European Americans than like members of their own ethnic groups.

But change may be coming. In 1997, 20-year-old Alek Wek emerged as one of the hottest international fashion models. She's stolen the scene in Paris, New York, and Milan. Born in Sudan, Wek is 5′11″, has dark ebony skin, full lips, a broad nose, and wears her hair closely cropped (Samuels, 1997, p. 68). She represents a traditional African form of beauty.

IMPLICATIONS OF GENDERED NONVERBAL COMMUNICATION

The concept of speech communities helps us understand gendered nonverbal codes. Just as male and female speech communities have alternative rules of talk, so do they include divergent rules for nonverbal communication. You will recall that masculine speech communities teach people to use talk to assert themselves, to compete for attention and status, and to control conversations. Feminine speech communities, on the other hand, teach people to use communication to create relationships, include and support others, and notice and respond to others' feelings. These principles also show up in the nonverbal styles of many girls and boys, women and men.

It is probably not wise to try to establish which style is better or more effective in an absolute sense because that depends on situations and purposes of communication. Instead, let's think about how each mode fits within the context of cultural values and what that implies for perceptions, opportunities, and self-concepts of men and women. Identifying cultural views doesn't necessarily mean we will accept them. If we find that social views restrict individuals, we may resist them and appreciate different nonverbal styles on their own terms. This allows us to act as agents of change who reform cultural understandings that evaluate one style as standard and all others as inferior.

■ The Cultural Context of Nonverbal Communication

The meanings of femininity and masculinity are sculpted through interactions and perpetuated through ongoing cultural activities. Given this, it's worthwhile to consider how feminine and masculine nonverbal communication styles fit within and reflect larger cultural values. We begin by noting that Western society values communality and agency differently. Agency, which involves power, activity, initiative, and achievement, is held to be more important, more significant than communality, which focuses on relationships and community. Thus, our culture accords unequal worth to feminine and masculine nonverbal styles. The values it confers on each reflect larger cultural patterns—in fact, the overall ethos of the culture.

The differential values assigned to agency and communality were dramatically illustrated in a classic study conducted three decades ago. A research team (Broverman, Broverman, Clarkson, Rosenkrantz, & Vogel, 1970) prepared a list of traits that reflected a broad range of human qualities. They then asked 79 male and female psychiatrists, psychologists, and social workers to check the attributes they thought described "normal, healthy women." Next, the clinicians checked traits they associated with "normal, healthy men." Finally, clinicians selected characteristics of "normal, healthy adults." The findings were clear and startling: Normal women were described as dependent, deferential, unassertive, concerned with appearance, submissive, emotional, and uncompetitive. In contrast, clinicians described normal men as independent, aggressive, competitive, not submissive, more rational than emotional, and ambitious. Associated with normal adults were the qualities used to describe normal men. From these clinical judgments, two conclusions follow. First, the clinicians perceived stereotypically masculine characteristics as the standard, or norm, for healthy adults. Second, being a normal, healthy woman was seen as incompatible with being a normal, healthy adult.

Unfortunately, the bias favoring masculine qualities, as described in the study by Inge Broverman and her colleagues, continues to linger in society (Basow, 1992;

Williams & Best, 1990). Western culture values agency, action, doing, achievement, and ambition—in short, the qualities encouraged in men and discouraged in women. The conflict between femininity and adulthood, between being a woman and being successful, creates a constant paradox for women. Some women feel they have to choose between being perceived as feminine and being perceived as effective—they cannot simultaneously meet both sets of standards because they are mutually exclusive (Campbell, 1973; Wood & Conrad, 1983).

Cultural beliefs are not sacred dogma etched in stone. Instead, they are constructed, sustained, and sometimes altered as members of a society interact in ways that constantly remake social values. We may either accept or challenge existing views of masculinity and femininity as well as the values currently attached to communality and agency.

■ Respecting Differences in Nonverbal Communication

We should recognize different nonverbal styles as simply different—not better or worse, just different. Because our culture emphasizes hierarchy and our language encourages polar thinking, it's hard to realize that different ways can be equally valid. If we cannot do this, however, we wind up operating from very egocentric perspectives that fail to respect others on their own terms.

Misinterpretation of nonverbal styles is frequent (Wood, 1998). Men may perceive a woman who defers as less confident of her own point of view than a man who advances his position assertively. Similarly, a woman might view a man as insensitive and domineering if he keeps an impassive face, offers little response to her talk, and promotes his agenda. Yet such judgments reflect the communication rules we have learned, ones that may not apply to others' ways of expressing themselves. If we impose our values on behaviors that emanate from an alternative standpoint that is not guided by the rules we take for granted, then we distort others' communication by viewing it within a perspective alien to it. Greater accuracy in interpreting others' nonverbal communication results from understanding and respecting differences in how people use nonverbal behaviors and the alternative goals promoted by different communicative modes.

Respecting differences calls on us to suspend judgment based on our own perspectives and to consider more thoughtfully what others mean *in their own terms,* not ours. This might lead you to ask for clarification of intent from conversational partners whose nonverbal communication patterns diverge from yours. For example, it might be constructive to say to someone less facially expressive than you, "I don't know how you're feeling about what I just said, because your face doesn't show any reaction. Could you tell me what you feel?" Conversely, understanding may be enhanced when someone with a masculine, assertive nonverbal style says to his or her more deferential partner, "I'm not sure where you stand, because you seem to be responding more to my ideas than expressing your own. I'm interested in your opinion." Communicative techniques such as these enable us to show respect for nonverbal differences and, at the same time, to transcend their potential to create misunderstandings.

Understanding and respecting different forms of nonverbal communication does not imply that you have to give up your own style. That would be as counterproductive as discounting a style different from yours. All that understanding and respect require is an honest effort to appreciate what another says on his or her own terms. At first this is difficult, because we have to get past our own egocentric ways of perceiving the world in order to interpret other people from their standpoints. People who commit to doing this say that it becomes easier with practice.

There's another benefit to learning to understand and respect alternative styles of nonverbal communication. It enhances your personal effectiveness by increasing the range of options you have for communicating with different people in diverse contexts and for varied reasons. Now that you are aware of gendered patterns in nonverbal communication, you may reflect on your own behaviors. Do you fit the patterns associated with your gender? Are you comfortable with your style and the effects it has, or would you like to alter your nonverbal behavior in some respects? By reflecting on your own nonverbal communication, you empower yourself to create consciously a style that reflects the identity you assign to yourself.

SUMMARY

In this chapter, we have seen that nonverbal communication expresses cultural views of gender. Social definitions of women as unaggressive, decorative, and relationship centered are reinforced through nonverbal communication that emphasizes their appearance, limits their space, and defines them as touchable. Views of men as independent, powerful, and in control are reflected in nonverbal behaviors that accord them larger territories and greater normative rights to invade others by entering their space and touching them. Consistent with how nonverbal communication defines men and women are differences in how they use it. Whereas women tend to embody femininity by being soft-spoken, condensing space and yielding territory, and being facially responsive, men are likely to command space and volume, defend their turf, and adopt impassive facial expressions to keep feelings camouflaged. These differences grow out of socialization in distinctive speech communities.

Recognizing the value of alternative styles of communication, both verbal and nonverbal, allows you to appreciate the richly diverse ways humans express themselves. It also enables you to reflect with increased insight on the patterns esteemed in our society and the extent to which different ones are assigned to women and men. In turn, this enables you to resist those social meanings you find unconstructive, to revise your own nonverbal communication to reflect the identity you want, and to work toward changing the values our society assigns to masculine and feminine modes of expression. In doing this, you speak back to society and claim your right to participate in the processes of constructing the meanings of masculinity and femininity and the values assigned to different forms of communication.

DISCUSSION QUESTIONS

1. Observe people in your classes, in restaurants and stores, walking around campus, and in the media. Do you see gendered patterns of nonverbal communication that were identified in this chapter? Do women smile, hold eye contact, and use condensed space more than men? Do men use larger motions and more relaxed posture and command more space than women? What is the cumulative impact of gender-linked nonverbal styles in influencing perceptions of women and men?

2. Think back to the years when you were growing up. What artifacts were part of your environment? What kinds of toys did you have? What colors were your room, bedspread, and so on? What sort of clothes did you have?

3. Do your parents have their own special territories—ones others were not supposed to use or interrupt? Do your father and mother or stepparents have equal amounts of space? Is there a head seat at your dining table? If so, who generally occupies it?

4. Violate one of the nonverbal expectations for nonverbal communication for your sex. If you are a woman, you might try to go a day without smiling or refuse to make eye contact when others are talking to you. If you are a man, you might try to smile constantly or hold very steady eye contact with others in conversation. Notice how people respond, both in things they say to you and in their nonverbal reactions to your behavior.

5. Choose PowerTrac on your InfoTrac College Edition, then select key word in the search index. Type "Women and Weight and Magazine Covers." Read the article "Women and Weight: Gendered Messages on Magazine Covers" by Amy Malkin, Kimberlie Wornian, and Joan Chrisler, which was published in a 1999 issue of the journal *Sex Roles*. Are the authors' findings consistent with your experiences? How might symbolic interaction theory (discussed in Chapter 2) explain their findings about the influence of magazine covers and women's feelings about weight?

6 Gendered Family Dynamics

Before reading this chapter, imagine yourself and your life 10 years from now. Write a one- or two-paragraph description of a perfect day in the life you want to have 10 years from now.

Our experiences during the early years of life profoundly influence our identities. Although we continue to evolve throughout our lives, the foundations of our self-concepts, values, attitudes, and perspectives are established through communication during the formative years between birth and age 5.

This chapter explores the communicative processes by which many children learn and internalize society's views of gender and how these views then affect their identities and lives. Children learn social values through communicating with others, who introduce them to the definitions, meanings, and values of the culture. Having learned these, the majority of women and men embody them in their own communication, thereby reproducing existing social views of gender.

To launch our discussion, we will first examine how individual identities are created through interactions with others. We will then trace how parents' communication teaches children the cultural gender code. Finally, we will trace the implications of gendering processes by considering how they are reflected in contemporary college students' views of what it means to be masculine or feminine in America today. By understanding the origins and implications of gender roles, we should gain clearer insight into our own identities—and perhaps options to them.

ENTERING A GENDERED SOCIETY

We are born into a gendered society. From the pink and blue blankets hospitals frequently use to swaddle newborns, to parents' distinctive interactions with sons and daughters, gender messages besiege infants from the moment of birth. Key players in the gender drama are parents, teachers, and peers, who teach cultural expectations and prescriptions to newcomers in the society so that they may understand and participate in a common social world.

According to Mead (1934), we have no self at birth. Instead, we develop an identity through communication with others who are significant to us. Newborn infants experience themselves as blurred with the rest of their environment. A baby interacts with family members and others who are part of a larger social world; these interactions facilitate two processes central to developing a personal identity: conceiving the self-as-object and monitoring.

■ Self-as-Object

As we noted in Chapter 4, humans are able to reflect on themselves. We are simultaneously the subjects and objects of our own experience. We are able to stand outside of ourselves in order to perceive, describe, and evaluate our activities, much as we would those of others. For instance, we say "I am attractive" or "I am strong." **Self-as-object,** which is our ability to self-reflect, enables us to define ourselves and exercise some choice over who we will become.

At first, others' views of us are external; but we gradually internalize them so that they influence how we see ourselves. Mead, in fact, insisted that we can *experience self only after experiencing others.* The emphasis others place on assigning gender to children explains why this is one of the first clear senses of self that we develop.

■ Monitoring

Because we learn to view the self as an object, we are able to monitor ourselves, which means we observe and regulate our attitudes and behaviors. We use symbols, usually language, to define who we are (*son, student, mother, attorney, kind, independent,* and so on). **Monitoring** is an internal process people use to regulate how they fit with external norms. Mead spoke of *internal dialogues* to indicate that monitoring happens inside of us, but it involves the perspectives of others we have imported into our own thinking. Thus, in our private self-talk, we engage in a dialogue with the social world. As we do so, we remind ourselves what we are supposed to think, do, and feel in various situations—that is, we tell ourselves what the social codes stipulate as appropriate for our age, sex, and so forth. For instance, a 5-year-old girl might think "I want to go play in the yard" and then monitor that wish by repeating something she has heard from her mother: "but nice girls don't get dirty." The little girl's voice and the mother's voice engage in an internal dialogue through which the child decides what to do.

With this background on the process by which identity reflects social meanings, we may now consider in more depth how communication from families contributes to forming gender identities.

GENDERING COMMUNICATION IN THE FAMILY

The family is a primary source of gender identity. Through overt instruction and subtle, unconscious communication, families contribute in major ways to the formation of gender identity. To understand how families gender children, we will focus on two dimensions of communication between parents and children. First, we will elaborate on the largely unconscious process of internalizing gender, which was introduced in Chapter 2. Second, we will examine more overt ways in which children learn gender from parents. Taken together, the unconscious and conscious processes call our attention to the fundamental importance of parent–child communication in creating gendered identities.

■ Unconscious Processes: Identification and Internalization

The conscious level of human experience does not fully explain human personality, including gender identity. Insight into unobservable yet very important unconscious dynamics comes primarily from psychoanalytic theories, the basic principle of which is that core personality is shaped by family relationships in the early years of life.

Sigmund Freud is famous for claiming "anatomy is destiny," by which he meant that biology, particularly the genitals, determines with which parent a child will identify and, thus, how the child will develop. According to Freud, at an early age children of both sexes focus on the penis. Boys identify with their fathers, who also have penises, whereas girls recognize their similarity with mothers, who do not have a penis. Freud theorized that girls regard their mothers as responsible for their "lack" of penises, whereas boys view their fathers as having the power to castrate them.

By identifying with the same-sex parent, each child aligns himself or herself with an adult in the hope of gaining that person's protection. Freud argued that boys' fear of castration is more formidable than girls' penis envy, so males develop stronger and more intense gender identities. Following identification with the same-sex parent, children internalize the gendered behaviors and attitudes of their primary models. Interesting as Freud's theory is, there has been little empirical support for

EILEEN

I don't buy this stuff about penis envy. I've never envied my brother his penis. I remember when we were both little, we took baths together sometimes, and I saw that he was made differently than I was. I thought it looked strange, but I didn't want it myself. But I do remember being jealous of him, or of the freedoms my parents allowed him but not me. They let him go off all day long to play, but I had to stay in the yard unless my mother was with me. He could play rough and get dirty, but I'd get a real fussin' if I did it. I remember wishing I were a boy so that I could do all of the fun things, but I didn't wish I had a penis. Definitely not.

ADRIENNE

I helped Mom a lot with cooking and cleaning when I was little. I used to really enjoy that because it made me feel like an adult. I remember thinking "I'm just like Mommy" when I'd be cleaning or doing stuff in the kitchen. I wanted to be like her, and doing what she did made me feel we were the same.

it, and some studies indicate that at least parts of the theory are not valid (Basow, 1992; Pleck, 1981; Williams, 1973).

Lack of support for Freud's ideas and the growing realization that he misrepresented female development led to alternative explanations of the psychic bases of gender. Newer theories reject Freud's assertion that anatomy is destiny and his claim that females are preoccupied with penis envy. According to more recent thinkers (Chodorow, 1978, 1989; Goldner, Penn, Sheinberg, & Walker, 1990; Miller, 1986), females do not literally envy the penis. What they may envy is what the penis symbolizes—the privilege and power that our society bestows on males.

Although current psychoanalytic theorists reject some of Freud's ideas, they agree with his fundamental claim that family psychodynamics are critical to the formation of gender identity. During the earliest stage of life, children of both sexes are in a similar state of "infantile dependence" (Chodorow, 1989, p. 47) in which they depend on and identify with the person who takes care of them. Usually this is a woman, typically the mother. This implies that children of both sexes customarily form their first primary identification with an adult woman.

Yet common identification with a female does not mean boys and girls pursue similar developmental paths. Because mothers and daughters have a sameness that mothers and sons do not, boys and girls form different relationships with their mothers. Mothers tend to identify with daughters more closely than with sons; they seem to experience daughters more as part of themselves, and they encourage daughters to feel connected to them (Apter, 1990; Chodorow, 1989). With sons, mothers are inclined to emphasize the difference between them and to encourage sons to differentiate from them. Through a variety of verbal and nonverbal communications, mothers fortify identification with daughters and curb it with sons.

According to psychodynamic theory, by age 3, male and female development diverges dramatically. You'll recall that this is the age at which gender constancy is secured so that children realize their sex is an unchanging, continuous part of their identity. For most girls, development proceeds along the path initially established—identification with the mother. Through concrete, daily interactions with her mother, a daughter continues to crystal-lize her sense of self within the original primary relationship.

To develop masculine gender identity, however, boys typically sever the early identification with the mother and replace it with an identification with a male, often the father. This process is complicated by the fact that fathers are generally less physically present in boys' everyday lives and often are emo-tionally remote as well (Banerji, 1998; Keen, 1991; U.S. Census, 2000; Way, 1998). In fact, the number of American households headed by single mothers increased by 25% in the 1990s (Schmitt, 2001). Thus, a masculine gender model with whom boys can identify is sometimes more abstract in their daily lives than is a feminine model for girls. The absence of fathers is particularly high in African American families, of which only 36% have two parents (U.S. Census, 2000). Because a number of boys lack a strong, personal relationship with the person they are supposed to become like (Ingrassia, 1993), masculine gender can be elusive and difficult to grasp. This may help explain why boys typically define their masculinity predominantly in negative terms—as not feminine, not like mother. They re-

RICH

My father left us before I was even a year old, so I didn't know him at all. My mom worked all day and was too tired to date or anything else, so there wasn't a man around. I tried to help Mom, but she'd tell me I didn't have to do this stuff because I was "her little man." I used to watch Mom doing stuff around the house and I'd think, "That's not what I'm supposed to do," but I had a lot of trouble figuring out what it was that I *was* supposed to do. I just knew it wasn't girl stuff. Then I got a Big Brother through a program at school. He was 17, and he spent most every Saturday with me and sometimes some time after school dur-ing the week. Michael was great. He'd let me hang out with him, and he'd show me how to do stuff like play ball and use tools to make things. Finally I had a sense of what I was supposed to be like and what I should do. Michael really helped me figure out who I was.

press the original identification with mothers and deny any feminine tendencies or feelings in themselves. By extension, this may be the source of boys' tendencies to devalue whatever is feminine in general ("Ugh, girls are icky"), a pattern not paral-leled by girls' views of masculinity. Scholars who study family dynamics note that many young boys feel compelled to disparage what is feminine to assure themselves that they are truly masculine (Chodorow, 1989; Gaylin, 1992; Kantrowitz & Kalb, 1998; Miller, 1986).

As development continues, girls are encouraged to be "Mommy's helper" and to interact continuously with their mothers. Boys, however, begin to roam away from home to find companions. Boys' social development typically occurs in larger groups with temporary and changing memberships; for many girls, it unfolds within continuing, personal relationships with individuals, including mothers. These different developmental paths encourage boys to become achieving and in-dependent and girls to become nurturing and relationally oriented (Chodorow, 1989; Gilligan, 1982; Miller, 1986).

Nancy Chodorow (1989) theorizes that, because girls develop feminine identity within personal, ongoing relationships, throughout life they continue to seek close relationships with particular individuals and to place importance on personal com-

JUMP START reprinted by permission of United Feature Syndicate, Inc.

munication with others. Because boys separate from their initial relationship with mothers to form masculine identities, and because they tend to interact in activity-specific groups with changing members, they learn to define themselves relatively independently and to maintain some distance between themselves and others. They tend to engage more in instrumental activities with others than in personal communication. For example, if you observe young children, you're likely to notice that girls typically engage in conversation or talk-oriented games (for example, playing house), whereas boys usually favor activities that require little relational talk (for example, baseball).

The different styles typical of males and females—whether children or adults—have been described as *agentic* and *communal,* respectively (Bakan, 1966, 1968). Explaining these differences, one researcher wrote that agency and communion

> characterize two fundamental modalities in the existence of living forms. . . . Agency manifests itself in self-protection, self-assertion, and self-expansion; communion manifests itself in the sense of being at one with other organisms. Agency manifests itself in the formation of separations; communion in the lack of separations. Agency manifests itself in isolation, alienation, and aloneness; communion in contact, openness, and union. Agency manifests itself in the urge to master; communion in noncontractual cooperation. (Bakan, 1966, p. 15)

Although others have used different terms, Bakan's association of agency with masculine identity and communion with feminine identity is widely accepted by clinicians and researchers. Various studies confirm the generalizations that femininity tends to be relationally oriented, whereas masculinity tends to pivot more centrally on independence (Belenky et al., 1986; Gilligan, 1982; Gilligan & Pollack, 1988; Mulac, 1998; Thompson & Walker, 1989). It's important to understand that these are generalizations about gender, not sex. In the process of developing identities, children move from identification with a sex (male or female) to identification with a gender (masculine, feminine, androgynous). Women as well as men with masculine inclinations value independence and prefer distance from others. Conversely, men as well as women with feminine orientations place a premium on relationships and interpersonal closeness. How is identity formation affected when men, not women, are primary caregivers? Research on this is just beginning, but it might encourage a more relational, communal identity in male children, because they could define themselves within the first relationship with another male.

■ Ego Boundaries

Concurrent with the process of constructing gender identity is a second intrapsychic development: formation of **ego boundaries** (Chodorow, 1989; Surrey, 1983). Ego boundaries define the point at which an individual stops and the rest of the world begins. They distinguish the self—more or less distinctly—from everyone and everything else. Because they are linked to gender identity and evolve concurrently with it, masculine and feminine ego boundaries tend to differ. Individuals who develop feminine gender identity, which emphasizes interrelatedness with others, tend to have relatively thin or permeable ego boundaries. Because girls are encouraged to identify with mothers and not to differentiate, they often do not perceive clear-cut or absolute lines between themselves and others.

The relatively thin ego boundaries cultivated in females may partially explain why they tend to be more empathic—to sense the feelings of those close to them and to experience those feelings almost as their own. It may also explain why women, more than men, sometimes become so involved with others that they neglect their own needs. Finally, this may shed light on the feminine tendency to feel responsible for others and for situations that are not one's own doing. When the lines between self and other are blurred, it's hard to tell what *your* responsibilities and *your* needs are. To the extent that others merge with you, helping them is helping you.

In most cases, masculine gender identity is premised on differentiating from a female caregiver and defining self as "not like her." It makes sense, then, that masculine individuals tend to have relatively thick or rigid ego boundaries. They generally have a clear sense of where they stop and others begin, and they are less likely to experience others' feelings as their own. The thicker ego boundaries encouraged in masculine socialization help us understand why later in life men generally keep some distance from others. Rigid ego boundaries also suggest why men in general are unlikely to feel deeply involved in others' problems and why they

> ### ⏰ VINCE
>
> My girlfriend is so strange about her friends. Like, the other night I went by her apartment and she was all upset and crying. When I asked her what was wrong she told me Linda, her best friend, had just been dumped by her boyfriend. I said she acted like it was her who'd broken up, not Linda, and she didn't need to be so upset. She got even more upset and said it felt like her problem too; couldn't I understand what Linda was going through? I said I could, but that *she* wasn't going through it; Linda was. She told me it was the same thing because when you're really close to somebody else you hurt when they hurt. It didn't make sense to me, but maybe this concept of ego boundaries is what that's all about.

tend not to experience another's feelings as their own. Contrary to some accusations, people with masculine identities are not necessarily unconcerned about others; instead, it is more likely that men generally experience others' feelings as separate from their own.

After measuring ego boundaries in nearly 1,000 people, Ernest Hartmann (1991) concluded that there are "clear-cut differences between men and women.... Overall, women scored significantly thinner than men—thinner by about twenty points, or 8% of the overall score" (p. 117). He also found that women tend to be comfortable feeling connected to others, sensing that their lives are interwoven with those close to them, and they may be uneasy with too much autonomy. Most men, on the other hand, tend to feel secure when autonomy and self-sufficiency are high, and they may feel suffocated in relationships that are extremely close. This may explain why women typically want more togetherness than men find comfortable and men tend to desire more separation than women enjoy. Some theorists (Rubin, 1985; Schaef, 1981) see these distinct preferences for closeness as a reason why women create more emotionally intense same-sex friendships than do men. With other women, they find the kind of intimate, personal connection they value. These patterns, which are particularly evident in adult life, have their roots in childhood socialization processes.

Important as childhood socialization is, we should remind ourselves it is not an absolute determinant of adult personality. Gender, like other important aspects of ourselves, is not resolutely fixed by age 3 and then constant and unchanging throughout the rest of our lives. Our understanding of gender and of our personal gender identity changes over time as we experience different situations and diverse people who embody alternative versions of masculinity and femininity.

■ Parental Attitudes About Gender

Among the people who influence our gender identities, parents are especially prominent. Children learn gender roles through the rewards and punishments they receive for various behaviors and through observing and emulating others. Typically, girls are encouraged to be communal through communication that reinforces cooperation, helpfulness, nurturance, and other behaviors consistent with social meanings of femininity. In boys, agentic tendencies are promoted by rewarding them for behaving competitively, independently, and assertively (Bruess & Pearson, 1996; Leaper, Anderson, & Sanders, 1998; Leaper, Leve, Strasser, & Schwartz, 1995). In addition, children learn about gender by watching parents. Children observe what mothers and fathers do, using parents as models for themselves.

One understanding of gender that most children learn through early communication is that males are generally more valued than females. According to Susan Basow (1992, p. 129), "Nearly everywhere in the world, most couples prefer male children to female children," a preference that is communicated indirectly and directly to children. In fact, preference for males is so strong that in some cultures female fetuses are aborted and female infants are killed immediately after birth (French, 1992; Pollitt, 1999; Steinbacher & Holmes, 1987). As Mala and Bonita's commentaries indicate, this bias is present in our society as well as others.

Parents' attitudes toward sons and daughters often reflect gender stereotypes. Social scientists have shown that labeling a baby male or female affects how parents perceive and respond to it. In a classic study, within just 24 hours of birth, parents responded to their babies in terms of gender stereotypes (Rubin, Provenzano, & Luria, 1974). Although male and female babies were matched for size, weight, and level of activity, parents described boys with words such as *strong, hardy, big, active,* and *alert.* Parents of equally large and active girls described their daughters with adjectives such as *small, dainty, quiet,* and *delicate.* More recent experiments show the persistence of parental tendencies to gender-stereotype children (Delk, Madden, Livingston, & Ryan, 1986; Stern & Karraker, 1989).

Parents have been shown to act toward children on the basis of gender labels. In general, boys are treated more roughly and encouraged to be more aggressive, whereas girls are treated gently and urged to be emotional and physically reserved (Antill, 1987). One study found that parental gender stereotypes prompt parents to expect boys to excel at math and science but do not expect or encourage this in girls (Eccles, 1989). Another report (National Public Radio, 1992) notes that parents praise

MALA

Males are favored over females in Indian culture. It is custom for a girl's family to give a dowry to a man who marries the girl to make it worth his while. As a result, many poor families in India kill a newborn baby if it is female and rejoice if the baby is male. When my third sister was born, my great grandmother expressed her disappointment that we had no boys and so many girls.

BONITA

You asked us to think about whether we ever got the message that males are more valued than females. I know I did. I guess I got it in a lot of ways, but one really stands out. I remember when I was 9 my mother was pregnant for the third time. When she went into labor, Daddy took her to the hospital with me and my sister. We all sat in the waiting room while they took Mom down the hall. Later the doctor came in and went to my father. I still remember his exact words. He said, "I'm sorry, Mr. Chavis, it's another girl. Guess you'll have to try again."

sons more than daughters for accomplishments, a pattern that encourages boys to aim for achievement and to tie their successes to what they are able to do. Finally, researchers report that parents respond more approvingly to assertiveness in sons than in daughters and react more positively to interpersonal and social skills in daughters than in sons (Fagot, Hagan, Leinbach, & Kronsberg, 1985; Leaper, Anderson, & Sanders, 1998).

■ **Parental Communication About Gender**

In addition to parents' responses to children's behaviors, gender stereotypes are communicated by the toys and clothes parents give children and the chores they assign to them. Despite evidence that rigid gender socialization restricts children's development (Morrow, 1990), many parents continue to select toys and clothes that are gender specific. When a group of researchers surveyed the rooms of 120 boys and girls who were under 2 years old (Pomerleau et al., 1990), they found that girls' rooms were populated by dolls and children's furniture and the color pink was prominent. Boys' rooms most often were decorated in the colors blue, red, and white, and in them were various vehicles, tools, and sports gear. Although boys and girls themselves show little difference in toy preference during the preschool years, they are often taught to develop gendered preferences. Thus, by age 5, most boys prefer action toys and most girls prefer dolls (Pereira, 1994).

Further investigations have shown that many parents actively discourage their children's interest in toys and games that are associated with the other sex (Antill, 1987; Fagot, 1978; Lytton & Romney, 1991). For instance, boys may be persuaded not to play house or cook, and girls may be dissuaded from engaging in vigorous, competitive games. Different types of toys and activities promote distinct kinds of thinking and interaction. More "feminine" toys such as dolls encourage quiet, nurturing interaction with another, physical closeness, and verbal communication. More typically "masculine" toys such as sporting equipment and train sets promote independent or competitive activities that require little verbal interaction. Because the toys children play with can affect how they think and interact, some researchers caution parents not to limit children to toys for one sex (Basow, 1992; Fagot, 1985).

Another way parents communicate gender expectations is through the household chores they assign to sons and daughters. As you might expect, domestic duties such as cleaning and cooking are most often designated for girls, and more active chores such as outdoor work, painting, and simple repairs are assigned to boys (Burns & Homel, 1989; Goodnow, 1988; McHale, Bartko, Crouter, & Perry-Jenkins, 1990). There are several implications of delegating different responsibilities to girls and boys. First, like toys, various tasks encourage particular types of thinking and activity. Domestic chores emphasize taking care of others and taking responsibility for them (cleaning their clothes, shopping for their needs, and so on), whereas maintenance jobs encourage independent activity and emphasize taking care of things rather than people. Domestic chores also tend to occur in small, interior spaces, whereas maintenance chores are frequently done in open spaces.

Aggression in children tends to be greeted with distinct responses from mothers and fathers. When daughters act aggressively, mothers often warn them that aggression will hurt others or diminish others' caring for them. Aggressive behavior from sons is less likely to be met with threats that it might endanger relationships (Hogan, Simpson, & Gillis, 1988). Thus girls more than boys are taught that acting aggressively may jeopardize relationships. Also, many fathers tend to condone and sometimes encourage aggressiveness in sons (A. Campbell, 1993). It appears that the sexes don't differ a great deal with respect to feelings of anger or aggression. Because of gender socialization, however, they do differ in whether and how they express those feelings.

In general, boys are more rigidly gender socialized than girls. This is more true of Caucasian than African American families, because the latter tend to socialize children of both sexes toward autonomy and nurturing of children (Bardewell, Cochran, & Walker, 1986; DeFrancisco & Chatham-Carpenter, 2000; Hale-Benson, 1986). It's much more acceptable for girls to be tomboys than for boys to play house or cuddle dolls. Similarly, it's considered more suitable for girls to be strong than for boys to cry, for girls to act independently than for boys to need others, and for girls to touch and show tenderness toward other girls than for boys to demonstrate closeness to male peers.

These differential gender latitudes are evident in how parents communicate with sons and daughters. Sons tend to receive more encouragement to conform to masculinity and more rewards for doing so than daughters receive for femininity. In addition, boys are more directly and strongly discouraged from any feminine inclinations than girls are from masculine behaviors and interests. It's also been shown that fathers are more insistent on gender-stereotyped toys and activities, especially for sons, than are mothers (Caldera, Huston, & O'Brien, 1989; Fagot & Leinbach, 1987; Lamb, 1986). The overall picture is that boys are more intensively and rigidly pushed to become masculine than girls are to become feminine.

FYI

Nature Versus Nuture

It's an old debate but one that's hard to resolve: Is nature (biology) or nurture (socialization) more important in shaping gender identity and other aspects of who we are?

Research shows that there are some biological differences between most males and females, and they are evident early in life. Males tend to be more aggressive than females, and females tend to be more oriented toward relationships. For instance, when researchers placed a barrier between 1-year-olds and something they wanted, the infant boys were more likely to knock down the barrier. The infant girls were more likely to try to get their mothers to help them.

Yet nature isn't the whole story. Research also shows clearly that many parents reinforce gender stereotypes with their children. Parents, especially fathers, encourage children to engage in activities and to play with toys that are "gender appropriate." Parents, again especially fathers, encourage boys to be more autonomous and encourage girls to be more interactive with others. Peers also encourage sex-stereotyped behavior—teasing boys who cry or show fear, shunning girls who don't accommodate others. A self-fulfilling prophecy takes hold when girls are encouraged to act feminine and boys are encouraged to act masculine.

After many years of debate and much research, the bottom-line conclusion remains the same: Gender, as well as other aspects of identity, is shaped by complicated interactions between nature and nurture.

Sources: Bryant, A., & Check, E. (2000, Fall/Winter). How parents raise boys and girls. *Newsweek,* pp. 64–65; Haag, P. (2000). *Voices of a generation: Teenage girls report about their lives.* New York: Marlowe and Company.

Why are boys more vigorously socialized into gender, especially by a majority of fathers? Some researchers believe this pattern reflects cultural and parental preferences for males and a general valuing of masculinity (Feinman, 1984) and a corresponding devaluation of femininity (French, 1992; Miller, 1986). It makes sense that boys would be encouraged to become what the culture esteems, whereas girls would not be so strongly urged to become something less valued. It's also possible that being masculine is more difficult than being feminine because the former promotes repressing some feelings, vulnerabilities, and needs (Maccoby & Jacklin, 1974; Pleck, 1981). If so, then stronger socialization would be required to overcome natural inclinations.

■ Parental Modeling

Another way parents communicate gender is through modeling masculinity and femininity and male–female relationships. Parents are powerful models for gender—they are perhaps the single most visible, constantly present examples of how to be a man and a woman. We have already discussed children's tendencies to identify with their same-sex parents. As a daughter identifies with her mother, she begins imitating her mother to become feminine herself. Boys tend to use mothers as a negative example of what they are *not* supposed to be and do (Chodorow, 1989). In addition, boys look to fathers for a definition of masculinity; a father is his son's primary model of manhood, one he emulates in his own efforts to become masculine.

Children also learn about gender by watching who does what in their families. By observing parents, children gain understanding of the roles socially prescribed for females and males. In families that adhere to traditional sex roles, children of both sexes are likely to learn that women are supposed to nurture others, clean, cook, and show emotional sensitivity, and men are supposed to earn money, make decisions, and be emotionally controlled. Not all families, however, adopt traditional sex roles. Single mothers provide children with a broad model of women's roles. The fact that a large number of African American families are headed by a single mother (Ingrassia, 1993; U.S. Census, 2000) may explain why African American women, in general, are more self-reliant and assertive than many European American women. In two-parent African American families, men are generally more involved with family, especially sons, and with extended kin than are White men (Gaines, 1995). In African American families, more than in European American ones, the breadwinning role is viewed as part of, not distinct from, the role of mother.

Parents also model attitudes about gender and physical appearance. Fathers who work out and engage in vigorous physical activities may impart the message that physical strength is masculine. Mothers who make disparaging remarks about their weight or eating communicate that women should be thin. Mothers powerfully influence daughters' body images and attitudes toward food (Davison & Birch,

2001). Debra Waterhouse, a nutritionist, says that "our daughters hear us making comments like 'I hate my thighs' or 'I ate like a pig' . . . and that forms their definition of womanhood" ("The Wrong Weight," 1997, p. 7).

One particularly striking example of gender roles that children learn from parents involves mothers' and fathers' responsibility for child care. Research consistently shows that mothers invest considerably more time in taking care of children than do fathers (Hochschild, 1989; Goldstein, 2000; Okin, 1989; Riessman, 1990; Steil, 2000). Even when both parents hold full-time jobs outside of the home, fewer than one third of male partners do half of the child care and homemaking chores (Steil, 2000). This holds true for Black and White

 DAVID

We used to wait for Dad to come home, because he'd always spend a half hour or so before dinner playing with us—tossing a ball or working with the trains or whatever. Mom never did that. Now I can see that she was really doing more for us all of the time—fixing our meals, buying us clothes, taking care of our doctor's appointments, and just generally being there for us. Maybe Dad was more special to us because he was around less than Mom. Anyway, he was the one we looked forward to playing with.

men alike (Hyde & Texidor, 1994). Further, mothers and fathers engage in different kinds of child care. Mothers do the constant day-in, day-out activities of feeding, bathing, dressing, supervising, and so forth. Fathers more typically engage in occasional activities and ones that are more enjoyable for both children and parents, such as playing games or taking weekly trips to the bagel shop or zoo (Burns & Homel, 1989; Hochschild, 1989). Given this, it's not surprising that most children turn to their mothers when they need help or comforting and to their fathers when they want to play. Fathers are the preferred playmates (Thompson & Walker, 1989). Learning these gender roles through observing parental models prepares children to reproduce the roles in their own lives as they grow into adulthood.

Fathers appear to be particularly important in shaping gender in children, especially sons. Interestingly, young girls generally use both parents as models, but boys tend to rely almost exclusively on their fathers or other males (Basow, 1992). Further, the extent to which fathers themselves hold strong gender stereotypes affects the attitudes about gender that children develop. Children of fathers with traditional gender beliefs tend to be conservative and hold rigid gender stereotypes themselves. They also seem to have narrower views of what males and females can do (Fagot & Leinbach, 1989). African American fathers, like European American ones, tend to interact more with their sons than with their daughters (Hyde & Texidor, 1994). Children of androgynous parents tend to have more androgynous and flexible attitudes and behaviors themselves (Sedney, 1987).

■ Different Contributions of Mothers and Fathers

As we've seen, both parents contribute to children's gender development. Although mothers' and fathers' contributions are equally important, they tend to be distinct in some ways.

Fathering: Past, Present, and Future

Throughout most of human history, women and men have lived and worked together with both sexes sharing the responsibilities of providing and caring for families. The Industrial Revolution drew men away from their families and led to a division between public and private spheres of life.

In our time, fatherhood is once again being recognized as a major part of men's lives and as an important relationship for children. Typically, father–child interaction has focused on discipline and play, whereas mothers have tended to engage more in caregiving activities with children (Snarey, 1994; Yogman, Cooley, & Kindlon, 1988). Yet, play and discipline are not the only—or necessarily the most important—aspects of father–child relationships. Research (Palm, 1993; Secunda, 1992) indicates that men who are actively involved with their children foster social and emotional development in their sons and daughters.

In a 1996 Princeton survey, men reported increasing commitment to fathering. More than half of the fathers surveyed said that being a parent is more important to them than it was to their fathers. Fully 70% of fathers surveyed said they spend more time with their children than their fathers spent with them (Adler, 1996).

And not all fathers share parenting with mothers. In 1999, there were 2.1 million single dads in the United States (Wellington, 1999). Many of these single dads report that parenting is their most important role. Yet, they also note that society doesn't always respect men who place parenting ahead of career advancement (Jackson, 1999). To combat negative social attitudes, some single dads belong to virtual support groups on the Internet. Others find support by belonging to Promise Keepers or other organized groups that emphasize the importance of men's role in families (Milbank, 1997).

It also appears that active fathering cultivates personal growth in men (Palm, 1993; Smith, 1995), giving them opportunities to expand their patience, compassion, and nurturing abilities. Studies of single fathers reveal that they can be as committed to parenting and as nurturing and loving as mothers (Greif, 1990; Hanson, 1988).

To learn more about groups that support active fathering, visit this Web site:

 American Federation for Fathers: **http://www.acfc.org**

In general, mothers emphasize relationships in their interactions with children. Mothers typically devote a lot of time to caring for children—providing comfort, security, and acceptance. They engage in more eye contact and face-to-face interaction with children than do fathers. Further, mothers tend to repeat infant daughters' vocalizations more than those of infant sons (Trudeau, 1996), perhaps because of the bond of likeness mothers feel with daughters. More than fathers, mothers tend to play with children at the children's level, which develops children's confidence and security in play.

Fathers typically focus more on playing with than taking care of children (Popenoe, 1996). They tend to engage in play that is physically stimulating and exciting, and they encourage children to develop skills and meet challenges. Fathers, more than mothers, stretch children by urging them to take risks and move beyond their current level of ability (Stacey, 1996). Fathers also tend to emphasize competition, achievement, and initiative in play.

The contributions of fathers and mothers tend to be different yet highly complementary. Fathers generally help children, especially sons, develop a sense of personal agency—independence, initiative, and achievement. Mothers are more likely to foster the value of communion in children—making connections with others and feeling emotionally secure. A fully developed, healthy person has an integrated sense of both agency and communion.

In summary, parents play a major role in shaping children's understandings of gender in general and their own gender in particular. Through unconscious identification and internalization of gender to more overt learning from communication of parents and modeling, most children's initial views of masculinity and femininity reflect their parents' attitudes, behaviors, and interactions. The gender socialization begun in early years is sustained and reinforced by other cultural influences such as media. We will examine some of these in later chapters. Before moving on, however, we should translate the research we've considered into more personal terms that illuminate the implications of gender socialization for later life.

THE PERSONAL SIDE OF THE GENDER DRAMA

Theory and research regarding how we become gendered are only part of the story. Equally important is understanding how gender socialization affects us as we move beyond childhood. To grasp this, we will consider what it means to grow up masculine and feminine in present-day America.

■ Growing Up Masculine

What does it mean to be masculine in the United States in the twenty-first century? Pervasive references to male privilege suggest that men, particularly heterosexual White men in the middle and upper classes, have special access to the opportunities and rewards of our society. Yet this tells us little about how masculinity constrains and affects individual men. To understand the advantages, challenges, and issues of masculinity, let's first consider what several college men say. In the commentaries by Jake, Charles, Randy, Henry, and Kevin, we hear of the pressures, expectations, and constraints of manhood as much as the prerogatives and privi-

ℰ JAKE

You asked what it means to be a man today. For me, it means that I can expect to get a job and keep it as long as I do decent work. It also means I'll probably have a family to support—or I'll be the major breadwinner for it. It means I don't have to worry about somebody thinking I'm not serious about my work because of my sex. My girlfriend keeps running into this in her job interviews—being treated as if she's not serious about working, when her GPA is higher than mine. I guess going through interviews together has made me aware of how much bias there still is against women. And, yeah, it's made me glad I'm a man.

leges. In his book *The Male Experience,* James A. Doyle (1997) identifies five themes of masculinity, which are woven throughout the commentaries of these five men. We will consider each of these elements of the male role as well as a sixth that seems to have emerged since Doyle made his analysis.

The prime directive is *don't be female.* Doyle believes that the most fundamental requirement for manhood is not being womanly. Early in life, most boys learn they must not think, act, or feel like girls and women. Because this prohibition teaches boys that girls are inferior, it is thought to be one of the sources of the general attitude that females are inferior to males. Any male who shows sensitivity or vulnerability is ridiculed as a sissy, a crybaby, a mama's boy, or a wimp (Kantrowitz & Kalb, 1998; Pollack, 2000). The antifemale directive is at least as strong for African American men as for European American ones.

The second element of the male role is the command *be successful,* which surfaces when men discuss the concept of masculinity. Men are expected to achieve status in their professions, to *be successful,* to "make it." Men may not be respected if they choose to stay home with children or if their wives earn more money than they do. Warren Farrell (1991) writes that men are regarded as "success objects," and their worth as marriage partners, friends, and men is judged by how successful they are at what they do. Training begins early with sports, where winning is stressed. As Alfie Kohn (1986) remarks, "The general rule is that American males are simply trained to win. The object, a boy soon gathers, is not to be liked but to be envied, . . . not to be part of a group but to distinguish himself from the others in that group" (p. 168).

Later in life, this translates into not just being good at what you do but being better than others, more powerful than peers, pulling in a bigger salary than your neighbors, and having a more expensive home, car, and so on, than your friends. Success for men, we might tell Randy, is a comparative issue—it means being better than others. Year after year, a national survey has reported that being a good provider is regarded as the primary requirement for manhood—an internalized requirement that appears to cut across lines of race and economic class (Cazenave & Leon, 1987; Faludi, 1991).

A third injunction for the male role is *be aggressive.* Even in childhood, boys are often encouraged to be roughnecks or at least are seldom scolded for being so (Cohen, 1997). They are expected to fight and not to run from battles and confrontations (Nelson, 1994b; Newburger, 1999; Pollack, 2000). Later, sports reinforce early training by emphasizing aggression, violence, and toughness (Messner, 2000). Coaches psych teams up with demands that they "make the other team hurt, hurt, hurt" or "make them bleed." Perhaps the ultimate training for aggression comes in military service, especially during times of war. "We'll make you into men" promises a recruiting poster. The pledge is to teach men to fight, to inflict pain on others, to endure it stoically themselves, and to win, win, win.

Men's training in aggression may be linked to violence (Gordon, 1988; Messner, 1997; Thompson & Walker, 1989), especially violence against women. Because males are taught that women are inferior (remember the prime directive of masculinity: don't be female) and that aggressiveness is good, it's not surprising that some men believe they are entitled to dominate women. This belief surfaces in studies of men who rape (Costin & Schwartz, 1987; Scott & Tetreault, 1987). The same belief that "I have a right to do my will on her" is evident in studies of men who abuse their girlfriends and wives (Dobash & Dobash, 1979; Gelles & Straus, 1988; Wood, 2001b). One study (Thompson, 1991) reports that both college women and men who are violent toward their dates have masculine gender orientations, reminding us again that gender and sex are not equivalent terms.

RANDY

Women have a choice about whether to "make their mark" on the world and be successful. I don't. I have to be successful at work, or I am a failure as a man. But I can't figure out exactly what it means to be successful. I see men who are successful, like my father, and they're slaves to their bosses and their jobs. They don't enjoy life. They're not free to do what they want. They always have to be making it, proving they're successful. Last year my uncle had a heart attack. He was only 51. He was successful, and look what it got him.

HENRY

My father died last year, and suddenly I was the head of my family. I have to be strong for my family, especially my mother. I can't show my fears or sadness, because everyone else is leaning on me. I have to hide my feelings and just keep going for everyone else. I hear the talk about men being emotionally repressed, but I don't have an option. All that is keeping me going is my ability to hold in my emotions and focus on supporting my family.

A fourth element of the male role is captured in the injunction *be sexual.* Men should be interested in sex—all the time, anytime. They are expected to have a number of sexual partners; the more partners a man has, the more of a stud he is (Gaylin, 1992). Some fraternities still have rituals such as recognizing brothers who "made it" at the last fraternity event. During rush, one fraternity recently issued invitations with the notation B.Y.O.A., which one of my students translated for me: Bring your own ass. Research indicates that brothers in some fraternities encourage drinking and sexual activity as signs of masculinity (Martin & Hummer, 1989). A number of writers (Brownmiller, 1993; Faludi, 1991; French, 1992; Russell, 1993) have criticized men's inclination to treat women as sex objects, which clearly de-

KEVIN

I'm a man, a normal man, okay? I mean I like girls, and I like sex. Sometimes. But that's not all I think about. And frankly, sometimes I'm not in the mood. But a man can't say that. If he does, then people think there's something wrong with him. You have to be on—always ready, always drooling for sex—to prove you're a man. We don't have any freedom to say "I'm not in the mood" or "I'm not interested." Once when a girl came on to me, I told her I wasn't interested, and she asked me if I was gay. I'm not gay. But I'm not a constant sex machine either.

DEREK

It's really frustrating to be a man today. My girlfriend wants me to open up and show my feelings and talk about them and stuff like that. But the guys on the team get on my case whenever I show any feelings other than about winning a game. I'm supposed to be sensitive and not. I'm supposed to keep my feelings to myself and not. I'm supposed to open doors for girls and pay for dates but then respect them as equals. A lot of times it feels like a no-win situation.

means women. Less often noted is that the injunction to be sexual also turns men into sex objects. Sex isn't a free choice when you have to perform to be a man. Some men resent the expectation that they should always be interested in sexual activity.

Finally, Doyle says the male sex role demands that men *be self-reliant.* Men are expected to be confident, independent, autonomous. The Marlboro Man was an extremely effective advertising image because he symbolized the independence and toughness of masculinity. A "real man" doesn't need others, particularly women. He depends on himself, takes care of himself, and relies on nobody. Autonomy is central to social views of manliness. As we noted earlier, male self-development typically begins with differentiation from others, and from infancy most boys are taught to be self-reliant and self-contained (Newburger, 1999; Thompson & Pleck, 1987). Men are expected to be emotionally controlled, not to let feelings control them, and not to need others.

In addition to the five themes of masculinity identified by Doyle, a sixth seems to have emerged. This theme highlights the mixed messages about being men that confront many boys and men today: *Embody and transcend traditional views of masculinity.* This theme expresses the paradox that many men feel today as they confront pressures both to be "real men" in traditional ways and simultaneously to defy traditional views of men by being sensitive and egalitarian (Kindlon & Thompson, 1999). For many men today, the primary source of pressure to be conventionally masculine is from other men who enforce what psychologist William Pollack (2000) calls the "boy code." Boys and, later, men encourage each other to be silent, tough, and independent and to take risks. Boys and men who don't measure up often face peer shaming ("You're a wuss," "Do you do everything she tell you to do?"). At the same time, many men feel other pressures—often from romantic partners, female friends, and mothers—to be more sensitive and emotionally open and to be a full partner in running a home and raising children. It's hard to be both traditionally male and not traditionally male, and it's hard to avoid criticism or shaming from someone for being either. These conflicting expectations for men reflect shifting gender identities and changes in relationships between women and men in our era. Just as women in the

Is There a War Against Boys?

In a recent book, Christina Sommers declares there is a "war against boys" in America. According to Sommers, the source of the war is that we've begun to think of normal boyhood as something pathological. Once, society considered it perfectly normal for boys to be aggressive, noisy, crude, and highly active. Now, claims Sommers, boys who act in these ways are diagnosed as hyperactive or as suffering from attention deficit disorder. She criticizes the suspension of a young boy who kissed a girl in school without her permission. Sommers asks, Why should he be punished when he was just being a normal boy? According to Sommers, the source of the war against boys is "misguided feminists" who have put too much emphasis on discrimination and other problems faced by girls. The result, says Sommers, is that boys have been shortchanged.

Michael Kimmel disagrees with Sommers. He says that two things are fundamentally wrong with Sommers's arguments. First, she creates a false opposition between the interests of boys and girls and suggests that we can't be equally concerned with both. Kimmel says that Sommers makes it seem as if anything done to benefit girls (equity in sports, for example) harms boys. The second problem with Sommers's work is that it conveniently overlooks incontrovertible evidence of real problems—not ones made up by "misguided feminists"—that are harming boys. He notes that boys commit suicide four times more often than girls, get into more fights, and do less well in school. Kimmel also notes that, in every case of school shootings, boys were the shooters who murdered classmates and teachers. Kimmel believes that unhealthy and outdated ideals of masculinity are the problem—are the source of the *real* war against boys. He thinks the solution is to challenge ideals of masculinity that encourage boys to believe that violence is a measure of masculinity.

Sources: Edmundson, M. (2000). Bad boys, Whatcha gonna do? *The Nation*, pp. 39–43. Kimmel, M. (2000, January 12). What about the boys? Keynote address at the 6th Annual Gender Equity Conference. Sommers, C. (2000). *The war against boys: How misguided feminism is harming our young men.* New York: Simon & Schuster.

1960s and 1970s were confronted with mixed messages about being traditionally female and not, men today are having to negotiate new terrain and new ways of defining themselves.

What happens when men don't measure up to the social expectations of manhood? One answer comes from a study of men in the military (Richissin, 1997). Army documents reveal that high-ranking officers sometimes refuse to allow mental health workers to approach soldiers who are having emotional problems. Further, army psychiatrists and psychologists cannot guarantee confidentiality to soldiers. Thus, to avoid the risk of being perceived as unable to handle their problems, many soldiers don't seek the help they need. Admitting personal problems goes against what reporter Todd Richissin calls the "Army's culture of bravado, of sucking it up and toughing it out" (p. 12-A).

Some counselors believe men's striving to live up to social ideals of masculinity has produced an epidemic of hidden male depression (Kahn, 1997). Terrence Real is a psychotherapist who specializes in treating men who are depressed. According to Real (1997), male depression is widespread, and so is society's unwillingness to recognize it. He believes that society's unwillingness to recognize male depression motivates many men to deny depression when they experience it personally. Whereas depressed women suffer the social stigma of having emotional problems, Real says men who admit they are depressed suffer the double stigma of having emotional problems and being unmanly by society's standards.

The first five themes of masculinity clearly reflect gender socialization in early life and lay out a blueprint for what being a man means. Yet this image of masculinity is not necessary or healthy. Perhaps that is why a sixth theme is emerging to challenge the adequacy of traditional views of "real men." Individual men have options about embodying society's traditional definition of masculinity, and many men are crafting alternative identities for themselves. In later chapters, we'll discover examples of ways to revise masculine identity.

■ Growing Up Feminine

What does it mean to be feminine in the United States in the twenty-first century? Casual talk and media offer us two quite different versions of modern women. One suggests that women now have it all. They can get jobs that were formerly closed to them and rise to the top levels of their professions; they can have egalitarian marriages with liberated men and raise nonsexist children. At the same time, other communication from the culture intones a quite different message. It tells us that women may be able to get jobs, but fewer than 20% will actually be given opportunities to advance to the highest levels of professional life. Crime statistics warn us rape is rising, as is battering of women. We discover that married women may have careers, but more than 80% of them still do the majority of housework and child care. Medical researchers warn that eating disorders among women are epidemic, and media relentlessly carry the message that youth and beauty are women's tickets to success. Prevailing images of women are conflicting and confusing. The commentaries by Jeanne, Jana, Bernadette, and Debbie give us a better understanding of what femininity means, as these women explain how they feel about being a woman. These women recognize cultural expectations of women that have been noted by researchers and social commentators. We can identify five themes in current views of femininity and womanhood.

The first theme is that *appearance still counts*. Women are still judged by their looks. They are urged to be pretty, slim, and well dressed to be desirable. The focus on appearance begins in the early years of life, when girls are given dolls and clothes, both of which invite them to attend to appearance. Gift catalogues for children regularly feature makeup kits, adornments for hair, and even wigs so that girls learn early to spend time and effort on looking good. Dolls, like the ever-popular

Barbie, come with accessories such as extensive wardrobes so that girls learn that clothes and jewelry are important. Teen magazines for girls feature fashion and grooming sections and are saturated with ads for makeup, diet aids, and hair products. As Jeanne says, nearly every magazine, film, and television show spotlights a beautiful woman. The cultural injunction that women should be physically attractive remains unambiguous and unabated (Haag, 2000; Tavris & Baumgartner, 1983; Wolf, 1991). Central to current cultural expectations for women is thinness. Jeanne's comments powerfully show how tyrannical this expectation can be. Millions of women suffer from chronic dieting and eating disorders, and thousands die each year in their quest to meet the cultural demand for excessive thinness (Davies-Popelka, 2000; Rodin, Silberstein, & Striegel-Moore, 1985; Wooley & Wooley, 1984).

The cultural ideals of feminine beauty continue to reflect primarily White standards (Lont, 2001). This can create special tension for women of color who may be unable, on the one hand, to meet White standards of beauty and, on the other hand, to reject the standards that the culture as a whole prescribes. In a critique of Blacks' acceptance of White standards of beauty, bell hooks (1994, 1995) describes the color caste system among Blacks whereby lighter skin is considered more desirable. She also points out that Black children learn early to devalue dark skin, and many Black men regard biracial women as the ideal against which other

> ### ֎ JEANNE
>
> Hungry. That's what being a woman means to me. I am hungry all of the time. Either I'm dieting, or I'm throwing up because I ate too much. I am scared to death of being fat, and I'm just not made to be thin. I gain weight just by smelling food. I think about food all the time—wanting it but being afraid to eat, eating but feeling guilty. It's a no-win situation. I'm obsessed, and I know it, but I can't help it. How can I not think about my weight all the time, when every magazine, every movie, every television show I see screams at me that I have to be thin to be desirable?

> ### ֎ JANA
>
> I like being a woman today. It's the best time ever to be female, because we can have it all. When I finish my B.A., I plan to go to law school, and then I want to practice. I also want to have a family with two children. My mother couldn't have had the whole package, but I can. I love the freedom of being a woman in this time—there's nothing I can't do.

Black women are measured. Most women of color who are successful models resemble White women more than they resemble people of their race–ethnicity in features, hair, and skin tone. In a society as ethnically diverse as ours, we need to question and challenge standards that reflect and respect only the identities of some groups.

A second cultural expectation of women is *be sensitive and caring*. Girls and women are supposed to care about and for others and to be nice, responsive, supportive, and friendly. It's part of their role as defined by the culture. A number of studies (Aronson, 1992; Fabes & Laner, 1986; Hochschild, 1989; Okin, 1989; Wood, 1994b) reveal that women do the majority of caregiving for others. From assuming primary responsibility for young children to taking care of elderly, often sick or disabled relatives, women do the preponderance of hands-on caring. In interviews

I think expectations of women today are impossible. I read magazines for working women, since I plan to work in business when I graduate. They tell me how to be a good leader, how to make tough decisions and keep others motivated, how to budget my time and advance in an organization. Then in the same magazines there's an article on how to throw a great dinner party with a three-course meal plus appetizers and dessert. Am I supposed to do that after working from 8 to 6 every day? Somehow the husband's role in all of this never gets mentioned. It's all supposed to come together, but I don't see how. It seems to me that a career is a full-time responsibility and so is running a home, yet I get the feeling I'm supposed to do both and keep my cool all the time. I just don't see how.

with adult daughters who care for their aging mothers, Jane Aronson (1992) found that daughters thought this was required to meet society's definition of being "good women." Giving care to others is part of being a woman.

At the opening of this chapter, I asked you what an ideal day would be like for you 10 years in the future. The question is one that psychologist Barbara Kerr (1997, 1999) uses to learn about undergraduate students' expectations. She reports a striking sex difference in responses to the question (1999). College men tend to describe their perfect day like this:

> "I wake up and get into my car—a really nice, rebuilt '67 Mustang—and then I go to work—I think I'm some kind of manager of a computer firm—and then I go home, and when I get there, my wife is there at the door (she has a really nice figure), she has a drink for me and she's made a great meal. We watch TV or maybe play with the kids." (p. B7)

Contrast the men's perfect day with this typical description from college women:

> "I wake up, and my husband and I get in our twin Jettas, and I go to the law firm where I work. Then after work, I go home, and he's pulling up in the driveway at the same time. We go in and have a glass of nice wine, and we make an omelet together and eat by candlelight. Then the nanny brings the children in and we play with them until bedtime." (p. B7)

One major difference between the ideal day fantasies of Kerr's male and female students concerns the expectation of who takes care of the home and partners. Many heterosexual college men assume that their wives will work but will also be waiting for them at home with drinks and a prepared meal. Fewer and fewer college women see this as an ideal day—or life. Yet, women's fantasy of shared responsibilities for home and family are not likely to be met unless there are major changes in current patterns.

Major responsibilities for children and needy relatives are not the only care burdens expected of women: They are also supposed to be nice, deferential, and helpful in general, whereas men are not held to the same requirements (Hochschild, 1975, 1979, 1983). In their survey of schoolchildren, Carol Tavris and Alice Baumgartner (1983) found that both boys and girls recognized there were greater restrictions on girls' activities than on those of boys, they perceived that girls have to do more for others and less for themselves. The girls said that if they were to wake up male, they'd be able to "do anything." They would have more freedom because they wouldn't have to focus on others' needs.

There is one activity that both boys and girls in the study of schoolchildren saw as a female advantage. Girls and women are allowed to express feelings more openly than are boys and men. Males are expected to be "calm and cool," as one of the schoolchildren remarked; they cannot let on how they really feel, especially if they are afraid of things. Cultural views of femininity include expressiveness, which may explain why women often seem more aware of and comfortable talking about feelings than men are.

A third persistent theme of femininity is *negative treatment by others.* According to substantial research, this still more or less goes with the territory of being female. Supporting this theme are the differential values our culture attaches to masculinity and femininity. Elizabeth Janeway's (1971) early findings that devaluation is built into the feminine role in our culture remain true three decades after she first reported them. It's not only built into cultural views, but typically is internalized by individuals, including women. Through communication with parents, teachers, peers, and others and through media and education, girls learn that boys get more respect and more opportunities. It is a lesson retained as girls mature into womanhood. For instance, Arlie Hochschild (1983) has shown that

 DEBBIE

To me, being a woman means I'd better include the expenses of cosmetics, beauty salons, health clubs, and super clothes in my budget from now on. I have to worry about being attractive. Guys don't face that. If a guy looks bad, it's okay, but it's not okay for a girl. I've seen this in classes a lot. In one class I had last term, we had a woman professor who was really fabulous. She really knew her stuff, and she was interesting, funny, and smart. But her clothes were out of style and sometimes rumpled like she didn't iron them. I heard a lot of comments about how "sloppy" she was. In another class of mine, the man who taught it wore the same jacket almost every day. It was frayed at the sleeves and just kind of ratty, and his shirts were usually wrinkled. So I said something once about his sloppy dress, and my friend just laughed at me and said I ought to appreciate his "eccentric" style. See what I mean? It's a real double standard that you don't hear about much. Whatever else may have changed about views of women, the demand to look good hasn't.

female flight attendants are more often verbally abused by passengers than are their male peers. Further, Hochschild reveals that both male and female flight attendants understand this pattern and accept it.

The knowledge that U.S. society values males more than females is imparted early as responses from schoolchildren make clear. Girls who imagined waking up as boys said (Tavris & Baumgartner, 1983, p. 94), "My dad would respect me more if I were a boy" and "My father would be closer because I'd be the son he always wanted." Early awareness of cultural disregard for women, coupled with ongoing elaboration of that theme, erodes the foundations of self-esteem and self-confidence. Given this, it's no wonder that girls and women generally suffer more depression and have lower self-confidence and belief in themselves than males: From birth they've been told that they *are* worth less than their male peers (French, 1992).

Is Adolescence a Danger Zone for Girls?

What is it that causes so many confident, happy 8- and 9-year-old girls to become unsure of themselves and unhappy when they are 11 to 14? Surely, adolescence is a confusing time for both boys and girls, but researchers report that girls suffer greater assaults on self-esteem and confidence than boys (Gilligan et al., 1988; Lally, 1996).

The Carnegie Council on Adolescent Development documented an alarming rise in the suicide rate for girls between ages 10 and 14. A less dramatic and more common problem faced by girls at this age is the loss of confidence in their own identities and a related emphasis on pleasing others. As girls enter puberty, society, peers, and sometimes family encourage them to focus on pleasing others. Girls are encouraged to lose weight, dress well, and use makeup so that others will find them attractive. They're taught to soften their opinions and to accommodate the wishes of others, particularly males. In an extensive interview study, one 15-year-old said that if she stood up to males at school and spoke her mind, they immediately called her a "bitch" (Haag, 2000). In the early teens, girls get the message that it's more important to make others feel good than to ask for what they want or speak up honestly. Anxiety about measuring up to stereotypical ideals of beauty was greater in White than in Black girls (Garrod, Ward, Robinson, & Kilkenny, 1999; Haag, 2000). The upshot is that, for many girls, adolescence means shifting attention from becoming personally competent to pleasing others. What's at stake is loss of self.

Another aspect of negative treatment of women is the violence inflicted on them. They are vulnerable in ways men generally are not to battering, rape, and other forms of abuse (Goldner et al., 1990; Gordon, 1988; Thompson, 1991; Wood, 2001b). Tavris and Baumgartner (1983) found that even 9-year-old boys and girls realize women are subject to violence from others. Contemplating waking up female, the boys said (p. 94), "I'd have to know how to handle drunk guys and rapists" (8th grader); "I would have to be around other girls for safety" (6th grader); "I would always carry a gun for protection" (4th grader). Vulnerability to violence is part of femininity in Western culture. Chapter 11 explores gendered violence in detail.

Be superwoman is a fourth theme emerging in cultural expectations of women, one well expressed by Bernadette. Jana's sense of exhilaration at "being able to have it all" is tempered by the realization that the idea that women *can* have it all appears to be transformed into the command that they *must* have it all. It's not enough to be just a homemaker and mother or to just have a career—young women seem to feel they are expected to do it all.

Women students talk with me frequently about the tension they feel in trying to figure out how to have a full family life and a successful career. They tell me that, in interviewing for jobs, they have to make compromises to locate where their romantic partners have jobs. They ask me how to stay on the fast track in business when they foresee taking off at least some time to have one or more children. How, they ask, can I advance in business like a man when I also have to be a mother? The physical and psychological toll on women who try to do it all is well documented (Coltrane & Adams, 2001; Greenberg, 2001; Orenstein, 2000), and it is growing steadily as women find that changes in the workplace are not paralleled by changes in home responsibilities. Perhaps it would be wise to realize that superwoman, like superman, is a comic-book character, not a viable model for real life. Recent reports suggest a number of women are deciding that they don't want to be superwoman. Instead of wanting to have it all, a number of young women seem to be aiming to have some of it all—some career, some family (Greenberg, 2001; Orenstein, 2000).

A final theme of femininity in the 1990s is one that reflects all of the others and the contradictions inherent in them: *There is no single meaning of "feminine" anymore.* Society no longer has a consensual view of who women are or what they are supposed to do, think, and be. A woman who is assertive and ambitious in a career is likely to meet with approval, disapproval, and curiosity from some people and be applauded by others. At the same time, a woman who chooses to stay home while her children are young will be criticized by some women and men, envied by others, respected by some, and disregarded by still others. Currently, multiple views of femininity are vying for legitimacy. This makes being a woman very confusing. Yet it also underlines the excitement and possibilities open to women of this era to validate multiple versions of femininity. Perhaps, as Sharon suggests in her commentary, there are many ways to be feminine, and we can respect all of them.

Prevailing themes of femininity in North America reveal both constancy and change. Traditional expectations of attractiveness and caregiving to others persist, as does the continuing devaluation of anything considered feminine. Change, however, is signaled by expanding opportunities and less consensus on what a woman must do and be. There are different options, which may allow women with different talents, interests, and gender orientations to define themselves in diverse ways and to chart life courses that suit them as individuals.

SUMMARY

In this chapter, we have considered formative influences on gender identity and how they are reflected later in adult life. Beginning with Mead's symbolic interactionist theory, we saw that children are literally talked into membership in the human community. Through interaction, we learn how others see us and import their views into our self-conception so that how we view ourselves is inevitably laced with social overtones. We rely on internal dialogues to resist social views of gender or to conform to them by guiding thought, feeling, and action. Interactions with others also affect the structure of the psyche, which is the core of human identity. Because this process occurs in our first stage of life, it profoundly shapes our sense of who we are as gendered individuals. We build on the psychic understanding of gender through interaction with parents, teachers, peers, and others whose communication provides us with both direct instruction and models of femininity and masculinity.

Theory and research about gender identity have practical, personal implications. Communication about being masculine and feminine in childhood affects how we define ourselves as adults, what feelings we allow and suppress, what constraints we experience on our activities, and how we judge our basic self-worth. Communication plays a primary role in shaping gender identity. Through interaction with others, we come to understand how society defines masculinity and femininity and what specific individuals such as parents, teachers, and peers expect of us. Communication creates gendered identities by transforming us from biological males and females into gendered individuals.

Before we leave our discussion of influences on gender identity, it's important to reiterate the role of personal choice in defining ourselves. Socialization is not as relentless and deterministic a force as it may sometimes seem. Clearly, we are influenced by the expectations of our culture as those are communicated to us in interaction with individuals and institutions. Yet we also contribute to social understandings of gender. By reflecting on how our society views masculinity and femininity and how those expectations of gender are communicated to us, we enlarge our capacity to think critically about the desirability of cultural views in general and their appropriateness for each of us in particular.

It's also important to remember that social views of gender are not self-sustaining. They endure only to the extent that individuals and institutions persist in reproducing them through their own activities. Through our own communication and the ways that we embody masculinity and femininity, we participate in reinforcing or altering cultural views of masculinity and femininity. Shifts in social expectations of gender that emerged in students' descriptions of the meaning of manliness and womanliness clue us to the important realization that what gender means is not fixed—it changes. How it changes and what sorts of revisions it includes depend on individual and social practices that question existing views of gender and argue for new views that enable us to define ourselves and live our lives as we choose.

DISCUSSION QUESTIONS

1. Use InfoTrac's College Edition's EasyTrac option. Type in "Single fathers," then access the 2001 *Time* article, "Father makes two: Unmarried men who raise children are one of the fastest-growing groups in America." What reasons are given for the increase in unmarried single fathers? Do their challenges seem similar to those of unmarried single mothers?

2. Would you describe your ego boundaries as relatively permeable or rigid? How did you develop a sense of yourself as more connected to others or independent of them? How do your ego boundaries influence your current relationships with others? How do permeable ones enrich life and relationships? How might they constrain and limit someone? What are the advantages of rigid ego boundaries? How might they restrict a person? How do you perceive Western culture values permeable and rigid ego boundaries? Do you think other cultures, particularly ones that are more collectivist than the West, would perceive permeable and rigid boundaries differently?

3. What kinds of toys did you receive as a child? Were you encouraged to like and play with "gender-appropriate" toys? Did you ever ask for a toy that your parents told you was not appropriate for you? Are there differences in how parents responded to men and women students' interest in cross-gender toys?

4. What kinds of chores and responsibilities did you have growing up in your family? Were they consistent with social definitions of your gender? Did you help with outside work or activities inside the home? Did you ever resent what you were told to do and what you were told was not your job?

5. How did your parents model masculinity and femininity? Explain how parents (mother, stepmother, father, stepfather) represent what it means to be feminine and masculine. Does your own embodiment of gender reflect influences from them?

6. Think back to your childhood. What do you recall about your interactions with each of your parents or stepparents? Did your parents follow the patterns typical of each sex that were discussed in this chapter? Did your mother emphasize relationships and emotional security and your father emphasize risk taking and achievement?

7. Do you think the themes of masculinity discussed in this chapter apply to men today? If you are a man, do you feel you're expected to be successful, aggressive, sexual, self-reliant, and not feminine? Do you feel pressures both to conform to and to depart from traditional views of manhood? How do these social expectations affect your options and your comfort as a person? If you are a woman, are these themes ones you associate with masculinity and expect in men? How might this be limiting for your relationships?

8. Do you think the five themes of femininity identified in this chapter still apply to women? If you are a woman, do you feel you are supposed to be attractive and sensitive to others? Do you expect to be treated negatively (from being trivialized to being vulnerable to rape) because of your sex? To what extent do you feel pressured to be superwoman—be it all, do it all? If you are a man, are the themes of femininity ones that are part of your thinking and expectations about women? How might endorsing these themes limit your relationships with women?

9. Write a page or so describing what it means to you to be a man or a woman today. Specify what you like and dislike about being a woman or a man. As a class, discuss your views of femininity and masculinity and the ways in which they are comfortable and inhibiting in your lives.

7 | Gendered Close Relationships

Perhaps you have found yourself in situations such as those Paige and Mark describe. If you are a heterosexual man, Mark's predicament may remind you of ones in your own life. If you are a heterosexual woman, Paige's (see p. 182) frustration may be more familiar to you. What they describe reflects gendered orientations toward close relationships. For Mark, as for most people socialized into masculinity, the purpose of talking is to accomplish some goal or solve some problem; for his partner, talking about the relationship is a primary means to intimacy. Paige cannot understand how Ed could concentrate on his paper when there is a problem between them; for Ed, the paper is a way to distract himself from something that matters very much. If Paige and Ed and Mark and Ellen do not figure out that their gendered viewpoints are creating misunderstandings, they will continue to find themselves at cross-purposes.

In this chapter, we will focus on gender dynamics in close relationships. To begin our discussion, we will consider masculine and feminine ways of experiencing and expressing closeness. Next we'll explore gendered dynamics in friendships and romantic relationships. As we explore interaction in close relationships, we want not only to understand masculine and feminine inclinations but also to ap-

---

 PAIGE

Honestly, I almost left my boyfriend when we had our first fight after moving in together. It was really a big one about how to be committed to our relationship and also do all the other stuff that we have to do. It was major. And after we'd yelled for a while, there seemed to be nothing else to do—we were just at a stalemate in terms of conflict between what each of us wanted. So Ed walked away, and I sat fuming in the living room. When I finally left the living room, I found him working away on a paper for one of his courses, and I was furious. I couldn't understand how he could concentrate on work when we were so messed up. How in the world could he just put us aside and get on with his work? I felt like it was a really clear message that he wasn't very committed.

preciate each on its own terms. Equally important, we want to consider alternatives to cultural prescriptions for how men and women should interact in their significant relationships.

THE MEANING OF PERSONAL RELATIONSHIPS

◼ Defining Personal Relationships

Of the many relationships we form, only a few become close and personal. These are the ones that occupy a special place in our lives and affect us more than other, less important associations we have. **Personal relationships** are those that endure over time and in which participants depend on one another for various things from affection to material assistance. Not all relationships marked by continuing interdependence are personal. For instance, two colleagues might work together for many years and help each other in varied ways without ever becoming personally involved. The essence of a close personal relationship is the strong feelings the individuals have for each other (Blumstein & Kollock, 1988; Brehm, 1992). If a social partner leaves or dies, a replacement may be found, and the functional relationship continues. When a personal partner leaves or dies, however, the relationship ends, although we may continue to feel connected to the person who is no longer with us.

◼ Gender and Closeness

There are notable differences in masculine and feminine approaches to close relationships, which generally—but not universally—coincide with male and female approaches to relationships. Yet researchers disagree about how to interpret the differences. Although some scholars argue that masculine interpersonal styles are inferior to feminine ones, others think the two styles are distinct yet equally valid. So that you may evaluate these two viewpoints, we will consider each.

The male deficit model. Based on a long-standing cultural definition of women as relationship experts, our society tends to regard women as more interpersonally sensitive and competent than men. Because women are perceived as relationship experts, their ways of forming relationships and interacting with others are presumed to be "the right ways." Operating from this premise, a number of researchers consider men's ways of relating to be inadequate. This view, the **male deficit model,** maintains that men are not adept at intimacy because they are less interested or able than women to disclose emotions, reveal personal information, and engage in communication about intimate topics.

The central assumption of the male deficit model is that personal, emotional talk is the hallmark of intimacy. With this assumption in mind, researchers began to study how women and men interacted in close relationships. A classic investigation (Caldwell & Peplau, 1982) measured the intimacy of men's and women's friendships by how much intimate information was confided—a kind of communication generally used more by women than by men. Given this measure of intimacy, it is not surprising that women were found to be more intimate than men. Findings such as this led to judgments that men's ways of relating are inadequate. Some researchers (Balswick & Peek, 1976) argued that men's inexpressiveness is a tragedy of our society. The solution recommended was for men to overcome masculine socialization by getting in touch with their feelings and learning to communicate openly and expressively (Pleck & Sawyer, 1974; Tognoli, 1980).

The trend to privilege women's ways of relating and disparage men's was heightened in the 1960s by the rhetorical movements that we discussed in Chapter 3. Early male feminists thought that men were emotionally repressed and would be enriched by becoming more aware and expressive of their feelings, and many men worked on developing and expressing emotions more openly in their relationships. In the 1980s, the male deficit model continued to prevail. Researchers claimed that men "feel threatened by intimacy" (Mazur & Olver, 1987, p. 533); men are "lacking in mutual self-disclosure, shared feelings and other demonstrations of emotional closeness" (Williams, 1985, p. 588); men suffer from "stunted emotional development" (Balswick, 1988); men do not know how to experience or communicate feelings (Aukett, Ritchie, & Mill, 1988); and men should learn to talk openly about their emotions (Tognoli, 1980).

Much academic and popular sentiment still holds that men are unskilled in expressing emotions and caring (Burleson, 1997; Oliker, 2001). A number of books written in the late 1990s and early part of this century state that personal disclosures are the crux of intimacy, that women have more intimate relationships than men, that boys' friendships lack the emotional depth of girls' friendships, and that males focus on activities to avoid intimacy (see Wood & Inman, 1993). What needed to be asked, however, is whether we should assume that activities cannot lead to intimacy and whether emotional and personal disclosures are the only way to create closeness. Questions like these have led to a second interpretation of differences between how men and women, in general, create and experience closeness.

The alternate paths model. The **alternate paths model** agrees with the male deficit model that gendered socialization is the root of differences in

 EDWIN

I don't have any problem being emotionally sensitive or expressing my feelings. I may not go on forever about my feelings, but I know what they are, and I can express them fine. It's just that the way I express my feelings is different from the way most girls I know express their feelings. I'm not dramatic or sentimental or gushy, but I have ways of showing how I feel.

women's and men's typical styles of interacting. It departs from the deficit model, however, in important ways. First, the alternate paths viewpoint does not presume that men lack feelings or emotional depth or that relationships and feelings are unimportant in men's lives. Rather, the alternate paths explanation suggests that masculine socialization constrains men's comfort in verbally expressing some feelings and, further, that it limits men's opportunities to practice emotional talk. A second important distinction is that the alternate paths model argues that men *do* express closeness in ways that they value and understand—ways that may differ from women's but that are nonetheless valid.

Françoise Cancian (1987, 1989) calls attention to the "feminization of love," meaning that the ways we have learned to think about close, personal relationships are heavily gendered. As a culture, she suggests, we use a "feminine ruler" to define and measure closeness. She also argues that using a specifically feminine standard (emotional talk) automatically misrepresents and devalues masculine modes of caring in the same way that using male standards to measure women's speech distorts the unique qualities of women's communication. Cancian argues that men's and women's ways of demonstrating affection, however different, are both valid when judged on their own terms. She states (1987, p. 78), "There is a distinctive masculine style of love, . . . but it is usually ignored by scholars and the general public."

Influenced by this viewpoint, Scott Swain (1989) studied men's perceptions of their close friendships. He discovered that men develop a closeness "in the doing"—a kind of connection that grows out of engaging in activities. His research suggests that men engage in activities not as a substitute for intimacy but, in fact, as an alternate path to closeness. Other scholars (Clark, 1998; Paul & White, 1990; Tavris, 1992; Wright, 1988) agreed and began to study how men express closeness and what they appreciate from others as demonstrations of caring. Drury Sherrod's (1989) research led him to conclude that men's friendships are no less intimate than women's, but "men generally do not express intimacy through self-disclosure" (p. 168). There is also some evidence that talking about problems may be less effective than diversionary activities in relieving men's stress and enhancing their feelings of closeness (Riessman, 1990; Swain, 1989; Tavris, 1992).

Recent research provides further insight into gendered communication in close relationships. In a study of how men and women communicate support, Daena Goldsmith and Susan Dun (1997) found that women tend to engage in both emotional and instrumental forms of communication. Similarly, Françoise Cancian and Stacey Oliker (2000) found that women friends enjoy doing things together and helping each other out. In general, most men engage in less emotional forms of communication, preferring instead to provide support in the form of trying to deny, minimize, or solve others' problems. Yet men do experience and express emotions in a range of ways, and they can be very sentimental (Chapman & Hendler, 1999).

The sex of the person needing support may be as important as the sex of the person offering support. Communication scholars Jerold Hale, Rachael Tighe, and Paul Mongeau (1997) report that women typically engage in more sensitive comforting messages than men. However, both sexes are more overtly sensitive and feeling when trying to comfort women than when trying to comfort men. Further, these researchers found that men offer more sensitive comforting communication in response to major stresses, whereas women tend to provide sensitive comfort for both major stresses and daily events.

The safest conclusion may be that males less often express their feelings in feminine ways, just as women less frequently express theirs in masculine ways. This suggests some men may find that intimate talk doesn't make them feel close, just as some women find instrumental demonstrations of commitment unsatisfying. If so, then becoming "bilingual" is a necessity for healthy relationships. Understanding alternative ways of creating and sustaining intimacy empowers us to create and participate in a range of ways of communicating with others who matter to us.

GENDERED FRIENDSHIPS

As we explore women's and men's communication in friendships and romantic commitments, keep in mind the possibility that we may be seeing only different, not differently valuable, orientations toward closeness. The goal is not to judge which is better but to understand and learn from each orientation.

◼ Commonalities in Women's and Men's Friendships

Before we consider differences between the genders, we should note that there are some important commonalities in masculine and feminine views of friendship. Both women and men value intimate same-sex friends, and both agree on basic qualities of close friendships: intimacy, acceptance, trust, and help (Reis, 1998; Sherrod, 1989). Other researchers concur that in many respects there are few substantial differences between the sexes' friendships (Berscheid, Snyder, & Omoto, 1989; Duck & Wright, 1993; Jones, 1991; Umberson, Chen, House, Hopkins, & Slaten, 1996).

◼ Differences Between Women's and Men's Friendships

Against the backdrop of commonalities in the genders' understandings of friendships, we now explore general differences in how women and men typically—but not invariably—create friendships and interact within them. As we consider this topic, we want to be careful not to misinterpret distinct styles by assuming that one is superior.

As early as 1982, Paul Wright pointed to interaction style as a key difference between women's and men's friendships. He noted that women tend to engage each other face to face, whereas men usually interact side by side. By this, Wright meant that women are more likely than men to communicate directly and verbally with each other in order to share themselves and their feelings. Men more typically engage in activities with friends. Wright suggested that the crux of friendship differs between the sexes: For men, it tends to be doing things together; for women, being and talking together is the essence.

The fact that women use talk as a primary way to develop relationships and men generally rely less on talk to relate to friends underlies four gender-linked patterns in friendship. First, communication is typically central to women friends, whereas activities tend to be the primary focus of men's friendships. Second, talk between women friends tends to be expressive and disclosive, focusing on details of personal lives, people, relationships, and feelings; talk in men's friendships generally revolves around less personal topics such as sports, events, money, music, and politics. Third, in general, men assume a friendship's value and seldom discuss it, whereas women are likely to talk about the dynamics of their relationship. Finally, women's friendships generally appear to be broader in scope than those of men. Let's now see how these differences lead to unique kinds of friendship between women, between men, and between men and women.

■ Women's Friendships: Closeness in Dialogue

In an early study, Elizabeth Aries and Fern Johnson (1983) reported that women use talk to build connections with friends. They share their personal feelings, experiences, fears, and problems in order to know and be known by each other. In addition, Aries and Johnson note, women exchange information about their daily lives and activities. By sharing details of lives, women feel intimately and continuously connected to one another (Rubin, 1985; Schaef, 1981). To capture the special quality of friendship that women create through talking, Caroline Becker (1987) describes women's friendships as "an evolving dialogue" through which initially separate worlds are woven together into a common one. Becker writes (p. 65), "As time spent together continues and each woman brings important parts of her life into the friendship, a world of shared meanings and understanding is created." The common world of women friends grows directly out of ongoing communication that is the crux of closeness between women.

In general, for women feeling close is facilitated by knowing each other in depth. To achieve this, women tend to talk about personal feelings and disclose intimate information (Aries & Johnson, 1983; Buhrke & Fuqua, 1987; Johnson, 1996; Oliker, 1989; Reisman, 1990). They act as confidantes for each other, respecting the courage required to expose personal vulnerabilities and inner feelings. Consistent with gender socialization, women's communication also tends to be expressive and supportive (Aukett, Ritchie, & Mill, 1988; Maccoby, 1998; Schaef, 1981; Wright &

Scanlon, 1991). Typically, there is a high level of re- sponsiveness and caring in women's talk, which en- hances the emotional quality of women's friend- ships (Aries & Johnson, 1983). The more permeable ego boundaries encouraged by feminine socializa- tion cultivate women's ability to empathize and to feel a part of each other's life.

Because women are socialized to be attentive, emotionally supportive, and caring, certain prob- lems may arise in their relationships. Clinicians have pointed out that feminine norms of commu- nication make it difficult for women to deal with feelings of envy and competition (Eichenbaum & Orbach, 1987; Rubin, 1985). It is not that women do not experience envy and competitiveness, but rather that they think it's wrong to have such feel- ings. Being jealous of a friend lies outside of cultural prescriptions for femininity, so women may repress or avoid talking with each other about these taboo feelings. Avoidance, however, may harm friend-

> ### ♀ JANICE
>
> One of the worst things about being female is not having permission to be selfish or jealous or *not* to care about a friend. Usually, I'm pretty nice; I feel good for my friends when good things happen to them, and I want to sup- port them when things aren't going well. But sometimes I don't feel that way. Like right now, all my friends and I are interviewing for jobs, and my best friend just got a great offer. I've had 23 interviews and no job offers so far. I felt good for Sally, but I also felt jeal- ous. I couldn't talk about this with her, because I'm not supposed to feel jeal- ous or to be selfish like this. It's just not allowed, so my friends and I have to hide those feelings.

ships by creating barriers and distance. For this reason, clinicians like Luise Eichen- baum and Suzie Orbach advise women to recognize and learn to deal openly with envy and competition. It's also the case that women may find it difficult to override socialization's message that they are supposed to be constantly available and caring. Thus, when women lack the time or energy required to nurture others, they may feel guilty and self-critical (Eichenbaum & Orbach, 1983; Miller, 1986). The re- sponsiveness and caring typical of women's friendships both enrich and constrain people socialized into feminine rules of relating.

Another quality of communication between women friends is explicit talk about their relationship. The friendship itself and the dynamics between women are mat- ters of interest and discussion (Winstead, 1986). It is not unusual for women to state affection explicitly or to discuss tensions within a friendship. The ability to recognize and deal with interpersonal difficulties allows women to monitor their friendships and improve them in ways that enhance satisfaction.

A final quality typical of women's friendships is breadth (Caldwell & Peplau, 1982; Wright, 1982; Wright & Scanlon, 1991). With close friends, women tend not to restrict their disclosures to specific areas but invite each other into many aspects of their lives. Because women talk in detail about varied aspects of their lives, they know each other in complex and layered ways (Aries & Johnson, 1983; Buhrke & Fuqua, 1987; Rubin, 1983, 1985). Typically, this renders close friendships between women broad in scope. In summary, women's friendships tend to develop out of the central role accorded to communication, which allows disclosures, expressive-

ness, depth and breadth of knowledge, and attentiveness to the evolving nature of the relationships. Because they know the basic rhythms of each other's lives, women friends often feel interconnected even when they are not physically together.

Men's Friendships: Closeness in the Doing

Like women, men value friendships and count on friends to be there for them. However, many men create and express closeness more through action than through talk. Activities, rather than conversation, are generally the center of most men's friendships (Aries & Johnson, 1983; Duck, 1988; Mazur & Olver, 1987; Paul & White, 1990; Reisman, 1990; Riessman, 1990; Wood & Inman, 1993). Beginning in childhood, interaction between males often revolves around shared activities, particularly sports. Scott Swain's (1989) phrase "closeness in the doing" captures the way most men create and experience friendships. More than two-thirds of men in Swain's study described activities other than talking as the most meaningful times with friends. Engaging in sports, watching games, and doing other things together cultivate a sense of camaraderie and closeness between men (Sherrod, 1989; Williams, 1985). Whereas women tend to look for confidantes in friends, men more typically seek companions (Inman, 1996). Much of the research on men's friendships suggests they perceive talking as only one way—and maybe not the best one—to be close to others (Cancian, 1987; Monsour, 1992; Swain, 1989).

Growing out of the emphasis on activities is a second feature of men's friendships: an instrumental focus. Many men like to do things for people they care about (Cancian, 1987; Sherrod, 1989). Swain (1989) describes men's friendships as involving a give-and-take of favors, skills, and assistance. Instead of being the focus of interaction, for many men talk tends to accompany activities and to be

⚡ KEITH

My best friend and I almost never sit and just talk. Mainly we do things together, like go places or shoot hoops or watch games on TV. When we do talk, we talk about what we have done or plan to do or what's happening in our lives, but we don't say much about how we feel. I don't think we need to. You can say a lot without words.

about impersonal topics, especially sports (Aries & Johnson, 1983; Sherman & Haas, 1984). Between men, there is often a sense of reciprocity, for example, one offers expertise in repairing cars and the other provides computer skills—an exchange of favors that allows each man to hold his own while showing he cares about the other. The masculine inclination toward instrumentality also surfaces in how men help each other through rough times. Rather than engaging in explicit, expressive conversation about problems as women often do, men are more likely to help a friend out by distracting him from troubles with diversionary activities (Cancian, 1987; Riessman, 1990; Tavris, 1992).

The masculine emphasis on doing things together may explain why men's friendships are less likely to last if one friend moves away. According to Mary Rohlfing (1995), women friends can sustain their closeness in dialogue through phone calls, letters, and electronic mail. It's more difficult to shoot hoops or go to concerts with someone who lives miles away.

Third, men's relationships are distinguished by what Swain (1989) labels "covert intimacy." In contrast to the overt expressions of caring between women, men tend to signal affection through indirect, nonverbal means. These include joking, engaging in friendly competition, razzing, and being together in comfortable companionship. Perhaps because men are socialized not to express personal feelings, most find it awkward to say "I care about you" or "Our relationship really matters to me," or

 LEE

I don't know what girls get out of sitting around talking about problems all the time. What a downer. When something bad happens to me, like I blow a test or break up with a girl, the last thing I want is to talk about it. I already feel bad enough. What I want is something to distract me from how lousy I feel. That's where having buddies really matters. They know you feel bad and help you out by taking you out drinking or starting a pickup game or something that gets your mind off the problems. They give you breathing room and some escape from troubles; girls just wallow in troubles.

JOEL

The best thing about guys' friendships is that you can just relax and hang out together. With women you have to be on—intense, talking all the time—but with guys you can just be comfortable. It's not like we're not close, but we don't have to talk about it or about our lives all the time like girls do. It's more laid back and easygoing. I don't know about other guys, but I feel a lot closer to guys than to girls.

to hug, all of which are comfortable for many women. Instead, men tease, interact without explicitly discussing their friendship, and touch each other in sports or in playful punches and backslapping (Mazur & Olver, 1987; Swain, 1989). An exception to this is androgynous men, who, more than their sex-typed brothers, engage in expressive, emotional communication (Williams, 1985).

Communication scholar Kory Floyd studies sex differences in communicating affection. From a series of studies (1995, 1996a, 1996b, 1997a, 1997b), Floyd concludes that both women and men consider expressions of affection important, yet men are likely to restrict these expressions to opposite-sex relationships, whereas women employ them in both same-sex and opposite-sex relationships. Floyd thinks that expressing affection is considered less appropriate in male friendships than in male–female friendships or romantic relationships (1997b). Floyd notes, however, that the infrequency of overt expressions of affection between men does not mean that men don't have and value close friendships. He concludes that men "simply communicate affection in different, more 'covert' ways, so as to avoid the possible ridicule that more overt expression might invite" (1997b, p. 78).

Finally, men's friendships are often, although not always, more restricted in scope than women's. A number of researchers (Bell, 1981; Buhrke & Fuqua, 1987; Davidson & Duberman, 1982) report that men tend to have different friends for various spheres of interest rather than doing everything with any one friend. Another study (Wright & Scanlon, 1991) reports that men's relationships tend to center around specific, structured activities. Thus, Jim might meet Ed for racquetball matches, get together with Bob for poker, and go out drinking with Randy. Because they tend to limit friendship to particular areas, men may not share as many dimensions of their lives as is typical of women friends. Overall, then, men's friendships involve shared activities, instrumental demonstrations of commitment, covert intimacy, and limited spheres of interaction.

In summary, distinctive patterns of communication define unique qualities of men's and women's friendships. Women tend to see closeness as sharing themselves and their lives through personal communication. Men more typically create closeness by sharing particular activities and interests and by doing things with and for others. Describing these gender differences, Lillian Rubin (1985) writes that men tend to bond nonverbally through sharing experiences, whereas women typically become intimate through communicating verbally.

■ Friendships Between Women and Men

Differences typical of how women and men experience and express closeness make friendships between the sexes particularly interesting. They pose unique challenges and offer special opportunities for growth. Because our culture so heavily emphasizes gender, it is difficult for women and men not to see each other in sexual terms (Bingham, 1996; Johnson, Stockdale, & Saal, 1991; O'Meara, 1989). Even when cross-sex friends are not sexually involved, an undertone of sexuality often punctuates their friendship.

Another impediment to friendship between women and men is sex segregation in our society. Beginning in childhood, males and females are often separated, as are their activities (Cohen, 1997; Thorne, 1986). We have Boy Scouts and Girl Scouts, rather than Scouts, and most athletic teams are sex segregated. As boys and girls interact with same-sex peers and enter into distinct speech communities, differences are compounded by learning different styles of interaction. Because males and females generally learn alternative rules for communicating, there is greater potential for misunderstanding and awkwardness in mixed-sex friendships. This seems true for African Americans as well as for Caucasians (Gary, 1987).

Despite these difficulties, many women and men do form friendships with each other and find them rewarding (West, Anderson, & Duck, 1996). In mixed-sex friendships, each partner has something unique to offer as the expert in particular areas. Women may lead the way in providing personal

 RAUL

Last year I got to be /
a girl who was in one of m/
I felt I could tell her things I wou.
tell my guy friends. She was always willing to listen and empathize with my problems, and she never put me down if I felt bad or hurt or anything. I always felt better about whatever was wrong after I talked with her because she was so accepting and supportive, and in later situations she never threw up weaknesses I revealed.

support, whereas men tend to have more skill in using activities to increase closeness. Years ago, an insightful psychiatrist (Sullivan, 1953) claimed that intimacy and companionship are basic needs of all humans, ones that men and women are differentially encouraged to cultivate in themselves. For many women, a primary benefit of friendships with men is fun——companionship that is less emotionally intense than that with women friends. For men, an especially valued benefit of closeness with women is access to emotional and expressive support, which tends to be less overtly communicated in friendships between men. Men say they receive more emotional support and therapeutic release with women than with men friends. The greater supportiveness of women also is reported by women, who say they receive less of it from men than from women friends (Aries & Johnson, 1983; Aukett, Ritchie, & Mill, 1988; Reisman, 1990). This may explain why both sexes seek a woman friend in times of stress and why both women and men are generally more comfortable self-disclosing to women than to men (Buhrke & Fuqua, 1987; Rubin, 1985). Research also shows that people who interact with women more than with men tend to be healthier (Reis, Senchak, & Soloman, 1985). These patterns reflect cultural views that it is women who nurture, support, and care for others.

Differences in men's and women's communication styles show up in friendships between them. In general, men talk more and get more attention, response, and support than they offer to women with whom they are friends. Women often find there is less symmetry in their friendships with men than with other women, a pattern that echoes the male-dominant model in society at large. Thus, both women and men perceive women as more attentive, caring, and responsive, and a majority of both sexes report that friendships with women are closer and more satisfying than those with men (Aries & Johnson, 1983; Buhrke & Fuqua, 1987; Werking, 1997).

Differences in men's and women's ways of creating and sustaining friendships also surface in other kinds of close relationships. As we will see, the basic gendered patterns discussed here are prominent in dating and romantic commitments.

GENDERED ROMANTIC RELATIONSHIPS

Nowhere else are cultural expectations of masculinity and femininity so salient as in heterosexual romantic relationships. The cultural script for romance stipulates a number of rules that are well known to us: First, the romantic ideal promoted by our culture is decidedly heterosexual, which excludes transsexuals, intersexed people, gays, and lesbians, although they make up at least 10% of the population. The cultural script also specifies other things:

- Feminine women and masculine men are desirable.

- Men should initiate, plan, and direct activities and have greater power within the relationship.

- Women should facilitate conversation, generally defer to men, but control sexual behavior.

- Men should excel in status and earning money, and women should assume primary responsibility for the relationship, the home, and the children.

This heavily gendered cultural script is well understood by most people. In fact, in one study (Rose & Frieze, 1989), college students were asked to define the content of men's and women's roles on a first date, and there was virtually unanimous agreement on who did various things and when they were appropriate. The elements of this script are evident in both dating relationships and enduring commitments.

GINA

I consider myself a very independent, untraditional woman. I plan a career in law, and I am very assertive. But when it comes to dating relationships, I fall into some really conventional patterns. I think a woman should be able to call a guy she likes and ask him out, but I can't bring myself to do that. I also kind of expect guys to pay for dates, at least until a relationship gets serious, even though I think it's more fair to split expenses. I expect the guy I'm with to make plans and decisions about a date, and I expect myself to be more interpersonally sensitive. I guess some of the old roles do persist.

■ Developing Romantic Intimacy

Insight into what heterosexual men and women seek in romantic partners may be gleaned from reading personal advertisements. Ads written by men often emphasize the importance of stereotypically feminine physical qualities using words such as *attractive, slender, petite,* and *sexy.* Women's ads for male partners frequently emphasize status and success and include words such as *secure, ambitious, professional,* and *successful* (S. Davis, 1990; Smith, Waldorf, & Trembath, 1990). As in personal ads, in reality women's and men's views of desirable partners often reflect cultural gender expectations, emphasizing success in males and beauty in females (Stewart, Stinnett, & Rosenfeld, 2000).

The conventional heterosexual dating script

calls for men to take the initiative. Although many people, especially women, claim not to accept this pattern, research suggests that most heterosexuals conform to it (Cochran & Peplau, 1985; Riessman, 1990; Rubin, 1983). Conformity seems to reflect both our internalized sense of how we are supposed to be and the belief that the other sex expects us to meet cultural gender ideals. Thus, women tend to play feminine and men tend to play masculine, each reflecting and perpetuating established social views of gender. However, what counts as "playing feminine" or "playing masculine" is not fixed. Scripts, including sexual scripts, are changing, as the FYI box on this page shows.

There are exceptions to compliance with cultural scripts. Androgynous individuals, who break from rigid cultural definitions of masculinity and femininity, behave in more flexible, less stereotypical ways (DeLucia, 1987). There is also less role playing between gay men and even less between lesbian women (Kurdek & Schmitt, 1986b, 1986c, 1987). Because gays and lesbians are of the same sex and usually the same gender, gender differences tend to be less salient than in heterosexual romances. The tendency for greater role playing between gay men than be-

---

FYI

Changing Views of Feminine Sexuality

For most of America's history, there have been double standards for sexual activity. Men could be sexually active before marriage without risking serious disapproval. In fact, sexual experience and conquests were generally expected of men and respected by other men. For women, historically the rules were different. Having sex before marriage, or at least outside of a very serious relationship, would lead to widespread disapproval and disrespect. Men who "did it" were studs; women were tramps and sluts.

That seems to be changing. Paula Kamen, an academic and veteran journalist, interviewed young women to find out how they viewed their sexual identity and appropriate sexual conduct. Kamen reports that personal comfort and morality are the standards by which a majority of young women today make decisions about sexual identity and activity. Sexual choices ranging from remaining a virgin until marriage to engaging in group sex are evaluated against the standards of what individual women find comfortable and moral. For many young women today, morality is not measured primarily by religious prescriptions. Women whom Kamen interviewed accepted those religious teachings that were consistent with their sense of themselves and their sexuality and disregarded those that didn't support their personal identity.

Kamen also found that increasingly young women judge it comfortable and moral to have sex earlier and before marrying. Further, they are more likely than previous generations to know what turns them on sexually, to expect partners to satisfy them, and to have sex with multiple partners. Some young women today are comfortable having sex only with partners they love, but others enjoy casual sex in which sex and emotions are disconnected.

Sources: Kamen, P. (2001). *Her way: Young women remake the sexual revolution.* New York: New York University Press; McMillan, T. (2001, May 28). Generation sex. *In These Times*, pp. 24–25.

---

tween lesbian women, however, may reflect masculine socialization's emphasis on power (Blumstein & Schwartz, 1983; Kurdek & Schmitt, 1986c; Wood, 1993e).

Is one gender more romantic than the other? Contrary to folklore, research (Brehm, 1992) indicates that men tend to fall in love sooner and harder than women do. There are also differences in what love generally means to women and men. For men, it tends to be more active, impulsive, sexualized, and game playing than for women, whose styles of loving are more pragmatic and friendship focused (Cancian, 1987; Hendrick & Hendrick, 1986, 1996; Riessman, 1990). For instance, men may see love as taking trips to romantic places, spontaneously making love, and engaging in ploys to surprise a partner. Women might more typically think of quiet, extended conversation in front of a fire or comfort in each other's presence.

In romantic relationships, women are generally expected to assume the role of "relationship expert." This has long been recognized in heterosexual relationships (Cancian, 1987; Tavris, 1992; Wood, 1993a, 1998). Further evidence of the belief that women take care of relationships comes from studies of homosexual commitments. In lesbian couples, partners tend to take mutual responsibility for nurturing the dyad and for providing emotional direction and support (Eldridge & Gilbert, 1990; Kurdek & Schmitt, 1986c; Wood, 1993e). Because both women are likely to have internalized feminine identities, both are attentive to intimate dynamics. Gay couples, on the other hand, are least likely to have a partner who focuses on nurturing the dyad and provides emotional leadership (Kurdek & Schmitt, 1986b; Wood, 1993e).

Despite efforts to increase equality between the sexes, enduring heterosexual love relationships, in general, continue to reflect traditional gender roles endorsed by the culture (Riessman, 1990; Wood, 1993a). Men tend to be perceived as the head of the family and the major breadwinner; women tend to assume primary responsibility for domestic labor and child care; and men tend to have greater power.

Because gender distinctions are not as salient, gay and lesbian relationships depart from the roles characteristic of heterosexual couples. Research (Brehm, 1992; Huston & Schwartz, 1996) suggests that both gay and lesbian commitments resemble best-friend relationships with the added dimensions of sexuality and romance. Following the best-friends model, lesbian relationships tend to be monogamous and high in emotionality, disclosure, and support, and partners have the most equality of all types of relationships (Blumstein & Schwartz, 1983; Eldridge & Gilbert, 1990; Kurdek & Schmitt, 1986c). Gay couples are less monogamous (and more tolerant of extrarelationship sexual involvements), keenly sensitive to power issues, and lowest of all relationships in expressiveness and nurturance (Blumstein & Schwartz, 1983; Kurdek & Schmitt, 1986b; Wood, 1993e).

▇ Engaging in Committed Relationships

Gendered orientations influence four primary dimensions of couple involvement: modes of expressing care, needs for autonomy and connection, responsibility for relational maintenance, and power balance. As we will discover, these dynamics are

When Focusing on Feelings Backfires

In general, women have a greater tendency to pay attention to feelings than men. In many ways, this is positive. It can allow women to be in touch with their emotions and to work through feelings.

But there may be a down side. Susan Nolen-Hoeksema, a professor of psychology at the University of Michigan, has devoted more than 10 years to studying depression. According to Nolen-Hoeksema, women have a greater tendency than men to focus inwardly and brood about bad feelings. Her studies show that this can lead women to get stuck in unhappy feelings and to spiral downward emotionally. Such brooding is a major predictor of depression.

What does Nolen-Hoeksema suggest as more constructive ways of dealing with melancholy and sadness? She notes that distracting ourselves from gloomy feelings is a powerful antidote. Do something. Go somewhere. Get involved in an activity. Focus thoughts elsewhere. In other words, instrumental coping strategies may be helpful.

Source: Shea, C. (1998, January 30). Why depression strikes more women than men: "Ruminative coping" may provide answers. *Chronicle of Higher Education*, p. A14.

influenced by distinctive assumptions, styles, and preferences emphasized by masculine and feminine socialization.

Gendered modes of expressing care. As we have seen, women generally rely heavily on talk to create and express closeness, whereas men rely predominantly on instrumental activities. Anne Wilson Schaef (1981) notes that "women are often hurt in relationships with men because they totally expose their beings and do not receive respect and exposure in return" (p. 150). Conversely, men may sometimes feel uneasy or resentful when women pressure them to be emotionally expressive. To some men, intensely personal talk feels more intrusive than loving.

For many women, ongoing conversation about feelings and daily activities is a primary way to express and enrich connections between people. The masculine speech communities in which most men are socialized, however, regard the primary reasons to talk as solving problems and achieving goals. Thus, unless there is some problem, men often find talking about a relationship unnecessary, whereas women are more likely to feel that continuing conversation is the best way to keep problems from developing. These mismatched views about communication pave the way for misunderstandings, hurt, and dissatisfaction.

Modes of expressing closeness further reflect and reproduce gender by the different ways men and women tend to demonstrate they care. Catherine Riessman (1990) maintains that women and men often have different views of what intimacy means. For many women, she says (p. 24), closeness is identified with "communicating deeply and closely," whereas for most men "talk is not the centerpiece." This creates a likelihood that women and men may not recognize each other's styles of

PHIL

What does my girlfriend want? That's all I want to know. She says if I really loved her, I'd want to be together and talk all the time. I tell her all I do for her. I fix her car when it's broken; I give her rides to places; I helped her move last semester. We've talked about marriage, and I plan to take care of her then, too. I will work all day and overtime to give her a good home and to provide for our family. But she says, "Don't tell me what you *do* for me," like *do* is a bad word. Now, why would I do all this stuff if I didn't love her? Just tell me that.

SHARON

Most of this course has been a review of stuff I already knew, but the unit on how men and women show they love each other was news to me. I'm always fussing at my boyfriend for not showing me he cares. I tell him he takes me for granted and if he really loved me he'd want to talk more about personal, deep stuff inside him. But he bought me a book I'd been wanting, and a couple of weeks ago he spent a whole day fixing my car because he was worried about whether it was safe for me—I thought of that when we talked about the guy in the experiment who washed his wife's car. I guess he *has* been showing he cares for me, but I haven't been seeing it.

communicating care. The feminine style of loving seems important in romantic relationships. A study of 174 college dating couples found that both men and women were more satisfied with partners who embodied traditionally feminine qualities (Lamke, Sollie, Durbin, & Fitzpatrick, 1994). Specific communication skills valued by dating partners of both sexes included being willing to engage in intimate self-disclosure, giving emotionally supportive responses, and expressing one's own feelings clearly.

According to Françoise Cancian (1989, p. 18), "With the split between home and work and the polarization of gender roles, love became a feminine quality." Since that time, love has been measured by a "feminine ruler," which assumes that women's ways of loving are *the right ways*. The cultural bias favoring feminine modes of expressing love is illustrated by a classic study (Wills, Weiss, & Patterson, 1974) on the effects of increased demonstrations of affection between spouses. Husbands were instructed to engage in affectional behaviors toward their wives, and then the wives' responses were measured. When one wife showed no indication of receiving more affection, the researchers called the husband to see if he had followed instructions. Somewhat irately, the husband said he certainly had—that he had thoroughly washed his wife's car. Not only did his wife not experience this as affection, but the researchers themselves claimed he had "confused" instrumental with affectional behaviors. Doing something for someone was entirely disregarded as a valid way to express affection! This exemplifies the cultural bias toward feminine views of loving. It also illustrates a misunderstanding that plagues many heterosexual love relationships.

Gay and lesbian couples tend to have less discrepant understandings of the purpose of communication. Gay men, like their heterosexual counterparts, tend to engage in limited emotional and intimate dialogue and do not process their relationship constantly (Wood, 1993e). Lesbians, on the other hand, generally create the most expressive and nurturant communication climates of any type of couple, because both partners typically are socialized into feminine forms of interaction and, thus, value talk as a means of expressing feelings and creating closeness (Blumstein & Schwartz,

1983; Wood, 1993e). Lesbian partners' mutual attentiveness to nurturing and emotional openness may explain why researchers consistently find that lesbians report being more satisfied with their romantic relationships than gays or heterosexuals do (Eldridge & Gilbert, 1990; Kurdek & Schmitt, 1986c). Further, lesbian couples generally create intensely close and highly verbal intimacy (Kirpatrick, 1989).

Gendered preferences for autonomy and connection. Researchers and clinicians (Baxter, 1990; Bergner & Bergner, 1990; Goldner et al., 1990; Scarf, 1987; Thompson & Walker, 1989) state that autonomy and connection are two basic needs of all

> ## 𝒞 SHANNON
>
> I don't think I should be *the* one to take care of my marriage or children. I think that Vince and I should do that equally. But what I *think* and what I *feel* are different things. I feel I should be the one the kids count on. I feel I should take care of Vince and our home. The feelings are not so much from Vince as from me. I expect myself to be a caretaker. I hope the next generation of women doesn't feel as compelled to be caretakers as I and my peers do.

humans. We all need to feel we have both personal freedom and meaningful interrelatedness with others (Wood, 1995). What may differ is how much of each of these we want and how partners coordinate preferences. Masculine individuals tend to want greater autonomy and less connection than feminine persons, whose relative priorities are generally reversed. It is not that men want *only* autonomy and women want *only* connection. Both sexes tend to want both, yet the proportionate weights women and men assign to autonomy and connection generally differ.

Desires for different degrees of autonomy and connection frequently generate friction in close relationships, particularly in heterosexual ones. Many couples are familiar with a pattern called "demand–withdraw" (Christensen & Heavey, 1990) or "pursuer–distancer" (James, 1989). The dynamic of this pattern is that one partner seeks emotional closeness through disclosive, intimate communication, and the other partner withdraws from a degree of closeness that stifles his or her need for autonomy. The more one pursues, the more the other distances; the more one withdraws from interaction, the more the other demands talk and time together. Socialized toward independence, masculine individuals need some distance to feel comfortable, whereas feminine persons feel that closeness is jeopardized and that they are being rejected when a partner retreats from intimate talk (Wood, 1993a). Both men and women are more likely to demand changes they want in a partner and to withdraw when partners request changes in them. However, the intensity of withdrawal is greater when a woman requests change in a man than when a man requests change in a woman (Sagrestano, Heavey, & Christensen, 1998). British scholar Elizabeth Mapstone (1998) suggests this may be because many men are uncomfortable arguing with women. The irony is that the very thing that creates closeness for one partner impedes it for the other. As you might suspect, this pattern is less prominent in gay and lesbian relationships, in which both partners tend to have congruent desires for autonomy and connection.

More hurtful than the pattern itself, however, are partners' tendencies to inter-

LUANN reprinted by permission of United Features Syndicate, Inc.

pret each other according to rules that distort the other's behavior. For instance, to think that a man who wants time alone doesn't care for his partner or value a relationship is to interpret his actions through the rules of femininity. Similarly, to perceive a woman who wants intimate conversation as intrusive is to misjudge her by applying masculine standards. Although the pursuer–distancer pattern may persist in relationships, we can eliminate the poison of misinterpretation by respecting different needs for autonomy and connection (Bergner & Bergner, 1990).

Gendered responsibility for relational health. Lesbian partners generally share responsibility for keeping their relationship healthy. Because most lesbians, like the majority of heterosexual women, learn feminine ways of thinking and acting, both partners tend to be sensitive to interpersonal dynamics and willing to work out conflicts to enrich their bond (Blumstein & Schwartz, 1983; Kirpatrick, 1989; Wood, 1993e). Sharing responsibility for safeguarding a relationship lessens the pressure on each partner and also reduces the potential for conflict over investing in the relationship.

Against the standard set by lesbians, heterosexual couples do not fare so well in distributing responsibility for relational health. Women are widely expected to be relationship specialists, and both men and women tend to assume that women are more responsible for relationships and better at keeping them on track (Miller, 1986; Okin, 1989; Ragsdale, 1996; Rubin, 1985; Stafford, Dutton, & Haas, 2000). Because relationships and interpersonal sensitivity are not promoted in masculine socialization, some men are less aware of and less skilled in reading the nuances of personal interaction (Christensen & Heavey, 1990; Wamboldt & Reiss, 1989; Wood & Lenze, 1991b). Two scholars (Thompson & Walker, 1989) summarize much re-

> ### ✆ HAL
>
> My former girlfriend definitely wanted more connection than I was comfortable with. When we first started dating, we would call each other and talk on the phone for hours on end. After a while, though, I wasn't interested in long talks unless there was something important to say. But she kept calling and wanting to talk about all kinds of trivial things. I would have rather gone out, done something, gone somewhere, but she was happiest just talking on the phone or sitting around talking in person.

search in this area, concluding that wives "have more responsibility than their husbands for monitoring the relationship, confronting disagreeable issues, setting the tone of conversation, and moving toward resolution when conflict is high" (p. 849).

The expectation that one person should take care of relationships often cultivates problems. It inequitably burdens one partner while exempting the other person from responsibility (Cancian, 1987; Miller, 1986; Thompson & Walker, 1989). In addition, it is difficult for one person to meet relationship responsibilities if a partner does not acknowledge and work on matters that jeopardize relational health. What can happen is that the partner expected to safeguard the relationship is perceived as a nag by someone who fails to recognize problems until they become very serious (Tavris, 1992). Not surprisingly, research shows that the highest levels of couple satisfaction result when both partners follow the lesbian pattern of sharing responsibility (Gunter & Gunter, 1990; Peterson, Baucom, Elliott, & Farr, 1989; Steil & Turetsky, 1987).

Gendered power dynamics. The social view of women as less powerful than men shapes how many romantic relationships operate. A majority of both women and men still believe that men should be more powerful, and this holds true even when a female partner's job equals a male's in prestige and salary (Anderson & Leslie, 1991; Hochschild with Machung, 1989; Loscocco, 1997; Risman & Godwin, 2001; Steil & Weltman, 1991).

Consistent with social prescriptions for masculinity, men are expected to have higher job status and earn greater salaries than women. When this expectation is not met, many heterosexual couples either experience dissatisfaction or engage in a variety of rationalizations to convince themselves the husbands are of greater status and value (Anderson & Leslie, 1991; Hochschild with Machung, 1989; Steil & Weltman, 1991).

As you might predict, problems fostered by believing that men should be more powerful are absent in lesbian relationships, which tend to be highly egalitarian. On the other hand, power issues are accentuated in gay relationships, where partners may engage in constant competition for dominance (Blumstein & Schwartz, 1983; Kurdek & Schmitt, 1986a, 1986b). The expectation of male dominance in heterosexual relationships is reflected in three important ways: division of labor, patterns of influence and decision making, and violence between partners.

One of the clearest indicators of power is how equitably labor is divided between partners. On this matter, deeply gendered patterns prevail in heterosexual relationships. Few families today have a single male wage earner; the vast majority have dual workers. What has not changed with the times, however, is the distribution of responsibility for domestic chores and care of children and other relatives (Goldstein, 2000; Greenstein, 1996; Nussbaum, 1992; Risman & Godwin, 2001). By and large, these responsibilities are still carried entirely or predominantly by women, regardless of whether they work outside of the home. Dubbing this the "second shift," so-

My mother works all day at her job. She also cooks all of the meals for the family, does all of the housework, and takes care of my younger brother and sister. When my mother goes out of town on business, she fixes all of the family meals and freezes them before she leaves. She also arranges for day care and cleans very thoroughly before she leaves. My father expects this of her, and she expects it of herself.

Ⓔ GLORIA

I'm a mother and a professional and a part-time student, but I am not the only one who takes care of my home and family. That's a shared responsibility in our house. My daughter and son each cook dinner one night a week, and they switch off on chores like laundry and vacuuming. My husband and I share the other chores 50–50. Children don't resist a fair division of labor if their parents model it and show that it's expected of them.

ciologist Arlie Hochschild (1989) found that the majority of wives employed outside of their homes have a **second-shift** job when they get home. In dual-worker families without children, women spend an average of 5 hours more than men per week on homemaking and housework. In dual-worker families with children, the women spend an average of 17 more hours per week than men on homemaking and child care (Goldstein, 2000). Further, it is almost always women who assume responsibility for parents and in-laws who need assistance (Wood, 1994b). According to *Newsweek* ("The Daughter Track," 1990), the average woman in the United States will spend 17 years raising children and 18 years caring for elderly parents and in-laws. From all reports, she will also do the bulk of cleaning, cooking, and shopping, regardless of her job responsibilities outside of the home. In stark contrast to the rise in the number of women working outside of their homes, the amount of housework and child care that husbands do has risen only about 10% (from 20% to 30%) in nearly three decades (Morin & Rosenfeld, 1998; Pleck, 1987).

Not only do women work more than men at home, but the work they do is generally more taxing and less gratifying. For instance, whereas many of the contributions men typically make are sporadic, variable, and flexible in timing (for example, repairing an appliance, mowing the lawn), the work women typically do is repetitive, routine, and constrained by deadlines. Further, more than men, women engage simultaneously in multiple tasks. For example, many women help a child with homework while preparing dinner. These features render women's work in the home less gratifying. This is also true of child care. Whereas mothers tend to be constantly on duty—performing repetitive caretaking such as fixing meals, giving baths, and supervising activities—fathers more typically volunteer for irregular and fun child-care activities such as a trip to the zoo. Sporadic excursions for recreation and adventure are more fun for both parents and children than the constant, necessary activities of caretaking.

Another way in which women's contributions to home life are greater is in terms of what Hochschild (1989) terms **psychological responsibility,** which is the responsibility to remember, plan, and make sure things get done. For instance, it may be that partners agree to share responsibility for taking a child to medical and dental visits, but it is typically the woman who is expected to remember when various

FYI

Making Room for Daddy

A 1992 study by the Du Pont Company found that 57% of men want to spend more time with their kids. That's up substantially from the 37% of men who wanted more time with kids in 1988. Further, 68% of fathers in one survey think their companies should offer paternity leave, and 92% of the men say they would take it.

Fathers' desires, however, are at odds with professional norms and the views of high-ranking personnel. When chief executive officers (CEOs) in one large study were asked how much paternity leave would be reasonable for companies to offer fathers, 63% of the CEOs said "none." Men for whom fathering is a priority may have to pick their jobs carefully. Chris Jolliffe, a Boston social worker, for instance, turned down a major career advancement because the new position wouldn't allow him enough time with his first child.

Forbes reporter Mary Beth Grover (1999) observes that men who want to spend more time with families are often at a disadvantage in the workplace because "corporations expect and tolerate women who publicly push for balance in their lives and work" (p. 203). The same does not always hold true for men. Her interviews with working fathers led her to conclude that men who devote more time to family life "do it fearful that they're putting their careers [in] peril" (p. 203).

Newsweek columnist Robert Samuelson agrees that men need to assume active roles as fathers—and not just for the children. Samuelson says that fathering profoundly changed him and made him a better man. He writes that "fatherhood is a powerful antidote to self-centeredness. . . . It made me do things . . . it has connected me with others . . . and it has made me happier" (1996, p. 43).

Yet not all men feel as Samuelson does. West Shell, who runs Netcentives, says he doesn't feel Daddy stress. He loves working in a high-power job that requires long hours and much travel. He explains, "My wife gets a little nuts, but this is what CEOs do. We like to run companies and lead large groups of people" (quoted in Grover, 1999, p. 208). Not all men have the same priorities. Like women, some want to be highly involved with families and others prefer less involvement.

Sources: Brott, A. (1993, June). Will men take paternity leave? *Redbook*, p. 131; Grover, M. B. (1999, September 6). Daddy stress. *Forbes*, pp. 202–208; Samuelson, R. (1996, April 8). Why men need family values. *Newsweek*, p. 43; Shellenbarger, S. (1993, December 17). More dads take off to look after baby. *Wall Street Journal*, p. B1.

inoculations are due, schedule appointments, notice when the child needs attention, and keep track of whose turn it is to take the child. Similarly, partners may share responsibility for preparing meals, but women take charge of planning menus, keeping an inventory of what's in the home, making shopping lists, and going to the grocery store. All of this planning and organization is a psychological responsibility that is often not counted in couples' agreements for sharing the work of a family.

The consequences of women's second shift are substantial. Women who do the majority of homemaking and child-care tasks are often extremely stressed, fatigued,

As a male who was reared by a single mother, I see women differently than most of the White men I know. I and a lot of Blacks see women as our equals more than most White men do. We treat the women in our lives with a lot more respect than middle-class White males. Being raised by a single mother, which is the case in many Black households, I think we understand women and their plight better than most White men. We know we and Black women are in it together.

and susceptible to illness (Hochschild, 1989). Frustration, resentment, and conflict are also likely outcomes when only one person in a partnership is meeting the double responsibilities of jobs inside and outside of the home (Kluwer, Heesink, & Vliert, 1996; Knudson-Martin & Mahoney, 1996). In addition, the inequity of the arrangement is a primary source of relationship dissatisfaction and instability. Marital stability is more closely tied to equitable divisions of housework and child care than to a couple's income (Fowers, 1991; Hochschild, 1989; Suitor, 1991).

Another clue to power dynamics is whose preferences prevail when partners differ. Research on marriages repeatedly finds that in both spouses' minds, husbands' preferences usually count more than those of wives on everything from how often to engage in sexual activity to who does the housework (Paul & White, 1990; Schneider & Gould, 1987; Thompson & Walker, 1989). Further, we know that masculine individuals (whether female or male) tend to use more unilateral strategies to engage in and to avoid conflicts (Snell, Hawkins, & Belk, 1988; Stafford et al., 2000). Feminine individuals more typically try to please, defer, submit, or compromise to reduce tension, and they employ indirect strategies when they do engage in conflict (Howard, Blumstein, & Schwartz, 1986; Miller, 1986; Mulac, 1998; White, 1989).

More than feminine or androgynous persons, individuals with masculine identities tend to deny problems or to exit situations of conflict, thus enacting the masculine tendency to maintain independence and protect the self. Feminine persons, in contrast, tend to initiate discussion of problems and stand by in times of trouble (Rusbult, 1987; Stafford et al., 2000). As you might expect, the tension between masculine and feminine ways of exerting influence is less pronounced in lesbian relationships, where equality is particularly high. For gay partners, power struggles are especially common and are sometimes a continual backdrop in the relationship (Blumstein & Schwartz, 1983; Kurdek & Schmitt, 1986b).

Finally, gendered power dynamics underlie violence and abuse, which are means of exercising dominance over others. Not confined to any single group, violence cuts across race, ethnic, and class lines. Researchers estimate that at least 28% and possibly as many as 50% of women suffer physical abuse from partners, and even more suffer psychological abuse (Brock-Utne, 1989; French, 1992; Roberts, 1983; Wood, 2001b).

Violence is strongly linked to gender. First, it is inflicted primarily by those socialized into masculine identities: Less than 5% of reported violence against a partner is committed by women (Kurtz, 1989). In the United States, every 12 to 18 seconds a woman is beaten by a man; four women are reported beaten to death daily;

and women are 600% more likely to be brutalized by an intimate than are men (Wood, 2001b). Violence is also linked to masculine identity and cultural ideologies of male dominance. Cross-cultural research indicates that partner abuse, like rape, is lowest in societies that have ideologies of sexual equality and harmony among people and with nature; it is most frequent in cultures that are stratified by sex and believe in male dominance of women (Levinson, 1989). Clinical studies of men who batter women have convinced many researchers and counselors that abusive relationships reflect gender roles and expectations between women and men generally (Jacobson & Gottman, 1998). Like rape, battering and abuse seem to be promoted by cultural ideals that link masculinity with aggression, strength, control, and domination (Jhally & Katz, 2001; Messner, 2001).

Convincing evidence that violence is more connected to gender than sex comes from a study by Edwin Thompson (1991). Based on reports from 336 undergraduates, Thompson found a high degree of violence in dating relationships. Sex alone, however, did not explain the violence. What Thompson discovered is that violence is linked to gender, with abusers—both male and female—being more masculine and less feminine in their gender orientation. This led Thompson to conclude that physical aggression is associated with traditional views of masculinity and a self-definition based on control, domination, and power. Many women stay in abusive situations to fulfill the feminine ideals of caring for others and keeping their families together (Wood, 2001b).

Close relationships reflect the distinctive expectations and interpersonal orientations encouraged by feminine and masculine socialization. In turn, these are evident in four processes central to intimacy: how partners express and experience caring, preferences for balances of autonomy and connection, responsibility for maintaining relationships, and power dynamics. Each of these dimensions of close relationships is deeply influenced by the gendered identities of participants in friendships and romantic commitments.

SUMMARY

So, what are close relationships? What is caring? Is it one kind of activity and orientation that women are better at than men? Or, like so many human experiences, are there multiple forms of caring, and does it mean different things to different people? We have seen that widely held social views of friendships and love relationships reflect primarily feminine values and marginalize or dismiss masculine styles of enacting closeness. Whether we wish to accept these cultural views is up to us.

Social definitions of friendship and intimacy reflect traditional stereotypes of men's and women's roles; men are expected to have more power and status, require more autonomy, and assume less responsibility for domestic and caretaking duties than women. Although these gendered patterns may work for some, to growing numbers of people they are not satisfying. As friends and committed partners discover the limits and disadvantages of traditional gender roles, they are experimenting with new ways to form and sustain relationships.

Many who resist prevailing cultural gender scripts discover new and exciting dimensions of personal identity and close relationships. For instance, men who are single fathers or who devote themselves to caring for their parents heighten their abilities to empathize and provide comfort, and they create rich, intimate relationships with others that traditional prescriptions for masculinity preclude. Women who pursue careers outside the home develop increased personal agency and confidence in their judgment and value. Examples such as these remind us that we can venture beyond conventional definitions of identity and relationships if we choose to. In so doing, we edit cultural scripts, using our own lives as examples of alternative visions of women, men, and the kinds of relationships they may form with each other. By contributing these to the cultural collage, we enrich our individual and interpersonal lives and the social fabric as a whole.

DISCUSSION QUESTIONS

1. Sign on to InfoTrac College Edition, and select PowerTrac to access Jennifer Thomas and Kimberly A. Daubman's 2001 article, "The relationship between friendship quality and self-esteem in adolescent girls and boys." How are males' and females' self-esteem affected by friendships with people of the same and other sex? Based on what you've learned in this chapter, how would you explain the findings reported in this article?

2. Do you think that men really are less able to engage in closeness than women, as the male deficit model claims, or that men and women simply have different ways of experiencing and communicating closeness? How does the theory you accept affect your behaviors and interpretations of others?

3. Think about your friendships with women and men. How are they different from one another? In what ways are they similar? Are your experiences with friends consistent with general patterns identified in the chapter?

4. Keep experimenting with expanding your personal repertoire. If you have relied primarily on talk to build closeness, see what happens when you do things with friends. Do you experience a "closeness in the doing"? If your friendships have tended to grow out of shared activities, check out what happens if you talk with friends without some activity to structure time.

5. Do you see gendered patterns of interaction in your romantic relationships? Think about gender-linked differences in how partners express caring, power, interest in the relationship, and needs for autonomy and connection. Are these points of difference and perhaps tension in your romantic relationships? Does knowing about gender-linked patterns regarding these issues affect how you interpret what happens in your own relationships?

6. To learn more about the second shift, sign on to InfoTrac College Edition, select PowerTrac, and select Susan Lang's 2000 article, "Working couples make time for their families." What does Lang report about the amount of time that fathers and mothers make for families? What is the "neotraditional" arrangement that Lang describes? Do you think this arrangement alters or perpetuates the second shift discussed in this chapter?

7. Sign on to InfoTrac College Edition, and select PowerTrac to access Donna Pawlow- ski's 1998 article, "Dialectial tensions in marital partners' accounts of their relation- ships." Where did husbands and wives differ in their perceptions of dialectical ten- sions in their marriages?

8

Gendered Education:
Communication in Schools

Schools are powerful agents of socialization. They teach us about our culture's history, traditions, practices, beliefs, and values. In addition, schools teach us who is important and who is not; who has influenced the directions of history, science, literature, and social organization; and what possibilities and responsibilities exist for various individuals in the society. Also, schools teach us how smart, competent, and valuable we ourselves are. By implication, schools join with other socializing agents to communicate what identities we are expected to assume and what personal, civic, and professional opportunities are open to us. Finally, schools teach by example. The organization of educational institutions and the roles of males and females in schools implicitly communicate how social systems work and which people have more and less status within them.

Historically and today, schools reflect social views of women and men. In the first centuries of America's life, women were excluded from higher education because it was believed they were too fragile to withstand the rigors of serious study. Further, thinking at that time cautioned that exposure to higher education might "unsex" women, since an educated woman was "unnatural" (Gordon, 1998). Although some women were allowed to pursue education beyond high school, they were sent to finishing schools, which aimed to teach women how to be good wives, mothers, and homemakers. Today, women and men have relatively equal opportunities to pursue education in the United States. Even so, many school environments continue to reflect and reproduce unequal views of and expectations for women and men. From preschool through graduate programs, communication within educational institutions reproduces cultural views of women as supportive of others and unambitious and of males as dominant, independent, and achieving. This is

A Short History of Gendered Educational Practices

As views of women and men have changed in America, so have educational institutions. In America's earliest years, women whose families could afford higher education sent daughters to finishing schools, where they were taught womanly skills such as sewing and cleaning. In addition, women were given firm moral education, since they were expected to be the moral anchor for families. In the 1800s, some female academies were established to train women as nurses or teachers, two professions considered appropriate for women.

From America's beginning through the 1800s, many people considered it dangerous for women to have too much education. Popular wisdom held that women's brains weren't large enough to learn a great deal. Worse yet, it was feared that too much education would harm women's reproductive systems by "unsexing" them and making them unfit for their "proper" roles as women.

The Morrill Act of 1862 established coeducational state universities and land grant colleges to educate women and men in the liberal arts and practical skills. Practical education for men included agriculture and mechanics, while practical education for women was home economics. By 1870, 30% of U.S. colleges enrolled students of both sexes. In 1920, fully 70% of U.S. higher education institutions enrolled women and men. The Progressive Education Movement in the 1920s and 1930s led to development of women's colleges that stressed intellectual development, personal independence, and creativity—educational emphases not offered to women at most coeducational institutions.

Throughout most of America's history, many colleges practiced various types of sex discrimination. For instance, for years Stanford had a quota system that accepted three males for every one female. Even in the 1960s, many schools accepted only women applicants who were better qualified than male applicants. Title IX of the Education Act Amendments of 1972 became law. As a result, all educational institutions that receive federal funds are required to treat boys and girls, men and women, equally.

Sources: Gordon, L. (1998). Women's colleges. In Mankiller, et al., *The reader's companion to U.S. women's history* (pp. 642–644). New York: Houghton Mifflin; Minnich, E. (1998). Education. In Mankiller, et al. (Eds.), *The reader's companion to U.S. women's history* (pp. 163–167). New York: Houghton Mifflin.

not the intended purpose of education, and it is one of which many educators are not consciously aware. Nonetheless, as we will see, schools provide powerful lessons in gender.

In addition to the explicit agenda of education, a **hidden curriculum** (Lee & Gropper, 1974), reinforces social views of women and men. This hidden curriculum consists of institutional organization, content, and teaching styles that reflect gender stereotypes and sustain gender inequities by privileging White males and marginalizing and devaluing female and minority students. After we have explored these three dimensions of the hidden curriculum, we will identify their implications for women's and men's personal and professional lives. Examining these issues may give us insight into the reasons that males' self-esteem and aspirations rise and females' decline in proportion to the extent of their participation in education.

THE ORGANIZATION OF SCHOOLS

As we have noted in previous chapters, social institutions and practices organize cultural life and normalize certain values so that we come to see a particular organization as natural, right, and just the "way things are." As we participate in cultural institutions, most of us come to see as natural the prevailing order they embody. Without conscious reflection, we then reproduce it in our own identities and actions (West & Zimmerman, 1987). Thus, institutions normalize cultural values and instill them in individuals. Among the organizations that embody and perpetuate the social order, schools are particularly important. As you read this chapter, keep in mind that schools are also a major site of change. Classes such as the one you are taking now enable you to recognize gendered patterns and inequities and, if you choose, to challenge them.

■ Schools Perpetuate Gender Inequities

Educational institutions reflect our culture's views of gender and encourage us to see as normal the unequal status and value assigned to women and men. The actual organization of schools communicates strong messages about relationships among

Gender Stratification in Higher Education

Below is a summary of findings from the U.S. Department of Education's most recent survey of full-time faculty and instructional staff in institutions of higher education (Wilson, 2001).

Type of Institution	Men	Women
All Institutions	63.7	36.3
Public Research	70.5	29.5
Private Research	73.9	26.1
Public Doctoral	66.7	33.3
Private Doctoral	63.6	36.4
Public Comprehensive	61.7	38.3
Private Comprehensive	63.3	36.7
Private Liberal Arts	62.2	37.8
Public 2-year	50.1	49.9

gender, identity, value, and opportunities. Think about your elementary and high schools. Who were the teachers? Who were the principals? Which of the two had more authority? Who were the aides, cafeteria workers, and secretaries? From our earliest experiences in schools, we learn that males have authority—the principal is the primary authority figure in elementary and secondary schools, and the chancellor or provost is in charge at colleges and universities. The head person is usually male, whereas most women are in subordinate positions—teachers and support staff. Further, at higher levels of education, where the position of teacher has more status, the number of women decreases (AAUW, 1998; Spade, 2001).

School athletics also are typically organized so that far more males than females have positions of higher status and authority. Before passage of Title IX, which mandated equal sporting opportunities for women and men, more than 90% of coaches of women's sports were women. Ironically, today fewer women's sports are coached by women, and all Division I colleges pay male coaches more than they pay women coaches (Suggs, 1999; Zimbalist, 2000).

Schools Limit Career Aspirations

Although most students are not consciously aware of the disproportionate number of men in positions of authority in schools, they nonetheless may pick up the gender message that men are authorities and women are subordinates. In an interesting study (Paradise & Wall, 1986), researchers compared 1st-graders' perceptions of male and female principals. They found that students were much more likely to think that both women and men could be principals when they had a woman principal than when they had a man principal. In mirroring gender stereotypes of our society, the organization of schools instills in students the belief that it's more "normal" for men than for women to hold positions of status and authority.

At higher levels, gendered school organization continues to affect perceptions of career opportunities and appropriate roles for women and men. At colleges and universities, faculty are predominantly male, especially at the highest ranks. Nationwide, slightly more than one third of faculty in higher education are female (Wilson, 2001). The racial imbalance is even more dramatic than the gender imbalance: 85% of full-time faculty in higher education are White (Wilson, 2001).

Schools Have Too Few Female and Minority Role Models

A primary consequence of the prominence of male and White faculty is a lack of role models for women and people of color. In 1999, reporter Jane Stancill summarized current data on women in higher education: Women represent 34% of all faculty (up from 23% in 1974–1975) but only 19% of faculty at the rank of full professor. Across the United States, women are presidents of only 20% of colleges, mostly smaller schools and community colleges. In 2000, 11 of the 61 schools in the

Title IX: Fiction and Fact

Title IX prohibits sex discrimination in schools that receive tax dollars. Although Title IX has been around for a good while, it is still widely misunderstood. Check your knowledge of what it means and doesn't mean.

Fiction: Title IX is binding on all schools in the United States.

Fact: Title IX is binding only on schools that accept federal funds. All citizens' taxes support these schools, so they should provide equality of education to all students. Private schools are not required to abide by Title IX.

Fiction: Title IX bans sex discrimination only in athletic opportunities at schools that receive federal financial support.

Fact: Title IX bans sex discrimination of all sorts in federally supported schools. This applies to academics as well as athletics.

Fiction: Before Title IX, discrimination by schools was mainly in admissions.

Fact: Prior to passage of Title IX, some schools had separate entrances for males and females, and female students were not allowed to take courses in auto mechanics or criminal justice in some schools.

Fiction: The greater athletic opportunities that Title IX makes available to women students come at the expense of male students.

Fact: It's true that some college men's teams now have caps on their numbers of players, and a few men's sports have been eliminated at specific schools. In the overall picture, however, men's college sports are thriving. Since the passage of Title IX, college

Association of American Universities had women as their chief academic officers (Lively, 2000). Further, the few women and minority faculty members are overburdened with disproportionate requests for committee service and advising (Phillips, Gouran, Kuehn, & Wood, 1993; Welch, 1992). Several studies have confirmed the relationship between the presence of women and minorities in schools and the career aspirations of minority and women students. Female faculty are important role models for women students, providing concrete examples of the fact that women can hold positions of authority (Gilbert & Evans, 1985). Not surprisingly, women students' levels of ambition and self-confidence are highest in women's high schools (Lee & Marks, 1990) and colleges (Rice & Hemmings, 1988; Tidball, 1989), where women hold nearly all positions of status and authority. Similarly, African American faculty serve as role models who influence the likelihood that African American students will pursue further education and ambitious pro-men's sports opportunities have actually increased. In 1997–1998, there were 203,686 male athletes and 135,110 female athletes playing college sports.

Fiction: Today, colleges that receive federal money must provide fully equal support to women's and men's sports.

Fact: Women athletes receive significantly less financial and other support than male athletes. In 1997–1998, the latest year for which results are published, 40% of Division I scholarship athletes were women. They received 41% of the athletics scholarship budget, 30% of the recruiting budget, 33% of the total team operating budget, and 27% of the base salaries given to coaches. When on the road, female athletes stay in less expensive hotels and eat in cheaper restaurants.

Fiction: Most Americans don't support Title IX.

Fact: In a 2000 poll, 79% of Americans said that they approve of Title IX. The poll also asked whether people would approve of cutting men's sports to increase athletic opportunities for women. Fully 76% of people said they would support such cuts. The strong support for Title IX didn't vary much by sex. 79% of women and 73% of men supported cutting men's sports to increase women's sports.

Sources: Goodman, E. (1997, June 22). An act to strengthen women. *Raleigh News and Observer*, p. 29A; Ransom, L. (1997, June 29). Title IX is more than athletics. *Cincinnati Enquirer*, p. D1; Roe, M. (1997, June 29). Female athletes not going away. *Cincinnati Enquirer*, p. D1; Suggs, W. (1999, May 21). More women participate in collegiate sports. *Chronicle of Higher Education*, pp. A44–A49; Suggs, W. (2000, July 7). Poll finds strong public backing for gender equity in college athletics. *Chronicle of Higher Education*, p. A40; Zimbalist, A. (2000, March 3). Backlash against Title IX: An end run around female athletes. *Chronicle of Higher Education*, pp. B9–10.

fessions (Fleming, 1984; Freiberg, 1991; Lee & Marks, 1990). White male students are given an advantage: In most schools they are provided with more role models who underline their value and encourage them to establish high personal, social, and professional goals.

Persisting gender inequities in education lead some people to advocate single-sex education. Despite some evidence that single-sex education has benefits (Riechmann, 1996), not everyone is jumping on the bandwagon. David Sadker, a professor of education at American University and co-author of *Failing at Fairness: How America's Schools Cheat Girls,* warns that creating separate schools for males and females is a flawed solution for two reasons. First, he notes, it diverts attention from identifying and solving the problems that make coeducational schools less than equitable. Second, he says, single-sex schools aren't available to most people. Nearly all single-sex schools are private and charge tuitions that most families can't

Is Separate Equal in Education?

In October 1992, a federal appeals court ruled that single-sex education is justifiable because it results in greater student learning. Yet, that ruling didn't end the controversy over single-sex education. Proponents of women's schools claim that women receive better educations in all-women institutions. The facts on graduates of women's schools are persuasive: Although women's colleges produce less than 5% of all female college graduates, 25% of all women who are on boards of Fortune 500 companies and 50% of women in Congress graduated from women's colleges. When South Carolina's military academy, the Citadel, was all male, its graduation rate was 70%—much higher than the 48% national average.

But single-sex education in public institutions may be on limited time. Recently, the Citadel was forced by courts to open its doors to women, and now women have graduated from that school. Likewise, traditionally all-women schools have admitted male students in recent years.

Maggie Ford, president of the American Association of University Women, argues that sex-segregated education isn't the answer to gender inequities in schools. She says that a better solution is to make sure that teachers in all schools treat *all* students equally so that males and females have the same educational opportunities and support.

Then there's the case of Heather Sue Mercer, who decided separate wasn't equal on the football team. In August of 1994, Mercer enrolled in Duke after an all-state career as a kicker and asked to be a walk-on player for the school's football team. The coach—then Fred Goldsmith—agreed to let her try out. Although her tryout didn't go well, Mercer persisted. She went to practices and games in the role of manager and went through winter conditioning. That spring, she scored a winning field goal in an intersquad game, and Coach Goldsmith told reporters she was on the team. However, Goldsmith refused to let Mercer attend summer preseason camp and, in a telephone conversation, he said Mercer should enter beauty pageants instead of playing football. Later, he formally dismissed her from the team and refused to let her participate in winter conditioning. Mercer hired a lawyer and sued. A jury awarded her a two-million-dollar verdict. Duke appealed the decision. The original decision against Duke was upheld, and Duke was also ordered to pay Mercer's attorney fees—nearly $400,000. As this book goes to press, Duke is appealing again.

Sources: AAUW. (2001). *Beyond the "gender wars": A conversation about girls, boys, and education.* Washington, DC: AAUW; Beck, M., & Biddle, N. (1995, December 11). Separate, not equal. *Newsweek,* pp. 86–87; Brant, M. (1994, April 25). Far beyond white gloves and teas. *Newsweek,* pp. 57–59; Leslie, C. (1998, March 23). Separate and unequal? *Newsweek,* p. 55; Mace, N., & Ross, M. (2001). *In the company of men: A woman at The Citadel.* New York: Simon & Schuster; Suggs, W. (2001, March 30). Woman who wanted to play football at Duke wins another round in court. *Chronicle of Higher Education,* p. A51.

afford. Thus, although single-sex schools may benefit girls from well-to-do families, they won't do much to help the majority of female students (Nelson, 1996).

CURRICULAR CONTENT

The actual content of much education also reflects the hidden curriculum. Beginning in the 1970s, researchers examined educational content to determine what it communicates about women and men. For more than 25 years, reports have documented pervasive and persistent gender stereotyping in instructional materials and particularly in the language used in teaching and learning settings.

■ Misrepresentation of White Men as Standard

Readers in elementary school perpetuate gender stereotypes in several ways. First, they represent males as standard by overrepresenting men and underrepresenting women. Misrepresentation of the sexes was first discovered in a classic investigation conducted in 1972 (Women on Words and Images, 1972). Titling their study "Dick and Jane as Victims," the researchers reported that, in the 2,760 stories examined, there were approximately three males for every female. In biographies, males outnumbered females by an even higher percentage—

> **SCARLETT**
>
> I always liked science. Right from the first grade, it was my favorite subject. The older I got, though, the more I felt odd in my science classes. Especially in college after the required courses, I felt odd. Sometimes I was the only woman in a class. I was majoring in early education and just took science electives for fun. That changed when I had a woman professor in a course about unsolved problems in biology. She was really good and so was the course, but to me the main thing was seeing a woman teaching science. That's when I decided to change my major and become a science teacher.

> **KEVIN**
>
> I don't buy the stuff about history being distorted, and I don't think we should rewrite all of our books to make it look like women have done more just because that's politically correct. I'm fed up with all of this stuff in my classes that tries to convince us women and minorities did things. History is history, science is science, and saying women did things doesn't make it so.

approximately six to one. When males are the focus of the majority of stories, students are led to believe males are the norm, the standard, in society.

Perhaps you are thinking that "Dick and Jane as Victims" is interesting but irrelevant to education today. The same idea occurred to two communication scholars (Purcell & Stewart, 1990), so they replicated the 1972 study. They found that, although the numbers of male and female characters are more nearly equal now, other sex stereotypes persist. Males are still featured in two-thirds of the pictures and photographs in books, so they are still more visible and more the standard than females. Perhaps more important, the researchers found that both sexes were portrayed in sex-stereotyped ways: Females were shown depending on males to help and rescue them; males were portrayed as engaging in more adventurous

🎔 TERESA

When I went home over break, I was telling my daddy about this class, and he got all upset when I started explaining the distortions in education. He started ranting that education was being ruined by a bunch of misguided liberals who are putting political correctness before truth. So I said to him that it's just a matter of *whose* politics are in control. It seems to me that it was pretty political to write books in the first place that ignored what a lot of women and minorities did, but that kind of political correctness is consistent with my father's values.

activities than females, and males continue to be depicted in a wider range of careers. A related study (Tetenbaum & Pearson, 1989) of elementary readers found that male characters are more visible, more active, and more involved in areas of life that are considered important in our society. Other researchers also report gender biases in textbooks. One study (Balzer & Simonis, 1991) found a three-to-one ratio of male to female images in high school chemistry texts. Other investigations revealed that high school history texts feature four times as many photos of men as women (Sadker & Sadker, 1994), and in top-selling college psychology texts, males significantly outnumbered females as authors and reviewers as well as in the examples in the books (Peterson & Kroner, 1992).

The male-standard bias in our society is further reflected in theories taught in schools. For instance, prominent theories of human moral and cognitive development are based on research that relied exclusively on male subjects. Thus, the ways in which males develop morally were universalized to members of both sexes (Gilligan, 1982; Wood & Lenze, 1991b). As we learned in earlier chapters, however, many males and females are socialized in different contexts and in ways that lead to distinctly different cognitive and moral orientations. In general, feminine socialization prioritizes caring for others and responding to their needs, whereas masculine socialization emphasizes being fair to others and respecting their rights. Not surprisingly, when women were measured by a theory that excluded their experiences, they were judged to be less mature than men, on whom the theory is based. By representing male moral development as standard, instruction has distorted understanding of the range and forms of human morality. Until recently, science textbooks routinely described the process of human reproduction in ways that glaringly reflect social views of women and men: the active sperm "invade" the passively waiting egg. When scientists proved that the egg is also very active in the process, many science books revised their description of the process (Hammonds, 1998).

■ The Invisibility of Women

Sex-stereotypical portrayals of men as standard, active, and successful and women as invisible or marginal, passive, and dependent continue to appear in secondary and college-level books. Consider how history is presented and who figures prominently in making it. Accounts of wars, for instance, focus on battles and military leaders. Seldom noted are the contributions of women both on the battlefields and at home. Who kept families intact and food on the table while men fought? Who manufactured supplies for troops on the front? Chronicles of important events, such as the civil rights movement, focus on male leaders' speeches and press conferences and obscure the ways in which women contributed to the movements. We are taught about the activities of Stokely Carmichael, Malcolm X, and the Reverend Martin Luther King, Jr., but most of us didn't learn in schools about Ella Baker's pivotal efforts to organize neighborhoods in support of civil rights. The few women who are presented tend to be exceptional cases who distinguished themselves on men's terms and in masculine contexts, whereas women who made an impact in other ways and other settings remain hidden (Spitzack & Carter, 1987). Women virtually disappear in historical accounts of our country and the world (Kramarae, Schultz, & O'Barr, 1984).

Women and their experiences and perspectives are similarly neglected in other academic disciplines. For instance, Karlyn Campbell (1991) notes that women are significantly underrepresented in public address anthologies and public speaking textbooks. She argues that in omitting women's speeches and women speakers, the field has undermined the goal of public speaking courses, which is to empower students to speak. Women, she observes, are not empowered when their courses teach them that only men and masculine ways of speaking merit study.

■ Misrepresentation of Human Experiences

When education makes women invisible and distorts their experiences by relying on male standards, our overall understanding of social life is distorted. It is (mis)represented from the perspective of one group: White heterosexual males, who had and still have the greatest status in Western society. In one history book, the six-shooter receives six pages of discussion whereas the role and experiences of frontier women merit a mere six lines (Bate, 1988). Another widely used history text devotes a scant two sentences to the movement for women's right to vote. The male bias in curricular materials is further detected in the practice of defining historical epochs by their effects on men while totally neglecting their impact on the lives of women. It is ironic that the Renaissance is known as the period of rebirth and progress in human life when, in fact, it reduced the status and opportunities of most women (Kelly-Gadol, 1977).

As in other areas we have discussed, sexism in education intersects with other forms of discrimination: racism, classism, and heterosexism. Not just any males are presented as the standard: White, heterosexual, able-bodied, middle- and upper-class men are depicted as the norm. How often have you studied important people who were lesbian or gay? How much of your education has focused on describing and explaining the lives and contributions of economically disadvantaged people? Have your courses taught you about Black women and men in journalism, Asian women and men in music, Hispanic scientists, or gifted African writers? Criticizing the White bias in education, Linda Carty (1992) notes that Blacks are neglected in college education, where the reference point has been and remains White males.

Gender-biased curricular material diminishes education. Students are given partial and therefore false understandings of the subjects they study and the world in which they live. When they learn primarily or only about men and their experiences and accomplishments, they may internalize social views that men matter more than women (Gastil, 1990; Hamilton, 1991; Sheldon, 1990; Switzer, 1990). This deprives men, as well as women, of knowledge both about women's contributions to culture and about areas of life in which, historically, women have predominated. On a more personal level, gender biases in instructional content encourage men to see themselves as able to fulfill high ambitions and affect the course of events, and discourage women from those self-perceptions. By implication, both women and men are taught to see women as less able to lead, affect, and influence the world (AAUW, 1998; Henley, 1989; Spade, 2001).

E DUCATIONAL PROCESSES

A third dimension of the hidden curriculum consists of communication processes that devalue women and their ways of learning and expressing knowledge. Through inequitable expectations of and responses to male and female students, and through privileging masculine forms of communication, educators often unintentionally communicate that women students are inferior to male students.

▦ Unequal Attention to Male and Female Students

The most obvious way in which teachers' communication expresses the view that males are more important than females is the sheer amount of attention given to students of each sex. From preschool through graduate education, many teachers pay more attention to male students. Further, research (Epperson, 1988; Sadker & Sadker, 1994; Sandler, Silverberg, & Hall, 1996) indicates that teachers often give male students more individual instruction and time than they give female students.

Educational processes also reinforce different qualities in male and female students. Whereas teachers praise males for academic interest and achievement, they offer more support to female students for being quiet and compliant (Fagot, 1984; Gold, Crombie, & Noble, 1987; Lister, 1997; Sadker & Sadker, 1986). This pattern was first noticed in elementary classrooms, but later research has shown that it continues throughout all levels of education (Hall & Sandler, 1982; Sandler & Hall, 1986; Sandler et al., 1996).

▦ Not Taking Women Students Seriously

In a classic essay titled "Taking Women Students Seriously," Adrienne Rich (1979) called attention to the fact that men routinely are treated as serious students, whereas women sometimes are not. Women students are frequently praised for

Reprinted with special permission of King Features Syndicate.

their appearance, personalities, and nurturing inclinations, whereas their academic abilities and achievements receive little notice or encouragement (Brant, 1994; Hall & Sandler, 1982, 1984). When professors show an interest in men's ideas and encourage them to work further but do not extend this attention to women students, the clear message is that males are more academically serious—and worthwhile.

Compounding this are differences in how academic advisors and faculty mentors often counsel male and female students. More time, effort, and mentoring typically are given to males than to females (Hall & Sandler, 1984; Sandler et al., 1996). Women are sometimes discouraged from pursuing challenging careers and encouraged instead to focus on family life or undemanding careers. Further, as we noted earlier, the limited number of women in positions of authority in education reduces the likelihood that female students will find role models who could support their aspirations (Marshall, 1996; "Where Have All the Smart Girls Gone?" 1989).

Sexual harassment is a particularly reprehensible form of devaluing women students. Indicative of the overall lack of regard for women as students and persons, sexual harassment is widespread on college campuses (Haag, 2000; Hughes & Sandler, 1986). Women faculty and staff report being sexually harassed by male colleagues and administrators (Kreps, 1992; Wood, 1992b). Women students from elementary school to college report that some males routinely jeer, make lewd suggestions, and touch them without invitation or consent (Haag, 2000; Malovich & Stake, 1990). One fraternity at a Southern university has an annual tradition of making up a "pig book," which contains new women students they think are most attractive, and inviting them to fraternity parties called "cattle drives," at which the brothers and pledges encourage them to drink excessively and then take sexual liberties with the women.

Sexual harassment is not confined to peer interactions. Some faculty treat women in classes in gender-stereotyped ways rather than as serious stu-

℮ BAILEY

It's so unfair how professors treat women. I'm a serious student, and I plan a business career, but my professors have never asked me about my career plans. Even when I bring the subject up, all I get is really superficial stuff—like they really don't want to talk to me. One of my boyfriend's teachers invited him to have coffee and talk about graduate school. My boyfriend didn't even have to ask! They spent over an hour just talking about what he would do after undergraduate school. And my grades are better than his!

dents. Ranging from provocative remarks to offers of higher grades for sexual favors, these actions create a climate of intimidation in which many women students' sex is made more salient than their intellectual abilities and interests. In treating women as sexual objects, harassment ignores and undermines their status as students and tells them they are not taken seriously as members of an intellectual community.

■ Classroom Communication

Education further devalues women students through communication practices that favor and reward male students more than female ones. We will consider three of these practices: different ways teachers communicate to male and female students, communication among peers, and instructional styles that benefit males more than females.

Gender biases in teachers' communication. More than two decades ago, a pioneering study (Hall & Sandler, 1982) called attention to a variety of verbal and nonverbal communication practices that convey the hidden curriculum by providing less recognition and encouragement for female students than for male students. That investigation identified the following communication behaviors of teachers—both male and female—as ones that devalue female students:

- Professors are more likely to know the names of male students than of female students.

- Professors maintain more eye contact and more attentive postures when talking to male students than when addressing female students.

- Professors ask more challenging questions of male students.

- Professors give longer and more significant verbal and nonverbal responses to males' comments than to those of females. When male students cannot respond to a question, they tend to be given additional time along with encouragement and coaching until they come up with a good answer; when female students do not answer correctly, instructors frequently move on.

- Faculty call on male students more often.

- Faculty are more willing to make time and to devote longer periods of time to confer with male students than with female students.

- Female students' contributions are interrupted, ignored, or dismissed more often than those of males.

- Faculty extend and pursue comments by male students more than those of female students.

You may be thinking that a 20-year-old study is irrelevant to education in the 21st century. Unfortunately, that's not true. Numerous studies since the original one show that teachers continue to engage in a range of behaviors that take male students more seriously than female students (Krupnick, 1985; "Researcher," 1990; Sadker & Sadker, 1986; Spender, 1989; Sandler et al., 1996). In 1992, the American Association of University Women Educational Foundation commissioned a comprehensive review of 1,331 studies of gender and educational practices. The result was a report titled "How Schools Shortchange Girls" ("Sexism in the Schoolhouse," 1992), in which evidence was amassed to show that female students continue to receive less attention, encouragement, and serious regard than their male peers.

Not coincidentally, this report also found that "girls enter first grade with the same or better skills and ambitions as boys. But, all too often, by the time they finish high school, 'their doubts have crowded out their dreams'" ("Sexism in the Schoolhouse," 1992, p. 62). The evidence from this study led to the conclusion that the hidden curriculum creates a downward intellectual mobility cycle in which "girls are less likely to reach their potential than boys" (p. 62). The reasons for this pattern seem to lie in the cumulative effects of communication that devalues women students, presents White heterosexual males as normal and important, and considers females, gays, lesbians, and people of color as marginal.

Another way some teachers reinforce traditional gender roles is by encouraging and discouraging gender-stereotypical behaviors in male and female students. Consistent with cultural views of femininity, teachers typically reward female students for being quiet, obedient, and cooperative. Equally consistent with cultural views of masculinity, teachers often reward male students for accomplishments, assertion, and dominance in classrooms (Hall & Sandler, 1982; Sadker & Sadker, 1986). Whereas teachers tend to accept answers that boys shout out, they routinely reprimand female students for "speaking out of turn." This communicates to students that boys are expected to assert themselves, whereas girls are supposed to be quiet and polite.

Teacher expectations are particularly striking in their effects on African American students. When they begin school, African American girls tend to be active, ambitious, and independent—results of their familial socialization—but teachers encourage them to be more nurturing and less autonomous. By age 10, these girls have often learned that independence and achievement are not rewarded. To gain teachers' approval, many African American girls become more passive and dependent ("Study of Black Females," 1985). Many teachers also communicate low expectations of African American males. More than their White peers, African American males are disproportionately targets of teacher disapproval and unfavorable treatment (Grant, 1985). Even when actual behaviors don't differ according to students' race, some teachers perceive African American males as more disruptive and less intellectually able than White males or females of either race (Ross & Jackson, 1991). When these attitudes infect the everyday life of schools, it's small wonder that

African Americans' academic motivation often declines the longer they stay in
school and that they drop out in higher numbers than their White peers. This is another illustration of relationships between gender and race oppression.

Are there differences in male and female teachers' expectations and behaviors?
At least at higher education levels, there seem to be rather consistent differences.
Compared with their male counterparts, female university and college professors
tend to be less biased against female students, are more able to recognize females'
contributions and intellectual talents, and are more generous in giving them academic and career encouragement. In general, female students participate more
actively and more equally with their male peers in classes taught by women than
in those instructed by men. Unfortunately, substantial influence on gender identity has taken place by the time a student enters college. Further, although female faculty may be less likely to gender-stereotype students, they remain scarce in
higher education, so there are fewer women teachers with whom to take classes. Research also indicates that differences in teachers parallel those found in parents,
with male teachers tending to have stronger, more rigid gender-stereotypes than female teachers (Fagot, 1981; Weiler, 1988).

Communication among peers. Communication among peers in school settings
also influences gender identity. The power attributed to peer pressure is no myth.
Once children begin interacting with other children, peers exercise strong influence
on attitudes and identities. Children are simultaneously recipients and enforcers of
gender socialization. Acceptance by peers is higher when children conform to gender stereotypes (Maccoby, 1998; Martin, 1989), and this is especially true for boys
(Fagot, 1984; Messner, 2001). Males are much more insistent that boys do boy
things than females are that girls do girl things, which continues the more rigid gender socialization imposed on males.

Looking back on your own experiences, you can probably confirm the lesser tolerance for boys to engage in feminine activities than for girls to engage in masculine ones. Most young girls, in fact, do play rough sports, but boys generally don't engage in playing house, for instance. Those who do are likely to hear the cardinal insult for a young boy: "You're a sissy!" Peers communicate gender expectations for aggressiveness and passivity, although once again there is greater acceptance of girls who deviate from feminine prescriptions for passivity than for boys who don't measure up to the rules for masculinity ("How Boys and Girls Teach," 1992; Maccoby & Jacklin, 1987). Peers make it quite clear that boys are supposed to act like boys, which means, above all, they must not show any signs of femininity. Once again, this reinforces the cultural message that masculine is more valuable than feminine: Boys may not act feminine, but girls may act masculine.

Although peers are important to both sexes, they seem more critical to boys' gender identity (Maccoby & Jacklin, 1987). Male bonding tends to occur in adolescence and is extremely important to reinforcing and refining masculine identity (Gaylin, 1992; Kerr, 1999; Messner, 2001; Raphael, 1988; Rubin, 1985; Wood & Inman, 1993). Males' greater reliance on peers for gender identity may reflect the difference in parental same-sex models available to boys and girls. In most families, the mother is more constantly present in the home than the father, so a female child can learn how to be feminine within an ongoing, continuous relationship with another person. Because fathers tend to be more physically and psychologically removed from family life, they are less available as concrete models. Young boys may need to find other tangible examples of masculinity in order to define their own identities. Because peer acceptance is extremely important in the first two decades of life, fitting in with school friends and chums is a cornerstone of esteem. Thus, children and adolescents generally do what is necessary to gain the approval and acceptance of their companions. This is a source of considerable frustration to many parents, who try to eliminate stereotypes in how they raise their children only to find that peers quickly and effectively undo their efforts. From age 5 to the early twenties, peers typically have influence at least equal to that of families, and this influence seems particularly pronounced in encouraging gender-stereotypical attitudes, behaviors, and identities (Huston, 1985; Martin, 1989).

Instructional style. Teaching processes also disadvantage women students by favoring a classroom climate more conducive to male modes of learning and achievement. In Chapter 4, we discussed the speech communities in which men and women are socialized, and we discovered that these communities encourage distinctive understandings of how to communicate. In general, males learn to use talk to assert themselves and compete, whereas females see talk as a way to build cooperative relationships with others. Relatedly, research (Belenky et al., 1986) suggests that women may also learn in more interactive, collaborative ways than most men prefer. With these differences in mind, consider what kind of classroom climate would foster learning and involvement for each gender.

The expected and rewarded patterns of classroom participation are consistent with masculine rules of communication and inconsistent with feminine forms

(Hall & Sandler, 1982, 1984; "Sexism in the Schoolhouse," 1992; Wood & Lenze, 1991a). Given this, it is not surprising that males are more comfortable and find learning easier than females, because classroom climates so often employ masculine communication styles (Gabriel & Smithson, 1990; Tannen, 1991). From grade school to graduate school, classroom climates typically emphasize assertion, competition, and individual initiative. Students are encouraged to compete with one another in class discussions, performances, and tests. Further, assignments emphasize individual efforts and seldom allow for collaborative work. Assertion and self-confidence are more rewarded than are questioning and tentative statements. In all of these respects, the traditional educational climate reflects and enables men's participation and achievement more than women's. Many classrooms are actually masculine speech communities, which renders them ineffective in empowering individuals who employ feminine styles of communication. People who have learned to use communication to build relationships and collaborate with others find it uncomfortable to compete, to assert themselves over others, and to speak in absolute terms that don't invite others to participate. This may explain why many women students in coeducational institutions speak up less often in classrooms.

The effects of instruction favoring one gender's communication style are linked to the sex of students and teachers. In 1983, Paula Treichler and Cheris Kramarae reported on an experimental class that used primarily styles of interaction and learning reflective of women's speech communities: discussion, group projects, interactive teaching and learning, cooperative review sessions, and interaction in which students collaborate rather than compete with one another. Women students particularly responded to this learning environment, and men in the class at first found it uncomfortable but came to realize it had distinctive values and enlarged their learning. Later research (Crawford & MacLeod, 1990; Statham, Richardson, & Cook, 1991) indicates that women college faculty tend to encourage more participatory classroom climates than do male instructors. Not surprisingly, in classroom environments that are inclusive and invite collaboration, women students take more active roles, participating in relative equity with their male peers. These findings suggest that women, like men, excel in settings that favor and affirm their ways of thinking and communicating. By implication, the ideal instructional style might blend masculine and feminine modes of communicating, which would enable all students to participate comfortably some of the time and stretch all students to supplement their styles of interacting by learning additional ones.

The difference between instructional styles in which each sex flourishes is one of the issues fueling the controversy about women in military training schools (Beck & Biddle, 1995). Formerly all-male South Carolina's Citadel and the Virginia Military Institute were known for lack of privacy, harsh discipline, and punitive treatment, and for encouraging competitiveness and unflinching fortitude. But the all-female Virginia Women's Institute for Leadership and South Carolina's Institute for Leadership at Converse College, just 200 miles away from the Citadel, have a very different style of training. These schools rely on positive reinforcement and nurturing to develop women's leadership ability. Recent court rulings have made it illegal for military schools supported by taxpayers to remain single sex. The challenge now is for these schools to develop instructional styles that benefit both sexes equally.

The hidden curriculum creates inequitable educational settings that are often more hospitable to men than to women. Although some of the issues we have noted here appear small, in tandem they work to disempower women students. Although each specific form of gender inequity in education might seem minor, the *cumulative* impact can be overwhelming in communicating constantly that women are less valued, less respected, and less able than their male peers.

Certainly not all women students are derailed by gender biases that permeate education. Probably you know some women students who are very successful academically; perhaps you are one yourself. It's also likely that you have been in classes where teachers didn't favor male students and perhaps were even biased toward female students. The gender inequities in education we have discussed, like other gender patterns, have predictable *general* consequences for women and men as groups. This doesn't mean some individual women and men aren't exceptions. Clearly, some are. Those who are may not accept limiting social views of gender, or they may be able to overcome the general biases that operate in schools, or they personally may not have experienced gender bias in their educations. But exceptions to the rule don't negate the rule—the general patterns that make schools more hospitable to boys and men than to girls and women. The point is that no student—woman or man—should have to work against the odds to gain an education. Learning should be equally accessible to all.

SUMMARY

In this chapter, we have gone beneath the surface of education to examine the hidden curriculum, which creates unequal educational opportunities for women and men. The hidden curriculum consists of three elements. First, in mirroring the gender stratification of society in which men are defined as superior and women subordinate, educational institutions model these as normal to students, a process that re-creates inequity. Second, curricular content devalues women by excluding them and their experiences, perspectives, and contexts from instruction. In so doing, it represents men and male experiences as the norm, or standard, and women and their experiences as marginal, unimportant, or deviant. Third, communication in schools contributes to gendered education by giving men students greater attention, respect, and recognition than women students. In a number of ways, teachers and staff of educational institutions communicate to women that they are less valued and less able than their male peers. The combination of these three elements reproduces gender inequities within school settings, making education a process that generally enables men more than women.

Noteworthy trends, such as those we have discussed, indicate that many educators are becoming more aware of the hidden curriculum and the covert, subtle ways in which it creates inequitable learning climates for males and females. Further, increasing numbers of teachers are reading articles on gender sensitivity and attending workshops that help them discover subtle biases in their own instruction. It is also encouraging to see the wealth of materials being written by scholars to provide resources for those who wish to include women's contributions and perspectives along with those of men to make educational content representative of the range and diversity of people who compose and participate in cultural life.

Finally, we should realize that a number of students are taking active roles to challenge and change sexism, racism, and heterosexism in education. Many students, including a number of men, are taking courses in women's studies and African American studies to enrich the breadth of their education. Further, they often use what they learn in those classes to call attention to White male standards in other courses they take. More than once my students have helped me see where my teaching inadvertently excluded some groups, and they've frequently given me resources so that I could learn about people and issues I should include. After taking my course in gender and communication, students sometimes report back to me that they have used what they learned in our course to challenge sexism in other classes. For instance, one man told me he had asked a professor to stop using male generic language, and the professor had stopped. Another student said she had used her knowledge to intervene in a class where males interrupted females and where the professor paid more attention to male students' comments. Whenever a woman was interrupted, she would say, "I'd like to hear what Jane was saying"; whenever a woman student's ideas were dismissed, she would find a way to credit the woman in her own comments: "I think Mary had a good point when she said, . . . and I'd like to extend it." Students are powerful agents of change and a major force in charting the future of education.

DISCUSSION QUESTIONS

1. How many role models have you found in the schools you've attended? Which of your teachers have given you ideas about who you might become and what you might do in life?

2. Sign on to InfoTrac College Edition and select EasyTrac. Type the key words: "single sex education."Access Connie Leslie's 1998 article, "Separate and unequal." Why does the American Association of University Women not support single-sex education? Do

you agree with the reservations discussed in this article? How does this article affect your judgment about the appropriateness of single-sex education?

3. Examine one or more of the textbooks used in other courses you are taking this term. Do you see examples of the hidden curriculum in these books? Are men represented as standard by male generic language, disproportionate references to men and their activities, and theories that reflect masculine more than feminine interests and orientations?

4. As you attend classes this term, notice patterns of communication in them. Do teachers call on male and female students equally? Do they respond with equivalent interest and encouragement to students of both sexes?

5. If you have both women and men as professors, do you see differences in their styles of teaching? Do they rely equally on lecture and participative discussion? Do they engage students in similar ways, or are there differences in the formality, friendliness, and so forth of their interactions with students?

6. Think about your experiences as a student. In elementary and secondary school, what did your teachers praise about your work? What did they criticize? Are your experiences consistent with patterns identified in this chapter?

7. Sign on to InfoTrac College Edition and select EasyTrac. Select the subject guide search and type: "education amendments of 1972." Read John Thelin's 2000 article, "Good sport?" What is the significance of the *Brown v. Cohen* case discussed in the article? Does Thelin think that colleges have generally tried to comply with the 1972 amendments?

9 Gendered Organizational Communication

"Would you want a woman with PMS to be able to take the country to war?"

"If he really cared about his family, he'd be putting in extra time to make money, not asking for time off to be home."

"She may get results from her sales team, but she's one hard woman."

"He must feel awful having a wife who makes so much more money than he does."

These four comments illustrate some of the ways in which gender stereotypes surface in organizational settings. The first question, asked during a discussion of political candidates, reflects the widespread myth that women's hormonal fluctuations disqualify them for positions of leadership and authority. The second comment, uttered when a new father took advantage of his firm's family leave policy, discloses the still prevalent view that men's primary role is that of provider, and parenting is less important. The third statement reveals a paradox experienced by many women who pursue careers in which men have historically dominated: They may meet the requirements of their jobs or those of femininity, but they cannot achieve both simultaneously. In this example, the qualities that made the woman an effective manager are at odds with those prescribed for femininity. The final remark illustrates a tension for partners in some dual-career relationships whose roles conflict with the traditional view of men as the breadwinners.

All four of the comments underscore powerful ways in which cultural views of women and men permeate organizations. In this chapter, we will explore how gendered perceptions and expectations surface in institutional settings. We begin by examining stereotypes of women, men, and professional communication that are communicated through concrete practices, such as hiring, placement, promotion, and interaction patterns. We will also evaluate the evidence supporting these stereotypes. Next, we consider organizational communication systems that reflect and perpetuate limiting views of women and men. As we discuss gender stereotypes, we will try to understand how they affect the personal and professional lives of working people. Finally, we'll consider alternative legal and institutional efforts to redress gender inequity.

INSTITUTIONAL STEREOTYPES OF WOMEN AND MEN

Institutions, like individuals, operate according to beliefs, values, and goals. Collectively, these form a framework that organizes interaction among people who participate in organizations—employees as well as those who use institutions (for example, students in schools, plaintiffs and defendants in courts, customers of businesses). When these beliefs involve broad generalizations about women and men as groups, they are gender stereotypes. In this section, we analyze how stereotypes reflect and perpetuate gendered attitudes and identities.

■ Stereotypes of Women

Writing in 1977, Rosabeth Kanter, who specializes in organizational dynamics, observed that four basic stereotypes of women in our society also operate in organizations. Since Kanter first made this claim, other researchers (Garlick, Dixon, & Allen, 1992; Aries, 1998; Jamieson, 1995; Wood & Conrad, 1983) have corroborated it. According to Kanter, many members of organizations tend to classify women into one of four stereotypical roles: sex object, mother, child, or iron maiden.

Sex object. This stereotype defines women in terms of their sex or sexuality. Frequently, it is expressed in expectations that a woman's appearance and actions should conform to cultural views of femininity. The view that women must be conventionally pretty was highlighted in the summer of 1990 when one airline fired a woman from her job as ticketing agent for not wearing makeup. The ticketing agent brought and won a suit on the grounds of sex dis-

> ### ⌀ KEENA
>
> The sex-object stereotype really gets to me. I work as a waitress to pay my way through school, okay? So my manager has really been on my case lately about how I should fix my hair nicer and wear more makeup in order to please the customers. Is my job to serve them, or to provide them with artistic material? I do my job, and I do it well. I am polite, I check on customers during their meals—nobody's complained about my service. But my supervisor keeps telling me that I'm such a nice-looking girl and that I really should fix myself up more.

crimination, claiming that makeup was not required of male employees and was irrelevant to her job performance. Even though she won the case, the incident dramatically illustrates the institutional expectation that women should be attractive.

The stereotype of women as sex objects is also evident in how some co-workers and supervisors interact with women employees. In the workplace, women are more likely than men to receive comments about their appearance, reflecting the cultural tendency to perceive women in terms of physical attractiveness. Regarding women as sex objects contributes to sexual harassment, which at least 50%, and possibly as much as 90%, of the female workforce has experienced in some form (Rundblad, 2001). If someone defines a woman by her sex and sees her primarily as a woman, not a co-worker, then flirting, lewd remarks, and other inappropriate communication may follow.

The sex-object stereotype is also used to define and devalue gay men and lesbians. Like heterosexual women, gays and lesbians are often perceived primarily in terms of their sexuality, which is not the sum of their identities any more than it is of heterosexuals' identities. Stereotyping gays and lesbians can lead to gay bashing, in which lesbians and gays are devalued because of their sexual orientation, whereas their job performance goes unnoticed. Stereotyping gays and lesbians is particularly prevalent in the military (Bourg & Segal, 2001; J. Gross, 1990), which historically has barred known homosexuals from service. Sexual harassment in the military is exemplified by the Tailhook scandal in 1991, in which male military personnel mauled, violated, and verbally harassed female personnel. Incidents like Tailhook and charges against men of high status and power (Senator Bob Packwood and President Bill Clinton, for example) reflect the continuing tendency to perceive and treat women as sex objects in the workplace.

Mother. In institutional life, the stereotype of women as mothers has both figurative and literal forms. The figurative version of this stereotype is expressed when others expect women employees to take care of the "emotional labor" for everyone—to smile, exchange pleasantries, be accessible, and listen to, support, and help others (Basinger, 2001; Bellas, 2001). Regarding women as motherly sources of comfort may explain the tendency to communicate with women co-workers more than with men when support and sympathy are wanted. The figurative mother stereotype is also evident when people expect women employees to prepare coffee, arrange for snacks and meals, and so forth. As Charlotte points out in her commentary, the mother stereotype underlies the expectation that women will fix coffee, take notes, and arrange social activities.

Stereotyping women as mothers is a source of job segregation by gender, a subtle and pervasive form of discrimination. The growing number of women employed outside of the home suggests greater gender equality in the workforce than really exists. By and large, women and men are not competing equally in a single job market but are segregated into two distinct arenas of employment—his and hers (Jacobs, 1989). Approximately three-fourths of women working outside the home fall into one of three types of jobs: clerical/administrative support, service, and administrative/managerial (Matthaie, 1998; U.S. Department of Labor, 1991). Although approximately half of the workforce is female, women make up only 11.9% of the corporate officers of America's 500 largest companies (Armas, 2000; Erkut, 2001; "Forum," 1997). Thus, we see a pattern in which gender stereotypes of women's roles spill over into the workplace, limiting the positions for which women are considered qualified. More than 90% of employed women work in what is sometimes called the "pink collar ghetto"—jobs predominantly or entirely filled by women (Hoffman, 1998; Woody, 1989). The jobs into which women are segregated generally have the least prestige and the lowest salaries. Gender and race intersect to influence job segregation, with African American women more often expected to fill mothering jobs than European American women (Matthaie, 1998; Segal & Zellner, 1992; Woody, 1989, 1992).

> ### 🦶 CHARLOTTE
>
> I know the mother role all too well. Before coming back to college, I worked as an adjuster for an insurance company. In my office, there were 11 men and one other woman, Anne. I'll bet there weren't more than 10 days in the three years I worked there that one of the guys didn't come in to talk with me or Anne about some personal problem. Sometimes they wanted a lot of time and sympathy; sometimes they just wanted a few minutes, but always it was Anne and me they came to— never one of the other guys. What really burns is that they went to each other to consult about professional matters, but they never came to Anne and me about those. They treated us like mothers, not colleagues.

The woman-as-mother stereotype also has a literal manifestation. Women employees who have children are often classified as "not serious professionals." Because mothering is consistent with established images of women, this role overshadows perceptions of women's professional skills. The mother stereotype can become a self-fulfilling prophecy. For instance, if a manager decides not to offer Maria Constanza a new assignment because he assumes she is preoccupied with her children, then Ms. Constanza is deprived of professional experience. She will not have opportunities to learn what she needs to advance in her job. Later, when the manager is looking for someone who has background and experience in a certain area, he notes that Ms. Constanza is not qualified and attributes this to her being a mother.

Child. A third stereotype that is sometimes imposed on women defines them as children or pets, both of which are cute but not to be taken seriously. This stereotype reflects a view of women as less mature, competent, or capable of making decisions than men. Stereotyping women as children often masquerades as "protecting" women. Less than 10 years ago, a company tried to bar women of childbearing age from working in positions that exposed them to lead because lead may affect fetuses. (It may also affect males' reproductive capacities, but men were not restricted from these jobs.) Regardless of whether women employees planned to have children, the company insisted on "protecting women" from the dangers of these jobs (which, incidentally, were higher-paying jobs in that company). The policy was

I wanted to be in ROTC and then to go into a military career. My dad was a lifer, and I liked the lifestyle and opportunities the military offers. I found out, however, that women are treated as infantile and helpless in ROTC. One of my ROTC teachers actually said to me, "You shouldn't worry about understanding the details of military history. I'm sure you have more pleasant things to occupy your mind." Why did he think I was taking the class in military history if I didn't want to learn about it? And the male students treat me as if I'm delicate and need help—a man's help—all the time. On one outing, this guy kept offering to carry my knapsack, despite my telling him I could handle it. After a year of being made to feel like a 2-year-old, I left the program.

struck down when a court ruled that a company could not act as the parent of women employees, because women are adults, capable of assessing risks and making their own choices.

The medical profession has been criticized strongly for patronizing women patients. Women's complaints about physiological problems and symptoms are too often dismissed by doctors as "female hysteria," with sometimes serious, even deadly, consequences (Calderone, 1990; Zimmerman & Hall, 2001). Women report being told "Don't worry" or "You're imagining things" when they discuss symptoms with doctors. Far more often than men, women are given sedatives and tranquilizers, which reduce anxiety but do nothing to correct physiological conditions that may be legitimate cause for worry (Calderone, 1990; Gomberg, 1986).

In job-related situations, stereotypes of women as children may restrict women's opportunities so they are less able to demonstrate abilities and to grow professionally. Within the military, one argument against allowing women in combat is that they should be protected from the gruesome realities of war. This is somewhat ironic, because women have been involved in and killed in every war fought by our nation. In "protecting" women from challenging work, employers often exclude them from experiences that lead to promotion and salary raises, as well as from the personal development that comes with rising to meet new challenges. Within the military, for instance, combat duty is virtually essential for advancement to the highest levels.

Stereotyping of women workers as sex objects, mothers, and children contributes to inequities in pay. Today women continue to earn less than men working in similar or equivalent jobs. On average, full-time working women earn 72 cents for every dollar men earn (Moberg, 2001). There is a substantial disparity in salary when experience and other qualifications are equivalent for women and men. Level of education does not explain the disparity, because female college graduates earn about what male high school graduates do. Recent studies show that experience, performance, and other qualifications fail to explain at least much of the difference between women's and men's salaries (Aaronson & Hartmann, 1998; Steinberg, 2001).

Iron maiden. A final stereotype defines a woman as being unwomanly. She is unfeminine, manly, or, as the opening example stated, "one hard woman." This stereotype reflects the idea that it is unfeminine to be independent, ambitious, di-

Gendered Wages

In 1963, the U.S. Congress passed the Equal Pay Act. At the time, women earned 59 cents for every dollar men earned. That's changed. Today, the average woman earns 72 cents for every dollar the average man earns. But averages don't tell the whole story. Women in the top 20% of the workforce have made most of the gains, while women in the lower half are paid about what they were 25 years ago. The wage gap between mothers and women without children is even greater than the gap between women and men.

When analysts first identified the wage gap, they thought the difference was based on experience—maybe men were paid more because they had worked longer and gained more skills. But experience didn't account for the difference. How about education? Maybe men are paid more because they have more education. That didn't explain the difference either. In fact, women with college educations earned about what men with high school educations earned. After an extensive analysis of available data, the President's Council of Economic Advisors reported that the differences between men's and women's pay can't be accounted for by training, experience, type of occupation, or business size. After the Council adjusted for these and other factors, a 12% difference remained that could be explained only by the presence of discriminatory attitudes and practices.

A recent report suggests that attitudes that lead to paying women less start early and are equally likely in women and men. In an experiment, students were given money that they had to offer to share with another player. Half of the students didn't know the sex of the other player; the other half of the students were told the sex of the other player. When the other player's sex was known, men and women made lower offers to women. On the receiving end, players who got offers insisted on a higher amount when the offer came from a woman.

Sources: Crittenden, A. (2001). *The price of motherhood.* New York: Metropolitan Books; Moberg, D. (2001, January 8). Bridging the gap. *In These Times,* pp. 24–26. She's a woman, offer her less. (2001, May 7). *Business Week,* p. 12.

rective, competitive, and tough at times. A woman who engages in these behaviors may be labeled an "iron maiden" (Garlick, Dixon, & Allen, 1992). Communication scholars Majia Nadesan and Angela Trethewey (2000) interviewed women who were successful in corporate positions. They asked the women if they perceived any conflict between being professional and feminine. The women answered "yes." They said they had to be very careful not to be unfeminine yet simultaneously not to act "too much like women."

An example of this occurred in 1990, when Ann Hopkins sued the accounting firm of Price Waterhouse for sex discrimination (Fiske, Bersoff, Borgida, Deaux, & Heilman, 1991; Hopkins, 2001; Hopkins & Walsh, 1996). Ms. Hopkins brought in more money in new accounts than any of her 87 male peers, yet 47 of the men were made partner whereas Ms. Hopkins was not. Executives refused to promote Ms. Hopkins because they perceived her as unfeminine. Describing her as "author-

Bully Broads

What's a business to do when one of its managers is a bully? That depends on whether the manager is a man or a woman. According to Jean Hollands, a Silicon Valley executive coach, nobody likes a bully, but a man can get away with being one, whereas a woman can't. Bullying behaviors, such as demanding results and yelling at subordinates whose work is poor, are tolerated in men because they are consistent with cultural views that men are aggressive. The same behaviors are inconsistent with Western culture's view of femininity, so women who bully subordinates tend to be judged as ineffective managers.

The solution, says Hollands, is anti-assertiveness training for managerial women—training that teaches them to be more feminine. She claims that the rules for effective management are different for women and men. Men can bully subordinates and get results; women who bully subordinates get only resentment. Her company, Growth and Leadership Center, offers "Bully Broad" training programs that teach women managers how to be more soft, nurturing, friendly, tentative, and unaggressive. Women who want to succeed in executive positions are advised to use verbal and nonverbal communication that is considered feminine. In the program, Hollands coaches women to stutter, wear ruffles, smile, soften their voices, use self-deprecating humor, and cry—yes, cry, because it has tactical value for women, says Hollands. So far, Bully Broads has coached clients sent by premier companies such as Intel, Cisco, Hewlett-Packard, Sun Microsystems, and Lockheed-Martin.

Source: Hollands, J. (2001). *Same game, different rules: How to get ahead without being a bully broad, ice queen, or other Ms. Understood.* New York: McGraw-Hill.

itative" and "too tough," they suggested she could improve her chances for promotion if she looked and behaved more femininely. I met with Ann Hopkins to discuss her case. In our conversation, she recalled that a senior man in the firm had advised her to fix her hair and wear more jewelry (2001). Ms. Hopkins was promoted after a federal district court ruled that she was the target of gender stereotyping, which is a form of sex discrimination and therefore illegal. Yet there are many women like Ms. Hopkins who are underpaid and not promoted and who lack the funds or confidence to go to court to fight for their rights. Hillary Rodham Clinton is another example of a successful woman who has been called unfeminine, because she is assertive, has an agenda, and doesn't present herself in typically feminine ways.

As you can see, all four of these stereotypes define women as undesirable employees. Either women are incompetent (sex object, child), or they are only able to support others in positions but not to be leaders themselves (mother), or they are too unfeminine to be acceptable (iron maiden). Each stereotype entails some reason for discounting women as workers; each defines women by sex and gender rather than by job qualifications and performance.

■ Stereotypes of Men

Within institutional settings, men are also stereotyped. As was true of stereotypes of women, those applied to men reflect entrenched cultural views of masculinity and men's roles. We will discuss three stereotypes of men that limit them in institutional settings: sturdy oaks, fighters, and breadwinners.

Sturdy oak. The sturdy oak stereotype defines men as self-contained, self-sufficient pillars of strength who should not appear weak or reliant on others. In politics, we see dramatic examples of the extent to which men are expected to be sturdy oaks. Ronald Reagan ran and ruled as a man's man, catapulting his role in Western movies into political life. One of George H. Bush's greatest handicaps as both a candidate and a president was the perception that he was a wimp. He was perceived as whining, leaning on others, and failing to appear to be his own man. President George W. Bush is trying to avoid being seen as weak as his father was.

The stereotype of the sturdy oak can also affect men's professional performance. If it is not manly to admit doubts or fears, then men may take risks that are unwise at times. Similarly, if asking for help is prohibited, then consulting with others for advice or assistance may be ruled out, and decision making may be impeded by lack of important input. If a man does make a mistake, he may feel compelled to hide it.

Fighter. Cultural stereotypes also cast men as fighters—brave warriors who go to battle, whether literally in war or metaphorically in fighting the competition in business. Childhood training to be aggressive, to "give 'em hell," and to win at all costs translates into professional expectations that men should go out there and beat the other guys on Wall Street or in the courtroom. There is no room for being less than fully committed to the cause (your country, team, or company), less than aggressive, less than eager for combat, or less than ruthless in defeating the competition.

The stereotype of men as fighters echoes other themes of masculinity: dominance, force, and violence. Some interesting research suggests that this cultural definition of manhood may have influenced military engagements. Records on foreign

⚖ FORREST

Last summer, I took a job selling encyclopedias to make money for the fall. So every morning I set out on my territory, knocked on doors, and tried to sell people these encyclopedias. My supervisor asked me why I hadn't sold more in one neighborhood, and I told him the people there were really pressed to make ends meet, and they needed food more than encyclopedias. So he read me the riot act—told me those were the very folks who could be talked into buying encyclopedias because they wanted to help their kids get ahead. He told me to pressure them with a line of talk about what they owed their kids and how these books were the whole foundation of their children's lives and success. I told him I couldn't do that, that it was just too pushy. He told me that was what I was supposed to do—push, strong-arm people if I have to, but sell the books. When I checked around with some of the other reps, I found out they do that and they have contests to see who can push the most people into buying books. Maybe I'm not cut out to be a salesman.

policy suggest that the single greatest goal of U.S. involvement in Vietnam was to avoid a humiliating defeat that would make our country (and the commander in chief) appear weak. A mere 30% of our official reasons for being at war involved commitments to helping the Vietnamese people or saving their country from Chinese rule (Fasteau, 1974). President Reagan's invasion of Grenada and President Bush's invasions of Panama and the Persian Gulf have also been questioned by scholars who think these were premature acts of aggression. Social views of masculinity encourage such aggressiveness as a way to prove manliness (Messner, 2001).

One implication of this is that men are often not able to take time from work for family matters without risking disapproval from colleagues and supervisors. Although reports indicate that over half of men working outside the home would like to reduce their hours in order to spend more time with families (Schellhardt, 1997; Worley & Vannoy, 2001), very few companies and firms in America allow men to take time off from paid work to care for children. Even firms that technically allow paternity leaves often disapprove of men who take it (Rapoport, Bailyn, Kolb, & Fletcher, 1998). Men who do take time are often looked down upon by co-workers and superiors.

Breadwinner. Perhaps no other stereotype so strongly defines men in our society as does that of breadwinner. Men are expected to be the primary or exclusive wage earners for their families, and achieving this is central to how our society views men's success. Since the Industrial Revolution, maleness has been equated with being a good provider; to be a man is to earn a good income (Worley & Vannoy, 2001). If a man's ability to earn a good salary ends, then he may be emotionally at risk. This was dramatically illustrated when the Great Depression befell America in 1929. Men who lost their jobs often also forfeited respect for themselves as men, as breadwinners. Feeling psychologically emasculated (Komarovsky, 1940), many men became clinically depressed, and a number committed suicide. They could not live up to the stereotype imposed by the culture.

In our own era, there are risks for men who link their identity and worth to earning a big income. First, the economy is uncertain, and job security is not assured. Increasingly, companies are cutting staff to reduce expenses. Further, many workers are being replaced by machines, which may render today's qualifications irrelevant five years down the road. Because many families are unable to live on a single income, both partners work—an arrangement that lessens men's roles as providers for their families. Finally, in some couples, the woman's salary exceeds the man's, which may create tension between gendered expectations and daily life. Similarly, men who define themselves as earners may feel threatened by women colleagues who advance ahead of them. Psychiatrist Willard Gaylin (1992) reports that suicide rates for men are seven to eight times higher than for women and that most men who commit suicide do so because of business failures. Gaylin warns that making a salary define manhood is a dangerous foundation for identity and self-esteem,

Dual Workers, Dual Breadwinners

The stereotype of men as breadwinners is no longer supported by facts. Today, 51% of all married couples of childbearing age consist of two breadwinners. Increasing numbers of women bring in half or more of their household income—currently, approximately 1 in 3 wives who work outside the home are paid more than their husbands. Fully 48% of women who work outside the home say they would choose to work even if they didn't need the income, and this attitude is stronger among women aged 18 through 34 than older women. Whereas only 31% of women with children under 1 year old worked outside the home in 1976, the latest census found that 59% of new mothers choose to keep working. Most women work for the same reasons that most men do—not just income but also challenge, stimulation, and feelings of accomplishment.

And the breadwinner role isn't the only one that's reaching for gender equity. Twenty-one percent of men would prefer to stay home caring for family members. In fact, slightly more men than women (27% versus 26%) say that family time makes them feel like successful people.

Many couples are involved in dual careers of equal status and demands. In 1998, there were 28 million dual-earning couples in the United States—that's 45% of the workforce. Men and women involved in dual-worker families in 1998 are nearly equally eager for flexible, family-friendly work policies. These trends suggest that men and women are increasingly sharing the responsibilities for earning incomes and caring for families.

Sources: Aaronson, S., & Hartmann, H. (1998). Wage gap. In W. Mankiller, et al. (Eds.), *A reader's companion to U.S. women's history* (pp. 614–615). New York: Houghton Mifflin; Goldstein, A. (2000, February 27). Breadwinning wives alter marriage equation. *The Washington Post*, p. A1; Hattery, A. (2000). *Women, work and family: Balancing and weaving.* Thousand Oaks, CA: Sage; Jackson, M. (1998, January 21). His career, her career. *Raleigh News and Observer*, p. D3; Shellenbarger, S. (1995, May 11); Steinberg, R. (2001). How sex gets into your paycheck and how to get it out: The gender gap in pay and comparable worth. In D. Vannoy (Ed.), *Gender mosaics* (pp. 258–268). Los Angeles: Roxbury; Women indicate satisfaction with role of big breadwinner. *Wall Street Journal*, p. 81; U.S. Bureau of the Census (2000). Washington, DC; Wilson, T. (2000, October 4). Census: More mothers return to work. *Raleigh News & Observer*, pp. 1A, 9A.

and he encourages men to resist cultural pressures to define their worth by their paychecks.

■ Evaluation of Stereotypes

The stereotypes of working women and men that we have discussed are not supported by research on real women and men in the workforce. Decades of intensive study show that women are as motivated to achieve and are as committed to work as men are (Aries, 1998; Kahn & Yoder, 1989; Williams, 2000). Research also demonstrates that working men aren't always fighters, sturdy oaks, and breadwinners (Eyer, 1992; Rapoport et al., 1998). As we have seen in previous chapters, men can be nurturing and supportive of others—behaviors that are not consistent with the stereotypes of men. Even those sex stereotypes that are not well grounded in facts can powerfully influence working women's and men's professional status, salary, and advancement.

MISUNDERSTANDINGS OF PROFESSIONAL COMMUNICATION

Because men have historically dominated institutional life, masculine forms of communication are the standard in most work environments. Defining men and masculine patterns as normative leads to perceptions that women and feminine styles are not just different but inferior. In this section, we will examine three misunderstandings about communication in the workplace: first, that masculine communication is equivalent to professional communication; second, that communication styles are stable; and third, that men and women cannot work together effectively. Before doing that, however, let's briefly consider the male norms that define institutional life in general, because these establish the foundation of stereotypes of professional communication.

Male Standards in Institutions

Throughout this book, we have seen that communication, gender, and culture interact to affect one another and that they exert their combined effects on individuals and relationships. The cultural view of men as standard, or normative, is reflected throughout institutional life in the United States. Male standards are evident in our judicial system. Designed to provide equal justice for all, our legal system's assumption that masculinity is normative leads to inequitable treatment of women. From local levels to the Supreme Court, most judges are men who typically lack experiences that provide insight into some of the issues and conditions in women's lives. This was particularly evident during the Hill–Thomas hearings in 1991. During these proceedings, a roomful of male congressmen interrogated Anita Hill about her charge that Supreme Court nominee Clarence Thomas had sexually harassed her when she worked for him years earlier. The questioners could not understand (and thus did not believe) why, if this had happened, Hill did not object at the time. Men who have not been sexually harassed may be unable to understand sexual harassment and ways women react to it. If you have never been sexually harassed, and if you have not been taught to be passive, deferential, and friendly, then it may be impossible to understand why many victims of sexual harassment do not firmly, forcefully, and immediately protest harassment.

Other issues that affect women exclusively or primarily may also be issues that some men cannot fully understand and to which they would respond differently. For instance, there are cases in which women who have been chronically brutalized by their partners finally defend themselves by killing the men while the men are asleep. Because the murder takes place when the man is not actually attacking the woman, it fails to fit the legal definition of self-defense. But, argue an increasing number of attorneys, a person who is physically weaker and who has been repeatedly overcome by her partner may not be able to defend herself during an episode of violence. Her homicide may be the only reasonable self-defense, given the circumstances and relative strengths of the two partners. Cases of this sort, along with sexual harassment trials, are forcing the legal system to consider whether its standard, which is literally that of "a reasonable man" (What would a reasonable man do if . . . ?), is fair to women. The "reasonable woman" standard defines different courses of action as reasonable for women, based on their distinctive physical strength and socialization (Lamb, 1999; Wood, 1994a).

The male standard is also evident in religious systems. Not only has God historically been defined as male, but until very recently, only men have been allowed to occupy the highest offices, such as minister, priest, rabbi. In 1968, feminist theologian Mary Daly critiqued sexism in the church in her book *The Church and the Second Sex*, and she pursued this theme further in later books titled *Gyn/ecology* (1978), *Beyond God the Father* (1973), and *Outercourse* (1992). Although many churches and synagogues continue to discriminate against women, these sexist practices are being challenged (Kamionkowski & Rosenbaum, 2001; Nesbitt, Baust, & Bailey, 2001). Many denominations now ordain women into the ministry, although the Catholic Church has reiterated its belief that women should not be priests. Some religions have begun to speak of God as "motherlove and fatherlove" and to revise interpretations of the Bible so that women's presence, contributions, and value are more fully recognized.

With this broad understanding of the male standard that infuses institutional life in our culture, we may now consider three specific implications of assuming that men—White heterosexual, middle-class, able-bodied men—are the normal and best model for professional communication.

■ Masculine Norms for Professional Communication

The male-as-standard norm defines expected communication in professional settings. Leadership, a primary quality associated with professionals, is typically linked with masculine modes of communication—assertion, independence, competitiveness, and confidence, all of which are emphasized in masculine speech communities. Deference, inclusivity, collaboration, and cooperation, which are prioritized in feminine speech communities, are linked with subordinate roles rather than with leadership. To the extent that women engage in traditionally feminine communication, then, they may not be recognized as leaders or marked for advancement in settings where masculine standards prevail. The validity of equating leadership with masculinity is open to question, as we will see. Bias against feminine forms of communication assumes that these are not effective in leading others. This bias devalues important communication skills such as supportiveness, attentiveness, and collaboration, all of which appear to enhance morale and productivity in work settings (Fletcher, 1999; Fletcher, Jordan, & Miller, 2000; Helgesen, 1990; Natalle, 1996).

Women and men leaders act similarly in many respects: Both are able to direct and organize collective efforts, and many subordinates judge male and female leaders to be equally effective (Eagly & Johnson, 1990; O'Leary, 1988). Yet there are differences. Consistently, studies reveal that women, more than men, help others. This explains, at least in part, why women with high achievement goals tend to select professions such as teaching, social work, medicine, and human services, whereas men with strong motivation to achieve are more likely to choose high-status occupations (Bridges, 1989). Comparisons of women and men in the same professional roles reveal that women tend to employ more caring, personal styles (Lunneborg, 1990). In a four-year study of college seniors, 60% of women were upset when others were treated unfairly, whereas the unfair treatment troubled only 40% of the men. Women, more than men, also felt a responsibility to help others who had problems (Otten, 1995). For instance, female doctors tend to be more compassionate and patient centered than their male counterparts, and female attorneys tend to be more concerned with clients' needs and feelings (Gilligan & Pollack, 1988; Rosener, 1990). The desire to help others is a major factor in both African American and European American women's choices of jobs and styles of communication in their work (Fletcher, 1999; Murrell, Frieze, & Frost, 1991; Woody, 1992).

Similar differences have been found between the managerial styles of women and those of men. Women leaders are more likely to use collaborative, participative communication that enables others, reflecting how their speech communities have taught them to interact (Aries, 1987; Helgesen, 1990; Lunneborg, 1990; Rosener, 1990). Men, in general, engage in more directive, unilateral communication to exercise leadership, which is consistent with their learned view of talk as a way to as-

---

FYI

Gender and Peer Relationships in the Workplace

Both women and men form relationships on the job, but there are some general differences in the kinds of relationships they form and what happens in them. Communication researchers report that women and men say they have an equal number of relationships with colleagues but that women are more likely to build peer relationships that provide emotional support, whereas men build peer relationships that furnish information. Women also report talking with co-workers about job-related problems and issues more than do men.

Sources: Cahill, D., & Sias, P. (1997). The perceived social costs and importance of seeking emotional support in the workplace: Gender differences and similarities. *Communication Research Reports, 14*, 231–240; Fritz, J. (1997). Men's and women's organizational peer relationships: A comparison. *Journal of Business Communication, 34*, 27–46.

---

sert self and achieve status (Eagly & Karau, 1991). This suggests that there may be different tones to women's and men's leadership.

Does this mean that women are less professional and less able to lead than men? We could draw that conclusion only if research indicated that the style more characteristic of male leaders is also more effective in motivating followers and accomplishing results. Research, however, does not support the belief that masculine qualities are the only ones that yield good leadership. Although instrumentality and assertiveness are valued in leaders, so are supportiveness and collaboration, which are communication skills at which women tend to excel. Further, studies indicate that the most effective leadership style incorporates both relationship-building and instrumental qualities (Cann & Siegfried, 1990; Fletcher, 1999).

There's one further insight to add to this picture. Men and women may be judged differently for enacting the *same* communication. This highlights the importance of distinguishing between how women and men actually behave and how others perceive them. If communication is perceived through gender stereotypes, then women and men may need to communicate differently to be equally effective. Because cultural views hold that women should be supportive and friendly, not being so may be regarded as a violation of gender role and may result in negative evaluations of women. Relatedly, because highly assertive and instrumental communication is socially defined as masculine, women who engage in it may be branded "iron maidens," a perception that jeopardizes their acceptance and effectiveness (Aries, 1998; Butler & Geis, 1990; Carli, 1989). Research confirms that others may negatively evaluate women—but not men—whose communication is directive and unresponsive to feelings (Basow, 1990; Bradley, 1981; Gervasio & Crawford, 1989). Because emphatic, directive communication by women is viewed negatively, a more participative, supportive leadership style is likely to be most effective for women leaders (Statham, 1987). Thus, it may well be that the ways in which men and women enact leadership are different yet equally appropriate and effective in light of gendered expectations that others bring to professional settings.

> ## 🍀 TARA
>
> When I first started working, I tried to act like the men at my level. I was pleasant to people, but I didn't talk with co-workers about my life or their lives. I did my work, led my team with firm, directive communication, and stressed results. When I had my first performance review, I got great marks on achieving tasks, but there was serious criticism of "my attitude." A number of people—both my peers and staff I supervised—complained that I was unfriendly or even cold. People criticized me for not caring about them and their lives. I pointed out to my supervisor that nobody made those complaints about men, and she told me that I couldn't act like a man if I wanted to succeed in business.

■ Static (or Unchanging) Views of Communication

Earlier chapters in this book demonstrated that our communication styles are learned. We are taught to communicate in particular ways; females are encouraged to create and sustain interpersonal connections and respond to others, and males are encouraged to emphasize independence and status. Are we bound forever by

Dad died when I was just 11, and up until then Mom had been gentle and not at all pushy or demanding. But then she had to go to work to support us. She took a job in a factory in our town, and she was so good at her work she got promoted to supervisor in a couple of years. I watched her become more independent, more sure of herself, and more willing to lay down the law to me and my sisters. Before, she would let us get away with just about anything, but she became stricter and more willing to enforce her rules. I also saw changes in how she dealt with others, like salesmen. She used to let them push her around, but that was history after she went to work. She became a stronger person in a lot of ways.

what we learned in childhood? Are the communication styles we have at the moment set in stone?

To answer this question, we return to standpoint theory, introduced in Chapter 2. According to this perspective, our ways of knowing and acting are influenced by the circumstances of our lives. Thus, the different standpoints of women's and men's lives lead them to distinctive ways of exercising influence and interacting with others, ways that are reflected in how they communicate in their jobs. Yet standpoint theory also suggests that, as our standpoints change, so will our ways of thinking and communicating. If this is true, then as women enter into positions requiring forms of communication not fostered in feminine socialization, they should become proficient in new skills. Similarly, as institutions discover that cooperative, supportive communication is important in leadership, men should develop skills in these areas.

It appears that the requirements of jobs influence styles of communication—more so, in fact, than personal styles affect the structure of jobs. A series of studies (Epstein, 1968, 1981, 1982) showed that women attorneys who were not assertive, self-confident, or ambitious at the start of their careers became

---

FYI

Should Women Be in Combat Roles?

Even before *G.I. Jane* hit the box office, women's place in combat was a highly controversial topic. Although many people believe that women cannot manage the rigors of combat, Marine veteran Tim Brown disagrees. He cites the effectiveness of women commandos in the Nicaraguan Contras as evidence of women's fitness for combat.

Nicaraguan women commandos made up 7% of the Contra army. Two thousand of them were volunteers who fought on the front lines. Another 2,000 also served as *correos*, unarmed intelligence runners.

Brown concludes, "Whether the women of the Gulf War, those who served with me in the Marines, or women police officers I know . . . American women have clearly demonstrated ample dedication, stamina and just plain guts. . . . [W]hether women can do the job is no longer in doubt." In the 1990s, increasing numbers of women joined the armed forces.

Sources: Brown, T. (1997, September 30). Women unfit for combat? Au contraire! *Wall Street Journal*, p. A22; Enloe, C. (1998). Armed forces. In W. Mankiller, et al. (Eds.), *A reader's companion to U.S. women's history* (pp. 38–39). New York: Houghton Mifflin.

more so as a result of engaging in work that required those qualities. Other investigations (Aries, 1998; Hochschild, 1975; McGowen & Hart, 1990) demonstrate that women develop communication skills that respond to the conditions of their employment. Some research indicates that women managers may develop even more autonomous and instrumental communication styles than their male peers (Gordon, 1991; Hatcher, 1991).

This suggests that, as men and women enter into new settings and take on new roles, they reform their identities and communication patterns to reflect and respond to the norms and requirements of their contexts. Both sexes can develop communication skills that advance leadership as they find themselves in positions requiring abilities not emphasized in their earlier socialization.

■ Misperceptions of Men's and Women's Ability to Work Together

Because our culture defines women and men as opposites, some people believe that the sexes cannot work together well in the workplace. This misunderstanding boils down to a belief that we work best with "our own kind," a rationale that has been used to justify excluding minorities, lesbians, and gay men from many environments. Extending these two ideas, we run into the stereotype of women and men as sexual or romantic partners. Because the sexes historically have related in romantic and sexual ways, these overtones sometimes seep into workplace interaction between women and men. This leads some people to think that men and women are so focused on each other as romantic or sexual beings that they cannot work together as colleagues.

Studies of mixed-sex task groups shed light on the validity of these beliefs. Although women and men may feel awkward initially when they work together (Murphy & Zorn, 1996), this is usually overcome in a short time, and mixed-sex groups develop comfortable routines for interacting. Second, not only are mixed-sex groups not disruptive to productivity, they actually may enhance the quality of much decision making. Some researchers (W. Wood, 1987) report that groups of men and women are more effective than groups made up only of women or only of men. Why might this be so? Researchers suspect that, when men and women are together, each contributes in important ways to high-quality decision making. Women may specialize in communication that supports and builds

 PERRY

I'll admit I was against having a woman promoted to our executive board, but I'll also admit that I was wrong. I thought Linda wouldn't fit in or have anything to add. I voted for a junior male who I thought would fit in with the rest of us executives. But Linda is just superb. She knows the company inside and out, and she has lots of good ideas for refining policies and developing new lines of products. But what I like most about having her in our group is that she's a real consensus builder and nobody else is. Linda's first concern always seems to be finding common ground among us, and she has an absolutely amazing lack of ego invested in decisions. I'm not sure it's flattering to admit this, but the guys in the group, including me, operate from ego. Sometimes winning a point is more important than crafting the best decision. Linda moves us away from that mindset.

team cohesion, and men may initiate more communication focused on logistics of the task. Effective groups need both kinds of communication. Although androgynous individuals might well supply both kinds of communication, people who are more sex-typed specialize. Thus, mixing women and men often improves the quality of decision making and heightens members' satisfaction.

The research relevant to institutional stereotypes of men, women, and professional communication shows that for the most part the stereotypes are not well founded. Both sexes seem motivated to work and achieve in their jobs, and both seem able to develop the communication skills required in their roles. Further, it appears that not only are women and men able to work together effectively, but they may actually complement and enhance each other's competence in professional settings.

GENDERED COMMUNICATION SYSTEMS IN ORGANIZATIONS

Communication occurs in formal and informal structures and practices of institutions. Formal structures include communication designated by policies, and accountability among members of an organization: leave policies, work schedules, performance reviews, who reports to whom, who has authority to authorize and evaluate whom, and so on. Informal structures, which are at least as important as formal ones, concern interactions and norms beyond or in addition to those that are explicitly defined: becoming part of networks, caucusing with colleagues about issues, learning what is required to be on the fast track, trading favors, gossiping and exchanging information, advising, mentoring, and so forth. Taken together, formal and informal structures define the culture, or values and understandings, of an organization. As we will see, many organizations have gendered cultures (Nicotera & Cushman, 1992) that affect the professional and personal lives of employees. We will focus on leave policies and schedules, communication climates in organizations, and glass ceilings.

■ Leave Policies and Work Schedules

Leave policies. In 1993, the Family and Medical Leave Act was passed so that employees could care for newborns or sick family members. The act, however, doesn't cover all workers. Only companies with 50 or more workers are required to grant family leaves, and some employees can be exempted from leave. Further, the act does not require employers to pay for family leaves, so many workers cannot afford family leave even if they qualify for it. Some individual states, however, do require companies with as few as 25 employees to grant family and medical leave. Most small companies have reported no problems and little, if any, additional administrative expense in providing this benefit (Bernstein, 1999). These results suggest that it is possible to structure work environments so that they do not impose exorbitant costs on families.

Better family leave laws and policies are imperative. In 1999, Catalyst ("Statistics on Mothers," 1999), a nonprofit organization based in New York, reported that more than 60% of mothers with children under 3 are in the workforce, and nearly 80% of women with children under 17 work outside the home. Catalyst also reported that 77% of all single mothers have jobs outside the home. In most of these cases, fathers are not staying home to care for children, often because they feel the pressure to earn a salary and because there is less social approval for men who care for families. Even when companies do allow paternity leave, only one man in five takes it, because they know that men who do take it are not regarded as top-notch professionals (Adler, 1996). One new father reported that, when his daughter was born, he turned down a paternity leave because of "subtle, unspoken, never-in-print" assumptions that define being on the job as what it takes "to be a player." Another new father said, "It's socially unacceptable. The stigma is still there. . . . Society says a man shouldn't do it" ("Fears for Careers," 1990).

Companies that establish maternity leaves but not paternity or family leaves symbolically define women as those who do and should care for children. Fathers and fathering remain unnamed and therefore unrecognized as integral to family life

---

FYI

The Derailed Daddy Track

In fall 1993, Houston Oilers tackle David Williams learned a very expensive lesson—that men who put families above work get little support. Williams missed a game to be with his wife when she gave birth. He was fined a hefty $125,000 for his absence (Rubin, 1994). Like Williams, many men who want to be involved in raising their children encounter resistance at work. Fathering is still devalued in most workplaces, and men who make time to do it often lose out in terms of professional advancement and status.

Part of the reason for resistance is that many senior executives are men who grew up in an era when the norm was for professional men's wives to be full-time homemakers and mothers. The standpoint of the old guard makes it difficult for them to understand younger men who want to share family responsibilities. This problem showed up when John Kostouros asked for a parenting leave. Kostouros's boss told him, "I can't figure why a grown man would want to be with his baby" (Rubin, 1994, p. 19A).

Despite resistance, many men express strong desires to be actively involved in their families. In a 1997 survey (Gerson, 1994, 1998; Shellenbarger, 1997), nearly equal numbers of women and men who work outside of the home said balancing work and family was a major priority in their lives—74% of men and 78% of women. Says Jay Menario, 37-year-old vice president of Unum Life Insurance Company, "As devoted as I am to Unum's success, it isn't going to come at the expense of my children" (quoted in Shellenbarger, 1997).

(Cornell, 1991; Mann, 1989). The view of women as mothers combines with the stereotype of men as breadwinners to create a situation in which it is exceedingly difficult for men to become full partners in raising children. As long as men remain unrepresented in the language of caregiving, their roles in the process will be marginal, devalued, and discouraged.

The language of leave policies also poses another dilemma. When companies name only maternity, paternity, or parental leaves, they include newborn and newly adopted children among those for whom it is legitimate to care, but they exclude all others who might need care. Few U.S. organizations have policies that allow workers time to care for disabled or dying parents. As medical technology expands the human life span, there will be a growing number of older citizens, many of whom will need various degrees of assistance. Who will care for these people? How can children take in parents and provide care when they have their own children to care for and when employers make no provisions for family responsibilities? Will we be forced to choose among our children, our parents, and our livelihoods? The fact that generous parental and family leave policies are working in other countries—every industrialized nation except America has a national policy—provides reason to think they could work here also (Crittenden, 2001; Gerson, 1986; Hewlett, 1986, 1991; Okin, 1989).

Work schedules. Another way in which formal organizational rules affect men and women employees stems from rigid working schedules generally mandated. In-

---

FYI

Maternity Leaves in Various Countries

	Minimum Weeks Allowed	Percent Salary
Sweden*	51	90
France	16–38	84
Italy	20	80
Britain	18	90
Canada	15	60
Germany	14	100
Japan	14	60
Netherlands	7	100
United States	**None	**None

*For both parents combined.
**The 1993 Family and Medical Leave Act does not require all organizations to provide leaves, and it does not apply to all workers.
Source: Child care. (1992, August 10). *Fortune*, pp. 50–54.

---

creasingly, the 9-to-5 model of the workday is giving way to the expectation that 7 or 8 A.M. to 7 or 8 P.M. is normal for "really committed professionals." Obviously, this model—or even the 9-to-5 one—does not accommodate family needs and schedules (Williams, 2000). Day care is expensive, prohibitively so for many single parents. And day care is not a complete solution, because children are sometimes too sick to attend, and arrangements fall through periodically, making it necessary for a parent to take responsibility for child care. Women bear the majority of these responsibilities, taking time off when children are sick or when day care is unavailable. Often this forces them into part-time positions, which imperils their advancement in careers. This pattern (and its costs to women's careers) reflects the stereotype that women are the primary caregivers of children and men who are serious about their careers do not interrupt their work for family matters.

> ## 🐾 JOAN
>
> I'm a single mother, and it's really hard to be that and a worker too. It's not fair that women so often have to sacrifice career advancement because businesses won't create more flexible work hours. When my daughter was young, I had to use my lunch hour to pick her up from preschool. Often I had to ask a neighbor of the day-care provider to stay with her until the preschool opened because I had to attend early morning meetings.

Every study of the costs of providing more leave and flexible working hours shows that, not only do they not cost businesses, but they frequently save money! In states where employers are required to provide leave time (unpaid) for family

---

FYI

The Report Card on Family-Friendly Policies

The bipartisan Commission on Family and Medical Leave studied what happened in the workplace in the three years following passage in 1993 of the Family and Medical Leave Act (Meckler, 1996). Other researchers have also studied the effects of family-friendly practices in the workplace (Worley & Vannoy, 2001). Among the findings:

- Fewer than 4% of eligible workers took family leaves.

- Ninety percent of employers surveyed reported little or no increase in costs as a result of the Family and Medical Leave Act.

- More than 86% of employers said the Family and Medical Leave Act did not affect business productivity.

An increasing number of employers are providing family-friendly policies beyond the Family and Medical Leave Act. These policies include child-care subsidies, flexible work hours, on-site day care for young children, and reimbursement of child-care costs while employees are traveling. Why are companies providing all of these new benefits? The reason is simple, according to Tom Chappel, who founded Tom's of Maine: "In return we get deep gratitude. And along with that you get motivation, productivity, commitment, and loyalty" (Walt, 1997, p. 14).

---

care, there has been virtually no hardship for businesses (Ball, 1991). Surveys of the cost of allowing family leaves show that most businesses find it less expensive to grant leaves than to replace employees ("Hope for Working Families," 1991; Walt, 1997). Costs vary for firms, but the trend is clear: Providing leave for family responsibilities is not prohibitively expensive for most organizations. Companies such as Aetna, Corning, IBM, and Johnson & Johnson that have pioneered in family-friendly policies report that their employee turnover has dropped dramatically and morale has risen comparably ("Mommy Tracks," 1991). Companies also find that establishing family-friendly policies allows them to recruit and keep talented workers they would otherwise lose (Quinn, 2000). Unfortunately, policies that support family involvement, including the 1993 act, are usually available only to highly paid professionals, leaving the majority of workers without a safety net ("Child Care," 1992; Cowell, 1992; Okin, 1989; Quinn, 2000). Here again, we see the intersection of race, class, and gender oppression, because women workers and minorities in blue-collar jobs are least likely to have family leave policies.

■ Communication Climates in Organizations

An organization's communication climate includes interaction patterns and communication style. Communication climates are gendered to the extent that they emphasize gender differences, regard one gender as standard, or provide differential opportunities to women and men. Mentor relationships and collegial networks, a major aspect of communication climates, are seldom formally defined, yet these can make or break careers.

Unwelcoming environments for women. In our earlier discussion of gender inequities in educational settings, we identified a range of ways in which some schools marginalize, devalue, and discriminate against women students. A similar pattern occurs in some organizations. Because historically workplaces have been designed by and for men, some include language and behavior that men find familiar and comfortable but some women do not.

A key contributor to organizational climates in which some women feel devalued is language that emphasizes men's experiences and interests. Pervading most workplaces are terms taken from sports (*hit a home run, huddle on strategy, ballpark figures, second-string player, come up with a game plan, be a team player, line up, score a touchdown*), sexuality (*hit on a person, he has balls, he is a real prick, screw the competition; enter into a pissing contest; stick it to them;* such language also includes calling women employees "hon" or referring to women generally in sexual ways), and the military (*battle plan, mount a campaign, strategy, plan of attack, under fire, get the big guns*). Whether intentional or not, language related to sports, sexuality, and military functions to bind men together into a masculine community in which some women feel unwelcome (Hamilton, 1988; Messner, 2001).

Even today, there is often resistance—and occasionally outright hostility—to women who enter fields where men predominate (Forum, 1997; Palmer & Lee, 1990; Schroedel, 1990; Strine, 1992). Women may be given unrewarding assignments, isolated from key networks of people and information, and treated stereotypically as sex objects, mothers, or children. Each of these techniques contributes to a communication climate that defines women as "not real members of the team." Sexual harassment further devalues women's professional abilities and highlights their sex, which complicates women's work lives in ways men seldom experience (Morin & Rosenfeld, 1998; Strine, 1992; Taylor & Conrad, 1992; Wood, 1993d, 1993f).

The informal network. Relationships among colleagues are important in creating a sense of fit and providing access to essential information that may not come through formal channels. Because men have predominated in the workplace, most informal networks are largely or exclusively male, giving rise to the term *old boy network*. Hiring and promotion decisions are often made through informal communication within these networks. For example, Bob knows of a good job prospect and tells Nathan about it while they are golfing; over drinks, Ed comments to Joel about an impressive trainee, so that trainee stands out later when Ed selects people for an important assignment; Mike talks with Ben, John, and Frank about his new marketing plan, so when Mike introduces it formally in a meeting, he has support lined up. Informal communication networks are vital to professional success.

Women tend to be less involved than men in informal networks. They often feel unwelcome, and feminine socialization does not encourage them to assert themselves and claim a position in a group. Further, women may feel out of place because of their minority status. When only one or two women are in a company or at a particular level, they stand out and are aware of their token status (Kanter, 1977; O'Leary & Ickovics, 1991). A sense of difference also is experienced by people of color who confront a sea of White when they enter predominantly White professions. Co-workers' behaviors often compound women's and minority people's feeling of being different. When a woman enters an all-male group, men sometimes intensify masculine behaviors, talking more loudly, crudely, and perhaps profanely in what is probably an unconscious male-bonding process (Kanter, 1977). Similarly, Mary Strine (1992) has shown how sexual harassment in the workplace, in addition to violating women, communicates the message that "you are not wanted here." In the face of communication that defines them as outsiders, women may avoid informal networks, thus losing out on a key source of information and support.

 REGGIE

I've tried to get into the informal network at my job, but I'm the only Black guy there. After I first started work, when I saw a group of the White men standing around talking, I would go over to join them. One of two things happened: Either they stopped talking and the group broke up, or they kept talking but made no effort to include me, nor even to acknowledge I'd joined them. I don't think they meant to dis me, but they sure communicated that I wasn't one of them. Now I just do my work and don't try to be one of them.

Mentor relationships. A mentor is a senior colleague who advises and assists a junior employee in building a career. Often, faculty mentor graduate students and sometimes undergraduates. Coaches sometimes mentor players. In the past, fathers frequently tutored sons in running the family business. A mentor is at least helpful and sometimes indispensable to career advancement. Both women and minorities are less likely to have mentors than are men of the majority race.

Several factors account for the low number of women and minority people who have the benefit of mentors. First, the numbers game works against them. Most of us prefer to interact with people with whom we identify rather than with people who seem different from us. The paucity of women and minorities in senior positions means that there are few who identify with new female and/or minority employees. Research indicates that African American women are least likely of all groups to be mentored (Morrison & Von Glinow, 1990). Men are sometimes reluctant to mentor young women for a variety of reasons: fear of gossip about sexual relations, their assumption that women are less serious than men about careers, or feeling less comfortable with women than with men as colleagues. This pattern perpetuates the status quo in which White men gain assistance in climbing the corporate ladder, whereas women and minorities receive little help.

In an effort to compensate for the lack of networks and mentors available to women, several innovations have arisen. Professional women's networks allow women to share ideas, contacts, strategies for advancement, and information. In addition to furnishing information, these networks provide women with support and a sense of fit with other professionals like them. A number of established professional women also mentor younger women in their fields, even though doing so requires heavy investments of time and energy. Because even women who have earned professional status report that they must continue to work harder than their male colleagues to prove themselves, finding time to mentor is difficult. As men and women become accustomed to interacting as colleagues, they may become more comfortable mentoring one another and forming sex-integrated communication networks.

■ Glass Ceilings—and Walls

Finally, we consider what has been called the **glass ceiling,** which is an invisible barrier that limits advancement of women and minorities. In 1991, *U.S. News and World Report*'s lead business story concerned the glass ceiling that blocks women's progress in professions ("Trouble at the Top," 1991). Labeling her report the "glass ceiling initiative," Labor Secretary Lynn Martin revealed that gender discrimination pervades the workplace, particularly at the upper levels. Since that report was published over a decade ago, other research has confirmed the persistence of glass ceilings that limit women's careers (Armas, 2000; Ekrut, 2001; Valian, 1998). Most often, women's progress is impeded by subtle discrimination that limits women's opportunities. It might be the stereotype of women as mothers that leads an exec-

By permission of Dave Coverly and Creators Syndicate, Inc.

utive to assume that a working mother would not be interested in a major new assignment, one that could advance her career. It might be seeing a woman in sexual terms so that her competence is overlooked. It might be misinterpreting an inclusive, collaborative style of communication as indicating lack of initiative. All of these stereotypes and misperceptions pose subtle barriers—a glass ceiling that keeps women out of the executive suite.

But glass ceilings may be only part of the problem. As a 1992 report ("Study Says Women Face Glass Walls," 1992, p. B2) first noted, "If the ceiling doesn't stop today's working woman, the walls will." The term **glass walls** is a metaphor to describe sex segregation on the job, in which stereotypes lead to placing women in positions that require traditionally feminine skills (assistant to . . . , clerical roles, counseling, human relations). Typically, areas such as human resources do not include a career ladder in which doing well at one level allows advancement to the next. In essence, many of the positions that women are encouraged to take have no advancement paths (Hoffman, 1998).

Recognizing that subtle, unintentional discrimination is no more acceptable than overt prejudice, some companies are taking steps to break through

 TANGIA

Where I used to work, the boss was always dropping in on the men who held positions at my level, but he never dropped in to talk with any of the women at that level. He also had a habit of introducing males in our division to visitors from the main office, but he never introduced women to them. It was like there was a closed loop and we weren't part of it.

Microinequities

Microinequities are one of the most pervasive and subtle forms of discrimination. These are verbal comments and behaviors that devalue members of a group but are not specific violations of laws prohibiting discrimination. Examples are speaking to male colleagues but not speaking to female ones, asking only a male worker to fill in as supervisor when the supervisor has to be away from the office, and not telling women workers what they need to do to improve job performance and qualify for promotions. Mary Rowe (1990) reports that although microinequities don't cross the line of illegal actions, they have negative impact on morale, job performance, and opportunities for promotion and training.

Source: Rowe, M. (1990). Barriers to equality: The power of subtle discrimination to maintain unequal opportunity. *Employee Responsibilities and Rights Journal, 3,* 153–163.

glass ceilings and walls that unfairly hinder women's career advancement. Du Pont, for example, has initiated a rotation policy that moves women and men employees through different jobs so that all employees have opportunities to learn about the company and qualify for advancement ("Study Says Women Face Glass Walls," 1992, p. B2). This is a model of institutional efforts to accommodate diverse workers and in the process enlarge the pool of talent available to organizations.

EFFORTS TO REDRESS GENDERED INEQUITY IN INSTITUTIONS

A desire to correct gender and sex discrimination (as well as other types of discrimination) has led to a variety of solutions. Four particular means to end discrimination are equal opportunity, affirmative action, quotas and goals, and increasing sensitivity to gender issues in educational content and processes. Understanding the methods of redressing inequities and how they differ is important so that we can evaluate arguments for and against them and decide our own positions. Although this chapter focuses specifically on the workplace, our discussion will address discrimination in both professional and educational settings. These are the two contexts in which methods to lessen discrimination have been most pronounced.

■ Equal Opportunity Laws

Laws prohibiting discrimination began with the landmark *Brown v. Board of Education* case in 1954. In deciding the case for Brown, the U.S. Supreme Court overturned the "separate but equal" doctrine that allowed separate educational systems for White and African American citizens. Although this was the start of laws to guarantee civil liberties, equal opportunity legislation is not confined to racial discrimination. Following *Brown v. Board of Education,* a number of laws were passed in the 1950s and 1960s to prohibit discrimination against individual members of minority groups, including racial minorities and women. Two primary examples of **equal opportunity laws** are Title VII of the Civil Rights Act of 1964, which prohibits discrimination in employment on the basis of race, color, religion, sex, or national origin, and the 1972 Title IX, which forbids discrimination in educational programs receiving federal aid. Although Title IX is considered the primary federal law regarding discrimination on the basis of sex, it is not the only one. Others are Title IV of the 1964 Civil Rights Act, the Women's Educational Equity Act of 1974 and 1978, an amendment to the 1976 Vocational Education Act, and laws pertaining to specific institutes and foundations (Klein, 1985; Salomone, 1986).

Equal opportunity laws focus on discrimination against *individual* members of groups. For instance, complaints filed with the Equal Employment Opportunity Commission (EEOC) must claim that a particular person suffered discrimination because of sex, race, or other criteria named in laws (Public Agenda Foundation, 1990). Equal opportunity does not ask whether a group (for example, women or Hispanics) is underrepresented or has been treated inequitably; instead, it focuses specifically on discrimination against individuals. Further, the equal opportunity strategy focuses on *present* practices, so historical patterns of discrimination are irrelevant. For example, a university with a record of not admitting women into a particular program is not subject to suit unless a particular individual can prove she personally and currently suffered discrimination on the basis of her sex. Governmental obligation extends only to present, individual equality of opportunity. Equal opportunity is assessed on a case-by-case basis.

Although Title IX prohibits sex discrimination, for years it lacked regulations to ensure its implementation (Mickelson & Smith, 1992). Further, the scope of this law was weakened in 1984 when the Supreme Court narrowed its application from whole institutions to only specific programs and activities that receive federal money. Despite laws, sexism and discrimination against women persist in educational settings. In Chapter 8, we saw how curricular materials, school organization, and educational processes unequally benefit women and men. Equal opportunity legislation fails to address the impact of historical patterns of discrimination and covert biases, so these continue to riddle educational institutions and the workplace.

◼ Affirmative Action Policies

President Lyndon Johnson used his 1965 commencement address at Howard University to inaugurate a new strategy for combating discrimination. Saying that recent passage of civil rights legislation was important but insufficient to end discrimination, Johnson called for policies that address the weight of historical

RAY

I'm really glad to see affirmative action being rolled back. Ever since I was in high school, I've felt that as a White man I was going to suffer reverse discrimination. I think it was unfair that for so long women and minorities got preferential treatment and qualified White men couldn't get jobs or promotions.

SHERETTA

I get so ripped off when I hear White guys badmouth affirmative action. They don't know what they're talking about. They speak totally from their self-interest and their ignorance. The first thing they say is that qualified White men are losing jobs to unqualified Blacks. That's not true. Affirmative action doesn't require (or even suggest) that a job should go to an unqualified person, even if the individual is a green lesbian from Istanbul! Another thing White guys say a lot is that they didn't hold Blacks down in the past, so they shouldn't be penalized today. To that I'd like to say they sure as hell don't mind taking a heap of advantages they didn't earn, like good schools and clothes and financial support. Do they think they earned those things? How do they think their daddies and granddaddies earned them? I'll tell you how: off the labor of Black people that they were holding back, that's how.

prejudice. He said, "You do not take a person who for years has been hobbled by chains and liberate him, bring him to the starting line of a race, and then say, 'you are free to compete with all the others.'" Johnson went on to argue that equality of opportunity, which is the guarantee of civil rights legislation, must be matched with equality in results. To do this, he claimed, there must be measures to compensate for historical patterns of discrimination against groups as well as subtle forms of discrimination such as institutional racism and sexism.

Affirmative action hinges on three key ideas (Public Agenda Foundation, 1990). First, because discrimination has systematically restricted the opportunities of *groups* of people, remedies must apply to entire groups, not just to individuals. Second, there must be *preferential treatment* for members of groups that have suffered discrimination in order to compensate for the legacy of discrimination. Third, the effectiveness of remedies is judged by *results,* not intent. If a law does not result in greater presence of women and minorities, then it is ineffective in producing the result of equality.

The goal of affirmative action is to increase the representation in education and in the workplace of available and qualified women, minorities, and other historically marginalized groups. This focus causes some to question the fairness of affirmative action policies (summarized in Witt, 1990). They argue that insisting on greater numbers of women and minorities in companies and academic programs results in excluding better-qualified White males. Yet the claim that affirmative action deprives Whites of admission to schools is challenged by a recent study by William Bowen, president of the Mellon Foundation and former president of Princeton, and Derek Bok, former president of Harvard University (1998). After analyzing grades, SAT scores, and other data for 93,000 students of all races, Bowen and Bok found that eliminating affirmative action would raise Whites' chances of admission by a mere 1.5%. What many people do not realize is that affirmative action includes two important limitations. First, the goal is to increase the number of *qualified* members of historically marginalized groups, so there is no pressure to admit, hire, or promote women and minorities who lack necessary qualifications. Affirmative action policies also recognize the *limited availability* of historically underrepresented groups. Because of long-standing discriminatory practices, there may be fewer women and minorities who are qualified to participate in certain programs and activities. Affirmative action attempts only to increase the number of qualified members of minority groups commensurate with their availability.

To understand how affirmative action policies work, it's important to distinguish between *qualified* and *most qualified*. Consider an example: Jane Evans and John Powell are the final two candidates for the single remaining opening in a medical school that requires a 3.2 undergraduate grade point average and a 1200 on the medical aptitude exam. Jane's undergraduate average is 3.4, whereas John's is 3.6. On the entrance exam, she scores 1290, and he scores 1300. Although his qualifications are slightly better than hers, both individuals clearly meet the school's requirements; both are adequately qualified. In such a case, affirmative action would require admitting Jane instead of John because she meets the qualifications and does so despite historical patterns that discourage women from studying sciences and math, which are primary in pre-med schooling. The fact that she overcame disadvantages to become qualified suggests that Jane will succeed in medical studies if she is given the opportunity.

As columnist William Raspberry (1990) points out, affirmative action was an attempt to translate goals of equality from empty theory into concrete realities. Unlike equal opportunity legislation, affirmative action recognizes the impact of historical patterns of discrimination and the ways in which they disadvantage whole groups of people. Thus, this remedy aims to make up for the effects of a long heritage of bias by giving slight preference to individuals whose qualification was achieved despite obstacles and discrimination.

In recent years, affirmative action has been challenged. The first instance was Proposition 209, a California initiative that banned state and local governments from considering race or gender in public hiring, contracting, and enrollment in institutions of higher education. Since Proposition 209 passed, similar legislation has been voted into effect in other areas around the United States. At the same time, strong support for affirmative action has been expressed, and efforts to diminish it have been resisted. Students in California recently persuaded schools there not to remove affirmative action considerations from policies governing enrollment. In recent years, the courts have tended to support affirmative action admissions policies. In several cases, the courts have ruled that the goal of increasing diversity is an adequate basis for considering race in admissions decisions (Gose, 2001).

Extensive polling reveals that substantial majorities of students say they benefit educationally from ethnic and racial diversity on their campuses. Surveys of faculty similarly conclude that faculty think racial diversity is educationally advantageous (Schmidt, 2001).

Ever since affirmative action policies were enacted, public debate about them has been vigorous. Yet until recently there has been little hard evidence about the effects of affirmative action. That changed with a 1997 study that compared the careers of 356 students admitted to medical schools under affirmative action with a matched sample of students admitted using standard admission criteria (Dreier & Freer, 1997). On a 4.0 grading scale, the mean GPA of the affirmative action students was 3.06 compared with a 3.5 mean average for students who did not receive special consideration for admission. Students admitted under affirmative action had lower grades during their first years in medical school, but graduation rates were very similar: Ninety-four percent of the affirmative action students graduated, and 97% of the regularly admitted students graduated. Evaluations of the graduates years later showed that members of the two groups did equally well in their residencies and became equally qualified physicians. Further, Black men who graduated from selective schools were more likely than their White peers to become civic and community leaders (Bowen & Bok, 1998).

■ Quotas and Goals

Quotas. Perhaps the most controversial effort to redress discrimination is the **quota system.** Building on affirmative action's focus on end results, quotas specify that a number or percentage of women and/or minorities must be admitted to schools, hired in certain positions, or promoted to defined levels in institutions. For instance, a company might stipulate that it has a quota of 50% women in upper-management positions. A binding quota requires a specified number or percentage of women regardless of circumstances such as merit. If a medical school has an unmet quota of women to be admitted, it must admit women applicants even if they lack the required academic averages and entrance exam scores.

A famous case relevant to quotas was brought in 1978 when Allan Bakke sued a school, claiming that he had suffered discrimination when the University of California rejected him, a White male, in favor of less qualified minority applicants. Bakke won his case on the grounds that he had been a victim of "reverse discrimination." However, the court did not outlaw using race as one factor in admissions decisions. It only ruled that schools may not set aside specific numbers of spaces for minorities. In her 1990 race for the California governorship, Dianne Feinstein pledged that, if she won, she would appoint women to half of the offices in her administration. She reasoned that women are more than half of the voters in California, so a representative number—half—of state administrators should be women. This stand cost Feinstein votes because many people viewed her quotas as reverse discrimination. As one writer (Beck, 1990) notes, "Laws and policies that discriminate in favor of one race or sex or ethnic group discriminate against other people."

Goals. **Goals** are different from quotas, although the two are frequently confused. A goal states an institution's intention to achieve representation of minorities or women. For instance, a company could establish the goal of having women make up 30% of its workforce by the year 2005. Goals call for no flexibility on qualifications, and they do not require results. If the company in our example had only 13% women by 2005, there would be no penalty nor even any need to develop new strategies. The company could simply announce that its new goal is to have 30% women by the year 2010. Goals are more flexible than quotas, which many consider an advantage. However, goals also lack enforcement provisions, which means their effectiveness depends entirely on the commitment of those charged to pursue them. For this reason, groups that have been victims of discrimination are often skeptical of goals as a serious effort to increase equity (Witt, 1990).

Ironically, both quotas and goals can work *against* women and minorities. One researcher (Maraniss, 1991) points out that, just as they function to let in minorities, so too can they exclude people. The numbers specified by quotas and goals

> ## ℰ NICOLA
>
> The quota system is the only thing that can work. The laws aren't enforced, so they don't help, and affirmative action is just a bunch of talk. I've watched both my parents discriminated against all of their lives just because of their skin color. All the laws and pledges of affirmative action haven't done a damned thing to change that. Quotas cut through all of the crap of intentions and pledges and say point-blank there will be so many African Americans in this company or this school or whatever. That's the only way change is ever going to happen. And when I hear White dudes whining about how quotas are unfair to them, I want to throw up. They know *nothing* about unfair.

can be interpreted and used as a maximum number of women and minorities rather than a minimum. In our example, the 30% number established for women could be used to keep more than 30% of the workforce from being female, even if 40% of qualified applicants were women. Departments may hire an African American or woman scholar and then cease to consider other female and minority applicants for future openings—they've met their quota by employing one. Because

---

FYI

When Quotas Raise Questions—and When They Don't

Some people who oppose affirmative action policies, quotas, and goals say it's unfair to reserve places for members of a group—in this case, women and minorities. They argue that all applicants should be evaluated on individual merit and not be given special favors because they belong to some group.

It's interesting that questions aren't raised about a long-standing quota system that has benefited White students. Many, if not most, universities have legacy policies, which accord preferential consideration to the children of alumnae and alumni. At Harvard, for example, 44% of the class that entered in 1992 were legacies.

Sources: Marble, M. (1994). Reconciling race and reality. *Media Studies Journal, 8,* 11–18; Schmidt, P. (1998, October 30). U. of Michigan prepares to defend. *Chronicle of Higher Education,* pp. A32–A34.

both quotas and goals establish limits, they can be used to exclude as well as include.

Goals and quotas can work against women and minorities in a second way. When goals or quotas are in effect, members of institutions may assume women and minorities got in only because of their sex or race. When this happens, individual women and people of color are not regarded as capable members of the school, business, or trade. Others may overlook their qualifications and accomplishments and simply discount them as "quota fillers." One implication of this is that women and minorities—regardless of their qualifications—may be resented by peers who think they didn't earn membership in the institution. In addition, if others discount the abilities of minorities and women, they are unlikely to take them seriously and give them important responsibilities that allow achievement and opportunities that lead to advancement.

■ Increasing Sensitivity to Gender Issues

A final remedy for persistent discrimination is enhancing sensitivity to gender discrimination through training and through creating curricular and professional materials that do not foster inequity. This strategy assumes that many people are unaware of the range of ways in which institutions devalue and disadvantage women. If lack of awareness is the problem, then a promising solution is to make people conscious of practices that inadvertently devalue and marginalize women and to provide materials that incorporate women and their experiences.

Implementing this solution requires developing programs that inform educators and professionals of subtle biases and introduce them to alternative styles of behaving and interpreting others. For instance, a program of nonsexist education for 3- to 5-year-olds was developed (Koblinsky & Sugawara, 1984) and implemented. Both girls and boys who participated in the special program had substantially fewer sex-stereotypical views than they had before the program and than their peers in regular programs manifested. At some universities, faculty and staff have developed workshops on sexual harassment and gender discrimination in classrooms. Students, staff, and faculty who attend these workshops learn how some of their communication and course content may exclude women and people of color. In addition, participants in these workshops are introduced to methods for making their classrooms more inclusive and equitable for people of color and women. Of course, not everyone cares about inequities, and many people are not willing to make changes, especially changes that may limit some of their own privileges. Thus, an important drawback of gender-sensitivity programs is that they require the personal commitment and interest of administrators and participants in the programs.

A complementary way to decrease gender bias in education is to provide teachers with materials that allow them to teach more inclusively. For instance, Karlyn Campbell (1989a, 1989b, 1993) followed her call to include women speakers in public address courses by producing three volumes of material on the lives and speeches of important women orators. Helen Tierney has published a series of books that document women's contributions in the sciences (1989); literature, arts, and education (1990); and history, philosophy, and religion (1991). A colleague and I (Wood & Lenze, 1991b) published an article in which we explained how to incorporate both women's and men's developmental paths into instruction on communication and self-development. Similarly, another colleague and I (Wood & Inman, 1993) published an essay that showed ways to include masculine modes of creating and expressing closeness in curricular units on communication and romantic relationships.

 GEORGE

I like the idea of training in gender sensitivity. Part of the orientation program when I came here was a program in sexism and racism. Until I attended that, it never occurred to me that words like *girl* could offend, and I had never realized Confederate flags would seem like bigotry to Blacks. Maybe I was naive, but I really didn't understand those things, and now that I do, I don't do them anymore. And then courses like this one make me aware of other things, like how I interrupt women and how men dominate communication. I think a lot of the discrimination is really insensitivity and is really not deliberate. Once people understand that certain words and actions hurt, they'll stop.

The national debate over ways of redressing inequity is heated. Efforts to roll back affirmative action policies are being greeted with cheers from some Americans and dire warnings from others who fear that, without mandated efforts to prevent discrimination, organizations and schools will do nothing to ensure equity across sex and race–ethnicity. The conversation about remedies for inequities will remain on the national agenda for some time to come (Mickelson & Smith, 1998).

SUMMARY

In this chapter, we have considered a variety of ways in which institutional life intersects with cultural understandings of gender and communication. Views of masculinity and femininity endorsed by society seep into the workplace in the form of stereotypes of women, men, and professional communication and in communication systems that reflect and perpetuate gendered attitudes. Although overt and subtle gender bias persists in institutional life, we should remember that only recently have substantial numbers of women sought extended professional careers. As women and men gain experience in communicating with each other as colleagues, and as organizations recognize the distinctive contributions each gender makes to productivity and climate, we should see erosion in some of the barriers that exist today.

Clearly, organizations need to adapt to the nature of the contemporary workforce. This will involve recognizing family responsibilities as part of most employees' lives and increasing efforts to accommodate family commitments. In addition, institutions should identify and alter communication practices and climates that create inequitable working environments for diverse employees. Both organizations and individuals will benefit by climates that are equally hospitable to women, men, minority races, and gays and lesbians.

Reforming institutional structures and practices is a priority for young people who are now entering the workforce. You and your peers will make up and define the workplace of the future. Through attention to legislation that affects the workplace and through your own participation in it, you may take an active role in reforming the nature of institutional life in America so that it is more equitable and humane for all employees and so that it is actively enriched by the diversity of humans who make up our society.

Our focus on gendered communication in present-day organizations might lead you to feel overwhelmed by the serious problems that exist. Yet there is good reason to believe we can bring about changes. For instance, in 1979 only about 100 employers provided any kind of child-care support; a decade later, well over 4,000 did ("Firms Design Benefits," 1989), and we now have a national family leave policy. Between 1987 and 1989, about 100 firms adopted some kind of elder-care assistance programs ("Firms Design Benefits," 1989). More and more organizations are experimenting with flextime, telecommuting, and other options that allow employees to arrange schedules to accommodate both family and job responsibilities. Other changes are happening, and still more can be realized through our efforts.

For innovations to occur, we need to resist gender stereotypes in our own thinking and to challenge them in the thinking and actions of others. One of the most pressing challenges for your generation is to revise institutional gender stereotypes and communication systems that restrict the possibilities open to men and women for full lives as professionals and members of families. In short, we need to remake our institutions to correspond to the lives of today's men and women. By recognizing inequities that exist and the stereotypes behind them, you empower yourself to instigate changes that can improve the conditions in which we live and work.

DISCUSSION QUESTIONS

1. Have you observed instances of classifying women into the four sex stereotypes identified in the text: sex object, mother, child, and iron maiden? Have you observed or experienced these in environments where you have worked? Think about how working women are represented in television shows and in movies. Are they depicted in sex-stereotypical roles?

2. How might being classified as a sex object, mother, or child affect a woman's career opportunities and effectiveness? How might the iron maiden role influence them? What do you see as options for how women might resist being cast into these stereotypes?

3. Have you seen examples of men being classified as sturdy oaks, fighters, or breadwinners? Have you seen men classified as wimps? How do such sex stereotypes limit career opportunities and effectiveness for men? What happens to men who don't measure up to stereotypes of masculinity?

4. Do you agree with the chapter's claim that professionalism generally is defined by masculine standards? Is this a problem? How does defining normative behavior from the standpoint of a particular group affect people who are not members of that group? Should professionalism be defined more inclusively to incorporate diverse styles of communication?

5. If you have worked for both men and women, draw on your experience to identify similarities and differences in female and male supervisors' expectations of employees, communication styles, and relationships with co-workers and employees. Do they use power differently? Does one sex tend to encourage more participation than the other? Do they build different kinds of connections with others in work settings?

6. Use your InfoTrac College Edition's PowerTrac to access Alan Saltzstein, Yuan Ting, and Grace Hall Saltzstein's 2001 article, "Work-family balance and job satisfaction." According to this article, why do some policies intended to be "family friendly" actually increase work–family tension? Which family-friendly policies seem most effective for most workers?

7. Do you think organizations should accommodate families beyond what is required in the 1993 act? Specifically, should organizations adapt their policies and practices to provide more than 12 weeks leave when employees have or adopt children? Should organizations encourage men to be more actively involved in family life? Should organizations support workers who need time off to care for parents or other dependents? Should leaves be paid?

8. Interview some people involved in careers to discover how important networks are. Do women and men professionals report they are equally welcomed into informal networks in their organizations and fields? Do they report receiving equal guidance and mentoring from more established colleagues?

9. Use your InfoTrac College Edition's PowerTrac search engine to access Gillian Flynn's 1998 article, "The harsh reality of diversity programs." What evidence does she cite to support her claim that efforts to diversify the American workforce have not been successful? What role does she think communication can play in more effective efforts to diversify the workforce?

10. The chapter mentions gender-awareness programs that some organizations now provide to their employees. Do you think these are a good idea? Thinking about all that you have learned in this course, what would you include in a gender-awareness training program for a company? What understandings of gender and communication would assist people in working together comfortably and provide equally friendly

working environments to women and men? As a class, design the content of what you think would be an effective program in gender awareness.

11. Now that you understand distinctions among the equal opportunity laws, affirmative action, goals, quotas, and sensitivity training, which do you perceive to be most appropriate? Do you think different methods of redressing discrimination are advisable for short-term and long-term goals?

 12. Use your InfoTrac College Edition's PowerTrac search engine to access Candy Tymson's 2001 article, "Business communication: how to bridge the gender gap." Is her information on gender communication in the workplace consistent with material presented in this chapter? How does she recommend addressing miscommunications between women and men?

10

Gendered Media

Bruce Willis plays a sensitive psychologist in The Sixth Sense; *a devoted husband and father in* The Story of Us; *a decisive, confident, aggressive businessman in* Armageddon, *and an authoritarian, cold-blooded general in* The Siege.

Julia Roberts portrays a flighty, flirty woman who is waiting for the right man to complete her life in Runaway Bride *and a smart, assertive, sexy investigator in* Erin Brockovitch.

hat do you notice about the roles played by Willis and Roberts? How do they depart from established views of gender? How do they reinforce traditional views of gender? These examples, as well as others we'll discuss in this chapter, illustrate two key points about gender and contemporary media. First, in recent years there have been some significant changes in how women and men are represented in mainstream media. Today major actors embody traditional gender stereotypes: men as aggressive, independent, and violent; women as sexy and dependent on men. At the same time, major stars portray nontraditional versions of the sexes: men as sensitive and nurturing; women as assertive and independent. Media today offer a fascinating stage on which different, sometimes opposing images of women and men are played out. Conventional images of women and men are matched by very unconventional images of each sex.

The second point the opening examples reveal is more subtle: Underneath the new images of women and men lie some very traditional gender stereotypes. Erin Brockovitch can defy traditional views of femininity by being assertive and independent as long as she also embodies traditional ideals of femininity by being sexy.

Audiences find Elizabeth Corday on *ER* acceptable as a brilliant surgeon as long as she is also in a committed relationship with Mark Green. Ainsley Hayes appears as a strong, independent-thinking attorney on *The West Wing*, but viewers also note she is "the blonde Republican sex kitten." The Powerpuff girls are smart and strong, yet also very soft and nurturing. Bruce Willis can be gentle because he is clearly very masculine in traditional ways. Tony Soprano can be sensitive, but he's also a mobster who doesn't hesitate to kill his enemies. Jed Bartlett can be a kind, caring man, but as the President of the United States, he's also the most powerful man in the world. Underneath what appear to be radically different images of women and men are some very familiar, very traditional themes. In this chapter we explore what is happening in contemporary media and what it says about gender. We'll take note of how media representations of men and women have changed as well as how they stay the same.

Media are among the most important ways that society defines gender as well as other aspects of personal identity and collective life. From newspapers to MTV, media shape our understandings of women, men, and relationships between the sexes. Media tend to reflect and reproduce cultural ideals and expectations about gender. By defining "normal" women, men, and relationships, media suggest who we personally should be as women and men.

At the same time, media provide a stage upon which challenges to established views of gender are enacted and explored. Media are also gatekeepers of information and images. To a significant extent, they control what we see and know by deciding what programs to air, what news stories to feature, how to represent issues and events, and how to depict women and men. By selectively regulating what we see, media influence how we perceive gender issues, ourselves, and men and women in general.

To launch our exploration of how media reflect and shape understandings of gender, we will first establish the significance of media in cultural life. Next, we will identify basic themes and trends in media portrayals of women, men, and relationships between the sexes. Third, we will examine media's role as a gatekeeper of information on issues related to gender. Finally, we will ask how media portrayals of men, women, and gender issues contribute to misconceptions of issues, violence against women, psychological and physical problems of men and women, and limited views of our human possibilities.

THE PREVALENCE OF MEDIA IN CULTURAL LIFE

We live in an era saturated by media. Our views of ourselves and gender are influenced by the films and television we watch, the radio programs we hear, the music we listen to, and the magazines and newspapers we read. Recent demographic information (U.S. Bureau of the Census, 2000) reveals how much media are part of our lives. Televisions are in more than 98% of U.S. households. Two-thirds of households today have cable, and four of five households have VCRs. Fully 99% of homes have radios. In the average home, at least one television is on more than seven hours a day. Children between two and seven years old spend an average of 3½ hours a day with media (Weiner, 1999). MTV is the number 1 cable network for 12- to 24-year-olds (Ali & Gordon, 2001). By age 6, the average child in the United States has watched more than 5,000 hours of television (Leaper, 2000). Viewing time soars to 19,000 hours for the average 18-year-old person.

Beyond television, media continue to pervade our lives. While walking or riding through any area, we take in an endless procession of billboards that advertise various products, services, people, and companies. Magazines abound, and each one is full of stories and advertisements that portray men and women and their relationships. Advertisements, which make up nearly half of some magazines, tell us what products we need and where to buy them if we are to meet cultural standards for women and men. Radios, Walkmans, and stereo systems allow us to hear music as much of the time as we wish, whereas home videos are doing a record business as Americans see more films than ever.

> **STEPHANI**
>
> I don't think the media influence who I am or what I do. I mean, sure, I watch a lot of shows and movies and read magazines like *Cosmo* and *Self,* but I think for myself. I like to see new styles of clothes and hair and makeup and then I try them out for myself. That doesn't make me a dupe of the media.

> **FRED**
>
> I don't think my generation is very critical of media. Whatever it shows, we try to copy. Look at the "yard" (jail-yard) look that everyone's wearing now, with jeans falling off our butts. We saw rap stars wearing jeans that way, and now we're all doing it. I remember when I was a kid and *Charlie's Angels* was on TV and Farrah Fawcett was so hot. My mom got the Farrah hairdo. So did a lot of her friends. Now the girls I know are copying Britney or Ally or whoever is hot at the moment.

Newspapers, news programming, and talk shows establish the horizons of our world, contemporary issues, and the roles of various people in shaping cultural life. Popular advice books and gothic novels are best-sellers, and pornographic print and visual media are readily available to anyone who is interested.

THEMES IN MEDIA

Media communicate images of the sexes. Despite some changes in media representations of women and men, media continue to give prominence to unrealistic, stereotypical, and limiting perceptions of who we are and can be. Three themes describe how media represent gender. First, women and minorities are underrepresented, which falsely implies that White men are the cultural standard and that women and minorities are unimportant or invisible. Second, men and women are often portrayed in stereotypical ways that reflect and sustain socially endorsed views of gender. Third, depictions of relationships between men and women emphasize traditional roles and unequal power between men and women. We will consider each of these themes in this section.

■ Underrepresentation of Women and Minorities

A primary way in which media distort reality is in underrepresenting women and minorities. Whether it is prime-time television, children's programming, or newscasts, males outnumber females. Because this is inconsistent with the proportions of males and females in the actual world, media misrepresent actual proportions of men and women in the population. This constant distortion tempts us to believe that there really are more men than women and, further, that men are the cultural standard.

Minorities are even less visible than women, with African Americans appearing only rarely (Holtzman, 2000; Merritt, 2001) and other ethnic minorities virtually nonexistent. When members of minority groups do appear, they are typically in supporting roles, and they are likely to be shown in predominantly White cultures with their own racial culture and values obscured (Merritt, 2001; Rhodes, 1995). The prime-time schedule for fall 1999 dramatically demonstrates the underrepresentation of minorities in media. Of the 26 new entertainment programs that the major broadcast networks (ABC, CBS, Fox, NBC) announced in the late summer, not a single one featured a minority person in a leading role (Braxton, 1999). Although criticism of the lack of minorities led to some revisions in programming, media's tendency to underrepresent minorities persists. In children's programming, African Americans usually appear in supporting roles (O'Connor, 1989). Black characters are scarce and often stereotyped as subordinate, bad, or exotic. Ellen Seiter (1995), a professor of telecommunications, points out that in Saturday-morning commercials on children's television, Whites outnumber Blacks, speaking roles are reserved almost entirely for Whites, and Blacks are usually on the sides of the screen, whereas Whites occupy the center screen.

David Evans (1993) criticizes television for stereotyping Black males as athletes and entertainers. These roles, writes Evans, mislead young Black male viewers into thinking success "is only a dribble or dance step away" (p. 10) and blind them to other, more realistic ambitions. African Americans are also underrepresented in news programming. Sixty percent of news stories on Blacks portray them negatively, and reports of crimes in which Blacks are accused are less likely to include prodefense sound bites than are reports of crimes in which Whites are accused (Entman, 1994; Meyers, 1997). Hispanics and Asians are nearly absent in prime-time television, and when they are presented, it is usually as villains or criminals (Holtzman, 2000).

Also underrepresented is the single fastest-growing group of Americans—older people. As a country, we are aging such that people over 60 now make up a major part of our population; within this group, women significantly outnumber men. In contrast to demographic realities, media consistently show fewer older women than men, presumably because cultural ideals of femininity center on youth and beauty. Further, elderly individuals are frequently portrayed as sick, dependent, fumbling, and passive—images not borne out in real life. Distorted depictions of older people, especially older women, in media can delude us into thinking they are a small, sickly, and unimportant part of our population.

Portrayals of Men and Women

Media are powerful in shaping our views of women and men. Historically, media have emphasized stereotyped and highly traditional images of women, men, and relationships between the sexes. These stereotypical portrayals continue today. Men are most often represented as active, adventurous, powerful, sexually aggressive, and largely uninvolved in human relationships, and women are represented as maternal, childish, or sex objects who are young, thin, beautiful, passive, dependent, and often incompetent and dumb. Although these remain the dominant media images of the sexes, new versions of men and women are appearing in films, on television, in music, and in print media. Contemporary media, then, comprise a stage on which diverse, sometimes contradictory, images of gender are presented and negotiated.

Portrayals of men. Although contemporary media offer some nontraditional images of men, the majority of men on prime-time television are independent, aggressive, and in charge. Television programming for all ages disproportionately depicts men, particularly White heterosexual men, as serious, confident, competent, powerful, and in high-status positions. Gentleness in men, which was briefly evi-

---

FYI

Resurgence of the Military Man

Have you noticed the resurgence of wartime movies and, with them, the popularity of the traditional military man? Film critic Michael Medved (2000) has. He thinks Americans are renewing their admiration of the military man—in his most traditional form. In the wake of Vietnam, many Americans were disillusioned with war and military values, including the macho man embodied by John Wayne in *Sands of Iwo Jima*, which was produced in 1949. Now, half a century later, we're getting updated but not really different military stories and military heroes. *Gladiator* exemplifies the most traditional military values—courage, strength, decisiveness, and honor. The same is true of *Rules of Engagement*, in which a court-martial leads to an embrace of the military warrior's code. Reflecting on what this means, Medved says, "The John Wayne military image may become an icon again. . . . The comeback of the military personality may also connect with a reborn interest in manliness in general."

---

dent in the 1970s, has receded as established male characters are redrawn to be more tough and distanced from others. Highly popular films such as *Fight Club, Armageddon,* and *Gladiator,* exalt men who embody extreme stereotypes of masculinity: hard, tough, independent, sexually aggressive, unafraid, violent, totally in control of all emotions, and—above all—in no way feminine.

Equally interesting is how males are *not* typically presented. Specifically, they are seldom portrayed as nurturers. If they are presented this way, it is typically as a subordinant theme, not the central aspect of masculine identity. Men are rarely shown doing housework. Men are typically represented as uninterested in and incompetent at homemaking, cooking, and child care. Television continues to present ads for cooking and cleaning supplies that caricature men as incompetent buffoons who are klutzes in the kitchen and no better at taking care of children. Popular magazines similarly emphasize images of men in traditional roles and activities and far less frequently present images of men engaged in homemaking, child care, or other nurturing activities (Pendergast, 2000). Although children's books sometimes depict women engaged in activities outside the home, there has been little parallel effort to show men involved in family and home life. When someone is shown taking care of a child, it is usually the mother, not the father.

Another negative portrayal of men shows them as lazy dolts who are interested only in beer and sports. A good example of this representation of men is a commercial for Ameritrade that aired frequently in 2001 and more recently 2002. In the commercial, a woman is heading to work while her husband is dressed in grungy clothes and is slouching on the sofa with the remote control in his hand. She tells him that the only thing she needs for him to do that day is to open an Ameritrade account. Viewers see the man watching TV and eating junk food throughout the day until he drifts off to sleep. He is awakened by the sound of his wife's car in the garage. Quickly, he dashes to the computer and opens the Ameritrade account so that he has done what she asked by the time she walks in the door. In this commercial, the man is portrayed as a lazy, irresponsible child who must be made to behave by his wife.

Yet traditional representations of men are not the whole story. In *When a Man Loves a Woman,* Andy Garcia played a man who was both sensitive and sexy, both nurturing and assertive. During the course of *As Good As It Gets,* Jack Nicholson's character was transformed from a homophobic, sexist, egocentric jerk into a man who took care of others and displayed gentleness and compassion. In *Nobody's Fool,* Paul Newman played a man who embodied both traditional and nontraditional masculinity. He was independent, largely self-reliant, interested in women, and a bit of a rogue. At the same time, he took care of many people—his family of choice—and didn't need to dominate others.

Contradictory images of masculinity are also embodied by rock and rap artists and their music. While Eminem celebrates violent, homophobic men who dominate and harm women, other rock and rap artists present alternative images of masculinity. A 1997 video by LL Cool J opens with a gospel choir and portraits of young children. In his video, "Retrospect for Life," 25-year-old Common shows a young, pregnant Black woman who is facing single motherhood until the father returns to stay with her. What accounts for the change? In an interview with *Newsweek*'s Veronica Chambers, Common says, "A lot of my friends were getting turned off to hip-hop music because we were growing up" (Chambers, 1998, p. 66). LL Cool J, who had children with a woman to whom he wasn't married, offers a different answer: "I went to see my kids and my son asked me, 'Daddy, are you going to marry Mommy?' That was deep to listen to. That told me he was yearning for a family" (Chambers, 1998, p. 67). Since LL Cool J married, Snoop Doggy Dogg and Coolio have followed suit. Family values and men's roles as husbands and fathers are a new, if not dominant, theme in the hip-hop community.

Portrayals of women. Media's images of women parallel those of men. Although there are increasing instances of women in nontraditional roles or with nontraditional qualities, a majority of media images of women and girls reflect long-established cultural stereotypes. Women are portrayed as younger and thinner than women in the population as a whole, and most are depicted as dependent on and preoccupied with men and enmeshed in relationships or housework (Davis, 1990; Holtzman, 2000). The requirements of youth and beauty in women even influence news shows, where female newscasters are expected to be younger, more physically attractive, and less outspoken than males (Craft, 1988; Sanders & Rock, 1988). From children's programming, in which a majority of female characters typically spend their time watching males do things (Thompson & Zerbinos, 1995, 1997), to MTV, which routinely pictures men dominating women and women enjoying it

---

FYI

WANTED: NEWS ANCHOR FOR CNN. QUALIFICATIONS: FEMALE, BLONDE, YOUNG, AND GORGEOUS; NO JOURNALISTIC OR NEWS EXPERIENCE NEEDED.

As part of revamping its *Headline News,* CNN decided to hire a new anchor. Did they look for veteran journalists or people who had experience working with the news? No. Instead, they hired Andrea Thompson, best known for her role as a detective on *NYPD Blue,* if not for her erotic appearances in films such as *Jag* and *A Gun, a Car, a Blonde* (Levesque, 2001). Although Thompson never completed high school, she's confident viewers will accept her as a news anchor, despite what she refers to as "creative decisions" about her artistic career (Stroup, 2001). Besides, after CNN hired her, she worked with KRQE-TV in Albuquerque to learn how to write broadcast copy and do stand-up work in front of cameras.

(Jhally & Katz, 2001), media repeat the cultural image of women as dependent, ornamental objects whose primary functions are to look good, to please men, and to be sexually desirable and available.

Media have created two opposing images of women: good women and bad ones. These polar opposites are often juxtaposed to dramatize differences in the consequences that befall good and bad women. Good women are pretty, deferential, sexually restrained, and focused on home, family, and caring for others. Subordinate to men, they are usually cast as victims, angels, martyrs, and loyal wives and helpmates. Some newer shows, such as *ER, Judging Amy,* and *NYPD Blue,* feature women who are professionally competent and also attractive. The rule seems to be that a woman may be strong and successful if and only if she also exemplifies traditional stereotypes of femininity—subservience, beauty, and an identity linked to one or more men (Simonton, 1995).

Popular magazines aimed at women are another source of stereotypical portrayals. According to research on the effects of women's magazines (Kato, 1993), many women find them discouraging and devaluing. In a study of 75 women students at Stanford University, the women reported they felt worse about their appearance after reading women's magazines. Debbie Then, who conducted the study, reported that women's self-esteem is substantially diminished by the unrealistic standards for female beauty fostered by many women's magazines (cited in Kato, 1993).

Stereotyping women according to traditional roles seems especially persistent in popular magazines aimed at women, such as *Seventeen, Family Circle, Sassy, Lear, Self, Essence, Working Woman, Mirabella,* and *New Woman.* Although current popular magazines provide better coverage than women's magazines of a decade earlier on issues such as abortion, social projects, and obtaining credit, they continue to emphasize how to look better, lose weight, appeal to men, cook nice meals, maintain relationships, and care for families (Kuczynski, 2001; Rapping, 1994).

The other image of women the media offer us is the evil sister of the good homebody. Versions of this image are the witch, bitch, whore, or nonwoman, who is represented as hard, cold, aggressive—all of the things a good woman is not supposed to be. Exemplifying the evil woman was Alex in *Fatal Attraction,* which grossed more than $100 million in its first four months (Faludi, 1991). Yet Alex was only an extreme version of how bad women are generally portrayed in television shows such as *Melrose Place.* In 1995, Elisabeth Shue was a call girl (*Leaving Las Vegas*), and Sharon Stone appeared as an alcoholic (*Casino*). Four years later, in 1999, Sharon Stone played Gloria, a former "bad girl" (an ex-mistress and ex-convict) who developed maternal inclinations that made her a "good girl" when she took care of a young orphan. Amazingly, in *Gloria,* Stone did all this while running from bad guys in high heels and revealing clothes. In chil-

 MYRA

I have a love-hate affair with magazines. I always read *Cosmopolitan,* but it makes me feel horrible. I think I read it to figure out how I'm doing—like whether I am thin enough or have the right clothes. I know it's not realistic to compare myself to the women in *Cosmo,* but I do it anyway. I can't help myself. It makes me feel like I need to improve myself because I don't measure up.

Virgin or Whore; Virgin and Whore

Sut Jhally is a professor of communication at the University of Massachusetts. Jackson Katz is a former all-star football player and founder-director of the U.S. Marine Corps gender violence prevention program. Both men are committed to research and education that reduces men's violence. In a recent comment on pop culture's normalization of violence, they made these observations (Jhally & Katz, 2001, p. 30):

> While the forced choice between "virgin" and "whore" has been around for a long time—at least as far back as the Old Testament—in the contemporary period a new twist has been added: Girls now have to be *both* virgin and whore. Along with the cultural imperative that "sexuality is everything" is the equally powerful message that "good girls don't." In popular culture this contradiction is manifested in the figure of teenage pop star Britney Spears—highly sexualized in everything from appearance to vocals but "saving herself for marriage." Young women caught in this catch-22 are constantly negotiating an impossible balance between virgin and slut, constantly concerned that admiration may change to contempt. If girls are confused about their sexual identities and appropriate ways to behave, it is because the culture itself tells a contradictory story about female identity.

dren's literature, we encounter witches and mean stepmothers as villains, with beautiful and passive females like Snow White and Sleeping Beauty as their good counterparts.

In the early 1990s, more women were featured in prime-time television, and they were main characters who exemplified strength, competence, and success (Seplow, 1996). CBS's popular *Chicago Hope* featured Christine Lahti as Dr. Kathryn Austin. Unlike most female characters in prior television shows, Dr. Austin was a brilliant cardiac surgeon who earned and got the positions of chief of staff and then chief of surgery. Women portrayed the top officers on NBC's *Law & Order* and Fox's *New York Undercover*. This trend has continued with women in strong roles on *The Practice, Any Day Now, X-Files, The West Wing,* and *ER* (Liner, 2001). Recently, women warriors have become prominent on television, as in shows such as *Xena, Dark Angel, Buffy the Vampire Slayer,* and *Witchblade*. Women on these shows take charge and take care of themselves—and they manage to do it while simultaneously being at least attractive and often sexy. *Sailor Moon* is a popular children's show in which a woman is the lead character who gets involved in amazing adventures (Leaper, 2000). Even the image of good women as beautiful has been challenged in some recent media portrayals. For instance, Princess Fiona in *Shrek* is an overweight green ogre who doesn't ever change into a beautiful princess. Likewise, Camryn Manheim on *The Practice* is considerably heavier than social ideals of femininity prescribe. The character of Dr. Melfi on *The Sopranos*, while attractive, is middle aged and not stunningly thin or sexy.

Praise and Criticism for *Ally McBeal*

A lly McBeal is one of the most watched television programs in America. Not only do people watch it, but they are so involved with it they support over 30 Web sites, a bevy of chat rooms, and a handful of newsletters (Heywood, 1998). Critics of the show assert that Ally is petty (fighting other women over a can of Pringles), dependent on men for her identity ("I am a strong, working career girl who feels empty without a man"), and incredibly egocentric and self-obsessed ("I'm nothing without my face") (Heywood, 1998, p. B9).

Yet Ally has strong appeal for the 18-to-34 age group. In Ally, many young women see their own confusions. Like them, Ally is part feminist and part antifeminist, part modern woman and part nostalgic romantic, part career oriented and part relationship focused. Dana Hagerty, who manages one of the most popular *McBeal* Web sites, says, "Lots of women feel like they *are* Ally, or their lives are a lot like hers" (Heywood, 1998, p. B9). Ally experiences frustrations just like we do, and if some of hers are petty, so are some of ours.

Gloria Steinem praises Flockhart for portraying a character who doesn't give up her sexuality to be a professional (Johnson, 2000). Flockhart also doesn't give up her feminist activism. In 2000, she visited several African countries to add her voice and power to worldwide efforts to end violence against women, particularly genital mutilation (Turner, 2000).

At the same time that women are moving into nontraditional roles in some television programs, other programs continue to promote highly traditional images of women. For instance, although Ally McBeal is an attorney, we seldom see her engaging in professional activities. Instead, we see her mainly as an embodiment of stereotypes of women—unsure of herself, preoccupied with her appearance and social life, and very, very thin (Hass, 1998). With the exception of Dr. Melfi, the women on *The Sopranos* are dependent on men, and their primary identity is as sex objects for men. Tony Soprano and other men on the show have wives and mistresses, and a favorite gathering place for the men on the show is Da Bing, a strip club. In a bow to traditional views of femininity, the women members of the Soprano family aren't allowed to work in the family business.

Commercial films also offer competing images of women and femininity. The majority continue to emphasize traditional images of women. For example, in *Charlie's Angels,* the three women characters appear frequently in sexy, partially nude scenes—dancing around in underwear, wrapped in bath towels, and exposing cleavage even as they engage in fights. Rose, the character played by Kate Winslet in *Titanic,* was initially very passive—engaged to a man she didn't love or want to marry, going on a cruise her mother planned and forced on her. Rose gained personal power and voice only when rescued by Jack and brought alive by his attentions.

Yet some recent films offer images of women and femininity that depart from established social conventions. For instance, the women in *Charlie's Angels* manage

TANK MCNAMARA © Miller/Hinds. Reprinted with permission of UNIVERSAL PRESS SYNDICATE. All rights reserved.

to call the shots and succeed in dangerous missions even as they look and act sexy. The runaway hit *Crouching Tiger, Hidden Dragon* featured Zhang Ziyi playing Jen Yu, a strong woman character who resists the marriage that was arranged for her. Jen Yu fights fiercely, never needs rescuing, and calls her own shots. Although Jen Yu, like Thelma and Louise, goes over a cliff to avoid being controlled by others, she is nonetheless a strong, self-made character. When director Ang Lee accepted the Golden Globe award in 2001 for this film, he said he had modeled his female characters after "my wife, who is the strongest person I know." In *Star Trek Voyager* a woman is the captain of the ship. Erin Brockovitch is smart, assertive, and unwilling to let others define or control her. Susan Sarandon has taken a number of unglamorous roles, successfully portraying women who are strong, serious, capable, and not particularly young or beautiful.

Perhaps the most interesting trend in media is combining traditional and nontraditional images of masculinity in a single male character or femininity in a single female one. For instance, Erin Brockovitch met the conventional feminine image of sexiness, but she defied prevailing expectations of femininity by not putting her children ahead of her own goals. On *Star Trek Voyager,* Captain Katherine Janeway transcends traditional views of women by commanding a spaceship while she also conforms to established images of femininity by referring to the crew as "a family." Jack in *Titanic* is traditionally masculine in his adventurous spirit and independence, yet he is also nurturing and gentle. In *Saving Private Ryan,* Tom Hanks's character fulfilled dominant views of masculinity by being a soldier and engaging in the violence of war. At the same time, he disputed conventional views of masculinity by showing nurturance and tenderness.

■ Images of Relationships Between Men and Women

Because media portrayals of women and men predominantly reflect and reinforce traditional stereotypes, we shouldn't be surprised to find that relationships between women and men also reprise stereotypes about relations between women and men. Four themes demonstrate how media reflect and promote traditional relations between the sexes. As we discuss these, we'll also note exceptions that challenge traditional views of relationships between the sexes.

Women's dependence/men's independence. Historically, media have depicted women as dependent on men, who took care of women but were otherwise independent. This is still the dominant portrayal of power between the sexes, but it's no longer the only view. New views of more equal relationships—and occasionally relationships in which men are dependent—are included in current media.

Consider first the prevalence of depictions of girls and women as dependent and boys and men as independent. Disney's award-winning animated film *The Little Mermaid* vividly embodies females' dependence on males for identity. In this feature film, the mermaid quite literally gives up her identity as a mermaid in order to become acceptable to her human lover. In this children's story, we see a particularly obvious illustration of the asymmetrical relationship between women and men that is more subtly conveyed in other media productions. Similarly, Disney's *The Lion King* featured female lions that depended on a male lion to save them, and the heroine of *Pocahontas* was portrayed as a beautiful, sexy maiden, not the brave young Native American girl she actually was.

Women as well as minorities are still most often cast in supporting roles rather than leading ones in both children's shows and the commercials interspersed within them (O'Connor, 1989). The vast majority of MTV portrays females as passive and waiting for men's attention, whereas males are shown ignoring, exploiting, or directing women (Jhally & Katz, 2001). Gangsta male rap musicians sometimes refer to women as "bitches" and "hos" (whores), terms that invite disregard, disrespect, and violence toward women. News programs that have male and female hosts routinely cast the female as deferential to her male colleague (Craft, 1988; Sanders & Rock, 1988). Similarly, Blacks are unlikely to be represented as experts on topics other than Black affairs (Entman, 1994), and Blacks are still too often cast in racially stereotyped roles (Kern-Foxworth, 1994; Merritt, 2000). Commercials, too, manifest power cues that echo the male dominance/female subservience pattern. For instance, men are usually shown positioned above women, and women are more frequently pictured in varying degrees of undress (Masse & Rosenblum, 1988; Nigro, Hill, Gelbein, & Clark, 1988). Such nonverbal cues represent women as vulnerable and more submissive, whereas men stay in control.

In a brief departure from this pattern in the 1970s, films and television responded to the second wave of feminism by showing women who were independent but not hard, embittered, or without close relationships. Films such as *Alice Doesn't Live Here Anymore, Up the Sandbox, The Turning Point, Diary of a Mad Housewife,* and *An Unmarried Woman* offered realistic portraits of women who sought and found their own voices independent of men. *My Brilliant Career* particularly embodied this focus by telling the story of a woman who chooses work over marriage. During this period, television followed suit, offering viewers primetime fare such as *Maude* and *The Mary Tyler Moore Show,* which starred women who were able and achieving in their own rights (Dow, 1996). *One Day at a Time,* which premiered in 1974, was the first prime-time program about a divorced woman.

By the 1980s, however, traditionally gendered arrangements resurged as the backlash movement against feminism was embraced by media (Haskell, 1988; Maslin, 1990). Film fare in the 1980s and 1990s included *Pretty Woman,* the story of a prostitute who became a good woman when she was saved from her evil ways by a rigidly stereotypical man complete with millions to prove his success. At the same time, the prostitute conformed to conventional expectations of women by bringing out the man's tender side. Meanwhile, *Tie Me Up, Tie Me Down* trivialized abuse of women and underlined women's dependence on men with a story of a woman who is bound by a man and colludes in sustaining her bondage. *Crossing Delancey* showed successful careerist Amy Irving talked into believing she needs a man to be complete, a theme reprised by Cher in *Moonstruck.*

Joining the campaign to restore traditional dominant–subordinate patterns of male–female relationships were magazines, which reinvigorated their focus on women's role as the helpmate and supporter of husbands and families (Peirce, 1990). In 1988, that staple of Americana, *Good Housekeeping,* did its part to revive women's traditional roles with a full-page ad ("The Best in the House," 1988) for its new demographic edition marketed to "the new traditionalist woman." A month later, the magazine followed this up with a second full-page ad in national newspapers that saluted the new traditionalist woman, with this copy ("The New Traditionalist," 1988): "She has made her commitment. Her mission: create a more meaningful life for herself and her family. She is the New Traditionalist—a contemporary woman who finds her fulfillment in traditional values." The longstand-

Move Over, *Playboy*

Magazines such as *Playboy* and *Hustler* have been around for years, but most of the magazines generally aimed at men have not been so blatant in sexualizing women. That changed with one of the newest entries into the men's magazine market. *Maxim*'s recipe is to mix humor (often at women's expense) with very revealing pictures of women and very sexist advice on how to behave toward women. The first issue urged men to "leave that toilet seat up proudly!" Less than a year after its debut, *Maxim* seems to be an incredible success. It has a circulation of 800,000, which exceeds that of long-established men's magazines such as *Esquire* and *GQ*. What makes it so successful? According to *Maxim*'s current editor, Mark Golin, the magazine is a hit because "guys know they have their inner swine rooting around in there somewhere and they're dying to let it out" (Turner, 1999, p. 53). *Maxim* caters to the inner swine that Golin says men have.

ing dominant–submissive model for male–female relationships was largely restored in the 1980s. Even magazines such as *Working Woman* and *Savvy*, which are aimed at professional women, have articles on dress, hairstyle, dieting, cooking, and personal relationships along with articles on career topics. The same is true of magazines for pre-adolescent and adolescent girls (Kuczynski, 2001).

Recently, we've seen a few challenges to the traditional depiction of power relations between males and females. In the children's cartoon show *Dexter's Laboratory*, a little boy is a genius in his basement laboratory. However, his big sister usually outsmarts him. Captain Janeway on *Star Trek Voyager* is in charge of all the men and women on her spaceship. A number of women play characters who are fully equal to men on shows such as *ER*, *Law and Order*, *X-Files*, and *NYPD Blue*. In departing from the predominant media images of women as dependent on men and subservient to them, these views of gendered relationships offer us new possibilities for individual identity and interpersonal interaction.

Women's incompetence/men's authority. A second still prevalent theme in media representations of relationships is that men are the competent authorities who save women from their incompetence. Children's literature vividly implements this motif by casting females as helpless and males as coming to their rescue. Sleeping Beauty's resurrection depends on Prince Charming's kiss; this theme appears in the increasingly popular gothic romance novels and soap operas for adults.

One of the most pervasive ways in which media define males as authorities is in commercials. Women are routinely shown anguishing over dirty floors and bathroom fixtures only to be relieved of their distress when Mr. Clean shows up to tell them how to keep their homes spotless. Even when commercials are aimed at women, selling products intended for them, up to 90% of the time a man's voice is used to explain the value of what is being sold (Basow, 1992; Bretl & Cantor, 1988).

Spice Girls or Space Girls

Spice Girls burst on the scene with the cry for girl power and slogans such as "Silence is golden but shouting is fun." What is the girl power this group offers? Many young women see the Spice Girls as sassy, sexy gals who are redefining female power. But Kim Gordon, bassist and guitarist for Sonic Youth, doesn't agree. She says, "I think they're totally ridiculous. They're masquerading as little girls. It's repulsive" (Schoemer, 1998, p. 90).

Popular-music critic Patrick MacDonald (1998) thinks the Spice Girls have picked up the Riot Grrrls' battle cry without their strength, talent, or intelligence. After all, points out MacDonald, the Spice Girls were picked at an audition to create a woman's rock group composed of women who fit various niches in the market and various stereotypes of women—spicy, sexy, baby, and so on.

Comments made by the Spice Girls during interviews lead some to question their intelligence. For instance, one Spice Girl told interviewer Kathy Acker (1997), "I didn't really know that much, you know, history, but I knew about the sufragettes. They fought. It wasn't long ago." The Spice Girls—or the Space Girls, according to another critic, Nancy Hass (1998)—don't write lyrics or play instruments, and some critics think they don't sing very well.

The Spice Girls may present themselves as little girls, but they're involved in some very adult ideas. Spice Girls wallpaper was recalled when the manufacturer was flooded with objections from parents who discovered Baby Spice's nightgown said, "F— off." Defiant sexuality is not unique to Spice Girls. Girl rockers such as Ani DeFranco and Tori Amos advocate sexual freedom and fun for women. Although this may seem new to the current generation, women's sexual liberation was a major theme in the late 1960s and 1970s. Most women of that earlier time later reflected that women's sexual liberation was far more liberating for men than for women. This leads to the question of whether there might be ways of defining women's power that depart from traditional themes such as sexuality.

Using male voice-overs reinforces the cultural view that men are authorities and women depend on men to tell them what to do.

Television further communicates the message that men are authorities and women are not. One means of doing this is sheer numbers. As we have seen, men vastly outnumber women in television programming. In addition, the dominance of White men as news anchors and experts who inform us of happenings in the world underlines their authority. Prime-time television contributes to this image by showing women who need to be rescued by men and by presenting women as incompetent (Lichter, Lichter, & Rothman, 1986).

As with other stereotypes, this one is being challenged. Jen Yu in *Crouching Tiger, Hidden Dragon* takes care of herself without waiting for or needing a man to rescue her. The same is true of Queen Amidala in *Star Wars–Episode I*, Erin Brockovitch, Buffy, Abigail Bartlet on *The West Wing*, and Eleanor Frutt on *The*

Practice. As we see multiple ways that women and men can be, we gain freedom to imagine and create ourselves in the unique ways we choose.

Women as primary caregivers/men as bread-winners. A third perennial theme in media is that women are caregivers and men are providers. Since the 1980s, in fact, this gendered arrangement has been promulgated with renewed vigor. Once again, as in the 1950s, we see women devoting themselves to getting rings out of collars, gray out of their hair, and meals on the table. Corresponding to this is the restatement of men's inability in domestic and nurturing roles. For instance, in commercials men are regularly the butt of jokes for their ignorance about nutrition, child care, and housework.

When media portray women who work outside the home, the women's career lives often receive little or no attention. Although these characters have titles such as lawyer or doctor, they are shown predominantly in their roles as homemakers, mothers, and wives. The professional women in the sitcom *Designing Women* typically interacted in a cozy living room—not an office (Dow, 1996).

Magazines play a key role in promoting the pleasing of others as a primary focus of women's lives. Magazines aimed at women and girls stress looking good and doing things to please others (Kuczynski, 2001; Peirce, 1990). Thus, advertising tells women how to be "me, only better" by dyeing their hair to look younger; how to lose weight so "you'll still be attractive to him"; and how to prepare gourmet meals so "he's always glad to come home." The ads and articles emphasize that women need to change themselves to be adequate— they need to fix, improve, repair, rejuvenate, disguise, and correct some or all parts of themselves. These advertisements constantly emphasize pleasing others, especially men, as central to being a woman, and the message is fortified with the thinly veiled warning that if a woman fails to look good and please, her man might leave (Kang, 1997; Lont, 1995).

There is a second, less well-known way in which advertisements contribute to stereotypes of women as focused on others and men as focused on work. Sometimes advertisers control the *content* in magazines. In exchange for placing an ad, a company sometimes receives "complementary copy," one or more articles that increase the market appeal of its product (Turner, 1998). So a soup company that places an ad might be given a three-page story on how to prepare meals using that brand of soup; an ad for hair coloring products might be accompanied by interviews with famous women who choose to dye their hair. Thus, the message of advertisers is multiplied by magazine content, which readers often mistakenly assume is independent of advertising. *Ms.* is the only popular magazine that refuses to accept advertising so that it can control content.

Women's role in the home and men's role outside of it are reinforced by newspapers and news programming. Both emphasize men's independent activities and, in fact, define news almost entirely as stories about and by men. Stories about men focus on work and on their achievements (Luebke, 1989), reiterating the cultural message that men are supposed to *do,* to perform. Meanwhile, the few stories about women tend to emphasize their roles as wives, mothers, and homemakers. Even stories about women who are in the news because of achievements and professional activities typically mention marriage, family life, and other aspects of women's traditional role.

Women as victims and sex objects/men as aggressors. A final theme in mediated representations of relationships between women and men is the view of women as subject to men's sexual desires. The paradox of this representation is that the very qualities women are encouraged to develop (beauty, sexiness, passivity, and powerlessness) in order to meet cultural ideals of femininity contribute to objectifying and dehumanizing them (Jhally & Katz, 2001). Also, the qualities that men are urged to exemplify (aggressiveness, dominance, sexuality, and strength) are identical to those linked to abuse of women (Messner, 2001; Wood, 2001b).

Prevalent in media of all types are images of desirable men as aggressive and dominant and of desirable women as young, pretty, sexual, and helpless (Kang, 1997). Advertising directed at men often links products with ultra-masculinity and even violence. For example, the two leading brands of condoms bear the names of ancient warriors (Trojans) and kings (Rameses). Super-athlete Michael Jordan advertises Hanes underwear for men. Other athletes are used to advertise yogurt, deodorant, and light beers—if a star athlete will eat yogurt and and drink light beer, these products must be manly (Katz, 1995)!

Media continue to give priority to representing women as sexual objects. Whereas men are seldom pictured nude or even partially unclothed, women habitually are (Ansen & Bunn, 1995). Advertisements for makeup, colognes, hair products, and clothes often show women attracting men because they got the right products and made themselves irresistible. Perhaps you've seen the commercial for a particular shampoo. First we see an attorney doing her work in a courtroom. When the judge says the word "urge," she goes into a highly eroticized fantasy in which buff men shampoo her hair with the product being advertised. The message is that the woman's sexuality is uncontained and overpowers her work as an attorney. Stars on prime time and films, who are beautiful and dangerously thin, perpetuate the idea that women must starve themselves to meet cultural ideals (Holtzman, 2000; Silverstein et al., 1986).

Portrayals of women as sex objects and of men as sexual aggressors often occur in music videos and other programming. Typically, MTV portrays females dancing provocatively in scanty or revealing clothing. Frequently, men are seen coercing women into sexual activities or physically abusing them. Male dominance and sexual exploitation of women are themes in virtually all R- and X-rated films, which almost anyone may now rent for home viewing (Cowan, Lee, Levy, & Snyder, 1988; Cowan & O'Brien, 1990). Horror movies, especially slasher films, consistently represent women as distressed, helpless, passive victims (Clover, 1995). These media images carry to extremes long-standing cultural views of masculinity as aggressive and femininity as passive. They also encourage us to see violence as sexy (Arnold, 2001; Clover, 1995; Jhally & Katz, 2001; Russell, 1993).

One of the more interesting challenges to stereotypes of women as sex objects comes from some women's fashion subcultures and some women musical artists.

FYI

MADONNA

Who is Madonna? Whatever else she may be, she is a lightning rod for views of women, femininity, and power relations between the sexes. She has been called

a feminine icon	resistant to conventional views
an immoral opportunist	of women
a knowing virgin	consistent with conventional views
a pervert	of women
a feminist	a purveyor of soft porn
a whore	an embodiment of female-defined
a brilliant artist	sexuality
a gender politician	

Maybe she's all of that and more. She's presented herself as a material girl, traditionally feminine, erotically charged, a submissive victim of male aggression, a dominatrix, a mother, and . . . stay tuned, because it's a good bet that she will continue to reinvent herself. Madonna flaunts her sexuality, radically and repeatedly changes her identity, inverts and subverts any stable notion of femininity. In so doing, she insists that women who are ultrafeminine and ultra-sexy are both intimidating and seductive. Sheila Whiteley, professor of popular music, says the key to how people see Madonna is whether they perceive her work as ironic. If you see her videos, music, and films as ironic, you see her as deliberately playing with and disrupting any conventional notion of femininity, including the division of women into "good girls" and "bad girls." If you don't view her work as irony—if you regard it more literally—you're likely to regard her as reproducing entrenched views of women as sex objects. Perhaps the question is whether Madonna flirts with the camera or manipulates it to fit her own will and whims.

Sources: Whiteley, S. (2000). *Women and popular music: Sexuality, identity, and popular culture.* New York: Routledge; Arnold, R. (2001). *Fashion, desire, and anxiety: Image and morality in the 20th century.* New Brunswick, NJ: Rutgers University Press.

In the videogame Tomb Raider, Lara Croft is a digitally voluptuous, sexy female who carries and uses weapons. In combining conventional femininity (sexuality) and masculinity (weapons and violence), she challenges sex/gender dualities and personifies erotic fantasies that merge sex and power. Punk subculture also disputes and disrupts traditional views of women and femininity. Women wear ripped fishnet tops and combat boots; they deliberately use makeup and create hairstyles to create a garish, unnatural look that mocks traditional views of women even as it plays with them (Arnold, 2001; Whiteley, 2000). And then, there's Madonna, who uses, abuses, and changes all of the rules!

 TIFFANY

It makes Black guys angry when I say it, but I think gangsta rap is totally sexist and destructive. Some of my girlfriends say they like rap and don't take the antiwoman lyrics personally. The way I see it, though, calling women bitches and whores is as hateful as you can get. It totally disses women. If Black men talk that way about Black women, how can we respect ourselves or expect others to?

Tiffany's response (see commentary) to gangsta rap is not unusual. A number of commentators of different sexes and races have strongly criticized gangsta rap. According to Leonard Pitts, Jr., an African American music critic, "There's something vile and evil moving beneath the surface of this music. Something that hates you. And shames me" (1993, p. 7E). The National Political Congress of Black Women (NPCBW) agrees and has pressured record companies to stop distributing gangsta rap that uses street language to applaud drug use, impersonal sex, rape, and murder. C. Delores Tucker, chair of the NPCBW, says that the lyrics of gangsta rap "offer negative images of human relationships [that] too often teach African American men how to mistreat African American women. For our women to accept this is nothing short of mental and spiritual contamination" (cited in Ransom, 1993, p. A6). Scholar and social critic bell hooks (1994) agrees, and she urges African American women to speak out against the violence toward women that is glorified in much gangsta rap.

In sum, we have identified basic images and themes in media's representations of women, men, and relationships between the two. Individually and in combination, these images sustain and reinforce socially constructed views of the genders, views that have restricted both men and women and that appear to legitimize destructive behaviors ranging from anorexia to battering. Later in this chapter, we will probe more closely how media versions of gender are linked to such problems.

BIAS IN NEWS COVERAGE

Television is the primary source of news for most Americans, with newspapers ranking second. This suggests that our understanding of issues, events, and people is shaped substantially by what television and newspapers define as news and the manner in which they present it. As gatekeepers of information, news reporting selectively shapes our perceptions of issues related to gender.

Signe Wilkinson, Cartoonist and Writers Syndicate/cartoonweb. com.

Beginning with the second wave of U.S. feminism in the 1960s, media have consistently misrepresented the goals, activities, and members of women's movements. In the early days of radical feminism, media portrayed feminists as man-hating, bra-burning extremists. In fact, the famous bra-burning never happened but was erroneously reported by a journalist who misunderstood the facts (Faludi, 1991). In the early 1970s, an editor at *Newsday* gave these instructions to a reporter he assigned to research and write a story on the women's movement (Faludi, 1991): "Get out there and find an authority who'll say it's all a crock of shit" (pp. 75–76). Little wonder that the story that later appeared reported that the women's movement was a minor ripple without much validity or support.

One of the most famous—or infamous—media stunts of the 1980s was another manifestation of the backlash movement against feminism, which consistently received more favorable press than the women's movement itself. The cover story for the June 21, 1986, issue of *Newsweek* was about the so-called man shortage. With dramatic charts showing that chances for marrying plunge precipitously as a working woman ages, *Newsweek* proclaimed that, after age 40, a woman was more likely to be killed by a terrorist than to marry. Behind the headlines, the facts were shaky. The predictions of women's opportunities to marry were based on a study by researchers at Harvard and Yale, but the data of the study were discredited, and the study was withdrawn from publication. Did the flaws in the study and its withdrawal get headlines? No way. When the accurate U.S. Census Bureau's figures were released some months later and disproved the bogus study, *Newsweek* relegated that information to a mere two paragraphs in a minor column (Faludi, 1991).

Another incident illustrative of media's distortion of feminism came in 1989, when Felice Schwartz, a management consultant, published an article in the prestigious *Harvard Business Review,* in which she argued that women who want to have children cost businesses too much money and should be placed on a separate track in which they do not get the opportunities for advancement that go to men and women who are career oriented. Dubbing this "the mommy track," newspapers and magazines took Schwartz's article as occasion to reassert the viewpoint that women's place really is in the home and that they are lesser players in professional life. Once again, though, facts to support the claim were scant. Schwartz's article was speculative, as was her opinion that most women would willingly trade promotions and opportunities for more time with their families. When the annual Virginia Slims Opinion Poll (1990) directly asked women working outside of the home whether they favored mommy tracks, nearly three-fourths thought such a policy was regressive and discriminatory. Schwartz later retracted her suggestions, saying she had erred in

> ## *Ĉ* LOUISE
>
> Talk about biased coverage. Last year a group of us went to Washington, DC, for a pro-choice march. The turnout was fabulous and showed that a lot of women support freedom to choose what happens to our bodies. But was it given coverage? It got less than one minute on the nightly news that night, but a big business deal got over two minutes, and an athlete's decision to switch teams was the newsmaker interview that night. The march didn't even make the first section in some papers. If you just tuned in the news, you could think the whole march never happened. In fact, my mother and father told me they'd heard nothing about it when I got home.

claiming that women were more expensive as employees than men. Her retraction, however, got little coverage, because Schwartz's revised point of view did not support the media's bias regarding women's roles. Because there was virtually no coverage of Schwartz's change of opinion (Faludi, 1991), many people read only the first article and continue to believe it.

Communication scholars Lauren Danner and Susan Walsh (1999) reported an especially clear example of media distortion of women and their rights. They analyzed newspaper coverage of the United Nations Fourth World Conference on Women and discovered that barely one-fourth of the stories focused on substantive issues at the conference. The majority of coverage emphasized conflicts among women at the conference (referred to as "bickering"), conferees' appearances (criticized for "letting themselves go" and having no sense of style), and feminism as the root problem for women. Further, most stories were placed in the inside pages or lifestyle sections—a location that would never be considered for stories on other United Nations conferences.

Coverage of other gender issues reflects media biases. Two instances of bending events to fit gender stereotypes occurred in the 1990 Gulf War. As substantial numbers of women joined men in fighting, traditional values were shaken. Throughout the war, newspapers and magazines featured melodramatic pictures of children watching mothers go to war, while talk shows asked the question "Should a woman leave her baby to go to war?" (Flanders, 1990). Surely, this is a reasonable question to ask about any parent, but it was rarely applied to fathers. In focusing on women's roles as mothers, the media communicated two gender messages. First, they im-

Day Care = Aggression in Children. Read All About It!

In April 2001, newspapers all over the country carried headlines such as "Day Care Causes Aggression in Children, Study Reports." The articles that followed the headlines were about a study of the effects of day care on children. The study was particularly noteworthy because it took place over 10 years, included more than 1,000 children in 10 different locations, and was conducted by researchers at the highly respected National Institute of Child Health and Human Development. The finding that was highlighted by media was that 17% of kindergarten-aged children who had spent 30 or more hours in day care each week were highly aggressive. News accounts went on to note than only 6% of children who had spent fewer than 10 hours weekly in day care were highly aggressive by the time they reached kindergarten age.

The finding is startling, and it supports social views that women should be stay-at-home mothers. But several of the researchers who conducted the study say their research doesn't support that conclusion. They say the news reports misrepresented their investigation by distorting some findings and choosing not to report other findings that do not support the idea that stay-at-home moms are best for children. What did the media leave out in its gatekeeping? For starters:

■ Children who were in quality day care had better developed language and cognitive skills than children who spent little or no time in day care.

■ Fully 83% of children who spent 30+ hours a week in day care were *not* highly aggressive, so the majority didn't show the effect announced by the headline.

■ The researchers who conducted the study reported that the 17% of children who were labeled "highly aggressive" were in the upper range of "normal."

■ The researchers stated that the proportion of aggressive children who spend 30+ hours a week in day care is equivalent to the proportion of the overall population that is highly aggressive.

■ Many young children who aren't in day care don't have opportunities to play—or fight!—with peers. They might be judged more aggressive if they interacted with peers.

■ The research report states that family interactions are a greater influence on children's behavior than hours spent in day care.

■ And, by the way, why were fathers never mentioned in the reports? Do no fathers take care of children? Do only mothers have impact on children?

Sources: Garrison, J. (2001, April 28). Researchers scramble over day-care study. *Raleigh News and Observer*, p. 6A. Goodman, E. (2001, April 28). Playing with the numbers in child care. *Raleigh News and Observer*, p. 18A.

plied that women—real women—don't leave their children. The second gender message was that fathers are not able to take care of children while mothers were overseas.

A second gender issue relating to the Gulf War came when an American woman in the military, along with several men, was taken as a prisoner of war. Rather than presenting this as straightforward news, however, media focused on her femininity rather than on her military role. Newspapers showing photographs of all POWs featured the male ones in military uniform and the female in a glamour shot from her school yearbook. In highlighting her femininity, media ignited powerful public sentiment about women's fragility, vulnerability, and, therefore, inappropriateness in positions of danger. All attention focused, as the media directed it to, on possibilities of sexual assault of women POWs, thereby reinforcing images of women as sex objects. Only a year later, we learned of the Tailhook scandal, in which numerous male naval personnel sexually harassed female personnel. This made it clear that women are at least as likely to suffer sexual assault from male peers in the service as from enemies who capture them.

 THELMA

I never really thought much about how television affects children until I noticed changes in my son when he started watching television. After I returned to school, we hired someone to take care of Jimmy during the day. She let him watch TV a lot of the time, I guess so she wouldn't have to supervise him. My husband and I noticed that, right after he started watching a lot of TV, he started calling his sister "a stupid girl" and telling her she couldn't be on his soccer team because girls aren't good at sports. They'd been playing soccer together for years and, in fact, she was better than him. When I asked Jimmy why he thought that, he'd tell me about some program he'd seen on TV and how the boys in it didn't let girls on their team.

Do media representations of events shape our perceptions? To find out, I asked students to answer four questions on the first day of class:

Did feminists burn bras in the 1960s to protest the objectification of women?

Do women who have children cost more to employ than men?

Do men have hormonal cycles that affect their behavior?

Do women's hormonal swings affect their behavior?

In every case, the majority of students believed the myths created by media, with nearly all students thinking that women burned bras in the 1960s, that women are more expensive to employ and are subject to severe hormonal swings, and that men either do not have hormonal cycles or are not affected by them. Too often the messages media create misinform us about issues that affect our lives and perceptions.

IMPLICATIONS OF MEDIA REPRESENTATIONS OF GENDER

We have seen that media present limited and sometimes distorted images of men, women, and relationships. We've also noted that they act as gatekeepers, regulating what issues related to gender are covered and how they are presented. From childhood throughout our lives, media reinforce and reproduce gendered identities.

Media potentially hamper our understandings of ourselves as women and men in three ways. First, media perpetuate unrealistic ideals of what each gender should be, implying that normal people are inadequate by comparison. Simultaneously, because cultural ideals promoted by media are rigid, they limit views of each gender's abilities and opportunities, which may discourage us from venturing into areas outside those that media define for our sex. Second, media pathologize the bodies of men and especially of women, prompting us to consider normal physical qualities and functions as abnormal and requiring corrective measures. Third, media contribute significantly to normalizing violence against women, making it possible for men to believe they are entitled to abuse or force women to engage in sex and for women to consider such violations acceptable.

■ Fostering Unrealistic and Limited Gender Ideals

Many of the images dispensed by media are unrealistic. Most men are not as strong, bold, and successful as males on the screen. Few women are as slender, gorgeous, and well dressed as stars and models, whose photographs are airbrushed and retouched to create their artificial beauty. Most people will not reach executive positions by the age of 35, and those who do are unlikely to be as glamorous, stress free, and joyous as the atypical few featured in magazines like *Savvy, Business Week, Fortune,* and *Working Woman.* Further, no woman who is healthy can avoid turning 40, the age at which women virtually disappear from media. The relationships depicted in media also defy realistic possibilities, because most of us will encounter problems that cannot be solved in 30 minutes (minus time for commercial interruptions), and most of us will not be able to pursue a demanding career and still be as relaxed and available to family and friends as media characters are.

You might think that because we all know the difference between fantasy and reality, we don't accept media images as models for our own lives and identities. Research, however, suggests that the unrealistic ideals in popular media do influence how we feel about ourselves and our relationships. In 1999 Anne Becker, an anthropologist and psychiatrist, reported very disturbing research that suggests media are very powerful in shaping—or distorting—body images. For centuries, the people of Fiji had been a food-loving society. People enjoyed eating and considered fleshy bodies attractive in both women and men. In fact, when someone seemed to be losing weight, acquaintances would chide her or him for "going thin." All of that changed in 1995 when television stations in Fiji began broadcasting American programs such as *Melrose Place, Seinfeld,* and *Beverly Hills 90210.* Within three years, an astonishing number of Fijian women began dieting and developing eating disorders. When asked why they were trying to lose weight, young Fijian women cited characters such as Amanda (Heather Locklear) on *Melrose Place* as their model (Becker, 1999; Becker & Burwell, 1999; "Fat-Phobia," 1999; Goodman, 1999).

In one interesting study, Kimball (1986) compared the sex-stereotypical attitudes of children who lived in areas without television and those in similar areas who watched television. He found that children who watched television had more stereotyped views of the sexes; further, when television was introduced into communities that had not had it, the children's beliefs became more sex typed. Other research confirms the finding that television is linked to sex-typed attitudes in children and adolescents (Leaper, 2000; Morgan, 1987), especially ones in working-class families (Nikken & Peeters, 1988). One exception is programming that presents nonstereotypical portrayals of males and females, which tends to decrease, not fortify, sex stereotypes (Rosenwasser, Lingenfelter, & Harrington, 1989).

The effects of media are not limited to childhood. Radio is a major influence for adolescents, whose average listening time is five hours a day—slightly less for Caucasians and slightly more for African Americans, especially African American females (Brown, Childers, Bauman, & Koch, 1990). Although most popular music reflects sex stereotypes (Lont, 1990, 2001), this is less true of work composed and/or sung by some contemporary women artists such as Lauryn Hill, Melissa Etheridge, Tori Amos, Lorrie Morgan, and Ani DiFranco. However, because most songs are written and sung by males, rock and rap music generally reflects a male point of view in which women are depicted sexually and passively (St. Lawrence & Joynder, 1991). Other media stereotypes have similar distorting effects on our identities. For instance, popularized images of men as independent and women as nurturing and as relationship experts encourage women to feel responsible for others and men to regard caring as a low priority.

Mediated myths of relationships contribute to socializing people into unrealistic views of normal relationships. MTV's and rock music's emphasis on eroticism and sublime sex is linked to an expectation of sexual perfection in real relationships. Further, research shows that readers of self-help books tend to have less realistic ideals for relationships than do nonreaders of such books. Consequently, those who read self-help books experience more than typical amounts of frustration and disappointment when their relationships fail to meet the ideals promoted by media (Shapiro & Kroeger, 1991).

Of the many influences on our feelings about ourselves and our expectations of our relationships, media are substantial. Unrealistic images of what we and our relationships should be contribute significantly to dissatisfaction, which may lead to emotional difficulties, feelings of inadequacy, anorexia, and cosmetic surgery (Cooper, 1998; Mazzarella & Pecora, 1999; Posavac, Posavac, & Posavac, 1998). Media's images of women, men, and relationships are *ideals*—they are not real, and few of us can even approximate the standards they establish. Yet when we are constantly besieged with ideals of how we should look, feel, act, and be, it's difficult

 KALYN

If movies are going to show explicit sex scenes, I wish they would at least show normal sex like ordinary people have. Have you ever noticed that films and TV never show a woman being unaroused by a man or a man being less than a superstar stud in bed? Nobody on screen ever has to deal with an average sexual experience, much less a disappointing one. I think watching super sex all the time makes us think something is wrong in our own relationships when fireworks don't go off every time. And they don't every time.

not to feel inadequate. Men as well as women may feel woefully deficient if they rely on media characters as models. If we use media as a reference point for what is normal and desirable, we may find ourselves constantly feeling that we and our relationships are inferior by comparison.

■ Pathologizing the Human Body

One of the most damaging consequences of media images of women and men is that these images encourage us to perceive normal bodies and normal physical functions as problems. It's understandable to wish we weighed a little more or less, had better-developed muscles, and never had pimples or cramps. What is neither reasonable nor healthy, however, is to regard healthy, functional bodies as abnormal and unacceptable. Yet this is precisely the negative self-image cultivated by the predominant portrayals of women and men in media.

Not only do media encourage us to measure ourselves against artificial standards, they also encourage us to see normal bodies and normal bodily functions as pathologies. A good example is the media's construction of premenstrual syndrome (PMS). Historically, PMS has not been a problem. In fact, a good deal of research (Parlee, 1973, 1987) indicates that, in earlier eras, PMS affected very few women. After World War II, when women were no longer needed in the workforce, opinion changed, and the term *premenstrual tension* was coined (Greene & Dalton, 1953) and used to support the idea that women were inferior employees. In 1964, only one article on PMS appeared; from 1988 to 1989, a total of 425 were published (Tavris, 1992). Drug companies funded research and publicity because selling PMS meant selling their remedies for the newly created problem. Behind the hoopla, however, there was and is little evidence to support the currently widespread belief that PMS is a serious problem for a significant portion of the female population. Facts aside, the myth has caught on, carrying in its wake many women and men who now perceive normal monthly changes as abnormal and as support for the idea that women are unfit for positions of leadership and authority.

Menopause is similarly pathologized. Books and articles describe menopause "in terms of deprivation, deficiency, loss, shedding, and sloughing" (Tavris, 1992, p. 159), language that defines a normal process as negative. The cover of the May 25, 1992, *Newsweek* featured an abstract drawing of a tree in the shape of a woman's head. The tree was stripped of all leaves, making it look lifeless and barren. Across the picture was the cover-story headline "Menopause." From first glance, menopause was represented negatively—as desolate and unfruitful. The article focused primarily on the problems and losses of menopause. Only toward the end did readers find reports from anthropologists, whose cross-cultural research reveals that in many cultures menopause is not an issue or is viewed positively. Women in Mayan villages and the Greek island of Evia do not understand questions about hot flashes and depression, symptoms often associated with menopause in Western societies ("Menopause," 1992). These are not part of their experience in

Fixing the Pathologized Body

Once it was rare for people to have plastic surgery. Not anymore. Once, young people didn't consider plastic surgery, except for reconstruction following accidents. Not anymore. In 1998, the American Society of Plastic and Reconstructive Surgeons performed more than 25,000 elective procedures on teenagers. This is almost a 100% increase over the number of cosmetic surgeries performed in 1992. Nearly 2,000 teenage females had breast implants, and another 1,645 had liposuction. Once favored only by small numbers of wealthy women, plastic surgery is now sought by increasing numbers of both sexes who are not particularly rich—65% of people having cosmetic surgery have annual family incomes of less than $50,000.

In 2001, there was a news report about a London doctor who refused to perform breast enhancement on a 16-year-old female. He told the insistent parents that she was too young and her breasts were not fully developed. The parents stated that "the operation would give their daughter greater confidence and remove any 'hangups' she felt about her body" ("Doctor," 2001, p. 18A).

Psychologist Kris Gowen says, "You are a victim of this crazy ideal body image that is impossible to achieve unless you create it yourself. And it's fake" (quoted in Gerhart, 1999, p. 4E).

Sources: Bordo, S. (1999). *The male body: A new look at men in public and private.* New York: Farrar, Straus & Giroux; Doctor: Girl not ready for breast implants. (2001, January 6). *Raleigh News & Observer*, p. 18A; Gerhart, A. (1999, August 5). Young women increasingly choose plastic surgery. *Raleigh News and Observer*, p. 4E; Gilman, S. (1999). *Making the body beautiful: A cultural history of aesthetic surgery.* Princeton, NJ: Princeton University Press.

---

cultures that do not define a normal change in women as pathological. Because Western countries stigmatize menopause and define it as "the end of womanhood," Western women are likely to feel negatively about the cessation of menstruation (Greer, 1992).

Media also pathologize normal male bodies. No longer is it good enough to be healthy and active. The bodybuilding trend has created unrealistic ideals for masculine bodies. Today, abuse of steroids is an increasing problem among men. Surveys show that about 18% of male high school athletes use anabolic steroids (Angier, 1999). Although media's adulation for extreme musculature and strength is not the only cause of dangerous use of steroids, we should not dismiss the influence of portrayals of muscle-bound men as ideal. Media's increasing glorification of unrealistic male bodies is also reflected in action toys marketed to young boys. Since the G.I. Joe doll was introduced in 1964, each new version of the doll has been more muscular and more sharply cut than its predecessor.

Advertising is very effective in convincing us that we need products to solve problems we are unaware of until some public relations campaign persuades us that something natural about us is really unnatural and unacceptable. Media have convinced millions of U.S. women that what every medical source considers "normal body weight" is really abnormal and cause for severe dieting (Mazzarella & Pecora, 1999; Rogers, 1999; Wolf, 1991). Similarly, gray hair, which naturally develops with age, is now something all of us, especially women, are encouraged to cover up (Sharkey, 1993). Facial lines, which indicate a person has lived a life and accumulated experiences, can be removed so that we look younger—a prime goal in a culture that glorifies youth (Bordo, 1999; Greer, 1992; Gilman, 1999).

Body hair is another interesting case of media's convincing us that something normal is really abnormal. Beginning in 1915, a sustained marketing campaign informed women that underarm hair was unsightly and socially incorrect. (The campaign against leg hair came later.) *Harper's Bazaar,* an upscale magazine, launched the crusade against underarm hair with a photograph of a woman whose raised arms revealed clean-shaven armpits. Underneath the photograph was this caption: "Summer dress and modern dancing combine to make necessary the removal of objectionable hair" (Adams, 1991). Within a few years, ads promoting removal of underarm hair appeared in most women's magazines, and by 1922, razors and depilatories were firmly ensconced in middle America, as evidenced by their inclusion in the women's section of the Sears Roebuck catalogue.

Media efforts to pathologize natural physiology can be very serious. As we have seen in previous chapters, the emphasis on excessive thinness contributes to severe and potentially lethal dieting and eating disorders, especially in Caucasian women. Nonetheless, most of the top female models are skeletal. Phillip Myers and Frank Biocca (1992), professors of journalism, report that women in media advertisements are significantly thinner than average, healthy women, and that models are getting thinner. Approximately one in five college women deliberately eats less food than is required to meet requirements for adequate daily nutrition (Finstein, 1993).

CHRISTI

When I used to diet, I remember thinking that I was in control. I believed what all the ads said about taking charge of myself, exerting control. But I was totally *not* in control. The advertisers and the companies making diet products were in control. So was society with the idea that "you can't be too thin" and that it's more important for girls to look good (read thin) than to feel good (read not hungry). Society and its views of women were in control, not me. What I was was totally a puppet who was just doing what they told me to do.

Women who diet excessively do so to force their bodies to fit a socially constructed feminine ideal—an ideal that is unrealistic and unhealthy. Dangers—including heart attacks, strokes, and liver disease—also exist for men who use steroids in an effort to meet the ideal masculine form promoted by media (Angier, 1999).

Many women's natural breast size exceeded the cultural ideal in the 1960s, when thin, angular bodies were represented as ideal. Thus, breast reduction surgeries increased. By the 1980s, cultural standards had changed to define large breasts as the feminine ideal. Consequently, breast augmentation surgeries accelerated, and fully 80% of implants were for cosmetic reasons ("The Implant Circus," 1992). In an effort to meet the cultural standards for beautiful bodies, many women endured and continue to endure unnecessary surgery, leading to disfigurement, loss of feeling, and sometimes death.

Harming the body in an effort to meet social ideals for the feminine form is not new. In the 19th century, when a tiny waist and large bosom were ideals of womanliness, most middle- and upper-class women wore corsets. These garments forcefully pushed women's natural bodies into unnatural forms. Corsets often crushed women's ribs, interfered with breathing, sometimes injured lungs, and squeezed and injured internal organs (Lauer & Lauer, 1981). Accepting media messages about our bodies and ourselves, however, is not inevitable: We can reflect on the messages and resist those that are inappropriate or harmful.

■ Normalizing Violence Against Women

Violence is so pervasive in modern life that all of Chapter 11 is devoted to examining it. Yet it would be irresponsible not to mention violence in the context of media. Recall that, on average, a 6-year-old in the United States has watched 5,000 hours of television, and an 18-year-old has watched a stunning 19,000 hours. What do we watch in all of those hours of viewing? According to one estimate, by the age of 18 the average person in this country has viewed 200,000 acts of violence on television, including 40,000 murders (Zuckerman, 1993). In a *TV Guide* investigation, 1,846 acts of violence occurred on 10 channels in an 18-hour period (Zuckerman, 1993).

But, you may ask, is watching violence related to engaging in violence? The answer seems to be yes. Although it would be naïve to claim that media *causes* violence, there is mounting evidence that violence in media contributes to increasing violence in real life. According to one critic of media violence (Gelman, 1993, p. 48), "Teenagers don't invent violence, they learn it." From *Die Hard*, *Rambo*, and *Fight Club* to violent video games, children learn to perceive violence as part of normal social life (Dietz, 1998; Jhally & Katz, 2001). Children who watch a lot of television violence in their early years are more likely to commit violent crimes as adults (Zuckerman, 1993). The relationship between media violence and actual violence is one of the most studied aspects of media (Gelman, 1993).

As we will see in the next chapter, the media, along with other social structures and practices, tend to normalize violence in our culture. When we continuously see aggression, physical assault, murder, rape, and other forms of violence depicted in media, it is small wonder that we become desensitized to violence. In sum, media offer us a view of

> **❦ MIRIAM**
>
> My kids are so much more violent than I was or than my friends were when we were young, and I think the violence they see on television is a big part of the reason. When I caught my 3-year-old trying to hit our dog, he told me that he'd seen that on a cartoon show—a cartoon show! I try to screen what my children watch, but it's getting so there are very few programs that don't include violence. How can kids think it is anything but normal when they see it every day?

Should we ban violent, homophobic, sexist music such as that of rap artist Eminem? Should we regulate the content of MTV and films? Even those who are most outraged by the objectification and sexism of media seldom advocate censorship. The Constitution provides strong protections of freedom of speech, and for good reason. The problem with censoring is that somebody decides what all of us can watch, hear, see. Who has the right to make this decision for all of us? And if Eminem is banned today, who and what will be banned tomorrow?

A better answer may be to demand that media offer us multiple, diverse images of women and men. Instead of banning what we don't like, perhaps we work to enlarge the ways in which people and relationships are portrayed. In a conversation among Black professional women, MTV veejay and talk show host Ananda Lewis said, "I don't want just one image of women to exist. I want to see something and go, 'I shouldn't be like that.' Sometimes learning what not to do is much more important than being told what the right thing is" (Clemetson & Samuels, 2000, p. 57).

the world, and that view is of a world in which violence is commonplace, normal, and increasingly acceptable as part of ordinary life.

Substantial violence toward women punctuates movies, television—including children's programming—rock music, and music videos, desensitizing men and women alike to the *un*naturalness and unacceptability of force and brutality between human beings. We will explore violence, particularly gendered violence, in more depth in Chapter 11.

SUMMARY

Ranging from children's cartoons to pornography, media influence how we perceive men and women in general and ourselves and others in particular. Media also shape our views of what's normal and right in relationships between women and men. Historically, media have represented both women and men in highly stereotypical ways. This trend continues in media, but it is sometimes challenged by alternative images of women, men, and relationships. For the most part, even media representations that on the surface don't seem to conform to gender stereotypes reflect traditional views of women and men at a basic level. Three implications of media representations of gender are that they foster unrealistic gender ideals in men and women, they encourage us to pathologize normal human bodies and functions, and they normalize violence against women. These implications are likely as long as the media define masculinity and femininity in ways that limit us and our possibilities as human beings. Understanding the overt and subtle gender messages in media empowers us to be more critical about what we hear and see and to raise our voices in resistance to media messages we find harmful. As individuals, parents, and citizens, we have opportunities and responsibilities to criticize media representations that demean men and women and that contribute to attitudes that harm all of us and our relationships with one another.

DISCUSSION QUESTIONS

1. Sign on to InfoTrac College Edition. Select PowerTrac, select author index, then type: "Nancy Signorielli and Aaron Bacue." Read their article, "Recognition and Respect: A Content Analysis of Prime-Time Television Characters Across Three Decades," which appeared in the April 1999 issue of the journal *Sex Roles.* Do their findings suggest that sex stereotypes on television are increasing, decreasing, or staying fairly stable?

2. Watch children's programming on Saturday morning. Are male characters more prominent than female characters? Are there differences in the activities, integrity, intelligence, and so forth of male and female characters? How do you think commercial children's programming influences children's ideas about gender?

3. Focus on relationships between women and men in television programming. How many relationships seem relatively egalitarian? How often are male and female partners shown equally involved in work outside the home and inside it? Do they participate equally in making decisions that affect them both, or does one partner exercise more influence than the other?

4. Sign on to InfoTrac College Edition. Select PowerTrac and access the 1999 article by Adrian Furnham and Twiggy Mak, "Sex role stereotyping in television commercials: A review and comparison of fourteen studies done on five continents over 25 years." Do the authors report that sex-role stereotyping varies across the cultures studied? What roles and activities are generally associated with males and females in advertising?

5. Watch morning and evening news programming. What kinds of stories do male and female reporters and newscasters present? Are there differences in story content? Are there differences in the communication styles of male and female newscasters?

6. Bring advertisements from magazines to class and discuss the images of women, men, and relationships in them. Are these healthy? What are your options as a reader and consumer?

7. Sign on to InfoTrac College Edition. Select PowerTrac, select author index, then type: "Beverly A. Browne." Read her 1998 article, "Gender Stereotypes in Advertising on Children's Television in the 1990s: A Cross-National Sample." What does Browne report regarding how males and females are depicted in television advertising? Do her findings suggest that there have been substantial changes in how the sexes are represented?

11 Gendered Power and Violence

The FBI reported that, in 2000, rates declined for most violent crimes, such as murder and robbery; rates for forcible rape increased.

Twenty-five percent of American women will be victims of rape in their lifetimes.

Over 100 million women around the world have suffered genital mutilation.

Males who suffer abuse are less likely than female victims to report the abuse, because social prescriptions for masculinity specify that men should be able to take care of themselves.

According to the Centers for Disease Control, violence between intimates is the leading cause of injury for U.S. women between the ages of 15 and 44.

Thousands of women in India have been burned to death so that their husbands could collect their dowries.

Thirty to 50% of women students and as many as 75% of women workers have been sexually harassed.

Gendered violence is pervasive. Currently, it's estimated that every 12 seconds in the United States a woman is battered by an intimate, and each day ten women die from violence committed by intimates (Hasenauer, 1997; May, 1998a). Many more women are battered and killed by intimates, but their cases are unreported or are mislabeled as accidental injuries and deaths. In the United States, every five minutes a woman reports a rape, and the FBI estimates that only 36% of rapes are reported. In the time it has taken you to read this far in the chapter, at least one woman has been raped and at least two have been beaten by a friend, lover, or family member.

In this chapter, we'll focus on the distressing topic of gendered violence. In advance, I caution you that I found it difficult to research and write this chapter, and you may find parts of it upsetting to read. Yet if we wish to lessen gendered violence, we must first understand the many forms it takes and the social attitudes and practices that permit it to continue. In the pages that follow, we'll discuss the nature and extent of gendered violence and the ways in which it is related to communication. We'll also identify social structures, practices, and attitudes that underlie gendered violence. To close the chapter, we'll consider how we can use our voices to diminish violence in our lives.

THE SOCIAL CONSTRUCTION OF GENDERED VIOLENCE

Just as our views of gender, race, and other phenomena are socially constructed, so too are our understandings of violence shaped and sustained by our culture. For example, most societies disapprove of killing in general but approve of killing during war. What killing means depends on how a society defines it and the circumstances in which it takes place. Our society approves of brutal force against others if it occurs in war, on a football field, or in a boxing ring (Nelson, 1994a, 1994b; Messner, 1998). We also condone violence, even killing, if it is done to defend ourselves or our families.

Yet violence occurs outside of war, sports, and self-defense. It occurs on dates, in homes, and on the streets. Isolated incidents of violence may occur because of unique personal and situational factors. Widespread violence, however, cannot be explained by individual circumstances. Violence that is pervasive and disproportionately inflicted on certain groups exists only if a society allows or endorses it and communicates that acceptance to individuals. In other words, the epidemic of gendered violence reflects cultural values and social definitions of femininity and masculinity.

Media bombard us with violent images, especially acts of violence against women. Police officers sometimes avoid interfering in violence between intimates, and judges often fail to impose firm sentences on proven batterers. From families to courtrooms, many institutions in our culture communicate that violence against women is acceptable. This suggests that the alarming extent of gendered violence in our era is normalized by some of the very structures and practices that organize social life.

Social acceptance of domination of and violence against women is not new. As you learned in previous chapters, in the United States women were originally regarded as the property of men—of fathers or husbands. Men had the legal right to do to women largely what they wished. During the early years of U.S. history, wife beating and other abuses of women were legal (Deed, 1998; Wriggins, 1998; Zinn, 1995). Many of the first-wave feminists in the 1800s condemned violence against women, but their objections won little public support or legal protection. According to Cheris Kramarae (1995), by the 1870s most states had laws against wife beating, but they were weakly enforced.

Gendered violence is also not confined to the United States or to only a few societies. It is practiced and socially permitted around the world. Because gendered violence is a global problem, this chapter's discussion includes both the developing nations and developed countries. My students sometimes ask why they need to learn about dowry deaths in India or infibulations in Africa. "This isn't part of my life," they claim. "It's not relevant to me." I respond that these practices *are* relevant to all of us because we belong to a world that is larger than our own country.

THE MANY FACES OF GENDERED VIOLENCE

What comes to your mind when you hear terms such as *gendered violence* or *sexual violence*? Most people think of rape, battering, and perhaps sexual harassment. That trilogy of abuses, however, doesn't include all of the forms gendered violence takes. The term **gendered violence** refers to physical, verbal, emotional, sexual, and visual brutality that is inflicted disproportionately or exclusively on members of one sex. In the following pages we'll discuss six types of gendered violence.

■ Gender Intimidation

Gender intimidation occurs when members of one sex are treated in ways that make them feel humiliated, unsafe, or inferior because of their sex (Kramarae, 1992). Probably all of us, male and female, have had good reason to feel unsafe or humiliated at times. Gender intimidation, however, exists when members of one sex have greater reason to feel vulnerable than members of the other sex.

In her commentary, Sharon is right about the reality of dangers to women. When current statistics tell us that one in four women will be raped in her lifetime, there's reason for a woman to be wary, even afraid, of going out alone. The fear of being raped or assaulted is a major constraint on women's freedom. Even when there is no specific wish to go somewhere or do something, the knowledge that it would be dangerous to go out alone restricts

 SHARON

I'm not what you'd call a timid person, but I am scared to go out alone at night. Last year one of the girls in my suite was raped when she was walking to the library. She's not the only one—just the only one I know personally. Every week I read stories about women who are assaulted and raped just because they're out alone.

women. It's a continuous concern—always there, always part of the way many women feel they must plan their lives and activities.

Gender intimidation takes many forms. One example is lewd remarks and requests made to women as they walk on streets or on campuses. A number of women students at my university often take longer, less direct routes around campus to avoid construction workers who assault them with sexual comments and suggestions. They feel unsafe and uncomfortable in areas where others can violate them with verbal propositions, comments, and evaluations.

Gender intimidation also occurs when space is invaded and individuals are forced to tolerate unwelcome sexual conduct. One fraternity had a "prank" that promoted bonding among brothers at the expense of women. The brothers broke into the dining room of a sorority at dinnertime. While one fraternity brother delivered a vivid explanation of Freud's theory of penis envy, his cohort demonstrated masturbation with an artificial penis (Lyman, 1987). On another campus, a group of men arranged themselves into two lines on each side of one of the main paths to classrooms. Any women who passed through the lines were subjected to hearing the men rate their attractiveness and sexual desirability. In 2001, education reporter Eric Hoover described a more extreme form of gender intimidation. At Dartmouth, members of one fraternity printed and distributed two sex newsletters that offered detailed accounts of sexual activities between brothers and female students, some of whom were identified by name. Some women who were named were described as "loose" and "guaranteed hookups" (p. A36). The newsletters promised a future issue that would provide "patented date rape techniques" (p. A35). Not all students thought the sex newsletters were "just good fun." One student informed the deans of the newsletters, and the fraternity's charter was revoked. The response to her actions was mixed. Some students, faculty, and administrators praised her for speaking out. Others shunned her, and she has been told she is no longer welcome on fraternity row.

Some people think that gender intimidation is trivial and shouldn't be criticized or regulated. Katie Roiphe (1993), for instance, claims that making sexual comments, peeking down women's blouses, and so forth are natural and acceptable behaviors. Others argue that sexual banter, "pranks," and touching are insignificant and harmless activities that we shouldn't disapprove of or try to change. Certainly, sexual curiosity and interest are natural. How we do or don't act on sexual impulses, however, is shaped not only by hormones but also by cultural and moral standards that regulate social life. The issue is whether some people have a right to impose their sexual interests on others who have not invited it.

■ Sexual Assault

Sexual assault is sexual activity that occurs without the informed consent of at least one person. Rape is one type of sexual assault, but it isn't the only one. In fact, what rape means isn't as clear-cut as you might think. In many states, my own included, first-degree rape involves forced vaginal intercourse. This means that forced anal and oral intercourse are not considered first-degree rape. It also means that a group of boys who repeatedly thrust a broomstick into the vagina of a retarded girl were not prosecuted for rape. A man who is forced to have sex with another man has not been raped, according to laws that define rape as vaginal intercourse. Whether or not the law defines acts such as these as rape, they are egregious violations that can have long-lasting consequences.

Sexual assault includes rape and other forced sexual activities with strangers; sex that is coerced by "friends" or dates; forced sex in marriage; incest; and sexual activities with children. In other words, sexual assault occurs whenever one sexual partner doesn't consent knowledgeably to having sex or is unable to give **informed consent.** Informed consent can be given only by an adult who has normal mental abilities and whose judgment is not impaired by circumstances, including use of drugs and alcohol. Informed consent cannot be given by children, so the sexual abuse of at least 33% and perhaps as many as 66% of children, both boys and girls, under age 18 is sexual assault (Clutter, 1990; Trexler, 1997). Informed consent also cannot be given by individuals with mental limitations or people who have passed out from alcohol or other drugs. Consequently, having sex with anyone in these categories is sexual assault.

Rape is increasing in the United States. In the last decade, the overall rate of violent crimes in the U.S. has declined, but rates for rape have increased (Jhally & Katz, 2001; "Violent Crime's Era of Decline," 2001). The FBI states that rape is the single most underreported violent crime in the United States (Fuentes, 1998). Not confined to assaults between strangers, rape occurs with tragic frequency between dates and acquaintances. More than 75% of rapes are committed by men who know their victims (Fuentes, 1998; Wriggins, 1998). Research indicates that one reason for the prevalence of rape is that a substantial number of men regard forced sex as acceptable. In one study, a shocking 50% of college men reported that they had coerced, manipu-

---

👣 KENDALL

My father started doing things to me when I was 5 years old—maybe even before that, but that's as far back as I remember. At first he would come into my bedroom when Mom wasn't home and touch me in private places. When I was 12, he raped me the first time, and he made me promise to keep it our secret. I kept "our secret" until about two years ago when the shame overwhelmed me and began to interfere with my schoolwork. Now I'm in counseling to get my life on track.

👣 KILLIAN

The first week I was on campus I went to a fraternity mixer and had too much to drink. I never drank at home, so I didn't know what alcohol could do. I passed out, and when I woke up the next morning, I was in a guy's room—he wasn't even my date—and naked in bed and bleeding. That was rape.

---

lated, or pressured a woman to have sex or have had sex with a woman after getting her drunk. As many as 1 out of 12 men at some colleges admitted engaging in behaviors that met the legal definition of rape or attempted rape (Koss, Gidycz, & Wisniewski, 1987). In a study of 520 undergraduate students, Grace Kim and Michael Roloff (1999) found that both women and men tend not to judge forced intercourse as rape if it occurs with an acquaintance or friend and is not violent. This may reflect a "rape script" (Kahn & Mathie, 1994; Truman, Tokar, & Fischer, 1996) that maintains dates and friends can't rape because rape is a violent act imposed by a stranger. The law, however, requires informed, voluntary consent for sexual activity not to be assault.

Rape is not confined to civilian contexts. A 1996 report based on congressional hearings estimated that between 60,000 and 200,000 women in the military have been sexually assaulted by American servicemen. For years, military women remained silent about the sexual abuse they suffered from their colleagues in the service. By 1995, Veterans Affairs trauma specialists were talking to thousands of victims. In an interview, Lawrence Korb, former president Reagan's assistant secretary of defense, acknowledged that the government and services "treated military women like prostitutes in a foreign country" (Moniz & Pardue, 1996, p. 22A).

Many people think that rapists are psychologically abnormal. Although they may not meet your or my definition of normal, rapists as a group are

ℰ CLARENCE

I don't believe that a man can rape his wife or girlfriend. Maybe it's rape if a guy wants sex and a woman he doesn't know well doesn't, and he forces her. But a guy has a right to have sex in a relationship that is established. All this talk about date rape and marital rape is baloney. No woman I'm going with had better believe that baloney.

not distinguishable from other men on standardized tests of psychological adjustment, emotional well-being, involvement in heterosexual relationships, and frequency of sexual activity (Koss & Dinero, 1988; Muehlenhard & Falcon, 1990; Scully, 1990; Segel-Evans, 1987). The only clear difference between men who force women to have sex and men who don't is that rapists have what clinicians call "hypermasculine" self-concepts. They believe that men should dominate women and that men have a right to have sex (Allgeier, 1987; Koss & Dinero, 1988; Lisak & Roth, 1988; Spitzberg, 1998).

In the United States, many women are raped or sexually assaulted. More than one-third of all women have been sexually abused in some way before reaching age 18 (Fuentes, 1998). More than half of women in college report they have been coerced into some type of unwanted sex at least once (Poppen & Segal, 1988; Ullman, Karabatsos, & Koss, 1999; Warshaw, 1988). The immediate and long-term consequences of rape can be devastating. Fully a third of women who survive rape contemplate suicide (Koss, Dinero, Seibel, & Cox, 1988). Once past the initial trauma, many women who survive rape are haunted by enduring anger, fear, and depression (Marhoefer-Dvorak, Resick, Hutter, & Girelli, 1988).

Rape isn't caused by love or lust. Although rape involves sex, it isn't motivated primarily by sexual desire. Instead, rape is an act of aggression that is designed to humiliate and dominate another person (Costin & Schwartz, 1987; Jhally & Katz, 2001; Scott & Tetreault, 1987; Scully, 1990; South & Felson, 1990). The goal of exerting power explains why rape is one way that male prison inmates brutalize one another and establish a power hierarchy (Rideau & Sinclair, 1982).

Sexual assault includes forced prostitution, also called sexual slavery. During World War II, the Japanese forced countless women to be "comfort women" for Japanese soldiers. They were compelled to have sex with any and all Japanese soldiers who wanted them. Even today, in countries such as the Philippines and Thailand, some women are kidnapped and forced to be prostitutes (Barry, 1998b; French, 1992).

> **BELINDA**
>
> I don't know why guys think that because you have sex sometimes, you have to do it whenever they want. Once when my boyfriend wanted to mess around, I wasn't in the mood so I said no, but he wouldn't take that for an answer. He kept insisting and then tried to force me. I screamed to get him to stop, and he was furious. He still doesn't get it that having a relationship doesn't mean he has an automatic right to sex whenever it suits him. It's my body, after all.

■ Abuse Between Intimates

The trial of O. J. Simpson in 1995 focused the nation's attention on abuse in intimate relationships. At least 28% and possibly as many as 50% of women suffer physical abuse from their partners, and even more suffer emotional abuse, including verbal violence, which can be devastating (Brock-Utne, 1989; French, 1992; May, 1998a; Murphy-Milano, 1996; Roberts, 1993; "The Wounds of Words," 1992). National surveys report that nearly 25% of women and 30% of men regard violence

FYI

Comfort Women

In 1942, Pak Kumjoo was a happy 17-year-old. Then officials in her hometown of Hamun, Korea, complied with orders from the Japanese to recruit women for factory work to help in the war effort. When Korean officials sent Pak and other young women to the Japanese, the women were not given factory jobs. Instead, they were taken into China and, from there, to "comfort stations," where they were forced to have sex with 20 to 30 soldiers a day. Japanese Lieutenant-General Okamura Yasuji ordered that what he called "comfort women" be recruited to put a stop to the rapes being committed by Japanese troops stationed in China.

The comfort women—many of whom were torn from their families in their early teens—suffered profound abuse. The repeated and sometimes brutal rapes caused some of them to become sterile. Those who became pregnant were given injections of Terramycin, which caused their bodies to swell and usually induced abortions. Many were beaten, leaving permanent scars and injuries. Many committed suicide.

After the war, the Japanese government denied that women had been forced to work at comfort stations. In 1991, however, three Korean women sued the Japanese government for having forced them to serve as comfort women. In 1992, Professor Yoshimi Yoshiaki at Chuo University found wartime documents that confirmed that Japanese forces had operated comfort stations.

Sources: Berndt, C. (1997). *The Story of Pak Kumjoo*. Honors thesis in Asian Studies. University of North Carolina, Chapel Hill; Horn, D. (1997). Comfort women. *Endeavors*. Chapel Hill, NC: Office of Graduate Studies and Research, pp. 8–9.

as a normal and even positive part of marriage (Jacobson & Gottman, 1998; Straus, 1977), which suggests that acceptance of marital violence is widespread in our culture (Gelles, 1987; Hampton, Gullotta, Adams, Potter, & Weissberg, 1993; Jones, 1994, 1998a, 1998b; Wood, 2001b). Abuse is also on the rise in dating relationships, including those of very young people. In the most comprehensive study of dating violence ever conducted, 20% of girls between the ages of 14 and 18 reported they had been hit, slapped, shoved, or forced to have sex by a dating partner (Goode, 2001).

Increasingly, stalking is recognized as a form of abuse between intimates. As yet, there is no consensual definition of stalking. Lawmakers and administrators on campuses are wrestling with how to define something that is ambiguous and variable. The best current definition of stalking is repeated behavior that is uninvited and unwanted and that seems obsessive and makes the respondent afraid or concerned for her or his safety (Brownstein, 2000). The National Institute of Justice estimates that 8% of American women have been the object of at least one stalker (Brownstein, 2000). On college campuses, the figures are even higher: 13% of women students report being stalked in the last year (Brownstein, 2000). Accord-

Myths and Facts About Rape

Myth	Fact
Rape is a sexual act that results from sexual urges.	Rape is an aggressive act used to dominate another person.
Rapists are abnormal.	Rapists have not been shown to differ from nonrapists in personality, psychology, adjustment, or involvement in interpersonal relationships.
Most rapes occur between strangers.	More than 75% of rapes are committed by a person known to the victim.
Most rapists are African American men, and most victims are European American women.	More than three-fourths of all rapes occur within races, not between races. This myth reflects racism.
The way a woman dresses affects the likelihood she will be raped.	The majority—up to 90%—of rapes are planned in advance and without knowledge of how the victim will dress.
False reports of rapes are frequent.	False reports of rapes comprise only 2% of all reported rapes.
Rape is a universal problem.	The incidence of rape varies across cultures. It is highest in societies with ideologies of male dominance and a disregard for nature; it is lowest in cultures that respect women and feminine values.

ing to the National Institute of Justice, 2% of American men report having been stalked (Brownstein, 2000). Researchers who have studied stalking (Meloy, 1998; Orion, 1997; Spitzberg, Nicastro, & Cousins, 1998) state that about half of female victims are stalked by ex-partners and another 25% by men they dated at least once. All 50 states have laws against stalking (Murphy-Milano, 1996).

Physical and sexual violence between intimates is inflicted primarily by men and primarily on women. Females experience seven times as many nonfatal assaults by intimates as males do. According to the FBI, 26% of all female murder victims

PAULA

I think the worst thing I ever went through was being stalked by my ex-boyfriend. We'd dated for about a year when I broke up with him. He was so jealous—wouldn't let me go out with friends or anything, so I just decided to end the relationship. But he didn't want it to end. He followed me around campus, showed up at movies when I was out with other guys, and called at all hours of the night. Sometimes he would tell me he loved me and beg to get back together; other times he would threaten me. I finally called the police, and that put an end to his terrorism.

BRICE

Growing up, I saw my father shove Mom around whenever he was having a rough time at work. Sometimes it was more than shoving—he would actually hit her. Always the next day, he would be Mr. Nice, and things would go along fine for a while until he got upset about something else; then it would start all over again. I hated him because of what he did to Mother, and I swore I would never be like him. But last year when I was going through a really rough time, the girl I was dating kept nagging me, and I hauled off and hit her. I never thought I could do that.

in 1995 were killed by husbands or boyfriends, whereas only 3% of male murder victims were killed by wives or girlfriends ("Women Usually Attacked," 1996). Neil Jacobson and John Gottman (1998) agree. Their long-term study of violence between intimates demonstrates that women are battered more often and more seriously than are men. Sex is, however, less important than gender in explaining violence between intimates. A study of 336 undergraduates showed that both men and women who abused their partners had strong masculine gender orientations that esteemed control and domination (Thompson, 1991).

Violence in intimate relationships typically follows a cyclical pattern (Jacobson & Gottman, 1998; Walker, 1984). In the first stage, the batterer experiences mounting tension. Perhaps the individual has problems at work or feels insecure or frustrated. As tension mounts, verbal and emotional abuse may occur. In the second stage, there is a violent explosion involving physical assault—kicking, beating, wrenching arms or legs, throwing the victim against a wall, or using a weapon such as a knife or gun. The third stage in the cycle of abuse is called remorse because the batterer typically acts ashamed and is worried that the partner will leave. In this stage, the abuser apologizes and promises never to do it again. In the fourth stage, the honeymoon phase, the abuser is loving and often brings gifts to the battered partner. The apologies of stage 3 and the loving acts of stage 4 often convince victims to stay with abusive partners. Thus, the cycle continues.

Brice's experience, as expressed in his commentary, is not unusual. Clinicians have documented a strong relationship between growing up in a family with one or more abusive adults and becoming an abuser (Ingrassia & Beck, 1994). Just as we learn social values and codes of conduct through communication in our families, so too, it seems, we learn what is normal and allowable in relationships between men and women. Our parents are important models of how intimates should treat one another. What we learn in families, however, need not be the blueprint for our lives. We can choose to change destructive patterns in our lives.

Are women always the victims and men always the perpetrators of violence in in-

FYI

The Cycle of Violence Between Intimates

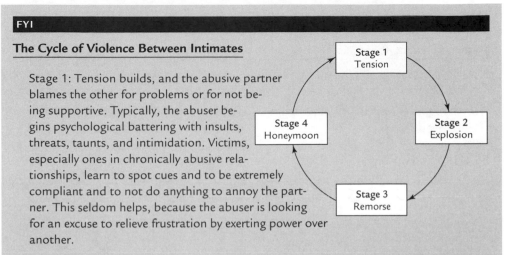

Stage 1: Tension builds, and the abusive partner blames the other for problems or for not being supportive. Typically, the abuser begins psychological battering with insults, threats, taunts, and intimidation. Victims, especially ones in chronically abusive relationships, learn to spot cues and to be extremely compliant and to not do anything to annoy the partner. This seldom helps, because the abuser is looking for an excuse to relieve frustration by exerting power over another.

Stage 2: An explosion occurs. Tension erupts into physical violence, and one or more battering incidents occur. The abuser may wait until the victim is relaxing quietly or even asleep and then attack. Often victims require hospital care. Sometimes they are pregnant and miscarry.

Stage 3: The abuser appears contrite and remorseful. The abuser may apologize to the victim and typically promises it will never happen again. The victim sees the "good person" inside and remembers what led to commitment or marriage.

Stage 4: This is the honeymoon phase. The abuser acts courtly and lovingly. The victim becomes convinced the abuse was an aberration that will not recur—even if it has repeatedly.

And then the whole cycle begins anew.

For information, write to the National Coalition Against Domestic Violence, Department P, Post Office Box 18749, Denver, CO 80218-0749.

timate relationships? No—both women and men can be victims and abusers. Family violence experts Murray Straus and Richard Gelles report that some men are abused by their wives or girlfriends but keep silent because they fear others will question their manhood (Cose, 1994). Yet in some states, 25% of arrests for domestic assaults are of women ("Abuse by Women," 1999).

There are differences, however, in the frequency, motivation, and type of violence committed by women and men, in general. FBI statistics on violence between intimates, which cover only reported cases, indicate that women are 2.4 times more likely to be killed by husbands than husbands are to be killed by wives (Cose, 1994). Richard Gelles ("Husbands Are Battered," 1994) estimates that, cumulatively, about 100,000 men have been battered by women. As horrible as that statistic is, it

Myths and Facts About Violence Between Intimates

Myth	Fact
Victims of battering can just leave the abusive relationship.	Many victims of battering have nowhere to go and no means of supporting themselves and their children.
Abuse of intimates often stops on its own.	Abuse of intimates seldom stops without intervention or other radical measures.
Abuse is confined primarily to working and poverty classes.	Abuse occurs in relationships between members of the upper and middle classes as well as members of the working and poverty classes.
Victims of battering would be safer if they left abusive relationships.	Victims of battering are more likely to be murdered by abusive partners if they try to leave.
Abusers don't love their partners.	Many abusers do love their partners despite brutal behavior.
Abusers have deviant personalities	There is no evidence that abusers differ from nonabusers on standard measures of mental health and personality.

pales before the fact that each year at least 2 million women in the United States are beaten by their partners (Ingrassia & Beck, 1994; White & Bondurant, 1996).

Men and women also differ in the severity of violence they inflict on others. A study conducted by the National Institute of Mental Health found that abusive women most often verbally abuse or push, slap, or shove partners. In contrast, abusive men were more likely to commit brutal, sometimes deadly, assaults (Cose, 1994). This pattern cuts across lines of race and class (Uzzell & Peebles-Wilkins, 1989). Murray Straus, who heads a national investigation of family violence, says that, although both sexes may engage in violence, men are far more likely to inflict serious bodily harm. He reports that women are seven times more likely than men to suffer moderate to severe physical injury ("Husbands Are Battered," 1994).

In comparing women's and men's abusive tendencies, we should also consider differences in motives. Many women engage in violent acts in self-defense. Many

Women are not the only victims of violence from intimates. Men are, too (Lucal, 1995; McFarlane & Wilson, 2000; Mignon, 1998). There is heated debate about the extent of violence by women against men. We know it occurs, but men are less likely to report it than women. Thus, it's hard to tell how widespread it is. Phillip Cook (1997) estimates that each year 2 million men in the United States are victims of violence from women. In his book, Cook offers real-life stories from men who have been abused by wives and girlfriends. Cook and others also show clearly that many men are reluctant to report women's violence against them because it goes against socially endorsed views of masculinity to be a victim or to complain to others about being hurt.

women slap a partner who has beaten them or throw an object at a partner who has slugged them (Jacobson & Gottman, 1998).

Even beyond self-defense, women's reasons for physical aggression are often distinct from those of men. After studying violence and reviewing the work of other researchers, Anne Campbell (1993) concludes that women generally aggress only when they can't resolve issues through strategies prescribed for women such as crying, talking with friends, and turning anger inward. For most women, physical aggression toward others is a method of last resort when all else has failed (O'Connell, 1995).

Men generally enact violence for different reasons. Many use physical aggression to gain or sustain self-esteem, win the respect of others, and maintain control over others and situations. Among children aged 4 to 7, girls aggress to protect themselves and their property, whereas boys aggress to dominate others and increase their status (Bordo, 1998; Hartup, 1974). As boys become men, they are most likely to resort to violence when they feel unsure of themselves, want to prove their toughness, or feel they need to gain control (May, 1998a; Messner, 2001). The patterns of sex difference in use of violence are evident in marriages, cohabiting relationships, and dating relationships. These patterns are wholly consistent with social prescriptions for gender that we have discussed throughout this book. The gendered identities reflected in violence between intimates have led some counselors to conclude that abusive relationships exemplify extreme versions of standard gender expectations in Western culture (Goldner et al., 1990).

■ Sexual Harassment

You may recall that, in 1991, law professor Anita Hill came forward to testify that Clarence Thomas, then a nominee for the Supreme Court, had sexually harassed her when she worked with him. The Hill–Thomas hearings riveted national attention on the long silenced issue of sexual harassment. Gendered violence in the form of **sexual harassment** is widespread in workplaces and schools. Sexual harassment is unwanted and unwelcome verbal or nonverbal behavior of a sexual nature that links academic or professional standing and success to sexual favors or that interferes with work or learning.

Prior to the 1970s, the term *sexual harassment* was not commonly used (Wise & Stanley, 1987). Our language gave victims no socially recognized way to label what happened to them as wrong and unacceptable. Since the term was coined, people who suffer unwelcome sexual conduct have had a way to name their experiences and to demand institutional and legal redress. The Supreme Court has recognized that men and women can be victims of sexual harassment. Although entrenched gender roles in Western culture make women the predominant targets and men the predominant harassers, either sex can be the target or perpetrator of harassment. Increasing numbers of men are filing charges of sexual harassment, citing both women and other men as the harassers. In 2001, men's charges account for 13.5% of all sexual harassment charges brought to the EEOC (Abelson, 2001). Two broad categories of sexual harassment are widely recognized today.

Quid pro quo. **Quid pro quo harassment** is the actual or threatened use of professional or academic rewards and/or punishments to gain sexual compliance from a subordinate or student. *Quid pro quo* is a Latin phrase that means "this for that" or "something for something." Quid pro quo sexual harassment involves an exchange of academic or career benefits for sexual favors. For instance, a professor might promise a student a good grade in exchange for a date, or a manager might offer a subordinate a promotion in exchange for sex. Quid pro quo harassment may also involve punishing someone for not providing sexual favors. For example, a manager might withhold an earned raise or promotion from an employee who refuses to have sex.

FYI

Same-Sex Harassment Recognized by Supreme Court

In the spring of 1998 the U.S. Supreme Court unanimously ruled that federal law protects employees from being sexually harassed by people of their own sex in the workplace. This ruling moves sexual harassment laws beyond the conventional domain of male–female interaction. In stating the court's opinion, Justice Antonin Scalia said that sexual harassment laws should address conduct itself, not the sex or motivation of the individuals involved. Within the intent of Title VII of the Civil Rights Act of 1964, stated Scalia, equal protection exists for victims of heterosexual or homosexual harassment.

Source: Greenhouse, L. (1998, March 5). Same-sex harassment recognized. *Raleigh News and Observer*, p. 4A.

Hostile environment. In 1986, the courts recognized a second type of sexual harassment, one at least as common as quid pro quo. **Hostile environment harassment** is unwelcome conduct of a sexual nature that interferes with a person's ability to perform a job or gain an education and/or that creates a hostile, intimidating, or offensive working environment because of sexualized conduct (Bordo, 1997; Paetzold & O'Leary-Kelly, 1993). Both women and men have brought suits for hostile environment sexual harassment. In one of the more recent cases, a jury awarded $3.75 million to a male prison guard. He sued because, despite his complaints, his employer did nothing to stop a female co-worker who harassed him by calling his home, following him at work, and making repeated sexual comments and invitations to him ("Sexually Harassed Male," 1999). Hostile environment sexual harassment includes a much broader range of behaviors than quid pro quo harassment. Hostile environment sexual harassment may involve making lewd remarks, using language that demeans one sex, hanging pinups, and circulating rumors about an individual's real or speculated sexual activities.

I sometimes consult with attorneys who are trying sexual harassment cases. In one instance, a woman sued her former supervisor for subjecting her to continuous comments about her body and questions about her sexual activities. The supervisor's constant sexualized communication interfered with the woman's ability to concentrate on her job and to feel safe in her work environment. In another case on which I consulted, the first woman in a region to be a high school principal was ridiculed and trivialized in a sexual way by a group of male faculty members. On her first day, the new principal was greeted by one faculty member who told her, "We're renaming the school Hen-House High because you're principal." Another male faculty member said that "having a woman in charge is like a cancer on our school." A subscription to *Playboy* was anonymously given to her by faculty members. These and other incidents formed a pattern of abusive conduct of a sexual nature that undercut the principal's authority and created a climate that was offensive to her and other women in the school.

Hostile environment sexual harassment involves a pattern of behavior. A single action, even if it is unwelcome and inappropriate, is unlikely to meet the legal standard for sexual harassment. Instead, there must be a pervasive pattern of unwelcome conduct of a sexual nature (Bingham, 1996; Shoop & Edwards, 1993). This standard ensures that isolated misconduct, which might be deliberate or inadvertent, doesn't result in excessive penalties.

Whose perspective counts? Perhaps you are thinking that people may differ in what they consider offensive. How can we have a common standard of what is offensive or intimidating sexual conduct when people vary in their perceptions? The courts have struggled with this issue ever since sexual harassment cases first appeared on trial dockets. Within Western legal traditions, the conventional standard for judging behavior has been that of "a reasonable man." Thus, to determine whether a homeowner who shot a burglar used appropriate force, the court would ask, "What would a reasonable man do if someone broke into his home?"

The reasonable man standard prevailed in early sexual harassment cases. For example, in *Rabidue v. Osceola Refining Company* (1986), the majority opinion of the court was that behavior that might offend many women was "an everyday occurrence . . . [that] is natural, acceptable, and part of the fabric of society's morality" (Pollack, 1990, p. 65). In *Rabidue,* male perceptions were declared to be the generic standard for social conduct. Dissenting from the majority opinion in *Rabidue,* Judge Damon Keith asserted that differences in the conditions of women's and men's lives may lead them to perceive events in distinct ways and, specifically, to find different behaviors intimidating and offensive (Forell, 1993). Although Judge Keith's opinion was the minority in *Rabidue,* he inaugurated judicial awareness of the reasonable woman standard.

A few years after *Rabidue,* the appropriateness of the reasonable man standard was rejected in a trial involving the question of whether pinups in public areas of a workplace created an offensive working environment. In this case, the judge ruled that, although nude and near-nude photos of women might not offend a reasonable man, they could well be offensive to a reasonable woman (Tiffs & VanOsdol, 1991). Since that ruling, the reasonable woman standard has been used to judge sexual harassment in a number of cases (Farrell & Matthews, 2000). This legal criterion draws on the logic of standpoint theory, which we discussed in Chapter 2.

Regardless of which standard is used, the law insists on the criterion of reasonableness. This provides a safeguard against frivolous charges and strictly subjective perceptions. Bernice Sandler, who has studied sexual harassment for years, emphasizes that laws governing sexual harassment cases do not favor purely subjective judgments of what is offensive. Instead, the courts assess whether or not perceptions of behaviors as harassing are warranted in light of general, reasonable perceptions of particular behaviors (Sandler, 1996).

◼ Genital Mutilation

Some people have never heard of genital mutilation. Of those who have, many think it is an ancient procedure that is no longer practiced. Yet as we begin the 21st century, genital mutilation continues in many parts of the world. Estimates are that more than 100 million women have been genitally mutilated (Lorber, 1997). In parts of Africa, female genital mutilation is routinely performed on young girls (Dreifus, 2000; Gruenbaum, 2001). In this section, we'll discuss forms of genital mutilation and their consequences. I'll warn you in advance that you may find the pages that follow uncommonly disturbing. It isn't possible to discuss genital mutilation accurately in a way that isn't distressing.

Male circumcision. Male circumcision is the removal of the sheath, or prepuce, of the penis. In many countries, including the United States, male babies are routinely circumcised shortly after birth. The rationale for male circumcision is that it makes it easier to keep the penis clean and reduces the likelihood of infections. Medical research, however, has not demonstrated any clear health advantages to male circumcision. Thus, this procedure may endure because of tradition, not sound scientific evidence.

Sunna. The word *sunna* comes from the Arabic word for "religious duty" (Trangsrud, 1994) and describes a form of female genital mutilation that is practiced in many parts of Africa and the Middle East as well as in some parts of India, Malaysia, and Indonesia (Hosken, 1992). This procedure involves removing both the sheath and the tip of the clitoris. Although you might think sunna and male circumcision are equivalent, they are different in severity and consequence. Removal of the foreskin of a penis doesn't preclude a man's sexual pleasure, but removal of the prepuce and tip of the clitoris usually leaves a woman unable to experience sexual excitement or orgasm. Sunna also has greater potential for medical complications.

Excision or clitoridectomy. A second type of genital mutilation of females is **excision** or **clitoridectomy,** which involves removal of the entire clitoris and parts of the labia minora (Toubia, 1994). This operation greatly diminishes women's ability to experience sexual pleasure, so it is thought to reduce the likelihood of sexual passions that would jeopardize women's virginity or their fidelity to husbands after marriage. Of lesser concern to those who endorse clitoridectomies is that they are medically dangerous, and they increase pain and danger in childbirth.

It might surprise you to learn that clitoridectomies were common in the United States and Europe through the latter part of the 19th century. In the United States, some physicians extended the procedure to remove women's ovaries in the belief that eliminating all sources of women's sexual sensation would "cure" masturbation and prevent nymphomania, not to mention orgasm, which was considered an "ailment" that could be cured by removing the clitoris (Dreifus, 2000; Lightfoot-Klein, 1989). This rationale reminds us of the power of social constructions of gender—views that women should be sexually "pure" were, and still are, used to justify mutilation of women. Even in the 20th century, some U.S. doctors performed clitoridectomies to discourage women from masturbating (Spitz, 1952). Until the mid-1940s, clitoridectomies were routine for female patients in many mental hospitals.

Infibulation. The most radical and brutal form of genital mutilation is **infibulation.** In this operation, the clitoris and labia minora are removed. Next, the flesh of the labia majora is scraped raw and then sewn together to form a hood over the opening to the vagina, with a small opening left for urination and menstruation (Toubia, 1994). When a female who has been infibulated marries, an opening is cut to permit intercourse. Sometimes the opening is deliberately made extremely small to increase male sexual pleasure. In fact, the Arabic term for infibulation is *adlat el rujal,* which means "men's circumcision," because it is designed to increase men's sexual pleasure. This practice increases women's pain during intercourse. Husbands may order their wives resewn when they go on journeys or to prevent pregnancy.

This technique seems to have been first used by ancient Upper Egyptians who fastened a clasp (fibula) through the large genital lips of slave women to keep them from having children, which would interfere with their work. Wealthy Romans also sometimes fastened a fibula through the foreskin of gladiators and other males whom they didn't want to have sex (French, 1992). Today, infibulation is practiced primarily in some Muslim and West African societies (Trangsrud, 1994). Somalians regard infibulation as a rite of passage that transforms young girls into virgins, an identity based on having undergone infibulation and not on having refrained from sexual intercourse (Van der Kwaak, 1992). After giving birth or losing a husband, some women recapture their status as virgins by being reinfibulated (Slack, 1988).

Women who have been genitally mutilated report that the process is excruciatingly painful (Finnerty, 1999; Ziv, 1997). A woman from Somalia who was circumcised at 7 years old reports her horror at watching her clitoris being sliced off. She bled for a week after the procedure. A woman from Somalia who was infibulated at the age of 6 reported that four women held her down and a razor blade was used to amputate her clitoris and all of her vaginal lips. Then thorns were used to close the wound, and her legs were bound together from her heels to her thighs.

Genital mutilation is seldom practiced in sterile settings with the benefit of anesthesia and precise surgical instruments. Infibulation, sunna, and excision are generally performed by people with little or no medical training, in unsanitary conditions, and with dirty, imprecise implements, including shards of glass, rusty razors, and lids of tin cans (Trangsrud, 1994). The immediate consequences of genital mutilation may include excruciating pain (anesthesia is not used), hemorrhage, tetanus, gangrene, blood poisoning, and fractured bones from the force needed to hold girls down during the operation. Longer term consequences include sterility, increased difficulty in delivering babies, permanent incontinence from bad "surgery," and stillbirths of babies who cannot emerge through birth canals that have been scarred and deformed by genital operations.

To many people, the idea of genital mutilation seems barbaric and unjustifiable. Yet that opinion

---

🎧 SUCHUNA

I know American college students cannot understand our ways. In Africa, we do not call it mutilation. We call it the custom. My friends here ask why mothers let this be done to their daughters. It is because men will not marry women who do not follow the custom. A mother who doesn't have the custom for her daughter dooms the daughter to being a social outcast and unmarriageable.

🎧 KYENOLA

In my home of Djibouti [East Africa], almost all women are infibulated. In America, I am told it is primitive and vicious. But here women put holes in their ears for jewelry and go to the hospital to have breasts made bigger or lips made more full. These things do not mutilate the body?

reflects a social standpoint that differs from the standpoint of members of cultures who surgically alter women's genitals. Within the standpoint of societies that do practice genital operations, the procedures affect a woman's status. Girls who have not undergone genital surgery are often ridiculed and made to feel unclean. Dr. Nahid Toubia (1993), one of the international authorities on female genital surgery, says a young girl who had not been infibulated told him that she felt ashamed in front of her friends who had been infibulated, and that her friends refused to let her touch them because she was unclean.

When we acknowledge religious and cultural traditions that uphold the practice of altering female genitalia, we realize it would be ineffective to try to legislate changes without first understanding cultural traditions and providing education about alternative ways to honor traditions (Gruenbaum, 2001; Trangsrud, 1994). We might gain greater perspective on this tradition by inspecting some of the ways we modify our bodies in the West, as Kyenola points out in her commentary.

Even though we should be hesitant to apply the standards of our culture to the practices of other cultures, troubling questions about genital surgery cannot be ignored. Even highly respected figures such as Alice Walker have been condemned for being ethnocentric when they criticized genital alteration. Critics have pointed out that genital surgery increases a woman's status in societies that endorse this practice. Yet, just as important as understanding that genital alteration increases a woman's

---

FYI

Changing Customs

Female genital mutilation is waning in many places. Senegal, Togo, and five other African countries have recently banned clitoridectomy (Pollitt, 1999), although the ban is still unevenly enforced. Waris Dirie, a Somali woman who suffered genital mutilation at 5 years old and later fled Somalia to escape an arranged marriage, became a celebrated high-fashion model in London. She also is the United Nations special ambassador on female genital mutilation (Dirie, 1998). Dirie says Westerners should not try to change African customs—changes must come from within the countries themselves. She believes female genital mutilation is coming to an end in Africa: "I've heard the chief of a village say, 'We know it is wrong and we've got to stop it'" (Finnerty, 1999, p. 22).

Sociologist Judith Lorber (1997) points out another example of cultural traditions that changed only when members of the culture organized to oppose established practices. In China, the cruel and crippling process of binding women's feet was standard for centuries. Yet it was eliminated in a mere 17 years (1895–1912) in urban China when progressive Chinese launched an education campaign to demonstrate the disadvantages of foot binding. Also critical to ending the practice was the formation of associations of fathers who refused to bind their daughters' feet and prohibited their sons from marrying women whose feet had been bound. When enough fathers made these commitments, it affected marriage patterns and created a demand for women with unbound feet.

Defining Human Rights

Fauziya Kasinga grew up in Togo, Ghana. Unlike most men in Togo, Fauziya's father was progressive. He didn't believe in polygamy, forced marriage, or denying education to women. He also refused to let any of his five daughters be circumcised, which was the custom in Togo. But when her father died, Fauziya was scheduled for ritual genital mutilation. She managed to escape and came to the United States, where she asked for asylum on the grounds that she would be subjected to genital mutilation if she returned home.

The immigration judge who heard her case concluded that her story was "unbelievable" and that Fauziya was not credible. Her case was investigated and then supported by Amnesty International and other human rights groups. On appeal, she was granted asylum—the first time the United States acknowledged that genital mutilation is a form of human rights abuse. This is a landmark decision that defines abuses based on gender as violations equal to those based on race, religion, or politics.

Sources: Goodman, E. (1996, April 9). Freedom from mutilation. *Raleigh News and Observer*, p. 9A; Kassindja, F. (1998). *Do they hear you when you cry?* New York: Delacorte; Pollitt, K. (1996, May 13). Women's rights, human rights. *Progressive*, p. 9.

status is asking why this painful and limiting procedure is needed for a woman to have status. We should also recognize the gender inequity that exists when men don't have to suffer genital surgery to gain status.

▪ Gender-Based Murder

Consider two facts: (1) When both sexes are given adequate care, more females than males survive; and (2) in many countries today, men substantially outnumber women. How can both of these facts be true? According to Amartya Sen (1990), the answer is that women are being systematically killed around the world. She estimates that more than 100 million women have disappeared or been killed.

One way to reduce the number of women is selective abortion of female fetuses, a common practice in some countries today (Pollitt, 1999). Female infanticide involves active or passive killing of female children. Active female infanticide is sometimes practiced by drowning newborn female babies in a bucket of water kept by the birthing bed. More passive methods of killing female babies include not feeding them enough or not feeding them at all and denying them essential medical care. The deliberate and systematic killing of women is evident in demographic trends. For example, infant mortality for girls in China rose from 37.7 per 1,000 in 1978 to 67.2 per 1,000 in 1984 (Sen, 1990). United Nations studies of countries such as India, Pakistan, Albania, and United Arab Emirates reveal similar evidence of women who have disappeared or been killed (*World's Women*, 1991).

Women who survive to adulthood aren't necessarily safe. In recent years, we have learned of the horrifying practice of dowry deaths, or bride burnings. Some groups in India still follow the custom wherein a woman's parents give a sum of money or other goods to the bridegroom when he marries their daughter. After the marriage, new husbands sometimes make additional demands for payments from the bride's parents. If the demands aren't met, the husband's family may hold the bride near the cooking stove until her sari catches fire and she burns to death. The husband is then free to get another wife and another dowry. Hundreds of thousands of women have been victims of bride burning, which the culture has condoned by not investigating cases in which women "accidentally" burn to death (French, 1992). Traditionally, in parts of India *suttee* was practiced—a custom in which a widow is expected to commit suicide by throwing herself on the funeral pyre of her husband.

From abortions of female fetuses to killing of female babies to dowry deaths, females around the world are being murdered daily. These practices are dramatic evidence of the devaluation of girls, women, and femininity. By now, the body count produced by these values is in the millions and still growing.

Throughout this book, we have seen that certain attitudes, behaviors, and values are naturalized, or made to seem natural, by social practices. What is considered acceptable or natural is a matter of social negotiation and communication in a culture. We construct views of what is normal and acceptable, and we communicate those views through social institutions and practices. Years ago it was considered normal for women not to have the right to vote or pursue higher education and careers. It was also considered normal for women to be men's property and for men to control everything from women's living conditions to decisions about medical procedures performed on women. Today in some countries genital mutilation, female infanticide, and the murder of women are regarded as normal.

We've seen that what is considered normal is not a matter of objective truth. Moral standards and codes of behavior are constructed and sustained by public and private communication throughout the world. This suggests that we need to understand social processes that allow or encourage gendered violence around the world.

SOCIAL FOUNDATIONS OF GENDERED VIOLENCE

We can't understand gendered violence by analyzing only individual motives. Although particular individuals commit violent acts and should be held responsible for them, we have to consider causes beyond individual psychology and circumstances. To unravel cultural forces that cultivate tolerance for violence against women, we will consider how media, institutions, and language normalize gendered violence.

■ Normalization of Violence in Media

One of the most obvious signs of widespread acceptance of violence is the amount of it that routinely appears in media. As we noted in Chapter 10, violence is customary—not unusual—in films, MTV, television programs, and popular music. Violence is also wired into video games, which many children and adolescents play for hours a day. One popular video for 10- to 14-year-olds is "Carnal Sins," which is extremely violent.

Gangsta rap has been especially criticized for its violence and sexism. Typical of gangsta rap are lyrics that refer to women as "hos" (whores) and "bitches" and that glorify killing for sport. Some critics of gangsta rap have suggested it reflects the pathological lifestyle and values of many young Black males. Yet this analysis fails to recognize that the musicians and the lyrics they compose exist in and are accepted by larger social systems. In other words, gangsta rap reflects a widespread and deeply ensconced cultural ideology that esteems violence (Dyson, 1995, 1996).

bell hooks (1994) strongly denounces the misogyny, sexism, and violence of gangsta rap, but she does not make the mistake of thinking it reflects values that are distinctive of Black youth culture. Although hooks acknowledges that "black male sexism is real and a serious problem in our communities" (p. 118), she also points out that a lot of White people produce, market, and listen to gangsta rap. Addressing Black women like herself, hooks says it's wrong to believe they must support vi-

---

FYI

Mediated Violence

Mass media are significant influences on identity and behavior. The media offer us ideas of who we are and should be—they give us stories of what it means to be a man, to be a woman, to be in a relationship. And the stories they give us increasingly tell us that to be a man is to dominate women, to be a woman is to be submissive to men, and to be in a relationship is to expect a degree of violence. Television and films offer image after image, story after story of men who are violent in general and violent toward women in particular. Media sexualize violence, making it appear erotic, desirable, and normal. Rap and rock music frequently refer to women as "bitches" and "hos," while country music urges women to "stand by your man." Newspapers and television news sometimes include titillating and entirely irrelevant details about victims of sexual assaults—what they were wearing, how they looked, where pants were found after a rape. The stream of violence against women in media encourages us to perceive violence as acceptable and to think it normal that men harm women and women tolerate it.

Sources: Jhally, S., & Katz, J. (2001, Winter). Big trouble, little pond: Reflections on the meaning of campus pond rapes. *Umass*, pp. 26–31; Meyers, M. (1997). *News coverage of violence against women: Engendering blame.* Thousand Oaks, CA: Sage; Wood, J. T. (2001b). The normalization of violence in heterosexual romantic relationships: Women's narratives of love and violence. *Journal of Social and Personal Relationships, 18,* 239–261.

---

olence and sexism "under the guise of standing by our men. If black men are betraying us through acts of male violence, we save ourselves and the race by resisting" (p. 123).

By now there is fairly convincing evidence that exposure to sexual violence in media is linked to increased tolerance, or even approval, of violence in actual relationships (Cuklanz, 1997; Hansen & Hansen, 1988). Women who view sexually violent MTV are more likely to accept violence in their own relationships than women who don't view sexually violent MTV (Dieter, 1989). Philosophy professor Larry May sees a connection between violence in media and violence against women. He notes that there is a "resurgence of the 'tough guy' image in movies and sports, and it is sometimes reflected in the way that boys intimidate girls on their co-ed grad school soccer or baseball teams" (1998a, p. B7).

Research on **pornography** further confirms the link between exposure to portrayals of violence in media and willingness to engage in or accept violence in real relationships (Russell, 1993). Before we discuss this research, however, it's important to distinguish pornography and **erotica.** Pornography is not simply sexually explicit material. Rather, it is material that favorably shows subordination and degradation of individuals by presenting sadistic behaviors as pleasurable, pain as enjoyable, and forced sex as positive. Erotica, on the other hand, depicts consensual activities that are desired by and pleasurable to all parties. Erotic material doesn't seem to cultivate violence in relationships, whereas pornographic media are linked to violence between intimates (Donnerstein, Linz, & Penrod, 1987; Mac-Kinnon, 1987).

Pornography is a multibillion-dollar business in the United States. Pornographic videos account for 50% to 60% of all videos selected (Fox-Genovese, 1991). One study of pornographic films found that more than 80% of X-rated films included scenes in which one or more men dominate and exploit one or more women; 75% of these films portray physical aggression against women, and 50% explicitly depict rape (Cowan et al., 1988). A number of researchers have concluded that viewing sexually violent films tends to desensitize men to rape and increases their predictions that they themselves might commit rape (Demare, Briere, & Lips, 1988; Donnerstein et al., 1987; Malamuth & Briere, 1986). A number of people who study violence against women think there is convincing evidence that repeated exposure to sexual violence may lead viewers to see it as acceptable and enticing (Jhally & Katz, 2001). Confirming this is the finding that the single best predictor of rape is the circulation of pornographic materials that glorify violence against women (Baron & Straus, 1989).

■ Normalization of Violence by Institutions

There is growing consensus that many of the basic structures and institutional practices of Western culture tolerate or uphold violence, especially violence against women. They do this in a variety of ways such as refusing to interfere in domestic disputes, advising victims not to prosecute batterers, and encouraging women to fulfill social prescriptions for femininity by standing by their men.

Family. One of the most important institutions shaping cultural consciousness, including perspectives on violence, is the family (Noddings, 2002). In families where violence exists, parents may teach daughters to expect it. One woman in a recent study I conducted explained why she stayed with a man who physically and sexually brutalized her: "Once when I told my mama that Gerald was sometimes mean, she said that all men are and that's just how they are—that all of them have bad spells—that's what Mama called them—and sometimes you just have to overlook those" (Wood, 2001b, p. 254). Many parents still encourage girls to be physically reserved, sensitive to relationships, and deferential to others. Boys are encouraged to be physically aggressive, to compete and win, and to control others. The combination of these two gender scripts lays the groundwork for men to be sexually aggressive and for women to defer or tolerate abuse from men (Messner, 2001). A man who internalizes social prescriptions for masculinity may regard it as appropriate to dominate and inflict violence on women. Further, researchers have shown that some men who engage in abuse justify their violence by saying their partners deserved it, their partners provoked them, or they had to use force to get what they were entitled to have (Christopher & McQuaid, 1998; Stamp & Sabourin, 1995). A woman who embodies femininity may be deferential and loyal even to someone who batters her. It is erroneous to think that women who follow social prescriptions for femininity enable abusers if they defer to abusive partners. To believe this is to make the mistake of holding victims responsible for violence against them.

When masculine socialization is extreme, it can promote appalling violence, such as that engaged in by members of the Spur Posse. In 1993, media attention focused on a group of high school athletes in a California suburb who dubbed themselves the Spur Posse and whose claims to status were the number of sexual encounters they could score and the disdain with which they treated women with whom they had sex. Although some parents of the Spur Posse members were upset when they learned of their sons' exploits, other parents weren't. In fact, some parents shared their sons' pride in numerous sexual conquests. As one father remarked, "Nothing my boy did was anything that any red-blooded American boy wouldn't do at his age" (Quindlen, 1994, p. A23). Parents who condone males' sexual abuse of females turn families into breeding grounds for violence against women.

A more recent incident of mob violence against women was the wilding in Central Park at the National Puerto Rican Day Parade on June 11, 2000. Four or five dozen men groped and stripped at least 47 women while yelling "Get that bitch" and "You know you want it" (Campo-Flores & Rosenberg, 2000). Over 900 police officers were on duty in the park at the time, but they were unresponsive to pleas for help. In response to public outcry, within a week Mayor Rudy Giuliani had promised an intense inquiry into police response, and 17 men had been arrested.

One of the men arrested shrugged off what he and others did to women, saying that it was "an innocent water fight that got out of hand" (Cloud, 2000, p. 32). The June 26 issue of *Time* included a 2-page story on the Central Park wilding. The same issue gave 5 pages to coverage of an architect and 7 pages to television voyeurism.

Law enforcement. Families are not the only social institution that upholds tolerance of violence. Practices by some law-enforcement agencies also reflect and sustain cultural acceptance of violence. Police officers are often reluctant to intervene in violence in families. As two reporters noted, "Bluntly put, cops hate domestic calls" (Ingrassia & Beck, 1994, p. 31). Some police officers regard domestic cases as less important than "real crime."

When they fail to treat abusers harshly, the courts also communicate that violence against women is not serious. According to Albert Hunt (1994), most spouse abusers receive lenient treatment in U.S. courts. In 1991, Juanita Leonard testified in divorce court that her husband, Sugar Ray Leonard, had repeatedly hit her, thrown her around, and harassed her in front of their children. The world-famous boxer denied none of his wife's claims. He did, however, say his violence was a private matter between him and his wife, a view that the court found credible (Nelson, 1994a).

Another case that dominated headlines was that of O. J. Simpson and Nicole Brown Simpson (Bordo, 1997). In 1989, police entered the Simpsons' home and found Nicole Brown Simpson badly beaten and fearful for her life. The officers accepted O. J.'s statement that he and his wife were involved in "a family matter . . . we can handle it" (Hunt, 1994). Judge Ronald Schoenberg didn't sentence repeated abuser O. J. Simpson to any prison time or even counseling. Another case, this one in New Hampshire in 1993, involved a man who smashed his partner's face so badly that she needed 17 stitches. Acknowledging that the man had battered the woman, the judge nonetheless ruled, "I can't conclude that it was completely unprovoked" (Hunt, 1994). Judgments such as this one communicate dramatically that it is acceptable to batter women. In so doing, they perpetuate violence against women and the values that underlie it.

Based on interviews with 80 survivors of violence at the hands of intimates, James West (1995) reported that women who are abused by partners often face strong social pressure to stay in relationships. West found that some judges, prosecutors, and other officers of the courts advise victims of battering to return home, not to press charges, or to "work things out." These messages from people in powerful institutional positions communicate that abuse of women is unimportant in the eyes of the law and the society.

Counseling. Compounding the legal system's contribution to normalizing violence against women is the advice given by some clergy and lay counselors to victims of violence. They may urge women to return to their battering partners in order to "be

I said, "I can't [go home]. What am I supposed to do if he's cheating on me and hits me?" He [the priest] said, "You should forgive him." And I said, "What if he continues to do it?" Then he said, "You should pray that he'll stop." I said, "I'm sorry, I'm sorry, I've waited for a long time for him to stop and he hasn't and I'm not going back." Then he told me that I was very selfish and all I cared about was myself and what I was doing.

When I was a sophomore, an instructor in my chemistry class tried to hit on me. He asked me to come to his office to discuss my work. But when I got there, he started touching me and asking if I'd go out with him. I don't remember what I said, but I got out of there as fast as I could. When I went to the chair of the department, he told me I was overreacting to "a misunderstanding." My advisor said the same thing, so I finally figured I must be wrong to think it was such a big deal. I quit going to the class because I wanted to avoid the instructor, so I failed. No big deal, right?

a good wife," "keep the family together," and "not be selfish" (West, 1995). The commentary by Jenni is not from a student but from a battered woman (West, 1995, p. 129). Jenni describes what happened after she turned to her church for help when her husband beat her and the priest advised her to return home.

Some institutions also perpetuate violence against women by suggesting that women are wrong to object to brutality and harassment. In her studies of responses to women who have been sexually harassed, Robin Clair (1994) found that victims' protests are often dismissed ("You misunderstood"), trivialized ("Don't make a mountain out of a molehill"), or defined as inappropriate ("All the guys around here do that"). Each of these responses defines the victim—not the sexual harasser—as wrong or at fault. By routinely treating sexual harassment and other forms of violence against women as unimportant, institutions sustain a cultural ideology that licenses violence against women.

Language. Another cultural practice that reflects and sustains tolerance of violence is language. Throughout this book and especially this chapter, we've noted ways in which communication reflects and sustains cultural views of gender and gender-related behavior, including violence. Sharon Lamb (1991, 1999) claims that much of the language used to describe violence between intimates conceals the brutality of what happens. She asks why we use inappropriately gentle terms such as *domestic dispute* or *spousal conflict* to camouflage actions such as smashing women's faces with fists and hammers, slashing women with knives, and breaking bones by throwing or stomping on women. In her historical account of the movement to aid women who are abused by their partners, Susan Schechter (1982) criticizes the shift in language that occurred when "battered women" and "battering men" were transformed into "domestic violence." Concurring with Schechter's analysis, James West (1995) notes that the term *domestic violence* "provides an image of the violence in a family as somehow less severe than violence between strangers" (p. 140).

Lamb also points out that language about gendered violence often obscures moral responsibility. Terms such as *spousal conflict* and *family problems* distort reality by representing the issue as one for which partners share culpability. Responsibility for violence is also diminished by passive language that fails to name aggressors—for example, "The battery occurred on Sunday," "Women are abused frequently," or "Many women are beaten." The horror of gendered violence is also diminished when the language of love is used to describe physical abuse. Media accounts of battering of women often include phrases such as "He loved her too much," "She was the victim of love," and "It was love that went too far" (Jones, 1994; Meyers, 1994, 1997).

It's clear that many of our cultural institutions reflect and sustain acceptance of violence as normal. It would be nice to believe that individuals don't necessarily share institutional views that violence is acceptable. If that were true, however, during O. J.'s frantic attempt to elude capture, why did drivers on the Los Angeles freeway stop their cars to let him pass, all the while chanting "Go, O. J., go"? They cheered on a known wife batterer and an accused murderer in his flight from justice.

Cultural acceptance of gendered violence is supported—subtly and overtly, deliberately and inadvertently—by a number of social practices and institutions. Particularly compelling evidence of cultural foundations for gendered violence comes from cross-cultural studies that reveal pronounced differences among societies in the extent of rape and other violations of women. Rape is most common in societies that embrace ideologies of male toughness and that disrespect women and nature (Basow, 1992; Coltrane, 1996, 1998; Sanday, 1986; Wriggins, 1998). On the other hand, rape is rare in cultures that respect women, that value feminine qualities such as nurturance, and that seek harmony with nature (Griffin, 1981; Sanday, 1986). Of 95 tribal societies studied, approximately one-half have virtually no rape (West Sumatra, for example) (Basow, 1992; Griffin, 1981). The existence of societies in which rape and other forms of gendered violence are rare demonstrates that violence against women is not innate in male sexuality and acceptance of violence is not inevitable. Attitudes toward gendered violence reflect particular cultural ideologies that can be transformed.

RESISTING GENDERED VIOLENCE: WHERE DO WE GO FROM HERE?

I suspect that this chapter has been as distressing for you to read as it was for me to research and write. It is disheartening to realize that violence against women is a persisting problem around the world. However, merely being distressed about the extent of gendered violence will not lessen it. We must ask how we can be agents of change who resist violence and who compel revisions in cultural attitudes toward it.

■ Personal Efforts to Reduce Gendered Violence

There is a great deal that each of us can do to lessen gendered violence. The most basic personal choice is to decide that you will not engage in or tolerate violence in your relationships. You can also make conscious choices about the language you use to speak about gendered violence. You can heighten others' awareness of the extent and brutality of violence against women by selecting words that accurately represent the ugliness and inhumanity of violent actions. An extension of this is to speak out against violence. For instance, if a woman you know verbally abuses her boyfriend, you can either be silent or let her know that you think what she's doing is wrong. You can also assume a voice by speaking against others who violate or threaten to violate women. There may be situations in which you, like Denny (see commentary), can intervene to prevent others from harming women.

There are other ways you personally can take a stand against gendered violence. You might volunteer to work with battered women or women who have been raped. Most campuses and communities have a number of women's groups that offer outreach programs to educate citizens about violence against women. Men on many campuses work to get other men involved in combatting violence against women. Being a community educator is one way you can be an active agent of change. You can also make a personal statement by writing to magazines, television stations, and companies that feature gendered violence.

You can use your voice to resist gendered violence by supporting friends and acquaintances who are victims of violence. For too many years, people have looked away from sexual harassment and violence between intimates. We've pretended not to see bruises, not to notice on-the-job harassment. If you suspect that a friend or colleague is experiencing violence, don't assume "it's none of my business." It *is* your business. Speaking up to support someone who is being harmed is a concrete way that you can use your voice to reduce the violence in our world.

If you are or plan to be a parent, you can make a difference by communicating to your children that they should respect their own bodies and those of others. All young children should learn that nobody has a right to touch them in a violent or sexual way without their permission. And all children should learn that it is not appropriate or acceptable to be violent toward others, including girls and women, and it is not acceptable to coerce women into sexual activities.

■ Social Efforts to Reduce Gendered Violence

We must also change cultural practices and structures. Here, too, there are many ways to be an agent of change. Our educational and social service institutions need to do a better job of educating and counseling both victims and perpetrators of violence. Some universities now offer an interdisciplinary minor in Violence Studies that allows students to prepare for careers working to reduce violence (Reisberg, 1999). You can also vote for bonds and tax increases necessary to underwrite more education and counseling. If you have skills as an educator or administrator, you may be able to help design and implement educational programs. In Wai'anae, Hawaii, women developed Peace Education, a two-week curriculum that helps students learn nonviolent ways to manage anger and frustration (French, 1992).

In India, a group of women formed *Vimochana,* an organization that assists battered women in getting legal help. In addition to responding to the symptoms of violence (battered women), *Vimochana* tackles structural causes of it by organizing consciousness-raising groups that allow women to work together to redefine battering and dowry murders as unacceptable. Groups patterned after *Vimochana*

FYI

Realizing the American Dream

In March 1995, President Clinton formed the Violence Against Women Office. In announcing the new office, President Clinton noted that violence against women is increasing significantly faster than the overall crime rate. He said, "If children aren't safe in their homes, if college women aren't safe in their dorms, if mothers can't raise their children in safety, then the American Dream will never be real for them." The Violence Against Women Office will fund state efforts to improve law enforcement, prosecution, and victims' services related to violence against women.

Source: Clinton forms office focusing on violence against women. (1995, March 22). *Raleigh News and Observer,* p. A4.

The Bandit Queen of India

Phoolan Devi was born into Dalit, a low caste of boat rowers in India. At 11, she was married to a man 20 years her elder who was chosen by her parents. Her husband beat her, and later while under detention, Devi was raped. Instead of accepting this as the fate of women in her society, Devi rebelled. She took up a gun and formed a gang that killed men who harmed women. In 1983 she turned herself in in exchange for the government's promise of an 8-year jail sentence. Devi was jailed without trial for 11 years, then released without comment in 1994. Within a year of her release, women elected her to federal parliament.

She became a very powerful advocate for women in India. To her followers, she was the reincarnation of Kali, a Hindu goddess, and a symbol for women's rights in a country that historically has not recognized that women have rights. In 2001, at the age of 38, Devi was gunned down in India by Sher Singh Rana, a 22-year-old student.

Source: Schmetzer, U. (1997, August 13). From abused wife to India's avenging angel. *Raleigh News and Observer*, p. 13A.

could begin to erode the foundations of gendered violence in other countries, including the United States.

You can also choose to become involved with international efforts to reduce violence against women. There are many organizations that work against violence, and they welcome volunteers and financial support. For example, Southeast Asian women formed *Saheli*, which protests dowry deaths. *Saheli* was successful in getting a law passed that requires thorough investigation of any "accidental death" of a woman in the first 7 years of marriage (French, 1992). Chilean women are risking imprisonment and death to demand that *desaparecidos*, "disappeared women," be returned. In Afghanistan courageous women quietly worked for women's rights, even under the oppressive Taliban rule (Herlinger, 2001). Groups such as these could use support, both personal and financial, from women and men in less hazardous circumstances.

There are many ways you can be an agent of change. All that is required is for you to decide you will assume an active role in constructing social life. You can use your knowledge of how gendered violence is normalized to make a difference in the world that you and others inhabit.

SUMMARY

In this chapter, we've examined forms of gendered violence and some of the ways in which communication sustains and normalizes violence, especially violence against women. It's difficult, painful, and upsetting to have to confront and think about the topics in this chapter. Yet, the distress that you and I feel in dealing with these issues pales in contrast to the agony felt by women around the world who are victims of unspeakable violations.

We do not have to accept the current state of affairs. There is much that we can do to reduce gendered violence in our personal lives and to contribute to broader changes in the social structures and practices that sustain cultural acceptance of gendered violence. We need to work together to provide safe refuges for victims of violence and to provide counseling to both victims and abusers. In addition, we need to develop educational programs that teach children at very young ages that it is not acceptable to sexually or physically abuse other people. These and other changes in social structures and practices can reform cultural attitudes toward gendered violence. The changes will not be easy, but they are possible. Continuing to live with pervasive and relentless violence is not.

DISCUSSION QUESTIONS

1. What are the values and shortcomings of various legal standards for judging whether sexual harassment occurs? Do you support the reasonable man, reasonable woman, or another standard? How is this issue linked to our discussion of generic language?

2. How we should perceive and respond to genital mutilation is more complex than it might first seem. Would Western efforts to end clitoridectomies and infibulations result in unmutilated women being outcasts who could never marry? (Reread Suchuna's commentary on page 310.) Is it ethnocentric to condemn practices that differ from those in our own culture? Do we have any right to impose the values of our particular social world on people with different standpoints? On the other hand, is it immoral to do nothing when human beings are being maimed (following custom) and killed?

3. Currently, most states will prosecute batterers only if a victim will press charges. However, because fear of retribution and other factors constrain many victims from pressing charges, some jurisdictions have redefined battering as a crime against the state, for which an individual victim doesn't need to press charges. These jurisdictions have a "pro-arrest" policy. Do you think batterers should be arrested if the victims don't want to press charges?

4. Sign on to InfoTrac College Edition. Select PowerTrac, select author index, then type: "Tracy Dietz." Read the 1998 article, "An Examination of Violence and Gender Role Portrayals in Video Games: Implications for Gender Socialization and Aggressive Behavior," which appeared in the journal *Sex Roles*. Based on Dietz's article, do you think violence on television promotes violence in children? Is there any evidence that the effects of violence on television are stronger for boys than for girls?

5. To understand how sexual harassment affects individuals, read the stories of people who have personally experienced it. The fall 1992 issue of the *Journal of Applied Communication Research* includes a special symposium that features stories from survivors of sexual harassment.

6. Now that you have learned about the extent of gendered violence, reread the discussion of power feminism in Chapter 3 (p. 78). In light of what you've learned in this chapter, do you think that "victim psychology is all in women's heads"? Do you think that women can avoid violence by exercising their individual wills?

7. Sign on to InfoTrac College Edition. Select EasyTrac, select key words, then type: "sexual harassment." Reread the article that appeared in an August 2000 issue of *USA Today*, "Violence against women in the military." What factors increase the likelihood that women in the military will experience physical assault?

8. Sign on to InfoTrac College Edition. Select PowerTrac to access Jill Elaine Hasday's 2000 article, "Contest and consent: A legal history of marital rape." According to Hasday's analysis, why have efforts to enact strong laws against marital rape been unsuccessful? Does she offer a solution to the problem she discusses?

Epilogue
Looking Backward, Looking Forward

he cultural conversation about gender is ongoing. It is carried on in barrooms and living rooms, college classes and beauty pageants, Saturday-morning cartoons and newspaper stories, private relationships and public platforms. It is a conversation in which we all participate, with each generation adding new themes to the overall dialogue. Even though this book is ending, what you've learned about communication, gender, and culture will affect your personal future and how you contribute to our collective horizons. In this epilogue, I want to look backward at major changes that have occurred and forward to choices that are open to us as we engage in the conversation through which we continuously re-create ourselves, gender, and the social world.

THE CULTURAL CONSTRUCTION AND RECONSTRUCTION OF GENDER

Throughout this book, we've seen that social order and meanings are created in daily messages that remind us what society regards as feminine and masculine, what it expects of women and men, and what rights, value, opportunities, and constraints it bestows on each gender. We are encouraged to accept these standards by continuous communication that normalizes prevailing views of gender and entices us to regard them as natural. Yet we are not only receivers of cultural communication about gender. We are also active communicators who shape our culture's views of men and women. We fortify or resist prevailing views as we enact our own gendered identities and as we express our own beliefs about what is normal, inferior, and superior.

Remaking Ourselves

Freedom . . . is characterized by a constantly renewed obligation to remake the Self, which designates the free being.

Source: Sartre, J. P. (1966). *Being and nothingness: An essay in phenomenological ontology* (pp. 34–35). New York: Citadel.

A central theme of *Gendered Lives* is that the currently prevalent views of gender are not the only possible ones, nor are they necessarily the best ones. In this book, I've invited you to become an active, critical member of our society, which means to reflect on its values and to challenge those that limit the quality of our individual and collective lives. We must not be lulled into believing that the views and values our culture seeks to normalize are, in fact, inevitable or absolutely right. As symbol-using beings, we have the ability to question, reflect, and remake the social world and ourselves in ever-new ways.

Regardless of whether you personally identify with one of the men's or women's movements and regardless of whether you embrace traditional or less conventional views of men and women, you live in a gendered society and a gendered world. By implication, not only are you affected by social perspectives on men and women, but you are also part of shaping those perspectives. This implies that you and others of your generation will revise cultural understandings of gender. Given the pervasive and profound impact of gender on individual and social life, this is no small responsibility.

LOOKING BACKWARD, LOOKING FORWARD

You have inherited opportunities and definitions of gender that were crafted by the generations that preceded you. Women and some men in the 1800s and early 1900s changed laws and the Constitution so that women gained full legal status and rights. My generation challenged restrictive definitions of women and men and social practices that limited the opportunities available to both sexes. We devoted much of our energy to identifying gender inequities and fighting to change economic, political, professional, and social subordination of women. The legacy of our efforts is substantial, and it has altered the educational, social, professional, and legal rights that are available to you.

Your generation faces its own distinct issues, and you will need to define priorities different from those that motivated my generation. Framing the issues of your era is growing awareness of how intersections among communication, gender, and culture privilege some people and oppress others. All around us are inequities—some glaringly obvious and others more subtle. In shaping the future, your generation will decide how to respond to social practices that produce decisive differences in the standpoints, quality of life, and opportunities available to various groups in our culture. To explore these, we'll ask what changes have been made and what issues invite our attention in the various contexts this book addresses.

■ Communication

Views of communication have altered considerably over the history of our society. Most notably, recent decades have heightened our awareness of differences in how women and men generally communicate and have enlarged understanding of the distinctive strengths of each style. As our knowledge of gender-linked communication and its effects has grown, many women have become more assertive, and some men have worked to become more responsive and inclusive.

Women's communication. In recent decades, increasing numbers of women have challenged inequities based on sex and gender. Many women are no longer willing to accept harassment on the job and in schools. Women are also speaking strongly on other issues, naming as government priorities support of family life, continued protection of women's rights to reproductive choice, and education for children, particularly disadvantaged ones. Clearly, many women have incorporated more vocal, less deferential forms of communication into their rhetorical repertoires. Films and television programs now feature girls and women who are powerful and independent along with girls and women in more traditionally decorative, powerless roles. The girl power movement that is part of the third wave of U.S. feminism is a prominent influence on and embodiment of women's bolder, stronger voices.

Men's communication. We've also seen some changes in men's communication patterns. Historically, the open, collaborative style that attempts to include others has been associated with women and devalued. Men have been expected to engage in more competitive, powerful forms of rhetoric. Yet the 1992 and 1996 presidential campaigns turned this stereotype on its head when candidate Bill Clinton consistently relied on an interactive, conversational mode of communication. He appeared on talk shows to engage in relaxed conversations with hosts and audience members. He fomented change in the traditional format of debates, which had relied on sequential speeches by individual candidates. Instead, he favored an open format that allowed him to interact directly with citizens by letting them pose questions that he would answer. In blending assertion and responsiveness, confidence and openness, and power and sensitivity, Bill Clinton altered stereotypes of how successful men communicate. George W. Bush followed Clinton's lead by adopting a conversational, folksy style of communication. Beyond the political realm, many men today are engaging in collaborative, responsive communication with colleagues and friends. Men are also showing that it is possible to combine tenderness and toughness, as exemplified by firefighters who rescued people from the twin towers after the terrorist attack in 2001. These men demonstrated very traditional masculine strenth and courage, and they also cried publicly, unafraid to express the depths of their pain.

Gender and communication in the future. Looking ahead, how will women's and men's communication continue to evolve? Will there be more men who demonstrate that a man can be simultaneously sensitive and strong? Will we see more women who show us that assertiveness and compassion are compatible? As your generation experiments with styles of interaction that depart from the rigid dichotomies of sex stereotypes, you will redefine the range of human communication that we see as appropriate for both sexes.

■ Women's and Men's Movements

Another context of change in views of gender has been women's and men's movements. Here we have seen remarkable developments, and additional ones promise to emerge in the coming years.

Feminism. Prior to the second wave of feminism in this country, there was no national organization dedicated to securing rights for women. Today NOW is more than 30 years old, and it has accomplished major changes in the material, political, and social conditions of women's lives. As a political voice for women, NOW has led the way on a number of pivotal issues. Liberal feminism isn't the only branch of the women's movement. Challenges to that branch's prominence have come from other groups, especially multiracial feminists and third-wave feminists. The past 10 years have been a time in which different, sometimes competing views and visions of women have been played out in rhetorical movements. These different branches of the women's movement have given birth to changes in public policy and private thinking.

The future of feminism. Yet more needs to be done if we are to remake our world so that all members may participate fully in a range of roles and contexts. What will be the shape and focus of women's movements in the coming decades? One important issue is whether the dominant branch of feminism will be the liberal one, which seeks to expand women's rights to participate equally in all spheres of life. Many people in their twenties and thirties do not see the liberal feminism of the second wave as viable today. Some criticisms of second-wave liberal feminism come from the backlash. Danielle Crittenden (1999), for example, argues that liberal feminism duped women into thinking that they could have jobs as well as families and told them men would desire them even if they let their hair go gray and allowed lines in their faces. Another backlash treatise comes from Wendy Shalit (1999), who claims that liberal feminism corrupted women, making them immodest and interested in their own lives and futures. She advises women to return to traditional, conservative principles of womanhood.

A very different criticism of second-wave liberal feminism is that it did not go far enough and that a feminism for the new millennium must be broader and more inclusive, more respectful of differences among women and the diverse conditions of their lives. This seems to be a major impulse propelling the third wave of feminism in the United States. Many young women who identify with the third wave want to build on the advances of the second wave. High in their priorities is transcending some of the divisions that have arisen between women and men. The better relationships between the sexes that many third-wave feminists seek will require more equality not just in the public realm but also in the home. In the coming years, we will see and be part of the conversation about where feminism is and should be heading.

Men's movements. Beginning in the 1980s, we have seen increasing interest in exploring men and men's issues. There has been an explosion of books on men and the ways in which culture shapes masculinity (Heller, 1993; May, 1998a). Simultaneously, we've seen the emergence of a number of men's movements that reflect widely different views of who men are and should be. Some movements seek to reinscribe highly traditional masculine identities, whereas others encourage men to redefine manhood in ways that do not simply repeat old images.

How will men's movements evolve in the years ahead? Will one of the current movements eclipse others to become dominant, as liberal feminism did in the second wave? Will the movements converge in ways that allow a unified men's movement, perhaps one rooted in spiritual principles and commitments (Stoltenberg, 1995)? Will entirely new men's movements emerge to offer yet other views of masculinity? The next 10 to 20 years may be pivotal for men if they, like many women in the 1960s and 1970s, work together to define their interests, needs, and

 AMY

I can't imagine not having had the chance to take courses about gender and women's studies. I'm not majoring in that or anything, but I have taken three courses, and I've really learned a lot about discrimination. Even more important to me is what I've learned about myself, like not to take femininity as a given. I've had to reflect a lot on why I am like I am and whether that's how I want to be. And I've started noticing things I wouldn't have seen before—like when my English literature course included only two women authors and 18 male ones. Before, I would never have even noticed this, much less questioned it. Now I do.

TAFT

I wonder if it's possible that we'll see a movement for gender equality that involves a lot of men and women. It seems to me that it would be good for us to work together instead of in separate movements. After all, a lot of the issues men face have to do with women and vice versa. Couldn't we get a lot more accomplished by talking with each other and combining forces to work for change?

problems and to build organizations that can change gender ideologies that hamper their lives.

Gender in Education

Within educational contexts, we have seen some significant changes in gender and communication. At the same time, there is still much to be done if we wish our schools to equally empower all students.

Reducing gender discrimination. Most basic among changes that have transpired is that we now have laws that make it illegal for schools that receive federal funding to discriminate on the basis of sex. Other changes of note include the growing number of female faculty members and the rising presence of women in formerly masculine majors such as science and in graduate and professional schools.

Another major change in the past two decades has been expansion of the curriculum to include the study of gender, both in its own right and as it interacts with all other areas of social life. Women's studies programs exist on most campuses today, whereas 30 years ago they were virtually nonexistent. Equally important, many courses not specifically focused on gender incorporate coverage of gender, race, and class. This enhances students' opportunities to learn how gender is implicated deeply in history, sociology, psychology, literature, and other areas formerly defined as independent of gender.

Future gender issues in education. Yet important as these developments are, educational contexts need further reform if they are to live up to the espoused ideal of equal opportunity for all students. It's evident that sexism persists when a report in the mid-1990s confirms that educational practices identified in the early 1980s as contributing to a chilly climate for girls and women still exist in classrooms across the country. Research on gendered dimensions of education has also shown us that boys and men can be disadvantaged when they are not encouraged to develop collaborative, cooperative modes of interacting with others. Further evidence of continuing gender discrimination lies in the gaps between salaries of women and men faculty with equivalent experience, records, and seniority, as well as in the paucity of qualified women faculty who are promoted to the higher ranks in academic institutions. Will the coming years bring further progress in eradicating gender discrimination in educational settings? If you continue your education, will you speak out against educational practices that disadvantage women? If you have children, will your daughters get as much intellectual encouragement and attention as your sons? Will you be active in making this happen, for instance, by learning how candidates running for school boards stand on gender equity issues? Will you perhaps run for such a position yourself so that you can work more directly toward gender equity in education?

Gendered Wages

In 1963, the U.S. Congress passed the Equal Pay Act. At the time, women earned 59 cents for every dollar men earned. That's changed. Today, the average woman earns 72 cents for every dollar the average man earns. But averages don't tell the whole story. Women in the top 20% of the workforce have made most of the gains, while women in the lower half are paid about what they were 25 years ago. The wage gap between mothers and women without children is even greater than the gap between women and men.

When analysts first identified the wage gap, they thought the difference was based on experience—maybe men were paid more because they had worked longer and gained more skills. But experience didn't account for the difference. How about education? Maybe men are paid more because they have more education. That didn't explain the difference either. In fact, women with college educations earned about what men with high school educations earned. After an extensive analysis of available data, the President's Council of Economic Advisors reported that the differences between men's and women's pay can't be accounted for by training, experience, type of occupation, or business size. After the Council adjusted for these and other factors, a 12% difference remained that could be explained only by the presence of discriminatory attitudes and practices.

A recent report suggests that attitudes that lead to paying women less start early and are equally likely in women and men. In an experiment, students were given money that they had to offer to share with another player. Half of the students didn't know the sex of the other player; the other half of the students were told the sex of the other player. When the other player's sex was known, men and women made lower offers to women. On the receiving end, players who got offers insisted on a higher amount when the offer came from a woman.

Sources: Crittenden, A. (2001). *The price of motherhood.* New York: Metropolitan Books; Moberg, D. (2001, January 8). Bridging the gap. *In These Times*, pp. 24–26. She's a woman, offer her less. (2001, May 7). *Business Week*, p. 12.

rective, competitive, and tough at times. A woman who engages in these behaviors may be labeled an "iron maiden" (Garlick, Dixon, & Allen, 1992). Communication scholars Majia Nadesan and Angela Trethewey (2000) interviewed women who were successful in corporate positions. They asked the women if they perceived any conflict between being professional and feminine. The women answered "yes." They said they had to be very careful not to be unfeminine yet simultaneously not to act "too much like women."

An example of this occurred in 1990, when Ann Hopkins sued the accounting firm of Price Waterhouse for sex discrimination (Fiske, Bersoff, Borgida, Deaux, & Heilman, 1991; Hopkins, 2001; Hopkins & Walsh, 1996). Ms. Hopkins brought in more money in new accounts than any of her 87 male peers, yet 47 of the men were made partner whereas Ms. Hopkins was not. Executives refused to promote Ms. Hopkins because they perceived her as unfeminine. Describing her as "author-

Bully Broads

What's a business to do when one of its managers is a bully? That depends on whether the manager is a man or a woman. According to Jean Hollands, a Silicon Valley executive coach, nobody likes a bully, but a man can get away with being one, whereas a woman can't. Bullying behaviors, such as demanding results and yelling at subordinates whose work is poor, are tolerated in men because they are consistent with cultural views that men are aggressive. The same behaviors are inconsistent with Western culture's view of femininity, so women who bully subordinates tend to be judged as ineffective managers.

The solution, says Hollands, is anti-assertiveness training for managerial women—training that teaches them to be more feminine. She claims that the rules for effective management are different for women and men. Men can bully subordinates and get results; women who bully subordinates get only resentment. Her company, Growth and Leadership Center, offers "Bully Broad" training programs that teach women managers how to be more soft, nurturing, friendly, tentative, and unaggressive. Women who want to succeed in executive positions are advised to use verbal and nonverbal communication that is considered feminine. In the program, Hollands coaches women to stutter, wear ruffles, smile, soften their voices, use self-deprecating humor, and cry—yes, cry, because it has tactical value for women, says Hollands. So far, Bully Broads has coached clients sent by premier companies such as Intel, Cisco, Hewlett-Packard, Sun Microsystems, and Lockheed-Martin.

Source: Hollands, J. (2001). *Same game, different rules: How to get ahead without being a bully broad, ice queen, or other Ms. Understood*. New York: McGraw-Hill.

itative" and "too tough," they suggested she could improve her chances for promotion if she looked and behaved more femininely. I met with Ann Hopkins to discuss her case. In our conversation, she recalled that a senior man in the firm had advised her to fix her hair and wear more jewelry (2001). Ms. Hopkins was promoted after a federal district court ruled that she was the target of gender stereotyping, which is a form of sex discrimination and therefore illegal. Yet there are many women like Ms. Hopkins who are underpaid and not promoted and who lack the funds or confidence to go to court to fight for their rights. Hillary Rodham Clinton is another example of a successful woman who has been called unfeminine, because she is assertive, has an agenda, and doesn't present herself in typically feminine ways.

As you can see, all four of these stereotypes define women as undesirable employees. Either women are incompetent (sex object, child), or they are only able to support others in positions but not to be leaders themselves (mother), or they are too unfeminine to be acceptable (iron maiden). Each stereotype entails some reason for discounting women as workers; each defines women by sex and gender rather than by job qualifications and performance.

Changes in gender relations. Among the changes achieved in personal relationships during recent decades, three stand out. First, marital rape, date rape, and acquaintance rape have been named as crimes. This gives victims of these crimes a socially recognized vocabulary for seeking justice. Second, divorce laws have been rewritten in many states so that nonfinancial investments in marriage are better recognized and accommodated in making property settlements. This is a pivotal change because it means that contributions to relationships, family life, and support of another's public career are legally recognized as having value. Third, many men and women of previous generations pioneered new forms of friendship and committed romantic relationships, and we worked out more equitable partnerships with our mates than those modeled by our parents (Blumstein & Kollock, 1988; Maccoby, 1990; Schwartz, 1994; Schwartz & Rutter, 1998). Yet there is much work still to be done in remaking our close relationships so that they are workable in the present era.

Addressing gender divisions. One of the greatest urgencies facing your generation is divisions between women and men. To make women's oppression visible, discrepancies between the rights of women and men had to be articulated and changed. That, however, was only the first stage in the larger effort to create a truly equitable society.

We have been much more successful in moving toward equality in the public realm than in the private realm of home and family. The second shift that we discussed earlier exemplifies gender inequity in personal relationships. It is neither fair nor loving when one partner in a dual-worker family assumes the majority of domestic and child care responsibilities. Although some men today are doing more inside the home than their fathers did, it's still the case that a minority of men in dual-worker relationships assume a full share of responsibilities. After years of studying marriages, Barbara Risman and Sandra Godwin conclude that marriage represents "a stalled revolution" (2001, p. 139). They mean that the second wave of feminism's aim to revolutionize gender relations only progressed so far. It stalled at the front door to home and family life.

You will make choices in your private relationships that belie or enact a commitment to equity. What kind of family responsibilities will you assume, and what will you expect of your partner? If you are a man, will you contribute equally to cleaning, cooking, and child care, including the repetitive, less satisfying tasks of bathing, feeding, and transporting children? If you are a woman, will you be more assertive than many members of the current generation of women in insisting on equity in home life? You will answer these questions not with statements of intent, but in daily practices through which you reinforce or reconfigure existing cultural patterns.

Will your generation find ways to overcome the divisiveness that too often poisons relationships between women and men? Recent decades have tended to portray women's interests as opposed to those of men, and gains in women's opportunities as losses for men. Too often, any negative comments about men are dismissed as "male bashing," with no reflection on their validity. All of us—men and women alike—need to realize that critically challenging sexism, sex discrimination, and gendered violence is not the same thing as male bashing.

Perhaps your generation will redefine issues so that they are not seen as win–lose. Your voice will fuel or defuse divisions between women and men. Will you be part of identifying interests, goals, rights, and needs that are common to both sexes? Will you find ways to cooperate and collaborate in creating relationships that are fair and satisfying to men and women? Can we begin to discover what is common to us—the needs we share, the dreams we have—without erasing what is unique about us as individuals?

■ Gender and Violence

Also on your generation's agenda is further work to identify and eliminate crimes of violence, of which women are disproportionately the victims worldwide. From activities that demean and violate women to battering, incest, rape, and gendered murder, there is a long and shameful list of crimes of violence that have too long contaminated life in our society. Legal sanctions against rape need to be broadened to include acquaintance and date rape. Carl Fox, the district attorney in my county, told me that juries are reluctant to convict a man of rape when a victim knew him and had been friendly with him. In short, rape is still widely considered assault by a stranger. This means that knowing a person functionally negates a woman's right to say no and have her refusal respected by our legal system.

Another important area in which views of gendered violence have changed and will change further is sexual harassment. In recent years, much progress has been made in creating laws and institutional policies that condemn sexual harassment and levy penalties for its commission. Yet inequities persist. Men who are sexually harassed are sometimes ridiculed, a response that reflects cultural views that men should be strong and self-sufficient. There is still too much willingness to excuse sexual harassment because of "extenuating circumstances." When charges of sexual harassment forced Bob Packwood of Oregon to resign from the Senate in 1995, he claimed that his problems with alcohol were responsible but that he personally wasn't. Where do we draw the line regarding personal responsibility for actions?

■ Gender in Institutional Settings

Although feminist efforts of the past three decades have increased women's entry into professional and public life, the majority of women have been excluded from top positions of leadership and power. Laws that have diminished discrimination in hiring have had little impact on the more informal structures that govern promotion and advancement. For instance, the Pregnancy Discrimination Act, passed in 1978 with NOW's support, makes it illegal to discriminate against pregnant women. Nonetheless, working women are reporting in increasing numbers that they are discriminated against when they become pregnant. They suddenly receive a bad evaluation after years of positive ones, or their jobs are filled or erased during a pregnancy leave (Noble, 1993). These and other informal forms of discrimination create grave inequities for the 85% of working women likely to become pregnant at some point in their lives.

Women's positions in institutions. Elections in the past 10 years have increased the number of minorities and women in the U.S. Congress. In addition, many companies have learned that they benefit by including people with varied backgrounds and perspectives at all levels of organizations. As it becomes clear that organizations are likely to benefit from diversity, they are making stronger efforts to identify and dismantle subtle barriers that have limited the professional growth of women and minorities (Worley & Vannoy, 2001). In the coming years, we will see how the increased participation and status of diverse people change organizations and national policies.

Social support for families. Finally, the future of gender in institutional contexts includes government and business policies regarding family life. Despite passage of the 1993 Family and Medical Leave Act, we still have no national policies that guarantee *all* workers leaves to care for newborns and newly adopted children or for partners, parents, children, or other relatives who need care. Unlike *every other* developed country in the world, the United States has not designed government and business regulations that enable women and men to be both involved professionals and responsible members of families.

In your professional life, you will have opportunities to influence what your company or field does to make it possible for people to participate responsibly in both careers and families. In influencing government and business policies regarding families, your generation will play a critical role in redesigning institutional practices that have an impact on every citizen.

C REATING THE FUTURE

All of the issues we've discussed in this epilogue converge to influence individual and social views of gender. Each generation has to define femininity and masculinity anew. As we begin the 21st century, how will you and your peers redraw cultural images of men and women? Historically, efforts to change views of women and men have resulted in pitting one vision of manhood or womanhood against another.

Should men be strong or sensitive? Should women be traditional homemakers or fast-track careerists? Is the ideal first lady embodied by Hillary Rodham Clinton or Laura Bush, or can it be either? Is Madonna or Ally McBeal the exemplar of modern women, or can they and others comprise a range of exemplars? Creating polar views of women and men does little to expand options, and it promotes divisiveness. Your generation has the opportunity to lead us away from oppositional images and embrace a flexible perspective that recognizes as valid the substantial variability within each gender and even within each individual. You could depart from established models to build altogether new understandings of masculinity, femininity, and the relationships possible between people.

■ Defining Masculinity and Femininity

What will you define as the crux of being a man? Will it be physical strength as in the 1800s or salary and position as it is today? Consider recent media emphasis on men as sex objects, whose value is contingent on muscles and wardrobe, and media images of men as incompetent in housework and child care. If you are a man, you might increase the salience of friendships between men and men's involvement in family life, particularly fathering, making these part of what we understand it means to be a man. Likewise, you can choose to assume an equitable share of responsibilities for relationship health and for domestic work in your private life. In refashioning masculinity, you will also need to consider the traditional relationship between violence and manhood. Like all social views, that can be changed, but only if you and others take a role in renouncing violence as part of what it means to be a man (Kirby & Krone, 2002). Another aspect of masculinity that will need rethinking will become clear as an increasing number of men of your generation have partners who earn higher salaries, prestige, and public position than you. If your view of manhood remains tied to status and power, this will create enormous tension in your relationships and your identity. Through your personal and collective choices, your generation will author its own vision of manhood, one that has the potential to revise and enlarge how women and men view masculinity (May, 1998b; Peterson et al., 1989).

You will also recast what femininity means. If you are a woman, think about how you will define your identity; if you are a man, think about what you will expect and value in women. Will you work to create healthier images that do not encourage women to starve themselves or to seek breast surgery in order to meet cultural standards? Will you recognize women for their minds and hearts more than their bodies? You have the capacity to resist cultural images of women that oppress you and others. By embodying a different view of women in your personal identity, you become part of creating new alternatives for everyone. As women and men, you can change what it means to be either in our society—that's an exciting opportunity.

Responding to Differences

Growing out of what we have discussed is perhaps the most urgent challenge for your generation: enlarging recognition and respect for differences that include and go beyond those between men and women. Diversity can be a source of strength or divisiveness, and you will choose which one it comes to mean in the future. Will you respect men who give up careers to be homemakers and primary parents and men who find their fulfillment in intense entrepreneurial ventures? Will you encourage your sons and daughters to be caring and strong? Understand that your real answers to these questions are not what you say but how you live your life. There is a saying that "those who talk the talk should also walk the walk," which means that we should practice what we say we believe. In living out answers to these questions, you will define your views of women, men, and differences.

Also relevant to the issue of defining differences is the ongoing debate about whether women and men really are different and, by implication, whether they should be treated differently. How we resolve this question has profound effects on our material lives, particularly in terms of legal rights and institutional policies. For example, our courts are currently hearing cases in which one attorney argues for equal treatment of women and opposing counsel argues for special treatment that is responsive to women's distinct nature. A specific example is pregnancy: Should it be defined as a uniquely female condition that requires special provisions, or should pregnancy be classified as one of many temporary human medical conditions?

Your generation will have an impact on the debate over sexual equality versus sexual difference. There are philosophical and practical arguments that support each side of the debate. Working out an answer to this issue may depend in part on our ability to discern which aspects of women's and men's lives are actually biologically based and which ones are socially constructed and therefore amenable to interpretation and change.

Redefining Culture

Throughout this book, we have seen that communication, gender, and culture interact constantly to affect one another. One implication of this is that, as your generation transforms social meanings of women, men, and differences, you will simultaneously influence our collective vision of who we are as a culture.

Our country has always consisted of people of varied gender identities, sexual orientations, socioeconomic classes, and races. Yet our language and the dominant cultural ideology advocate a single cultural ideal that some people embody more fully than others. Within this perspective, differences are matters of better and worse, and we are encouraged to evaluate ourselves and others in terms of a single standard. Historically, of course, the White, middle-class, heterosexual male has been that standard. The quest for a single cultural ideal is the impulse behind the melting pot metaphor that has long reigned in North America. We have encouraged people to erase their differences and become alike—to assimilate into a single culture based on a single denominator. The painful divisions in our society suggest that the melting pot is an inappropriate ideal for us. It no longer works—if indeed it ever did.

Perhaps it is time to abandon the melting pot metaphor and inaugurate a new one that acclaims difference as valuable and desirable, one that remakes the cultural ideal to incorporate all citizens instead of trying to remake diverse citizens to fit a single, noninclusive ideal. Maybe your generation will discard the melting pot metaphor and compose one that recognizes commonality without obliterating real and valuable differences among people. To create a new vision, we must realize that we participate in a common world, yet each of us experiences it somewhat differently from standpoints shaped by intersections among gender, race, class, and sexual orientation. What sort of metaphor might capture this as our national character?

In her history of the second wave of feminism in North America, Flora Davis (1991) uses the metaphor of a salad bowl to describe our society. Davis argues that a salad consists of many different ingredients that retain their individual tastes, textures, and colors and at the same time contribute to a whole that is more complex, interesting, and enjoyable than the individual parts or some fusion of those parts. The Reverend Jesse Jackson offered the compelling metaphor of our nation as a family quilt made up of patches of various colors and design. Another metaphor is that of a collage, in which distinct patterns stand out in their individual integrity while simultaneously contributing to the character and complexity of the whole. If your generation is able to affirm diversity in women and men, as well as in race, class, ethnicity, and affectional preference, then you will have inaugurated a bold new theme in the cultural conversation—one with the potential to make our society richer and more equitable for all. That is a responsibility and an opportunity that belongs to each of you.

■ Taking a Voice

Men and women like you will provide the leadership in the next stage of the cultural conversation about gender. You cannot avoid participation or the responsibilities it entails. Just as speaking out against discrimination is a choice, so too is silence. If you don't exercise your voice, you reinforce the status quo. You can't avoid influence; instead, you only have the options of what influence you will exert and how you will communicate it.

Society is a human creation that we continuously remake through communication in private and public settings. Your voice will join those of others to shape the meaning of gender and the concrete realities of being men and women in the coming years. You will also influence attitudes toward diversity either by reinscribing the view that differences are divisive or by affirming them as a source of individual and collective enrichment, regeneration, and growth. What gender and culture will mean in the future is up to you. In your personal relationships, professional interactions, and civic activities, you will create and communicate new visions of who we can be and how we can live.

DISCUSSION QUESTIONS

1. What do you see as the future of women's movements? Do you think one branch will come to predominate in each movement? Will new kinds of movements emerge?

2. What kind of evolution do you predict in men's movements during the coming decade? Do you think they will gain in popularity and visibility? What do you see as the primary issues to be addressed by contemporary men and men's movements? Do you plan to take part in these movements?

3. At the moment, very different images of women are embodied by visible public figures like Madonna, Sister Souljah, Oprah Winfrey, Ellen DeGeneris, Laura Bush, and Hillary Rodham Clinton. What do these diverse visions of women imply about cultural views of femininity? Are equally diverse images of men embodied in public figures? Do Denzel Washington, Bruce Willis, Colin Powell, George W. Bush, and the Reverend Jesse Jackson represent different models of masculinity? Do you think alternative versions of womanhood and manhood will continue to emerge, or will we as a society settle on one or two we consider normal and right? Do you find the diversity in women and men exciting, empowering, frustrating?

4. Think about your parents' or stepparents' marriages and those of other relatives and people with whom you have spent a lot of time. If you commit to an enduring romantic relationship, do you plan to model it after any of these? If not, how do you want to design your committed relationships? How does what you have learned in this course affect your thinking and dreaming about your ideal relationship?

5. How can you be part of changing social attitudes and policies regarding gender? Do you plan to take a voice on public issues such as laws to ensure family leave policies for men and women who work outside the home? Do you plan to make commitments within your personal relationships that lead to greater gender equity than traditional norms for relationships have? In the places you work, will you speak out for policies that provide equitable opportunities, working environments, and rewards for women and men on the job?

6. If you could write the script, how would you define masculinity and femininity in the year 2020? Ideally, what would each gender be like—or would there not be any need for two distinct genders? If gender is a linchpin of culture, then changing gender changes culture. How would the ideals you have in mind affect the character of social life?

7. The textbook closes by discussing metaphors for the United States that might replace the melting pot metaphor. Do you like the alternatives suggested in the Epilogue: a family quilt, a salad bowl, or a collage? Can you come up with other metaphors that simultaneously represent diversity and commonality among members of our society?

affirmative action Collective term for policies that go beyond equal opportunity laws to redress discrimination. Affirmative action assumes that historical patterns of discrimination against groups of people justify preferential treatment for members of those groups; focuses on results, not intent of efforts to redress inequities; and attempts to increase the number of qualified members of minorities in education and the workplace, commensurate with their availability.

alternate paths model A view of relationships that claims that masculine and feminine ways of creating and expressing closeness are distinct and that both are valid.

androgyny A psychological, as distinct from biological, sex-type. Androgynous people tend to identify with and enact qualities socially ascribed to both women and men.

artifacts Personal objects that influence how we see ourselves and how we express our identities.

backlash A countermovement that seeks to repudiate and contain feminism by arguing two contradictory claims: (1) that women have never had it so good, so there is no longer any need for feminism; and (2) that feminism has caused serious problems in women's lives and family relationships.

biological theory Theory that maintains that biological characteristics of the sexes are the basis of gender differences such as ways of thinking, communicating, and feeling.

clitoridectomy Removal of the entire clitoris in women. Part or all of the labia minora may also be removed.

cognitive development theory Theory that claims that children participate actively in defining their genders by acting on internal motivations to be competent, which lead children to seek out models of gender that allow them to sculpt their own femininity or masculinity.

communication A dynamic, systemic process in which meanings are created and reflected in and through humans' interactions with symbols.

content level of meaning The literal meaning of communication. Content-level meanings are the formal, or denotative, meanings of messages.

cultural feminism A branch of feminism that holds that women and men differ in fundamental ways, including biology, and because, in general, women and men have distinct standpoints that foster different experiences, perspectives, skills, and knowledge (for instance, nurturance in women and independence in men). Also called *structural* or *difference feminism.*

culture The structures and practices, especially relating to communication, through which a culture produces and reproduces a particular social order by legitimizing certain values, expectations, meanings, and patterns of behavior.

ecofeminism Launched in 1974, a movement that integrates the intellectual and political bases of feminist theorizing with ecological philosophy. The result is a movement focused on the large issue of oppression, of which the specific oppression of women is seen as a particular instance of a larger ideology that esteems violence and domination of women, children, animals, and the earth.

ego boundary The point at which an individual stops and the rest of the world begins; an individual's sense of the line between her or his own self and others. Ego boundaries exist on a continuum from permeable (a sense of self that includes others and their issues, problems, and so on) to rigid (a sense of self more distinct from others).

equal opportunity laws Laws that prohibit discrimination on the basis of race, color, religion, sex, or national origin. Equal opportunity laws seek to protect *individual* members of groups that have been targets of discrimination, and they confine their efforts to current discrimination, not historical bias.

erotica Depictions of sexual activities that are agreed to and enjoyed by all parties.

essentializing The tendency to reduce any phenomenon to essential characteristics, which are generally presumed to be innate and/or unchangeable. Essentializing the sexes implies that all women are alike in basic respects, that all men are alike in basic respects, and that the two sexes are distinct from each other because of fundamental, essential qualities.

excision See *clitoridectomy.*

father hunger From the mythopoetic men's movement, refers to men's yearning to be close to other men and to build deep, enduring bonds with other men. Based on mythopoetic belief that most young boys have distant relationships with the primary man in their lives, the father, and that the hunger for a meaningful contact with men of which they were deprived in youth continues through life.

Free Men A branch of the men's movement that seeks to restore the traditional, macho image of men by reviving competitive, independent, and rugged qualities in men.

gender A social, symbolic construction that expresses the meanings a society confers on biological sex. Gender varies across cultures, over time within any given society, and in relation to the other gender.

gender constancy A person's understanding, usually developing by 3 years of age, that her or his sex is relatively fixed and unchanging.

gender intimidation The treatment of members of one sex in ways that make them feel humiliated, unsafe, or inferior because of their sex.

gendered violence Physical, verbal, emotional, sexual, or visual brutality inflicted disproportionately or exclusively on members of one sex. Includes gender intimidation, sexual assault, violence between intimates, sexual harassment, genital mutilation, and gender-based murder.

glass ceiling An invisible barrier that limits the advancement of women and minorities, made up of subtle, often unconscious prejudices and stereotypes that limit women's and minorities' opportunities.

glass walls Metaphor for sex segregation on the job. Glass walls exist when members of a group, such as women, are placed in positions based on stereotypes of the group. Typically, the positions do not entail advancement ladders.

goals Statements of intention for the representation of women and minorities. Goals do not require results, nor do they require measures to increase the number of women and minorities hired by or admitted into institutions.

haptics Touch as a form of nonverbal communication.

hermaphrodite A person whose internal and external genitalia are inconsistent.

hidden curriculum The organization, content, and teaching styles of educational institutions that reflect gender stereotypes and sustain gender inequities by marginalizing and devaluing female and minority students.

hostile environment harassment Conduct of a sexual nature that interferes with a person's ability to perform a job or gain an education and/or that creates a hostile, intimidating, or offensive working environment.

hypothetical thought Consciousness of things that do not exist in the moment.

infibulation Genital mutilation involving removal of the clitoris and labia minora and joining the lips of the labia majora.

informed consent Consent given by an adult with normal mental abilities whose judgment is not impaired by circumstances, including drugs and alcohol.

lesbian feminists Feminists whose sexual preference is women and who define themselves as woman identified and committed to fighting for legal rights for all woman-identified women.

liberal feminism (also called *equality feminism, middle-class feminism,* and *White feminism*) Liberal feminism, as distinct from structural feminism, maintains that women and men are alike in important respects and that women should have the same economic, political, professional, and civic opportunities and rights as men. NOW is the best-known organization representing liberal feminism.

male circumcision Removal of the sheath, or prepuce, of the penis.

male deficit model A view of friendship that claims men are deficient in forming and participating in close relationships. According to the male deficit model, most men's ways of experiencing and expressing closeness are not simply different from, but inferior to, those typical of women.

male feminists (also called *profeminist men, New Age men,* and *sensitive men*) Male feminists believe that women and men are alike in important respects and that, therefore, the sexes should enjoy the same privileges, rights, opportunities, and status in society. Male feminists join liberal women feminists in fighting for equitable treatment for women. In addition, many male feminists seek to rid themselves of what they regard as toxic masculinity promoted in men by socialization and to develop in themselves sensitivities and tenderness more typically socialized into women.

male generic language Words and phrases that claim to include both women and men yet refer only to men. Examples of male generic terms are *mailman, mankind,* and *chairman.*

Marxist feminism Focuses on how the capitalist system creates economic inequities between the sexes by sustaining a sexual division of labor that subordinates women and privileges men.

matriarchal Of or pertaining to matriarchy, literally "rule by the mothers." The term *matriarchy* is generally used to refer to systems of ideology, social structures, and practices, created by women, that reflect the values, priorities, and views of women as a group.

microinequities Verbal comments and behaviors that devalue members of a group but do not violate antidiscrimination laws; can affect morale, job performance, and career advancement.

Million Man March A branch of men's movement that began with a march in Washington, DC, in 1995, at which Black men atoned for sins and committed themselves to spiritual transformation and political action. Annual marches were also held in later years.

Million Woman March Grassroots-organized gathering of African American women that was launched in 1997 in Philadelphia to celebrate and foster solidarity among Black women.

monitoring The process of observing and regulating our own attitudes and behaviors; possible because humans are able to reflect on themselves from the perspective of others (self as object).

multiracial feminism A branch of the women's movement that highlights race and racial oppression of women.

mythopoetic movement A branch of the men's movement headed by poet Robert Bly. Mythopoetics believe men need to rediscover their distinctively masculine modes of feeling rooted largely in myth.

nonverbal communication All elements of communication other than words themselves. Estimated to carry 65% to 93% of the total meaning of communication; includes visual, vocal, environmental, and physical aspects of interaction.

paralanguage Vocal cues that accompany verbal communication, such as accent, volume, and inflection.

patriarchal Of or pertaining to patriarchy, literally, "rule by the fathers." The term *patriarchy* is generally used to refer to systems of ideology, social structures, and practices, created by men, that reflect the values, priorities, and views of men as a group.

personal relationships Relationships that endure over an extended period of time, in which partners depend on and consider each other irreplaceable—they are strongly and specifically connected to each other.

physical characteristics Aspects of personal appearance, which are evaluated according to cultural standards.

polarized thinking Conceiving things as opposites, e.g., good or bad, right or wrong.

pornography Materials that vividly depict subordination and degradation of a person; for example, sadistic assaults presented as pleasurable. Pornographic presentations do not feature activities involving mutual agreement and mutual benefit.

power feminism A movement that emerged in the 1990s as a reaction to feminist emphasis on women's oppression. Urges women to take the power that is theirs and not to see themselves as victims of men or society.

promasculinist A category of men's movements that sees feminism as in conflict with men's interests.

Promise Keepers Begun in 1990, a Christian branch of the men's movement that calls men together to pray and commit to Christ-centered living.

proxemics Space and the human use of space, including personal territories.

psychodynamic theory Claims that family relationships, especially between mother and child during the formative years of life, have a pivotal and continuing impact on the development of self, particularly gender identity.

psychological responsibility Responsibility to remember, plan, think ahead, organize, and so forth. In most heterosexual relationships, even when physical labor is divided between partners, women have greater psychological responsibility for the home and children.

quid pro quo harassment Actual or threatened use of professional or academic rewards and/or punishments to gain sexual compliance from a subordinate or student.

quota system Rules that specify that a particular number or percentage of women and/or minorities must be admitted to schools, hired in certain positions, or promoted to certain levels in institutions.

radical feminism A branch of feminism that grew out of New Left politics and demanded the same attention to women's oppression as New Left organizations gave to racial oppression and other ideological issues. Radical feminists pioneered revolutionary communication techniques such as consciousness raising, leaderless group discussion, and guerrilla theater.

relationship level of meaning The nonliteral meaning of communication. The relationship level of meaning expresses how a speaker sees self and other and the relationship between them. In addition, it may provide cues about how to interpret the literal meaning of the message, for instance, as a joke.

revalorists Feminists who focus on valuing traditionally feminine skills, activities, and perspectives and their contributions to personal, interpersonal, and cultural life.

role Social definitions of expected behaviors and the values associated with them, which are internalized by individuals in the process of socialization.

second shift The work of homemaking and child care that a member of a dual-worker family does after and in addition to the work of the job in the paid labor force.

self-as-object The ability to reflect on the self from the standpoint of others. Because humans are able to take others' perspectives, their views of self are necessarily social.

separatists Group of feminists who believe patriarchal culture cannot be changed or reformed and so women who find it oppressive must create and live in their own women-centered communities separated from the larger culture.

sex A personal quality determined by biological and genetic characteristics. *Male, female, man,* and *woman* indicate sex.

sexual assault Sexual activity occurring without the informed consent of at least one person.

sexual harassment Unwelcome conduct of a sexual nature.

socialist feminism Argues that inequality between the sexes grows out of women's unpaid labor in the home and family and that patriarchy is inseparable from other systems of oppression such as racism and class oppression.

social learning theory Theory that claims that individuals learn to be masculine and feminine (among other things) by observing and imitating others and by reacting to the rewards and punishments others give in response to their imitative behaviors.

speech communities A group of people who share assumptions regarding how, when, and why to communicate as well as understandings of how to interpret others' communication.

spotlighting Highlighting the sex of a person rather than other characteristics that may be more relevant to why the person is being discussed. For example, in a headline that reads, "Woman Elected Mayor."

standpoint theory Theory that focuses on how gender, race, class, and other social categories influence the circumstances of people's lives, especially their social positions and the kinds of experiences fostered within those positions.

stereotype A broad generalization about an entire class of phenomena based on some knowledge of limited aspects of certain members of the class.

sunna Also called *female circumcision;* genital mutilation involving removal of the sheath and tip of the clitoris.

symbolic interactionism Theory that claims individuals develop self-identity and an understanding of social life, values, and codes of conduct through communicative interactions with others in a society.

territoriality An aspect of proxemics that concerns an individual's sense of personal space that one does not want others to invade.

theory A way to describe, explain, and predict relationships among phenomena.

third-wave feminism Emergent movement that asserts feminism for the current era is not just an extension of second-wave feminism. Aims (1) to be inclusive of diverse people; (2) to focus more on practice than theory; and (3) to work to improve relationships between women and men.

womanists Group of feminists who define their identity and goals as reflecting both race and gender oppression. The womanist movement arose out of dissatisfaction with mainstream feminism's focus on White, middle-class women and their interests.

women's rights Movement lasting from the mid-1800s to the 1920s that focused on gaining basic rights for women, such as the rights to vote, to pursue higher education, and to enter professions.

REFERENCES

Aaronson, S., & Hartmann, H. (1998). Wage gap. In W. Mankiller, G. Mink, M. Navarro, B. Smith, & G. Steinem (Eds.), *The reader's companion to U.S. women's history* (pp. 615–616). Boston: Houghton Mifflin.

Abdullah, H. (1999, January 22). Gender roles, new rules. *Raleigh News and Observer,* pp. E1, E3.

Abelson, R. (2001, June 10). More men taking same-sex harassment charges to EEOC. *Raleigh News and Observer,* p. 8A.

Abuse by women may be up. (1999, November 23). *Raleigh News and Observer,* p. 14A.

Acitelli, L. (1988). When spouses talk to each other about their relationship. *Journal of Social and Personal Relationships, 5,* 185–199.

Acker, K. (1997, May 3). All girls together. *Weekend Guardian,* p. 16.

Adams, C. (1991, April). The straight dope. *Triangle Comic Review,* p. 26.

Addington, D. W. (1968). The relationship of selected vocal characteristics to personality perceptions. *Speech Monographs, 35,* 492–503.

Adler, J. (1996, June 17). Building a better dad. *Newsweek,* 58–64.

Adler, J., with Duignan-Cabrera, A., & Gordon, J. (1991, June 24). Drums, sweat and tears. *Newsweek,* 46–54.

Adler, L. L. (1991). *Women in cross-cultural perspective.* Westport, CT: Praeger.

Adler, T. (1989, June). Early sex hormone exposure studied. *APA Monitor,* p. 9.

Adler, T. (1990, January). Differences explored in gays and straights. *APA Monitor,* p. 27.

Ali, L., & Gordon, D. (2001, July 23). We still want our mtv. *Newsweek,* pp. 50–53.

An all-consuming passion. (1991, May 13). *Newsweek,* p. 58.

Allen, K. (1999, May 24). Third wave versus second wave. *http://www.io.com/~wwwave/*

Allgeier, E. R. (1987). Coercive versus consensual sexual interactions. In V. P. Makosky (Ed.), *The G. Stanley Hall Lecture Series* (Vol. 7, pp. 7–63). Washington, DC: American Psychological Association.

American Association of University Women (AAUW). (1991). *Shortchanging girls, short-changing America.* Washington, DC: Greenberg-Lake Analysis Group.

American Association of University Women (AAUW). (1995). *How schools shortchange girls: The AAUW report.* New York: Marlowe.

American Association of University Women (AAUW). (1998). *Gender gaps: Where schools still fail our children.* Washington, DC: American Association of University Women Educational Foundation.

American Association of University Women (AAUW). (2001). *Beyond the "gender wars": A conversation about girls, boys, and education.* Washington, DC: American Association of University Women Educational Foundation.

Andelin, H. (1975). *Fascinating womanhood.* New York: Bantam.

Anderson, E. A., & Leslie, L. A. (1991). Coping with employment and family stress: Employment arrangement and gender differences. *Sex Roles, 24,* 223–237.

Anderson, K., & Leaper, C. (1998). Meta-analyses of gender effects on conversational interruption: Who, what, when, where, and how. *Sex Roles, 39,* 225–252.

Angier, N. (1995, November 19). Where woman was, there gal shall be. *New York Times,* p. 2E.

Angier, N. (1999, March 27). Not your average Joe: Dangers of the superman ideal. *Fairbanks Daily News-Miner,* p. C-1.

Ansen, D., & Bunn, A. (1995, September 18). Goodbye to the kids' stuff. *Newsweek,* pp. 74–76.

Antill, J. K. (1987). Parents' beliefs and values about sex roles, sex differences, and sexuality: Their sources and implications. In P. Shaver & C. Hendrick (Eds.), *Sex and gender* (pp. 294–328). Newbury Park, CA: Sage.

Anzaldúa, G. (1999). *Borderlands/la frontera: The new mestiza.* San Francisco: Spinsters/Aunt Lute.

Apter, T. (1990). *Altered loves: Mothers and daughters in adolescence.* New York: St. Martin's.

Aptheker, B. (1998). Cultural feminism. In W. Mankiller, G. Mink, M. Navarro, B. Smith, & G. Steinem (Eds.), *The reader's companion to*

U.S. women's history (pp. 205–206). New York: Houghton Mifflin.

Aries, E. (1987). Gender and communication. In P. Shaver & C. Hendrick (Eds.), *Sex and gender* (pp. 149–176). Newbury Park, CA: Sage.

Aries, E. (1998). Gender differences in interaction. In D. Canary & K. Dindia (Eds.), *Sex differences and similarities in interaction: Critical essays and empirical investigations* (pp. 65–81). Mahwah, NJ: Erlbaum.

Aries, E. J., & Johnson, F. L. (1983). Close friendship in adulthood: Conversational content between same-sex friends. *Sex Roles, 9,* 1183–1196.

Armas, G. (2000, April 24). Gender equality at work improving, statistics show. *Raleigh News and Observer,* p. 4A.

Arnold, R. (2001). *Fashion, desire and anxiety: Image and morality in the 20th century.* New Brunswick, NJ: Rutgers University Press.

Aronson, J. (1992). Women's sense of responsibility for the care of old people: "But who else is going to do it?" *Gender and Society, 6,* 8–29.

Aukett, R., Ritchie, J., & Mill, K. (1988). Gender differences in friendship patterns. *Sex Roles, 19,* 57–66.

Austin, A. M. B., Salehi, M., & Leffler, A. (1987). Gender and developmental differences in children's conversations. *Sex Roles, 16,* 497–510.

Avery, S. (1999, November 19). Whatever happened to the men's movement? *Raleigh News and Observer,* pp. 1E, 3E.

Bailey, A. (1994). Mothering, diversity, and peace politics. *Hypatia, 9,* 188–198.

Bailey, C. (1997). Making waves and drawing lines: The politics of defining the vicissitudes of feminism. *Hypatia, 12,* 17–29.

Bakan, D. (1966). *The duality of human existence: Isolation and communion in Western man.* Boston: Beacon.

Bakan, D. (1968). *Disease, pain and sacrifice.* Boston: Beacon.

Ball, K. (1991, May 23). Family leave poses few problems, study finds. *Morning Call,* p. B23.

Balswick, J. O. (1988). *The inexpressive male.* Lexington, MA: Lexington Books.

Balswick, J. O., & Peek, C. W. (1976). The inexpressive male: A tragedy of American society. In D. Brannon & R. Brannon (Eds.), *The forty-nine percent majority: The male sex-role* (pp. 55–57). Reading, MA: Addison-Wesley.

Balzer, J. A., & Simonis, D. A. (1991). Are high school chemistry books gender free? *Journal of Research in Science Teaching, 28,* 353–362.

Bandura, A., & Walters, R. H. (1963). *Social learning and personality development.* New York: Holt, Rinehart & Winston.

Banerji, A. (1998, July 10). Telling the stories of everyday youths. *Chronicle of Higher Education,* p. A7.

Barash, D. (1979). *The whisperings within.* New York: Harper & Row.

Bardewell, J. R., Cochran, S. W., & Walker, S. (1986). Relationship of parental education, race, and gender to sex role stereotyping in 5-year-old kindergartners. *Sex Roles, 15,* 275–281.

Baron, L., & Straus, M. A. (1989). *Four theories of rape in American society.* New Haven, CT: Yale University Press.

Barry, K. (1998a). Radical feminism. In W. Mankiller, G. Mink, M. Navarro, B. Smith, & G. Steinem (Eds.), *The reader's companion to U.S. women's history* (pp. 217–218). New York: Houghton Mifflin.

Barry, K. (1998b). Sexual slavery. In W. Mankiller, G. Mink, M. Navarro, B. Smith, & G. Steinem (Eds.), *The reader's companion to U.S. women's history* (pp. 539–540). New York: Houghton Mifflin.

Basinger, J. (2001, April 27). Struggling for a balanced life as a president. *Chronicle of Higher Education,* pp. A37–A39.

Basow, S. A. (1990). Effects of teacher expressiveness: Mediated by sex-typing? *Journal of Educational Psychology, 82,* 599–602.

Basow, S. A. (1992). *Gender: Stereotypes and roles* (3rd ed.). Pacific Grove, CA: Brooks/Cole.

Basow, S. A., & Kobrynowicz, D. (1990, August). *How much is she eating? Impressions of a female eater.* Paper presented at the meeting of the American Psychological Association, Boston. (ERIC Document Reproduction Service No. ED 326 827).

Bass, A. (1995). Do slasher films breed real-life violence? In G. Dines & J. Humez (Eds.), *Gender, race and class in media* (pp. 185–189). Thousand Oaks, CA: Sage.

Bate, B. (1988). *Communication between the sexes.* New York: Harper & Row.

Baumgardner, J., & Richards, A. (2000). *ManifestA: Young women, feminism, and the future.* New York: Farrar, Straus and Giroux.

Baxter, L. A. (1990). Dialectical contradictions in relational development. *Journal of Social and Personal Relationships, 7,* 143–158.

Beck, A. T. (1988). *Love is never enough.* New York: Harper & Row.

Beck, J. (1990, September 5). Calling them "balance laws" doesn't make quotas right. *Raleigh News and Observer,* p. 17A.

Beck, M., & Biddle, N. (1995, December 11). Separate, not equal. *Newsweek,* pp. 86–87.

Becker, A., & Burwell, R. (1999, May 19). *Acculturation and disordered eating in Fiji.* Paper presented at the American Psychiatric Association Conference, Washington, DC.

Becker, C. S. (1987). Friendship between women: A phenomenological study of best friends. *Journal of Phenomenological Psychology, 18,* 59–72.

Begley, S. (1995, March 27). Gray matters. *Newsweek,* pp. 48–54.

Begley, S. (2000, March 27). The nature of nurturing. *Newsweek,* pp. 64–66.

Behling, L. (2001). *The masculine woman in America, 1890–1935.* Urbana, IL: University of Illinois Press.

Belenky, M. F., Clinchy, B. M., Goldberger, N. R., & Tarule, J. M. (1986). *Women's ways of knowing: The development of self, voice, and mind.* New York: Basic.

Bell, R. R. (1981). Friendships of women and men. *Psychology of Women Quarterly, 5,* 402–417.

Bellas, M. (2001). The gendered nature of emotional labor in the workplace. In D. Vannoy (Ed.), *Gender mosaics* (pp. 269–278). Los Angeles: Roxbury.

Bellinger, D. C., & Gleason, J. B. (1982). Sex differences in parental directives to young children. *Sex Roles, 8,* 1123–1139.

Bem, S. (1993). *The lenses of gender: Transforming the debate on sexual inequality.* New Haven: Yale University Press.

Bergner, R. M., & Bergner, L. L. (1990). Sexual misunderstanding: A descriptive and pragmatic formulation. *Psychotherapy, 27,* 464–467.

Berndt, C. (1997). *The story of Pak Kumjoo.* Honors thesis in Asian studies, University of North Carolina, Chapel Hill.

Bernstein, A. (1999, February 1). Why the law should adopt more family leave. *Business Week,* p. 48.

Berscheid, E., Snyder, M., & Omoto, A. M. (1989). Issues in studying close relationships. In C. Hendrick (Ed.), *Close relationships* (pp. 63–91). Newbury Park, CA: Sage.

The best in the house. (1988, October 19). *New York Times,* p. 52Y.

Bettelheim, B. (1943). Individual and mass behavior in extreme situations. *Journal of Abnormal and Social Psychology, 38,* 417–452.

Bingham, S. (Ed.). (1994). *Conceptualizing sexual harassment as discursive practice.* Westport, CT: Praeger.

Bingham, S. (1996). Sexual harassment on the job, on the campus. In J. T. Wood (Ed.), *Gendered relationships: A reader* (pp. 233–252). Mountain View, CA: Mayfield.

Birdwhistell, R. (1970). *Kinesics and context.* Philadelphia: University of Pennsylvania Press.

Blankenship, J., & Robson, D. (1995). A "feminine style" in women's political discourse: An exploratory study. *Communication Quarterly, 43,* 353–366.

Bleier, R. (1986). Sex differences research: Science or belief? In R. Bleier (Ed.), *Feminist approaches to science* (pp. 147–164). New York: Pergamon.

Bloom, A. (1987). *The closing of the American mind: How higher education has failed democracy and impoverished the souls of today's students.* New York: Simon & Schuster.

Blum, D. (1997). *Sex on the brain: The biological differences between women and men.* New York: Penguin.

Blum, D. (1998, September/October). The gender blur: Where does biology end and society take over? *Utne Reader,* pp. 45–48.

Blumer, H. (1969). *Symbolic interactionism: Perspective and method.* Englewood Cliffs, NJ: Prentice-Hall.

Blumstein, P., & Kollock, P. (1988). Personal relationships. *Annual Review of Sociology, 14,* 467–490.

Blumstein, P., & Schwartz, P. (1983). *American couples: Love, sex, and money.* New York: Morrow.

Bly, R. (1990). *Iron John: A book about men.* Reading, MA: Addison-Wesley.

Bocella, K. (2001, January 31). Eating disorders spread among minority girls, women. *Raleigh News and Observer,* p. 5E.

Boling, P. (1991). The democratic potential of mothering. *Political Theory, 19,* 606–625.

Bonnett, A. (1996). The new primitives: Identity, landscape and cultural appropriation in the mythopoetic men's movement. *Antipode, 28,* 273–291.

Bordo, S. (1997). *Twilight zones: The hidden life of cultural images from Plato to O. J.* Berkeley: University of California Press.

Bordo, S. (1998, May 1). Sexual harassment is about bullying, not sex. *Chronicle of Higher Education,* p. B6.

Bordo, S. (1999). *The male body: A new look at men in public and in private.* New York: Farrar, Straus & Giroux.

Boston Women's Health Club Book Collective. (1976). *Our bodies/ourselves* (2nd ed.). New York: Simon & Schuster.

Bourg, C., & Segal, M. (2001). Gender, sexuality, and the military. In D. Vannoy (Ed.), *Gender mosaics* (pp. 332–342). Los Angeles: Roxbury.

Bowen, W., & Bok, D. (1998). *The shape of the river.* Princeton, NJ: Princeton University Press.

Bowman, K. K. (1994, January 10). Making the transition to "power feminism." *Wall Street Journal,* p. A10.

Bradley, P. H. (1981). The folk-linguistics of women's speech: An empirical examination. *Communication Monographs, 48,* 73–90.

Brandt, M. (1994, April 25). Far beyond white gloves and teas. *Newsweek,* pp. 57–59.

Braxton, G. (1999, June 5). Minorities glaringly absent from fall television lineup. *Richmond Times-Dispatch,* pp. F8–F9.

Brehm, S. S. (1992). *Intimate relationships* (2nd ed.). New York: McGraw-Hill.

Bretl, D., & Cantor, J. (1988). The portrayal of men and women in U.S. commercials: A recent content analysis and trend over 15 years. *Sex Roles, 18,* 595–609.

Bridges, J. S. (1989). Sex differences in occupational values. *Sex Roles, 20,* 205–211.

Brock-Utne, B. (1989). *Feminist perspectives on peace and peace education.* New York: Pergamon.

Brod, H. (1987). Introduction: Themes and theses of men's studies. In H. Brod (Ed.), *The making of masculinities: The new men's studies* (pp. 1–17). Boston: Allen and Unwin.

Brott, A. (1993, June). Will men take paternity leave? *Redbook,* p. 131.

Broverman, I., Broverman, D. M., Clarkson, F. E., Rosenkrantz, P. S., & Vogel, S. R. (1970). Sex-role stereotypes and clinical judgments of mental health. *Journal of Consulting and Clinical Psychology, 34,* 1–7.

Brown, C., & Shapiro, L. (1998, June 8). Woman warrior. *Newsweek,* pp. 64–65.

Brown, J. D., Childers, K. W., Bauman, K. E., & Koch, G. G. (1990). The influence of new media and family structure on young adolescents' television and radio use. *Communication Research, 17,* 65–82.

Brown, T. (1997, September 30). Women unfit for combat? Au contraire! *Wall Street Journal,* p. A22.

Brownmiller, S. (1993, January 4). Making female bodies the battlefield. *Newsweek,* p. 37.

Brownmiller, S. (2000). *In our time: Memoir of a revolution.* New York: Dial Press.

Brownstein, A. (2000, December 8). In the campus shadows, women are stalkers as well as the stalked. *Chronicle of Higher Education,* pp. A40–A42.

Bruess, C., & Pearson, J. (1996). Gendered patterns in family communication. In J. T. Wood (Ed.), *Gendered relationships: A reader* (pp. 59–78). Mountain View, CA: Mayfield.

Brumberg, J. (1997). *The body project: An intimate history of American girls.* New York: Random House.

Brumberg, J. J. (1988). *Fasting girls: The emergence of anorexia nervosa as a modern disease.* Cambridge, MA: Harvard University Press.

Bryant, A., & Check, E. (2000, Fall / Winter). How parents raise boys and girls. *Newsweek,* pp. 64–65.

Buhrke, R. A., & Fuqua, D. R. (1987). Sex differences in same- and cross-sex supportive relationships. *Sex Roles, 17,* 339–352.

Burgoon, J. K., Buller, D. B., Hale, J. L., & deTurck, M. A. (1988). Relational messages associated with nonverbal behaviors. *Human Communication Research, 10,* 351–378.

Burgoon, J. K., Buller, D. B., & Woodall, G. W. (1989). *Nonverbal communication: The unspoken dialogue.* New York: Harper & Row.

Burgoon, J. K., & Hale, J. L. (1988). Nonverbal expectancy violations: Model elaborations and application to immediacy behaviors. *Communication Monographs, 55,* 58–79.

Burgoon, J. K., & Le Poire, B. (1999). Nonverbal cues and interpersonal judgments: Participant and observer perceptions of intimacy, dominance, and composure. *Communication Monographs, 66,* 105–124.

Burke, K. (1966). *Language as symbolic action.* Berkeley: University of California Press.

Burleson, B. (1997, November). *Sex-related differences in communicative behavior: A matter of social skills, not gender cultures.* Paper presented at the National Communication Convention, Chicago.

Burns, A., & Homel, R. (1989). Gender division of tasks by parents and their children. *Psychology of Women Quarterly, 13,* 113–125.

Buss, D. (1994). *The evolution of desire: Strategies of human mating.* New York: Basic.

Buss, D. (1995). Evolutionary psychology: A new paradigm for psychological science. *Psychological Inquiry, 6,* 1–30.

Buss, D. (1996). The evolutionary psychology of human social strategies. In E. Higgins & A. Druglanski (Eds.), *Social psychology: Handbook of basic principles* (pp. 3–38). New York: Guilford.

Buss, D. (1999). *Evolutionary psychology: The new science of the mind.* Boston: Allyn & Bacon.

Buss, D., & Kenrick, D. (1998). Evolutionary social psychology. In D. Gilbert, S. Fiske, & G. Lindzey (Eds.), *The handbook of social psychology: Vol. 2* (4th ed., pp. 982–1026). Boston: McGraw-Hill.

Butler, D., & Geis, F. L. (1990). Nonverbal affect responses to male and female leaders: Implications for leadership. *Journal of Personality and Social Psychology, 58,* 48–59.

Butler, J. (1990). Performative acts and gender constitution: An essay in phenomenology and feminist theory. In S. Case (Ed.), *Performing feminisms: Feminist critical theory and theater* (pp. 270–282). Baltimore: Johns Hopkins University Press.

Cahill, D., & Sias, P. (1997). The perceived social costs and importance of seeking emotional support in the workplace: Gender differences and similarities. *Communication Research Reports, 14,* 231–240.

Caldera, Y. M., Huston, A. C., & O'Brien, M. (1989). Social interactions and play patterns of parents and toddlers with feminine, masculine, and neutral toys. *Child Development, 60,* 70–76.

Calderone, K. L. (1990). The influence of gender on the frequency of pain and sedative medication administered to postoperative patients. *Sex Roles, 23,* 713–725.

Caldwell, M. A., & Peplau, L. A. (1982). Sex differences in same-sex friendship. *Sex Roles, 8,* 721–732.

Calhoun, C. (1995). *Critical social theory.* Oxford, England: Basil Blackwell.

Campbell, A. (1993). *Men, women, and aggression.* New York: Basic.

Campbell, K. K. (1973). The rhetoric of women's liberation: An oxymoron. *Quarterly Journal of Speech, 59,* 74–86.

Campbell, K. K. (1989a). *Man cannot speak for her: I. A critical study of early feminist rhetoric.* New York: Praeger.

Campbell, K. K. (1989b). *Man cannot speak for*

her: II. Key texts of the early feminists. New York: Greenwood.

Campbell, K. K. (1991). Hearing women's voices. *Communication Education, 40,* 33–48.

Campbell, K. K. (Ed.). (1993). *Women public speakers in the United States: A bio-critical sourcebook.* Westport, CT: Greenwood.

Campbell, K., & Jerry, E. (1988). Woman and speaker: A conflict in roles. In S. Brehm (Ed.), *Seeing female: Social roles and personal lives.* New York: Greenwood.

Campo-Flores, A., & Rosenberg, Y. (2000, June 26). A return to wilding. *Newsweek,* p. 28.

Cancian, F. (1987). *Love in America.* Cambridge, MA: Cambridge University Press.

Cancian, F. (1989). Love and the rise of capitalism. In B. Risman & P. Schwartz (Eds.), *Gender in intimate relationships* (pp. 12–25). Belmont, CA: Wadsworth.

Cancian, F., & Oliker, S. (2000). *Caring and gender.* Thousand Oaks, CA: Sage.

Cann, A., & Siegfried, W. D. (1990). Gender stereotypes and dimensions of effective leader behavior. *Sex Roles, 23,* 413–419.

Carli, L. L. (1989). Gender differences in interaction style and influence. *Journal of Personality and Social Psychology, 56,* 565–576.

Carter, C. (1998). Branston, G., & Allan, S. (Eds.), *News, gender and power.* New York: Routledge.

Carty, L. (1992). Black women in academia: A statement from the periphery. In H. Bannerji, L. Carty, K. Dehli, S. Heald, & K. McKenna (Eds.), *Unsettling relations* (pp. 13–44). Boston: South End.

Cassirer, E. (1978). *An essay on man.* New Haven, CT: Yale University Press.

Cazenave, N. A., & Leon, G. H. (1987). Men's work and family roles and characteristics: Race, gender, and class. In M. S. Kimmel (Ed.), *Changing men: New directions in research on men and masculinity* (pp. 244–262). Newbury Park, CA: Sage.

Cegela, D., & Sillars, A. (1989). Further examination of nonverbal manifestations of interaction involvement. *Communication Reports, 2,* 39–47.

Chaiken, S., & Pliner, P. (1987). Women, but not men, are what they eat: The effect of meal size and gender on perceived femininity and masculinity. *Personality and Social Psychology Bulletin, 13,* 166–176.

Chambers, V. (1998, January 19). Family rappers. *Newsweek,* pp. 66–67.

Chapman, M., & Hendler, G. (Eds.). (1999). *Sentimental men: Masculinity and the politics of affect in American culture.* Berkeley: University of California Press.

Chase, S. (Ed.). (1991). *Defending the earth: A dialogue between Murray Bookchin and Dave Foreman.* Boston: South End.

Chatham-Carpenter, A., & DeFrancisco, V. (1998). Women construct self-esteem in their own terms: A feminist qualitative study. *Feminism & Psychology, 8,* 467–489.

Chesler, E. (1992). *Woman of valor: Margaret Sanger and the birth control movement in America.* New York: Simon & Schuster.

Chesler, P. (1972). *Women and madness.* Garden City, NY: Doubleday.

Chethik, N. (2001). *FatherLoss: How sons of all ages come to terms with the deaths of their dads.* New York: Hyperion.

Child care. (1992, August 10). *Fortune,* pp. 50–54.

Chodorow, N. J. (1978). *The reproduction of mothering: Psychoanalysis and the sociology of gender.* Berkeley: University of California Press.

Chodorow, N. J. (1989). *Feminism and psychoanalytic theory.* New Haven, CT: Yale University Press.

Chodorow, N. J. (1999). *The power of feelings: Personal meaning in psychoanalysis, gender, & culture.* New Haven, CT: Yale University Press.

Christensen, A., & Heavey, C. (1990). Gender and social structure in the demand/withdraw pattern in marital conflict. *Journal of Personality and Social Psychology, 59,* 73–81.

Christopher, F., & McQuaid, S. (1998). *Dating relationships and men's sexual aggression.* Sarasota Springs, NY: ISSPR.

Clair, R. (1994). Hegemony and harassment: A discursive practice. In S. Bingham (Ed.), *Conceptualizing sexual harassment as discursive practice* (pp. 59–70). Westport, CT: Praeger.

Clark, R. A. (1998). A comparison of topics and objectives in a cross section of young men's and women's everyday conversations. In D. J. Canary & K. Dindia (Eds.), *Sex differences and similarities in communication: Critical essays and empirical investigations of sex and gender in interaction* (pp. 303–319). Mahwah, NJ: Erlbaum.

Clemetson, L., & Samuels, A. (2000, December 18). We have the power. *Newsweek,* pp. 54–60.

Clinton forms office focusing on violence against women. (1995, March 22). *Raleigh News and Observer,* p. A4.

Clinton, K. (2001, May). Unplugged: Surrendered wives. *The Nation,* p. 17.

Cloud, J. (2000, June 26). The bad Sunday in the park. *Time,* pp. 32–33.

Clover, C. (1995). Her body, himself: Gender in the slasher film. In G. Dines & J. Humez (Eds.), *Gender, race, and class in media: A text reader* (pp. 169–184). Thousand Oaks, CA: Sage.

Clutter, S. (1990, May 3). Gender may affect response and outrage to sex abuse. *Morning Call,* p. D14.

Coates, J. (1986). *Women, men, and language: Studies in language and linguistics.* London: Longman.

Coates, J. (Ed.). (1997). *Language and gender: A reader.* London: Blackwell.

Coates, J., & Cameron, D. (1989). *Women in their speech communities: New perspectives on language and sex.* London: Longman.

Cochran, S. D., & Peplau, L. A. (1985). Value orientations in heterosexual relationships. *Psychology of Women Quarterly, 9,* 477–488.

Cohen, L. (1997, Fall). Hunters and gatherers in the classroom. *Independent School,* pp. 28–36.

Collins, P. H. (1986). Learning from the outsider within. *Social Problems, 33,* 514–532.

Collins, P. H. (1987). The meaning of motherhood in black culture. *Sage: A Scholarly Journal on Black Women, 4,* 3–10.

Collins, P. H. (1990). *Black feminist thought: Knowledge, consciousness, and the politics of empowerment.* Boston: Unwin Hyman.

Collins, P. H. (1996). What's in a name? Womanism, black feminism, and beyond. *Black Scholar, 26,* 9–17.

Collins, P. H. (1998). *Fighting words: Black women and the search for justice.* Minneapolis: University of Minnesota Press.

Collins, R., & Coltrane, S. (1995). *Sociology of marriage and the family.* Chicago: Nelson-Hall.

Coltrane, S. (1996). *Family man: Fatherhood, housework, and gender equity.* New York: Oxford University Press.

Coltrane, S. (1998). *Gender and families.* Newbury Park, CA: Pine Forge.

Coltrane, S., & Adams, M. (2001). Men, women and housework. In D. Vannoy (Ed.), *Gender mosaics* (pp. 145–154). Los Angeles: Roxbury.

Condry, S. M., Condry, J. C., & Pogatshnik, L. W. (1983). Sex differences: A study of the ear of the beholder. *Sex Roles, 9,* 697–704.

Cook, P. (1997). *Abused men: The hidden side of domestic violence.* Westport, CT: Greenwood Publishers.

Cooper, L. (1998, Winter). Images of women in popular song lyrics. *Popular Music and Society,* pp. 28–41.

Cordes, H. (1994, September/October). There's no such thing as a mothering instinct. *Utne Reader,* pp. 15–16.

Cornell, D. (1991, Summer). Sex discrimination law and equivalent rights. *Dissent,* pp. 400–405.

Cose, E. (1994, August 8). Truths about spouse abuse. *Newsweek,* p. 49.

Cose, E. (1997, October 13). . . . Promises. *Newsweek,* pp. 30–31.

Costin, F., & Schwartz, N. (1987). Beliefs about rape and women's social roles: A four-nation study. *Journal of Interpersonal Violence, 2,* 46–56.

Cowan, G., Lee, C., Levy, D., & Snyder, D. (1988). Dominance and inequality in X-rated videocassettes. *Psychology of Women Quarterly, 12,* 299–311.

Cowan, G., & O'Brien, M. (1990). Gender and survival vs. death in slasher films: A content analysis. *Sex Roles, 23,* 187–196.

Cowell, S. (1992, September/October). Work and family: The missing movement. *Democratic Left,* pp. 14–15.

Craft, C. (1988). *Too old, too ugly, and not deferential to men: An anchor-woman's courageous battle against sex discrimination.* Rockland, CA: Prima.

Crawford, M. (1988). Agreeing to differ: Feminist epistemologies and women's ways of knowing. In M. Crawford & M. Gentry (Eds.), *Gender and thought: Psychological perspectives* (pp. 128–145). New York: Springer-Verlag.

Crawford, M., & MacLeod, M. (1990). Gender in the college classroom: An assessment of the "chilly climate" for women. *Sex Roles, 23,* 101–122.

Crittenden, A. (2001). *The price of motherhood: Why the most important job in the world is still the least valued.* New York: Metropolitan.

Crittenden, D. (1999). *What our mothers didn't tell us: Why happiness eludes the modern woman.* New York: Simon & Schuster.

Cuklanz, L. (1996). *Rape on trial: How the media construct legal reforms and social change.* Philadelphia: University of Pennsylvania Press.

Daly, M. (1968). *The church and the second sex.* New York: Harper & Row.

Daly, M. (1973). *Beyond God the father: Toward a philosophy of women's liberation.* Boston: Beacon.

Daly, M. (1978). *Gyn/ecology: The metaethics of radical feminism.* Boston: Beacon.

Daly, M. (1992). *Outercourse: The bedazzling voyage.* San Francisco: Harper & Row.

Danner, L., & Walsh, S. (1999). "Radical" feminists and "bickering" women: U.S. media coverage of the United Nations Fourth World Conference on Women. *Critical Studies in Mass Communication, 16,* 63–84.

The daughter track/trading places. (1990, July 16). *Newsweek,* pp. 48–54.

Davidson, L. R., & Duberman, L. (1982). Friendship: Communication and interactional patterns in same-sex dyads. *Sex Roles, 8,* 809–822.

Davies-Popelka, W. (2000). Mirror, mirror on the wall: Weight, identity, and self-talk in women. In D. O. Braithwaite & J. T. Wood (Eds.), *Case studies in interpersonal communication* (pp. 52–60). Belmont, CA: Wadsworth.

Davis, D. M. (1990). Portrayals of women in prime-time network television: Some demographic characteristics. *Sex Roles, 23,* 325–332.

Davis, F. (1991). *Moving the mountain: The women's movement in America since 1960.* New York: Simon & Schuster.

Davis, S. (1990). Men as success objects and women as sex objects: A study of personal advertisements. *Sex Roles, 23,* 43–50.

Davison, K., & Birch, L. (2001). Weight, status, parent reaction, and self-concept in five-year-old girls. *Pediatrics, 107,* 42–53.

Deaux, K. (1976). *The behavior of men and women.* Monterey, CA: Brooks/Cole.

Deed, M. (1998). Abuse. In W. Mankiller, G. Mink, M. Navarro, B. Smith, & G. Steinem (Eds.), *The reader's companion to U.S. women's history* (pp. 606–607). New York: Houghton Mifflin.

Deford, F. (2000, June 5). Anna Kournikova. *Sports Illustrated,* pp. 95–110.

DeFrancisco, V., & Chatham-Carpenter, A. (2000). Self in community: African American women's views of self-esteem. *Howard Journal of Communication, 11,* 73–92.

Degler, C. N. (1980). *At odds: Women and the family in America from the Revolution to the present.* New York: Oxford University Press.

Delk, J. L., Madden, R. B., Livingston, M., & Ryan, T. T. (1986). Adult perceptions of the infant as a function of gender labeling and observer gender. *Sex Roles, 15,* 527–534.

DeLucia, J. L. (1987). Gender role identity and dating behavior: What is the relationship? *Sex Roles, 17,* 153–161.

Demare, D., Briere, J., & Lips, H. M. (1988). Violent pornography and self-reported likelihood of sexual aggression. *Journal of Research in Personality, 22,* 140–153.

The Diagram Group. (1977). *Woman's body: An owner's manual.* New York: Bantam.

Diamond, I., & Orenstein, G. F. (Eds.). (1990). *Reweaving the world: The emergence of ecofeminism.* San Francisco: Sierra Club.

Dieter, P. (1989, March). *Shooting her with video, drugs, bullets, and promises.* Paper presented at the meeting of the Association of Women in Psychology, Newport, RI.

Dietz, T. (1998). An examination of violence and gender role portrayals in video games: Implications for gender socialization and aggressive behavior. *Sex Roles, 38,* 187–201.

Dirie, W. (1998). *Desert flower.* New York: Morrow.

Dobash, R. E., & Dobash, R. P. (1979). *Violence against wives: A case against the patriarchy.* New York: Free Press.

Doctor: Girl not ready for breast implants. (2001, January 6). *Raleigh News & Observer,* p. 18A.

Donnerstein, E., Linz, D., & Penrod, S. (1987). *The question of pornography: Research findings and policy implications.* New York: Free Press.

Donovan, J. (1985). *Feminist theory: The intellectual traditions of American feminism.* New York: Frederick Unger.

Douglas, A. (1977). *The feminization of American culture.* New York: Knopf.

Dow, B. (1996). *Prime-time feminism.* Philadelphia: University of Pennsylvania Press.

Dow, B. J. (1992). Femininity and feminism in "Murphy Brown." *Southern Journal of Communication, 57,* 143–155.

Dow, B., & Tonn, M. B. (1993). Feminine style and political judgment in the rhetoric of Ann Richards. *Quarterly Journal of Speech, 79,* 286–302.

Downey, D., Ainsworth-Darnell, J., & Dufur, M. (1998). Sex of parent and children's well-being in single-parent households. *Journal of Marriage and the Family, 60,* 878–893.

Doyle, J. (1989). *The male experience* (2nd ed.). Dubuque, IA: William C. Brown.

Doyle, J. A. (1997). *The male experience* (3rd ed.). Dubuque, IA: Brown & Benchmark.

Doyle, L. (2001). *Surrendered wife: A practical guide for finding intimacy, passion and peace with your man.* New York: Fireside.

Dreier, P., & Freer, R. (1997, October 24). Saints, sinners, and affirmative action. *Chronicle of Higher Education,* pp. B6, B7.

Dreifus, C. (2000, July 11). A conversation with Nawal Nour. *New York Times,* p. D7.

Drummond, K., & Hopper, R. (1993). Acknowledgment tokens in series. *Communication Reports, 6,* 47–53.

Duck, S. W. (1988). *Relating to others.* Chicago: Dorsey.

Duck, S. W., & Wright, P. (1993). Re-examining gender differences in same-gender friendships: A close look at two kinds of data. *Sex Roles, 28,* 709–727.

DuPlessis, R., & Snitow, A. (Eds.). (1999). *The feminist memoir project: Voices from women's liberation.* Three Rivers, MI: Three Rivers.

Dyson, M. E. (1995). *Between God and gangsta rap.* New York: Oxford University Press.

Dyson, M. E. (1996). *Race rules: Navigating the color line.* New York: Addison-Wesley.

Eagly, A. H., & Johnson, B. T. (1990). Gender and leadership style: A meta-analysis. *Psychological Bulletin, 108,* 233–256.

Eagly, A. H., & Karau, S. J. (1991). Gender and the emergence of leaders: A meta-analysis. *Journal of Personality and Social Psychology, 60,* 687–710.

Eakins, B., & Eakins, G. (1976). Verbal turn-taking and exchanges in faculty dialogue. In B. L. DuBois & I. Crouch (Eds.), *Papers in southwest English: IV. Proceedings of the conference on the sociology of the languages of American women* (pp. 53–62). San Antonio: Trinity University Press.

Eakins, B. W., & Eakins, R. G. (1978). *Sex differences in human communication.* Boston: Houghton Mifflin.

Eccles, J. S. (1989). Bring young women to math and science. In M. Crawford & M. Gentry (Eds.), *Gender and thought: Psychological perspectives* (pp. 36–58). New York: Springer-Verlag.

Eckman, P., Friesen, W., & Ellsworth, P. (1971). *Emotion in the human face: Guidelines for research and an integration of findings.* Elmsford, NY: Pergamon.

Edmundson, M. (2000, October 9). Bad boys, whatcha gonna do? *The Nation*, pp. 39–43.

Edrut, O. (Ed.). (2000). *Body outlaws*. Seattle, WA: Seal Press.

Ehrenreich, B. (1990, Fall). Sorry sisters, this is not the revolution (Special issue). *Time*, p. 15.

Eichenbaum, L., & Orbach, S. (1983). *Understanding women: A feminist psychoanalytic approach*. New York: Basic.

Eichenbaum, L., & Orbach, S. (1987). *Between women: Love, envy, and competition in women's friendships*. New York: Viking.

Eldridge, N. S., & Gilbert, L. A. (1990). Correlates of relationship satisfaction in lesbian couples. *Psychology of Women Quarterly, 14*, 43–62.

Elias, M. (1992, August 3). Difference seen in brains of gay men. *USA Today*, p. 8-D.

England, P., & Farkas, G. (1980). *Households, employment, and gender*. New York: Aldine de Gruyter.

Enloe, C. (1998). Armed forces. In W. Mankiller, G. Mink, M. Navarro, B. Smith, & G. Steinem (Eds.), *The reader's companion to U.S. women's history* (pp. 38–39). New York: Houghton Mifflin.

Entman, R. M. (1994). Representation and reality in the portrayals of blacks on network television news. *Journalism Quarterly, 71*, 509–520.

Epperson, S. E. (1988, September 16). Studies link subtle sex bias in schools with women's behavior in the workplace. *Wall Street Journal*, p. 27.

Epstein, C. (1988). *Deceptive distinctions: Sex, gender, and the social order*. New Haven, CT: Yale University Press.

Epstein, C. F. (1968, November). Women in professional life. *Psychiatric Spectator*, n.p.

Epstein, C. F. (1981). *Women in law*. New York: Basic.

Epstein, C. F. (1982). *Changing perspectives and opportunities and their impact on careers and aspirations: The case of women lawyers*. Paper presented at the Annual Scientific Meeting of the Gerontological Society of America, Boston.

Erkut, S. (2001, Spring/Summer). Learning from leaders. *Wellesley Center for Women Research Report*, pp. 7–10.

Espiritu, Y. L. (1997). *Asian American women and men*. Thousand Oaks, CA: Sage.

Evans, D. (1993, March 1). The wrong examples. *Newsweek*, p. 10.

Evans, G. W., & Howard, R. B. (1973). Personal space. *Psychological Bulletin, 80*, 334–344.

Evelyn, J. (2001, June 1). Changing times. *Chronicle of Higher Education*, p. A6.

Eyer, D. E. (1992). *Mother-infant bonding: A scientific fiction*. New Haven, CT: Yale University Press.

Fabes, R. (1994). Physiological, emotional, and behavioral correlates of sex segregation. In C. Leaper (Ed.), *Childhood sex segregation: Causes and consequences*. San Francisco: Jossey-Bass.

Fabes, R. A., & Laner, M. R. (1986). How the sexes perceive each other: Advantages and disadvantages. *Sex Roles, 15*, 129–143.

Fagot, B. I. (1978). The influence of sex of child on parental reaction to toddler behaviors. *Child Development, 49*, 459–465.

Fagot, B. I. (1981). Stereotypes versus behavioral judgments of sex differences in young children. *Sex Roles, 7*, 1093–1096.

Fagot, B. I. (1984). Teacher and peer reactions to boys' and girls' play styles. *Sex Roles, 11*, 691–702.

Fagot, B. I. (1985). A cautionary note: Parents' socialization of boys and girls. *Sex Roles, 12*, 471–476.

Fagot, B. I., Hagan, R., Leinbach, M. D., & Kronsberg, S. (1985). Differential reactions to assertive and communicative acts of toddler boys and girls. *Child Development, 56*, 1499–1505.

Fagot, B. I., & Leinbach, M. D. (1987). Socialization of sex roles within the family. In B. Carter (Ed.), *Current conceptions of sex roles and sex typing: Theory and research* (pp. 89–100). New York: Praeger.

Fagot, B. I., & Leinbach, M. D. (1989). The young child's gender schema: Environmental input, internal organization. *Child Development, 60*, 663–672.

Fagot, B., Leinbach, M. D., & Hagan, R. (1986). Gender labeling and the development of sex-typed behaviors. *Developmental Psychology, 4*, 440–443.

Faludi, S. (1991). *Backlash: The undeclared war against American women*. New York: Crown.

Faludi, S. (1999). *Stiffed: The betrayal of the American man*. New York: Morrow.

Farrell, C., & Matthews, D. (2000). *A law of her own*. New York: New York University Press.

Farrell, C., & Matthews, D. (2000). *The reasonable woman as a standard for men*. New York: New York University Press.

Farrell, W. (1991, May/June). Men as success objects. *Utne Reader*, pp. 81–84.

Fasteau, M. F. (1974). *The male machine*. New York: McGraw-Hill.

Fat-phobia in the Fijis: TV-thin is in. (1999, May 31). *Newsweek*, p. 70.

Fears for careers curb paternity leaves. (1990, August 24). *Wall Street Journal*, p. B1.

Feingold, A. (1990). Gender differences in effects of physical attractiveness on romantic attraction: A comparison across five research paradigms. *Journal of Personality and Social Psychology, 59*, 981–993.

Feinman, S. (1984). A status theory of the evaluation of sex-role and age-role behavior. *Sex Roles, 10,* 445–456.

Feldman, R. S., & White, J. B. (1980). Detecting deception in children. *Journal of Communication, 30,* 121–128.

Ferraro, S. (2001, February 15). Gender affects the course of disease, researchers say. *Raleigh News and Observer,* p. 2E.

Fiebert, M. (1987). Some perspectives on the men's movement. *Men's Studies Review, 4,* 8–10.

Findlen, B. (Ed.). (1995). *Listen up! Voices from the next feminist generation.* Seattle: Seal.

Finnerty, A. (1999, May 9). The body politic. *New York Times Magazine,* p. 22.

Finstein, K. (1993, fall). Media-made beauty. *Carolina Alumni Review,* pp. 74–83.

Firms design benefits with families in mind. (1989, September 4). *Raleigh News and Observer,* pp. A1, A4.

Fisher, J. D., & Byrne, D. (1975). Too close for comfort: Sex differences in response to invasions of personal space. *Journal of Personality and Social Psychology, 32,* 15–21.

Fishman, P. M. (1978). Interaction: The work women do. *Social Problems, 25,* 397–406.

Fiske, S. T., Bersoff, D. N., Borgida, E., Deaux, K., & Heilman, M. E. (1991). Social science on trial: Use of sex stereotyping research in *Price Waterhouse v. Hopkins. American Psychologist, 46,* 1049–1060.

Flanders, L. (1990, November/December). Military women and the media. *New Directions for Women,* pp. 1, 9.

Fleming, J. (1984). *Blacks in college.* San Francisco: Jossey-Bass.

Fletcher, J. (1999). *Disappearing acts: Gender, power and relational practice at work.* Cambridge, MA: MIT Press.

Fletcher, J., Jordan, J., & Miller, J. (2000). Women and the workplace: Applications of a psychodynamic theory. *American Journal of Psychoanalysis, 60,* 243–261.

Floyd, K. (1995). Gender and closeness among friends and siblings. *Journal of Psychology, 129,* 193–202.

Floyd, K. (1996a). Brotherly love I: The experience of closeness in the fraternal dyad. *Personal Relationships, 3,* 369–385.

Floyd, K. (1996b). Communicating closeness among siblings: An application of the gendered closeness perspective. *Communication Research Reports, 13,* 27–34.

Floyd, K. (1997a). Brotherly love II: A developmental perspective on liking, love, and closeness in the fraternal dyad. *Journal of Family Psychology, 11,* 196–209.

Floyd, K. (1997b). Communicating affection in dyadic relationships: An assessment of behavior and expectancies. *Communication Quarterly, 45,* 68–80.

Folb, E. (1985). Who's got room at the top? Issues of dominance and nondominance in intracultural communication. In L. A. Samovar & R. E. Porter (Eds.), *Intercultural communication: A reader* (4th ed., pp. 119–127). Belmont, CA: Wadsworth.

Foreit, K. G., Agor, T., Byers, J., Larue, J., Lokey, H., Palazzini, M., Patterson, M., & Smith, L. (1980). Sex bias in the newspaper treatment of male-centered and female-centered news stories. *Sex Roles, 6,* 475–480.

Forell, C. (1993, March). Sexual and racial harassment: Whose perspective should control? *Trial,* pp. 70–76.

Forum. (1997, December). *Harpers,* pp. 47–58.

Foss, K., Edson, B., & Linde, J. (2000). What's in a name? Negotiating decisions about marital names. In D. O. Braithwaite & J. T. Wood (Eds.), *Case studies in interpersonal communication* (pp. 18–25). Belmont, CA: Wadsworth.

Fowers, B. J. (1991). His and her marriage: A multivariate study of gender and marital satisfaction. *Sex Roles, 24,* 209–221.

Fowler, R., & Fuchrer, A. (1997). Women's marital names: An interpretive study of name retainers' concepts of marriage. *Feminism & Psychology, 7,* 315–320.

Fox-Genovese, E. (1991). *Feminism without illusions: A critique of individualism.* Chapel Hill: University of North Carolina Press.

Fox-Genovese, E. (1996). *Feminism is not the story of my life.* New York: Nan A. Talese/Doubleday.

Franek, M. (1994, March 30). Code of honor. *Independent Weekly,* p. 8.

Franzoi, S. L. (1991, August). *Gender role orientation and female body perception.* Paper presented at the meeting of the American Psychological Association, San Francisco.

Freedman, C. (1985). *Manhood redux: Standing up to feminism.* Brooklyn, NY: Samson.

Freiberg, P. (1991, May). Separate classes for black males? *APA Monitor,* p. 33.

French, M. (1992). *The war against women.* New York: Summit.

Freud, S. F. (1957). *The ego and the id* (J. Riviere, Trans.). London: Hogarth.

Friedan, B. (1963). *The feminine mystique.* New York: Dell.

Friedan, B. (1981). *The second stage.* New York: Summit.

Fritz, J. (1997). Men's and women's organizational peer relationships: A comparison. *Journal of Business Communication, 34,* 27–46.

Fuentes, A. (1998, January 14). Rape statistics too good to be true. *Raleigh News and Observer,* p. 13A.

Futuyama, D., & Risch, S. (1984). Sexual orientation, sociobiology, and evolution. *Journal of Homosexuality, 9,* 157–168.

Gaard, G., & Murphy, P. (Eds.). (1999). *Ecofemi-*

nist literary criticism. Urbana: University of Illinois Press.

Gabriel, S. L., & Smithson, I. (Eds.). (1990). Gender in the classroom: Power and pedagogy. Urbana: University of Illinois Press.

Gaines, S. O., Jr. (1995). Relationships between members of cultural minorities. In J. T. Wood & S. Duck (Eds.), Understanding relationship processes, 6: Understudied relationships: Off the beaten track (pp. 51–88). Thousand Oaks, CA: Sage.

Garbarino, M. (1976). Native American heritage. Boston: Little, Brown.

Garlick, B., Dixon, S., & Allen, P. (Eds.). (1992). Stereotypes of women in power: Historical perspectives and revisionist views. Westport, CT: Greenwood.

Garrison, J. (2001, April 28). Researchers scramble over day-care study. Raleigh News and Observer, p. 6A.

Garrod, A., Ward, J., Robinson, T., & Kilkenny, R. (Eds.). (1999). Souls looking back: Life stories of growing up Black. New York: Routledge.

Gary, L. E. (1987). Predicting interpersonal conflict between men and women: The case of black men. In M. S. Kimmel (Ed.), Changing men: New directions in research on men and masculinity (pp. 232–243). Newbury Park, CA: Sage.

Gastil, J. (1990). Generic pronouns and sexist language: The oxymoronic character of masculine generics. Sex Roles, 23, 629–643.

Gaylin, W. (1992). The male ego. New York: Viking/Penguin.

Gelernter, D. (1996, February). Why mothers should stay home. Commentary, pp. 25–28.

Gelles, R. (1987). Family violence (2nd ed.). Newbury Park, CA: Sage.

Gelles, R., & Straus, M. (1988). Intimate violence. New York: Simon & Schuster.

Gelman, D. (1993, August 2). The violence in our heads. Newsweek, p. 48.

Gender difference in how brain "reads." (1995, February 16). San Francisco Chronicle, p. A4.

Gerhart, A. (1999, August 5). Young women increasingly choose plastic surgery. Raleigh News and Observer, p. 4E.

Gerson, K. (1986). Hard choices. How women decide about work, career, and motherhood. University of California Press.

Gerson, K. (1994). No man's land: Men's changing connections to family and work. New York: Basic.

Gerson, K. (1998). Gender and the future of the family: Implications for the postindustrial workplace. In D. Vannoy & P. Dubeck (Eds.), Challenges for work and family in the twenty-first century (pp. 11–21). New York: Aldine de Gruyter.

Gervasio, A. H., & Crawford, M. (1989). Social evaluations of assertiveness: A critique and

speech act reformulation. Psychology of Women Quarterly, 13, 1–25.

Gilbert, L. A., & Evans, S. L. (1985). Dimensions of same-gender student–faculty role-model relationships. Sex Roles, 12, 111–123.

Gilligan, C. (1982). In a different voice: Psychological theory and women's development. Cambridge, MA: Harvard University Press.

Gilligan, C., & Pollack, S. (1988). The vulnerable and invulnerable physician. In C. Gilligan, J. V. Ward, & J. M. Taylor, with B. Bardige (Eds.), Mapping the moral domain (pp. 245–262). Cambridge, MA: Harvard University Press.

Gilligan, C., Ward, J. V., Taylor, J. M., with Bardige, B. (Eds.). (1988). Mapping the moral domain. Cambridge, MA: Harvard University Press.

Gilman, C. P. (1915/1979). Herland. New York: Harper & Row.

Gilman, S. (1999). Making the body beautiful: A cultural history of aesthetic surgery. Princeton, NJ: Princeton University Press.

Gold, D., Crombie, G., & Noble, S. (1987). Relations between teachers' judgments of girls' and boys' compliance and intellectual competence. Sex Roles, 16, 351–358.

Goldner, V., Penn, P., Sheinberg, M., & Walker, G. (1990). Love and violence: Gender paradoxes in volatile attachments. Family Process, 19, 343–364.

Goldsmith, D., & Dun, S. (1997). Sex differences and similarities in the communication of social support. Journal of Social and Personal Relationships, 14, 317–337.

Goldsmith, D., & Fulfs, P. (1999). "You just don't have the evidence": An analysis of claims and evidence in Deborah Tannen's You Just Don't Understand. In M. Roloff (Ed.), Communication Yearbook, 22, pp. 1–49.

Goldstein, A. (2000, February 27). Breadwinning wives alter marital equation. Washington Post, p. A1.

Gomberg, E. S. L. (1986). Women: Alcohol and other drugs. Drugs and Society, 1, 75–109.

Gonzales, A., & Kertész, J. (2001). Engendering power in Native North America. In D. Vannoy (Ed.), Gender mosaics (pp. 43–52). Los Angeles: Roxbury.

Goode, E. (2001, August 1). 20% of girls report abuse by a date. Raleigh News and Observer, p. 10A.

Goodman, E. (1996, April 9). Freedom from mutilation. Raleigh News and Observer, p. 9A.

Goodman, E. (1999, May 29). Western culture pounds away at paradise. Raleigh News and Observer, p. 24-A.

Goodman, E. (2001, April 28). Playing with the numbers in child care. Raleigh News and Observer, p. 18A.

Goodnow, J. J. (1988). Children's household

work: Its nature and functions. *Psychological Bulletin, 103,* 5–26.

Goodwin, M. H. (1990). *He said, she said: Talk as social organization among Black children.* Bloomington: Indiana University Press.

Gordon, L. (1976). *Woman's body, woman's right: A social history of birth control in America.* New York: Grossman.

Gordon, L. (1988). *Heroes of their own lives.* New York: Viking.

Gordon, L. (1998). Women's colleges. In W. Mankiller, G. Mink, M. Navarro, B. Smith, & G. Steinem (Eds.), *The reader's companion to U.S. women's history* (pp. 642–644). New York: Houghton Mifflin.

Gordon, S. (1991). *Prisoners of men's dreams: Striking out for a new feminine future.* Boston: Little, Brown.

Gose, B. (2001, June 8). Supreme Court rejects appeal of a decision that cited "Bakke" to defend affirmative action. *Chronicle of Higher Education,* p. A24.

Grant, L. (1985). Race–gender status, classroom interaction, and children's socialization in elementary school. In L. C. Wilkinson & C. B. Marrett (Eds.), *Gender influences in classroom interaction* (pp. 57–77). Orlando: Academic.

Gray, J. (1992). *Men are from Mars, women are from Venus: A practical guide for improving communication and getting what you want in your relationships.* New York: HarperCollins.

Gray, J. (1995). *Mars and Venus in the bedroom: A guide to lasting romance and passion.* New York: HarperCollins.

Gray, J. (1996a). *Mars and Venus in love.* New York: HarperCollins.

Gray, J. (1996b). *Mars and Venus together forever.* New York: HarperCollins.

Gray, J. (1998). *Mars and Venus on a date: A guide for navigating the five stages of dating to create a loving and lasting relationship.* New York: HarperCollins.

Greenberg, S. (2001, January 8). Time to plan your life. *Newsweek,* pp. 54–55.

Greene, R., & Dalton, K. (1953). The premenstrual syndrome. *British Medical Journal, 1,* 1007–1014.

Greenhouse, L. (1998, March 5). Same-sex harassment recognized. *Raleigh News and Observer,* p. 4A.

Greenstein, T. (1996). Husbands' participation in domestic labor: The interactive effects of wives' and husbands' gender ideologies. *Journal of Marriage and the Family, 58,* 585–595.

Greer, G. (1992). *The change: Women, aging, and menopause.* New York: Knopf.

Greif, G. (1990). *The daddy track and the single father.* Lexington, MA: Lexington Books.

Griffin, C. (1996). Review of *Listen up! Voices from the next feminist generation. Journal of Applied Communication Research, 24,* 116–119.

Griffin, S. (1981). *Pornography and silence: Culture's revenge against nature.* New York: Harper & Row.

Griffin, S. (1993, April 16). Double struggle. *San Diego Union Tribune,* pp. E1, E3.

Griffith, R. (1997, October 17). The affinities between feminists and evangelical women. *Chronicle of Higher Education,* pp. B6, B7.

Griggs, C. (1998). *S/he: Changing sex and changing clothes.* New York: Berg/NYU Press.

Grinalds, J. (2000, February 15). New look, proven values at The Citadel. *Raleigh News and Observer,* p. 9A.

Gross, D. (1990, April 16). The gender rap. *New Republic,* pp. 11–14.

Gross, J. (1990, September 2). Navy is urged to root out lesbians despite abilities. *New York Times,* p. A24.

Gross, M. (2000, June). The lethal politics of beauty. *George,* pp. 53–59, 99–100.

Grover, M. B. (1999, September 6). Daddy stress. *Forbes,* pp. 202–208.

Gruenbaum, E. (2001). *The female circumcision controversy: An anthropological perspective.* Philadelphia: University of Pennsylvania Press.

Guerrero, L. (1997). Nonverbal involvement across interactions with same-sex friends, opposite-sex friends, and romantic partners: Consistency or change? *Journal of Social and Personal Relationships, 14,* 31–58.

Guerrilla Girls. (1995). *Confessions of the Guerrilla Girls.* New York: HarperPerennial.

Gunter, N. C., & Gunter, B. G. (1990). Domestic division of labor among working couples: Does androgyny make a difference? *Sex Roles, 14,* 355–370.

Haag, P. (2000). *Voices of a generation: Teenage girls report about their lives today.* New York: Marlowe & Co.

Halberstadt, A. G., & Saitta, M. B. (1987). Gender, nonverbal behavior, and perceived dominance: A test of the theory. *Journal of Personality and Social Psychology, 53,* 257–272.

Hale, J., Tighe, R., & Mongeau, P. (1997). Effects of event type and sex on comforting messages. *Communication Research Reports, 14,* 214–220.

Hale-Benson, J. E. (1986). *Black children: Their roots, culture, and learning styles* (Rev. ed.). Provo, UT: Brigham Young University Press.

Hales, D. (1999). *Just like a woman.* New York: Bantam.

Hall, D., & Langellier, K. (1988). Storytelling strategies in mother–daughter communication. In B. Bate & A. Taylor (Eds.), *Women communicating: Studies of women's talk* (pp. 107–126). Norwood, NJ: Ablex.

Hall, E. T. (1959). *The silent language.* Greenwich, CT: Fawcett.

Hall, E. T. (1966). *The hidden dimension.* New York: Anchor/Doubleday.

Hall, J. A. (1987). On explaining gender differences: The case of nonverbal communication. In P. Shaver & C. Hendrick (Eds.), *Sex and gender* (pp. 177–200). Newbury Park, CA: Sage.

Hall, J. A. (1998). How big are nonverbal sex differences? The case of similarity and sensitivity to nonverbal cues. In D. Canary & K. Dindia (Eds.), *Sex differences and similarities in communication: Critical essays and empirical investigations of sex and gender in interaction* (pp. 155–178). Mahwah, NJ: Erlbaum.

Hall, J. A., & Taylor, M. C. (1985). Psychological androgyny and the masculinity–femininity interaction. *Journal of Personality and Social Psychology, 49*, 429–435.

Hall, R. M., with Sandler, B. R. (1982). *The classroom climate: A chilly one for women?* Washington, DC: Association of American Colleges, Project on the Status and Education of Women.

Hall, R. M., & Sandler, B. R. (1984). *Out of the classroom: A chilly campus climate for women.* Washington, DC: Association of American Colleges, Project on the Status and Education of Women.

Hamilton, M. C. (1988). Using masculine generics: Does generic *he* increase male bias in the user's imagery? *Sex Roles, 19*, 785–799.

Hamilton, M. C. (1991). Masculine bias in the attribution of personhood: People–male, male–people. *Psychology of Women Quarterly, 15*, 393–402.

Hammer, J. (2001). *What it means to be a daddy: Fatherhood for Black men living away from their children.* Columbia University Press.

Hammonds, E. (1998). Science and gender. In W. Mankiller, G. Mink, M. Navarro, B. Smith, & G. Steinem (Eds.), *The reader's companion to U.S. women's history* (pp. 521–522). New York: Houghton Mifflin.

Hampton, R., Gullotta, T., Adams, G., Potter, E., & Weissberg, R. (Eds.). (1993). *Family violence: Prevention and treatment.* Thousand Oaks, CA: Sage.

Hanisch, C. (1970). What can be learned? A critique of the Miss America protest. In L. Tanner (Ed.), *Voices from women's liberation* (pp. 132–136). New York: Signet Classics.

Hansen, C. H., & Hansen, R. D. (1988). How rock music videos can change what is seen when boy meets girl: Priming stereotypic appraisal of social interactions. *Sex Roles, 19*, 287–316.

Hanson, S. (1988). Divorced fathers with custody. In P. Bronstein & C. P. Cowan (Eds.), *Fatherhood today: Men's changing role in the family* (pp. 166–194). New York: Wiley.

Harding, S. (1991). *Whose science? Whose knowledge? Thinking from women's lives.* Ithaca, NY: Cornell University Press.

Harding, S. (1998). *Can feminism be multicultural?* Ithaca, NY: Cornell University Press.

Hare-Mustin, R. T., & Marecek, J. (1988). The

meaning of difference: Gender theory, postmodernism, and psychology. *American Psychologist, 43*, 455–464.

Harper, L. V., & Sanders, K. M. (1975). Preschool children's use of space: Sex differences in outdoor play. *Developmental Psychology, 11*, 119.

Harris, J. (1998). *The nurture assumption.* New York: Simon & Schuster/Free Press.

Harrison, C. E. (1988). *On account of sex: The politics of women's issues, 1945–1968.* Berkeley: University of California Press.

Hartlage, L. C. (1980, March). *Identifying and programming for differences.* Paper presented at the Parent and Professional Conference on Young Children with Special Needs, Cleveland.

Hartman, S. (1998). *The other feminists: Activists in the liberal establishment.* New Haven, CT: Yale University Press.

Hartmann, E. (1991). *Boundaries in the mind: A new psychology of personality.* New York: Basic.

Hartup, W. (1974). Aggression in childhood: Developmental perspectives. *American Psychologist, 29*, 336–341.

Hasenauer, H. (1997). Taking on domestic violence. *Soldiers, 52*, 34–36.

Haskell, M. (1988, May). Hollywood Madonnas. *Ms.*, pp. 84, 86, 88.

Hass, N. (1998, October 20). Space girls. *Raleigh News and Observer*, pp. 1E, 3E.

Hatcher, M. A. (1991). The corporate woman of the 1990s: Maverick or innovator? *Psychology of Women Quarterly, 15*, 251–259.

Hattery, A. (2000). *Women, work and family: Balancing and weaving.* Thousand Oaks, CA: Sage.

Hawkes, B., & Spade, J. (1998, July). Women and men engineering students: Anticipations of family and work roles. *Journal of Engineering Education, 1–8.*

Hearn, J. (1987). *The gender of oppression: Men, masculinity and the critique of Marxism.* New York: St. Martin's.

Heath, D. (1991). *Fulfilling lives: Paths to maturity and success.* San Francisco: Jossey-Bass.

Hegel, G. W. F. (1807). *Phenomenology of mind.* (J. B. Baillie, Trans.). Germany: Wurzburg & Bamburg.

Heilbrun, A. B. (1986). Androgyny as type and androgyny as behavior: Implications for gender schema in males and females. *Sex Roles, 14*, 123–139.

Heilbrun, A. B., & Han, Y. (1984). Cost-effectiveness of college achievement by androgynous men and women. *Psychological Reports, 55*, 977–978.

Helgesen, S. (1990). *The female advantage: Women's ways of leadership.* New York: Doubleday Currency.

Heller, S. (1993, February 3). Scholars debate the Marlboro Man: Examining stereotypes of masculinity. *Chronicle of Higher Education,* pp. A6–A8, A15.

Hemmer, J. D., & Kleiber, D. A. (1981). Tomboys and sissies: Androgynous children? *Sex Roles, 7,* 1205–1211.

Hendrick, C., & Hendrick, S. (1986). A theory and method of love. *Journal of Personality and Social Psychology, 50,* 392–402.

Hendrick, C., & Hendrick, S. (1996). Gender and the experience of heterosexual love. In J. T. Wood (Ed.), *Gendered relationships: A reader.* Mountain View, CA: Mayfield.

Henley, N. M. (1977). *Body politics: Power, sex and nonverbal communication.* Englewood Cliffs, NJ: Prentice-Hall.

Henley, N. M. (1989). Molehill or mountain? What we know and don't know about sex bias in language. In M. Crawford & M. Gentry (Eds.), *Gender and thought: Psychological perspectives* (pp. 59–78). New York: Springer-Verlag.

Hennesee, J. (1999). *Betty Friedan: A biography.* New York: Random House.

Herlinger, C. (2001, December 7). Afghan women seek new role. *Raleigh News and Observer,* p. 4E.

Hertz, S. H. (1977). The politics of the Welfare Mothers Movement: A case study. *Signs: Journal of Women in Culture and Society, 2,* 600–611.

Hewlett, S. (1986). *A lesser life: The myth of female liberation in America.* New York: Morrow.

Hewlett, S. (1991). *When the bough breaks: The cost of neglecting our children.* New York: Basic.

Heywood, L. (1998, September 4). Hitting a cultural nerve: Another season of "Ally McBeal," *Chronicle of Higher Education,* p. B9.

Heywood, L., & Drake, J. (Eds.). (1997). *Third wave agenda: Being feminist, doing feminism.* Minneapolis: University of Minnesota Press.

Hicks, J. (1998a, February 12). Eating disorders screening offered. *Raleigh News and Observer,* p. 2E.

Hicks, J. (1998b, November 5). A thin line. *Raleigh News and Observer,* pp. 1E, 3E.

Hine, D., & Thompson, K. (1998). *A shining thread of hope: The history of Black women in America.* New York: Broadway.

Hines, M. (1992, April 19). [Untitled report]. *Health Information Communication Network, 5,* 2.

Hochschild, A. (1975). The sociology of feeling and emotion: Selected possibilities. In M. Millman & R. M. Kanter (Eds.), *Another voice* (pp. 180–207). New York: Doubleday/Anchor.

Hochschild, A. (1979). Emotion work, feeling rules, and social structure. *American Journal of Sociology, 85,* 551–595.

Hochschild, A. (1983). *The managed heart: Commercialization of human feeling.* Berkeley: University of California Press.

Hochschild, A. (1989). The economy of gratitude. In D. Franks & E. D. McCarthy (Eds.), *The sociology of emotions: Original essays and research papers* (pp. 95–113). Greenwich, CT: JAI Press.

Hochschild, A., with Machung, A. (1989). *The second shift: Working parents and the revolution at home.* New York: Viking/Penguin.

Hoffman, B. (1998). Pink collar ghetto. In W. Mankiller, G. Mink, M. Navarro, B. Smith, & G. Steinem (Eds.), *The reader's companion to U.S. women's history* (pp. 450–451). New York: Houghton Mifflin.

Hogan, J., Simpson, J., & Gillis, A. R. (1988). Feminist scholarship, relational and instrumental control, and a power-control theory of gender and delinquency. *British Journal of Sociology, 39,* 301–336.

Hollands, J. (2001). *Same game, different rules: How to get ahead without being a bully broad, ice queen or other Ms. Understood.* New York: McGraw-Hill.

Holt, P. (1998, June 29). Unraveling the secret life of a man who was a woman. *San Francisco Chronicle,* pp. D1, D5.

Holtzman, L. (2000). *Media messages: What film, television, and popular music teach us about race, class, gender, and sexual orientation.* New York: M. E. Sharpe.

hooks, b. (1981). *Ain't I a woman? Black women and feminism.* Boston: South End.

hooks, b. (1990). Definitions of difference. In D. L. Rhode (Ed.), *Theoretical perspectives on sexual difference* (pp. 185–193). New York: Yale University Press.

hooks, b. (1994). *Outlaw culture.* New York: Routledge.

hooks, b. (1995, August). Appearance obsession: Is the price too high? *Essence, 26,* 69–71.

hooks, b. (2000). *Feminism is for everybody.* Boston: South End Press.

Hoover, E. (2001, June 8). New scrutiny for powerful Greek systems. *Chronicle of Higher Education,* pp. A35–A37.

Hope for working families. (1991, April 17). *Raleigh News and Observer,* p. A16.

Hopkins, A., & Walsh, M. (1996). *So ordered: Making partner the hard way.* Amherst: University of Massachusetts Press.

Horn, D. (1997). Comfort women. *Endeavors* (pp. 8–9). Chapel Hill, NC: Office of Graduate Studies and Research, University of North Carolina.

Horowitz, D. (1998). *Betty Friedan and the making of the feminine mystique: The American left, the cold war, and modern feminism.* Amherst: University of Massachusetts Press.

Hosken, F. (1992). *The Hosken report: Genital and sexual mutilation of females.* Lexington, KY: WIN News.

House, A., Dallinger, J., & Kilgallen, D. (1998). Androgyny and rhetorical sensitivity: The connection of gender and communicator style. *Communication Reports, 11,* 11–20.

How boys and girls teach each other. (1992, October). *Working Mother,* p. 116.

Howard, J. A., Blumstein, P., & Schwartz, P. (1986). Sex, power, and influence factors in intimate relationships. *Journal of Personality and Social Psychology, 51,* 102–109.

Howry, A. (1999). *The next feminist generation: Negotiating contradiction and ambiguity.* Unpublished master's thesis, University of North Carolina, Chapel Hill, North Carolina.

Hudson, L., & Jacot, B. (1992). *The way men think.* New Haven, CT: Yale University Press.

Hughes, J. O., & Sandler, B. R. (1986). *In case of sexual harassment: A guide for women students.* Washington, DC: Association of American Colleges, Project on the Status and Education of Women.

Hunt, A. (1994, June 23). O.J. and the brutal truth about marital violence. *Wall Street Journal,* p. A15.

Husbands are battered as often as wives. (1994, June 23). *USA Today,* p. D8.

Huston, A. C. (1985). The development of sex typing: Themes from recent research. *Developmental Review, 5,* 1–17.

Huston, M., & Schwartz, P. (1996). Gendered dynamics in gay and lesbian relationships. In J. T. Wood (Ed.), *Gendered relationships: A reader* (pp. 89–121). Mountain View, CA: Mayfield.

Hyde, B., & Texidor, M. (1994). Childbearing and parental roles: A description of the fathering experience among Black fathers. In R. Staples (Ed.), *The Black family: Essays and studies* (pp. 157–164). Belmont, CA: Wadsworth.

Hyde, J. S. (1984). Children's understanding of sexist language. *Developmental Psychology, 20,* 697–706.

The implant circus. (1992, February 18). *Wall Street Journal,* p. A20.

Ingraham, L. (1997, July 15). Feminists welcome the Promise Keepers. *Raleigh News and Observer,* p. 11A.

Ingrassia, M. (1993, August 30). Endangered family. *Newsweek,* pp. 17–29.

Ingrassia, M. (1995, April 24). The body of the beholder. *Newsweek,* pp. 66–67.

Ingrassia, M., & Beck, M. (1994, July 4). Patterns of abuse. *Newsweek,* pp. 26–33.

Inman, C. (1996). Friendships between men: Closeness in the doing. In J. T. Wood (Ed.), *Gendered relationships: A reader* (pp. 95–110). Mountain View, CA: Mayfield.

Jacklin, C. N. (1989). Female and male: Issues of gender. *American Psychologist, 44,* 127–133.

Jackson, L. A. (1983). The perception of androgyny and physical attractiveness: Two is better than one. *Personality and Social Psychology Bulletin, 9,* 405–430.

Jackson, M. (1998, January 21). His career, her career. *Raleigh News and Observer,* p. D3.

Jackson, M. (1999, February 14). For dads, "leave" has meant "stay." *Raleigh News and Observer,* p. 6E.

Jacobs, J. A. (1989). *Revolving doors: Sex segregation and women's careers.* Stanford, CA: Stanford University Press.

Jacobson, J. (2001, March 9). Why do so many female athletes enter ACL hell? *Chronicle of Higher Education,* p. A45.

Jacobson, N., & Gottman, J. (1998). *When men batter women: New insights into ending abusive relationships.* New York: Simon & Schuster.

James, K. (1989). When twos are really threes: The triangular dance in couple conflict. *Australian and New Zealand Journal of Family Therapy, 10,* 179–186.

Jamieson, K. H. (1995). *Beyond the double bind: Women and leadership.* New York: Oxford University Press.

Janeway, E. (1971). *Man's world, woman's place: A study in social mythology.* New York: Dell.

Jhally, S., & Katz, J. (2001, Winter). Big trouble, little pond: Reflections on the meaning of the campus pond rapes. *UMass,* pp. 26-31.

Johnson, A. (2000, April 5). The power and the Gloria. *Raleigh News and Observer,* p. 3E.

Johnson, C. B., Stockdale, M. S., & Saal, F. E. (1991). Persistence of men's misperceptions of friendly cues across a variety of interpersonal encounters. *Psychology of Women Quarterly, 15,* 463–465.

Johnson, F. (1996). Friendships among women: Closeness in dialogue. In J. T. Wood (Ed.), *Gendered relationships: A reader* (pp. 79–94). Mountain View, CA: Mayfield.

Johnson, F. (2000). *Speaking culturally: Language diversity in the United States.* Thousand Oaks, CA: Sage.

Johnson, F. L. (1989). Women's culture and communication: An analytical perspective. In C. M. Lont & S. A. Friedley (Eds.), *Beyond boundaries: Sex and gender diversity in communication* (pp. 301–316). Fairfax, VA: George Mason University Press.

Jones, A. (1994). *Next time she'll be dead: Battering and how to stop it.* Boston: Beacon.

Jones, A. (1998a). Battered women. In W. Mankiller, G. Mink, M. Navarro, B. Smith, & G. Steinem (Eds.), *The reader's companion to U.S. women's history* (pp. 607-609). New York: Houghton Mifflin.

Jones, A. (1998b). Domestic violence. In W. Mankiller, G. Mink, M. Navarro, B. Smith, & G. Steinem (Eds.), *The reader's companion to U.S. women's history* (p. 609). New York: Houghton Mifflin.

Jones, D. C. (1991). Friendship satisfaction and

gender: An examination of sex differences in contributors to friendship satisfaction. *Journal of Social and Personal Relationships, 8*, 167–185.

Joseph, G. I., & Lewis, J. (1981). *Common differences.* New York: Anchor.

Kahn, A., & Mathie, V. (1994). Rape scripts and rape acknowledgment. *Psychology of Women Quarterly, 18*, 53–66.

Kahn, A. S., & Yoder, J. D. (1989). The psychology of women and conservatism: Rediscovering social change. *Psychology of Women Quarterly, 13*, 417–432.

Kahn, J. (1997, April 11). Therapist says male depression widespread and widely denied. *Raleigh News and Observer*, p. 5D.

Kamen, P. (2001). *Her way: Young women remake the sexual revolution.* New York: New York University Press.

Kaminer, W. (1993, October). Whither feminism? Feminism's identity crisis. *Atlantic Monthly*, pp. 48–56.

Kamionkowski, S., & Rosenbaum, M. (2001). Gender and Hebrew Biblical studies. In D. Vannoy (Ed.), *Gender mosaics* (pp. 397–405). Los Angeles: Roxbury.

Kang, M. (1997). The portrayal of women's images in magazine advertisements: Goffman's gender analysis revisited. *Sex Roles, 37*, 979–997.

Kanter, R. M. (1977). *Men and women of the corporation.* New York: Basic.

Kantrowitz, B., & Kalb, C. (1998, May 11). How to build a better boy. *Newsweek*, pp. 55–60.

Kaplan, E. A. (1992). *Motherhood and representation.* New York: Routledge.

Karp, M., & Stoller, D. (1999). *The BUST guide to the new girl order.* New York: Penguin.

Kassindja, F. (1998). *Do they hear you when you cry?* New York: Delacorte.

Kato, D. (1993, March 9). Read 'em and weep, women. *Raleigh News and Observer*, pp. E1, E3.

Katz, J. (1995). Advertising and the construction of violent White masculinity. In G. Dines & J. Humez (Eds.), *Gender, race and class in media* (pp. 133-141). Thousand Oaks, CA: Sage.

Kaye, L. W., & Applegate, J. S. (1990). Men as elder caregivers: A response to changing families. *American Journal of Orthopsychiatry, 60*, 86–95.

Keen, S. (1991). *Fire in the belly: On being a man.* New York: Bantam.

Keller, E. F. (1983). *A feeling for the organism: The life and work of Barbara McClintock.* New York: Freeman.

Keller, E. F. (1985). *Reflections on gender and science.* New Haven, CT: Yale University Press.

Kelly-Gadol, J. (1977). Did women have a renaissance? In R. Bridenthal & C. Koonz (Eds.), *Becoming visible: Women in European history* (pp. 136–164). Boston: Houghton Mifflin.

Kemper, S. (1984). When to speak like a lady. *Sex Roles, 10*, 435–443.

Kern-Foxworth, M. (1994). *Aunt Jemima, Uncle Ben, and Rastus: Blacks in advertising, yesterday, today, and tomorrow.* Westport, CT: Greenwood.

Kerr, B. (1997). *Smart girls: A new psychology of girls, women, and giftedness.* Scottsdale, AZ: Gifted Psychology Press.

Kerr, B. (1999, March 5). When dreams differ: Male-female relations on campuses. *Chronicle of Higher Education*, pp. B7–B8.

Kessler, S. (1998). *Lessons from the intersexed.* New Brunswick, NJ: Rutgers University Press.

Kessler, S., & McKenna, W. (1978). *Gender: An ethnomethodological approach.* New York: Wiley.

Kim, G., & Roloff, M. (1999). Attributing sexual consent. *Journal of Applied Communication Research, 27*, 1–23.

Kimball, M. M. (1986). Television and sex-role attitudes. In T. M. Williams (Ed.), *The impact of television: A natural experiment in three communities* (pp. 265–301). Orlando: Academic.

Kimbrell, A. (1991, May/June). A time for men to pull together. *Utne Reader*, pp. 66–71.

Kimmel, M. (1995). (Ed.), *The politics of manhood: Profeminist men respond to the Mythopoetic men's movement (and the Mythopoetic leaders answer).* Philadelphia: Temple University Press.

Kimmel, M. (1996). *Manhood.* New York: Free Press.

Kimmel, M. (2000a). *The gendered society.* Cambridge, MA: Oxford Press.

Kimmel, M. (2000b, January 12). What about the boys? Keynote speech at the Center for Research on Women's 6th Annual Gender Equity Conference, Boston, MA.

Kimmel, M. (2002, February 8). Gender, class and terrorism. *Chronicle of Higher Education*, pp. B11–B12.

Kimmel, M., & Mosmiller, T. (Eds.). (1992). *Against the tide.* Collingdale, PA: Diane Publishing Company.

Kindlon, D., & Thompson, M. (1999). *Raising Cain: Protecting the emotional life of boys.* New York: Ballantine.

Kirby, E., & Krone, K. (2002). "The policy exists but you can't really use it": Communication and the structuration of work-family policies. *Journal of Applied Communication Research, 30*, 50–77.

Kirpatrick, M. (1989). Middle age and the lesbian experience. *Women's Studies Quarterly, 17*, 87–96.

Klein, E. (1984). *Gender politics: From consciousness to mass politics.* Cambridge: Harvard University Press.

Klein, S., Stafford, L., & Miklosovic, J. (1996). Women's surnames: Decisions, interpretations, and associations with relational qualities. *Journal of Social and Personal Relationships, 13,* 593–617.

Klein, S. S. (1985). *Handbook for achieving sex equity in education.* Baltimore: Johns Hopkins University Press.

Kluwer, E., Heesink, J., & Vliert, E. (1996). The marital dynamics of conflict over the division of labor. *Journal of Marriage and the Family, 59,* 635–653.

Knudson-Martin, C., & Mahoney, A. (1996). Gender dilemmas and myths in the construction of marital bargains: Issues for marital therapy. *Family Process, 35,* 137–153.

Koblinsky, S. A., & Sugawara, A. I. (1984). Nonsexist curricula, sex of teacher, and children's sex-role learning. *Sex Roles, 10,* 357–367.

Kohlberg, L. (1958). *The development of modes of thinking and moral choice in the years 10 to 16.* Unpublished doctoral dissertation, University of Chicago.

Kohlberg, L. (1966). A cognitive-developmental analysis of children's sex-role concepts and attitudes. In E. M. Maccoby (Ed.), *The development of sex differences* (pp. 82–173). Stanford, CA: Stanford University Press.

Kohn, A. (1986). *No contest: The case against competition.* Boston: Houghton Mifflin.

Komarovsky, M. (1940). *The unemployed man and his family.* New York: Dryden.

Koss, M. P., & Dinero, T. E. (1988). Predictors of sexual aggression among a national sample of male college students. In V. I. Quinsey & R. Orentky (Eds.), *Human sexual aggression* (pp. 133–147). New York: Academy of Sciences.

Koss, M. P., Dinero, T. E., Seibel, C. A., & Cox, S. L. (1988). Stranger and acquaintance rape: Are there differences in the victim's experience? *Psychology of Women Quarterly, 12,* 1–24.

Koss, M. P., Gidycz, C. J., & Wisniewski, N. (1987). The scope of rape: Incidence and prevalence of sexual aggression and victimization in a national sample of higher education students. *Journal of Consulting and Clinical Psychology, 55,* 162–170.

Kovacs, P., Parker, J., & Hoffman, L. (1996). Behavioral, affective and social correlates of involvement in cross-sex friendships in elementary school. *Child Development, 67,* 2269–2286.

Kramarae, C. (1981). *Women and men speaking: Frameworks for analysis.* Rowley, MA: Newbury House.

Kramarae, C. (1992). Harassment and everyday life. In L. F. Rakow (Ed.), *Women making meaning: New feminist directions in communication* (pp. 100–120). New York: Routledge.

Kramarae, C., Schultz, M., & O'Barr, W. (Eds.). (1984). *Language and power.* Beverly Hills: Sage.

Kramarae, C., Thorne, B., & Henley, N. (1978). Perspectives on language and communication. *Signs: Journal of Women in Culture and Society, 5,* 638–651.

Kreps, G. L. (Ed.). (1992). *Communication and sexual harassment in the workplace.* Cresskill, NJ: Hampton.

Krupnick, C. G. (1985, May). Women and men in the classroom: Inequality and its remedies. *On Teaching and Learning: The Journal of the Harvard-Danforth Center for Teaching and Learning, 18*–25.

Kuczynski, A. (2001, April 9). Magazines try to help teens. *Raleigh News and Observer,* p. 3E.

Kurdek, L. A., & Schmitt, J. P. (1986a). Early development of relationship quality in heterosexual married, heterosexual cohabiting, gay, and lesbian couples. *Developmental Psychology, 22,* 305–309.

Kurdek, L. A., & Schmitt, J. P. (1986b). Interaction of sex-role self-concept with relationship quality and relationship belief in married, heterosexual cohabiting, gay, and lesbian couples. *Journal of Personality and Social Psychology, 51,* 365–370.

Kurdek, L. A., & Schmitt, J. P. (1986c). Relationship quality of partners in heterosexual married, heterosexual cohabiting, and gay and lesbian relationships. *Journal of Personality and Social Psychology, 51,* 711–720.

Kurdek, L. A., & Schmitt, J. P. (1987). Partner homogamy in married, heterosexual cohabiting, gay, and lesbian couples. *Journal of Sex Research, 23,* 212–232.

Kurtz, D. (1989). Social science perspectives on wife abuse: Current debates and future directions. *Gender and Society, 3,* 489–505.

Labov, W. (1972). *Sociolinguistic patterns.* Philadelphia: University of Pennsylvania Press.

LaFrance, M., & Mayo, C. (1979). A review of nonverbal behaviors of women and men. *Western Journal of Speech Communication, 43,* 96–107.

Lakoff, R. (1975). *Language and woman's place.* New York: Harper & Row.

Lakoff, R. (1998). Language and power. In W. Mankiller, G. Mink, M. Navarro, B. Smith, & G. Steinem (Eds.), *The reader's companion to U.S. women's history* (pp. 314–316). New York: Houghton Mifflin.

Lally, K. (1996, January 7). For girls now, adolescence a perilous rite. *Richmond Times Dispatch,* pp. G1, G2.

Lamb, M. E. (1986). The changing roles of fathers. In M. E. Lamb (Ed.), *The father's role: Applied perspectives* (pp. 3–27). New York: Wiley.

Lamb, S. (1991). Acts without agents: An analysis of linguistic avoidance in journal articles on men who batter women. *American Journal of Orthopsychiatry, 61,* 87–102.

Lamb, S. (1999). (Ed.). *New versions of victims.* Thousand Oaks, CA: Sage.

Lamke, L. K. (1982). The impact of sexual orientation on self-esteem in early adolescence. *Child Development, 53,* 1530–1535.

Lamke, L., Sollie, D., Durbin, R., & Fitzpatrick, J. (1994). Masculinity, femininity, and relationship satisfaction: The mediating role of interpersonal competence. *Journal of Social and Personal Relationships, 11,* 535–554.

Lang, S. S. (1991, January 20). When women drink. *Parade,* pp. 18–20.

Langer, S. K. (1953). *Feeling and form: A theory of art.* New York: Scribner's.

Langer, S. K. (1979). *Philosophy in a new key: A study in the symbolism of reason, rite and art* (3rd ed.). Cambridge, MA: Harvard University Press.

Langreth, R. (1997, June 12). Hey guys, for the next party, try borrowing women's genes. *Wall Street Journal,* p. B1.

Lauer, R. H., & Lauer, J. C. (1981). *Fashion power: The meaning of fashion in American society.* Englewood Cliffs, NJ: Prentice-Hall.

Lawson, C. (1993, February 16). Genderbenders. *Raleigh News and Observer,* p. E1.

Leaper, C. (1991). Influence and involvement in children's discourse: Age, gender, and partner effects. *Child Development, 62,* 797–811.

Leaper, C. (Ed.). (1994). *Childhood gender segregation: Causes and consequences.* San Francisco: Jossey-Bass.

Leaper, C. (1996). The relationship of play activity and gender to parent and child sex-typed communication. *International Journal of Behavioral Development, 19,* 689–703.

Leaper, C. (2000). The social construction and socialization of gender. In P. Miller & E. Scholnick (Eds.), *Towards a feminist developmental psychology* (pp. 127–152). New York: Routledge.

Leaper, C., Anderson, K., & Sanders, P. (1998). Moderators of gender effects on parents' talk to their children: A meta-analysis. *Developmental Psychology, 34,* 3–27.

Leaper, C., Leve, L., Strasser, T., & Schwartz, R. (1995). Mother–child communication sequences: Play activity, child gender, and marital status effects. *Merrill-Palmer Quarterly, 41,* 307–327.

Leathers, D. G. (1986). *Successful nonverbal communication: Principles and applications.* New York: Macmillan.

Lee, P. C., & Gropper, N. B. (1974). Sex-role culture and educational practice. *Harvard Educational Review, 44,* 369–407.

Lee, S. (Director). (1997). *Get on the Bus.* (motion picture). United States: Columbia/Tristar.

Lee, V. E., & Marks, H. M. (1990). Sustained effects of the single-sex secondary school experience on attitudes, behaviors, and values in college. *Journal of Educational Psychology, 82,* 578–592.

Legato, M. (1998, May 15). Research on the biology of women will improve health care for men, too. *Chronicle of Higher Education,* pp. B4–B5.

Leo, J. (1997, March 31). Boy, girl, boy again. *Newsweek,* p. 17.

LePoire, B. A., Burgoon, J. K., & Parrott, R. (1992). Status and privacy restoring communication in the workplace. *Journal of Applied Communication Research, 4,* 419–436.

Lesak, M. (1976). *Neuropsychological assessment.* New York: Oxford University Press.

Leslie, C. (1998, March 23). Separate and unequal? *Newsweek,* p. 55.

Levesque, J. (2001, May 1). News flash: Pretty faces sell. *Raleigh News and Observer,* p. 5E.

Levinson, D. (1989). *Family violence in cross-cultural perspective.* Newbury Park, CA: Sage.

Levinson, R., Powell, B., & Steelman, L. C. (1986). Social location, significant others, and body image among adolescents. *Social Psychology Quarterly, 49,* 330–337.

Lewis, E. T., & McCarthy, P. R. (1988). Perceptions of self-disclosure as a function of gender-linked variables. *Sex Roles, 19,* 47–56.

Lichter, S. R., Lichter, L. S., & Rothman, S., (1986, September/October). From Lucy to Lacey: TV's dream girls. *Public Opinion,* pp. 16–19.

Lightfoot-Klein, H. (1989). *Prisoners of ritual: An odyssey into female genital circumcision in Africa.* New York: Harrington Park.

Liner, E. (2001, May 24). Women's TV enters a new golden age. *Raleigh News and Observer,* p. 9E.

Lingard, B., & Douglas, P. (1999). *Men engaging feminism: Profeminism, backlashes, and schooling.* Philadelphia: Open University Press.

Lisak, D., & Roth, S. (1988). Motivational factors in nonincarcerated sexually aggressive men. *Journal of Personality and Social Psychology, 55,* 795–802.

Lister, L. (1997, Fall). Among school girls. *Independent School,* pp. 42–45.

Lively, K. (2000, June 16). Women in charge. *Chronicle of Higher Education,* pp. A33–A35.

Logwood, D. (1997, Summer). Ghetto feminism. *Hues,* pp. 36–37.

Logwood, D. (1998, Winter). One million strong. *Hues,* pp. 15–19.

Lont, C. (Ed.). (1995). *Women and media: Content, careers, criticism.* Belmont, CA: Wadsworth.

Lont, C. (2001). The influence of media on gender images. In D. Vannoy (Ed.), *Gender mosaics* (pp. 114–122). Los Angeles: Roxbury.

Lont, C. M. (1990). The roles assigned to females and males in non-music radio programming. *Sex Roles, 22,* 661–668.

Lorber, J. (1997). A woman's rights/cultural conflict. *Democratic Left, 2,* 3–5.

Lorber, J. (2001). *Gender inequality: Feminist*

theories and politics, (2ⁿᵈ ed.). Los Angeles: Roxbury.

Loscocco, K. (1997). Work-family linkages among self-employed women and men. *Journal of Vocational Behavior, 50,* 204-226.

Lott, B. (1989). Sexist discrimination as distancing behavior: II. Prime-time television. *Psychology of Women Quarterly, 13,* 341–355.

Loury, G. (1996, January/February). Joy and doubt on the mall. *Utne Reader,* pp. 70–71.

Lucal, B. (1995). The problem with "battered husbands." *Deviant Behavior: An Interdisciplinary Journal, 16,* 95–112.

Luebke, B. F. (1989). Out of focus: Images of women and men in newspaper photographs. *Sex Roles, 20,* 121–133.

Lugones, M., & Spelman, E. (1983). Have we got a theory for you! Feminist theory, cultural imperialism, and the demand for "the woman's voice." *Women's Studies International Forum, 6,* 573–581.

Lunneborg, P. W. (1990). *Women changing work.* Westport, CT: Greenwood.

Lyman, P. (1987). The fraternal bond as a joking relationship: A case of the role of sexist jokes in male group bonding. In M. S. Kimmel (Ed.), *Changing men: New directions in research on men and masculinity* (pp. 148–163). Newbury Park, CA: Sage.

Lynn, D. B. (1969). *Parental and sex role identification: A theoretical formulation.* Berkeley, CA: McCutchan.

Lytton, H., & Romney, D. M. (1991). Parents' differential socialization of boys and girls: A meta-analysis. *Psychological Bulletin, 109,* 267–296.

Maccoby, E. E. (1990). Gender and relationships: A developmental account. *American Psychologist, 45,* 513–520.

Maccoby, E. E. (1998). *The two sexes: Growing up apart, coming together.* Cambridge, MA: Harvard University Press, Belknap.

Maccoby, E. E., & Jacklin, C. N. (1974). *The psychology of sex differences.* Stanford, CA: Stanford University Press.

Maccoby, E. E., & Jacklin, C. N. (1987). Gender segregation in childhood. *Advances in Child Development and Behavior, 20,* 239–287.

MacDonald, P. (1998, August 14). Sugar and spice feminism. *Raleigh News and Observer,* pp. 1E, 3E.

Mace, N., & Ross, M. (2001). *In the company of men: A woman at the Citadel.* New York: Simon & Schuster.

MacKinnon, C. A. (1987). *Feminism unmodified: Discourses on life and law.* Cambridge, MA: Harvard University Press.

Mahlstedt, D. (1992). *Female survivors of dating violence and their social networks.* Working paper.

Major, B. (1980). Gender patterns in touching behavior. In C. Mayo & N. M. Henley (Eds.), *Gender and nonverbal behavior* (pp. 3–37). New York: Springer-Verlag.

Major, B., Schmidlin, A. M., & Williams, L. (1990). Gender patterns in social touch: The impact of setting and age. *Journal of Personality and Social Psychology, 58,* 634–643.

Malamuth, N. M., & Briere, J. (1986). Sexual violence in the media: Indirect effects on aggression against women. *Journal of Social Issues, 42,* 75–92.

Malandro, L. A., & Barker, L. L. (1983). *Nonverbal communication.* Reading, MA: Addison-Wesley.

Male hormone causes killer hyena cubs. (1991, May 4). *Raleigh News and Observer,* p. A3.

Malovich, N. J., & Stake, J. E. (1990). Sexual harassment on campus: Individual differences in attitudes and beliefs. *Psychology of Women Quarterly, 14,* 63–81.

Maltz, D. N., & Borker, R. (1982). A cultural approach to male–female miscommunication. In J. J. Gumpertz (Ed.), *Language and social identity* (pp. 196–216). Cambridge, England: Cambridge University Press.

Mann, J. (1989, March 15). The demeaning "mommy track." *Washington Post,* p. C3.

Mapstone, E. (1998). *War of words: Women and men argue.* London: Random House.

Maraniss, D. (1991, June 23). Blacks see quotas working for Whites. *Raleigh News and Observer,* p. B7.

Marble, M. (1994). Reconciling race and reality. *Media Studies Journal, 8,* 11–18.

Marcus, I. (1998). Violence against women. In W. Mankiller, G. Mink, M. Navarro, B. Smith, & G. Steinem (Eds.), *The reader's companion to U.S. women's history* (pp. 602–606). New York: Houghton Mifflin.

Marhoefer-Dvorak, S., Resick, P., Hutter, C., & Girelli, S. (1988). Single- versus multiple-incident rape victims: A comparison of psychological reactions to rape. *Journal of Interpersonal Violence, 3,* 145–160.

Marshall, C. (Ed.). (1996). *Feminist critical policy analysis: A perspective from primary and secondary schooling.* Washington, DC: Falmer.

Martin, C. (1991). The role of cognition in understanding gender effects. In H. Reese (Ed.), *Advances in child development and behavior, 23.* (pp. 110–142). San Diego: Academic.

Martin, C. (1994). Cognitive influences on the development and maintenance of gender segregation. In C. Leaper (Ed.), *New directions for child development* (pp. 87–116). San Francisco: Jossey-Bass.

Martin, C. (1997). *Gender cognitions and social relationships.* Paper presented at the meeting of the American Psychological Association, Chicago.

Martin, C. L. (1989). Children's use of gender-related information in making social judgments. *Developmental Psychology, 25,* 80–88.

Martin, P. Y., & Hummer, R. A. (1989). Fraternities and rape on campus. *Gender and Society, 3,* 457–473.

Martin, T., & Doka, K. (2000). *Men don't cry . . . women do: Transcending gender stereotypes of grief.* Philadelphia: University of Pennsylvania Press.

Martyna, W. (1978). What does "he" mean—use of the generic pronoun. *Journal of Communication, 28,* 131–138.

Maslin, J. (1990, June 17). Bimbos embody retro rage. *New York Times,* pp. H13, H14.

Masse, M. A., & Rosenblum, K. (1988). Male and female created they them: The depiction of gender in the advertising of traditional women's and men's magazines. *Women's Studies International Forum, 11,* 127–144.

Matthaei, J. (1998). Double day. In W. Mankiller, G. Mink, M. Navarro, B. Smith, & G. Steinem (Eds.), *The reader's companion to U.S. women's history* (p. 156). New York: Houghton Mifflin.

Maume, D. (2001). Work-family conflict: Effects for job segregation and career perceptions. In D. Vannoy (Ed.), *Gender mosaics* (pp. 240–248). Los Angeles: Roxbury.

May, L. (1998a). Many men still find strength in violence. *Chronicle of Higher Education,* p. B7.

May, L. (1998b). *Masculinity and morality.* Ithaca, NY: Cornell University Press.

Mazur, E. (1989). Predicting gender differences in same-sex friendships from affiliation motive and value. *Psychology of Women Quarterly, 13,* 277–291.

Mazur, E., & Olver, R. R. (1987). Intimacy and structure: Sex differences in imagery of same sex relationships. *Sex Roles, 16,* 533–558.

Mazzarella, S., & Pecora, N. (Eds.). (1999). *Growing up girls: Popular culture and the construction of identity.* New York: Peter Lang.

McDowell, A. (1998, Winter). Making it big. *Hues,* p. 8.

McFarlane, J., & Wilson, P. (2000). Intimate partner violence: A gender comparison. *Journal of Interpersonal Violence, 15,* 158–169.

McGowen, K. R., & Hart, L. E. (1990). Still different after all these years: Gender differences in professional identity formation. *Professional Psychology: Research and Practice, 21,* 118–223.

McHale, S. M., Bartko, W. T., Crouter, A. C., & Perry-Jenkins, M. (1990). Children's housework and psychosocial functioning: The mediating effects of parents' sex-role behaviors and attitudes. *Child Development, 61,* 1413–1426.

McMillan, T. (2001, May 28). Generation sex. *In These Times,* pp. 24–25.

Mead, G. H. (1934). *Mind, self, and society.* Chicago: University of Chicago Press.

Mead, M. (1935/1968). *Sex and temperament in three primitive societies.* New York: Dell.

Mechling, E., & Mechling, J. (1994). The Jung and the restless: The mythopoetic men's movement. *Southern Communication Journal, 59,* 97–111.

Meckler, L. (1996, May 2). Report supports Family Leave Act. *Raleigh News and Observer,* p. 5A.

Medved, M. (2000, May 15). Macho military makes comeback. *USA Today,* p. 23A.

Mehrabian, A. (1981). *Silent messages: Implicit communication of emotion and attitudes* (2nd ed.). Belmont, CA: Wadsworth.

Mellor, M. (1998). *Feminism and ecology.* New York: NYU Press.

Meloy, R. (1998). *The psychology of stalking: Clinical and forensic perspectives.* New York: Academic.

Men use half a brain to listen, study finds. (2000, November 29). *Raleigh News and Observer,* p. 8A.

Menopause. (1992, May 25). *Newsweek,* pp. 71–80.

Merritt, B. (2000). Illusive reflections: African American women on primetime television. In A. González, M. Houston, & V. Chen (Eds.), *Our voices* (pp. 47–53). Los Angeles: Roxbury.

Messner, M. (1997). *Politics of masculinities: Men in movements.* Thousand Oaks, CA: Sage.

Messner, M. (1998). Masculinities and athletic careers. In M. Anderson & P. Collins (Eds.), *Race, Class and Gender* (3rd ed.) (pp. 195–208). Belmont, CA: Wadsworth.

Messner, M. (2001). When bodies are weapons: Masculinity and violence in sports. In D. Vannoy (Ed.), *Gender mosaics* (pp. 94–105). Los Angeles: Roxbury.

Meyers, M. (1994). News of battering. *Journal of Communication, 44,* 47–62.

Meyers, M. (1997). *News coverage of violence against women: Engendering blame.* Thousand Oaks, CA: Sage.

Mickelson, A., & Smith, S. (1992). Education and the struggle against race, class, and gender inequality. In M. Andersen & P. H. Collins (Eds.), *Race, class, and gender: An anthology* (pp. 359–376). Belmont, CA: Wadsworth.

Mickelson, A. & Smith, S. (1998). Can education eliminate race, class, and gender equality? In M. Anderson & P. Collins (Eds.), *Race, Class, and Gender* (3rd ed.) (pp. 328–340). Belmont, CA: Wadsworth.

Middlebrook, D. (1998). *Suits me: The double life of Billy Tipton.* New York: Houghton Mifflin.

Mignon, S. (1998). Husband battering: A review of the debate over a controversial social phenomenon. In N. Jackson & G. Oates (Eds.), *Violence in intimate relationships* (pp. 137–154). Boston: Butterworth-Heinemann.

Milbank, D. (1997, October 3). More dads raise families without mom. *Wall Street Journal,* pp. B1, B2.

Miller, C. L. (1987). Qualitative differences among gender-stereotyped toys: Implications for cognitive and social development. *Sex Roles, 16,* 473–487.

Miller, J. B. (1986). *Toward a new psychology of women* (2nd ed.). Boston: Beacon.

Million Family March picks up where men's march ended 5 years before. (2000, October 14). *Raleigh News and Observer*, p. 6B.

Mills, C. J., & Bohannon, W. E. (1983). Personality, sex-role orientation, and psychological health in stereotypically masculine groups of males. *Sex Roles, 9,* 1161–1169.

Mills, J. (1985, February). Body language speaks louder than words. *Horizon*, pp. 8–12.

Mills, S. (1999). Discourse competence: Or how to theorize strong women. In C. Hendricks & K. Oliver (Eds.), *Language and liberation* (pp. 81–97). Albany, NY: State University of New York Press.

Mink, G. (1998). Title IX. In W. Mankiller, G. Mink, M. Navarro, B. Smith, & G. Steinem (Eds.), *The reader's companion to U.S. women's history* (pp. 593–594). New York: Houghton Mifflin.

Minnich, E. (1998). Education. In W. Mankiller, G. Mink, M. Navarro, B. Smith, & G. Steinem (Eds.), *The reader's companion to U.S. women's history* (pp. 163–167). New York: Houghton Mifflin.

Mintz, L. B., & Betz, N. E. (1986). Sex differences in the nature, realism, and correlates of body image. *Sex Roles, 15,* 185–195.

Mischel, W. (1966). A social learning view of sex differences in behavior. In E. E. Maccoby (Ed.), *The development of sex differences* (pp. 93–106). Stanford, CA: Stanford University Press.

Mishkind, M. E., Rodin, J., Silberstein, L. R., & Striegel-Moore, R. H. (1987). The embodiment of masculinity: Cultural, psychological, and behavioral dimensions. In M. S. Kimmel (Ed.), *Changing men: New directions in research on men and masculinity* (pp. 37–52). Newbury Park, CA: Sage.

Moberg, D. (2001, January 8). Bridging the gap. *In These Times*, pp. 24–26.

Moller, L., & Serbin, L. (1996). Antecedents of toddler gender segregation: Cognitive consonance, gender-typed toy preferences and behavioral compatibility. *Sex Roles, 35,* 445–460.

Molloy, B., & Herzberger, S. (1998). Body image and self-esteem: A comparison of African-American and Caucasian women. *Sex Roles, 38,* 631–643.

Mommy tracks. (1991, November 25). *Newsweek*, pp. 48–49.

Monaghan, P. (1998, March 6). Beyond the Hollywood myths: Researchers examine stalkers and their victims. *Chronicle of Higher Education*, pp. A17, A20.

Money, J. (1986). *Venuses penuses: Sexology, sexosophy, and exigency theory*. Buffalo, NY: Prometheus.

Money, J. (1988). *Gay, straight, and in-between: The sexology of erotic orientation*. New York: Oxford University Press.

Money, J., & Ehrhardt, A. (1972). *Man and woman: Boy and girl*. Baltimore: Johns Hopkins University Press.

Moniz, D., & Pardue, D. (1996, June 23). Uncounted casualties. *Raleigh News and Observer*, pp. 21A, 22A.

Monsour, M. (1992). Meanings of intimacy in cross- and same-sex friendships. *Journal of Social and Personal Relationships, 9,* 277–295.

Morgan, M. (1973). *The total woman*. New York: Pocket.

Morgan, M. (1987). Television, sex-role attitudes, and sex-role behavior. *Journal of Early Adolescence, 7,* 269–282.

Morin, R., & Rosenfeld, M. (1998, April 19). Men and women: What still divides us? *Raleigh News and Observer*, pp. 23A, 24A.

Morrison, A. M., & Von Glinow, M. A. (1990). Women and minorities in management. *American Psychologist, 45,* 200–208.

Morrow, F. (1990). *Unleashing our unknown selves: An inquiry into the future of femininity and masculinity*. Westport, CT: Praeger.

Muehlenhard, C. L., & Falcon, P. L. (1990). Men's heterosocial skill and attitudes toward women as predictors of verbal sexual coercion and forceful rape. *Sex Roles, 23,* 241–259.

Mulac, A. (1998). The gender-linked language effect: Do language differences really make a difference? In D. J. Canary & K. Dindia (Eds.), *Sex differences and similarities in communication: Critical essays and empirical investigations of sex and gender in interaction* (pp. 127–153). Mahwah, NJ: Erlbaum.

Mulac, A., Wiemann, J. M., Widenmann, S. J., & Gibson, T. W. (1988). Male/female language differences and effects in same-sex and mixed-sex dyads: The gender-linked language effect. *Communication Monographs, 55,* 315–335.

Mullen, P., & Pathé, M. (2000). *Stalkers and victims*. MA: Cambridge University Press.

Murphy, B., & Zorn, T. (1996). Gendered interaction in professional relationships. In J. T. Wood (Ed.), *Gendered relationships: A reader* (pp. 213–232). Mountain View, CA: Mayfield.

Murphy-Milano, S. (1996). *Defending our lives*. New York: Anchor/Doubleday.

Murrell, A. J., Frieze, I. H., & Frost, J. L. (1991). Aspiring to careers in male- and female-dominated professions. A study of Black and White college women. *Psychology of Women Quarterly, 15,* 103–126.

Musician's death at 74 reveals he was a woman. (1989, February 2). *New York Times*.

Myers, P. N., & Biocca, F. A. (1992). The elastic body image: The effect of television advertising on body image distortion in young women. *Journal of Communication, 3,* 108–133.

Nadesan, M., & Trethewey, A. (2000). Performing the enterprising subject: Gendered strategies of success. *Text and Performance Quarterly, 20,* 223–250.

Natalle, E. (1996). Gendered issues in the workplace. In J. T. Wood (Ed.), *Gendered relationships: A reader* (pp. 253–274). Mountain View, CA: Mayfield.

National Coalition Against Domestic Violence. (1999, July 10). http:www.ncadv.org.

National Public Radio. (1992, July 23). Untitled report on parental responses to children.

Navarro, M. (1998, Winter). Fashion a la mode. *Hues,* p. 9.

Nearly half of teen girls trying to diet, survey says. (1991, November 11). *Morning Call,* p. A7.

Nelson, E. (1996, March 18). Why Johnny can't empathize: No girls in his class? *Wall Street Journal,* pp. B1, B6.

Nelson, M. B. (1994a, June 23). Violence from the locker room. *Raleigh News and Observer,* p. A13.

Nelson, M. B. (1994b). *The stronger women get, the more men love football: Sexism and the American culture of sports.* New York: Harcourt Brace.

Nesbitt, P., Baust, J., & Bailey, E. (2001). Women's status in the Christian church. In D. Vannoy (Ed.), *Gender mosaics* (pp. 386–396). Los Angeles: Roxbury.

Newburger, E. (1999). *The men they will become: The nature and nurture of male character.* Cambridge, MA: Perseus Books.

A new court decision. (1992, September). *The Newsletter,* p. 5.

The new traditionalist. (1988, November 17). *New York Times,* p. Y46.

Nichter, M. (2000). *Fat talk: What girls and their parents say about dieting.* Cambridge, MA: Harvard University Press.

Nicotera, A. M., & Cushman, D. P. (1992). Organizational ethics: A within-organization view. *Journal of Applied Communication, 4,* 437–462.

Nigro, G. N., Hill, D. E., Gelbein, M. E., & Clark, C. L. (1988). Changes in the facial prominence of women and men over the last decade. *Psychology of Women Quarterly, 12,* 225–235.

Nikken, P., & Peeters, A. L. (1988). Children's perceptions of television reality. *Journal of Broadcasting and Electronic Media, 32,* 441–452.

No sexism please, we're *Webster's.* (1991, June 24). *Newsweek,* p. 59.

Noble, B. P. (1993, January 2). Bias up against pregnant workers. *Raleigh News and Observer,* pp. A1, A8.

Noddings, N. (2002). *Starting at home: Caring and social policy.* Berkeley: University of California Press.

Noller, P. (1986). Sex differences in nonverbal communication: Advantage lost or supremacy regained? *Australian Journal of Psychology, 38,* 23–32.

Northrup, C. (1995). *Women's bodies, women's wisdom.* New York: Bantam.

Nussbaum, J. F. (1992). Effective teacher behaviors. *Communication Education, 41,* 167–180.

Nussbaum, M. (1992, October 18). Justice for women! *New York Review of Books,* pp. 43–48.

O'Connell, L. (1995, April 21). Internal, external: Women and men handle stress differently. *Raleigh News and Observer,* p. D5.

O'Connor, J. J. (1989, June 6). What are commercials selling to children? *New York Times,* p. 28.

O'Kelly, C. G., & Carney, L. S. (1986). *Women and men in society* (2nd ed.). Belmont, CA: Wadsworth.

Okin, S. M. (1989). *Justice, gender, and the family.* New York: Basic.

O'Leary, V. E., & Ickovics, J. R. (1991). Cracking the glass ceiling. Overcoming isolation and alienation. In U. Sekeran & F. Long (Eds.), *Pathways to excellence: New patterns for human utilization.* Beverly Hills: Sage.

Olien, M. (1978). *The human myth.* New York: Harper & Row.

Oliker, S. (1989). *Best friends and marriage: Exchange among women.* Berkeley: University of California Press.

Oliker, S. (2001). Gender and friendship. In D. Vannoy (Ed.), *Gender mosaics* (pp. 195–204). Los Angeles: Roxbury.

O'Meara, J. D. (1989). Cross-sex friendship: Four basic challenges of an ignored relationship. *Sex Roles, 21,* 525–543.

Orenstein, P. (2000). *Flux: Women on sex, work, love, kids and life in a half-changed world.* New York: Doubleday.

Orion, D. (1997). *I know you really love me: A psychiatrist's journal of erotomania, stalking, and obsessive love.* New York: Macmillan.

Orr, C. (1997). Charting the currents of the third wave. *Hypatia, 12,* 29–46.

Otten, A. L. (1995, January 27). Women and men still see things differently. *Wall Street Journal,* p. B1.

Paetzold, R., & O'Leary-Kelly, A. (1993). The legal context of sexual harassment. In G. L. Kreps (Ed.), *Sexual harassment: Communication implications* (pp. 63–77). Cresskill, NJ: Hampton.

Painter, N. (1996). *Sojourner Truth: A life, a symbol.* New York: Norton.

Palm, G. (1993). Involved fatherhood: A second chance. *Journal of Men's Studies, 2,* 139–155.

Palmer, H. T., & Lee, J. A. (1990). Female workers' acceptance in traditionally male-dominated blue-collar jobs. *Sex Roles, 22,* 607–625.

Panee, B. (1994). *Defending the "date-rape crisis": A critical discussion of Katie Roiphe's The mor-*

ing after: Sex, fear, and feminism on campus. Paper submitted in Communication Studies 111, Chapel Hill, University of North Carolina.

Paradise, L. V., & Wall, S. M. (1986). Children's perceptions of male and female principals and teachers. *Sex Roles, 14,* 1–7.

Parlee, M. B. (1973). The premenstrual syndrome. *Psychological Bulletin, 80,* 454–465.

Parlee, M. B. (1979, May). Conversational politics. *Psychology Today,* pp. 48–56.

Parlee, M. B. (1987). Media treatment of premenstrual syndrome. In B. E. Ginsburg & B. F. Carter (Eds.), *Premenstrual syndrome.* New York: Plenum.

Paul, E., & White, K. (1990). The development of intimate relationships in late adolescence. *Adolescence, 25,* 375–400.

Pearson, J. C. (1985). *Gender and communication.* Dubuque, IA: William C. Brown.

Pearson, J., West, R., & Turner, Ly. (1995). *Gender and communication* (3rd ed). Dubuque, IA: Brown and Benchmark.

Peirce, K. (1990). A feminist theoretical perspective on the socialization of teenage girls through *Seventeen* magazine. *Sex Roles, 23,* 491–500.

Pendergast, T. (2000). *Creating the modern man: American magazines and consumer culture, 1900–1950.* University of Missouri Press.

Pereira, J. (1994, September 23). Oh, boy! In toyland, you get more if you're male. *Wall Street Journal,* pp. B1, B3.

Peterson, C. D., Baucom, D. H., Elliott, M. J., & Farr, P. A. (1989). The relationship between sex role identity and marital adjustment. *Sex Roles, 21,* 775–787.

Peterson, S. B., & Kroner, T. (1992). Gender biases in textbooks for introductory psychology and human development. *Psychology of Women Quarterly, 16,* 17–36.

Phillips, G. M., Gouran, D. S., Kuehn, S. A., & Wood, J. T. (1993). *Professionalism: A survival guide for beginning academics.* Cresskill, NJ: Hampton.

Piaget, J. (1932/1965). *The moral judgment of the child.* New York: Free Press.

Pinsky, L., Erickson, R., & Schimke, R. (Eds.). (1999). *Genetic disorders of human sexual development.* New York: Oxford University Press.

Pitts, L., Jr. (1993, June 30). Music's new wave of sexism is especially discordant. *Miami Herald,* pp. 1E, 7E.

Pleck, E. (1987). *Domestic tyranny: The making of American social policy against family violence from colonial times to the present.* New York: Oxford University Press.

Pleck, J. H. (1981). *The myth of masculinity.* Cambridge, MA: MIT Press.

Pleck, J. H., & Sawyer, J. (Eds.). (1974). *Men and masculinity.* Englewood Cliffs, NJ: Prentice-Hall.

Polit, D., & LaFrance, M. (1977). Sex differences in reaction to spatial invasion. *Journal of Social Psychology, 102,* 59–60.

Pollack, W. (1990). Sexual harassment: Women's experience vs. legal definitions. *Harvard Women's Law Review, 13,* 35–85.

Pollack, W. (2000). *Real boys: Rescuing ourselves from the myths of boyhood.* New York: Owl Books.

Pollitt, K. (1994). *Reasonable creatures: Essays on women and feminism.* New York: Knopf.

Pollitt, K. (1996, May 13). Women's rights, human rights. *Progressive,* p. 9.

Pollitt, K. (1999, March 29). Women's rights: As the world turns. *The Nation,* p. 9.

Pollitt, K. (2000, May 1). Abortion history 101. *The Nation,* p. 8.

Pomerleau, A., Bolduc, D., Malcuit, G., & Cossette, L. (1990). Pink or blue: Environmental stereotypes in the first two years of life. *Sex Roles, 22,* 359–367.

Popenoe, D. (1996). *Life without father.* New York: Free Press.

Poppen, P. J., & Segal, N. J. (1988). The influence of sex and sex role orientation on sexual coercion. *Sex Roles, 19,* 689–701.

Posavac, H., Posavac, S., & Posavac, E. (1998). Exposure to media images of female attractiveness and concern with body weight among young people. *Sex Roles, 38,* 187–201.

Promise Keepers: "Men have dropped the ball." (1997, October 1). *USA Today,* p. 14A.

Public Agenda Foundation. (1990). *Remedies for racial inequality: Why progress has stalled, what should be done.* Dubuque, IA: Kendall/Hunt.

Puka, B. (1990). The liberation of caring: A different voice for Gilligan's different voice. *Hypatia, 5,* 59–82.

Purcell, P., & Stewart, L. (1990). Dick and Jane in 1989. *Sex Roles, 22,* 177–185.

Quindlen, A. (1994, March 20). The unending nightmare of violence against women. *Raleigh News and Observer,* p. A23.

Quinn, J. (2000, July 17). Revisiting the mommy track. *Newsweek,* p. 44.

Rabidue v. Osceola Refining Company. 805F 2nd 611, 626 Cir (6th Cir 1986).

Ragsdale, D. (1996). Gender, satisfaction level, and the use of relational maintenance strategies in marriage. *Communication Monographs, 63,* 354–369.

Rakow, L. F. (1992). "Don't hate me because I'm beautiful": Feminist resistance in advertising's irresistible meanings. *Southern Communication Journal, 57,* 132–141.

Ransom, F. (1993, December 23). Black women man the ramparts for war on "gangsta rap" sexism. *Raleigh News and Observer,* p. A6.

Ransom, L. (1997, June 29). Title IX is more than athletics. *Cincinnati Enquirer,* p. D1.

Raphael, R. (1988). *The men from the boys: Rites*

of passage in male America. Lincoln: University of Nebraska Press.

Rapoport, R., Bailyn, L., Kolb, D., & Fletcher, J. (1998). Relinking life and work: Toward a better future. *Innovations in Management Series.* Waltham, MA: Pegasus.

Rapping, E. (1994, May). Women are from Venus, men are from Mars. *Progressive,* pp. 40–42.

Rasmussen, J. L., & Moley, B. E. (1986). Impression formation as a function of the sex role appropriateness of linguistic behavior. *Sex Roles, 14,* 149–161.

Raspberry, W. (1990, December 13). Affirmative action is call for fairness. *Raleigh News and Observer,* p. A11.

Real, T. (1997). *I don't want to talk about it: Overcoming the secret legacy of male depression.* New York: Scribner's.

Reeder, H. (1996). A critical look at gender differences in communication research. *Communication Studies, 47,* 318–330.

Reis, H. T. (1998). Gender differences in intimacy and related behaviors: Context and process. In D. Canary & K. Dindia (Eds.), *Sex differences and similarities in communication* (pp. 203–232). Mahwah, NJ: Erlbaum.

Reis, H. T., Senchak, M., & Soloman, B. (1985). Sex differences in the intimacy of social interaction: Further examination of potential explanations. *Journal of Personality and Social Psychology, 48,* 1204–1217.

Reisberg, L. (1999, November 5). Violence-studies program takes aim at social evils and student attitudes. *Chronicle of Higher Education,* A60–A61.

Reisman, J. M. (1990). Intimacy in same-sex friendships. *Sex Roles, 23,* 65–82.

Reiss, D. (2000). *The relational code: Genetic and social influences on social development.* Cambridge, MA: Harvard University Press.

Researcher: Male students get more for their money in college. (1990, April 29). *Durham Morning Herald,* p. A10.

Reuther, R. (2001). Ecofeminism and healing ourselves, healing the earth. In D. Vannoy (Ed.), *Gender mosaics* (pp. 406–414). Los Angeles: Roxbury.

Reuther, R. R. (Ed.). (1974). *Religion and sexism: Images of woman in the Jewish and Christian traditions.* New York: Simon & Schuster.

Reuther, R. R. (1975). *New woman/new earth: Sexist ideologies and human liberation.* New York: Seabury.

Reuther, R. R. (1983). *Sexism and God-talk: Toward a feminist theology.* Boston: Beacon.

Rhodes, J. (1995). Television's realist portrayal of African-American women and the case of *L. A. Law.* In G. Dines & J. Humez (Eds.), *Gender, race, and class in media: A text reader* (pp. 424–429). Thousand Oaks, CA: Sage.

Rice, J. K., & Hemmings, A. (1988). Women's colleges and women achievers: An update. *Signs: Journal of Women in Culture and Society, 13,* 546–559.

Rich, A. (1979). *On lies, secrets and silences: Selected prose, 1966–1978.* New York: Norton.

Richissin, T. (1997, October 26). When "tough it out" backfires. *Raleigh News and Observer,* pp. 1A, 12A.

Rideau, W., & Sinclair, B. (1982). Prison: The sexual jungle. In A. Scacco, Jr. (Ed.), *Male rape* (pp. 3–29). New York: AMS Press.

Riechmann, D. (1996, February 22). Single-sex classes get a star for achievement. *Raleigh News and Observer,* p. 8A.

Riessman, C. K. (1990). *Divorce talk: Women and men make sense of personal relationships.* New Brunswick, NJ: Rutgers University Press.

Risman, B., & Godwin, S. (2001). Twentieth-century changes in economic work and family. In D. Vannoy (Ed.), *Gender mosaics* (pp. 134–144). Los Angeles: Roxbury.

Risman, B. J. (1989). Can men mother? Life as a single father. In B. J. Risman & P. Schwartz (Eds.), *Gender in intimate relationships* (pp. 155–164). Belmont, CA: Wadsworth.

Roberts, B. (1993). No safe place: The war against women. *Our Generation, 15,* 7–26.

Rodin, J., Silberstein, L., & Striegel-Moore, R. H. (1985). Women and weight: A normative discontent. In T. B. Sonderegger (Ed.), *Nebraska symposium on motivation 1984: Psychology and gender* (Vol. 32, pp. 267–307). Lincoln: University of Nebraska Press.

Roe, M. (1997, June 29). Female athletes not going away. *Cincinnati Enquirer,* p. D1.

Roe v. Wade at twenty-five. (1998, February). *The Progressive,* pp. 8–9.

Rogers, M. (1999). *Barbie culture.* Thousand Oaks, CA: Sage.

Rohlfing, M. (1995). "Doesn't anybody stay in one place anymore?" An exploration of the understudied phenomenon of long-distance relationships. In J. T. Wood & S. W. Duck (Eds.), *Understanding personal relationships, 6: Understudied relationships: Off the beaten track* (pp. 173–196). Thousand Oaks, CA: Sage.

Roiphe, K. (1993). *The morning after: Sex, fear, and feminism on campus.* Boston: Little, Brown.

Root, M. P. P. (1990). Disordered eating in women of color. *Sex Roles, 22,* 525–536.

Rose, S., & Frieze, I. H. (1989). Young singles' scripts for a first date. *Gender and Society, 3,* 258–268.

Rosen, R. (2001). *The world split open: How the modern women's movement changed America.* New York: Viking.

Rosener, J. (1990, November/December). Ways women lead. *Harvard Business Review,* pp. 119–125.

Rosenfeld, M. (2001, January 9). Sugar and spice and POW! *Raleigh News and Observer,* pp. 1E, 3E.

Rosengrant, T. J., & McCroskey, J. C. (1975). The effect of race and sex on proxemic behavior in an interview setting. *Southern Speech Communication Journal, 40,* 408–420.

Rosenthal, R., & DePaulo, B. M. (1979). Sex differences in eavesdropping on nonverbal cues. *Journal of Personality and Social Psychology, 37,* 273–285.

Rosenwasser, S. M., Lingenfelter, M., & Harrington, A. F. (1989). Nontraditional gender role portrayals on television and children's gender role perceptions. *Journal of Applied Developmental Psychology, 10,* 97–105.

Ross, S. I., & Jackson, J. M. (1991). Teachers' expectations for Black males' and Black females' academic achievement. *Personality and Social Psychology Bulletin, 17,* 78–82.

Roth, M. (1994). *Mother journey.* New York: Spinster's Ink.

Rothberg, P., Schafhausen, N., & Schneider, C. (Eds.). (2000). *Race, class and gender in the United States: An integrated study.* New York: Worth Publishing.

Rowe, M. (1990). Barriers to equality: The power of subtle discrimination to maintain unequal opportunity. *Employee Responsibilities and Rights Journal, 3,* 153–163.

Rubin, B. M. (1994, April 17). The daddy track. *Raleigh News and Observer,* p. A17.

Rubin, J. Z., Provenzano, F. J., & Luria, Z. (1974). The eye of the beholder: Parents' views on sex of newborns. *American Journal of Orthopsychiatry, 44,* 512–519.

Rubin, L. (1985). *Just friends: The role of friendship in our lives.* New York: Harper & Row.

Rubin, L. B. (1983). *Intimate strangers: Men and women together.* New York: Harper & Row.

Ruble, D., & Martin, C. (1998). Gender development. In W. Damon (Ed.), *The handbook of child psychology* (pp. 933–1017). New York: Wiley.

Ruddick, S. (1989). *Maternal thinking: Toward a politics of peace.* Boston: Beacon.

Rundblad, G. (2001). Gender, power, and sexual harassment. In D. Vannoy (Ed.), *Gender mosaics* (pp. 352-362). Los Angeles: Roxbury.

Rusbult, C. (1987). Responses to dissatisfaction in close relationships: The exit-voice-loyalty-neglect model. In D. Perlman & S. W. Duck (Eds.), *Intimate relationships: Development, dynamics, and deterioration* (pp. 209–238). London: Sage.

Russell, D. E. H. (Ed.). (1993). *Feminist views on pornography.* Cholchester, VT: Teachers College Press.

Ryan, M. (1979). *Womanhood in America: From colonial times to the present* (2nd ed.). New York: New Viewpoints.

Sadker, M., & Sadker, D. (1984). *The report card on sex bias.* Washington, DC: Mid-Atlantic Center for Sex Equity.

Sadker, M., & Sadker, D. (1986, March). Sexism in the classroom: From grade school to graduate school. *Phi Delta Kappan,* pp. 512–515.

Sadker, M., & Sadker, D. (1994). *Failing at fairness: How America's schools cheat girls.* New York: Simon & Schuster.

Safilios-Rothschild, C. (1979). Sex role socialization and sex discrimination: A synthesis and critique of the literature. Washington, DC: National Institute of Education.

Sagan, C., & Druyan, A. (1992). *Shadows of forgotten ancestors.* New York: Random House.

Sagrestano, L., Heavey, C., & Christensen, A. (1998). Theoretical approaches to understanding sex differences and similarities in conflict behavior. In D. J. Canary & K. Dindia (Eds.), *Sex differences and similarities in communication: Critical essays and empirical investigations of sex and gender in interaction* (pp. 287–302). Mahwah, NJ: Erlbaum.

Sales, K. (1987, September 26). Ecofeminism—a new perspective. *The Nation,* pp. 302–305.

Sallinen-Kuparinen, A. (1992). Teacher communicator style. *Communication Education, 41,* 153–166.

Salomone, R. (1986). *Equality of education under the law.* New York: St. Martin's.

Samovar, L., Porter, R., & Stefani, L. (1998). *Communication between cultures* (2nd ed). Belmont, CA: Wadsworth.

Samuels, A. (1997, November 24). Black beauty's new face. *Newsweek,* p. 68.

Samuelson, R. (1996, April 8). Why men need family values. *Newsweek,* p. 43.

Sanday, P. R. (1986). Rape and the silencing of the feminine. In S. Tomaselli & R. Porter (Eds.), *Rape* (pp. 84–101). Oxford, England: Basil Blackwell.

Sanders, M., & Rock, M. (1988). *Waiting for prime time: The women of television news.* Urbana: University of Illinois Press.

Sandler, B. (1996, June 27). Letter to the editor. *Wall Street Journal,* p. A19.

Sandler, B. R., & Hall, R. M. (1986). *The campus climate revisited: Chilly for women faculty, administrators, and graduate students.* Washington, DC: Association of American Colleges, Project on the Status and Education of Women.

Sandler, B. R., Silverberg, L. A., & Hall, R. M. (1996). *The chilly classroom climate: A guide to improve the education of women.* Washington, DC: National Association for Women in Education.

Sanger, M. (1914, June). *Suppression. The woman rebel,* p. 1.

Sartre, J. P. (1966). *Being and nothingness: An essay in phenomenological ontology.* New York: Citadel.

Saunders, B. (2001, March 24). The stomach grumbles at equal-opportunity eating ills. *Raleigh News and Observer,* p. 17A.

Saurer, M. K., & Eisler, R. M. (1990). The role of

masculine gender roles' stress in expressivity and social support network factors. *Sex Roles, 23*, 261–271.

Scarf, M. (1987). *Intimate partners.* New York: Random House.

Schaef, A. W. (1981). *Women's reality.* St. Paul, MN: Winston.

Schechter, S. (1982). *Women and male violence: The visions and the struggles of the battered women's movement.* Boston: South End.

Schellhardt, T. (1997, March 31). Dropping out. *Wall Street Journal,* p. 12.

Scheper-Hughes, N. (1994). *Death without weeping.* Berkeley: University of California Press.

Scheuble, L., & Johnson, D. R. (1993). Marital name change: Plans and attitudes of college students. *Journal of Marriage and the Family, 55*, 747–754.

Schmetzer, U. (1997, August 13). From abused wife to India's avenging angel. *Raleigh News and Observer,* p. 13A.

Schmidt, P. (1998, October 30). U. of Michigan prepares to defend admissions policy in court. *Chronicle of Higher Education,* pp. A32–A34.

Schmidt, P. (2001, May 18). Debating the benefits of affirmative action. *Chronicle of Higher Education,* pp. A25–A26.

Schmitt, E. (2001, May 15). For first time, nuclear families drop below 25% of households. *New York Times,* p. A1.

Schneider, B. E., & Gould, M. (1987). Female sexuality: Looking back into the future. In B. B. Hess and M. M. Ferree (Eds.), *Analyzing gender: A handbook of social science research* (pp. 120–153). Newbury Park, CA: Sage.

Schneider, J., & Hacker, S. (1973). Sex role imagery and use of the generic "man" in introductory texts: A case in the sociology of sociology. *American Sociologist, 8*, 12–18.

Schoemer, K. (1998, January 5). The selling of girl power. *Newsweek,* p. 90.

Schroedel, J. R. (1990). Blue-collar women: Paying the price at home and on the job. In H. Y. Grossman & N. L. Chester (Eds.), *The experience and meaning of work in women's lives* (pp. 241–260). Hillsdale, NJ: Erlbaum.

Schroeder, L. O. (1986). A rose by any other name: Post-marital right to use maiden name: 1934–1982. *Sociology and Social Research, 70*, 290–293.

Schrof, J. M. (1994, April 11). A sporting chance? *U.S. News and World Report,* pp. 51–53.

Schwalbe, M. (1996). *Unlocking the cage: The men's movement, gender, politics, and American culture.* Cambridge, MA: Oxford University Press.

Schwartz, B., & Cellini, H. (1995). Female sex offenders. In B. Schwartz & H. Cellini (Eds.), *The sex offender: Corrections, treatment, and legal practice* (Vol. 1, pp. 5-1–5-22). Kingston, NJ: Civic Research Institute.

Schwartz, F. (1989, January/February). Management women and the new facts of life. *Harvard Business Review,* pp. 65–76.

Schwartz, P. (1994). *Peer marriage: How love between equals really works.* New York: Free Press.

Schwartz, P., & Rutter, V. (1998). *The gender of sexuality.* Newbury Park, CA: Pine Forge.

Schwichtenberg, C. (1989). The "mother-lode" of feminist research: Congruent paradigms in the analysis of beauty culture. In B. Dervin, L. Grossberg, B. J. O'Keefe, & E. Wartella (Eds.), *Rethinking communication* (Vol. 2, pp. 291–306). Beverly Hills: Sage.

Schwichtenberg, C. (1992). Madonna's postmodern feminism: Bringing the margins to center. *Southern Communication Journal, 57*, 120–131.

Scott, R., & Tetreault, L. (1987). Attitudes of rapists and other violent offenders toward women. *Journal of Social Psychology, 124*, 375–380.

Scully, D. (1990). *Understanding sexual violence: A study of convicted rapists.* Boston: Unwin Hyman.

Secunda, V. (1992). *Women and their fathers.* New York: Delta.

Sedney, M. A. (1987). Development of androgyny: Parental influences. *Psychology of Women Quarterly, 11*, 311–326.

Segal, A. T., with Zellner, W. (1992, June 8). Corporate women: Progress? Sure. But the playing field is still far from level. *Business Week,* pp. 74–78.

Segel-Evans, K. (1987). Rape prevention and masculinity. In F. Abbott (Ed.), *New men, new minds: Breaking male tradition* (pp. 117–121). Freedom, CA: Crossing.

Segerstråle, U. (2000). *Defenders of the truth: The battle for science in the sociobiology debate and beyond.* UK: Oxford University Press.

Seiter, E. (1995). Different children, different dreams. In G. Dines & J. Humez (Eds.), *Gender, race and class in media* (pp. 99–108). Thousand Oaks, CA: Sage.

Seligmann, J. (1994, May 2). The pressure to lose. *Newsweek,* pp. 60–61.

Seligmann, J., Joseph, N., Donovan, J. B., & Gosnell, M. (1987, July 27). The littlest dieters. *Newsweek,* p. 48.

Sen, A. (1990, December 20). More than 100 million women are missing. *New York Review of Books,* pp. 7–11.

Seplow, S. (1996, January 19). "Old boy" networks fall. *Raleigh News and Observer,* pp. 1D, 5D.

Sexism in the schoolhouse. (1992, February 24). *Newsweek,* p. 62.

Sexually harassed male guard awarded $3.75 million. (1999, May 30). *Raleigh News and Observer,* p. 9A.

Shalit, W. (1999). *A return to modesty: Discovering the lost virtue.* New York: Free Press.

Shandler, S. (1999). *Ophelia speaks: Adolescent girls write about their search for self.* New York: Harper Perennial.

Shapiro, J., & Kroeger, L. (1991). Is life just a romantic novel? The relationship between attitudes about intimate relationships and the popular media. *American Journal of Family Therapy, 19,* 226–236.

Shapiro, L. (1990, May 28). Guns and dolls. *Newsweek,* pp. 56–65.

Sharkey, B. (1993, February). You've come a long way, Madison Avenue. *Lear's,* p. 94.

Sharpe, R. (1994, January 31). Education of girls trails that of boys in many countries. *Wall Street Journal,* p. B5.

Shea, C. (1998, January 30). Why depression strikes more women than men: "Ruminative coping" may provide answers. *Chronicle of Higher Education,* p. A14.

Sheehan, R. (1999, February 28). Mom's working doesn't harm child, study finds. *Raleigh News and Observer,* pp. 1A, 12A.

Sheldon, A. (1990, January). "Kings are royaler than queens": Language and socialization. *Young Children,* pp. 4–9.

Shellenbarger, S. (1993, December 17). More dads take off to look after baby. *Wall Street Journal,* p. B1.

Shellenbarger, S. (1995, May 11). Women indicate satisfaction with role of big breadwinner. *Wall Street Journal,* p. B1.

Shellenbarger, S. (1997, April 30). These top bosses may signal move to more family time. *Wall Street Journal,* p. B1.

Sherman, M. A., & Haas, A. (1984, June). Man to man, woman to woman. *Psychology Today,* pp. 72–73.

Sherrod, D. (1989). The influence of gender on same-sex friendships. In C. Hendrick (Ed.), *Close relationships* (pp. 164–186). Newbury Park, CA: Sage.

She's a woman, offer her less. (2001, May 7). *Business Week,* p. 12.

Shimron, Y. (1997, January 22). Men unite to live their faith. *Raleigh News and Observer,* pp. 1A, 6A.

Shoop, R. J., & Edwards, D. L. (1993). *How to stop sexual harassment in our schools.* Boston: Allyn & Bacon.

Siever, M. D. (1988, August). *Sexual orientation, gender, and the perils of sexual objectification.* Paper presented at the American Psychological Association, Atlanta.

Silverstein, B., Perdue, L., Peterson, B., & Kelly, E. (1986). The role of the mass media in promoting a thin standard of bodily attractiveness for women. *Sex Roles, 14,* 519–532.

Silverstein, L., Auerbach, C., Grieco, L., & Dunkel, F. (1999). Do Promise Keepers dream of feminist sheep? *Sex Roles, 40,* 665–688.

Simon, R. J., & Danziger, G. (1991). *Women's movements in America: Their successes, disappointments, and aspirations.* Westport, CT: Praeger.

Simonton, A. F. (1995). Women for sale. In C. Lont (Ed.), *Women and media: Content, careers, criticism* (pp. 143–177). Belmont, CA: Wadsworth.

Slack, A. (1988). Female circumcision: A critical appraisal. *Human Rights Quarterly, 10,* 432–446.

Smith, B. (1998). Black feminism. In W. Mankiller, G. Mink, M. Navarro, B. Smith, & G. Steinem (Eds.), *The reader's companion to U.S. women's history* (pp. 202–204). New York: Houghton Mifflin.

Smith, J. E., Waldorf, V. A., & Trembath, D. L. (1990). "Single White male looking for thin, very attractive . . ." *Sex Roles, 23,* 675–685.

Smith, L. (1995, March 21). How do fathers nurture? *Raleigh News and Observer,* p. E1.

Smith, N. (1998). Guerrilla girls. In W. Mankiller, G. Mink, M. Navarro, B. Smith, & G. Steinem (Eds.), *The reader's companion to U.S. women's history* (p. 250). New York: Houghton Mifflin.

Smith, V. (1998). *Not just race, not just gender: Black feminist readings.* New York: Routledge.

Snarey, J. (1994). *How fathers care for the next generation.* Cambridge, MA: Harvard University Press.

Snell, W. E., Jr., Hawkins, R. C., II, & Belk, S. S. (1988). Stereotypes about male sexuality and the use of social influence strategies in intimate relationships. *Journal of Clinical and Social Psychology, 7,* 42–48.

Sollie, D. L., & Fischer, J. L. (1985). Sex-role orientation, intimacy of topic, and target person differences in self-disclosure among women. *Sex Roles, 12,* 917–929.

Sommers, C. (2000). *The war against boys: How misguided feminism is harming our young men.* New York: Simon & Schuster.

Soroka v. Dayton Hudson Corporation, No. A052157. (1991, October 25). Calif. C. Apps.

South, S. J., & Felson, R. B. (1990). The racial patterning of rape. *Social Forces, 69,* 71–93.

Spade, J. (2001). Gender and education in the United States. In D. Vannoy (Ed.), *Gender mosaics* (pp. 85–93). Los Angeles: Roxbury.

Spain, D. (1992). *Gendered spaces.* Chapel Hill: University of North Carolina Press.

Spayde, J. (1998, September/October). Indefinable heroes. *Utne Reader,* pp. 52–55.

Spelman, E. V. (1988). *Inessential woman: Problems of exclusion in feminist thought.* Boston: Beacon.

Spender, D. (1984a). *Man made language.* London: Routledge and Kegan Paul.

Spender, D. (1984b). Defining reality: A powerful tool. In C. Kramarae, M. Schultz, & W. O'Barr (Eds.), *Language and power* (pp. 195–205). Beverly Hills: Sage.

Spender, D. (1989). *Invisible women: The schooling scandal.* London: Women's Press.

Spitz, R. (1952). Authority and masturbation. *Psychoanalytic Quarterly, 21,* 38–52.

Spitzack, C. (1990). *Confessing excess.* Albany: SUNY Press.

Spitzack, C. (1993). The spectacle of anorexia nervosa. *Text and Performance Quarterly, 13,* 1–21.

Spitzack, C., & Carter, K. (1987). Women in communication studies: A typology for revision. *Quarterly Journal of Speech, 73,* 401–423.

Spitzberg, B. (1998). Sexual coercion in courtship relations. In B. Spitzberg & W. Cupach (Eds.), *The dark side of close relationships* (pp. 179–232). Mahwah, NJ: Erlbaum.

Spitzberg, B., Nicastro, A., & Cousins, A. (1998). Exploring the interactional phenomenon of stalking and obsessive relational intrusion. *Communication Reports, 11,* 33–47.

Stacey, J. (1990). *Brave new families: Stories of domestic upheaval in late twentieth-century America.* New York: Basic.

Stacey, J. (1996). *In the name of the father: Rethinking family values in a postmodern age.* Boston: Beacon.

Stafford, L., Dutton, M., & Haas, S. (2000). Measuring routine maintenance: Scale revision, sex versus gender roles, and the prediction of relational characteristics. *Communication Monographs, 67,* 306–323.

Stafford, L., & Kline, S. (1996). Women's surnames and titles: Men's and women's views. *Communication Research Reports, 13,* 214–224.

Stamp, G., & Sabourin, T. (1995). Accounting for violence: An analysis of males' spousal abuse narratives. *Journal of Applied Communication Research, 23,* 284–307.

Stancill, J. (1999, April 17). In triangle, women rise to the top of higher-learning realm. *Raleigh News and Observer,* pp. 1A, 15A.

Stanley, J. P. (1977). Paradigmatic woman: The prostitute. In D. L. Shores & C. P. Hines (Eds.), *Papers in language variation* (pp. 303–321). Tuscaloosa: University of Alabama Press.

Statham, A. (1987). The gender model revisited: Differences in the management styles of men and women. *Sex Roles, 16,* 409–429.

Statham, A., Richardson, L., & Cook, J. A. (1991). *Gender and university teaching: A negotiated difference.* Albany: SUNY Press.

Statistics on mothers in the workforce. (1999, May 7). *San Francisco Chronicle,* p. B3.

Status Report. (2000, June). *Smart Money,* p. 82.

Stearney, L. (1994). Feminism, ecofeminism, and the maternal archetype. *Communication Quarterly, 42,* 145–159.

Steele, S. (1990). *The content of our character.* New York: St. Martin's.

Steil, J. M. (2000). Contemporary marriage: Still an unequal partnership. In C. Hendrick & C. Hendrick (Eds.), *Close relationships: A sourcebook* (pp. 125–136). Thousand Oaks, CA: Sage.

Steil, J. M., & Turetsky, B. A. (1987). Is equal better? The relationship between marital equality and psychological symptomology. In S. Oskamp (Ed.), *Applied social psychology annual* (Vol. 7, pp. 73–97). Newbury Park, CA: Sage.

Steil, J. M., & Weltman, K. (1991). Marital inequality: The importance of resources, personal attributes, and social norms on career valuing and the allocation of domestic responsibilities. *Sex Roles, 24,* 161–179.

Stein, R. (1995, August 15). Is affirmative action necessary? *Investor's Business Daily,* p. B1.

Steinbacher, R., & Holmes, H. B. (1987). Sex choice: Survival and sisterhood. In G. Corea, R. D. Klein, J. Hanmer, H. B. Holmes, B. Hoskins, M. Kishwar, J. Raymond, R. Rowland, & R. Steinbacher (Eds.), *Man-made women: How new reproductive technologies affect women* (pp. 52–63). London: Hutchinson.

Steinberg, C. (1999, May 9). Not doing what the Romans do. *New York Times,* p. 8.

Steinberg, R. (2001). How sex gets into your paycheck and how to get it out: The gender gap in pay and comparable worth. In D. Vannoy (Ed.), *Gender mosaics* (pp. 258–268). Los Angeles: Roxbury.

Stern, M., & Karraker, K. H. (1989). Sex stereotyping of infants: A review of gender labeling studies. *Sex Roles, 20,* 501–522.

Stewart, L. P., Stewart, A. D., Friedley, S. A., & Cooper, P. J. (1996). *Communication between the sexes: Sex differences, and sex role stereotypes* (3rd ed.). Scottsdale, AZ: Gorsuch Scarisbrick.

Stewart, S., Stinnett, H., & Rosenfeld, L. (2000). Sex differences in desired characteristics of short-term and long-term relationship partners. *Journal of Social and Personal Relationships, 17,* 843–853.

St. Lawrence, J. S., & Joynder, D. J. (1991). The effects of sexually violent rock music on males' acceptance of violence against women. *Psychology of Women Quarterly, 15,* 49–63.

Stoller, D., & Karp, M. (Eds.). (1999). *The Bust guide to the new girl order.* New York: Penguin.

Stoltenberg, J. (1995). Male virgins, blood covenants, and family values. *On the Issues, 4,* n.p.

Straus, M. (1977). Wife beating: How common and why? *Victimology, 2,* 443–458.

Strine, M. S. (1992). Understanding how things work: Sexual harassment and academic culture. *Journal of Applied Communication Research, 4,* 391–400.

Stroup, K. (2001, May 7). Newsmakers. *Newsweek,* p. 75.

Study links high testosterone to male urge for upper hand. (1991, July 17). *Raleigh News and Observer,* pp. A1, A8.

Study links men's cognitive abilities to seasonal

cycles. (1991, November 11). *Raleigh News and Observer*, p. A3.

Study of Black females cites role of praise. (1985, June 25). *New York Times*, p. C5.

Study says women face glass walls as well as ceilings. (1992, March 3). *Wall Street Journal*, pp. B1, B2.

Suggs, W. (1999, May 21). More women participate in collegiate sports. *Chronicle of Higher Education*, pp. A44–A49.

Suggs, W. (2000, July 7). Poll finds strong public backing for gender equity in college athletics. *Chronicle of Higher Education*, p. A40.

Suggs, W. (2001, May 4). Woman who wanted to play football at Duke wins another round in court. *Chronicle of Higher Education*, p. A51.

Suitor, J. J. (1991). Marital quality and satisfaction with the division of household labor across the family life cycle. *Journal of Marriage and the Family, 53*, 221–230.

Sullivan, H. S. (1953). *The interpersonal theory of psychiatry.* New York: Norton.

Surrey, J. L. (1983). The relational self in women: Clinical implications. In J. V. Jordan, J. L. Surrey, & A. G. Kaplan (Speakers), *Women and empathy: Implications for psychological development and psychotherapy* (pp. 6–11). Wellesley, MA: Stone Center for Developmental Services and Studies.

Swain, S. (1989). Covert intimacy: Closeness in men's friendships. In B. J. Risman & P. Schwartz (Eds.), *Gender and intimate relationships* (pp. 71–86). Belmont, CA: Wadsworth.

Switzer, J. Y. (1990). The impact of generic word choices: An empirical investigation of age- and sex-related differences. *Sex Roles, 22*, 69–82.

Tannen, D. (1986). *That's not what I meant! How conversational style makes or breaks relationships.* New York: Ballantine.

Tannen, D. (1990a). Gender differences in conversational coherence: Physical alignment and topical cohesion. In B. Dorval (Ed.), *Conversational organization and its development.* (Vol. XXXVIII, pp. 167–206). Norwood, NJ: Ablex.

Tannen, D. (1990b). *You just don't understand: Women and men in conversation.* New York: Morrow.

Tannen, D. (1991, June 19). Teachers' classroom strategies should recognize that men and women use language differently. *Chronicle of Higher Education*, pp. B1, B3.

Tannen, D. (1995). *Talking 9 to 5: Women and men in the workplace.* New York: Avon.

Tanouye, E. (1996, June 28). Heredity theory says intelligence in males is "like mother, like son." *Wall Street Journal*, p. B1.

Tavris, C. (1992). *The mismeasure of woman.* New York: Simon & Schuster.

Tavris, C., & Baumgartner, A. (1983, February). How would your life be different? *Redbook*, pp. 92–95.

Taylor, B., & Conrad, C. R. (1992). Narratives of sexual harassment: Organizational dimensions. *Journal of Applied Communication Research, 4*, 401–418.

Taylor, V., & Rupp, L. (1998). Lesbian organizations. In W. Mankiller, G. Mink, M. Navarro, B. Smith, & G. Steinem (Eds.), *The reader's companion to U.S. women's history* (pp. 330–332). New York: Houghton Mifflin.

Tetenbaum, T. J., & Pearson, J. (1989). The voices in children's literature: The impact of gender on the moral decisions of storybook characters. *Sex Roles, 20*, 381–395.

3rd Wave. (1999, May 24). http://www.io.com/~wwwave/

Thomas, V. G. (1989). Body-image satisfaction among Black women. *Journal of Social Psychology, 129*, 107–112.

Thomas, V. G., & James, M. D. (1988). Body image, dieting tendencies, and sex-role traits in urban Black women. *Sex Roles, 18*, 523–529.

Thompson, E. H., Jr. (1991). The maleness of violence in dating relationships: An appraisal of stereotypes. *Sex Roles, 24*, 261–278.

Thompson, E. H., Jr., & Pleck, J. H. (1987). The structure of male role norms. In M. S. Kimmel (Ed.), *Changing men: New directions in research on men and masculinity* (pp. 25–36). Newbury Park, CA: Sage.

Thompson, L., & Walker, A. J. (1989). Gender in families: Women and men in marriage, work, and parenthood. *Journal of Marriage and the Family, 51*, 845–871.

Thompson, T., & Zerbinos, E. (1995). Television cartoons: Do children notice it's a boy's world? *Sex Roles, 37*, 415–432.

Thompson, T., & Zerbinos, E. (1997). Gender roles in animated cartoons: Has the picture changed in 20 years? *Sex Roles, 32*, 651–673.

Thorne, B. (1986). Boys and girls together . . . but mostly apart: Gender arrangements in elementary schools. In W. Hartup & Z. Rubin (Eds.), *Relationships and development* (pp. 167–184). Hillsdale, NJ: Erlbaum.

Thorne, B., & Henley, N. (Eds.). (1975). *Language and sex: Difference and dominance.* Rowley, MA: Newbury House.

Thurer, S. L. (1994). *The myths of motherhood.* New York: Houghton Mifflin.

Tidball, M. E. (1989). Women's colleges: Exceptional conditions, not exceptional talent, produce high achievers. In C. S. Pearson, D. L. Shavlik, & J. G. Touchton (Eds.), *Educating the majority: Women challenge tradition in higher education* (pp. 157–172). New York: American Council on Education/Macmillan.

Tierney, H. (Ed.). (1989). *Volume I: Views from the sciences.* Westport, CT: Greenwood.

Tierney, H. (Ed.). (1990). *Volume II: Literature, arts, and learning.* Westport, CT: Greenwood.

Tierney, H. (Ed.). (1991). *Volume III: History,*

philosophy, and religion. Westport, CT: Greenwood.

Tiffs, S., & VanOsdol, P. (1991, February 4). A setback for pinups at work. *Time,* p. 61.

Tiggemann, M., & Rothblum, E. D. (1988). Gender differences in social consequences of perceived overweight in the United States and Australia. *Sex Roles, 18,* 75–86.

Tjaden, P., & Thoennes, N. (1998). *Prevalence, incidence, and consequences of violence against women: Findings from the National Violence Against Women Survey.* Atlanta, GA: Centers for Disease Control and Prevention, Center for Injury Prevention and Control.

Tobias, S. (1997). *The faces of feminism.* Boulder, CO: Westview.

Todd-Mancillas, W. (1981). Masculine generics—sexist language: A review of literature and implications for speech communication professionals. *Communication Quarterly, 29,* 107–115.

Tognoli, J. (1980). Male friendship and intimacy across the life span. *Family Relations, 29,* 273–279.

Toubia, N. (1993). *Female genital mutilation: A call for global action.* New York: Women, Ink.

Toubia, N. (1994). Female circumcision as a public health issue. *New England Journal of Medicine, 331,* 712–716.

Trangsrud, K. (1994). Female genital mutilation: Recommendations for education and policy. *Carolina Papers in International Health and Development, 1,* n.p.

Treichler, P. A., & Kramarae, C. (1983). Women's talk in the ivory tower. *Communication Quarterly, 31,* 118–132.

Trexler, R. (1997). *Sex and conquest.* Ithaca, NY: Cornell University Press.

Trinh, M. (1989). *Woman, native, other: Writing postcoloniality and feminism.* Bloomington: Indiana University Press.

Trouble at the top. (1991, June 17). *U.S. News and World Report,* pp. 40–48.

Trudeau, M. (1996, June 4). Morning news. Public Broadcasting System.

Truman, D., Ttokar, D., & Fischer, A. (1996). Dimensions of masculinity: Relations to date rape, supportive attitudes, and sexual aggression in dating situations. *Journal of Counseling and Development, 74,* 555–562.

Tucker, L. A. (1983). Muscular strength and mental health. *Journal of Personality and Social Psychology, 45,* 1255–1360.

Turner, M. (2000, August 19–25). Flockhart does her part to help womankind. *Channels,* p. 4.

Turner, R. (1998, December 14). Back in the Ms. biz. *Newsweek,* p. 67.

Turner, R. (1999, February 1). Finding the inner swine. *Newsweek,* pp. 52–53.

Ueland, B. (1992, November/December). Tell me more: On the fine art of listening. *Utne Reader,* pp. 104–109.

Ugwu-Ojo, D. (2000, December 4). My turn: Should my tribal past shape Delia's future? *Newsweek,* p. 14.

Ullman, S., Karabatsos, G., & Koss, M. (1999). Alcohol and sexual assault in a national sample of college women. *Journal of Interpersonal Violence, 14,* 603–625.

Umberson, D., Chen, M., House, K., Hopkins, & Slaten, E. (1996). The effect of social relationships on psychological well-being: Are men and women really so different? *American Sociological Review, 61,* 837–857.

U.S. Bureau of the Census. (2000). *Statistical abstract of the United States, 1999.* Washington, DC: U.S. Bureau of the Census.

U.S. Department of Labor, Bureau of Labor Statistics. (1991). *Employment and earnings, February 1991.* Washington, DC: U.S. Government Printing Office.

Uzzell, O., & Peebles-Wilkins, W. (1989). Black spouse abuse: A focus on factors and intervention strategies. *Western Journal of Black Studies, 13,* 10–16.

Valian, V. (1998). *Why so slow? The advancement of women.* Boston: MIT Press.

Van der Kwaak, A. (1992). Female circumcision and gender identity: A questionable alliance? *Social Science Medicine, 35,* 777–787.

Villarosa, L. (1994, January). Dangerous eating. *Essence,* pp. 19–21, 87.

Violent crime's era of decline is over, report says. (2001, May 31). *Raleigh News and Observer,* p. 7A.

The Virginia Slims Opinion Poll. (1990), pp. 79–81. (Cited in Faludi, 1991, p. 91)

Vobejda, B., & Perlstein, L. (1998, June 7). Girls catching up with boys in ways good and bad, study finds. *Raleigh News and Observer,* pp. 1A, 14A.

Wadsworth, B. (1996). *Piaget's theory of cognitive and affective development.* New York: Addison-Wesley.

Wagenheim, J. (1990, September/October). The secret life of men. *New Age Journal,* pp. 40–45, 106–118.

Wagenheim, J. (1996, January–February). Among the Promise Keepers. *Utne Reader,* pp. 74–77.

Waggoner, C., & O'Brien Hallstein, L. (2001). Feminist ideologies meet fashionable bodies: Managing the agency/constraint conundrum. *Text and Performance Quarterly, 21,* 26–46.

Walker, A. (1983). *In search of our mothers' gardens.* New York: Harcourt Brace Jovanovich.

Walker, L. E. (1984). *The battered woman syndrome.* New York: Springer-Verlag.

Walsh, K. (1978). *Neuropsychology.* Edinburgh/London: Churchill Livingstone.

Walt, V. (1997, March 31). The cutting edge. *Wall Street Journal*, p. 14.

Wamboldt, F. S., & Reiss, D. (1989). Defining a family heritage and a new relationship identity: Two central tasks in the making of a marriage. *Family Process, 28,* 317–335.

Warren, K. (2000). *Ecofeminist philosophy: A Western perspective on what it is and why it matters.* Rowan & Littlefield.

Warshaw, R. (1988). *I never called it rape.* New York: Harper & Row.

Waterman, A. S., & Whitbourne, S. K. (1982). Androgyny and psychological development among college students and adults. *Journal of Personality, 50,* 121–133.

Watzlawick, P., Beavin, J., & Jackson, D. D. (1967). *Pragmatics of human communication.* New York: Norton.

Way, N. (1998). *Everyday courage.* New York: NYU Press.

Weedon, C. (1987). *Feminist practice and post-structuralist theory.* New York: Basil Blackwell.

Weiler, K. (1988). *Women teaching for change: Gender, class and power.* New Haven, CT: Yale University Press.

Weiner, J. (1999, November 18). Youths' media time is mostly TV. *Raleigh News and Observer,* p. 7A.

Weisman, L. K. (1992). *Discrimination by design: A feminist critique of the man-made environment.* Chicago: University of Chicago Press.

Weiss, D. M., & Sachs, J. (1991). Persuasive strategies used by preschool children. *Sociology, 97,* 114–142.

Welch, L. B. (Ed.). (1992). *Perspectives on minority women in higher education.* Westport, CT: Praeger.

Wellington, E. (1999, May 12). The single dad. *Raleigh News and Observer,* pp. 1E, 3E.

Welter, B. (1966). The cult of true womanhood: 1820–1960. *American Quarterly, 18,* 151–174.

Werking, K. (1997). *We're just good friends: Women and men in nonromantic relationships.* New York: Guilford.

West, C., & Zimmerman, D. H. (1983). Small insults: A study of interruptions in cross-sex conversations between unacquainted persons. In B. Thorne, C. Kramarae, & N. Henley (Eds.), *Language, gender and society* (pp. 102–117). Rowley, MA: Newbury House.

West, C., & Zimmerman, D. H. (1987). "Doing gender." *Gender and Society, 1,* 125–151.

West, J. T. (1995). Understanding how the dynamics of ideology influence violence between intimates. In S. Duck & J. T. Wood (Eds.), *Understanding relationship processes, 5: Confronting relationship challenges* (pp. 129–149). Thousand Oaks, CA: Sage.

West, L., Anderson, J., & Duck, S. (1996). Crossing the barriers to friendship between women and men. In J. T. Wood (Ed.), *Gendered relationships: A reader* (pp. 111–127). Mountain View, CA: Mayfield.

What about this backlash? (1994, March 16). *Independent Weekly,* pp. 14–15.

Wheeler, D. (1998, April 24). Researchers explore gender-related differences in response to pain. *Chronicle of Higher Education,* p. A18.

Wheeless, V. E. (1984). A test of the theory of speech accommodation using language and gender orientation. *Women's Studies in Communication, 7,* 13–22.

Where have all the smart girls gone? (1989, April). *Psychology Today,* p. 20.

Whitaker, S. (2001). Gender politics in men's movements. In D. Vannoy (Ed.), *Gender mosaics* (pp. 343–351). Los Angeles: Roxbury.

White, B. (1989). Gender differences in marital communication patterns. *Family Process, 28,* 89–106.

White, J., & Bondurant, B. (1996). Gendered violence between intimates. In J. T. Wood (Ed.), *Gendered relationships: A reader* (pp. 197–210). Mountain View, CA: Mayfield.

Whitehead, B. (1997, October 3). Soccer dads march on Washington. *Wall Street Journal,* p. A10.

Whiteley, S. (2000). *Women and popular music: Sexuality, identity, and subjectivity.* New York: Routledge.

Whiting, B., & Edwards, C. (1973). A cross-cultural analysis of sex differences in the behavior of children aged three through eleven. *Journal of Social Psychology, 91,* 171–188.

Williams, D. G. (1985). Gender, masculinity, femininity, and emotional intimacy in same-sex friendship. *Sex Roles, 12,* 587–600.

Williams, J. (2000, December 15). What stymies women's academic careers? It's personal. *Chronicle of Higher Education,* p. B10.

Williams, J. E., & Best, D. L. (1990). *Measuring sex stereotypes: A multi-nation study* (Rev. ed.). Newbury Park, CA: Sage.

Williams, J. H. (1973). Sexual role identification and personality functioning in girls: A theory revisited. *Journal of Personality, 41,* 1–8.

Willis, E. (1992). *No more nice girls: Countercultural essays.* Hanover, NH: Wesleyan University Press.

Willis, F. N., Jr. (1966). Initial speaking distance as a function of the speaker's relationship. *Psychonomic Science, 5,* 221–222.

Wills, T. A., Weiss, R. L., & Patterson, G. R. (1974). A behavioral analysis of the determinants of marital satisfaction. *Journal of Consulting and Clinical Psychology, 42,* 802–811.

Wilson, E. (1975). *Sociobiology: The new synthesis.* Cambridge, MA: Belknap of Harvard University Press.

Wilson, R. (2001, May 4). Proportion of part-time faculty members leveled off from 1992 to 1998, data show. *Chronicle of Higher Education,* p. A14.

Wilson, T. (2000, October 24). Census: Mothers return to work. *Raleigh News and Observer,* pp. 1A, 9A.

Winkler, K. (1997, November 7). Girls at risk: A passionate history surveys culture and physiology. *Chronicle of Higher Education,* pp. A15, A16.

Winstead, B. A. (1986). Sex differences in same-sex friendships. In V. J. Derlega & B. A. Winstead (Eds.), *Friendship and social interaction* (pp. 81–99). New York: Springer-Verlag.

Wise, S., & Stanley, L. (1987). *Georgie Porgie: Sexual harassment in everyday life.* New York: Pandora.

Witt, S. L. (1990). *The pursuit of race and gender equity in American academe.* Westport, CT: Praeger.

Wolf, N. (1991). *The beauty myth.* New York: Morrow.

Wolf, N. (1993). *Fire with fire: The new female power and how it will change the 21st century.* New York: Random House.

Women on Words and Images. (1972). *Dick and Jane as victims.* Princeton, NJ: Author.

Women usually attacked by people they know. (1996, December 19). *Raleigh News and Observer,* p. 9A.

Wood, J. T. (1992a). *Spinning the symbolic web: Human communication and symbolic interaction.* Norwood, NJ: Ablex.

Wood, J. T. (1992b). Telling our stories: Narratives as a basis for theorizing sexual harassment. *Journal of Applied Communication Research, 4,* 349–363.

Wood, J. T. (1993a). Engendered relationships: Interaction, caring, power, and responsibility in close relationships. In S. Duck (Ed.), *Processes in close relationships: Contexts of close relationships* (Vol. 3, pp. 26–54). Beverly Hills: Sage.

Wood, J. T. (1993b). Engendered identities: Shaping voice and mind through gender. In D. Vocate (Ed.), *Intrapersonal communication: Different voices, different minds* (pp. 145–167). Hillsdale, NJ: Erlbaum.

Wood, J. T. (1993c). From "woman's nature" to standpoint epistemology: Gilligan and the debate over essentializing in feminist scholarship. *Women's Studies in Communication, 15,* 1–24.

Wood, J. T. (1993d). Issues facing non-traditional members of academe. In G. M. Phillips, D. S. Gouran, S. A. Kuehn, & J. T. Wood, *Professionalism: A survival guide for beginning academics* (pp. 55–72). Cresskill, NJ: Hampton.

Wood, J. T. (1993e). Gender and relationship crises: Contrasting reasons, responses, and relational orientations. In J. Ringer (Ed.), *Queer words, queer images: The (re)construction of homosexuality* (pp. 238–264). New York City: NYU Press.

Wood, J. T. (1993f). Defining and studying sexual harassment as situated experience. In G. L. Kreps (Ed.), *Communication and sexual harassment in the workplace* (pp. 6–23). Cresskill, NJ: Hampton.

Wood, J. T. (1994a). Saying it makes it so: The discursive construction of sexual harassment. In S. Bingham (Ed.), *Discursive conceptualizations of sexual harassment* (pp. 17–30). Greenwood, NJ: Praeger.

Wood, J. T. (1994b). *Who cares: Women, care, and culture.* Carbondale: Southern Illinois University Press.

Wood, J. T. (1995). *Relational communication: Continuity and change in personal relationships.* Belmont, CA: Wadsworth.

Wood, J. T. (1996a). Dominant and muted discourses in popular representations of feminism. *Quarterly Journal of Speech, 82,* 171–185.

Wood, J. T. (Ed.). (1996b). *Gendered relationships: A reader.* Mountain View, CA: Mayfield.

Wood, J. T. (1998). *But I thought you meant . . . : Misunderstandings in human communication.* Mountain View, CA: Mayfield.

Wood, J. T. (2000). He says/she says: Misunderstandings in communication between women and men. In D. O. Braithwaite & J. T. Wood (Eds.), *Case studies in interpersonal communication* (pp. 93–100). Belmont, CA: Wadsworth.

Wood, J. T. (2001a). A critical response to John Gray's Mars and Venus portrayals of men and women. *Southern Communication Journal, 67,* 201–210.

Wood, J. T. (2001b). The normalization of violence in heterosexual romantic relationships: Women's narratives of love and violence. *Journal of Social and Personal Relationships, 18,* 239–262.

Wood, J. T. (2002). *Interpersonal communication: Everyday encounters* (3rd ed.). Belmont, CA: Wadsworth.

Wood, J. T., & Conrad, C. R. (1983). Paradox in the experience of professional women. *Western Journal of Speech Communication, 47,* 305–322.

Wood, J. T., & Inman, C. (1993). In a different mode: Recognizing male modes of closeness. *Journal of Applied Communication Research, 21,* 279–295.

Wood, J. T., & Lenze, L. F. (1991a). Strategies to enhance gender sensitivity in communication education. *Communication Education, 40,* 16–21.

Wood, J. T., & Lenze, L. F. (1991b). Gender and the development of self: Inclusive pedagogy in interpersonal communication. *Women's Studies in Communication, 14,* 1–23.

Wood, W. (1987). Meta-analytic review of sex differences in group performance. *Psychological Bulletin, 102,* 53–71.

Woody, B. (1989). Black women in the emerging services economy. *Sex Roles, 21,* 45–67.

Woody, B. (1992). *Black women in the workplace: Impacts of structural change in the economy.* Westport, CT: Greenwood.

Wooley, S. C., & Wooley, O. W. (1984, February). Feeling fat in a thin society. *Glamour*, pp. 198–252.

The world's women: 1970–1990: Trends and statistics. (1991). United Nations Report. (Cited in French, 1992)

Worley, J., & Vannoy, D. (2001). The challenge of integrating work and family life. In D. Vannoy (Ed.), *Gender mosaics* (pp. 165–173). Los Angeles: Roxbury.

The wounds of words. (1992, October 12). *Newsweek*, pp. 90–91.

Wriggins, J. (1998). Rape. In W. Mankiller, G. Mink, M. Navarro, B. Smith, & G. Steinem (Eds.), *The reader's companion to U.S. women's history* (pp. 612–614). New York: Houghton Mifflin.

Wright, P. H. (1982). Men's friendships, women's friendships, and the alleged inferiority of the latter. *Sex Roles, 8,* 1–20.

Wright, P. H. (1988). Interpreting research on gender differences in friendship: A case for moderation and a plea for caution. *Journal of Social and Personal Relationships, 5,* 367–373.

Wright, P. H., & Scanlon, M. B. (1991). Gender role orientations and friendship: Some attenuation but gender differences still abound. *Sex Roles, 24,* 551–566.

The wrong weight. (1997, November). *Carolina Woman*, p. 7.

Yellin, J. F. (1990). *Women and sisters: Antislavery feminists in American culture.* New Haven, CT: Yale University Press.

Yogman, M., Cooley, J., & Kindlon, D. (1988). Fathers, infants, and toddlers: A developing relationship. In P. Bronstein & C. Cowan (Eds.), *Fatherhood today: Men's changing role in the family* (pp. 53–78). New York: Wiley.

Young, C. (1992, October 4). Female trouble. *Washington Post*, pp. C1, C4.

Zimbalist, A. (2000, March 3). Backlash against Title IX: An end run around female athletes. *Chronicle of Higher Education*, p. B9.

Zimmerman, D. H., & West, C. (1975). Sex roles, interruptions and silences in conversation. In B. Thorne & N. Henley (Eds.), *Language and sex: Difference and dominance* (pp. 105–129). Rowley, MA: Newbury House.

Zimmerman, M., & Hall, L. (2001). Men and women: Health and illness. In D. Vannoy (Ed.), *Gender mosaics* (pp. 426–435). Los Angeles: Roxbury.

Zinn, H. (1995). *A people's history.* New York: HarperCollins.

Zinn, M., & Dill, B. (1996). Theorizing difference from multiracial feminism. *Feminist Studies, 22,* 321–331.

Ziv, L. (1997, May). The horror of female genital mutilation. *Cosmopolitan*, pp. 242–245.

Zuckerman, M. B. (1993, August 2). The victims of TV violence. *U.S. News and World Report*, p. 64.

marital, 30, 298, 333
myths and facts about, 301
pornography and, 315
power and, 299
prevalence of, 294, 297–298, 299, 303–304
Rape script, 298
Real men, 87, 170–172
Reasonable man standard, 237, 307–308, 337–338
Reasonable person standard, 337–338
Reasonable woman standard, 237, 308
Re-covering, 74
Relationship(s), 181–205
commitment in, 181, 194–203
defined, 182
family. See Families
friendships. See Friendships
in future, 332–334
heterosexual, 2, 192–203, 332–334
meaning of, 182–185
mentor, 248
myths of, 285–286
responsibility for health of, 198–199
romantic, 192–203, 332–334
stereotypical images of, 272–279
workplace, 238, 241–250
Relationship experts, women as, 182, 194, 198
Relationship level of meaning, 32–33, 120–121, 124, 131, 132–135
Relationship talk, 127, 187
Religious systems, male standards in, 237
Reproductive rights, 64, 81
Responsibility
psychological, 200–201
for relationships, 198–199
for violence, 319
Responsiveness, 132–134, 187
Reuther, Rosemary Radford, 98, 99
Revalorists, 74–75
Reverse discrimination, 252
Rhetoric, 60
Rhetorical movements, 60–101
Rights, 312
civil, 250–251
equal, 84–85
of fathers, 88
of gays, 87, 89, 228
reproductive, 64, 81
voting, 62–65, 215
of women, 61–63
Role, 53–54
Role models
for adolescents, 48–49
of alternatives to traditional views, 24
in families, 157, 164–165
masculine, 157
in media, 48–49, 286
in schools, 209–213

Sanger, Margaret, 64
Schlafly, Phyllis, 84, 97
Schools. See Education

Script
gender, 54, 298, 316
rape, 298
for romance, 192–194
Second shift, 199–202, 333. See also Working women
Self, 52–54, 154
Self-as-object, 154
Self-defense, 304–305
Self-disclosure, 186, 191, 196
Self-esteem, 268, 305
androgyny and, 114
physical appearance and, 172–173
Self-reflection, 114–115
Self-reliance, 170
Self-talk, 154–155
Seneca Falls Convention, 62–63
Separate but equal doctrine, 212, 250–251
Separatism, 71–72
Sex, 19–21
Sex differences, 17–21, 40–43
in brain structure, 40–42
in chromosomal structure, 19, 20, 39
in friendships, 185–186
in hormones, 19–21, 40
sexual orientation and, 21
Sex discrimination. See Discrimination
Sex object, 227–228, 277–279
Sex segregation, 117, 190–191
in education, 211, 212, 213
in workplace, 229, 248–250
Sexism, 85, 330
awareness of, 68
in children's books, 70
in education, 215–216
Sexist language, 3, 104–105
Sexual, directive for men to be, 169–170
Sexual abuse, 297
Sexual assault, 297–299. See also Rape
Sexual harassment, 108–109, 139, 140, 217–218, 228, 305–308
in future, 334
in hostile environment, 307
institutions and, 318
quid pro quo, 306
same-sex, 306
standards for assessing, 237, 307–308
Sexual orientation, 21, 41–42, 192–203. See also Gay(s); Lesbian(s)
Sexuality, feminine, 193
Signals, 103
Single-sex schools, 211, 212, 213
Smiling, 133
Social construction
of heterosexuality as normal, 2
of inequality, 2–4
of normal, 23, 50–52, 313, 325–326
Social learning theory, 46–47
Social movements, 60–101
men's, 83–95, 329–330
women's, 60, 61–83, 280–283
Socialist feminism, 73

Weight, 143–147, 164–165, 173
White(s). *See* European Americans
Wife beating. *See* Abuse between intimates
Wollstonecraft, Mary, 21
Womanhood, ideals of, 15, 143, 331–332
Womanists, 75–77
Women
  caretaking role of, 53–54. *See also* Caregiving
  depression in, 172, 195
  devaluing of, 104, 111–112, 175, 178, 217, 218,
    228, 256, 268
  education of, 206–207
  friendships between, 184, 186–188
  physical appearance of, 175, 267–268, 269
  as relationship experts, 182, 194, 198
  rights of, 61–63
  speech of, 119–122
  stereotypes of, 110, 142, 227–232, 248–249,
    266, 267–279, 331–332
  underrepresentation of, 104–105, 209–213,
    263, 264, 265
  as victims, 78, 79, 80, 108, 277–279

  working, 65, 96, 172, 173, 174, 176–177, 199–
    202, 235, 240, 245, 248–250, 333, 335
  See also Femininity
Women's Educational Equity Act of 1974 and
  1978, 251
Women's movements, 60, 61–83, 280–283
Work schedules, 244–246
Working women, 65, 96, 172, 173, 174, 176–177,
  199–202, 235, 240, 245, 248–250, 333, 335
Workplace
  bias in, 234–235
  inequity in, 242–250
  relationships in, 238, 241–250
  sex discrimination in, 113, 227–228, 231–232,
    251
  sex segregation in, 229, 248–250
Wright, Martha Coffin, 62

X chromosome, 19, 20, 39, 42
X-rated films, 278

Y chromosome, 19, 20, 39